THE PORTABLE
James Joyce

THE PORTABLE

JAMES JOYCE

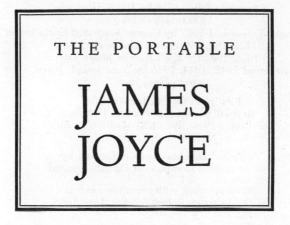

WITH AN INTRODUCTION & NOTES

BY HARRY LEVIN

The Viking Press

First published in January 1947
Revised edition published in 1966 by
The Viking Press, Inc., 625 Madison Avenue,
New York, N.Y. 10022

Published simultaneously in Canada by
The Macmillan Company of Canada Limited

Ninth printing, with corrections in text
of *Dubliners* by Robert Scholes, June 1968

Sixteenth printing January 1972

SBN 670-40998-7 (hardbound)
SBN 670-01030-8 (paperbound)

Library of Congress catalog card number: 47-1424

Printed in U.S.A.

Contents

Editor's Introduction

A LONG and hazardous period of probation seems to face a writer when, ceasing to be a contemporary, he becomes a classic. But in Joyce's case, perhaps because he was so rigorously tested during his lifetime, this further trial has been cut short. Already his work has weathered rejection by publishers, objection by printers, suppression by censors, confiscation by customs officials, bowdlerization by pirates, oversight by proofreaders, attack by critics, and defense by coteries—not to mention misunderstanding by readers. Meanwhile he has won the most significant kind of recognition: imitation by writers. His influence has been so pervasive that, to a large extent, it remains unacknowledged. How many of those who read John Hersey's *Hiroshima* recognize its literary obligation to *Ulysses?* There have been other demonstrations, but none so pertinent, of how an original mode of expression can help us to grasp a new phase of experience. Is it any wonder, when we live in such an explosive epoch, that even the arts have made themselves felt through a series of shocks?

Hence Joyce's books, which a few years ago we had to smuggle into this country, are today required reading in college courses. As we study them closely, we are less intimidated by their idiosyncrasies, and more impressed not only by the qualities they share with the great books of other ages, but by their vital concern for the problems of our own age. In the light of the political exile that has activated so many writers in recent years, Joyce's artistic expatriation no longer seems a willful gesture. His escape from his native island to the continent of Europe, as it turned out, was to merge his private career with what he called "the nightmare of history." It was easier for Flaubert, a sedentary bachelor with a comfortable estate and a regular income, to assume the stigmata of esthetic martyrdom. It was excruciating for Joyce, a nomadic foreigner struggling to support a family by other means than his writing, to be bound—as he put it—"to the cross of his own cruelfiction."

The temptations and distractions that sidetrack the artist have multiplied, and examples of intransigence are rarer now than they were in Flaubert's day. What he represented to his younger contemporaries, nonetheless, Joyce has become for us: the Writers' Writer. The characteristics that enabled him to sustain his purpose are apparent in his very death-mask. Delicately but firmly molded, the head is long and narrow, the forehead high, the chin strong, and the eyes are closed. It is the face of his Stephen Dedalus, of the perennial student, of a man who carries to the verge of his sixtieth year the agility, the curiosity, the sensibility of his youth. And, just as many of Joyce's fellow citizens are forever transfixed in the poses he caught—the priests saying mass, the barmaids pouring ale, the sandwich-men filing by, the midwives and undertakers plying their respective trades—so he has crystallized himself in our minds as the hero of *Stephen Hero,* the model for *A Portrait of the Artist as a Young Man.*

Setting down his memories of his brother in a current Italian journal, Professor Stanislaus Joyce would caution us against a too complete identification. James Joyce was a rather more filial son than Stephen Dedalus, it appears, and his actual adolescence was less dispiriting than his later depiction of it. This we might have gathered by comparing the account of his university days in *Stephen Hero* with the final chapter of the *Portrait*. The earlier version is more immediate, fully rounded and factually detailed; the definitive treatment is carefully shaded and dramatically sharpened. It is not enough for the novelist to possess, like a number of Joyce's characters, "an odd autobiographical habit." He must be able to trace a meaningful pattern through the welter of circumstances. Joyce has managed, by invoking an ancient myth, to conjure up a modern one. Deliberately he has struck the attitude of Icarus—the classical posture of flight, the artist's revulsion from his middle-class environment, the youthful effort to try one's father's wings.

The works of Joyce's maturity are less personal and more human: in his own terms, they are farther removed from his lyric self and closer to his godlike ideal of sympathetic detachment. Their emphasis shifts from flight to creation, accordingly, and from the son's role to the father-image: Dedalus, the fabulous artificer; Ulysses, the paternal wanderer; Finnegan, the builder of cities. The technical and psychological paradox is that Joyce, as his comprehension of ordinary humanity increased, became less comprehensible to the common reader. He is commonly remembered not as the mature creator—forging, in mingled arrogance and piety, "the uncreated conscience of his race"—but as a winged figure poised for a break with the dominating forces in his background. Language, religion, and nationality were envisaged by Stephen as a series of nets to restrain that initial impetus. When his trial flight succeeded, and the creative process began, the metaphor was calculated to change. For the irreducible substances out of which Joyce created his monumental achievement were nationality, religion, and language.

II

The first consideration, with an Irishman, is nationality. Joyce, like Stephen, was "all too Irish"—all the more Irish because he was a "wildgoose," because he resided mainly in foreign countries after his twentieth year, seldom as long as a year in the same domicile. From first to last, his underlying impulses were those of his racial endowment: humor, imagination, eloquence, belligerence. If other endemic traits are less in evidence, notably gregariousness and bibulousness, it is because they were so brilliantly exemplified in Joyce's father. A genial ne'er-do-well, a political job-holder, a man about Dublin —but there can be no substitute for the characterization of Simon Dedalus by his eldest son. The *Portrait* begins with the child's earliest reminiscence, a story told by his parent; it ends with the fledgling's departure from the parental roof. Its most dramatic episode occurs at the family's Christmas dinner. Here, in a vividly remembered argument, lies Joyce's basic premise: the long delayed hope of independence that was frustrated again with the downfall of Ireland's leading politician, Charles Stewart Parnell.

The latent blood-feud with England had come to the surface, a few months after Joyce's birth, when two high British officials were assassinated in the Phoenix Park. Though the attempt to incriminate Parnell had been legally exposed as a forgery, a private scandal was brewing which finally discredited him. The desertion of his clerical supporters, so vociferously defended by Stephen's Mrs. Riordan, was a particularly sore point. Parnell's death soon afterward was the occasion of Joyce's first literary effort—a poem echoed in "Ivy Day in the Committee Room," his own favorite among his stories.

The impact of the news upon Stephen, semi-delirious in the school infirmary, is registered in the *Portrait*. The state of the nation during the period that ensued, the period in which Joyce gathered his lasting impressions of it, he has diagnosed as a spiritual and temporal paralysis. The cure was further violence, which led to the founding of the Irish Free State; which had started with the uprising of Easter Week, 1916, four years after Joyce left Ireland for the last time.

He left too early for the Revolution; he arrived too late for the Renaissance. His undergraduate idol, the subject of his first published article, was not Yeats but Ibsen. He greeted the Irish Literary Theater with a polemic against folksy estheticism. He outraged his college debating society by expounding the iconoclasms of European drama. On several visits home from the Continent, between the ages of twenty and thirty, he considered whether some journalistic or pedagogical niche existed for him in the cultural life of his native city. In his single play, *Exiles*, as in actuality, he pushed this problem toward a negative conclusion. In his short stories, *Dubliners*, the recurrent situation is entrapment. Their timid protagonists are trapped into marriage ("The Boarding House"), kept from eloping ("Eveline"), wistfully envious of colleagues who get away ("A Little Cloud"). In "Counterparts" a father makes his son the victim of his own frustrations. The plight suggested in "The Dead" is that of a mill-horse harnessed to a carriage, pulling it round and round a public statue.

Escaping from the treadmill of Dublin, Joyce spent the rest of his life brooding upon it and writing about it. His insistence on calling its denizens by their names, and pointing out its local landmarks, held up the publication of *Dubliners* for several years. *Ulysses*, more comprehensively than *Dubliners* and more objectively than the *Portrait,* is saturated with "consciousness of place." The city is commemorated, street by street and hour by hour, as it stood on Thursday, June 16, 1904. The crones on Nelson's Pillar, spitting down plum-stones upon the pedestrians, sum up Stephen's departing attitude. His earlier description of Ireland, "the old sow that eats her farrow," is acted out in Circe's disorderly house, where men are figuratively turned into swine. No Dubliner will raise a hand to help the drunken Stephen, excepting Leopold Bloom, with whom he has nothing in common but humanity. Bloom, the ineffectual advertising man, the modern Ulysses, is "Everyman or Noman," every inch the Man in the Street. He is suspected, among many other devices, of having inspired the Home-Rule journalist, Arthur Griffith, with his *Sinn Fein* program.

Stephen departs for Europe promising "to write something in ten years." Joyce, living through the next decade in polyglot Trieste, finished the *Portrait* and began *Ulysses* in 1914. He lived through the First World War in neutral Zurich, a denaturalized British subject among exiles from many lands. In cosmopolitan Paris, during the period between wars, the appearance of *Ulysses* and the parturition of *Finnegans Wake* were international events. The latter coincided with the Second World War; and Joyce, returning to Zurich, died upon the operating table in 1941. In *Ulysses* he had looked upon battle as a teacher viewing a playing field. In *Finnegans Wake* all the world's great battles are reduced to a grand Irish free-for-all: "history as her is harped." But Ireland is Joyce's microcosm; his gigantic hero is compounded of many heroes; H. C. Earwicker stands for "Here Comes Everybody." "Easterheld," he enacts the regeneration of "Easter Island." Thus Joyce's feeling for his country, long dormant, is never dead. To cite his inimitable phraseology once more, it is merely "hiberniating."

III

But racial inheritance is guided and shaped by cultural tradition, even as Ireland has been by Catholicism. Where the father is the embodiment of nationality in Stephen's recollections, his mother embodies religion. Her unquestioning acceptance is contrasted with her son's developing skepticism; their naturally affectionate relationship has all but reached an impasse when he leaves for Paris in 1902. Six months later he is summoned home to her deathbed. His refusal to take part in the family's prayers for her seems to have stimulated that remorse of conscience, that "agenbite of inwit" which re-echoes through *Ulysses*. Here Stanislaus Joyce interposes a revealing detail. Mrs. Joyce, he informs us, was already past praying for; it was not her request, but an officious uncle's, that James Joyce refused. Retrospectively, then, he has gone out of his way to sharpen the issue and dramatize the incident. Loss of faith, for a Roman Catholic, can never mean a gradual and easy process of evaporation. In this case, it became a credo in itself. Enfranchisement brought its own exacting discipline.

"Why?" asks Stephen's friend, Buck Mulligan (Dr. Oliver Gogarty). "Because you have the cursed Jesuit strain in you, only it's injected the wrong way." The *Portrait* derives its pattern from the successive stages of a Jesuit education. Joyce was a prize student, albeit an embarrassing protégé, of zealous and thoroughgoing teachers. It was almost inevitable that they should suggest, and that he should very seriously consider, the possibility of entering the priesthood. That he felt the intellectual attraction of theology, as well as the emotional appeal of ritual, is evident in everything he wrote.

Both are submerged in the cold terror of Stephen's central dilemma between carnal sin and priestly absolution. Nature, which incites his heresies, inspires his true vocation. Pride of intellect ultimately ranges him with the forces of Satanic rebellion. The cry, *Non serviam!*, is his protest against Ireland's condition of servitude, against its many masters: Britain not less than Rome, Mammon not less than Caesar. The businessmen's retreat in "Grace" adds an ironic postscript to the schoolboys' sermon on hell.

With the self-dedication of the priest Joyce took the vows of the artist. His imaginative constructions are therefore grounded on the rock of his buried religious experience. His view of human nature is based upon the psychology of the confessional. His esthetic theory is a stimulating mixture of Flaubertian naturalism and neo-Thomism. His literary technique is richly colored by ecclesiastical symbolism; a series of notes on the liturgy of Holy Week, for example, accompanies the manuscript of *Stephen Hero*. There, too, he explains his conception of art as an "epiphany," a sudden illumination if not a divine revelation, a slight but definite insight into other lives, a fragmentary clue to the meaning of life as a whole. Even the stroke of the Ballast Office clock can have this effect, says Stephen, and we may regard *Ulysses* as an extended commentary on his remark. God is manifest, Stephen now believes, as "a noise in the street." The writer's vantage-point is that of "Araby": an acolyte bearing his chalice through the streets of Dublin.

Typical of Joyce's Dubliners is Mr. Duffy in "A Painful Case," whose suburban existence lacks "any communion with others." Shivering with loneliness, as he walks among the lovers on Magazine Hill, he resigns himself to being an "outcast from life's feast." But Joyce does not, like Thomas Mann, sentimentalize his artists by assuming their exclusion from a comfortable bourgeois world. Joyce knows his petty bourgeoisie too well for that; he knows that they too are outsiders, estranged from each other. An inveterate stranger, his wandering Jew, Mr. Bloom, is obscurely involved in the destiny of Throwaway, the "outsider" that wins the Ascot cup. The other event of Bloomsday, the sinking of a New York excursion steamer with five hundred passengers aboard, implies that the members of any community are all in the same boat. Pausing for a moment in a church, Bloom envies the communicants because they are "not so lonely." Later, in a tavern, an anti-Semitic nationalist, anonymously known as "the Citizen," attacks him as an apostle of international peace and universal love.

The problem of *Ulysses* is the age-old attempt to put Christian precept into practice. The consequence is all too palpably illustrated by the anecdote of two drunks in Glasnevin Cemetery, who confound a statue of Jesus with their lamented friend Mulcahy. Beginning as it does with the *Introit,* the book proceeds to a blasphemous climax with the celebration of the Black Mass. Yet, as Bloom foresees, "Longest way round is the shortest way home." The autobiographical hero of Joyce's earlier volumes is depicted awaiting the eucharist; the universalized hero of *Finnegans Wake,* who literally presides over a public house, is himself a host in more ways than one. Through the thickening intonations of his customers can be heard unexpected overtones of the Last Supper: "Pass the fish for Christ's sake!" The various rites of death and burial, which celebrate his wake, all culminate in some version of the Easter ceremony. Even the Phoenix, symbol of political desperation, fulfills its prophecy of resurrection. And the writer, expatriate and excommunicate, reasserts his sense of community and communion.

IV

Communication, however, brought further difficulties which it was his special triumph to overcome. If "his destiny was to be elusive of social or religious orders," it was because he reserved his energies for order of another kind. "The first principle of artistic economy," he had found, was isolation; he had detached himself from his nationality and his religion; but he found his medium, language, pointing back to them. In the somber background, liturgical and scholastic, hovered the Latinity of the Church. In the embattled foreground loomed the Gaelic revival, though it never elicited more than a half-hearted interest from Joyce. In his enthusiasm for Ibsen he had learned Norwegian, and had even used it to salute the dying playwright with a brave and touching letter. At University College he had specialized in Romance languages, and had shown such proficiency that there had been talk of a professorship. During his hardest years on the Continent, before a benefactor endowed his literary work, he worked as a commercial translator and a teacher in a Berlitz school.

It is a striking fact about English literature in the twentieth century that its most notable practitioners have seldom been Englishmen. The fact that they have so often been Irishmen supports Synge's belief in the reinvigorating suggestiveness of Irish popular speech. That English was not Joyce's native language, in the strictest sense, he was keenly aware; and it helps to explain his unparalleled virtuosity. But a more concrete explanation is to be discerned among his physical traits, one of which we normally classify as a serious handicap. Joyce lived much of his life in varying states of semi-blindness. To preserve what eyesight he had, he underwent repeated operations and counter-measures. A schoolboy humiliation, when he broke his glasses and failed to do his lessons, is painfully recollected in the *Portrait* and again in *Ulysses*. His writing tends more and more toward low visibility; his imagination is auditory rather than visual. If the artist is a man for whom the visible world exists, remarked George Moore, then Joyce is essentially a metaphysician; for he is less concerned with the seeing eye than with the thinking mind.

We may add that he is most directly concerned with the hearing ear. Doubtless the sonorities of Homer and Milton are intimately connected with their blindness. It is scarcely coincidental that Joyce, almost unique among modern prose-writers in this respect, must be read aloud to be fully appreciated. In addition to his linguistic aptitude, and in compensation for his defective vision, he was gifted with an especially fine tenor voice. Professional singing was one of the possible careers he had contemplated. His singer's taste inclined toward opera and *bel canto*, romantic ballads and Elizabethan airs: not music but song, he liked to say. His poems, except for a few excursions into Swiftian satire, are songs; lyrics which, without their musical settings, look strangely fragile. Yeats, upon first reading them, praised Joyce's delicate talent, and shrewdly wondered whether his ultimate form would be verse or prose. Operating within the broader area of fiction, he was to retain the cadenced precision of the poet. Above all he remained an accomplished listener, whose pages are continually animated by the accurate recording of overheard conversation.

Joyce's style is distinguished not only by the rise and fall of its rhythms but by its feeling for the texture of the particular word. Words assert a magical power over things. Treasured phrases enable Stephen to transform "the dull phenomenon of Dublin," to transcend "the decayed city" by communing with a rapturous seascape. Jotted impressions are conceived as epiphanies, mystical visions which link the beholder to the object beheld. Between the planes of inward speculation and external observation, Joyce maintains a serio-comic interplay. The narrative of *Ulysses* is identified with the internal monologue of three major characters; it also responds to such discursive influences as newspaper headlines and fugal variations; one chapter comprises parodies of the principal English stylists; and the whole may be studied as a comprehensive handbook of verbal techniques. In *Finnegans Wake* a universe of discourse, seemingly unlimited in space and time, is spanned by associations of thought and play upon words. Names of hundreds of rivers figure in the torrential dialogue, "Anna Livia Plurabelle," which took Joyce 1600 hours to concoct.

His pangs of composition have recently been described by Philippe Soupault as "a sort of daily damnation: the creation of the Joycean world." The perverse ingenuity of these later experiments has been deplored more frequently than deciphered. A long series of misunderstandings with the public inevitably reinforced those early vows of silence, exile, and cunning. Inhibited from writing naturally of natural instincts, Joyce ended by inventing an artificial language of innuendo and mockery. In *Finnegans Wake* he drew upon his linguistic skills and learned hobbies to contrive an optophone—an instrument which, for the benefit of the blind, converts images into sounds. Out of it come, not merely echoes of the past, but warnings of the future. Mr. Earwicker's worldly misfortunes are climaxed by a lethal explosion: *"the abnihilisation of the etym."* Pessimists may interpret this ambiguous phenomenon as the annihilation of all meaning, a chain reaction set off by the destruction of the atom. Optimists will emphasize the creation of matter *ex nihilo,* and trust in the Word to create another world.

V

The alternatives that Joyce suspends, the nihilistic and creative potentialities that now confront us, keep us in an ambivalent state of mind. He himself kept the balance by moving from a negative position to a positive accomplishment. But, because his self-portrait was so explicit, and his masterworks were so elaborate, this development has not clearly been understood. Readers are bound to remember Stephen, "the eternal son," stiff-kneed and self-doomed. They are less likely to think of the roistering alderman, the "folksforefather," who bears a closer resemblance to Simon Dedalus. Nor, until they penetrate *Finnegans Wake,* will they recognize that Joyce's attitude mellowed as his stature increased; that he is finally to be identified less with the prodigal than with the paterfamilias; he plays the demiurge, smiling down on his creations. Meanwhile, of course, the children continue to quarrel among themselves; the old issue between the civic and the esthetic is belabored through many rounds by the priest-politician, Shaun, and Shem —who is a veritable caricature of the artist as a young man.

Though the *Portrait* ends with a striking gesture of denial, we must not forget that the last word of *Ulysses* is an emphatic "yes," or that Mrs. Bloom's affirmation is echoed by the conclusion to *Finnegans Wake,* in which nothing is concluded. The waters of the River Liffey, by wending again to the sea, re-establish the natural pattern of fertility. Here was the horizon that first opened up before Stephen when, seeking the light, he walked along the shore. Flying, he then realized, involved the

risk of falling; but he was pledged, like Faust, to strive
and stray. The falling cadence at the end of "The Dead"
is characteristic of Joyce's early prose. His obsession
with death gradually yields in *Ulysses* to a new concern
with life; the fall of man, colliding with the law of falling bodies, is transposed into scientific terms: "thirty-
two feet per sec." No fall but a rising, the reawakening
of Finn MacCool and all the other sleeping heroes of
Irish legend, is the theme of Joyce's literary testament.

Unlike the leprechaun-fanciers of the Celtic Revival,
Joyce did not seek forgotten beauty; he evoked the past
to illuminate the present. The results of this continual
juxtaposition were an ironic attitude and an iconoclastic
technique which temporarily aligned him with Ibsen
and the naturalists. The shock aroused by his incidental
frankness is travestied in H. C. Earwicker, who reproaches himself for indecent exposure. Not exposure
but synthesis is Joyce's final intention. His deeper affin-
ities are with Dante, with the medieval iconographers,
with the symbolic structures that art once built upon
faith. But these, according to Aquinas, require wholeness, harmony, and radiance. How can they be constructed out of the fragments, the discords, and the
obscure details of modern life? By proceeding through
what William James termed "the stream of consciousness" to what Jung terms "the racial unconscious," beyond individual dream to collective myth. From two
Italian philosophers, from Giambattista Vico's cyclical
theory of history and Giordano Bruno's dialectical concept of nature, Joyce learned how to reconcile the principles of unity and diversity: "the same anew."

A phrase from his notebooks, "centripetal writing,"
seems to indicate his direction. The municipal motto of
Dublin, *Obedientia civium urbis felicitas*, gets rather

freely translated in *Finnegans Wake:* "Thine obesity, O civilian, hits the felicitude of our orb!" However, *urbi et orbi,* all roads lead homeward for Joyce. The world was his parish; his universe is parochial. The central human relationships, for him as for Proust, were warmly and tenderly domestic. Joyce's women tend to be either mothers or daughters, Goethean or Dantesque types like the rival heroines of *Exiles,* the maternal Bertha and the virginal Beatrice. His own outlook grew increasingly paternal, as he himself became intensively a family man. From 1904 his exile was lightened by the lifelong companionship of Nora Barnacle, who became his wife. He shared his musical interests with his son, and was especially devoted to his daughter, whose mental illness saddened his last years. His ripest and perhaps his finest poem, *"Ecce Puer,"* marks the double occasion of his father's death and the birth of his only grandchild, Stephen.

Those who confuse a writer with his material find it all too easy to make a scapegoat out of Joyce. They make Proust responsible for the collapse of France because he prophesied it so acutely; and, because Joyce sensed the contemporary need to create a conscience, they accuse him of lacking any sense of values. Of course it is he who should be accusing them.. His work, though far from didactic, is full of moral implications; his example of esthetic idealism, set by abnegation and artistry, is a standing rebuke to facility and venality, callousness and obtuseness. Less peculiarly Joycean, and therefore even more usable in the long run, is his masterly control of social realism, which ingeniously springs the varied traps of Dublin and patiently suffers rebuffs with Mr. Bloom. The heroine of *Stephen Hero,* who has almost disappeared from the *Portrait,* says farewell after "an in-

stant of all but union." By dwelling upon that interrupted nuance, that unconsummated moment, that un-
realized possibility, Joyce renews our apprehension of
reality, strengthens our sympathy with our fellow creatures, and leaves us in awe before the mystery of created things.

HARRY LEVIN

PUBLISHER'S NOTE ON THE TEXTS

The definitive text of *A Portrait of the Artist as a Young
Man* used in this volume was prepared for the 1964
Viking Press edition by Chester G. Anderson, who compared Joyce's final fair-copy manuscript, in his own
handwriting, with all the texts published in England
and America, and with lists of corrections and changes
noted by Joyce, some of which were never made in any
of the published versions. Mr. Anderson then prepared
an extensive list of possible corrections for the current
Viking edition. Richard Ellmann, Joyce's biographer
and the editor of his letters, was asked to act as arbiter,
and made the final selection, which was then incor-
porated in all Viking editions.

The new text of *Dubliners*, restoring Joyce's manuscript style and his later corrections, was prepared for
the 1968 Viking Press edition by Robert Scholes in
consultation with Richard Ellmann. A detailed note on
the text and a list of the emendations is available upon
request from the publisher.

Dubliners

The Definitive Text, restoring Joyce's
manuscript style and his later corrections

MOST of *Dubliners* was written, from earlier notes jotted down on the spot, during Joyce's first year in Trieste, 1905. The manuscript was accepted the following year by the English publisher, Grant Richards, but was not brought out until 1914 because of objections raised by his printers. Meanwhile Joyce had added three more stories to the original twelve and sent them all to the Dublin firm of Maunsel and Company, which printed them, then changed its mind, and destroyed the sheets. When Joyce's insistence finally triumphed over the long delay, the published text included the exceptionable matter: the repetition of "bloody," the innuendo against Edward VII, and—what was most offensive to the Irish publisher and most intrinsic to Joyce's method —the specific mention of local establishments and personalities. The book is not a systematic canvass like *Ulysses;* nor is it integrated, like the *Portrait,* by one intense point of view; but it comprises, as Joyce explained, a series of chapters in the moral history of his community; and the episodes are arranged in careful progression from childhood to maturity, broadening from private to public scope. The older technique of short-story writing, with Maupassant and O.Henry, attempted to make daily life more eventful by unscru-

pulous manipulation of surprises and coincidences. Joyce
—with Chekhov—discarded such contrivances, introducing a genre which has been so widely imitated that
nowadays its originality is not readily detected. The
open structure, which casually adapts itself to the flow
of experience, and the close texture, which gives precise
notation to sensitive observation, are characteristic of
Joycean narrative. The fact that so little happens, apart
from expected routines, connects form with theme: the
paralyzed uneventfulness to which the modern city re-
duces the lives of its citizens. Little of the actual story
need be told: the romance of "Two Gallants" is painfully implicit in conversations before and after. Not one
but many of these sketches might be titled "An Encounter." In calling his original jottings "epiphanies," Joyce
underscored the ironic contrast between the manifestation that dazzled the Magi and the apparitions that
manifest themselves on the streets of Dublin; he also
suggested that those pathetic and sordid glimpses, to
the sentient observer, offer a kind of revelation. As the
part, significantly chosen, reveals the whole, a word or
detail may be enough to exhibit a character or convey
a situation. From his characters and their environment,
from the churchgoers of "Grace" and the politicians of
"Ivy Day in the Committee Room," Joyce fastidiously
detaches himself. Yet the frustrated little people, and
especially the children, always enlist his sympathy. The
last and latest story, "The Dead," is closely identifiable
with his immediate background. Gabriel Conroy is what
Joyce might have become, had he remained in Ireland,
and the closing paragraphs are a valedictory. Many of
these Dubliners, notably Martin Cunningham, reappear
in *Ulysses*. It should not be forgotten that Mr. Bloom's
day first occurred to Joyce as the subject for another
short story.

The Sisters

THERE was no hope for him this time: it was the third stroke. Night after night I had passed the house (it was vacation time) and studied the lighted square of window: and night after night I had found it lighted in the same way, faintly and evenly. If he was dead, I thought, I would see the reflection of candles on the darkened blind for I knew that two candles must be set at the head of a corpse. He had often said to me: *I am not long for this world,* and I had thought his words idle. Now I knew they were true. Every night as I gazed up at the window I said softly to myself the word *paralysis.* It had always sounded strangely in my ears, like the word *gnomon* in the Euclid and the word *simony* in the Catechism. But now it sounded to me like the name of some maleficent and sinful being. It filled me with fear, and yet I longed to be nearer to it and to look upon its deadly work.

Old Cotter was sitting at the fire, smoking, when I came downstairs to supper. While my aunt was ladling out my stirabout he said, as if returning to some former remark of his:

—No, I wouldn't say he was exactly . . . but there was something queer . . . there was something uncanny about him. I'll tell you my opinion. . . .

He began to puff at his pipe, no doubt arranging his opinion in his mind. Tiresome old fool! When we knew him first he used to be rather interesting, talking of faints and worms; but I soon grew tired of him and his endless stories about the distillery.

—I have my own theory about it, he said. I think it was one of those . . . peculiar cases. . . . But it's hard to say. . . .

He began to puff again at his pipe without giving us his theory. My uncle saw me staring and said to me:

—Well, so your old friend is gone, you'll be sorry to hear.

—Who? said I.

—Father Flynn.

—Is he dead?

—Mr Cotter here has just told us. He was passing by the house.

I knew that I was under observation so I continued eating as if the news had not interested me. My uncle explained to old Cotter.

—The youngster and he were great friends. The old chap taught him a great deal, mind you; and they say he had a great wish for him.

—God have mercy on his soul, said my aunt piously.

Old Cotter looked at me for a while. I felt that his little beady black eyes were examining me but I would not satisfy him by looking up from my plate. He returned to his pipe and finally spat rudely into the grate.

—I wouldn't like children of mine, he said, to have too much to say to a man like that.

—How do you mean, Mr Cotter? asked my aunt.

—What I mean is, said old Cotter, it's bad for children. My idea is: let a young lad run about and play with young lads of his own age and not be . . . Am I right, Jack?

—That's my principle, too, said my uncle. Let him learn to box his corner. That's what I'm always saying to that Rosicrucian there: take exercise. Why, when I was a nipper every morning of my life I had a cold bath, winter and summer. And that's what stands to me now. Education is all very fine and large. . . . Mr Cotter might take a pick of that leg of mutton, he added to my aunt.

—No, no, not for me, said old Cotter.

My aunt brought the dish from the safe and laid it on the table.

—But why do you think it's not good for children, Mr Cotter? she asked.

—It's bad for children, said old Cotter, because their minds are so impressionable. When children see things like that, you know, it has an effect. . . .

I crammed my mouth with stirabout for fear I might give utterance to my anger. Tiresome old red-nosed imbecile!

It was late when I fell asleep. Though I was angry with old Cotter for alluding to me as a child I puzzled my head to extract meaning from his unfinished sentences. In the dark of my room I imagined that I saw again the heavy grey face of the paralytic. I drew the blankets over my head and tried to think of Christmas. But the grey face still followed me. It murmured; and I understood that it desired to confess something. I felt my soul receding into some pleasant and vicious region; and there again I found it waiting for me. It began to confess to me in a murmuring voice and I wondered why it smiled continually and why the lips were so moist with spittle. But then I remembered that it had died of paralysis and I felt that I too was smiling feebly as if to absolve the simoniac of his sin.

The next morning after breakfast I went down to look at the little house in Great Britain Street. It was an unassuming shop, registered under the vague name of *Drapery*. The drapery consisted mainly of children's bootees and umbrellas; and on ordinary days a notice used to hang in the window, saying: *Umbrellas Re-covered.* No notice was visible now for the shutters were up. A crape bouquet was tied to the door-knocker with ribbon. Two poor women and a telegram boy were reading the card pinned on the crape. I also approached and read:

July 1st, 1895

The Rev. James Flynn (formerly of S. Catherine's Church, Meath Street), aged sixty-five years.

R.I.P.

The reading of the card persuaded me that he was dead and I was disturbed to find myself at check. Had he not been dead I would have gone into the little dark room behind the shop to find him sitting in his arm-chair by the fire, nearly smothered in his great-coat. Perhaps my aunt would have given me a packet of High Toast for him and this present would have roused him from his stupefied doze. It was always I who emptied the packet into his black snuff-box for his hands trembled too much to allow him to do this without spilling half the snuff about the floor. Even as he raised his large trembling hand to his nose little clouds of smoke dribbled through his fingers over the front of his coat. It may have been these constant showers of snuff which gave his ancient priestly garments their green faded look for the red handkerchief, blackened, as it always was, with the snuff-stains of a week, with which he tried to brush away the fallen grains, was quite inefficacious.

I wished to go in and look at him but I had not the courage to knock. I walked away slowly along the sunny side of the street, reading all the theatrical advertisements in the shop-windows as I went. I found it strange that neither I nor the day seemed in a mourning mood and I felt even annoyed at discovering in myself a sen-

sation of freedom as if I had been freed from something
by his death. I wondered at this for, as my uncle had
said the night before, he had taught me a great deal. He
had studied in the Irish college in Rome and he had
taught me to pronounce Latin properly. He had told me
stories about the catacombs and about Napoleon Bona-
parte, and he had explained to me the meaning of the
different ceremonies of the Mass and of the different
vestments worn by the priest. Sometimes he had amused
himself by putting difficult questions to me, asking me
what one should do in certain circumstances or whether
such and such sins were mortal or venial or only imperfections. His questions showed me how complex and
mysterious were certain institutions of the Church which
I had always regarded as the simplest acts. The duties
of the priest towards the Eucharist and towards the secrecy of the confessional seemed so grave to me that I
wondered how anybody had ever found in himself the
courage to undertake them; and I was not surprised
when he told me that the fathers of the Church had
written books as thick as the *Post Office Directory* and
as closely printed as the law notices in the newspaper,
elucidating all these intricate questions. Often when I
thought of this I could make no answer or only a very
foolish and halting one upon which he used to smile and
nod his head twice or thrice. Sometimes he used to put
me through the responses of the Mass which he had
made me learn by heart; and, as I pattered, he used to
smile pensively and nod his head, now and then pushing
huge pinches of snuff up each nostril alternately. When
he smiled he used to uncover his big discoloured teeth
and let his tongue lie upon his lower lip—a habit which
had made me feel uneasy in the beginning of our acquaintance before I knew him well.

As I walked along in the sun I remembered old Cotter's words and tried to remember what had happened afterwards in the dream. I remembered that I had noticed long velvet curtains and a swinging lamp of antique fashion. I felt that I had been very far away, in some land where the customs were strange—in Persia, I thought. . . . But I could not remember the end of the dream.

In the evening my aunt took me with her to visit the house of mourning. It was after sunset; but the window-panes of the houses that looked to the west reflected the tawny gold of a great bank of clouds. Nannie received us in the hall; and, as it would have been unseemly to have shouted at her, my aunt shook hands with her for all. The old woman pointed upwards interrogatively and, on my aunt's nodding, proceeded to toil up the narrow staircase before us, her bowed head being scarcely above the level of the banister-rail. At the first landing she stopped and beckoned us forward encouragingly towards the open door of the dead-room. My aunt went in and the old woman, seeing that I hesitated to enter, began to beckon to me again repeatedly with her hand.

I went in on tiptoe. The room through the lace end of the blind was suffused with dusky golden light amid which the candles looked like pale thin flames. He had been coffined. Nannie gave the lead and we three knelt down at the foot of the bed. I pretended to pray but I could not gather my thoughts because the old woman's mutterings distracted me. I noticed how clumsily her skirt was hooked at the back and how the heels of her cloth boots were trodden down all to one side. The fancy came to me that the old priest was smiling as he lay there in his coffin.

But no. When we rose and went up to the head of the bed I saw that he was not smiling. There he lay, solemn and copious, vested as for the altar, his large hands loosely retaining a chalice. His face was very truculent, grey and massive, with black cavernous nostrils and circled by a scanty white fur. There was a heavy odour in the room—the flowers.

We blessed ourselves and came away. In the little room downstairs we found Eliza seated in his arm-chair in state. I groped my way towards my usual chair in the corner while Nannie went to the sideboard and brought out a decanter of sherry and some wine-glasses. She set these on the table and invited us to take a little glass of wine. Then, at her sister's bidding, she poured out the sherry into the glasses and passed them to us. She pressed me to take some cream crackers also but I declined because I thought I would make too much noise eating them. She seemed to be somewhat disappointed at my refusal and went over quietly to the sofa where she sat down behind her sister. No one spoke: we all gazed at the empty fireplace.

My aunt waited until Eliza sighed and then said:

—Ah, well, he's gone to a better world.

Eliza sighed again and bowed her head in assent. My aunt fingered the stem of her wine-glass before sipping a little.

—Did he . . . peacefully? she asked.

—O, quite peacefully, ma'am, said Eliza. You couldn't tell when the breath went out of him. He had a beautiful death, God be praised.

—And everything . . . ?

—Father O'Rourke was in with him a Tuesday and anointed him and prepared him and all.

—He knew then?

—He was quite resigned.

—He looks quite resigned, said my aunt.

—That's what the woman we had in to wash him said. She said he just looked as if he was asleep, he looked that peaceful and resigned. No one would think he'd make such a beautiful corpse.

—Yes, indeed, said my aunt.

She sipped a little more from her glass and said:

—Well, Miss Flynn, at any rate it must be a great comfort for you to know that you did all you could for him. You were both very kind to him, I must say.

Eliza smoothed her dress over her knees.

—Ah, poor James! she said. God knows we done all we could, as poor as we are—we wouldn't see him want anything while he was in it.

Nannie had leaned her head against the sofa-pillow and seemed about to fall asleep.

—There's poor Nannie, said Eliza, looking at her, she's wore out. All the work we had, she and me, getting in the woman to wash him and then laying him out and then the coffin and then arranging about the Mass in the chapel. Only for Father O'Rourke I don't know what we'd have done at all. It was him brought us all them flowers and them two candlesticks out of the chapel and wrote out the notice for the *Freeman's General* and took charge of all the papers for the cemetery and poor James's insurance.

—Wasn't that good of him? said my aunt.

Eliza closed her eyes and shook her head slowly.

—Ah, there's no friends like the old friends, she said, when all is said and done, no friends that a body can trust.

—Indeed, that's true, said my aunt. And I'm sure now that he's gone to his eternal reward he won't forget you and all your kindness to him.

—Ah, poor James! said Eliza. He was no great trouble to us. You wouldn't hear him in the house any more than now. Still, I know he's gone and all to that. . . .

—It's when it's all over that you'll miss him, said my aunt.

—I know that, said Eliza. I won't be bringing him in his cup of beef-tea any more, nor you, ma'am, sending him his snuff. Ah, poor James!

She stopped, as if she were communing with the past and then said shrewdly:

—Mind you, I noticed there was something queer coming over him latterly. Whenever I'd bring in his soup to him there I'd find him with his breviary fallen to the floor, lying back in the chair and his mouth open.

She laid a finger against her nose and frowned: then she continued:

—But still and all he kept on saying that before the summer was over he'd go out for a drive one fine day just to see the old house again where we were all born down in Irishtown and take me and Nannie with him. If we could only get one of them new-fangled carriages that makes no noise that Father O'Rourke told him about—them with the rheumatic wheels—for the day cheap, he said, at Johnny Rush's over the way there and drive out the three of us together of a Sunday evening. He had his mind set on that. . . . Poor James!

—The Lord have mercy on his soul! said my aunt.

Eliza took out her handkerchief and wiped her eyes with it. Then she put it back again in her pocket and gazed into the empty grate for some time without speaking.

—He was too scrupulous always, she said. The duties of the priesthood was too much for him. And then his life was, you might say, crossed.

—Yes, said my aunt. He was a disappointed man. You could see that.

A silence took possession of the little room and, under

cover of it, I approached the table and tasted my sherry and then returned quietly to my chair in the corner. Eliza seemed to have fallen into a deep revery. We waited respectfully for her to break the silence: and after a long pause she said slowly:

—It was that chalice he broke. . . . That was the beginning of it. Of course, they say it was all right, that it contained nothing, I mean. But still. . . . They say it was the boy's fault. But poor James was so nervous, God be merciful to him!

—And was that it? said my aunt. I heard something. . . .

Eliza nodded.

—That affected his mind, she said. After that he began to mope by himself, talking to no one and wandering about by himself. So one night he was wanted for to go on a call and they couldn't find him anywhere. They looked high up and low down; and still they couldn't see a sight of him anywhere. So then the clerk suggested to try the chapel. So then they got the keys and opened the chapel and the clerk and Father O'Rourke and another priest that was there brought in a light for to look for him. . . . And what do you think but there he was, sitting up by himself in the dark in his confession-box, wide-awake and laughing-like softly to himself?

She stopped suddenly as if to listen. I too listened; but there was no sound in the house: and I knew that the old priest was lying still in his coffin as we had seen him, solemn and truculent in death, an idle chalice on his breast.

Eliza resumed:

—Wide-awake and laughing-like to himself. . . . So then, of course, when they saw that, that made them think that there was something gone wrong with him. . . .

An Encounter

IT WAS Joe Dillon who introduced the Wild West to us. He had a little library made up of old numbers of *The Union Jack, Pluck* and *The Halfpenny Marvel*. Every evening after school we met in his back garden and arranged Indian battles. He and his fat young brother Leo the idler held the loft of the stable while we tried to carry it by storm; or we fought a pitched battle on the grass. But, however well we fought, we never won siege or battle and all our bouts ended with Joe Dillon's war dance of victory. His parents went to eight-o'clock mass every morning in Gardiner Street and the peaceful odour of Mrs Dillon was prevalent in the hall of the house. But he played too fiercely for us who were younger and more timid. He looked like some kind of an Indian when he capered round the garden, an old tea-cosy on his head, beating a tin with his fist and yelling:

—Ya! yaka, yaka, yaka!

Everyone was incredulous when it was reported that he had a vocation for the priesthood. Nevertheless it was true.

A spirit of unruliness diffused itself among us and, under its influence, differences of culture and constitution were waived. We banded ourselves together, some boldly, some in jest and some almost in fear: and of the number of these latter, the reluctant Indians who were afraid to seem studious or lacking in robustness, I was one. The adventures related in the literature of the Wild

West were remote from my nature but, at least, they opened doors of escape. I liked better some American detective stories which were traversed from time to time by unkempt fierce and beautiful girls. Though there was nothing wrong in these stories and though their intention was sometimes literary they were circulated secretly at school. One day when Father Butler was hearing the four pages of Roman History clumsy Leo Dillon was discovered with a copy of *The Halfpenny Marvel.*

—This page or this page? This page? Now, Dillon, up! *Hardly had the day . . .* Go on! What day? *Hardly had the day dawned . . .* Have you studied it? What have you there in your pocket?

Everyone's heart palpitated as Leo Dillon handed up the paper and everyone assumed an innocent face. Father Butler turned over the pages, frowning.

—What is this rubbish? he said. *The Apache Chief!* Is this what you read instead of studying your Roman History? Let me not find any more of this wretched stuff in this college. The man who wrote it, I suppose, was some wretched scribbler that writes these things for a drink. I'm surprised at boys like you, educated, reading such stuff. I could understand it if you were . . . National School boys. Now, Dillon, I advise you strongly, get at your work or . . .

This rebuke during the sober hours of school paled much of the glory of the Wild West for me and the confused puffy face of Leo Dillon awakened one of my consciences. But when the restraining influence of the school was at a distance I began to hunger again for wild sensations, for the escape which those chronicles of disorder alone seemed to offer me. The mimic warfare of the evening became at last as wearisome to me as the routine of school in the morning because I wanted real adventures to happen to myself. But real adventures, I reflected, do not happen to people who remain at home: they must be sought abroad.

The summer holidays were near at hand when I made up my mind to break out of the weariness of school-life for one day at least. With Leo Dillon and a boy named Mahony I planned a day's miching. Each of us saved up sixpence. We were to meet at ten in the morning on the Canal Bridge. Mahony's big sister was to write an excuse for him and Leo Dillon was to tell his brother to say he was sick. We arranged to go along the Wharf Road until we came to the ships, then to cross in the ferryboat and walk out to see the Pigeon House. Leo Dillon was afraid we might meet Father Butler or someone out of the college; but Mahony asked, very sensibly, what would Father Butler be doing out at the Pigeon House. We were reassured: and I brought the first stage of the plot to an end by collecting sixpence from the other two, at the same time showing them my own sixpence. When we were making the last arrangements on the eve we were all vaguely excited. We shook hands, laughing, and Mahony said:

—Till to-morrow, mates.

That night I slept badly. In the morning I was first-comer to the bridge as I lived nearest. I hid my books in the long grass near the ashpit at the end of the garden where nobody ever came and hurried along the canal bank. It was a mild sunny morning in the first week of June. I sat up on the coping of the bridge admiring my frail canvas shoes which I had diligently pipeclayed overnight and watching the docile horses pulling a tram-load of business people up the hill. All the branches of the tall trees which lined the mall were gay with little light green leaves and the sunlight slanted through them on to the water. The granite stone of the bridge was beginning to be warm and I began to pat it with my hands in time to an air in my head. I was very happy.

When I had been sitting there for five or ten minutes I saw Mahony's grey suit approaching. He came up the hill, smiling, and clambered up beside me on the bridge. While we were waiting he brought out the catapult which bulged from his inner pocket and explained some improvements which he had made in it. I asked him why he had brought it and he told me he had brought it to have some gas with the birds. Mahony used slang freely, and spoke of Father Butler as Bunsen Burner. We waited on for a quarter of an hour more but still there was no sign of Leo Dillon. Mahony, at last, jumped down and said:

—Come along. I knew Fatty'd funk it.

—And his sixpence . . . ? I said.

—That's forfeit, said Mahony. And so much the better for us—a bob and a tanner instead of a bob.

We walked along the North Strand Road till we came to the Vitriol Works and then turned to the right along the Wharf Road. Mahony began to play the Indian as soon as we were out of public sight. He chased a crowd of ragged girls, brandishing his unloaded catapult and, when two ragged boys began, out of chivalry, to fling stones at us, he proposed that we should charge them. I objected that the boys were too small, and so we walked on, the ragged troop screaming after us: *Swaddlers! Swaddlers!* thinking that we were Protestants because Mahony, who was dark-complexioned, wore the silver badge of a cricket club in his cap. When we came to the Smoothing Iron we arranged a siege; but it was a failure because you must have at least three. We revenged ourselves on Leo Dillon by saying what a funk he was and guessing how many he would get at three o'clock from Mr Ryan.

We came then near the river. We spent a long time walking about the noisy streets flanked by high stone walls, watching the working of cranes and engines and often being shouted at for our immobility by the drivers of groaning carts. It was noon when we reached the quays and, as all the labourers seemed to be eating their lunches, we bought two big currant buns and sat down to eat them on some metal piping beside the river. We pleased ourselves with the spectacle of Dublin's commerce—the barges signalled from far away by their curls of woolly smoke, the brown fishing fleet beyond Ringsend, the big white sailing-vessel which was being discharged on the opposite quay. Mahony said it would be right skit to run away to sea on one of those big ships and even I, looking at the high masts, saw, or imagined, the geography which had been scantily dosed to me at school gradually taking substance under my eyes. School and home seemed to recede from us and their influences upon us seemed to wane.

We crossed the Liffey in the ferryboat, paying our toll to be transported in the company of two labourers and a little Jew with a bag. We were serious to the point of solemnity, but once during the short voyage our eyes met and we laughed. When we landed we watched the discharging of the graceful three-master which we had observed from the other quay. Some bystander said that she was a Norwegian vessel. I went to the stern and tried to decipher the legend upon it but, failing to do so, I came back and examined the foreign sailors to see had any of them green eyes for I had some confused notion. . . . The sailors' eyes were blue and grey and even black. The only sailor whose eyes could have been called green was a tall man who amused the crowd on the quay by calling out cheerfully every time the planks fell:

—All right! All right!

When we were tired of this sight we wandered slowly
into Ringsend. The day had grown sultry, and in the
windows of the grocers' shops musty biscuits lay bleaching. We bought some biscuits and chocolate which we
ate sedulously as we wandered through the squalid
streets where the families of the fishermen live. We
could find no dairy and so we went into a huckster's
shop and bought a bottle of raspberry lemonade each.
Refreshed by this, Mahony chased a cat down a lane,
but the cat escaped into a wide field. We both felt
rather tired and when we reached the field we made
at once for a sloping bank over the ridge of which we
could see the Dodder.

It was too late and we were too tired to carry out our
project of visiting the Pigeon House. We had to be
home before four o'clock lest our adventure should be
discovered. Mahony looked regretfully at his catapult
and I had to suggest going home by train before he re-
gained any cheerfulness. The sun went in behind some
clouds and left us to our jaded thoughts and the crumbs
of our provisions.

There was nobody but ourselves in the field. When
we had lain on the bank for some time without speaking
I saw a man approaching from the far end of the field. I
watched him lazily as I chewed one of those green stems
on which girls tell fortunes. He came along by the bank
slowly. He walked with one hand upon his hip and in
the other hand he held a stick with which he tapped
the turf lightly. He was shabbily dressed in a suit of
greenish-black and wore what we used to call a jerry
hat with a high crown. He seemed to be fairly old for
his moustache was ashen-grey. When he passed at our
feet he glanced up at us quickly and then continued his
way. We followed him with our eyes and saw that when

he had gone on for perhaps fifty paces he turned about and began to retrace his steps. He walked towards us very slowly, always tapping the ground with his stick, so slowly that I thought he was looking for something in the grass.

He stopped when he came level with us and bade us good-day. We answered him and he sat down beside us on the slope slowly and with great care. He began to talk of the weather, saying that it would be a very hot summer and adding that the seasons had changed greatly since he was a boy—a long time ago. He said that the happiest time of one's life was undoubtedly one's schoolboy days and that he would give anything to be young again. While he expressed these sentiments which bored us a little we kept silent. Then he began to talk of school and of books. He asked us whether we had read the poetry of Thomas Moore or the works of Sir Walter Scott and Lord Lytton. I pretended that I had read every book he mentioned so that in the end he said:

—Ah, I can see you are a bookworm like myself. Now, he added, pointing to Mahony who was regarding us with open eyes, he is different; he goes in for games.

He said he had all Sir Walter Scott's works and all Lord Lytton's works at home and never tired of reading them. Of course, he said, there were some of Lord Lytton's works which boys couldn't read. Mahony asked why couldn't boys read them—a question which agitated and pained me because I was afraid the man would think I was as stupid as Mahony. The man, however, only smiled. I saw that he had great gaps in his mouth between his yellow teeth. Then he asked us which of us had the most sweethearts. Mahony mentioned lightly that he had three totties. The man asked me how many had I. I answered that I had none. He did not believe me and said he was sure I must have one. I was silent.

—Tell us, said Mahony pertly to the man, how many have you yourself?

The man smiled as before and said that when he was our age he had lots of sweethearts.

—Every boy, he said, has a little sweetheart.

His attitude on this point struck me as strangely liberal in a man of his age. In my heart I thought that what he said about boys and sweethearts was reasonable. But I disliked the words in his mouth and I wondered why he shivered once or twice as if he feared something or felt a sudden chill. As he proceeded I noticed that his accent was good. He began to speak to us about girls, saying what nice soft hair they had and how soft their hands were and how all girls were not so good as they seemed to be if one only knew. There was nothing he liked, he said, so much as looking at a nice young girl, at her nice white hands and her beautiful soft hair. He gave me the impression that he was repeating something which he had learned by heart or that, magnetised by some words of his own speech, his mind was slowly circling round and round in the same orbit. At times he spoke as if he were simply alluding to some fact that everybody knew, and at times he lowered his voice and spoke mysteriously as if he were telling us something secret which he did not wish others to overhear. He repeated his phrases over and over again, varying them and surrounding them with his monotonous voice. I continued to gaze towards the foot of the slope, listening to him.

After a long while his monologue paused. He stood up slowly, saying that he had to leave us for a minute or so, a few minutes, and, without changing the direction of

my gaze, I saw him walking slowly away from us towards the near end of the field. We remained silent
when he had gone. After a silence of a few minutes I
heard Mahony exclaim:

—I say! Look what he's doing!

As I neither answered nor raised my eyes Mahony
exclaimed again:

—I say . . . He's a queer old josser!

—In case he asks us for our names, I said, let you be
Murphy and I'll be Smith.

We said nothing further to each other. I was still
considering whether I would go away or not when the
man came back and sat down beside us again. Hardly
had he sat down when Mahony, catching sight of the
cat which had escaped him, sprang up and pursued her
across the field. The man and I watched the chase.
The cat escaped once more and Mahony began to throw
stones at the wall she had escaladed. Desisting from
this, he began to wander about the far end of the field,
aimlessly.

After an interval the man spoke to me. He said that
my friend was a very rough boy and asked did he get
whipped often at school. I was going to reply indignantly that we were not National School boys to be
whipped, as he called it; but I remained silent. He began
to speak on the subject of chastising boys. His mind,
as if magnetised again by his speech, seemed to circle
slowly round and round its new centre. He said that
when boys were that kind they ought to be whipped
and well whipped. When a boy was rough and unruly
there was nothing would do him any good but a good
sound whipping. A slap on the hand or a box on the ear
was no good: what he wanted was to get a nice warm
whipping. I was surprised at this sentiment and involun-

tarily glanced up at his face. As I did so I met the gaze of a pair of bottle-green eyes peering at me from under a twitching forehead. I turned my eyes away again.

The man continued his monologue. He seemed to have forgotten his recent liberalism. He said that if ever he found a boy talking to girls or having a girl for a sweetheart he would whip him and whip him; and that would teach him not to be talking to girls. And if a boy had a girl for a sweetheart and told lies about it then he would give him such a whipping as no boy ever got in this world. He said that there was nothing in this world he would like so well as that. He described to me how he would whip such a boy as if he were unfolding some elaborate mystery. He would love that, he said, better than anything in this world; and his voice, as he led me monotonously through the mystery, grew almost affectionate and seemed to plead with me that I should understand him.

I waited till his monologue paused again. Then I stood up abruptly. Lest I should betray my agitation I delayed a few moments pretending to fix my shoe properly and then, saying that I was obliged to go, I bade him good-day. I went up the slope calmly but my heart was beating quickly with fear that he would seize me by the ankles. When I reached the top of the slope I turned round and, without looking at him, called loudly across the field:

—Murphy!

My voice had an accent of forced bravery in it and I was ashamed of my paltry stratagem. I had to call the name again before Mahony saw me and hallooed in answer. How my heart beat as he came running across the field to me! He ran as if to bring me aid. And I was penitent; for in my heart I had always despised him a little.

Araby

NORTH RICHMOND STREET, being blind, was a quiet street except at the hour when the Christian Brothers' School set the boys free. An uninhabited house of two storeys stood at the blind end, detached from its neighbours in a square ground. The other houses of the street, conscious of decent lives within them, gazed at one another with brown imperturbable faces.

The former tenant of our house, a priest, had died in the back drawing-room. Air, musty from having been long enclosed, hung in all the rooms, and the waste room behind the kitchen was littered with old useless papers. Among these I found a few paper-covered books, the pages of which were curled and damp: *The Abbot,* by Walter Scott, *The Devout Communicant* and *The Memoirs of Vidocq.* I liked the last best because its leaves were yellow. The wild garden behind the house contained a central apple-tree and a few straggling bushes under one of which I found the late tenant's rusty bicycle-pump. He had been a very charitable priest; in his will he had left all his money to institutions and the furniture of his house to his sister.

When the short days of winter came dusk fell before we had well eaten our dinners. When we met in the street the houses had grown sombre. The space of sky above us was the colour of ever-changing violet and towards it the lamps of the street lifted their feeble lanterns. The cold air stung us and we played till our bodies glowed. Our shouts echoed in the silent street. The career of our play brought us through the dark muddy lanes behind the houses where we ran the gantlet of the rough tribes from the cottages, to the back doors of the dark dripping gardens where odours arose from the ashpits, to the dark odorous stables where a coachman smoothed and combed the horse or shook music from the buckled harness. When we returned to the street light from the kitchen windows had filled the areas. If my uncle was seen turning the corner we hid in the shadow until we had seen him safely housed. Or if Mangan's sister came out on the doorstep to call her brother in to his tea we watched her from our shadow peer up and down the street. We waited to see whether she would remain or go in and, if she remained, we left our shadow and walked up to Mangan's steps resignedly. She was waiting for us, her figure defined by the light from the half-opened door. Her brother always teased her before he obeyed and I stood by the railings looking at her. Her dress swung as she moved her body and the soft rope of her hair tossed from side to side.

Every morning I lay on the floor in the front parlour watching her door. The blind was pulled down to within an inch of the sash so that I could not be seen. When she came out on the doorstep my heart leaped. I ran to the hall, seized my books and followed her. I kept her brown figure always in my eye and, when we came near the point at which our ways diverged, I quickened my pace and passed her. This happened morning after morning. I had never spoken to her, except for a few casual words, and yet her name was like a summons to all my foolish blood.

Her image accompanied me even in places the most hostile to romance. On Saturday evenings when my aunt went marketing I had to go to carry some of the parcels. We walked through the flaring streets, jostled by drunken men and bargaining women, amid the curses of labourers, the shrill litanies of shop-boys who stood on guard by the barrels of pigs' cheeks, the nasal chanting of street-singers, who sang a *come-all-you* about O'Donovan Rossa, or a ballad about the troubles in our native land. These noises converged in a single sensation of life for me: I imagined that I bore my chalice safely through a throng of foes. Her name sprang to my lips at moments in strange prayers and praises which I myself did not understand. My eyes were often full of tears (I could not tell why) and at times a flood from my heart seemed to pour itself out into my bosom. I thought little of the future. I did not know whether I would ever speak to her or not or, if I spoke to her, how I could tell her of my confused adoration. But my body was like a harp and her words and gestures were like fingers running upon the wires.

One evening I went into the back drawing-room in which the priest had died. It was a dark rainy evening and there was no sound in the house. Through one of the broken panes I heard the rain impinge upon the earth, the fine incessant needles of water playing in the sodden beds. Some distant lamp or lighted window gleamed below me. I was thankful that I could see so little. All my senses seemed to desire to veil themselves and, feeling that I was about to slip from them, I pressed the palms of my hands together until they trembled, murmuring: *O love! O love!* many times.

At last she spoke to me. When she addressed the first words to me I was so confused that I did not know what to answer. She asked me was I going to *Araby*. I forget whether I answered yes or no. It would be a splendid bazaar, she said; she would love to go.

—And why can't you? I asked.

While she spoke she turned a silver bracelet round and round her wrist. She could not go, she said, because there would be a retreat that week in her convent. Her brother and two other boys were fighting for their caps and I was alone at the railings. She held one of the spikes, bowing her head towards me. The light from the lamp opposite our door caught the white curve of her neck, lit up her hair that rested there and, falling, lit up the hand upon the railing. It fell over one side of her dress and caught the white border of a petticoat, just visible as she stood at ease.

—It's well for you, she said.

—If I go, I said, I will bring you something.

What innumerable follies laid waste my waking and sleeping thoughts after that evening! I wished to annihilate the tedious intervening days. I chafed against the work of school. At night in my bedroom and by day in the classroom her image came between me and the page I strove to read. The syllables of the word *Araby* were called to me through the silence in which my soul luxuriated and cast an Eastern enchantment over me. I asked for leave to go to the bazaar on Saturday night. My aunt was surprised and hoped it was not some Freemason's affair. I answered few questions in class. I watched my master's face pass from amiability to sternness; he hoped I was not beginning to idle. I could not call my wandering thoughts together. I had hardly any patience with the serious work of life which, now that it stood between me and my desire, seemed to me child's play, ugly monotonous child's play.

On Saturday morning I reminded my uncle that I wished to go to the bazaar in the evening. He was fussing at the hallstand, looking for the hat-brush, and answered me curtly:

—Yes, boy, I know.

As he was in the hall I could not go into the front
parlour and lie at the window. I left the house in bad
humour and walked slowly towards the school. The air
was pitilessly raw and already my heart misgave me.

When I came home to dinner my uncle had not yet
been home. Still it was early. I sat staring at the clock
for some time and, when its ticking began to irritate me,
I left the room. I mounted the staircase and gained the
upper part of the house. The high cold empty gloomy
rooms liberated me and I went from room to room singing. From the front window I saw my companions playing below in the street. Their cries reached me weakened
and indistinct and, leaning my forehead against the cool
glass, I looked over at the dark house where she lived.
I may have stood there for an hour, seeing nothing but
the brown-clad figure cast by my imagination, touched
discreetly by the lamplight at the curved neck, at the
hand upon the railings and at the border below the dress.

When I came downstairs again I found Mrs Mercer
sitting at the fire. She was an old garrulous woman, a
pawnbroker's widow, who collected used stamps for
some pious purpose. I had to endure the gossip of the
tea-table. The meal was prolonged beyond an hour and
still my uncle did not come. Mrs Mercer stood up to go:
she was sorry she couldn't wait any longer, but it was
after eight o'clock and she did not like to be out late,
as the night air was bad for her. When she had gone
I began to walk up and down the room, clenching my
fists. My aunt said:

—I'm afraid you may put off your bazaar for this night
of Our Lord.

At nine o'clock I heard my uncle's latchkey in the
halldoor. I heard him talking to himself and heard the
hallstand rocking when it had received the weight of his
overcoat. I could interpret these signs. When he was

midway through his dinner I asked him to give me the money to go to the bazaar. He had forgotten.

—The people are in bed and after their first sleep now, he said.

I did not smile. My aunt said to him energetically:

—Can't you give him the money and let him go? You've kept him late enough as it is.

My uncle said he was very sorry he had forgotten. He said he believed in the old saying: *All work and no play makes Jack a dull boy.* He asked me where I was going and, when I had told him a second time he asked me did I know *The Arab's Farewell to his Steed.* When I left the kitchen he was about to recite the opening lines of the piece to my aunt.

I held a florin tightly in my hand as I strode down Buckingham Street towards the station. The sight of the streets thronged with buyers and glaring with gas recalled to me the purpose of my journey. I took my seat in a third-class carriage of a deserted train. After an intolerable delay the train moved out of the station slowly. It crept onward among ruinous houses and over the twinkling river. At Westland Row Station a crowd of people pressed to the carriage doors; but the porters moved them back, saying that it was a special train for the bazaar. I remained alone in the bare carriage. In a few minutes the train drew up beside an improvised wooden platform. I passed out on to the road and saw by the lighted dial of a clock that it was ten minutes to ten. In front of me was a large building which displayed the magical name.

I could not find any sixpenny entrance and, fearing that the bazaar would be closed, I passed in quickly through a turnstile, handing a shilling to a weary-looking man. I found myself in a big hall girdled at half its height by a gallery. Nearly all the stalls were closed and the greater part of the hall was in darkness. I recognised a silence like that which pervades a church after a service. I walked into the centre of the bazaar timidly. A few people were gathered about the stalls which were still open. Before a curtain, over which the words *Café Chantant* were written in coloured lamps, two men were counting money on a salver. I listened to the fall of the coins.

Remembering with difficulty why I had come I went over to one of the stalls and examined porcelain vases and flowered tea-sets. At the door of the stall a young lady was talking and laughing with two young gentlemen. I remarked their English accents and listened vaguely to their conversation.

—O, I never said such a thing!

—O, but you did!

—O, but I didn't!

—Didn't she say that?

—Yes. I heard her.

—O, there's a . . . fib!

Observing me the young lady came over and asked me did I wish to buy anything. The tone of her voice was not encouraging; she seemed to have spoken to me out of a sense of duty. I looked humbly at the great jars that stood like eastern guards at either side of the dark entrance to the stall and murmured:

—No, thank you.

The young lady changed the position of one of the vases and went back to the two young men. They began to talk of the same subject. Once or twice the young lady glanced at me over her shoulder.

I lingered before her stall, though I knew my stay was useless, to make my interest in her wares seem the more real. Then I turned away slowly and walked down the middle of the bazaar. I allowed the two pennies to fall against the sixpence in my pocket. I heard a voice call from one end of the gallery that the light was out. The upper part of the hall was now completely dark.

Gazing up into the darkness I saw myself as a creature driven and derided by vanity; and my eyes burned with anguish and anger.

Eveline

S HE sat at the window watching the evening invade the avenue. Her head was leaned against the window curtains and in her nostrils was the odour of dusty cretonne. She was tired.

Few people passed. The man out of the last house passed on his way home; she heard his footsteps clacking along the concrete pavement and afterwards crunching on the cinder path before the new red houses. One time there used to be a field there in which they used to play every evening with other people's children. Then a man from Belfast bought the field and built houses in it— not like their little brown houses but bright brick houses with shining roofs. The children of the avenue used to play together in that field—the Devines, the Waters, the Dunns, little Keogh the cripple, she and her brothers and sisters. Ernest, however, never played: he was too grown up. Her father used often to hunt them in out of the field with his blackthorn stick; but usually little Keogh used to keep *nix* and call out when he saw her father coming. Still they seemed to have been rather happy then. Her father was not so bad then; and besides, her mother was alive. That was a long time ago;

she and her brothers and sisters were all grown up; her mother was dead. Tizzie Dunn was dead, too, and the Waters had gone back to England. Everything changes. Now she was going to go away like the others, to leave her home.

Home! She looked round the room, reviewing all its familiar objects which she had dusted once a week for so many years, wondering where on earth all the dust came from. Perhaps she would never see again those familiar objects from which she had never dreamed of being divided. And yet during all those years she had never found out the name of the priest whose yellowing photograph hung on the wall above the broken harmonium beside the coloured print of the promises made to Blessed Margaret Mary Alacoque. He had been a school friend of her father. Whenever he showed the photograph to a visitor her father used to pass it with a casual word:

—He is in Melbourne now.

She had consented to go away, to leave her home. Was that wise? She tried to weigh each side of the question. In her home anyway she had shelter and food; she had those whom she had known all her life about her. Of course she had to work hard both in the house and at business. What would they say of her in the Stores when they found out that she had run away with a fellow? Say she was a fool, perhaps, and her place would be filled up by advertisement. Miss Gavan would be glad. She had always had an edge on her, especially whenever there were people listening.

—Miss Hill, don't you see these ladies are waiting?

—Look lively, Miss Hill, please.

She would not cry many tears at leaving the Stores.

But in her new home, in a distant unknown country, it would not be like that. Then she would be married—

she, Eveline. People would treat her with respect then. She would not be treated as her mother had been. Even now, though she was over nineteen, she sometimes felt herself in danger of her father's violence. She knew it was that that had given her the palpitations. When they were growing up he had never gone for her, like he used to go for Harry and Ernest, because she was a girl; but latterly he had begun to threaten her and say what he would do to her only for her dead mother's sake. And now she had nobody to protect her. Ernest was dead and Harry, who was in the church decorating business, was nearly always down somewhere in the country. Besides, the invariable squabble for money on Saturday nights had begun to weary her unspeakably. She always gave her entire wages—seven shillings—and Harry always sent up what he could but the trouble was to get any money from her father. He said she used to squander the money, that she had no head, that he wasn't going to give her his hard-earned money to throw about the streets, and much more, for he was usually fairly bad of a Saturday night. In the end he would give her the money and ask her had she any intention of buying Sunday's dinner. Then she had to rush out as quickly as she could and do her marketing, holding her black leather purse tightly in her hand as she elbowed her way through the crowds and returning home late under her load of provisions. She had hard work to keep the house together and to see that the two young children who had been left to her charge went to school regularly and got their meals regularly. It was hard work—a hard life—but now that she was about to leave it she did not find it a wholly undesirable life.

She was about to explore another life with Frank. Frank was very kind, manly, open-hearted. She was to go away with him by the night-boat to be his wife and to live with him in Buenos Ayres where he had a home waiting for her. How well she remembered the first time she had seen him; he was lodging in a house on the main road where she used to visit. It seemed a few weeks ago. He was standing at the gate, his peaked cap pushed back on his head and his hair tumbled forward over a face of bronze. Then they had come to know each other. He used to meet her outside the Stores every evening and see her home. He took her to see *The Bohemian Girl* and she felt elated as she sat in an unaccustomed part of the theatre with him. He was awfully fond of music and sang a little. People knew that they were courting and, when he sang about the lass that loves a sailor, she always felt pleasantly confused. He used to call her Poppens out of fun. First of all it had been an excitement for her to have a fellow and then she had begun to like him. He had tales of distant countries. He had started as a deck boy at a pound a month on a ship of the Allan Line going out to Canada. He told her the names of the ships he had been on and the names of the different services. He had sailed through the Straits of Magellan and he told her stories of the terrible Patagonians. He had fallen on his feet in Buenos Ayres, he said, and had come over to the old country just for a holiday. Of course, her father had found out the affair and had forbidden her to have anything to say to him.

—I know these sailor chaps, he said.

One day he had quarrelled with Frank and after that she had to meet her lover secretly.

The evening deepened in the avenue. The white of two letters in her lap grew indistinct. One was to Harry; the other was to her father. Ernest had been her favourite but she liked Harry too. Her father was becoming old lately, she noticed; he would miss her. Sometimes he could be very nice. Not long before, when she had been

laid up for a day, he had read her out a ghost story and
made toast for her at the fire. Another day, when their
mother was alive, they had all gone for a picnic to the
Hill of Howth. She remembered her father putting on
her mother's bonnet to make the children laugh.

Her time was running out but she continued to sit by
the window, leaning her head against the window curtain, inhaling the odour of dusty cretonne. Down far in
the avenue she could hear a street organ playing. She
knew the air. Strange that it should come that very
night to remind her of the promise to her mother, her
promise to keep the home together as long as she could.
She remembered the last night of her mother's illness;
she was again in the close dark room at the other side of
the hall and outside she heard a melancholy air of
Italy. The organ-player had been ordered to go away
and given sixpence. She remembered her father strutting back into the sickroom saying:

—Damned Italians! coming over here!

As she mused the pitiful vision of her mother's life
laid its spell on the very quick of her being—that life
of commonplace sacrifices closing in final craziness. She
trembled as she heard again her mother's voice saying
constantly with foolish insistence:

—Derevaun Seraun! Derevaun Seraun!

She stood up in a sudden impulse of terror. Escape!
She must escape! Frank would save her. He would give
her life, perhaps love, too. But she wanted to live. Why
should she be unhappy? She had a right to happiness.
Frank would take her in his arms, fold her in his arms.
He would save her.

.   .   .   .

She stood among the swaying crowd in the station at
the North Wall. He held her hand and she knew that
he was speaking to her, saying something about the pas-

sage over and over again. The station was full of soldiers
with brown baggages. Through the wide doors of the
sheds she caught a glimpse of the black mass of the boat,
lying in beside the quay wall, with illumined portholes.
She answered nothing. She felt her cheek pale and cold
and, out of a maze of distress, she prayed to God to
direct her, to show her what was her duty. The boat
blew a long mournful whistle into the mist. If she went,
to-morrow she would be on the sea with Frank, steaming towards Buenos Ayres. Their passage had been
booked. Could she still draw back after all he had done
for her? Her distress awoke a nausea in her body and
she kept moving her lips in silent fervent prayer.

A bell clanged upon her heart. She felt him seize her
hand:

—Come!

All the seas of the world tumbled about her heart.
He was drawing her into them: he would drown her.
She gripped with both hands at the iron railing.

—Come!

No! No! No! It was impossible. Her hands clutched
the iron in frenzy. Amid the seas she sent a cry of
anguish!

—Eveline! Evvy!

He rushed beyond the barrier and called to her to
follow. He was shouted at to go on but he still called to
her. She set her white face to him, passive, like a helpless animal. Her eyes gave him no sign of love or farewell or recognition.

After the Race

THE cars came scudding in towards Dublin, running evenly like pellets in the groove of the Naas Road. At the crest of the hill at Inchicore sightseers had gathered in clumps to watch the cars careering homeward and through this channel of poverty and inaction the Continent sped its wealth and industry. Now and again the clumps of people raised the cheer of the gratefully oppressed. Their sympathy, however, was for the blue cars—the cars of their friends, the French.

The French, moreover, were virtual victors. Their team had finished solidly; they had been placed second and third and the driver of the winning German car was reported a Belgian. Each blue car, therefore, received a double round of welcome as it topped the crest of the hill and each cheer of welcome was acknowledged with smiles and nods by those in the car. In one of these trimly built cars was a party of four young men whose spirits seemed to be at present well above the level of successful Gallicism: in fact, these four young men were almost hilarious. They were Charles Ségouin, the owner of the car; André Rivière, a young electrician of Canadian birth; a huge Hungarian named Villona and a neatly groomed young man named Doyle. Ségouin was in good humour because he had unexpectedly received some orders in advance (he was about to start a motor establishment in Paris) and Rivière was in good humour because he was to be appointed manager of the establishment; these two young men (who were cousins)

were also in good humour because of the success of the
French cars. Villona was in good humour because he
had had a very satisfactory luncheon; and besides he
was an optimist by nature. The fourth member of the
party, however, was too excited to be genuinely happy.

He was about twenty-six years of age, with a soft,
light brown moustache and rather innocent-looking grey
eyes. His father who had begun life as an advanced
Nationalist, had modified his views early. He had made
his money as a butcher in Kingstown and by opening
shops in Dublin and in the suburbs he had made his
money many times over. He had also been fortunate
enough to secure some of the police contracts and in the
end he had become rich enough to be alluded to in the
Dublin newspapers as a merchant prince. He had sent
his son to England to be educated in a big Catholic college and had afterwards sent him to Dublin University
to study law. Jimmy did not study very earnestly and
took to bad courses for a while. He had money and he
was popular; and he divided his time curiously between
musical and motoring circles. Then he had been sent
for a term to Cambridge to see a little life. His father,
remonstrative, but covertly proud of the excess, had paid
his bills and brought him home. It was at Cambridge
that he had met Ségouin. They were not much more
than acquaintances as yet but Jimmy found great pleasure in the society of one who had seen so much of the
world and was reputed to own some of the biggest hotels
in France. Such a person (as his father agreed) was
well worth knowing, even if he had not been the charming companion he was. Villona was entertaining also—a
brilliant pianist—but, unfortunately, very poor.

The car ran on merrily with its cargo of hilarious
youth. The two cousins sat on the front seat; Jimmy and
his Hungarian friend sat behind. Decidedly Villona was

in excellent spirits; he kept up a deep bass hum of melody for miles of the road. The Frenchmen flung their laughter and light words over their shoulders and often Jimmy had to strain forward to catch the quick phrase. This was not altogether pleasant for him, as he had nearly always to make a deft guess at the meaning and shout back a suitable answer in the teeth of a high wind. Besides Villona's humming would confuse anybody; the noise of the car, too.

Rapid motion through space elates one; so does notoriety; so does the possession of money. These were three good reasons for Jimmy's excitement. He had been seen by many of his friends that day in the company of these Continentals. At the control Ségouin had presented him to one of the French competitors and, in answer to his confused murmur of compliment, the swarthy face of the driver had disclosed a line of shining white teeth. It was pleasant after that honour to return to the profane world of spectators amid nudges and significant looks. Then as to money—he really had a great sum under his control. Ségouin, perhaps, would not think it a great sum but Jimmy who, in spite of temporary errors, was at heart the inheritor of solid instincts knew well with what difficulty it had been got together. This knowledge had previously kept his bills within the limits of reasonable recklessness and, if he had been so conscious of the labour latent in money when there had been question merely of some freak of the higher intelligence, how much more so now when he was about to stake the greater part of his substance! It was a serious thing for him.

Of course, the investment was a good one and Ségouin had managed to give the impression that it was by a favour of friendship the mite of Irish money was to be included in the capital of the concern. Jimmy had a respect for his father's shrewdness in business matters and in this case it had been his father who had first suggested the investment; money to be made in the motor business, pots of money. Moreover Ségouin had the unmistakable air of wealth. Jimmy set out to translate into days' work that lordly car in which he sat. How smoothly it ran. In what style they had come careering along the country roads! The journey laid a magical finger on the genuine pulse of life and gallantly the machinery of human nerves strove to answer the bounding courses of the swift blue animal.

They drove down Dame Street. The street was busy with unusual traffic, loud with the horns of motorists and the gongs of impatient tram-drivers. Near the Bank Ségouin drew up and Jimmy and his friend alighted. A little knot of people collected on the footpath to pay homage to the snorting motor. The party was to dine together that evening in Ségouin's hotel and, meanwhile, Jimmy and his friend, who was staying with him, were to go home to dress. The car steered out slowly for Grafton Street while the two young men pushed their way through the knot of gazers. They walked northward with a curious feeling of disappointment in the exercise, while the city hung its pale globes of light above them in a haze of summer evening.

In Jimmy's house this dinner had been pronounced an occasion. A certain pride mingled with his parents' trepidation, a certain eagerness, also, to play fast and loose for the names of great foreign cities have at least this virtue. Jimmy, too, looked very well when he was dressed and, as he stood in the hall giving a last equation to the bows of his dress tie, his father may have felt even commercially satisfied at having secured for his son qualities often unpurchasable. His father, therefore, was unusually friendly with Villona and his manner expressed a real respect for foreign accomplishments; but this subtlety of his host was probably lost upon the Hungarian, who was beginning to have a sharp desire for his dinner.

The dinner was excellent, exquisite. Ségouin, Jimmy decided, had a very refined taste. The party was increased by a young Englishman named Routh whom Jimmy had seen with Ségouin at Cambridge. The young men supped in a snug room lit by electric candle-lamps. They talked volubly and with little reserve. Jimmy, whose imagination was kindling, conceived the lively youth of the Frenchmen twined elegantly upon the firm framework of the Englishman's manner. A graceful image of his, he thought, and a just one. He admired the dexterity with which their host directed the conversation. The five young men had various tastes and their tongues had been loosened. Villona, with immense respect, began to discover to the mildly surprised Englishman the beauties of the English madrigal, deploring the loss of old instruments. Rivière, not wholly ingenuously, undertook to explain to Jimmy the triumph of the French mechanicians. The resonant voice of the Hungarian was about to prevail in ridicule of the spurious lutes of the romantic painters when Ségouin shepherded his party into politics. Here was congenial ground for all. Jimmy, under generous influences, felt the buried zeal of his father wake to life within him: he aroused the torpid Routh at last. The room grew doubly hot and Ségouin's task grew harder each moment: there was even danger of personal spite. The alert host at an opportunity lifted his glass to Humanity and, when the toast had been drunk, he threw open a window significantly.

That night the city wore the mask of a capital. The five young men strolled along Stephen's Green in a faint cloud of aromatic smoke. They talked loudly and gaily and their cloaks dangled from their shoulders. The people made way for them. At the corner of Grafton Street a short fat man was putting two handsome ladies on a car in charge of another fat man. The car drove off and the short fat man caught sight of the party.

—André.

—It's Farley!

A torrent of talk followed. Farley was an American. No one knew very well what the talk was about. Villona and Rivière were the noisiest, but all the men were excited. They got up on a car, squeezing themselves together amid much laughter. They drove by the crowd, blended now into soft colours, to a music of merry bells. They took the train at Westland Row and in a few seconds, as it seemed to Jimmy, they were walking out of Kingstown Station. The ticket-collector saluted Jimmy; he was an old man:

—Fine night, sir!

It was a serene summer night; the harbour lay like a darkened mirror at their feet. They proceeded towards it with linked arms, singing *Cadet Roussel* in chorus, stamping their feet at every:

—*Ho! Ho! Hohé, vraiment!*

They got into a rowboat at the slip and made out for the American's yacht. There was to be supper, music, cards. Villona said with conviction:

—It is beautiful!

There was a yacht piano in the cabin. Villona played a waltz for Farley and Rivière, Farley acting as cavalier and Rivière as lady. Then an impromptu square dance, the men devising original figures. What merriment! Jimmy took his part with a will; this was seeing life, at least. Then Farley got out of breath and cried *Stop!* A man brought in a light supper, and the young men sat down to it for form' sake. They drank, however: it was

Bohemian. They drank Ireland, England, France, Hungary, the United States of America. Jimmy made a speech, a long speech, Villona saying *Hear! hear!* whenever there was a pause. There was a great clapping of hands when he sat down. It must have been a good speech. Farley clapped him on the back and laughed loudly. What jovial fellows! What good company they were!

Cards! cards! The table was cleared. Villona returned quietly to his piano and played voluntaries for them. The other men played game after game, flinging themselves boldly into the adventure. They drank the health of the Queen of Hearts and of the Queen of Diamonds. Jimmy felt obscurely the lack of an audience: the wit was flashing. Play ran very high and paper began to pass. Jimmy did not know exactly who was winning but he knew that he was losing. But it was his own fault for he frequently mistook his cards and the other men had to calculate his I.O.U.'s for him. They were devils of fellows but he wished they would stop: it was getting late. Someone gave the toast of the yacht *The Belle of Newport* and then someone proposed one great game for a finish.

The piano had stopped; Villona must have gone up on deck. It was a terrible game. They stopped just before the end of it to drink for luck. Jimmy understood that the game lay between Routh and Ségouin. What excitement! Jimmy was excited too; he would lose, of course. How much had he written away? The men rose to their feet to play the last tricks, talking and gesticulating. Routh won. The cabin shook with the young men's cheering and the cards were bundled together. They began then to gather in what they had won. Farley and Jimmy were the heaviest losers.

He knew that he would regret in the morning but at present he was glad of the rest, glad of the dark stupor

that would cover up his folly. He leaned his elbows on
the table and rested his head between his hands, counting the beats of his temples. The cabin door opened and
he saw the Hungarian standing in a shaft of grey light:

—Daybreak, gentlemen!

Two Gallants

THE grey warm evening of August had descended
upon the city and a mild warm air, a memory of
summer, circulated in the streets. The streets, shuttered
for the repose of Sunday, swarmed with a gaily coloured
crowd. Like illumined pearls the lamps shone from the
summits of their tall poles upon the living texture below
which, changing shape and hue unceasingly, sent up
into the warm grey evening air an unchanging unceasing murmur.

Two young men came down the hill of Rutland
Square. One of them was just bringing a long monologue
to a close. The other, who walked on the verge of the
path and was at times obliged to step on to the road,
owing to his companion's rudeness, wore an amused
listening face. He was squat and ruddy. A yachting cap
was shoved far back from his forehead and the narrative
to which he listened made constant waves of expression
break forth over his face from the corners of his nose
and eyes and mouth. Little jets of wheezing laughter
followed one another out of his convulsed body. His
eyes, twinkling with cunning enjoyment, glanced at
every moment towards his companion's face. Once or
twice he rearranged the light waterproof which he had

slung over one shoulder in toreador fashion. His breeches, his white rubber shoes and his jauntily slung waterproof expressed youth. But his figure fell into rotundity at the waist, his hair was scant and grey and his face, when the waves of expression had passed over it, had a ravaged look.

When he was quite sure that the narrative had ended he laughed noiselessly for fully half a minute. Then he said:

—Well! . . . That takes the biscuit!

His voice seemed winnowed of vigour; and to enforce his words he added with humour:

—That takes the solitary, unique, and, if I may so call it, *recherché* biscuit!

He became serious and silent when he had said this. His tongue was tired for he had been talking all the afternoon in a public-house in Dorset Street. Most people considered Lenehan a leech but, in spite of this reputation, his adroitness and eloquence had always prevented his friends from forming any general policy against him. He had a brave manner of coming up to a party of them in a bar and of holding himself nimbly at the borders of the company until he was included in a round. He was a sporting vagrant armed with a vast stock of stories, limericks and riddles. He was insensitive to all kinds of discourtesy. No one knew how he achieved the stern task of living, but his name was vaguely associated with racing tissues.

—And where did you pick her up, Corley? he asked.

Corley ran his tongue swiftly along his upper lip.

—One night, man, he said, I was going along Dame Street and I spotted a fine tart under Waterhouse's clock and said good-night, you know. So we went for a walk round by the canal and she told me she was a slavey in a house in Baggot Street. I put my arm round her and squeezed her a bit that night. Then next Sunday, man, I met her by appointment. We went out to Donnybrook and I brought her into a field there. She told me she used to go with a dairyman. . . . It was fine, man. Cigarettes every night she'd bring me and paying the tram out and back. And one night she brought me two bloody fine cigars—O, the real cheese, you know, that the old fellow used to smoke. . . . I was afraid, man, she'd get in the family way. But she's up to the dodge.

—Maybe she thinks you'll marry her, said Lenehan.

—I told her I was out of a job, said Corley. I told her I was in Pim's. She doesn't know my name. I was too hairy to tell her that. But she thinks I'm a bit of class, you know.

Lenehan laughed again, noiselessly.

—Of all the good ones ever I heard, he said, that emphatically takes the biscuit.

Corley's stride acknowledged the compliment. The swing of his burly body made his friend execute a few light skips from the path to the roadway and back again. Corley was the son of an inspector of police and he had inherited his father's frame and gait. He walked with his hands by his sides, holding himself erect and swaying his head from side to side. His head was large, globular and oily; it sweated in all weathers; and his large round hat, set upon it sideways, looked like a bulb which had grown out of another. He always stared straight before him as if he were on parade and, when he wished to gaze after someone in the street, it was necessary for him to move his body from the hips. At present he was about town. Whenever any job was vacant a friend was always ready to give him the hard word. He was often to be seen walking with policemen in plain clothes, talking earnestly. He knew the inner side of all affairs and was fond of delivering final judgments. He spoke without listening to the speech of his companions. His conversation was mainly about himself: what he had said to such a person and what such a person had said to him and what he had said to settle the matter. When he reported these dialogues he aspirated the first letter of his name after the manner of Florentines.

Lenehan offered his friend a cigarette. As the two young men walked on through the crowd Corley occasionally turned to smile at some of the passing girls but Lenehan's gaze was fixed on the large faint moon circled with a double halo. He watched earnestly the passing of the grey web of twilight across its face. At length he said:

—Well . . . tell me, Corley, I suppose you'll be able to pull it off all right, eh?

Corley closed one eye expressively as an answer.

—Is she game for that? asked Lenehan dubiously. You can never know women.

—She's all right, said Corley. I know the way to get around her, man. She's a bit gone on me.

—You're what I call a gay Lothario, said Lenehan. And the proper kind of a Lothario, too!

A shade of mockery relieved the servility of his manner. To save himself he had the habit of leaving his flattery open to the interpretation of raillery. But Corley had not a subtle mind.

—There's nothing to touch a good slavey, he affirmed. Take my tip for it.

—By one who has tried them all, said Lenehan.

—First I used to go with girls, you know, said Corley, unbosoming; girls off the South Circular. I used to take them out, man, on the tram somewhere and pay the tram or take them to a band or a play at the theatre or buy them chocolate and sweets or something that way. I used to spend money on them right enough, he added, in a

convincing tone, as if he were conscious of being dis-
believed.

But Lenehan could well believe it; he nodded gravely.

—I know that game, he said, and it's a mug's game.

—And damn the thing I ever got out of it, said Corley.

—Ditto here, said Lenehan.

—Only off of one of them, said Corley.

He moistened his upper lip by running his tongue
along it. The recollection brightened his eyes. He too
gazed at the pale disc of the moon, now nearly veiled,
and seemed to meditate.

—She was . . . a bit of all right, he said regretfully.

He was silent again. Then he added:

—She's on the turf now. I saw her driving down Earl
Street one night with two fellows with her on a car.

—I suppose that's your doing, said Lenehan.

—There was others at her before me, said Corley
philosophically.

This time Lenehan was inclined to disbelieve. He
shook his head to and fro and smiled.

—You know you can't kid me, Corley, he said.

—Honest to God! said Corley. Didn't she tell me herself?

Lenehan made a tragic gesture.

—Base betrayer! he said.

As they passed along the railings of Trinity College,
Lenehan skipped out into the road and peered up at the
clock.

—Twenty after, he said.

—Time enough, said Corley. She'll be there all right. I
always let her wait a bit.

Lenehan laughed quietly.

—Ecod! Corley, you know how to take them, he said.

—I'm up to all their little tricks, Corley confessed.

—But tell me, said Lenehan again, are you sure you

can bring it off all right? You now it's a ticklish job.
They're damn close on that point. Eh? . . . What?

His bright, small eyes searched his companion's face
for reassurance. Corley swung his head to and fro as if
to toss aside an insistent insect, and his brows gathered.

—I'll put it off, he said. Leave it to me, can't you?

Lenehan said no more. He did not wish to ruffle his
friend's temper, to be sent to the devil and told that his
advice was not wanted. A little tact was necessary. But
Corley's brow was soon smooth again. His thoughts
were running another way.

—She's a fine decent tart, he said, with appreciation;
that's what she is.

They walked along Nassau Street and then turned
into Kildare Street. Not far from the porch of the club
a harpist stood in the roadway, playing to a little ring of
listeners. He plucked at the wires heedlessly, glancing
quickly from time to time at the face of each new-
comer and from time to time, wearily also, at the sky.
His harp too, heedless that her coverings had fallen
about her knees, seemed weary alike of the eyes of
strangers and of her master's hands. One hand played in
the bass the melody of *Silent, O Moyle*, while the other
hand careered in the treble after each group of notes.
The notes of the air throbbed deep and full.

The two young men walked up the street without
speaking, the mournful music following them. When
they reached Stephen's Green they crossed the road.
Here the noise of trams, the lights and the crowd released from their silence.

—There she is! said Corley.

At the corner of Hume Street a young woman was
standing. She wore a blue dress and a white sailor hat.
She stood on the curbstone, swinging a sunshade in one
hand. Lenehan grew lively.

—Let's have a squint at her, Corley, he said.

Corley glanced sideways at his friend and an unpleasant grin appeared on his face.

—Are you trying to get inside me? he asked.

—Damn it! said Lenehan boldly, I don't want an introduction. All I want is to have a look at her. I'm not going to eat her.

—O . . . A look at her? said Corley, more amiably. Well . . . I'll tell you what. I'll go over and talk to her and you can pass by.

—Right! said Lenehan.

Corley had already thrown one leg over the chains when Lenehan called out:

—And after? Where will we meet?

—Half ten, answered Corley, bringing over his other leg.

—Where?

—Corner of Merrion Street. We'll be coming back.

—Work it all right now, said Lenehan in farewell.

Corley did not answer. He sauntered across the road swaying his head from side to side. His bulk, his easy pace and the solid sound of his boots had something of the conqueror in them. He approached the young woman and, without saluting, began at once to converse with her. She swung her sunshade more quickly and executed half turns on her heels. Once or twice when he spoke to her at close quarters she laughed and bent her head.

Lenehan observed them for a few minutes. Then he walked rapidly along beside the chains to some distance and crossed the road obliquely. As he approached Hume Street corner he found the air heavily scented and his eyes made a swift anxious scrutiny of the young woman's appearance. She had her Sunday finery on. Her blue serge skirt was held at the waist by a belt of black leather. The great silver buckle of her belt seemed to depress the centre of her body, catching the light stuff of her white blouse like a clip. She wore a short black jacket with mother-of-pearl buttons and a ragged black boa. The ends of her tulle collarette had been carefully disordered and a big bunch of red flowers was pinned in her bosom, stems upwards. Lenehan's eyes noted approvingly her stout short muscular body. Frank rude health glowed in her face, on her fat red cheeks and in her unabashed blue eyes. Her features were blunt. She had broad nostrils, a straggling mouth which lay open in a contented leer, and two projecting front teeth. As he passed Lenehan took off his cap and, after about ten seconds, Corley returned a salute to the air. This he did by raising his hand vaguely and pensively changing the angle of position of his hat.

Lenehan walked as far as the Shelbourne Hotel where he halted and waited. After waiting for a little time he saw them coming towards him and, when they turned to the right, he followed them, stepping lightly in his white shoes, down one side of Merrion Square. As he walked on slowly, timing his pace to theirs, he watched Corley's head which turned at every moment towards the young woman's face like a big ball revolving on a pivot. He kept the pair in view until he had seen them climbing the stairs of the Donnybrook tram; then he turned about and went back the way he had come.

Now that he was alone his face looked older. His gaiety seemed to forsake him and, as he came by the railings of the Duke's Lawn, he allowed his hand to run along them. The air which the harpist had played began to control his movements. His softly padded feet played the melody while his fingers swept a scale of variations idly along the railings after each group of notes.

He walked listlessly round Stephen's Green and then

down Grafton Street. Though his eyes took note of many
elements of the crowd through which he passed they did
so morosely. He found trivial all that was meant to
charm him and did not answer the glances which invited
him to be bold. He knew that he would have to speak a
great deal, to invent and to amuse, and his brain and
throat were too dry for such a task. The problem of how
he could pass the hours till he met Corley again troubled
him a little. He could think of no way of passing them
but to keep on walking. He turned to the left when he
came to the corner of Rutland Square and felt more at
ease in the dark quiet street, the sombre look of which
suited his mood. He paused at last before the window
of a poor-looking shop over which the words *Refreshment Bar* were printed in white letters. On the glass of
the window were two flying inscriptions: *Ginger Beer*
and *Ginger Ale*. A cut ham was exposed on a great blue
dish while near it on a plate lay a segment of very light
plum-pudding. He eyed this food earnestly for some
time and then, after glancing warily up and down the
street, went into the shop quickly.

He was hungry for, except some biscuits which he
had asked two grudging curates to bring him, he had
eaten nothing since breakfast-time. He sat down at an
uncovered wooden table opposite two work-girls and a
mechanic. A slatternly girl waited on him.

How much is a plate of peas? he asked.

—Three halfpence, sir, said the girl.

—Bring me a plate of peas, he said, and a bottle of
ginger beer.

He spoke roughly in order to belie his air of gentility
for his entry had been followed by a pause of talk. His
face was heated. To appear natural he pushed his cap
back on his head and planted his elbows on the table.
The mechanic and the two work-girls examined him

point by point before resuming their conversation in a subdued voice. The girl brought him a plate of hot grocer's peas, seasoned with pepper and vinegar, a fork and his ginger beer. He ate his food greedily and found it so good that he made a note of the shop mentally. When he had eaten all the peas he sipped his ginger beer and sat for some time thinking of Corley's adventure. In his imagination he beheld the pair of lovers walking along some dark road; he heard Corley's voice in deep energetic gallantries and saw again the leer of the young woman's mouth. This vision made him feel keenly his own poverty of purse and spirit. He was tired of knocking about, of pulling the devil by the tail, of shifts and intrigues. He would be thirty-one in November. Would he never get a good job? Would he never have a home of his own? He thought how pleasant it would be to have a warm fire to sit by and a good dinner to sit down to. He had walked the streets long enough with friends and with girls. He knew what those friends were worth: he knew the girls too. Experience had embittered his heart against the world. But all hope had not left him. He felt better after having eaten than he had felt before, less weary of his life, less vanquished in spirit. He might yet be able to settle down in some smug corner and live happily if he could only come across some good simple-minded girl with a little of the ready.

He paid twopence halfpenny to the slatternly girl and went out of the shop to begin his wandering again. He went into Capel Street and walked along towards the City Hall. Then he turned into Dame Street. At the corner of George's Street he met two friends of his and stopped to converse with them. He was glad that he could rest from all his walking. His friends asked him had he seen Corley and what was the latest. He replied that he had spent the day with Corley. His friends talked very little. They looked vacantly after some figures in the crowd and sometimes made a critical remark. One said that he had seen Mac an hour before in Westmoreland Street. At this Lenehan said that he had been with Mac the night before in Egan's. The young man who had seen Mac in Westmoreland Street asked was it true that Mac had won a bit over a billiard match. Lenehan did not know: he said that Holohan had stood them drinks in Egan's.

He left his friends at a quarter to ten and went up George's Street. He turned to the left at the City Markets and walked on into Grafton Street. The crowd of girls and young men had thinned and on his way up the street he heard many groups and couples bidding one another good-night. He went as far as the clock of the College of Surgeons: it was on the stroke of ten. He set off briskly along the northern side of the Green, hurrying for fear Corley should return too soon. When he reached the corner of Merrion Street he took his stand in the shadow of a lamp and brought out one of the cigarettes which he had reserved and lit it. He leaned against the lamp-post and kept his gaze fixed on the part from which he expected to see Corley and the young woman return.

His mind became active again. He wondered had Corley managed it successfully. He wondered if he had asked her yet or if he would leave it to the last. He suffered all the pangs and thrills of his friend's situation as well as those of his own. But the memory of Corley's slowly revolving head calmed him somewhat: he was sure Corley would pull it off all right. All at once the idea struck him that perhaps Corley had seen her home by another way and given him the slip. His eyes searched the street: there was no sign of them. Yet it was surely half-an-hour since he had seen the clock of the College of Surgeons. Would Corley do a thing like

that? He lit his last cigarette and began to smoke it
nervously. He strained his eyes as each tram stopped at
the far corner of the square. They must have gone home
by another way. The paper of his cigarette broke and
he flung it into the road with a curse.

Suddenly he saw them coming towards him. He
started with delight and, keeping close to his lamp-post,
tried to read the result in their walk. They were walking
quickly, the young woman taking quick short steps,
while Corley kept beside her with his long stride. They
did not seem to be speaking. An intimation of the result
pricked him like the point of a sharp instrument. He
knew Corley would fail; he knew it was no go.

They turned down Baggot Street and he followed
them at once, taking the other footpath. When they
stopped he stopped too. They talked for a few moments
and then the young woman went down the steps into
the area of a house. Corley remained standing at the
edge of the path, a little distance from the front steps.
Some minutes passed. Then the hall-door was opened
slowly and cautiously. A woman came running down the
front steps and coughed. Corley turned and went towards her. His broad figure hid hers from view for a
few seconds and then she reappeared running up the
steps. The door closed on her and Corley began to walk
swiftly towards Stephen's Green.

Lenehan hurried on in the same direction. Some drops
of light rain fell. He took them as a warning and, glancing back towards the house which the young woman
had entered to see that he was not observed, he ran
eagerly across the road. Anxiety and his swift run made
him pant. He called out:

—Hallo, Corley!

Corley turned his head to see who had called him,
and then continued walking as before. Lenehan ran

after him, settling the waterproof on his shoulders with one hand.

—Hallo, Corley! he cried again.

He came level with his friend and looked keenly in his face. He could see nothing there.

—Well? he said. Did it come off?

They had reached the corner of Ely Place. Still without answering Corley swerved to the left and went up the side street. His features were composed in stern calm. Lenehan kept up with his friend, breathing uneasily. He was baffled and a note of menace pierced through his voice.

—Can't you tell us? he said. Did you try her?

Corley halted at the first lamp and stared grimly before him. Then with a grave gesture he extended a hand towards the light and, smiling, opened it slowly to the gaze of his disciple. A small gold coin shone in the palm.

The Boarding House

MRS MOONEY was a butcher's daughter. She was a woman who was quite able to keep things to herself: a determined woman. She had married her father's foreman and opened a butcher's shop near Spring Gardens. But as soon as his father-in-law was dead Mr Mooney began to go to the devil. He drank, plundered the till, ran headlong into debt. It was no use making him take the pledge: he was sure to break out again a few days after. By fighting his wife in the presence of customers and by buying bad meat he ruined

his business. One night he went for his wife with the
cleaver and she had to sleep in a neighbour's house.

After that they lived apart. She went to the priest and
got a separation from him with care of the children. She
would give him neither money nor food nor house-room;
and so he was obliged to enlist himself as a sheriff's man.
He was a shabby stooped little drunkard with a white
face and a white moustache and white eyebrows, pencilled above his little eyes, which were pink-veined and
raw; and all day long he sat in the bailiff's room, waiting
to be put on a job. Mrs Mooney, who had taken what
remained of her money out of the butcher business and
set up a boarding house in Hardwicke Street, was a big
imposing woman. Her house had a floating population
made up of tourists from Liverpool and the Isle of Man
and, occasionally, *artistes* from the music halls. Its resident population was made up of clerks from the city.
She governed her house cunningly and firmly, knew
when to give credit, when to be stern and when to let
things pass. All the resident young men spoke of her as
The Madam.

Mrs Mooney's young men paid fifteen shillings a week
for board and lodgings (beer or stout at dinner ex-
cluded). They shared in common tastes and occupations
and for this reason they were very chummy with one
another. They discussed with one another the chances
of favourites and outsiders. Jack Mooney, the Madam's
son, who was clerk to a commission agent in Fleet
Street, had the reputation of being a hard case. He was
fond of using soldiers' obscenities: usually he came
home in the small hours. When he met his friends he
had always a good one to tell them and he was always
sure to be on to a good thing—that is to say, a likely
horse or a likely *artiste*. He was also handy with the mits
and sang comic songs. On Sunday nights there would

often be a reunion in Mrs Mooney's front drawing-room.
The music-hall *artistes* would oblige; and Sheridan
played waltzes and polkas and vamped accompaniments.
Polly Mooney, the Madam's daughter, would also sing.
She sang:

> *I'm a . . . naughty girl.*
> *You needn't sham:*
> *You know I am.*

Polly was a slim girl of nineteen, she had light soft
hair and a small full mouth. Her eyes, which were grey
with a shade of green through them, had a habit of
glancing upwards when she spoke with anyone, which
made her look like a little perverse madonna. Mrs
Mooney had first sent her daughter to be a typist in a
corn-factor's office but, as a disreputable sheriff's man
used to come every other day to the office, asking to be
allowed to say a word to his daughter, she had taken
her daughter home again and set her to do housework.
As Polly was very lively the intention was to give her
the run of the young men. Besides, young men like to
feel that there is a young woman not very far away.
Polly, of course, flirted with the young men but Mrs
Mooney, who was a shrewd judge, knew that the young
men were only passing the time away: none of them
meant business. Things went on so for a long time and
Mrs Mooney began to think of sending Polly back to
typewriting when she noticed that something was going
on between Polly and one of the young men. She
watched the pair and kept her own counsel.

Polly knew that she was being watched, but still her
mother's persistent silence could not be misunderstood.
There had been no open complicity between mother
and daughter, no open understanding but, though
people in the house began to talk of the affair, still Mrs
Mooney did not intervene. Polly began to grow a little

strange in her manner and the young man was evidently perturbed. At last, when she judged it to be the right moment, Mrs Mooney intervened. She dealt with moral problems as a cleaver deals with meat: and in this case she had made up her mind.

It was a bright Sunday morning of early summer, promising heat, but with a fresh breeze blowing. All the windows of the boarding house were open and the lace curtains ballooned gently towards the street beneath the raised sashes. The belfry of George's Church sent out constant peals and worshippers, singly or in groups, traversed the little circus before the church, revealing their purpose by their self-contained demeanour no less than by the little volumes in their gloved hands. Breakfast was over in the boarding house and the table of the breakfast-room was covered with plates on which lay yellow streaks of eggs with morsels of bacon-fat and bacon-rind. Mrs Mooney sat in the straw arm-chair and watched the servant Mary remove the breakfast things. She made Mary collect the crusts and pieces of broken bread to help to make Tuesday's bread-pudding. When the table was cleared, the broken bread collected, the sugar and butter safe under lock and key, she began to reconstruct the interview which she had had the night before with Polly. Things were as she had suspected: she had been frank in her questions and Polly had been frank in her answers. Both had been somewhat awkward, of course. She had been made awkward by her not wishing to receive the news in too cavalier a fashion or to seem to have connived and Polly had been made awkward not merely because allusions of that kind always made her awkward but also because she did not wish it to be thought that in her wise innocence she had divined the intention behind her mother's tolerance.

Mrs Mooney glanced instinctively at the little gilt

clock on the mantelpiece as soon as she had become
aware through her revery that the bells of George's
Church had stopped ringing. It was seventeen minutes
past eleven: she would have lots of time to have the
matter out with Mr Doran and then catch short twelve
at Marlborough Street. She was sure she would win. To
begin with she had all the weight of social opinion on
her side: she was an outraged mother. She had allowed
him to live beneath her roof, assuming that he was a
man of honour, and he had simply abused her hospitality. He was thirty-four or thirty-five years of age, so
that youth could not be pleaded as his excuse; nor
could ignorance be his excuse since he was a man who
had seen something of the world. He had simply taken
advantage of Polly's youth and inexperience: that was
evident. The question was: What reparation would he
make?

There must be reparation made in such cases. It is
all very well for the man: he can go his ways as if nothing had happened, having had his moment of pleasure,
but the girl has to bear the brunt. Some mothers would
be content to patch up such an affair for a sum of
money; she had known cases of it. But she would not
do so. For her only one reparation could make up for
the loss of her daughter's honour: marriage.

She counted all her cards again before sending Mary
up to Mr Doran's room to say that she wished to speak
with him. She felt sure she would win. He was a serious
young man, not rakish or loud-voiced like the others.
If it had been Mr Sheridan or Mr Meade or Bantam
Lyons her task would have been much harder. She did
not think he would face publicity. All the lodgers in the
house knew something of the affair; details had been
invented by some. Besides, he had been employed for
thirteen years in a great Catholic wine-merchant's office

and publicity would mean for him, perhaps, the loss of his sit. Whereas if he agreed all might be well. She knew he had a good screw for one thing and she suspected he had a bit of stuff put by.

Nearly the half-hour! She stood up and surveyed herself in the pier-glass. The decisive expression of her great florid face satisfied her and she thought of some mothers she knew who could not get their daughters off their hands.

Mr Doran was very anxious indeed this Sunday morning. He had made two attempts to shave but his hand had been so unsteady that he had been obliged to desist. Three days' reddish beard fringed his jaws and every two or three minutes a mist gathered on his glasses so that he had to take them off and polish them with his pocket-handkerchief. The recollection of his confession of the night before was a cause of acute pain to him; the priest had drawn out every ridiculous detail of the affair and in the end had so magnified his sin that he was almost thankful at being afforded a loophole of reparation. The harm was done. What could he do now but marry her or run away? He could not brazen it out. The affair would be sure to be talked of and his employer would be certain to hear of it. Dublin is such a small city: everyone knows everyone else's business. He felt his heart leap warmly in his throat as he heard in his excited imagination old Mr Leonard calling out in his rasping voice: *Send Mr Doran here, please.*

All his long years of service gone for nothing! All his industry and diligence thrown away! As a young man he had sown his wild oats, of course; he had boasted of his free-thinking and denied the existence of God to his companions in public-houses. But that was all passed and done with . . . nearly. He still bought a copy of *Reynolds's Newspaper* every week but he attended to his religious duties and for nine-tenths of the year lived a regular life. He had money enough to settle down on; it was not that. But the family would look down on her. First of all there was her disreputable father and then her mother's boarding house was beginning to get a certain fame. He had a notion that he was being had. He could imagine his friends talking of the affair and laughing. She *was* a little vulgar; sometimes she said *I seen* and *If I had've known.* But what would grammar matter if he really loved her? He could not make up his mind whether to like her or despise her for what she had done. Of course, he had done it too. His instinct urged him to remain free, not to marry. Once you are married you are done for, it said.

While he was sitting helplessly on the side of the bed in shirt and trousers she tapped lightly at his door and entered. She told him all, that she had made a clean breast of it to her mother and that her mother would speak with him that morning. She cried and threw her arms round his neck, saying:

—O, Bob! Bob! What am I to do? What am I to do at all?

She would put an end to herself, she said.

He comforted her feebly, telling her not to cry, that it would be all right, never fear. He felt against his shirt the agitation of her bosom.

It was not altogether his fault that it had happened. He remembered well, with the curious patient memory of the celibate, the first casual caresses her dress, her breath, her fingers had given him. Then late one night as he was undressing for bed she had tapped at his door, timidly. She wanted to relight her candle at his for hers had been blown out by a gust. It was her bath night. She wore a loose open combing-jacket of printed flannel. Her white instep shone in the opening of her furry

slippers and the blood glowed warmly behind her perfumed skin. From her hands and wrists too as she lit
and steadied her candle a faint perfume arose.

On nights when he came in very late it was she who
warmed up his dinner. He scarcely knew what he was
eating, feeling her beside him alone, at night, in the
sleeping house. And her thoughtfulness! If the night was
anyway cold or wet or windy there was sure to be a
little tumbler of punch ready for him. Perhaps they
could be happy together. . . .

They used to go upstairs together on tiptoe, each with
a candle, and on the third landing exchange reluctant
good-nights. They used to kiss. He remembered well her
eyes, the touch of her hand and his delirium. . . .

But delirium passes. He echoed her phrase, applying
it to himself: *What am I to do?* The instinct of the
celibate warned him to hold back. But the sin was there;
even his sense of honour told him that reparation must
be made for such a sin.

While he was sitting with her on the side of the bed
Mary came to the door and said that the missus wanted
to see him in the parlour. He stood up to put on his coat
and waistcoat, more helpless than ever. When he was
dressed he went over to her to comfort her. It would
be all right, never fear. He left her crying on the bed
and moaning softly: *O my God!*

Going down the stairs his glasses became so dimmed
with moisture that he had to take them off and polish
them. He longed to ascend through the roof and fly away
to another country where he would never hear again of
his trouble, and yet a force pushed him downstairs step
by step. The implacable faces of his employer and of
the Madam stared upon his discomfiture. On the last
flight of stairs he passed Jack Mooney who was coming
up from the pantry nursing two bottles of *Bass.* They

saluted coldly; and the lover's eyes rested for a second or two on a thick bulldog face and a pair of thick short arms. When he reached the foot of the staircase he glanced up and saw Jack regarding him from the door of the return-room.

Suddenly he remembered the night when one of the music-hall *artistes,* a little blond Londoner, had made a rather free allusion to Polly. The reunion had been almost broken up on account of Jack's violence. Every-one tried to quiet him. The music-hall *artiste,* a little paler than usual, kept smiling and saying that there was no harm meant: but Jack kept shouting at him that if any fellow tried that sort of a game on with *his* sister he'd bloody well put his teeth down his throat, so he would.

.   .   .   .

Polly sat for a little time on the side of the bed, crying. Then she dried her eyes and went over to the looking-glass. She dipped the end of the towel in the water-jug and refreshed her eyes with the cool water. She looked at herself in profile and readjusted a hairpin above her ear. Then she went back to the bed again and sat at the foot. She regarded the pillows for a long time and the sight of them awakened in her mind secret amiable memories. She rested the nape of her neck against the cool iron bed-rail and fell into a revery. There was no longer any perturbation visible on her face.

She waited on patiently, almost cheerfully, without alarm, her memories gradually giving place to hopes and visions of the future. Her hopes and visions were so intricate that she no longer saw the white pillows on which her gaze was fixed or remembered that she was waiting for anything.

At last she heard her mother calling. She started to her feet and ran to the banisters.

—Polly! Polly!

—Yes, mamma?

—Come down, dear. Mr Doran wants to speak to you.

Then she remembered what she had been waiting for.

A Little Cloud

EIGHT years before he had seen his friend off at the North Wall and wished him godspeed. Gallaher had got on. You could tell that at once by his travelled air, his well-cut tweed suit and fearless accent. Few fellows had talents like his and fewer still could remain unspoiled by such success. Gallaher's heart was in the right place and he had deserved to win. It was something to have a friend like that.

Little Chandler's thoughts ever since lunch-time had been of his meeting with Gallaher, of Gallaher's invitation and of the great city London where Gallaher lived. He was called Little Chandler because, though he was but slightly under the average stature, he gave one the idea of being a little man. His hands were white and small, his frame was fragile, his voice was quiet and his manners were refined. He took the greatest care of his fair silken hair and moustache and used perfume discreetly on his handkerchief. The half-moons of his nails were perfect and when he smiled you caught a glimpse of a row of childish white teeth.

As he sat at his desk in the King's Inns he thought what changes those eight years had brought. The friend whom he had known under a shabby and necessitous guise had become a brilliant figure on the London Press. He turned often from his tiresome writing to gaze out of the office window. The glow of a late autumn sunset covered the grass plots and walks. It cast a shower of kindly golden dust on the untidy nurses and decrepit old men who drowsed on the benches; it flickered upon all the moving figures—on the children who ran screaming along the gravel paths and on everyone who passed through the gardens. He watched the scene and thought of life; and (as always happened when he thought of life) he became sad. A gentle melancholy took possession of him. He felt how useless it was to struggle against fortune, this being the burden of wisdom which the ages had bequeathed to him.

He remembered the books of poetry upon his shelves at home. He had bought them in his bachelor days and many an evening, as he sat in the little room off the hall, he had been tempted to take one down from the bookshelf and read out something to his wife. But shyness had always held him back; and so the books had remained on their shelves. At times he repeated lines to himself and this consoled him.

When his hour had struck he stood up and took leave of his desk and of his fellow-clerks punctiliously. He emerged from under the feudal arch of the King's Inns, a neat modest figure, and walked swiftly down Henrietta Street. The golden sunset was waning and the air had grown sharp. A horde of grimy children populated the street. They stood or ran in the roadway or crawled up the steps before the gaping doors or squatted like mice upon the thresholds. Little Chandler gave them no thought. He picked his way deftly through all that minute vermin-like life and under the shadow of the

gaunt spectral mansions in which the old nobility of
Dublin had roistered. No memory of the past touched
him, for his mind was full of a present joy.

He had never been in Corless's but he knew the value
of the name. He knew that people went there after the
theatre to eat oysters and drink liqueurs; and he had
heard that the waiters there spoke French and German.
Walking swiftly by at night he had seen cabs drawn up
before the door and richly dressed ladies, escorted by
cavaliers, alight and enter quickly. They wore noisy
dresses and many wraps. Their faces were powdered
and they caught up their dresses, when they touched
earth, like alarmed Atalantas. He had always passed
without turning his head to look. It was his habit to
walk swiftly in the street even by day and whenever he
found himself in the city late at night he hurried on his
way apprehensively and excitedly. Sometimes, however,
he courted the causes of his fear. He chose the darkest
and narrowest streets and, as he walked boldly forward, the silence that was spread about his footsteps
troubled him, the wandering silent figures troubled him;
and at times a sound of low fugitive laughter made him
tremble like a leaf.

He turned to the right towards Capel Street. Ignatius
Gallaher on the London Press! Who would have thought
it possible eight years before? Still, now that he reviewed
the past, Little Chandler could remember many signs of
future greatness in his friend. People used to say that
Ignatius Gallaher was wild. Of course, he did mix with
a rakish set of fellows at that time, drank freely and borrowed money on all sides. In the end he had got mixed
up in some shady affair, some money transaction: at
least, that was one version of his flight. But nobody
denied him talent. There was always a certain . . .
something in Ignatius Gallaher that impressed you in

spite of yourself. Even when he was out at elbows and at his wits' end for money he kept up a bold face. Little Chandler remembered (and the remembrance brought a slight flush of pride to his cheek) one of Ignatius Gallaher's sayings when he was in a tight corner:

—Half time, now, boys, he used to say light-heartedly. Where's my considering cap?

That was Ignatius Gallaher all out; and, damn it, you couldn't but admire him for it.

Little Chandler quickened his pace. For the first time in his life he felt himself superior to the people he passed. For the first time his soul revolted against the dull inelegance of Capel Street. There was no doubt about it: if you wanted to succeed you had to go away. You could do nothing in Dublin. As he crossed Grattan Bridge he looked down the river towards the lower quays and pitied the poor stunted houses. They seemed to him a band of tramps, huddled together along the river-banks, their old coats covered with dust and soot, stupefied by the panorama of sunset and waiting for the first chill of night to bid them arise, shake themselves and begone. He wondered whether he could write a poem to express his idea. Perhaps Gallaher might be able to get it into some London paper for him. Could he write something original? He was not sure what idea he wished to express but the thought that a poetic moment had touched him took life within him like an infant hope. He stepped onward bravely.

Every step brought him nearer to London, farther from his own sober inartistic life. A light began to tremble on the horizon of his mind. He was not so old—thirty-two. His temperament might be said to be just at the point of maturity. There were so many different moods and impressions that he wished to express in verse. He felt them within him. He tried to weigh his

soul to see if it was a poet's soul. Melancholy was the
dominant note of his temperament, he thought, but it
was a melancholy tempered by recurrences of faith and
resignation and simple joy. If he could give expression
to it in a book of poems perhaps men would listen. He
would never be popular: he saw that. He could not sway
the crowd but he might appeal to a little circle of kindred
minds. The English critics, perhaps, would recognise him
as one of the Celtic school by reason of the melancholy
tone of his poems; besides that, he would put in allusions. He began to invent sentences and phrases from
the notices which his book would get. *Mr Chandler has
the gift of easy and graceful verse.* . . . *A wistful sadness pervades these poems.* . . . *The Celtic note.* It was
a pity his name was not more Irish-looking. Perhaps it
would be better to insert his mother's name before the
surname: Thomas Malone Chandler, or better still. T.
Malone Chandler. He would speak to Gallaher about it.

He pursued his revery so ardently that he passed his
street and had to turn back. As he came near Corless's
his former agitation began to overmaster him and he
halted before the door in indecision. Finally he opened
the door and entered.

The light and noise of the bar held him at the doorway for a few moments. He looked about him, but his
sight was confused by the shining of many red and green
wine-glasses. The bar seemed to him to be full of people
and he felt that the people were observing him curiously. He glanced quickly to right and left (frowning
slightly to make his errand appear serious), but when
his sight cleared a little he saw that nobody had turned
to look at him: and there, sure enough, was Ignatius
Gallaher leaning with his back against the counter and
his feet planted far apart.

—Hallo, Tommy, old hero, here you are! What is it to

be? What will you have? I'm taking whisky: better stuff
than we get across the water. Soda? Lithia? No mineral?
I'm the same. Spoils the flavour. . . . Here, *garçon*,
bring us two halves of malt whisky, like a good fellow.
. . . Well, and how have you been pulling along since
I saw you last? Dear God, how old we're getting! Do
you see any signs of aging in me—eh, what? A little grey
and thin on the top—what?

Ignatius Gallaher took off his hat and displayed a
large closely cropped head. His face was heavy, pale
and clean-shaven. His eyes, which were of bluish slate-
colour, relieved his unhealthy pallor and shone out
plainly above the vivid orange tie he wore. Between
these rival features the lips appeared very long and
shapeless and colourless. He bent his head and felt with
two sympathetic fingers the thin hair at the crown. Little
Chandler shook his head as a denial. Ignatius Gallaher
put on his hat again.

—It pulls you down, he said, Press life. Always hurry
and scurry, looking for copy and sometimes not finding
it: and then, always to have something new in your
stuff. Damn proofs and printers, I say, for a few days.
I'm deuced glad, I can tell you, to get back to the old
country. Does a fellow good, a bit of a holiday. I feel a
ton better since I landed again in dear dirty Dublin.
. . . Here you are, Tommy. Water? Say when.

Little Chandler allowed his whisky to be very much
diluted.

—You don't know what's good for you, my boy, said
Ignatius Gallaher. I drink mine neat.

—I drink very little as a rule, said Little Chandler
modestly. An odd half-one or so when I meet any of the
old crowd: that's all.

—Ah, well, said Ignatius Gallaher, cheerfully, here's
to us and to old times and old acquaintance.

They clinked glasses and drank the toast.

—I met some of the old gang to-day, said Ignatius Gallaher. O'Hara seems to be in a bad way. What's he doing?

—Nothing, said Little Chandler. He's gone to the dogs.

—But Hogan has a good sit, hasn't he?

—Yes; he's in the Land Commission.

—I met him one night in London and he seemed to be very flush. . . . Poor O'Hara! Boose, I suppose?

—Other things, too, said Little Chandler shortly.

Ignatius Gallaher laughed.

—Tommy, he said, I see you haven't changed an atom. You're the very same serious person that used to lecture me on Sunday mornings when I had a sore head and a fur on my tongue. You'd want to knock about a bit in the world. Have you never been anywhere, even for a trip?

—I've been to the Isle of Man, said Little Chandler.

Ignatius Gallaher laughed.

—The Isle of Man! he said. Go to London or Paris: for choice. That'd do you good.

—Have you seen Paris?

—I should think I have! I've knocked about there a little.

—And is it really so beautiful as they say? asked Little Chandler.

He sipped a little of his drink while Ignatius Gallaher finished his boldly.

—Beautiful? said Ignatius Gallaher, pausing on the word and on the flavour of his drink. It's not so beautiful, you know. Of course, it is beautiful. . . . But it's the life of Paris; that's the thing. Ah, there's no city like Paris for gaiety, movement, excitement. . . .

Little Chandler finished his whisky and, after some

trouble, succeeded in catching the barman's eye. He ordered the same again.

—I've been to the Moulin Rouge, Ignatius Gallaher continued when the barman had removed their glasses, and I've been to all the Bohemian cafés. Hot stuff! Not for a pious chap like you, Tommy.

Little Chandler said nothing until the barman returned with the two glasses: then he touched his friend's glass lightly and reciprocated the former toast. He was beginning to feel somewhat disillusioned. Gallaher's accent and way of expressing himself did not please him. There was something vulgar in his friend which he had not observed before. But perhaps it was only the result of living in London amid the bustle and competition of the Press. The old personal charm was still there under this new gaudy manner. And, after all, Gallaher had lived, he had seen the world. Little Chandler looked at his friend enviously.

—Everything in Paris is gay, said Ignatius Gallaher. They believe in enjoying life—and don't you think they're right? If you want to enjoy yourself properly you must go to Paris. And, mind you, they've a great feeling for the Irish there. When they heard I was from Ireland they were ready to eat me, man.

Little Chandler took four or five sips from his glass.

—Tell me, he said, is it true that Paris is so . . . immoral as they say?

Ignatius Gallagher made a catholic gesture with his right arm.

—Every place is immoral, he said. Of course you do find spicy bits in Paris. Go to one of the students' balls, for instance. That's lively, if you like, when the *cocottes* begin to let themselves loose. You know what they are, I suppose?

—I've heard of them, said Little Chandler.

Ignatius Gallaher drank off his whisky and shook his head.

—Ah, he said, you may say what you like. There's no woman like the Parisienne—for style, for go.

—Then it is an immoral city, said Little Chandler, with timid insistence—I mean, compared with London or Dublin?

—London! said Ignatius Gallaher. It's six of one and half-a-dozen of the other. You ask Hogan, my boy. I showed him a bit about London when he was over there. He'd open your eye. . . . I say, Tommy, don't make punch of that whisky: liquor up.

—No, really.' . . .

—O, come on, another one won't do you any harm. What is it? The same again, I suppose?

—Well . . . all right.

—*François,* the same again. . . . Will you smoke, Tommy?

Ignatius Gallaher produced his cigar-case. The two friends lit their cigars and puffed at them in silence until their drinks were served.

—I'll tell you my opinion, said Ignatius Gallaher, emerging after some time from the clouds of smoke in which he had taken refuge, it's a rum world. Talk of immorality! I've heard of cases—what am I saying?— I've known them: cases of . . . immorality. . . .

Ignatius Gallaher puffed thoughtfully at his cigar and then, in a calm historian's tone, he proceeded to sketch for his friend some pictures of the corruption which was rife abroad. He summarised the vices of many capitals and seemed inclined to award the palm to Berlin. Some things he could not vouch for (his friends had told him), but of others he had had personal experience. He spared neither rank nor caste. He revealed many of the secrets of religious houses on the Continent and described some of the practices which were fashionable in high society and ended by telling, with details, a story about an English duchess—a story which he knew to be true. Little Chandler was astonished.

—Ah, well, said Ignatius Gallaher, here we are in old jog-along Dublin where nothing is known of such things.

—How dull you must find it, said Little Chandler, after all the other places you've seen!

—Well, said Ignatius Gallaher, it's a relaxation to come over here, you know. And, after all, it's the old country, as they say, isn't it? You can't help having a certain feeling for it. That's human nature. . . . But tell me something about yourself. Hogan told me you had . . . tasted the joys of connubial bliss. Two years ago, wasn't it?

Little Chandler blushed and smiled.

—Yes, he said. I was married last May twelve months.

—I hope it's not too late in the day to offer my best wishes, said Ignatius Gallaher. I didn't know your address or I'd have done so at the time.

He extended his hand, which Little Chandler took.

—Well, Tommy, he said, I wish you and yours every joy in life, old chap, and tons of money, and may you never die till I shoot you. And that's the wish of a sincere friend, an old friend. You know that?

—I know that, said Little Chandler.

—Any youngsters? said Ignatius Gallaher.

Little Chandler blushed again.

—We have one child, he said.

—Son or daughter?

—A little boy.

Ignatius Gallaher slapped his friend sonorously on the back.

—Bravo, he said, I wouldn't doubt you, Tommy.

Little Chandler smiled, looked confusedly at his glass and bit his lower lip with three childishly white front teeth.

—I hope you'll spend an evening with us, he said, before you go back. My wife will be delighted to meet you. We can have a little music and—

—Thanks awfully, old chap, said Ignatius Gallaher, I'm sorry we didn't meet earlier. But I must leave to-morrow night.

—To-night, perhaps . . . ?

—I'm awfully sorry, old man. You see I'm over here with another fellow, clever young chap he is too, and we arranged to go to a little card-party. Only for that . . .

—O, in that case. . . .

—But who knows? said Ignatius Gallaher consider-ately. Next year I may take a little skip over here now that I've broken the ice. It's only a pleasure deferred.

—Very well, said Little Chandler, the next time you come we must have an evening together. That's agreed now, isn't it?

—Yes, that's agreed, said Ignatius Gallaher. Next year if I come, *parole d'honneur.*

—And to clinch the bargain, said Little Chandler, we'll just have one more now.

Ignatius Gallaher took out a large gold watch and looked at it.

—Is it to be the last? he said. Because you know, I have an a.p.

—O, yes, positively, said Little Chandler.

—Very well, then, said Ignatius Gallaher, let us have another one as a *deoc an doruis*—that's good vernacular for a small whisky, I believe.

Little Chandler ordered the drinks. The blush which had risen to his face a few moments before was establishing itself. A trifle made him blush at any time: and now he felt warm and excited. Three small whiskies had gone to his head and Gallaher's strong cigar had confused his mind, for he was a delicate and abstinent person. The adventure of meeting Gallaher after eight years, of finding himself with Gallaher in Corless's surrounded by lights and noise, of listening to Gallaher's stories and of sharing for a brief space Gallaher's vagrant and triumphant life, upset the equipoise of his sensitive nature. He felt acutely the contrast between his own life and his friend's, and it seemed to him unjust. Gallaher was his inferior in birth and education. He was sure that he could do something better than his friend had ever done, or could ever do, something higher than mere tawdry journalism if he only got the chance. What was it that stood in his way? His unfortunate timidity! He wished to vindicate himself in some way, to assert his manhood. He saw behind Gallaher's refusal of his invitation. Gallaher was only patronising him by his friendliness just as he was patronising Ireland by his visit.

The barman brought their drinks. Little Chandler pushed one glass towards his friend and took up the other boldly.

—Who knows? he said, as they lifted their glasses. When you come next year I may have the pleasure of wishing long life and happiness to Mr and Mrs Ignatius Gallaher.

Ignatius Gallaher in the act of drinking closed one eye expressively over the rim of his glass. When he had drunk he smacked his lips decisively, set down his glass and said:

—No blooming fear of that, my boy. I'm going to have my fling first and see a bit of life and the world before I put my head in the sack—if I ever do.

—Some day you will, said Little Chandler calmly.

Ignatius Gallaher turned his orange tie and slate-blue eyes full upon his friend.

—You think so? he said.

—You'll put your head in the sack, repeated Little Chandler stoutly, like everyone else if you can find the girl.

He had slightly emphasised his tone and he was aware that he had betrayed himself; but, though the colour had heightened in his cheek, he did not flinch from his friend's gaze. Ignatius Gallaher watched him for a few moments and then said:

—If ever it occurs, you may bet your bottom dollar there'll be no mooning and spooning about it. I mean to marry money. She'll have a good fat account at the bank or she won't do for me.

Little Chandler shook his head.

—Why, man alive, said Ignatius Gallaher, vehemently, do you know what it is? I've only to say the word and to-morrow I can have the woman and the cash. You don't believe it? Well, I know it. There are hundreds—what am I saying?—thousands of rich Germans and Jews, rotten with money, that'd only be too glad. . . . You wait a while, my boy. See if I don't play my cards properly. When I go about a thing I mean business, I tell you. You just wait.

He tossed his glass to his mouth, finished his drink and laughed loudly. Then he looked thoughtfully before him and said in a calmer tone:

—But I'm in no hurry. They can wait. I don't fancy tying myself up to one woman, you know.

He imitated with his mouth the act of tasting and made a wry face.

—Must get a bit stale, I should think, he said.

. . . .

Little Chandler sat in the room off the hall, holding a child in his arms. To save money they kept no servant but Annie's young sister Monica came for an hour or so in the morning and an hour or so in the evening to help. But Monica had gone home long ago. It was a quarter to nine. Little Chandler had come home late for tea and, moreover, he had forgotten to bring Annie home the parcel of coffee from Bewley's. Of course she was in a bad humour and gave him short answers. She said she would do without any tea but when it came near the time at which the shop at the corner closed she decided to go out herself for a quarter of a pound of tea and two pounds of sugar. She put the sleeping child deftly in his arms and said:

—Here. Don't waken him.

A little lamp with a white china shade stood upon the table and its light fell over a photograph which was enclosed in a frame of crumpled horn. It was Annie's photograph. Little Chandler looked at it, pausing at the thin tight lips. She wore the pale blue summer blouse which he had brought her home as a present one Saturday. It had cost him ten and elevenpence; but what an agony of nervousness it had cost him! How he had suffered that day, waiting at the shop door until the shop was empty, standing at the counter and trying to appear at his ease while the girl piled ladies' blouses before him, paying at the desk and forgetting to take up the odd penny of his change, being called back by the cashier, and, finally, striving to hide his blushes as he left the shop by examining the parcel to see if it was

securely tied. When he brought the blouse home Annie
kissed him and said it was very pretty and stylish; but
when she heard the price she threw the blouse on the
table and said it was a regular swindle to charge ten and
elevenpence for that. At first she wanted to take it back
but when she tried it on she was delighted with it,
especially with the make of the sleeves, and kissed him
and said he was very good to think of her.

Hm! . . .

He looked coldly into the eyes of the photograph and
they answered coldly. Certainly they were pretty and
the face itself was pretty. But he found something mean
in it. Why was it so unconscious and lady-like? The
composure of the eyes irritated him. They repelled him
and defied him: there was no passion in them, no rapture. He thought of what Gallaher had said about rich
Jewesses. Those dark Oriental eyes, he thought, how full
they are of passion, of voluptuous longing! . . . Why
had he married the eyes in the photograph?

He caught himself up at the question and glanced
nervously round the room. He found something mean
in the pretty furniture which he had bought for his
house on the hire system. Annie had chosen it herself
and it reminded him of her. It too was prim and pretty.
A dull resentment against his life awoke within him.
Could he not escape from his little house? Was it too
late for him to try to live bravely like Gallaher? Could
he go to London? There was the furniture still to be
paid for. If he could only write a book and get it published, that might open the way for him.

A volume of Byron's poems lay before him on the
table. He opened it cautiously with his left hand lest he
should waken the child and began to read the first poem
in the book:

Hushed are the winds and still the evening gloom,
Not e'en a Zephyr wanders through the grove,
Whilst I return to view my Margaret's tomb
And scatter flowers on the dust I love.

He paused. He felt the rhythm of the verse about him
in the room. How melancholy it was! Could he, too,
write like that, express the melancholy of his soul in
verse? There were so many things he wanted to describe: his sensation of a few hours before on Grattan
Bridge, for example. If he could get back again into that
mood. . . .

The child awoke and began to cry. He turned from
the page and tried to hush it: but it would not be
hushed. He began to rock it to and fro in his arms but
its wailing cry grew keener. He rocked it faster while
his eyes began to read the second stanza:

Within this narrow cell reclines her clay,
That clay where once . . .

It was useless. He couldn't read. He couldn't do anything. The wailing of the child pierced the drum of his
ear. It was useless, useless! He was a prisoner for life.
His arms trembled with anger and suddenly bending to
the child's face he shouted:

—Stop!

The child stopped for an instant, had a spasm of
fright and began to scream. He jumped up from his
chair and walked hastily up and down the room with
the child in his arms. It began to sob piteously, losing
its breath for four or five seconds, and then bursting out
anew. The thin walls of the room echoed the sound. He
tried to soothe it but it sobbed more convulsively. He
looked at the contracted and quivering face of the child

and began to be alarmed. He counted seven sobs without a break between them and caught the child to his
breast in fright. If it died! . . .

The door was burst open and a young woman ran in,
panting.

—What is it? What is it? she cried.

The child, hearing its mother's voice, broke out into
a paroxysm of sobbing.

—It's nothing, Annie . . . it's nothing. . . . He began to cry . . .

She flung her parcels on the floor and snatched the
child from him.

—What have you done to him? she cried, glaring into
his face.

Little Chandler sustained for one moment the gaze of
her eyes and his heart closed together as he met the
hatred in them. He began to stammer:

—It's nothing. . . . He . . . he began to cry. . . .
I couldn't . . . I didn't do anything. . . . What?

Giving no heed to him she began to walk up and
down the room, clasping the child tightly in her arms
and murmuring:

—My little man! My little mannie! Was 'ou frightened,
love? . . . There now, love! There now! . . . Lamba-
baun! Mamma's little lamb of the world! . . . There
now!

Little Chandler felt his cheeks suffused with shame
and he stood back out of the lamplight. He listened
while the paroxysm of the child's sobbing grew less and
less; and tears of remorse started to his eyes.

Counterparts

THE bell rang furiously and, when Miss Parker went to the tube, a furious voice called out in a piercing North of Ireland accent:

—Send Farrington here!

Miss Parker returned to her machine, saying to a man who was writing at a desk:

—Mr Alleyne wants you upstairs.

The man muttered *Blast him!* under his breath and pushed back his chair to stand up. When he stood up he was tall and of great bulk. He had a hanging face, dark wine-coloured, with fair eyebrows and moustache: his eyes bulged forward slightly and the whites of them were dirty. He lifted up the counter and, passing by the clients, went out of the office with a heavy step.

He went heavily upstairs until he came to the second landing, where a door bore a brass plate with the inscription *Mr Alleyne*. Here he halted, puffing with labour and vexation, and knocked. The shrill voice cried:

—Come in!

The man entered Mr Alleyne's room. Simultaneously Mr Alleyne, a little man wearing gold-rimmed glasses on a clean-shaven face, shot his head up over a pile of documents. The head itself was so pink and hairless that it seemed like a large egg reposing on the papers. Mr Alleyne did not lose a moment:

—Farrington? What is the meaning of this? Why have I always to complain of you? May I ask you why you haven't made a copy of that contract between Bodley and Kirwan? I told you it must be ready by four o'clock.

—But Mr Shelley said, sir—

—*Mr Shelley said, sir.* . . . Kindly attend to what I say and not to what *Mr Shelley says, sir.* You have always some excuse or another for shirking work. Let me tell you that if the contract is not copied before this evening I'll lay the matter before Mr Crosbie. . . . Do you hear me now?

—Yes, sir.

—Do you hear me now? . . . Ay and another little matter! I might as well be talking to the wall as talking to you. Understand once for all that you get a half an hour for your lunch and not an hour and a half. How many courses do you want, I'd like to know. . . . Do you mind me, now?

—Yes, sir.

Mr Alleyne bent his head again upon his pile of papers. The man stared fixedly at the polished skull which directed the affairs of Crosbie & Alleyne, gauging its fragility. A spasm of rage gripped his throat for a few moments and then passed, leaving after it a sharp sensation of thirst. The man recognised the sensation and felt that he must have a good night's drinking. The middle of the month was passed and, if he could get the copy done in time, Mr Alleyne might give him an order on the cashier. He stood still, gazing fixedly at the head upon the pile of papers. Suddenly Mr Alleyne began to upset all the papers, searching for something. Then, as if he had been unaware of the man's presence till that moment, he shot up his head again, saying:

—Eh? Are you going to stand there all day? Upon my word, Farrington, you take things easy!

—I was waiting to see . . .

—Very good, you needn't wait to see. Go downstairs and do your work.

The man walked heavily towards the door and, as he
went out of the room, he heard Mr Alleyne cry after
him that if the contract was not copied by evening Mr
Crosbie would hear of the matter.

He returned to his desk in the lower office and
counted the sheets which remained to be copied. He
took up his pen and dipped it in the ink but he continued to stare stupidly at the last words he had written:
In no case shall the said Bernard Bodley be . . . The
evening was falling and in a few minutes they would
be lighting the gas; then he could write. He felt that he
must slake the thirst in his throat. He stood up from his
desk and, lifting the counter as before, passed out of the
office. As he was passing out the chief clerk looked at
him inquiringly.

—It's all right, Mr Shelley, said the man, pointing with
his finger to indicate the objective of his journey.

The chief clerk glanced at the hat-rack but, seeing
the row complete, offered no remark. As soon as he was
on the landing the man pulled a shepherd's plaid cap
out of his pocket, put it on his head and ran quickly
down the rickety stairs. From the street door he walked
on furtively on the inner side of the path towards the
corner and all at once dived into a doorway. He was
now safe in the dark snug of O'Neill's shop, and, filling
up the little window that looked into the bar with his
inflamed face, the colour of dark wine or dark meat, he
called out:

—Here, Pat, give us a g.p., like a good fellow.

The curate brought him a glass of plain porter. The
man drank it at a gulp and asked for a caraway seed.
He put his penny on the counter and, leaving the curate
to grope for it in the gloom, retreated out of the snug
as furtively as he had entered it.

Darkness, accompanied by a thick fog, was gaining

upon the dusk of February and the lamps in Eustace
Street had been lit. The man went up by the houses
until he reached the door of the office, wondering
whether he could finish his copy in time. On the stairs
a moist pungent odour of perfumes saluted his nose:
evidently Miss Delacour had come while he was out in
O'Neill's. He crammed his cap back again into his
pocket and re-entered the office, assuming an air of
absent-mindedness.

—Mr Alleyne has been calling for you, said the chief
clerk severely. Where were you?

The man glanced at the two clients who were standing at the counter as if to intimate that their presence
prevented him from answering. As the clients were both
male the chief clerk allowed himself a laugh.

—I know that game, he said. Five times in one day
is a little bit. . . . Well, you better look sharp and get
a copy of our correspondence in the Delacour case for
Mr Alleyne.

This address in the presence of the public, his run
upstairs and the porter he had gulped down so hastily
confused the man and, as he sat down at his desk to
get what was required, he realised how hopeless was
the task of finishing his copy of the contract before half
past five. The dark damp night was coming and he
longed to spend it in the bars, drinking with his friends
amid the glare of gas and the clatter of glasses. He got
out the Delacour correspondence and passed out of the
office. He hoped Mr Alleyne would not discover that the
last two letters were missing.

The moist pungent perfume lay all the way up to Mr
Alleyne's room. Miss Delacour was a middle-aged
woman of Jewish appearance. Mr Alleyne was said to be
sweet on her or on her money. She came to the office

often and stayed a long time when she came. She was sitting beside his desk now in an aroma of perfumes, smoothing the handle of her umbrella and nodding the great black feather in her hat. Mr Alleyne had swivelled his chair round to face her and thrown his right foot jauntily upon his left knee. The man put the correspondence on the desk and bowed respectfully but neither Mr Alleyne nor Miss Delacour took any notice of his bow. Mr Alleyne tapped a finger on the correspondence and then flicked it towards him as if to say: *That's all right: you can go.*

The man returned to the lower office and sat down again at his desk. He stared intently at the incomplete phrase: *In no case shall the said Bernard Bodley be* . . . and thought how strange it was that the last three words began with the same letter. The chief clerk began to hurry Miss Parker, saying she would never have the letters typed in time for post. The man listened to the clicking of the machine for a few minutes and then set to work to finish his copy. But his head was not clear and his mind wandered away to the glare and rattle of the public-house. It was a night for hot punches. He struggled on with his copy, but when the clock struck five he had still fourteen pages to write. Blast it! He couldn't finish it in time. He longed to execrate aloud, to bring his fist down on something violently. He was so enraged that he wrote *Bernard Bernard* instead of *Bernard Bodley* and had to begin again on a clean sheet.

He felt strong enough to clear out the whole office singlehanded. His body ached to do something, to rush out and revel in violence. All the indignities of his life enraged him. . . . Could he ask the cashier privately for an advance? No, the cashier was no good, no damn good: he wouldn't give an advance. . . . He knew

where he would meet the boys: Leonard and O'Halloran
and Nosey Flynn. The barometer of his emotional nature was set for a spell of riot.

His imagination had so abstracted him that his name
was called twice before he answered. Mr. Alleyne and
Miss Delacour were standing outside the counter and all
the clerks had turned round in anticipation of something. The man got up from his desk. Mr Alleyne began
a tirade of abuse, saying that two letters were missing.
The man answered that he knew nothing about them,
that he had made a faithful copy. The tirade continued:
it was so bitter and violent that the man could hardly
restrain his fist from descending upon the head of the
manikin before him.

—I know nothing about any other two letters, he said
stupidly.

—*You—know—nothing*. Of course you know nothing,
said Mr Alleyne. Tell me, he added, glancing first for
approval to the lady beside him, do you take me for a
fool? Do you think me an utter fool?

The man glanced from the lady's face to the little
egg-shaped head and back again; and, almost before he
was aware of it, his tongue had found a felicitous moment:

—I don't think, sir, he said, that that's a fair question
to put to me.

There was a pause in the very breathing of the clerks.
Everyone was astounded (the author of the witticism no
less than his neighbours) and Miss Delacour, who was
a stout amiable person, began to smile broadly. Mr
Alleyne flushed to the hue of a wild rose and his mouth
twitched with a dwarf's passion. He shook his fist in
the man's face till it seemed to vibrate like the knob of
some electric machine:

—You impertinent ruffian! You impertinent ruffian! I'll

make short work of you! Wait till you see! You'll apologise to me for your impertinence or you'll quit the office
instanter! You'll quit this, I'm telling you, or you'll
apologise to me!

.   .   .   .   .   .

He stood in a doorway opposite the office watching
to see if the cashier would come out alone. All the clerks
passed out and finally the cashier came out with the
chief clerk. It was no use trying to say a word to him
when he was with the chief clerk. The man felt that his
position was bad enough. He had been obliged to offer
an abject apology to Mr Alleyne for his impertinence
but he knew what a hornet's nest the office would be for
him. He could remember the way in which Mr Alleyne
had hounded little Peake out of the office in order to
make room for his own nephew. He felt savage and
thirsty and revengeful, annoyed with himself and with
everyone else. Mr Alleyne would never give him an
hour's rest; his life would be a hell to him. He had made
a proper fool of himself this time. Could he not keep his
tongue in his cheek? But they had never pulled together
from the first, he and Mr Alleyne, ever since the day Mr
Alleyne had overheard him mimicking his North of Ireland accent to amuse Higgins and Miss Parker: that had
been the beginning of it. He might have tried Higgins
for the money, but sure Higgins never had anything for
himself. A man with two establishments to keep up, of
course he couldn't. . . .

He felt his great body again aching for the comfort
of the public-house. The fog had begun to chill him and
he wondered could he touch Pat in O'Neill's. He could
not touch him for more than a bob—and a bob was no
use. Yet he must get money somewhere or other: he had
spent his last penny for the g.p. and soon it would be too
late for getting money anywhere. Suddenly, as he was

fingering his watch-chain, he thought of Terry Kelly's
pawn-office in Fleet Street. That was the dart! Why
didn't he think of it sooner?

He went through the narrow alley of Temple Bar
quickly, muttering to himself that they could all go to
hell because he was going to have a good night of it.
The clerk in Terry Kelly's said *A crown!* but the con-
signor held out for six shillings; and in the end the six
shillings was allowed him literally. He came out of the
pawn-office joyfully, making a little cylinder of the
coins between his thumb and fingers. In Westmoreland
Street the footpaths were crowded with young men and
women returning from business and ragged urchins ran
here and there yelling out the names of the evening editions. The man passed through the crowd, looking on
the spectacle generally with proud satisfaction and staring masterfully at the office-girls. His head was full of
the noises of tram-gongs and swishing trolleys and his
nose already sniffed the curling fumes of punch. As he
walked on he preconsidered the terms in which he
would narrate the incident to the boys:

—So, I just looked at him—coolly, you know, and
looked at her. Then I looked back at him again—taking
my time, you know. *I don't think that that's a fair
question to put to me,* says I.

Nosey Flynn was sitting up in his usual corner of
Davy Byrne's and, when he heard the story, he stood
Farrington a half-one, saying it was as smart a thing as
ever he heard. Farrington stood a drink in his turn.
After a while O'Halloran and Paddy Leonard came in
and the story was repeated to them. O'Halloran stood
tailors of malt, hot, all round and told the story of the
retort he had made to the chief clerk when he was in
Callan's of Fownes's Street; but, as the retort was after

the manner of the liberal shepherds in the eclogues, he had to admit that it was not so clever as Farrington's retort. At this Farrington told the boys to polish off that and have another.

Just as they were naming their poisons who should come in but Higgins! Of course he had to join in with the others. The men asked him to give his version of it, and he did so with great vivacity for the sight of five small hot whiskies was very exhilarating. Everyone roared laughing when he showed the way in which Mr Alleyne shook his fist in Farrington's face. Then he imitated Farrington, saying, *And here was my nabs, as cool as you please,* while Farrington looked at the company out of his heavy dirty eyes, smiling and at times drawing forth stray drops of liquor from his moustache with the aid of his lower lip.

When that round was over there was a pause. O'Halloran had money but neither of the other two seemed to have any; so the whole party left the shop somewhat regretfully. At the corner of Duke Street Higgins and Nosey Flynn bevelled off to the left while the other three turned back towards the city. Rain was drizzling down on the cold streets and, when they reached the Ballast Office, Farrington suggested the Scotch House. The bar was full of men and loud with the noise of tongues and glasses. The three men pushed past the whining match-sellers at the door and formed a little party at the corner of the counter. They began to exchange stories. Leonard introduced them to a young fellow named Weathers who was performing at the Tivoli as an acrobat and knockabout *artiste*. Farrington stood a drink all round. Weathers said he would take a small Irish and Apollinaris. Farrington, who had definite notions of what was what, asked the boys would they have an Apollinaris too;

but the boys told Tim to make theirs hot. The talk became theatrical. O'Halloran stood a round and then Farrington stood another round, Weathers protesting that the hospitality was too Irish. He promised to get them in behind the scenes and introduce them to some nice girls. O'Halloran said that he and Leonard would go but that Farrington wouldn't go because he was a married man; and Farrington's heavy dirty eyes leered at the company in token that he understood he was being chafed. Weathers made them all have just one little tincture at his expense and promised to meet them later on at Mulligan's in Poolbeg Street.

When the Scotch House closed they went round to Mulligan's. They went into the parlour at the back and O'Halloran ordered small hot specials all round. They were all beginning to feel mellow. Farrington was just standing another round when Weathers came back. Much to Farrington's relief he drank a glass of bitter this time. Funds were running low but they had enough to keep them going. Presently two young women with big hats and a young man in a check suit came in and sat at a table close by. Weathers saluted them and told the company that they were out of the Tivoli. Farrington's eyes wandered at every moment in the direction of one of the young women. There was something striking in her appearance. An immense scarf of peacock-blue muslin was wound round her hat and knotted in a great bow under her chin; and she wore bright yellow gloves, reaching to the elbow. Farrington gazed admiringly at the plump arm which she moved very often and with much grace; and when, after a little time, she answered his gaze he admired still more her large dark brown eyes. The oblique staring expression in them fascinated him. She glanced at him once or twice and, when the party was leaving the room, she brushed against his chair and said *O, pardon!* in a London accent. He watched her leave the room in the hope that she would look back at him, but he was disappointed. He cursed his want of money and cursed all the rounds he had stood, particularly all the whiskies and Apollinaris which he had stood to Weathers. If there was one thing that he hated it was a sponge. He was so angry that he lost count of the conversation of his friends.

When Paddy Leonard called him he found that they were talking about feats of strength. Weathers was showing his biceps muscle to the company and boasting so much that the other two had called on Farrington to uphold the national honour. Farrington pulled up his sleeve accordingly and showed his biceps muscle to the company. The two arms were examined and compared and finally it was agreed to have a trial of strength. The table was cleared and the two men rested their elbows on it, clasping hands. When Paddy Leonard said *Go!* each was to try to bring down the other's hand on to the table. Farrington looked very serious and determined.

The trial began. After about thirty seconds Weathers brought his opponent's hand slowly down on to the table. Farrington's dark wine-coloured face flushed darker still with anger and humiliation at having been defeated by such a stripling.

—You're not to put the weight of your body behind it. Play fair, he said.

—Who's not playing fair? said the other.

—Come on again. The two best out of three.

The trial began again. The veins stood out on Farrington's forehead, and the pallor of Weathers' complexion changed to peony. Their hands and arms trembled under the stress. After a long struggle Weathers again brought his opponent's hand slowly on to the table. There was a murmur of applause from the spectators. The curate, who was standing beside the table, nodded his red head towards the victor and said with loutish familiarity:

—Ah! that's the knack!

—What the hell do you know about it? said Farrington fiercely, turning on the man. What do you put in your gab for?

—Sh, sh! said O'Halloran, observing the violent expression of Farrington's face. Pony up, boys. We'll have just one little smahan more and then we'll be off.

A very sullen-faced man stood at the corner of O'Connell Bridge waiting for the little Sandymount tram to take him home. He was full of smouldering anger and revengefulness. He felt humiliated and discontented; he did not even feel drunk; and he had only twopence in his pocket. He cursed everything. He had done for himself in the office, pawned his watch, spent all his money; and he had not even got drunk. He began to feel thirsty again and he longed to be back again in the hot reeking public-house. He had lost his reputation as a strong man, having been defeated twice by a mere boy. His heart swelled with fury and, when he thought of the woman in the big hat who had brushed against him and said *Pardon!* his fury nearly choked him.

His tram let him down at Shelbourne Road and he steered his great body along in the shadow of the wall of the barracks. He loathed returning to his home. When he went in by the side-door he found the kitchen empty and the kitchen fire nearly out. He bawled upstairs:

—Ada! Ada!

His wife was a little sharp-faced woman who bullied her husband when he was sober and was bullied by him

when he was drunk. They had five children. A little boy
came running down the stairs.

—Who is that? said the man, peering through the
darkness.

—Me, pa.

—Who are you? Charlie?

—No, pa. Tom.

—Where's your mother?

—She's out at the chapel.

—That's right. . . . Did she think of leaving any
dinner for me?

—Yes, pa. I—

—Light the lamp. What do you mean by having the
place in darkness? Are the other children in bed?

The man sat down heavily on one of the chairs while
the little boy lit the lamp. He began to mimic his son's
flat accent, saying half to himself: *At the chapel. At the
chapel, if you please!* When the lamp was lit he banged
his fist on the table and shouted:

—What's for my dinner?

—I'm going . . . to cook it, pa, said the little boy.

The man jumped up furiously and pointed to the fire.

—On that fire! You let the fire out! By God, I'll teach
you to do that again!

He took a step to the door and seized the walking-
stick which was standing behind it.

—I'll teach you to let the fire out! he said, rolling up
his sleeve in order to give his arm free play.

The little boy cried *O, pa!* and ran whimpering round
the table, but the man followed him and caught him
by the coat. The little boy looked about him wildly but,
seeing no way of escape, fell upon his knees.

—Now, you'll let the fire out the next time! said the
man, striking at him viciously with the stick. Take that,
you little whelp!

The boy uttered a squeal of pain as the stick cut his thigh. He clasped his hands together in the air and his voice shook with fright.

—O, pa! he cried. Don't beat me, pa! And I'll . . . I'll say a *Hail Mary* for you. . . . I'll say a *Hail Mary* for you, pa, if you don't beat me. . . . I'll say a *Hail Mary*. . . .

Clay

THE matron had given her leave to go out as soon as the women's tea was over and Maria looked forward to her evening out. The kitchen was spick and span: the cook said you could see yourself in the big copper boilers. The fire was nice and bright and on one of the side-tables were four very big barmbracks. These barmbracks seemed uncut; but if you went closer you would see that they had been cut into long thick even slices and were ready to be handed round at tea. Maria had cut them herself.

Maria was a very, very small person indeed but she had a very long nose and a very long chin. She talked a little through her nose, always soothingly: *Yes, my dear*, and *No, my dear*. She was always sent for when the women quarrelled over their tubs and always succeeded in making peace. One day the matron had said to her:

—Maria, you are a veritable peace-maker!

And the sub-matron and two of the Board ladies had heard the compliment. And Ginger Mooney was always saying what she wouldn't do to the dummy who had charge of the irons if it wasn't for Maria. Everyone was so fond of Maria.

The women would have their tea at six o'clock and she would be able to get away before seven. From Balls-bridge to the Pillar, twenty minutes; from the Pillar to Drumcondra, twenty minutes; and twenty minutes to buy the things. She would be there before eight. She took out her purse with the silver clasps and read again the words *A Present from Belfast*. She was very fond of that purse because Joe had brought it to her five years before when he and Alphy had gone to Belfast on a Whit-Monday trip. In the purse were two half-crowns and some coppers. She would have five shillings clear after paying tram fare. What a nice evening they would have, all the children singing! Only she hoped that Joe wouldn't come in drunk. He was so different when he took any drink.

Often he had wanted her to go and live with them; but she would have felt herself in the way (though Joe's wife was ever so nice with her) and she had be-come accustomed to the life of the laundry. Joe was a good fellow. She had nursed him and Alphy too; and Joe used often say:

—Mamma is mamma but Maria is my proper mother.

After the break-up at home the boys had got her that position in the *Dublin by Lamplight* laundry, and she liked it. She used to have such a bad opinion of Protes-tants but now she thought they were very nice people, a little quiet and serious, but still very nice people to live with. Then she had her plants in the conservatory and she liked looking after them. She had lovely ferns and wax-plants and, whenever anyone came to visit her, she always gave the visitor one or two slips from her con-

servatory. There was one thing she didn't like and that
was the tracts on the walls; but the matron was such a
nice person to deal with, so genteel.

When the cook told her everything was ready she
went into the women's room and began to pull the big
bell. In a few minutes the women began to come in by
twos and threes, wiping their steaming hands in their
petticoats and pulling down the sleeves of their blouses
over their red steaming arms. They settled down before their huge mugs which the cook and the dummy
filled up with hot tea, already mixed with milk and
sugar in huge tin cans. Maria superintended the distribution of the barmbrack and saw that every woman
got her four slices. There was a great deal of laughing
and joking during the meal. Lizzie Fleming said Maria
was sure to get the ring and, though Fleming had said
that for so many Hallow Eves, Maria had to laugh and
say she didn't want any ring or man either; and when
she laughed her grey-green eyes sparkled with disappointed shyness and the tip of her nose nearly met the
tip of her chin. Then Ginger Mooney lifted up her mug
of tea and proposed Maria's health while all the other
women clattered with their mugs on the table, and said
she was sorry she hadn't a sup of porter to drink it in.
And Maria laughed again till the tip of her nose nearly
met the tip of her chin and till her minute body nearly
shook itself asunder because she knew that Mooney
meant well though, of course, she had the notions of a
common woman.

But wasn't Maria glad when the women had finished
their tea and the cook and the dummy had begun to
clear away the tea-things! She went into her little bedroom and, remembering that the next morning was a
mass morning, changed the hand of the alarm from
seven to six. Then she took off her working skirt and her

house-boots and laid her best skirt out on the bed and
her tiny dress-boots beside the foot of the bed. She
changed her blouse too and, as she stood before the
mirror, she thought of how she used to dress for mass on
Sunday morning when she was a young girl; and she
looked with quaint affection at the diminutive body
which she had so often adorned. In spite of its years
she found it a nice tidy little body.

When she got outside the streets were shining with
rain and she was glad of her old brown raincloak. The
tram was full and she had to sit on the little stool at the
end of the car, facing all the people, with her toes barely
touching the floor. She arranged in her mind all she
was going to do and thought how much better it was
to be independent and to have your own money in your
pocket. She hoped they would have a nice evening. She
was sure they would but she could not help thinking
what a pity it was Alphy and Joe were not speaking.
They were always falling out now but when they were
boys together they used to be the best of friends: but
such was life.

She got out of her tram at the Pillar and ferreted her
way quickly among the crowds. She went into Downes's
cakeshop but the shop was so full of people that it was
a long time before she could get herself attended to. She
bought a dozen of mixed penny cakes, and at last came
out of the shop laden with a big bag. Then she thought
what else would she buy: she wanted to buy something
really nice. They would be sure to have plenty of apples
and nuts. It was hard to know what to buy and all she
could think of was cake. She decided to buy some plumcake but Downes's plumcake had not enough almond
icing on top of it so she went over to a shop in Henry
Street. Here she was a long time in suiting herself and
the stylish young lady behind the counter, who was evi-

dently a little annoyed by her, asked her was it wedding-cake she wanted to buy. That made Maria blush and smile at the young lady; but the young lady took it all very seriously and finally cut a thick slice of plumcake, parcelled it up and said:

—Two-and-four, please.

She thought she would have to stand in the Drum-condra tram because none of the young men seemed to notice her but an elderly gentleman made room for her. He was a stout gentleman and he wore a brown hard hat; he had a square red face and a greyish moustache. Maria thought he was a colonel-looking gentleman and she reflected how much more polite he was than the young men who simply stared straight before them. The gentleman began to chat with her about Hallow Eve and the rainy weather. He supposed the bag was full of good things for the little ones and said it was only right that the youngsters should enjoy themselves while they were young. Maria agreed with him and favoured him with demure nods and hems. He was very nice with her, and when she was getting out at the Canal Bridge she thanked him and bowed, and he bowed to her and raised his hat and smiled agreeably; and while she was going up along the terrace, bending her tiny head under the rain, she thought how easy it was to know a gentle-man even when he has a drop taken.

Everybody said: *O, here's Maria!* when she came to Joe's house. Joe was there, having come home from business, and all the children had their Sunday dresses on. There were two big girls in from next door and games were going on. Maria gave the bag of cakes to the eldest boy, Alphy, to divide and Mrs Donnelly said it was too good of her to bring such a big bag of cakes and made all the children say:

—Thanks, Maria.

But Maria said she had brought something special for papa and mamma, something they would be sure to like, and she began to look for her plumcake. She tried in Downes's bag and then in the pockets of her raincoat and then on the hallstand but nowhere could she find it. Then she asked all the children had any of them eaten it—by mistake, of course—but the children all said no and looked as if they did not like to eat cakes if they were to be accused of stealing. Everybody had a solution for the mystery and Mrs Donnelly said it was plain that Maria had left it behind her in the tram. Maria, remembering how confused the gentleman with the greyish moustache had made her, coloured with shame and vexation and disappointment. At the thought of the failure of her little surprise and of the two and fourpence she had thrown away for nothing she nearly cried outright.

But Joe said it didn't matter and made her sit down by the fire. He was very nice with her. He told her all that went on in his office, repeating for her a smart answer which he had made to the manager. Maria did not understand why Joe laughed so much over the answer he had made but she said that the manager must have been a very overbearing person to deal with. Joe said he wasn't so bad when you knew how to take him, that he was a decent sort so long as you didn't rub him the wrong way. Mrs Donnelly played the piano for the children and they danced and sang. Then the two next-door girls handed round the nuts. Nobody could find the nutcrackers and Joe was nearly getting cross over it and asked how did they expect Maria to crack nuts without a nutcracker. But Maria said she didn't like nuts and that they weren't to bother about her. Then Joe asked would she take a bottle of stout and Mrs Donnelly said there was port wine too in the house if she would prefer that. Maria said she would rather they didn't ask her to take anything: but Joe insisted.

So Maria let him have his way and they sat by the fire talking over old times and Maria thought she would put in a good word for Alphy. But Joe cried that God might strike him stone dead if ever he spoke a word to his brother again and Maria said she was sorry she had mentioned the matter. Mrs Donnelly told her husband it was a great shame for him to speak that way of his own flesh and blood but Joe said that Alphy was no brother of his and there was nearly being a row on the head of it. But Joe said he would not lose his temper on account of the night it was and asked his wife to open some more stout. The two next-door girls had arranged some Hallow Eve games and soon everything was merry again. Maria was delighted to see the children so merry and Joe and his wife in such good spirits. The next-door girls put some saucers on the table and then led the children up to the table, blindfold. One got the prayer-book and the other three got the water; and when one of the next-door girls got the ring Mrs Donnelly shook her finger at the blushing girl as much as to say: *O, I know all about it!* They insisted then on blindfolding Maria and leading her up to the table to see what she would get; and, while they were putting on the bandage, Maria laughed and laughed again till the tip of her nose nearly met the tip of her chin.

They led her up to the table amid laughing and joking and she put her hand out in the air as she was told to do. She moved her hand about here and there in the air and descended on one of the saucers. She felt a soft wet substance with her fingers and was surprised that nobody spoke or took off her bandage. There was a pause for a few seconds; and then a great deal of scuffling and whispering. Somebody said something about the garden, and

at last Mrs Donnelly said something very cross to one
of the next-door girls and told her to throw it out at
once: that was no play. Maria understood that it was
wrong that time and so she had to do it over again: and
this time she got the prayer-book.

After that Mrs Donnelly played Miss McCloud's Reel
for the children and Joe made Maria take a glass of
wine. Soon they were all quite merry again and Mrs
Donnelly said Maria would enter a convent before the
year was out because she had got the prayer-book.
Maria had never seen Joe so nice to her as he was that
night, so full of pleasant talk and reminiscences. She
said they were all very good to her.

At last the children grew tired and sleepy and Joe
asked Maria would she not sing some little song before
she went, one of the old songs. Mrs Donnelly said *Do,
please, Maria!* and so Maria had to get up and stand
beside the piano. Mrs Donnelly bade the children be
quiet and listen to Maria's song. Then she played the
prelude and said *Now, Maria!* and Maria, blushing very
much, began to sing in a tiny quavering voice. She sang
I Dreamt that I Dwelt, and when she came to the
second verse she sang again:

> *I dreamt that I dwelt in marble halls*
> *With vassals and serfs at my side*
> *And of all who assembled within those walls*
> *That I was the hope and the pride.*
>
> *I had riches too great to count, could boast*
> *Of a high ancestral name,*
> *But I also dreamt, which pleased me most,*
> *That you love me still the same.*

But no one tried to show her her mistake; and when
she had ended her song Joe was very much moved. He

said that there was no time like the long ago and no
music for him like poor old Balfe, whatever other people might say; and his eyes filled up so much with tears
that he could not find what he was looking for and in
the end he had to ask his wife to tell him where the
corkscrew was.

A Painful Case

MR JAMES DUFFY lived in Chapelizod because he wished to live as far as possible from
the city of which he was a citizen and because he found
all the other suburbs of Dublin mean, modern and pretentious. He lived in an old sombre house and from his
windows he could look into the disused distillery or
upwards along the shallow river on which Dublin is
built. The lofty walls of his uncarpeted room were free
from pictures. He had himself bought every article of
furniture in the room: a black iron bedstead, an iron
washstand, four cane chairs, a clothes-rack, a coal-scut-
tle, a fender and irons and a square table on which lay
a double desk. A bookcase had been made in an alcove
by means of shelves of white wood. The bed was clothed
with white bed-clothes and a black and scarlet rug covered the foot. A little hand-mirror hung above the washstand and during the day a white-shaded lamp stood as
the sole ornament of the mantelpiece. The books on the
white wooden shelves were arranged from below upwards according to bulk. A complete Wordsworth stood
at one end of the lowest shelf and a copy of the *May-
nooth Catechism,* sewn into the cloth cover of a note-

book, stood at one end of the top shelf. Writing materials were always on the desk. In the desk lay a manuscript translation of Hauptmann's *Michael Kramer*, the stage directions of which were written in purple ink, and a little sheaf of papers held together by a brass pin. In these sheets a sentence was inscribed from time to time and, in an ironical moment, the headline of an advertisement for *Bile Beans* had been pasted on to the first sheet. On lifting the lid of the desk a faint fragrance escaped—the fragrance of new cedarwood pencils or of a bottle of gum or of an over-ripe apple which might have been left there and forgotten.

Mr Duffy abhorred anything which betokened physical or mental disorder. A mediæval doctor would have called him saturnine. His face, which carried the entire tale of his years, was of the brown tint of Dublin streets. On his long and rather large head grew dry black hair and a tawny moustache did not quite cover an unamiable mouth. His cheekbones also gave his face a harsh character; but there was no harshness in the eyes which, looking at the world from under their tawny eyebrows, gave the impression of a man ever alert to greet a redeeming instinct in others but often disappointed. He lived at a little distance from his body, regarding his own acts with doubtful side-glances. He had an odd autobiographical habit which led him to compose in his mind from time to time a short sentence about himself containing a subject in the third person and a predicate in the past tense. He never gave alms to beggars and walked firmly, carrying a stout hazel.

He had been for many years cashier of a private bank in Baggot Street. Every morning he came in from Chapelizod by tram. At midday he went to Dan Burke's and took his lunch—a bottle of lager beer and a small trayful of arrowroot biscuits. At four o'clock he was set free.

He dined in an eating-house in George's Street where he felt himself safe from the society of Dublin's gilded youth and where there was a certan plain honesty in the bill of fare. His evenings were spent either before his landlady's piano or roaming about the outskirts of the city. His liking for Mozart's music brought him sometimes to an opera or a concert: these were the only dissipations of his life.

He had neither companions nor friends, church nor creed. He lived his spiritual life without any communion with others, visiting his relatives at Christmas and escorting them to the cemetery when they died. He performed these two social duties for old dignity' sake but conceded nothing further to the conventions which regulate the civic life. He allowed himself to think that in certain circumstances he would rob his bank but, as these circumstances never arose, his life rolled out evenly —an adventureless tale.

One evening he found himself sitting beside two ladies in the Rotunda. The house, thinly peopled and silent, gave distressing prophecy of failure. The lady who sat next him looked round at the deserted house once or twice and then said:

—What a pity there is such a poor house to-night! It's so hard on people to have to sing to empty benches.

He took the remark as an invitation to talk. He was surprised that she seemed so little awkward. While they talked he tried to fix her permanently in his memory. When he learned that the young girl beside her was her daughter he judged her to be a year or so younger than himself. Her face, which must have been handsome, had remained intelligent. It was an oval face with strongly marked features. The eyes were very dark blue and steady. Their gaze began with a defiant note but was confused by what seemed a deliberate swoon of the pupil into the iris, revealing for an instant a temperament of great sensibility. The pupil reasserted itself quickly, this half-disclosed nature fell again under the reign of prudence, and her astrakhan jacket, moulding a bosom of a certain fulness, struck the note of defiance more definitely.

He met her again a few weeks afterwards at a concert in Earlsfort Terrace and seized the moments when her daughter's attention was diverted to become intimate. She alluded once or twice to her husband but her tone was not such as to make the allusion a warning. Her name was Mrs Sinico. Her husband's great-great-grandfather had come from Leghorn. Her husband was captain of a mercantile boat plying between Dublin and Holland; and they had one child.

Meeting her a third time by accident he found courage to make an appointment. She came. This was the first of many meetings; they met always in the evening and chose the most quiet quarters for their walks together. Mr. Duffy, however, had a distaste for underhand ways and, finding that they were compelled to meet stealthily, he forced her to ask him to her house. Captain Sinico encouraged his visits, thinking that his daughter's hand was in question. He had dismissed his wife so sincerely from his gallery of pleasures that he did not suspect that anyone else would take an interest in her. As the husband was often away and the daughter out giving music lessons Mr Duffy had many opportunities of enjoying the lady's society. Neither he nor she had had any such adventure before and neither was conscious of any incongruity. Little by little he entangled his thoughts with hers. He lent her books, provided her with ideas, shared his intellectual life with her. She listened to all.

Sometimes in return for his theories she gave out

some fact of her own life. With almost maternal solicitude she urged him to let his nature open to the full;
she became his confessor. He told her that for some time
he had assisted at the meetings of an Irish Socialist
Party where he had felt himself a unique figure amidst
a score of sober workmen in a garret lit by an inefficient
oil-lamp. When the party had divided into three sec-
tions, each under its own leader and in its own garret,
he had discontinued his attendances. The workmen's
discussions, he said, were too timorous; the interest they
took in the question of wages was inordinate. He felt
that they were hard-featured realists and that they resented an exactitude which was the product of a leisure
not within their reach. No social revolution, he told her,
would be likely to strike Dublin for some centuries.

She asked him why did he not write out his thoughts.
For what, he asked her, with careful scorn. To com-
pete with phrasemongers, incapable of thinking con-
secutively for sixty seconds? To submit himself to the
criticisms of an obtuse middle class which entrusted its
morality to policemen and its fine arts to impresarios?

He went often to her little cottage outside Dublin;
often they spent their evenings alone. Little by little,
as their thoughts entangled, they spoke of subjects less
remote. Her companionship was like a warm soil about
an exotic. Many times she allowed the dark to fall upon
them, refraining from lighting the lamp. The dark discreet room, their isolation, the music that still vibrated
in their ears united them. This union exalted him, wore
away the rough edges of his character, emotionalised
his mental life. Sometimes he caught himself listening
to the sound of his own voice. He thought that in her
eyes he would ascend to an angelical stature; and, as he
attached the fervent nature of his companion more and
more closely to him, he heard the strange impersonal

voice which he recognised as his own, insisting on the
soul's incurable loneliness. We cannot give ourselves, it
said: we are our own. The end of these discourses was
that one night during which she had shown every sign
of unusual excitement, Mrs Sinico caught up his hand
passionately and pressed it to her cheek.

Mr Duffy was very much surprised. Her interpretation of his words disillusioned him. He did not visit her
for a week; then he wrote to her asking her to meet him.
As he did not wish their last interview to be troubled
by the influence of their ruined confessional they met in
a little cakeshop near the Parkgate. It was cold autumn
weather but in spite of the cold they wandered up and
down the roads of the Park for nearly three hours. They
agreed to break off their intercourse: every bond, he
said, is a bond to sorrow. When they came out of the
Park they walked in silence towards the tram; but here
she began to tremble so violently that, fearing another
collapse on her part, he bade her good-bye quickly and
left her. A few days later he received a parcel containing his books and music.

Four years passed. Mr Duffy returned to his even
way of life. His room still bore witness of the orderliness
of his mind. Some new pieces of music encumbered the
music-stand in the lower room and on his shelves stood
two volumes by Nietzsche: *Thus Spake Zarathustra* and
The Gay Science. He wrote seldom in the sheaf of
papers which lay in his desk. One of his sentences, written two months after his last interview with Mrs Sinico,
read: Love between man and man is impossible because
there must not be sexual intercourse and friendship between man and woman is impossible because there must
be sexual intercourse. He kept away from concerts lest
he should meet her. His father died; the junior partner
of the bank retired. And still every morning he went

into the city by tram and every evening walked home from the city after having dined moderately in George's Street and read the evening paper for dessert.

One evening as he was about to put a morsel of corned beef and cabbage into his mouth his hand stopped. His eyes fixed themselves on a paragraph in the evening paper which he had propped against the water-carafe. He replaced the morsel of food on his plate and read the paragraph attentively. Then he drank a glass of water, pushed his plate to one side, doubled the paper down before him between his elbows and read the paragraph over and over again. The cabbage began to deposit a cold white grease on his plate. The girl came over to him to ask was his dinner not properly cooked. He said it was very good and ate a few mouthfuls of it with difficulty. Then he paid his bill and went out.

He walked along quickly through the November twilight, his stout hazel stick striking the ground regularly, the fringe of the buff *Mail* peeping out of a side-pocket of his tight reefer over-coat. On the lonely road which leads from the Parkgate to Chapelizod he slackened his pace. His stick struck the ground less emphatically and his breath, issuing irregularly, almost with a sighing sound, condensed in the wintry air. When he reached his house he went up at once to his bedroom and, taking the paper from his pocket, read the paragraph again by the failing light of the window. He read it not aloud, but moving his lips as a priest does when he reads the prayers *Secreto*. This was the paragraph:

DEATH OF A LADY AT SYDNEY PARADE

A Painful Case

To-day at the City of Dublin Hospital the Deputy Coroner (in the absence of Mr Leverett) held an inquest on the body of Mrs Emily Sinico, aged forty-three years, who was killed at Sydney Parade Station yesterday evening. The evidence showed that the deceased lady, while attempting to cross the line, was knocked down by the engine of the ten o'clock slow train from Kingstown, thereby sustaining injuries of the head and right side which led to her death.

James Lennon, driver of the engine, stated that he had been in the employment of the railway company for fifteen years. On hearing the guard's whistle he set the train in motion and a second or two afterwards brought it to rest in response to loud cries. The train was going slowly.

P. Dunne, railway porter, stated that as the train was about to start he observed a woman attempting to cross the lines. He ran towards her and shouted but, before he could reach her, she was caught by the buffer of the engine and fell to the ground.

A juror—You saw the lady fall?

Witness—Yes.

Police Sergeant Croly deposed that when he arrived he found the deceased lying on the platform apparently dead. He had the body taken to the waiting-room pending the arrival of the ambulance.

Constable 57E corroborated.

Dr Halpin, assistant house surgeon of the City of Dublin Hospital, stated that the deceased had two lower ribs fractured and had sustained severe contusions of the right shoulder. The right side of the head had been injured in the fall. The injuries were not sufficient to have caused death in a normal person. Death, in his opinion, had been probably due to shock and sudden failure of the heart's action.

Mr H. B. Patterson Finlay, on behalf of the railway company, expressed his deep regret at the accident.

The company had always taken every precaution to prevent people crossing the lines except by the bridges, both by placing notices in every station and by the use of patent spring gates at level crossings. The deceased had been in the habit of crossing the lines late at night from platform to platform and, in view of certain other circumstances of the case, he did not think the railway officials were to blame.

Captain Sinico, of Leoville, Sydney Parade, husband of the deceased, also gave evidence. He stated that the deceased was his wife. He was not in Dublin at the time of the accident as he had arrived only that morning from Rotterdam. They had been married for twenty-two years and had lived happily until about two years ago when his wife began to be rather intemperate in her habits.

Miss Mary Sinico said that of late her mother had been in the habit of going out at night to buy spirits. She, witness, had often tried to reason with her mother and had induced her to join a league. She was not at home until an hour after the accident.

The jury returned a verdict in accordance with the medical evidence and exonerated Lennon from all blame.

The Deputy Coroner said it was a most painful case, and expressed great sympathy with Captain Sinico and his daughter. He urged on the railway company to take strong measures to prevent the possibility of similar accidents in the future. No blame attached to anyone.

Mr Duffy raised his eyes from the paper and gazed out of his window on the cheerless evening landscape. The river lay quiet beside the empty distillery and from time to time a light appeared in some house on the Lucan road. What an end! The whole narrative of her death revolted him and it revolted him to think that he had ever spoken to her of what he held sacred. The threadbare phrases, the inane expressions of sympathy, the cautious words of a reporter won over to conceal the details of a commonplace vulgar death attacked his stomach. Not merely had she degraded herself; she had degraded him. He saw the squalid tract of her vice, miserable and malodorous. His soul's companion! He thought of the hobbling wretches whom he had seen carrying cans and bottles to be filled by the barman. Just God, what an end! Evidently she had been unfit to live, without any strength of purpose, an easy prey to habits, one of the wrecks on which civilisation has been reared. But that she could have sunk so low! Was it possible he had deceived himself so utterly about her? He remembered her outburst of that night and interpreted it in a harsher sense than he had ever done. He had no difficulty now in approving of the course he had taken.

As the light failed and his memory began to wander he thought her hand touched his. The shock which had first attacked his stomach was now attacking his nerves. He put on his overcoat and hat quickly and went out. The cold air met him on the threshold; it crept into the sleeves of his coat. When he came to the public-house at Chapelizod Bridge he went in and ordered a hot punch.

The proprietor served him obsequiously but did not venture to talk. There were five or six working-men in the shop discussing the value of a gentleman's estate in County Kildare. They drank at intervals from their huge pint tumblers and smoked, spitting often on the floor and sometimes dragging the sawdust over their spits with their heavy boots. Mr Duffy sat on his stool and gazed at them, without seeing or hearing them. After a while they went out and he called for another punch. He sat a long time over it. The shop was very quiet. The proprietor sprawled on the counter reading the *Herald* and yawning. Now and again a tram was heard swishing along the lonely road outside.

As he sat there, living over his life with her and evoking alternately the two images in which he now conceived her, he realised that she was dead, that she had ceased to exist, that she had become a memory. He began to feel ill at ease. He asked himself what else could he have done. He could not have carried on a comedy of deception with her; he could not have lived with her openly. He had done what seemed to him best. How was he to blame? Now that she was gone he understood how lonely her life must have been, sitting night after night alone in that room. His life would be lonely too until he, too, died, ceased to exist, became a memory—if anyone remembered him.

It was after nine o'clock when he left the shop. The night was cold and gloomy. He entered the Park by the first gate and walked along under the gaunt trees. He walked through the bleak alleys where they had walked four years before. She seemed to be near him in the darkness. At moments he seemed to feel her voice touch his ear, her hand touch his. He stood still to listen. Why had he withheld life from her? Why had he sentenced her to death? He felt his moral nature falling to pieces.

When he gained the crest of the Magazine Hill he halted and looked along the river towards Dublin, the lights of which burned redly and hospitably in the cold night. He looked down the slope and, at the base, in the shadow of the wall of the Park, he saw some human figures lying. Those venal and furtive loves filled him with despair. He gnawed the rectitude of his life; he felt that he had been outcast from life's feast. One human being had seemed to love him and he had denied her life and happiness: he had sentenced her to ignominy, a death of shame. He knew that the prostrate creatures down by the wall were watching him and wished him gone. No one wanted him; he was outcast from life's feast. He turned his eyes to the grey gleaming river, winding along towards Dublin. Beyond the river he saw a goods train winding out of Kingsbridge Station, like a worm with a fiery head winding through the darkness, obstinately and laboriously. It passed slowly out of sight; but still he heard in his ears the laborious drone of the engine reiterating the syllables of her name.

He turned back the way he had come, the rhythm of the engine pounding in his ears. He began to doubt the reality of what memory told him. He halted under a tree and allowed the rhythm to die away. He could not feel her near him in the darkness nor her voice touch his ear. He waited for some minutes listening. He could hear nothing: the night was perfectly silent. He listened again: perfectly silent. He felt that he was alone.

Ivy Day
in the Committee Room

OLD JACK raked the cinders together with a piece of cardboard and spread them judiciously over the whitening dome of coals. When the dome was thinly covered his face lapsed into darkness but, as he set himself to fan the fire again, his crouching shadow ascended the opposite wall and his face slowly re-emerged into light. It was an old man's face, very bony and hairy. The moist blue eyes blinked at the fire and the moist mouth fell open at times, munching once or twice mechanically when it closed. When the cinders had caught he laid the piece of cardboard against the wall, sighed and said:

—That's better now, Mr O'Connor.

Mr O'Connor, a grey-haired young man, whose face was disfigured by many blotches and pimples, had just brought the tobacco for a cigarette into a shapely cylinder but when spoken to he undid his handiwork meditatively. Then he began to roll the tobacco again meditatively and after a moment's thought decided to lick the paper.

—Did Mr Tierney say when he'd be back? he asked in a husky falsetto.

—He didn't say.

Mr O'Connor put his cigarette into his mouth and began to search his pockets. He took out a pack of thin pasteboard cards.

—I'll get you a match, said the old man.

—Never mind, this'll do, said Mr O'Connor.

He selected one of the cards and read what was printed on it:

MUNICIPAL ELECTIONS

Royal Exchange Ward

Mr Richard J. Tierney, P.L.G., respectfully solicits the favour of your vote and influence at the coming election in the Royal Exchange Ward

Mr O'Connor had been engaged by Mr Tierney's agent to canvass one part of the ward but, as the weather was inclement and his boots let in the wet, he spent a great part of the day sitting by the fire in the Committee Room in Wicklow Street with Jack, the old caretaker. They had been sitting thus since the short day had grown dark. It was the sixth of October, dismal and cold out of doors.

Mr O'Connor tore a strip off the card and, lighting it, lit his cigarette. As he did so the flame lit up a leaf of dark glossy ivy in the lapel of his coat. The old man watched him attentively and then, taking up the piece of cardboard again, began to fan the fire slowly while his companion smoked.

—Ah, yes, he said, continuing, it's hard to know what way to bring up children. Now who'd think he'd turn out like that! I sent him to the Christian Brothers and I done what I could for him, and there he goes boosing about. I tried to make him someway decent.

He replaced the cardboard wearily.

—Only I'm an old man now I'd change his tune for him. I'd take the stick to his back and beat him while I could stand over him—as I done many a time before. The mother, you know, she cocks him up with this and that. . . .

—That's what ruins children, said Mr O'Connor.

—To be sure it is, said the old man. And little thanks you get for it, only impudence. He takes th'upper hand of me whenever he sees I've a sup taken. What's the world coming to when sons speaks that way to their father?

—What age is he? said Mr O'Connor.

—Nineteen, said the old man.

—Why don't you put him to something?

—Sure, amn't I never done at the drunken bowsy ever since he left school? *I won't keep you,* I says. *You must get a job for yourself.* But, sure, it's worse whenever he gets a job; he drinks it all.

Mr O'Connor shook his head in sympathy, and the old man fell silent, gazing into the fire. Someone opened the door of the room and called out:

—Hello! Is this a Freemasons' meeting?

—Who's that? said the old man.

—What are you doing in the dark? asked a voice.

—Is that you, Hynes? asked Mr O'Connor.

—Yes. What are you doing in the dark? said Mr Hynes, advancing into the light of the fire.

He was a tall slender young man with a light brown moustache. Imminent little drops of rain hung at the brim of his hat and the collar of his jacket-coat was turned up.

—Well, Mat, he said to Mr O'Connor, how goes it?

Mr O'Connor shook his head. The old man left the hearth and, after stumbling about the room returned with two candlesticks which he thrust one after the other into the fire and carried to the table. A denuded room came into view and the fire lost all its cheerful colour. The walls of the room were bare except for a copy of an election address. In the middle of the room was a small table on which papers were heaped.

Mr Hynes leaned against the mantelpiece and asked:

—Has he paid you yet?

—Not yet, said Mr O'Connor. I hope to God he'll not leave us in the lurch to-night.

Mr Hynes laughed.

—O, he'll pay you. Never fear, he said.

—I hope he'll look smart about it if he means business, said Mr O'Connor.

—What do you think, Jack? said Mr Hynes satirically to the old man.

The old man returned to his seat by the fire, saying:

—It isn't but he has it, anyway. Not like the other tinker.

—What other tinker? said Mr Hynes.

—Colgan, said the old man scornfully.

—Is it because Colgan's a working-man you say that?

What's the difference between a good honest bricklayer and a publican—eh? Hasn't the working-man as good a right to be in the Corporation as anyone else—ay, and a better right than those shoneens that are always hat in hand before any fellow with a handle to his name? Isn't that so, Mat? said Mr Hynes, addressing Mr O'Connor.

—I think you're right, said Mr O'Connor.

—One man is a plain honest man with no hunker-sliding about him. He goes in to represent the labour classes. This fellow you're working for only wants to get some job or other.

—Of course, the working-classes should be represented, said the old man.

—The working-man, said Mr Hynes, gets all kicks and no halfpence. But it's labour produces everything. The working-man is not looking for fat jobs for his sons and nephews and cousins. The working-man is not going to drag the honour of Dublin in the mud to please a German monarch.

—How's that? said the old man.

—Don't you know they want to present an address of welcome to Edward Rex if he comes here next year? What do we want kowtowing to a foreign king?

—Our man won't vote for the address, said Mr O'Connor. He goes in on the Nationalist ticket.

—Won't he? said Mr Hynes. Wait till you see whether he will or not. I know him. Is it Tricky Dicky Tierney?

—By God! perhaps you're right, Joe, said Mr O'Connor. Anyway, I wish he'd turn up with the spondulics.

The three men fell silent. The old man began to rake more cinders together. Mr Hynes took off his hat, shook it and then turned down the collar of his coat, displaying, as he did so, an ivy leaf in the lapel.

—If this man was alive, he said, pointing to the leaf, we'd have no talk of an address of welcome.

—That's true, said Mr O'Connor.

—Musha, God be with them times! said the old man. There was some life in it then.

The room was silent again. Then a bustling little man with a snuffling nose and very cold ears pushed in the door. He walked over quickly to the fire, rubbing his hands as if he intended to produce a spark from them.

—No money, boys, he said.

—Sit down here, Mr Henchy, said the old man, offering him his chair.

—O, don't stir, Jack, don't stir, said Mr Henchy.

He nodded curtly to Mr Hynes and sat down on the chair which the old man vacated.

—Did you serve Aungier Street? he asked Mr O'Connor.

—Yes, said Mr O'Connor, beginning to search his pockets for memoranda.

—Did you call on Grimes?

—I did.

—Well? How does he stand?

—He wouldn't promise. He said: *I won't tell anyone what way I'm going to vote.* But I think he'll be all right.

—Why so?

—He asked me who the nominators were; and I told him. I mentioned Father Burke's name. I think it'll be all right.

Mr Henchy began to snuffle and to rub his hands over the fire at a terrific speed. Then he said:

—For the love of God, Jack, bring us a bit of coal. There must be some left.

The old man went out of the room.

—It's no go, said Mr Henchy, shaking his head. I

asked the little shoeboy, but he said: *O, now, Mr Henchy when I see the work going on properly I won't forget you, you may be sure.* Mean little tinker! 'Usha, how could he be anything else?

—What did I tell you, Mat? said Mr Hynes. Tricky Dicky Tierney.

—O, he's as tricky as they make 'em, said Mr Henchy. He hasn't got those little pigs' eyes for nothing. Blast his soul! Couldn't he pay up like a man instead of: *O, now, Mr Henchy, I must speak to Mr Fanning. . . . I've spent a lot of money?* Mean little shoeboy of hell! I suppose he forgets the time his little old father kept the hand-me-down shop in Mary's Lane.

—But is that a fact? asked Mr O'Connor.

—God, yes, said Mr Henchy. Did you never hear that? And the men used to go in on Sunday morning before the houses were open to buy a waistcoat or a trousers—moya! But Tricky Dicky's little old father always had a tricky little black bottle up in a corner. Do you mind now? That's that. That's where he first saw the light.

The old man returned with a few lumps of coal which he placed here and there on the fire.

—That's a nice how-do-you-do, said Mr O'Connor. How does he expect us to work for him if he won't stump up?

—I can't help it, said Mr Henchy. I expect to find the bailiffs in the hall when I go home.

Mr Hynes laughed and, shoving himself away from the mantelpiece with the aid of his shoulders, made ready to leave.

—It'll be all right when King Eddie comes, he said. Well, boys, I'm off for the present. See you later. 'Bye, 'bye.

He went out of the room slowly. Neither Mr Henchy

nor the old man said anything but, just as the door was closing, Mr O'Connor, who had been staring moodily into the fire, called out suddenly:

—'Bye, Joe.

Mr Henchy waited a few moments and then nodded in the direction of the door.

—Tell me, he said across the fire, what brings our friend in here? What does he want?

—'Usha, poor Joe! said Mr O'Connor, throwing the end of his cigarette into the fire, he's hard up like the rest of us.

Mr Henchy snuffled vigorously and spat so copiously that he nearly put out the fire which uttered a hissing protest.

—To tell you my private and candid opinion, he said, I think he's a man from the other camp. He's a spy of Colgan's if you ask me. *Just go round and try and find out how they're getting on. They won't suspect you.* Do you twig?

—Ah, poor Joe is a decent skin, said Mr. O'Connor.

—His father was a decent respectable man, Mr Henchy admitted. Poor old Larry Hynes! Many a good turn he did in his day! But I'm greatly afraid our friend is not nineteen carat. Damn it, I can understand a fellow being hard up but what I can't understand is a fellow sponging. Couldn't he have some spark of manhood about him?

—He doesn't get a warm welcome from me when he comes, said the old man. Let him work for his own side and not come spying around here.

—I don't know, said Mr O'Connor dubiously, as he took out cigarette-papers and tobacco. I think Joe Hynes is a straight man. He's a clever chap, too, with the pen. Do you remember that thing he wrote . . . ?

—Some of these hillsiders and fenians are a bit too

clever if you ask me, said Mr Henchy. Do you know what my private and candid opinion is about some of those little jokers? I believe half of them are in the pay of the Castle.

—There's no knowing, said the old man.

—O, but I know it for a fact, said Mr Henchy. They're Castle hacks. . . . I don't say Hynes. . . . No, damn it, I think he's a stroke above that. . . . But there's a certain little nobleman with a cock-eye—you know the patriot I'm alluding to?

Mr O'Connor nodded.

—There's a lineal descendant of Major Sirr for you if you like! O, the heart's blood of a patriot! That's a fellow now that'd sell his country for fourpence—ay—and go down on his bended knees and thank the Almighty Christ he had a country to sell.

There was a knock at the door.

—Come in! said Mr Henchy.

A person resembling a poor clergyman or a poor actor appeared in the doorway. His black clothes were tightly buttoned on his short body and it was impossible to say whether he wore a clergyman's collar or a layman's because the collar of his shabby frock-coat, the uncovered buttons of which reflected the candlelight, was turned up about his neck. He wore a round hat of hard black felt. His face, shining with raindrops, had the appearance of damp yellow cheese save where two rosy spots indicated the cheekbones. He opened his very long mouth suddenly to express disappointment and at the same time opened wide his very bright blue eyes to express pleasure and surprise.

—O, Father Keon! said Mr Henchy, jumping up from his chair. Is that you? Come in!

—O, no, no, no! said Father Keon quickly, pursing his lips as if he were addressing a child.

—Won't you come in and sit down?

—No, no, no! said Father Keon, speaking in a discreet indulgent velvety voice. Don't let me disturb you now! I'm just looking for Mr Fanning. . . .

—He's round at the *Black Eagle,* said Mr Henchy. But won't you come in and sit down a minute?

—No, no thank you. It was just a little business matter, said Father Keon. Thank you, indeed.

He retreated from the doorway and Mr. Henchy, seizing one of the candlesticks, went to the door to light him downstairs.

—O, don't trouble, I beg!

—No, but the stairs is so dark.

—No, no, I can see. . . . Thank you, indeed.

—Are you right now?

—All right, thanks. . . . Thanks.

Mr Henchy returned with the candlestick and put it on the table. He sat down again at the fire. There was silence for a few moments.

—Tell me, John, said Mr O'Connor, lighting his cigarette with another pasteboard card.

—Hm?

—What is he exactly?

—Ask me an easier one, said Mr Henchy.

—Fanning and himself seem to me very thick. They're often in Kavanagh's together. Is he a priest at all?

—'Mmmyes, I believe so. . . . I think he's what you call a black sheep. We haven't many of them, thank God! but we have a few. . . . He's an unfortunate man of some kind. . . .

—And how does he knock it out? asked Mr O'Connor.

—That's another mystery.

—Is he attached to any chapel or church or institution or—

—No, said Mr Henchy. I think he's travelling on his

own account. . . . God forgive me, he added, I thought he was the dozen of stout.

—Is there any chance of a drink itself? asked Mr O'Connor.

—I'm dry too, said the old man.

—I asked that little shoeboy three times, said Mr Henchy, would he send up a dozen of stout. I asked him again now but he was leaning on the counter in his shirt-sleeves having a deep goster with Alderman Cowley.

—Why didn't you remind him? said Mr O'Connor.

—Well, I couldn't go over while he was talking to Alderman Cowley. I just waited till I caught his eye, and said: *About that little matter I was speaking to you about. . . .That'll be all right, Mr H.,* he said. Yerra, sure the little hop-o'-my-thumb has forgotten all about it.

—There's some deal on in that quarter, said Mr O'Connor thoughtfully. I saw the three of them hard at it yesterday at Suffolk Street corner.

—I think I know the little game they're at, said Mr Henchy. You must owe the City Fathers money nowadays if you want to be made Lord Mayor. Then they'll make you Lord Mayor. By God! I'm thinking seriously of becoming a City Father myself. What do you think? Would I do for the job?

Mr O'Connor laughed.

—So far as owing money goes. . . .

—Driving out of the Mansion House, said Mr Henchy, in all my vermin, with Jack here standing up behind me in a powdered wig—eh?

—And make me your private secretary, John.

—Yes. And I'll make Father Keon my private chaplain. We'll have a family party.

—Faith, Mr Henchy, said the old man, you'd keep up

better style than some of them. I was talking one day to old Keegan, the porter. *And how do you like your new master, Pat?* says I to him. *You haven't much entertaining now,* says I. *Entertaining!* says he. *He'd live on the smell of an oil-rag.* And do you know what he told me? Now, I declare to God, I didn't believe him.

—What? said Mr Henchy and Mr O'Connor.

—He told me: *What do you think of a Lord Mayor of Dublin sending out for a pound of chops for his dinner? How's that for high living?* says he. *Wisha! wisha,* says I. *A pound of chops,* says he, *coming into the Mansion House. Wisha!* says I, *what kind of people is going at all now?*

At this point there was a knock at the door, and a boy put in his head.

—What is it? said the old man.

—From the *Black Eagle,* said the boy, walking in sideways and depositing a basket on the floor with a noise of shaken bottles.

The old man helped the boy to transfer the bottles from the basket to the table and counted the full tally. After the transfer the boy put his basket on his arm and asked:

—Any bottles?

—What bottles? said the old man.

—Won't you let us drink them first? said Mr Henchy.

—I was told to ask for bottles.

—Come back to-morrow, said the old man.

—Here, boy! said Mr Henchy, will you run over to O'Farrell's and ask him to lend us a corkscrew—for Mr Henchy, say. Tell him we won't keep it a minute. Leave the basket there.

The boy went out and Mr Henchy began to rub his hands cheerfully, saying:

—Ah, well, he's not so bad after all. He's as good as his word, anyhow.

—There's no tumblers, said the old man.

—O, don't let that trouble you, Jack, said Mr Henchy. Many's the good man before now drank out of the bottle.

—Anyway, it's better than nothing, said Mr O'Connor.

—He's not a bad sort, said Mr Henchy, only Fanning has such a loan of him. He means well, you know, in his own tinpot way.

The boy came back with the corkscrew. The old man opened three bottles and was handing back the corkscrew when Mr Henchy said to the boy:

—Would you like a drink, boy?

—If you please, sir, said the boy.

The old man opened another bottle grudgingly, and handed it to the boy.

—What age are you? he asked.

—Seventeen, said the boy.

As the old man said nothing further the boy took the bottle, said: *Here's my best respects, sir* to Mr Henchy, drank the contents, put the bottle back on the table and wiped his mouth with his sleeve. Then he took up the corkscrew and went out of the door sideways, muttering some form of salutation.

—That's the way it begins, said the old man.

—The thin end of the wedge, said Mr Henchy.

The old man distributed the three bottles which he had opened and the men drank from them simultaneously. After having drunk each placed his bottle on the mantelpiece within hand's reach and drew in a long breath of satisfaction.

—Well, I did a good day's work to-day, said Mr Henchy, after a pause.

—That so, John?

—Yes. I got him one or two sure things in Dawson Street, Crofton and myself. Between ourselves, you know, Crofton (he's a decent chap, of course), but he's not worth a damn as a canvasser. He hasn't a word to throw to a dog. He stands and looks at the people while I do the talking.

Here two men entered the room. One of them was a very fat man, whose blue serge clothes seemed to be in danger of falling from his sloping figure. He had a big face which resembled a young ox's face in expression, staring blue eyes and a grizzled moustache. The other man, who was much younger and frailer, had a thin clean-shaven face. He wore a very high double collar and a wide-brimmed bowler hat.

—Hello, Crofton! said Mr Henchy to the fat man. Talk of the devil. . . .

—Where did the boose come from? asked the young man. Did the cow calve?

—O, of course, Lyons spots the drink first thing! said Mr O'Connor, laughing.

—Is that that way you chaps canvass, said Mr Lyons, and Crofton and I out in the cold and rain looking for votes?

—Why, blast your soul, said Mr Henchy, I'd get more votes in five minutes than you two'd get in a week.

—Open two bottles of stout, Jack, said Mr O'Connor.

—How can I? said the old man, when there's no cork-screw?

—Wait now, wait now! said Mr Henchy, getting up quickly. Did you ever see this little trick?

He took two bottles from the table and, carrying them to the fire, put them on the hob. Then he sat down again by the fire and took another drink from his bottle. Mr Lyons sat on the edge of the table, pushed his hat towards the nape of his neck and began to swing his legs.

—Which is my bottle? he asked.

—This lad, said Mr Henchy.

Mr Crofton sat down on a box and looked fixedly at the other bottle on the hob. He was silent for two reasons. The first reason, sufficient in itself, was that he had nothing to say; the second reason was that he considered his companions beneath him. He had been a canvasser for Wilkins, the Conservative, but when the Conservatives had withdrawn their man and, choosing the lesser of two evils, given their support to the Nationalist candidate, he had been engaged to work for Mr Tierney.

In a few minutes an apologetic *Pok!* was heard as the cork flew out of Mr Lyons' bottle. Mr Lyons jumped off the table, went to the fire, took his bottle and carried it back to the table.

—I was just telling them, Crofton, said Mr Henchy, that we got a good few votes to-day.

—Who did you get? asked Mr Lyons.

—Well, I got Parkes for one, and I got Atkinson for two, and I got Ward of Dawson Street. Fine old chap he is, too—regular old toff, old Conservative! *But isn't your candidate a Nationalist?* said he. *He's a respectable man,* said I. *He's in favour of whatever will benefit this country. He's a big ratepayer,* I said. *He has extensive house property in the city and three places of business and isn't it to his own advantage to keep down the rates? He's a prominent and respected citizen,* said I, *and a Poor Law Guardian, and he doesn't belong to any party, good, bad, or indifferent.* That's the way to talk to 'em.

—And what about the address to the King? said Mr Lyons, after drinking and smacking his lips.

—Listen to me, said Mr Henchy. What we want in

this country, as I said to old Ward, is capital. The King's coming here will mean an influx of money into this country. The citizens of Dublin will benefit by it. Look at all the factories down by the quays there, idle! Look at all the money there is in the country if we only worked the old industries, the mills, the shipbuilding yards and factories. It's capital we want.

—But look here, John, said Mr O'Connor. Why should we welcome the King of England? Didn't Parnell himself . . .

—Parnell, said Mr Henchy, is dead. Now, here's the way I look at it. Here's this chap come to the throne after his old mother keeping him out of it till the man was grey. He's a man of the world, and he means well by us. He's a jolly fine decent fellow, if you ask me, and no damn nonsense about him. He just says to himself: *The old one never went to see these wild Irish. By Christ, I'll go myself and see what they're like*. And are we going to insult the man when he comes over here on a friendly visit? Eh? Isn't that right, Crofton?

Mr Crofton nodded his head.

—But after all now, said Mr Lyons argumentatively, King Edward's life, you know, is not the very . . .

—Let bygones be bygones, said Mr Henchy. I admire the man personally. He's just an ordinary knockabout like you and me. He's fond of his glass of grog and he's a bit of a rake, perhaps, and he's a good sportsman. Damn it, can't we Irish play fair?

—That's all very fine, said Mr Lyons. But look at the case of Parnell now.

—In the name of God, said Mr Henchy, where's the analogy between the two cases?

—What I mean, said Mr Lyons, is we have our ideals. Why, now, would we welcome a man like that? Do you think now after what he did Parnell was a fit man to

lead us? And why, then, would we do it for Edward
the Seventh?

—This is Parnell's anniversary, said Mr O'Connor, and
don't let us stir up any bad blood. We all respect him
now that he's dead and gone—even the Conservatives,
he added, turning to Mr Crofton.

Pok! The tardy cork flew out of Mr Crofton's bottle.
Mr Crofton got up from his box and went to the fire.
As he returned with his capture he said in a deep voice:

—Our side of the house respects him because he was
a gentleman.

—Right you are, Crofton! said Mr Henchy fiercely.
He was the only man that could keep that bag of cats
in order. *Down, ye dogs! Lie down, ye curs!* That's the
way he treated them. Come in, Joe! Come in! he called
out, catching sight of Mr Hynes in the doorway.

Mr Hynes came in slowly.

—Open another bottle of stout, Jack, said Mr Henchy.
O, I forgot there's no corkscrew! Here, show me one
here and I'll put it at the fire.

The old man handed him another bottle and he placed
it on the hob.

—Sit down, Joe, said Mr O'Connor, we're just talking
about the Chief.

—Ay, ay! said Mr Henchy.

Mr Hynes sat on the side of the table near Mr Lyons
but said nothing.

—There's one of them, anyhow, said Mr Henchy, that
didn't renege him. By God, I'll say for you, Joe! No, by
God, you stuck to him like a man!

—O, Joe, said Mr O'Connor suddenly. Give us that
thing you wrote—do you remember? Have you got it on
you?

—O, ay! said Mr Henchy. Give us that. Did you ever
hear that, Crofton? Listen to this now: splendid thing.

—Go on, said Mr O'Connor. Fire away, Joe.

Mr Hynes did not seem to remember at once the piece to which they were alluding but, after reflecting a while, he said:

—O, that thing is it. . . . Sure, that's old now.

—Out with it, man! said Mr O'Connor.

—'Sh, 'sh, said Mr Henchy. Now, Joe!

Mr Hynes hesitated a little longer. Then amid the silence he took off his hat, laid it on the table and stood up. He seemed to be rehearsing the piece in his mind. After a rather long pause he announced:

THE DEATH OF PARNELL

6th October 1891

He cleared his throat once or twice and then began to recite:

> *He is dead. Our Uncrowned King is dead.*
> *O, Erin, mourn with grief and woe*
> *For he lies dead whom the fell gang*
> *Of modern hypocrites laid low.*
>
> *He lies slain by the coward hounds*
> *He raised to glory from the mire;*
> *And Erin's hopes and Erin's dreams*
> *Perish upon her monarch's pyre.*
>
> *In palace, cabin or in cot*
> *The Irish heart where'er it be*
> *Is bowed with woe—for he is gone*
> *Who would have wrought her destiny.*
>
> *He would have had his Erin famed,*
> *The green flag gloriously unfurled,*

Her statesmen, bards and warriors raised
  Before the nations of the World.

He dreamed (alas, 'twas but a dream!)
  Of Liberty: but as he strove
To clutch that idol, treachery
  Sundered him from the thing he loved.

Shame on the coward caitiff hands
  That smote their Lord or with a kiss
Betrayed him to the rabble-rout
  Of fawning priests—no friends of his.

May everlasting shame consume
  The memory of those who tried
To befoul and smear th' exalted name
  Of one who spurned them in his pride.

He fell as fall the mighty ones,
  Nobly undaunted to the last,
And death has now united him
  With Erin's heroes of the past.

No sound of strife disturb his sleep!
  Calmly he rests: no human pain
Or high ambition spurs him now
  The peaks of glory to attain.

They had their way: they laid him low.
  But Erin, list, his spirit may
Rise, like the Phœnix from the flames,
  When breaks the dawning of the day,

The day that brings us Freedom's reign.
  And on that day may Erin well

Pledge in the cup she lifts to Joy
One grief—the memory of Parnell.

Mr Hynes sat down again on the table. When he had finished his recitation there was a silence and then a burst of clapping: even Mr Lyons clapped. The applause continued for a little time. When it had ceased all the auditors drank from their bottles in silence.

Pok! The cork flew out of Mr Hynes' bottle, but Mr Hynes remained sitting, flushed and bareheaded on the table. He did not seem to have heard the invitation.

—Good man, Joe! said Mr O'Connor, taking out his cigarette papers and pouch the better to hide his emotion.

—What do you think of that, Crofton? cried Mr Henchy. Isn't that fine? What?

Mr Crofton said that it was a very fine piece of writing.

A Mother

M R HOLOHAN, assistant secretary of the *Eire Abu* Society, had been walking up and down Dublin for nearly a month, with his hands and pockets full of dirty pieces of paper, arranging about the series of concerts. He had a game leg and for this his friends called him Hoppy Holohan. He walked up and down constantly, stood by the hour at street corners arguing the point and made notes; but in the end it was Mrs Kearney who arranged everything.

Miss Devlin had become Mrs Kearney out of spite. She had been educated in a high-class convent where she had learned French and music. As she was naturally pale and unbending in manner she made few friends at school. When she came to the age of marriage she was sent out to many houses where her playing and ivory manners were much admired. She sat amid the chilly circle of her accomplishments, waiting for some suitor to brave it and offer her a brilliant life. But the young men whom she met were ordinary and she gave them no encouragement, trying to console her romantic desires by eating a great deal of Turkish Delight in secret. However, when she drew near the limit and her friends began to loosen their tongues about her she silenced them by marrying Mr Kearney, who was a bootmaker on Ormond Quay.

He was much older than she. His conversation, which was serious, took place at intervals in his great brown beard. After the first year of married life Mrs Kearney perceived that such a man would wear better than a romantic person but she never put her own romantic ideas away. He was sober, thrifty and pious; he went to the altar every first Friday, sometimes with her, oftener by himself. But she never weakened in her religion and was a good wife to him. At some party in a strange house when she lifted her eyebrow ever so slightly he stood up to take his leave and, when his cough troubled him, she put the eider-down quilt over his feet and made a strong rum punch. For his part he was a model father. By paying a small sum every week into a society he ensured for both his daughters a dowry of one hundred pounds each when they came to the age of twenty-four. He sent the elder daughter, Kathleen, to a good convent, where she learned French and music and afterwards paid her fees at the Academy. Every year in the month of July Mrs Kearney found occasion to say to some friend:

—My good man is packing us off to Skerries for a few weeks.

If it was not Skerries it was Howth or Greystones.

When the Irish Revival began to be appreciable Mrs Kearney determined to take advantage of her daughter's name and brought an Irish teacher to the house. Kathleen and her sister sent Irish picture postcards to their friends and these friends sent back other Irish picture postcards. On special Sundays when Mr Kearney went with his family to the pro-cathedral a little crowd of people would assemble after mass at the corner of Cathedral Street. They were all friends of the Kearneys —musical friends or Nationalist friends; and, when they had played every little counter of gossip, they shook hands with one another all together, laughing at the crossing of so many hands and said good-bye to one another in Irish. Soon the name of Miss Kathleen Kearney began to be heard often on people's lips. People said that she was very clever at music and a very nice girl and, moreover, that she was a believer in the language movement. Mrs Kearney was well content at this. Therefore she was not surprised when one day Mr Holohan came to her and proposed that her daughter should be the accompanist at a series of four grand concerts which his Society was going to give in the Antient Concert Rooms. She brought him into the drawing-room, made him sit down and brought out the decanter and the silver biscuit-barrel. She entered heart and soul into the details of the enterprise, advised and dissuaded; and finally a contract was drawn up by which Kathleen was to receive eight guineas for her services as accompanist at the four grand concerts.

As Mr Holohan was a novice in such delicate matters as the wording of bills and the disposing of items for a programme Mrs Kearney helped him. She had tact. She knew what *artistes* should go into capitals and what *artistes* should go into small type. She knew that the first tenor would not like to come on after Mr Meade's comic turn. To keep the audience continually diverted she slipped the doubtful items in between the old favourites. Mr Holohan called to see her every day to have her advice on some point. She was invariably friendly and advising—homely, in fact. She pushed the decanter towards him, saying:

—Now, help yourself, Mr Holohan!

And while he was helping himself she said:

—Don't be afraid! Don't be afraid of it!

Everything went on smoothly. Mrs Kearney bought some lovely blush-pink charmeuse in Brown Thomas's to let into the front of Kathleen's dress. It cost a pretty penny; but there are occasions when a little expense is justifiable. She took a dozen of two-shilling tickets for the final concert and sent them to those friends who could not be trusted to come otherwise. She forgot nothing and, thanks to her, everything that was to be done was done.

The concerts were to be on Wednesday, Thursday, Friday and Saturday. When Mrs Kearney arrived with her daughter at the Antient Concert Rooms on Wednesday night she did not like the look of things. A few young men, wearing bright blue badges in their coats, stood idle in the vestibule; none of them wore evening dress. She passed by with her daughter and a quick glance through the open door of the hall showed her the cause of the stewards' idleness. At first she wondered had she mistaken the hour. No, it was twenty minutes to eight.

In the dressing-room behind the stage she was introduced to the secretary of the Society, Mr Fitzpatrick. She smiled and shook his hand. He was a little man with

a white vacant face. She noticed that he wore his soft
brown hat carelessly on the side of his head and that his
accent was flat. He held a programme in his hand and,
while he was talking to her, he chewed one end of it
into a moist pulp. He seemed to bear disappointments
lightly. Mr Holohan came into the dressing-room every
few minutes with reports from the box-office. The *artistes*
talked among themselves nervously, glanced from time
to time at the mirror and rolled and unrolled their music.
When it was nearly half-past eight the few people in
the hall began to express their desire to be entertained.
Mr Fitzpatrick came in, smiled vacantly at the room,
and said:

—Well now, ladies and gentlemen, I suppose we'd
better open the ball.

Mrs Kearney rewarded his very flat final syllable with
a quick stare of contempt and then said to her daughter
encouragingly:

—Are you ready, dear?

When she had an opportunity she called Mr Holohan
aside and asked him to tell her what it meant. Mr
Holohan did not know what it meant. He said that the
Committee had made a mistake in arranging for four
concerts: four was too many.

—And the *artistes!* said Mrs Kearney. Of course they
are doing their best, but really they are no good.

Mr Holohan admitted that the *artistes* were no good
but the Committee, he said, had decided to let the first
three concerts go as they pleased and reserve all the
talent for Saturday night. Mrs Kearney said nothing but,
as the mediocre items followed one another on the platform and the few people in the hall grew fewer and
fewer, she began to regret that she had put herself to
any expense for such a concert. There was something
she didn't like in the look of things and Mr Fitzpatrick's

vacant smile irritated her very much. However, she said nothing and waited to see how it would end. The concert expired shortly before ten and everyone went home quickly.

The concert on Thursday night was better attended but Mrs Kearney saw at once that the house was filled with paper. The audience behaved indecorously as if the concert were an informal dress rehearsal. Mr Fitzpatrick seemed to enjoy himself; he was quite unconscious that Mrs Kearney was taking angry note of his conduct. He stood at the edge of the screen, from time to time jutting out his head and exchanging a laugh with two friends in the corner of the balcony. In the course of the evening Mrs Kearney learned that the Friday concert was to be abandoned and that the Committee was going to move heaven and earth to secure a bumper house on Saturday night. When she heard this she sought out Mr Holohan. She buttonholed him as he was limping out quickly with a glass of lemonade for a young lady and asked him was it true. Yes, it was true.

—But, of course, that doesn't alter the contract, she said. The contract was for four concerts.

Mr Holohan seemed to be in a hurry; he advised her to speak to Mr Fitzpatrick. Mrs Kearney was now beginning to be alarmed. She called Mr Fitzpatrick away from his screen and told him that her daughter had signed for four concerts and that, of course, according to the terms of the contract, she should receive the sum originally stipulated for whether the society gave the four concerts or not. Mr Fitzpatrick, who did not catch the point at issue very quickly, seemed unable to resolve the difficulty and said that he would bring the matter before the Committee. Mrs Kearney's anger began to flutter in her cheek and she had all she could do to keep from asking:

—And who is the *Cometty*, pray?

But she knew that it would not be ladylike to do that: so she was silent.

Little boys were sent out into the principal streets of Dublin early on Friday morning with bundles of hand-bills. Special puffs appeared in all the evening papers reminding the music-loving public of the treat which was in store for it on the following evening. Mrs Kearney was somewhat reassured but she thought well to tell her husband part of her suspicions. He listened carefully and said that perhaps it would be better if he went with her on Saturday night. She agreed. She re-spected her husband in the same way as she respected the General Post Office, as something large, secure and fixed; and though she knew the small number of his talents she appreciated his abstract value as a male. She was glad that he had suggested coming with her. She thought her plans over.

The night of the grand concert came. Mrs Kearney, with her husband and daughter, arrived at the Antient Concert Rooms three-quarters of an hour before the time at which the concert was to begin. By ill luck it was a rainy evening. Mrs Kearney placed her daughter's clothes and music in charge of her husband and went all over the building looking for Mr Holohan or Mr Fitz-patrick. She could find neither. She asked the stewards was any member of the Committee in the hall and, after a great deal of trouble, a steward brought out a little woman named Miss Beirne to whom Mrs Kearney ex-plained that she wanted to see one of the secretaries. Miss Beirne expected them any minute and asked could she do anything. Mrs Kearney looked searchingly at the oldish face which was screwed into an expression of trustfulness and enthusiasm and answered:

—No, thank you!

The little woman hoped they would have a good house. She looked out at the rain until the melancholy of the wet street effaced all the trustfulness and enthusiasm from her twisted features. Then she gave a little sigh and said:

—Ah, well! We did our best, the dear knows.

Mrs Kearney had to go back to the dressing-room.

The *artistes* were arriving. The bass and the second tenor had already come. The bass, Mr Duggan, was a slender young man with a scattered black moustache. He was the son of a hall porter in an office in the city and, as a boy, he had sung prolonged bass notes in the resounding hall. From this humble state he had raised himself until he had become a first-rate *artiste*. He had appeared in grand opera. One night, when an operatic *artiste* had fallen ill, he had undertaken the part of the king in the opera of *Maritana* at the Queen's Theatre. He sang his music with great feeling and volume and was warmly welcomed by the gallery; but, unfortunately, he marred the good impression by wiping his nose in his gloved hand once or twice out of thoughtlessness. He was unassuming and spoke little. He said *yous* so softly that it passed unnoticed and he never drank anything stronger than milk for his voice' sake. Mr Bell, the second tenor, was a fair-haired little man who competed every year for prizes at the Feis Ceoil. On his fourth trial he had been awarded a bronze medal. He was extremely nervous and extremely jealous of other tenors and he covered his nervous jealousy with an ebullient friendliness. It was his humour to have people know what an ordeal a concert was to him. Therefore when he saw Mr Duggan he went over to him and asked:

—Are you in it too?

—Yes, said Mr Duggan.

Mr Bell laughed at his fellow-sufferer, held out his hand and said:

—Shake!

Mrs Kearney passed by these two young men and went to the edge of the screeen to view the house. The seats were being filled up rapidly and a pleasant noise circulated in the auditorium. She came back and spoke to her husband privately. Their conversation was evidently about Kathleen for they both glanced at her often as she stood chatting to one of her Nationalist friends, Miss Healy, the contralto. An unknown solitary woman with a pale face walked through the room. The women followed with keen eyes the faded blue dress which was stretched upon a meagre body. Someone said that she was Madam Glynn, the soprano.

—I wonder where did they dig her up, said Kathleen to Miss Healy, I'm sure I never heard of her.

Miss Healy had to smile. Mr Holohan limped into the dressing-room at that moment and the two young ladies asked him who was the unknown woman. Mr Holohan said that she was Madam Glynn from London. Madam Glynn took her stand in a corner of the room, holding a roll of music stiffly before her and from time to time changing the direction of her startled gaze. The shadow took her faded dress into shelter but fell revengefully into the little cup behind her collar-bone. The noise of the hall became more audible. The first tenor and the baritone arrived together. They were both well dressed, stout and complacent and they brought a breath of opulence among the company.

Mrs Kearney brought her daughter over to them, and talked to them amiably. She wanted to be on good terms with them but, while she strove to be polite, her eyes followed Mr Holohan in his limping and devious courses. As soon as she could she excused herself and went out after him.

—Mr Holohan, I want to speak to you for a moment, she said.

They went down to a discreet part of the corridor. Mrs Kearney asked him when was her daughter going to be paid. Mr Holohan said that Mr Fitzpatrick had charge of that. Mrs Kearney said that she didn't know anything about Mr Fitzpatrick. Her daughter had signed a contract for eight guineas and she would have to be paid. Mr Holohan said that it wasn't his business.

—Why isn't it your business? asked Mrs Kearney. Didn't you yourself bring her the contract? Anyway, if it's not your business it's my business and I mean to see to it.

—You'd better speak to Mr Fitzpatrick, said Mr Holohan distantly.

—I don't know anything about Mr Fitzpatrick, repeated Mrs Kearney. I have my contract, and I intend to see that it is carried out.

When she came back to the dressing-room her cheeks were slightly suffused. The room was lively. Two men in outdoor dress had taken possession of the fireplace and were chatting familiarly with Miss Healy and the baritone. They were the *Freeman* man and Mr O'Madden Burke. The *Freeman* man had come in to say that he could not wait for the concert as he had to report the lecture which an American priest was giving in the Mansion House. He said they were to leave the report for him at the *Freeman* office and he would see that it went in. He was a grey-haired man, with a plausible voice and careful manners. He held an extinguished cigar in his hand and the aroma of cigar smoke floated near him. He had not intended to stay a moment because concerts and *artistes* bored him considerably but he remained leaning against the mantelpiece. Miss Healy stood in front of him, talking and laughing. He was old enough to suspect one reason for her politeness but young enough in spirit to turn the moment to account. The warmth, fragrance and colour of her body appealed to his senses. He was pleasantly conscious that the bosom which he saw rise and fall slowly beneath him rose and fell at that moment for him, that the laughter and fragrance and wilful glances were his tribute. When he could stay no longer he took leave of her regretfully.

—O'Madden Burke will write the notice, he explained to Mr Holohan, and I'll see it in.

—Thank you very much, Mr Hendrick, said Mr Holohan. You'll see it in, I know. Now, won't you have a little something before you go?

—I don't mind, said Mr Hendrick.

The two men went along some tortuous passages and up a dark staircase and came to a secluded room where one of the stewards was uncorking bottles for a few gentlemen. One of these gentlemen was Mr O'Madden Burke, who had found out the room by instinct. He was a suave elderly man who balanced his imposing body, when at rest, upon a large silk umbrella. His magniloquent western name was the moral umbrella upon which he balanced the fine problem of his finances. He was widely respected.

While Mr Holohan was entertaining the *Freeman* man Mrs Kearney was speaking so animatedly to her husband that he had to ask her to lower her voice. The conversation of the others in the dressing-room had become strained. Mr Bell, the first item, stood ready with his music but the accompanist made no sign. Evidently something was wrong. Mr Kearney looked straight before him, stroking his beard, while Mrs Kearney spoke into Kathleen's ear with subdued emphasis. From the hall came sounds of encouragement, clapping and stamping of feet. The first tenor and the baritone and Miss Healy stood together, waiting tranquilly, but Mr Bell's nerves were greatly agitated because he was afraid the audience would think that he had come late.

Mr Holohan and Mr O'Madden Burke came into the room. In a moment Mr Holohan perceived the hush. He went over to Mrs Kearney and spoke with her earnestly. While they were speaking the noise in the hall grew louder. Mr Holohan became very red and excited. He spoke volubly, but Mrs Kearney said curtly at intervals:

—She won't go on. She must get her eight guineas.

Mr Holohan pointed desperately towards the hall where the audience was clapping and stamping. He appealed to Mr Kearney and to Kathleen. But Mr Kearney continued to stroke his beard and Kathleen looked down, moving the point of her new shoe: it was not her fault. Mrs Kearney repeated:

—She won't go on without her money.

After a swift struggle of tongues Mr Holohan hobbled out in haste. The room was silent. When the strain of the silence had become somewhat painful Miss Healy said to the baritone:

—Have you seen Mrs Pat Campbell this week?

The baritone had not seen her but he had been told that she was very fine. The conversation went no further. The first tenor bent his head and began to count the links of the gold chain which was extended across his waist, smiling and humming random notes to observe the effect on the frontal sinus. From time to time everyone glanced at Mrs Kearney.

The noise in the auditorium had risen to a clamour

when Mr Fitzpatrick burst into the room, followed by
Mr Holohan, who was panting. The clapping and
stamping in the hall were punctuated by whistling. Mr
Fitzpatrick held a few bank-notes in his hand. He
counted out four into Mrs Kearney's hand and said she
would get the other half at the interval. Mrs Kearney
said:

—This is four shillings short.

But Kathleen gathered in her skirt and said: *Now,
Mr Bell,* to the first item, who was shaking like an
aspen. The singer and the accompanist went out together. The noise in the hall died away. There was a
pause of a few seconds: and then the piano was heard.

The first part of the concert was very successful except for Madam Glynn's time. The poor lady sang
Killarney in a bodiless gasping voice, with all the old-
fashioned mannerisms of intonation and pronunciation
which she believed lent elegance to her singing. She
looked as if she had been resurrected from an old
stage-wardrobe and the cheaper parts of the hall made
fun of her high wailing notes. The first tenor and the
contralto, however, brought down the house. Kathleen
played a selection of Irish airs which was generously
applauded. The first part closed with a stirring patriotic
recitation delivered by a young lady who arranged
amateur theatricals. It was deservedly applauded; and,
when it was ended, the men went out for the interval,
content.

All this time the dressing-room was a hive of excitement. In one corner were Mr Holohan, Mr Fitzpatrick,
Miss Beirne, two of the stewards, the baritone, the bass,
and Mr O'Madden Burke. Mr O'Madden Burke said
it was the most scandalous exhibition he had ever witnessed. Miss Kathleen Kearney's musical career was

ended in Dublin after that, he said. The baritone was asked what did he think of Mrs Kearney's conduct. He did not like to say anything. He had been paid his money and wished to be at peace with men. However, he said that Mrs Kearney might have taken the *artistes* into consideration. The stewards and the secretaries debated hotly as to what should be done when the interval came.

—I agree with Miss Beirne, said Mr O'Madden Burke. Pay her nothing.

In another corner of the room were Mrs Kearney and her husband, Mr Bell, Miss Healy and the young lady who had recited the patriotic piece. Mrs Kearney said that the Committee had treated her scandalously. She had spared neither trouble nor expense and this was how she was repaid.

They thought they had only a girl to deal with and that, therefore, they could ride roughshod over her. But she would show them their mistake. They wouldn't have dared to have treated her like that if she had been a man. But she would see that her daughter got her rights: she wouldn't be fooled. If they didn't pay her to the last farthing she would make Dublin ring. Of course she was sorry for the sake of the *artistes*. But what else could she do? She appealed to the second tenor who said he thought she had not been well treated. Then she appealed to Miss Healy. Miss Healy wanted to join the other group but she did not like to do so because she was a great friend of Kathleen's and the Kearneys had often invited her to their house.

As soon as the first part was ended Mr Fitzpatrick and Mr Holohan went over to Mrs Kearney and told her that the other four guineas would be paid after the Committee meeting on the following Tuesday and that, in case her daughter did not play for the second part, the Committee would consider the contract broken and would pay nothing.

—I haven't seen any Committee, said Mrs Kearney angrily. My daughter has her contract. She will get four pounds eight into her hand or a foot she won't put on that platform.

—I'm surprised at you, Mrs Kearney, said Mr Holohan. I never thought you would treat us this way.

—And what way did you treat me? asked Mrs Kearney.

Her face was inundated with an angry colour and she looked as if she would attack someone with her hands.

—I'm asking for my rights, she said.

—You might have some sense of decency, said Mr Holohan.

—Might I, indeed? . . . And when I ask when my daughter is going to be paid I can't get a civil answer.

She tossed her head and assumed a haughty voice:

—You must speak to the secretary. It's not my business. I'm a great fellow fol-the-diddle-I-do.

—I thought you were a lady, said Mr Holohan, walking away from her abruptly.

After that Mrs. Kearney's conduct was condemned on all hands: everyone approved of what the Committee had done. She stood at the door, haggard with rage, arguing with her husband and daughter, gesticulating with them. She waited until it was time for the second part to begin in the hope that the secretaries would approach her. But Miss Healy had kindly consented to play one or two accompaniments. Mrs Kearney had to stand aside to allow the baritone and his accompanist to pass up to the platform. She stood still for an instant like an angry stone image and, when the first notes of the song struck her ear, she caught up her daughter's cloak and said to her husband:

—Get a cab!

He went out at once. Mrs Kearney wrapped the cloak round her daughter and followed him. As she passed through the doorway she stopped and glared into Mr Holohan's face.

—I'm not done with you yet, she said.

—But I'm done with you, said Mr Holohan.

Kathleen followed her mother meekly. Mr Holohan began to pace up and down the room, in order to cool himself for he felt his skin on fire.

—That's a nice lady! he said. O, she's a nice lady!

—You did the proper thing, Holohan, said Mr O'Madden Burke, poised upon his umbrella in approval.

Grace

TWO gentlemen who were in the lavatory at the time tried to lift him up: but he was quite helpless. He lay curled up at the foot of the stairs down which he had fallen. They succeeded in turning him over. His hat had rolled a few yards away and his clothes were smeared with the filth and ooze of the floor on which he had lain, face downwards. His eyes were closed and he breathed with a grunting noise. A thin stream of blood trickled from the corner of his mouth.

These two gentlemen and one of the curates carried him up the stairs and laid him down again on the floor of the bar. In two minutes he was surrounded by a ring

of men. The manager of the bar asked everyone who he
was and who was with him. No one knew who he was
but one of the curates said he had served the gentleman
with a small rum.

—Was he by himself? asked the manager.

—No, sir. There was two gentlemen with him.

—And where are they?

No one knew; a voice said:

—Give him air. He's fainted.

The ring of onlookers distended and closed again
elastically. A dark medal of blood had formed itself near
the man's head on the tessellated floor. The manager,
alarmed by the grey pallor of the man's face, sent for a
policeman.

His collar was unfastened and his necktie undone. He
opened his eyes for an instant, sighed and closed them
again. One of the gentlemen who had carried him upstairs held a dinged silk hat in his hand. The manager
asked repeatedly did no one know who the injured man
was or where had his friends gone. The door of the bar
opened and an immense constable entered. A crowd
which had followed him down the laneway collected
outside the door, struggling to look in through the glass
panels.

The manager at once began to narrate what he knew.
The constable, a young man with thick immobile
features, listened. He moved his head slowly to right
and left and from the manager to the person on the
floor, as if he feared to be the victim of some delusion.
Then he drew off his glove, produced a small book from
his waist, licked the lead of his pencil and made ready
to indite. He asked in a suspicious provincial accent:

—Who is the man? What's his name and address?

A young man in a cycling-suit cleared his way
through the ring of bystanders. He knelt down promptly

beside the injured man and called for water. The constable knelt down also to help. The young man washed the blood from the injured man's mouth and then called for some brandy. The constable repeated the order in an authoritative voice until a curate came running with the glass. The brandy was forced down the man's throat. In a few seconds he opened his eyes and looked about him. He looked at the circle of faces and then, understanding, strove to rise to his feet.

—You're all right now? asked the young man in the cycling-suit.

—Sha, 's nothing, said the injured man, trying to stand up.

He was helped to his feet. The manager said something about a hospital and some of the bystanders gave advice. The battered silk hat was placed on the man's head. The constable asked:

—Where do you live?

The man, without answering, began to twirl the ends of his moustache. He made light of his accident. It was nothing, he said: only a little accident. He spoke very thickly.

—Where do you live? repeated the constable.

The man said they were to get a cab for him. While the point was being debated a tall agile gentleman of fair complexion, wearing a long yellow ulster, came from the far end of the bar. Seeing the spectacle he called out:

—Hallo, Tom, old man! What's the trouble?

—Sha, 's nothing, said the man.

The new-comer surveyed the deplorable figure before him and then turned to the constable saying:

—It's all right, constable. I'll see him home.

The constable touched his helmet and answered:

—All right, Mr Power!

—Come now, Tom, said Mr Power, taking his friend by the arm. No bones broken. What? Can you walk?

The young man in the cycling-suit took the man by the other arm and the crowd divided.

—How did you get yourself into this mess? asked Mr Power.

—The gentleman fell down the stairs, said the young man.

—I' 'ery 'uch o'liged to you, sir, said the injured man.

—Not at all.

—'an't we have a little . . . ?

—Not now. Not now.

The three men left the bar and the crowd sifted through the doors into the laneway. The manager brought the constable to the stairs to inspect the scene of the accident. They agreed that the gentleman must have missed his footing. The customers returned to the counter and a curate set about removing the traces of blood from the floor.

When they came out into Grafton Street Mr Power whistled for an outsider. The injured man said again as well as he could:

—I' 'ery 'uch o'liged to you, sir. I hope we'll 'eet again. 'y na'e is Kernan.

The shock and the incipient pain had partly sobered him.

—Don't mention it, said the young man.

They shook hands. Mr Kernan was hoisted on to the car and, while Mr Power was giving directions to the carman, he expressed his gratitude to the young man and regretted that they could not have a little drink together.

—Another time, said the young man.

The car drove off towards Westmoreland Street. As it passed the Ballast Office the clock showed half-past nine. A keen east wind hit them blowing from the mouth of the river. Mr Kernan was huddled together with cold. His friend asked him to tell how the accident had happened.

—I 'an't, 'an, he answered, 'y 'ongue is hurt.

—Show.

The other leaned over the well of the car and peered into Mr Kernan's mouth but he could not see. He struck a match and, sheltering it in the shell of his hands, peered again into the mouth which Mr Kernan opened obediently. The swaying movement of the car brought the match to and from the opened mouth. The lower teeth and gums were covered with clotted blood and a minute piece of the tongue seemed to have been bitten off. The match was blown out.

—That's ugly, said Mr Power.

—Sha, 's nothing, said Mr Kernan, closing his mouth and pulling the collar of his filthy coat across his neck.

Mr Kernan was a commercial traveller of the old school which believed in the dignity of its calling. He had never been seen in the city without a silk hat of some decency and a pair of gaiters. By grace of these two articles of clothing, he said, a man could always pass muster. He carried on the tradition of his Napoleon, the great Blackwhite, whose memory he evoked at times by legend and mimicry. Modern business methods had spared him only so far as to allow him a little office in Crowe Street on the window blind of which was written the name of his firm with the address—London, E. C. On the mantelpiece of this little office a little leaden battalion of canisters was drawn up and on the table before the window stood four or five china bowls which were usually half full of a black liquid. From these bowls Mr Kernan tasted tea. He took a mouthful, drew it up, saturated his palate with it and then spat it forth into the grate. Then he paused to judge.

Mr Power, a much younger man, was employed in the Royal Irish Constabulary Office in Dublin Castle. The arc of his social rise intersected the arc of his friend's decline but Mr Kernan's decline was mitigated by the fact that certain of those friends who had known him at his highest point of success still esteemed him as a character. Mr Power was one of these friends. His inexplicable debts were a byword in his circle; he was a debonair young man.

The car halted before a small house on the Glasnevin road and Mr Kernan was helped into the house. His wife put him to bed while Mr Power sat downstairs in the kitchen asking the children where they went to school and what book they were in. The children—two girls and a boy, conscious of their father's helplessness and of their mother's absence, began some horseplay with him. He was surprised at their manners and at their accents and his brow grew thoughtful. After a while Mrs Kernan entered the kitchen, exclaiming:

—Such a sight! O, he'll do for himself one day and that's the holy alls of it. He's been drinking since Friday.

Mr Power was careful to explain to her that he was not responsible, that he had come on the scene by the merest accident. Mrs Kernan, remembering Mr Power's good offices during domestic quarrels as well as many small, but opportune loans, said:

—O, you needn't tell me that, Mr Power. I know you're a friend of his not like some of those others he does be with. They're all right so long as he has money in his pocket to keep him out from his wife and family. Nice friends! Who was he with to-night, I'd like to know?

Mr Power shook his head but said nothing.

—I'm so sorry, she continued, that I've nothing in the house to offer you. But if you wait a minute I'll send round to Fogarty's at the corner.

Mr Power stood up.

—We were waiting for him to come home with the money. He never seems to think he has a home at all.

—O, now, Mrs. Kernan, said Mr Power, we'll make him turn over a new leaf. I'll talk to Martin. He's the man. We'll come here one of these nights and talk it over.

She saw him to the door. The carman was stamping up and down the footpath and swinging his arms to warm himself.

—It's very kind of you to bring him home, she said.

—Not at all, said Mr Power.

He got up on the car. As it drove off he raised his hat to her gaily.

—We'll make a new man of him, he said. Good-night, Mrs Kernan.

.   .   .   .

Mrs Kernan's puzzled eyes watched the car till it was out of sight. Then she withdrew them, went into the house and emptied her husband's pockets.

She was an active, practical woman of middle age. Not long before she had celebrated her silver wedding and renewed her intimacy with her husband by waltzing with him to Mr Power's accompaniment. In her days of courtship Mr Kernan had seemed to her a not ungallant figure: and she still hurried to the chapel door whenever a wedding was reported and, seeing the bridal pair, recalled with vivid pleasure how she had passed out of the Star of the Sea Church in Sandymount, leaning on the arm of a jovial well-fed man who was dressed smartly in a frock-coat and lavender trousers and carried a silk hat gracefully balanced upon his other arm. After three weeks she had found a wife's life irksome and, later on, when she was beginning to find it unbearable, she had become a mother. The part of mother presented to her no insuperable difficulties and for twenty-five years she had kept house shrewdly for her husband. Her two eldest sons were launched. One was in a draper's shop in Glasgow and the other was clerk to a tea-merchant in Belfast. They were good sons, wrote regularly and sometimes sent home money. The other children were still at school.

Mr Kernan sent a letter to his office next day and remained in bed. She made beef-tea for him and scolded him roundly. She accepted his frequent intemperance as part of the climate, healed him dutifully whenever he was sick and always tried to make him eat a breakfast. There were worse husbands. He had never been violent since the boys had grown up and she knew that he would walk to the end of Thomas Street and back again to book even a small order.

Two nights after his friends came to see him. She brought them up to his bedroom, the air of which was impregnated with a personal odour, and gave them chairs at the fire. Mr Kernan's tongue, the occasional stinging pain of which had made him somewhat irritable during the day, became more polite. He sat propped up in the bed by pillows and the little colour in his puffy cheeks made them resemble warm cinders. He apologised to his guests for the disorder of the room but at the same time looked at them a little proudly, with a veteran's pride.

He was quite unconscious that he was the victim of a plot which his friends, Mr Cunningham, Mr M'Coy and Mr Power had disclosed to Mrs Kernan in the parlour. The idea had been Mr Power's but its development was entrusted to Mr Cunningham. Mr Kernan

came of Protestant stock and, though he had been converted to the Catholic faith at the time of his marriage,
he had not been in the pale of the Church for twenty
years. He was fond, moreover, of giving side-thrusts at
Catholicism.

Mr Cunningham was the very man for such a case.
He was an elder colleague of Mr Power. His own domestic life was not very happy. People had great sympathy with him for it was known that he had married
an unpresentable woman who was an incurable drunkard. He had set up house for her six times; and each
time she had pawned the furniture on him.

Everyone had respect for poor Martin Cunningham.
He was a thoroughly sensible man, influential and intelligent. His blade of human knowledge, natural astute-
ness particularised by long association with cases in the
police courts, had been tempered by brief immersions in
the waters of general philosophy. He was well informed. His friends bowed to his opinions and considered that his face was like Shakespeare's.

When the plot had been disclosed to her Mrs Kernan
had said:

—I leave it all in your hands, Mr Cunningham.

After a quarter of a century of married life she had
very few illusions left. Religion for her was a habit and
she suspected that a man of her husband's age would
not change greatly before death. She was tempted to
see a curious appropriateness in his accident and, but
that she did not wish to seem bloody-minded, she would
have told the gentlemen that Mr Kernan's tongue
would not suffer by being shortened. However, Mr Cunningham was a capable man; and religion was religion.
The scheme might do good and, at least, it could do
no harm. Her beliefs were not extravagant. She believed
steadily in the Sacred Heart as the most generally use-

ful of all Catholic devotions and approved of the sacraments. Her faith was bounded by her kitchen but, if
she was put to it, she could believe also in the banshee
and in the Holy Ghost.

The gentlemen began to talk of the accident. Mr
Cunningham said that he had once known a similar
case. A man of seventy had bitten off a piece of his
tongue during an epileptic fit and the tongue had filled
in again so that no one could see a trace of the bite.

—Well, I'm not seventy, said the invalid.

—God forbid, said Mr Cunningham.

—It doesn't pain you now? asked Mr M'Coy.

Mr M'Coy had been at one time a tenor of some reputation. His wife, who had been a soprano, still taught
young children to play the piano at low terms. His line
of life had not been the shortest distance between two
points and for short periods he had been driven to live
by his wits. He had been a clerk in the Midland Railway, a canvasser for advertisements for *The Irish Times*
and for *The Freeman's Journal,* a town traveller for a
coal firm on commission, a private inquiry agent, a clerk
in the office of the Sub-Sheriff and he had recently become secretary to the City Coroner. His new office
made him professionally interested in Mr Kernan's
case.

—Pain? Not much, answered Mr Kernan. But it's so
sickening. I feel as if I wanted to retch off.

—That's the boose, said Mr Cunningham firmly.

—No, said Mr Kernan, I think I caught a cold on the
car. There's something keeps coming into my throat,
phlegm or—

—Mucus, said Mr M'Coy.

—It keeps coming like from down in my throat; sickening thing.

—Yes, yes, said Mr M'Coy, that's the thorax.

He looked at Mr Cunningham and Mr Power at the same time with an air of challenge. Mr Cunningham nodded his head rapidly and Mr Power said:

—Ah, well, all's well that ends well.

—I'm very much obliged to you, old man, said the invalid.

Mr Power waved his hand.

—Those other two fellows I was with—

—Who were you with? asked Mr Cunningham.

—A chap. I don't know his name. Damn it now, what's his name? Little chap with sandy hair. . . .

—And who else?

—Harford.

—Hm, said Mr Cunningham.

When Mr Cunningham made that remark people were silent. It was known that the speaker had secret sources of information. In this case the monosyllable had a moral intention. Mr Harford sometimes formed one of a little detachment which left the city shortly after noon on Sunday with the purpose of arriving as soon as possible at some public-house on the outskirts of the city where its members duly qualified themselves as *bona-fide* travellers. But his fellow-travellers had never consented to overlook his origin. He had begun life as an obscure financier by lending small sums of money to workmen at usurious interest. Later on he had become the partner of a very fat short gentleman, Mr Goldberg, of the Liffey Loan Bank. Though he had never embraced more than the Jewish ethical code his fellow-Catholics, whenever they had smarted in person or by proxy under his exactions, spoke of him bitterly as an Irish Jew and an illiterate and saw divine disapproval of usury made manifest through the person of his idiot son. At other times they remembered his good points.

—I wonder where did he go to, said Mr Kernan.

He wished the details of the incident to remain vague. He wished his friends to think there had been some mistake, that Mr Harford and he had missed each other. His friends, who knew quite well Mr Harford's manners in drinking, were silent. Mr Power said again:

—All's well that ends well.

Mr Kernan changed the subject at once.

—That was a decent young chap, that medical fellow, he said. Only for him—

—O, only for him, said Mr Power, it might have been a case of seven days without the option of a fine.

—Yes, yes, said Mr Kernan, trying to remember. I remember now there was a policeman. Decent young fellow, he seemed. How did it happen at all?

—It happened that you were peloothered, Tom, said Mr Cunningham gravely.

—True bill, said Mr Kernan, equally gravely.

—I suppose you squared the constable, Jack, said Mr M'Coy.

Mr Power did not relish the use of his Christian name. He was not straight-laced but he could not forget that Mr M'Coy had recently made a crusade in search of valises and portmanteaus to enable Mrs M'Coy to fulfill imaginary engagements in the country. More than he resented the fact that he had been victim-ised he resented such low playing of the game. He answered the question, therefore, as if Mr Kernan had asked it.

The narrative made Mr Kernan indignant. He was keenly conscious of his citizenship, wished to live with his city on terms mutually honourable and resented any affront put upon him by those whom he called country bumpkins.

—Is this what we pay rates for? he asked. To feed and clothe these ignorant bostoons . . . and they're nothing else.

Mr Cunningham laughed. He was a Castle official only during office hours.

—How could they be anything else, Tom? he said.

He assumed a thick provincial accent and said in a tone of command:

—65, catch your cabbage!

Everyone laughed. Mr M'Coy, who wanted to enter the conversation by any door, pretended that he had never heard the story. Mr Cunningham said:

—It is supposed—they say, you know—to take place in the depot where they get these thundering big country fellows, omadhauns, you know, to drill. The sergeant makes them stand in a row against the wall and hold up their plates.

He illustrated the story by grotesque gestures.

—At dinner, you know. Then he has a bloody big bowl of cabbage before him on the table and a bloody big spoon like a shovel. He takes up a wad of cabbage on the spoon and pegs it across the room and the poor devils have to try and catch it on their plates: *65, catch your cabbage.*

Everyone laughed again: but Mr Kernan was somewhat indignant still. He talked of writing a letter to the papers.

—These yahoos coming up here, he said, think they can boss the people. I needn't tell you, Martin, what kind of men they are.

Mr Cunningham gave a qualified assent.

—It's like everything else in this world, he said. You get some bad ones and you get some good ones.

—O yes, you get some good ones, I admit, said Mr Kernan, satisfied.

—It's better to have nothing to say to them, said Mr M'Coy. That's my opinion!

Mrs Kernan entered the room and, placing a tray on the table, said:

—Help yourselves, gentlemen.

Mr Power stood up to officiate, offering her his chair. She declined it, saying she was ironing downstairs, and, after having exchanged a nod with Mr Cunningham behind Mr Power's back, prepared to leave the room. Her husband called out to her:

—And have you nothing for me, duckie?

—O, you! The back of my hand to you! said Mrs Kernan tartly.

Her husband called after her:

—Nothing for poor little hubby!

He assumed such a comical face and voice that the distribution of the bottles of stout took place amid general merriment.

The gentlemen drank from their glasses, set the glasses again on the table and paused. Then Mr Cunningham turned towards Mr Power and said casually:

—On Thursday night, you said, Jack?

—Thursday, yes, said Mr Power.

—Righto! said Mr Cunningham promptly.

—We can meet in M'Auley's, said Mr M'Coy. That'll be the most convenient place.

—But we mustn't be late, said Mr Power earnestly, because it is sure to be crammed to the doors.

—We can meet at half-seven, said Mr M'Coy.

—Righto! said Mr Cunningham.

—Half-seven at M'Auley's be it!

There was a short silence. Mr Kernan waited to see whether he would be taken into his friends' confidence. Then he asked:

—What's in the wind?

—O, it's nothing, said Mr Cunningham. It's only a little matter that we're arranging about for Thursday.

—The opera, is it? said Mr Kernan.

—No, no, said Mr Cunningham in an evasive tone, it's just a little . . . spiritual matter.

—O, said Mr Kernan.

There was silence again. Then Mr Power said, point-blank:

—To tell you the truth, Tom, we're going to make a retreat.

—Yes, that's it, said Mr Cunningham, Jack and I and M'Coy here—we're all going to wash the pot.

He uttered the metaphor with a certain homely energy and, encouraged by his own voice, proceeded:

—You see, we may as well all admit we're a nice collection of scoundrels, one and all. I say, one and all, he added with gruff charity and turning to Mr Power. Own up now!

—I own up, said Mr Power.

—And I own up, said Mr M'Coy.

—So we're going to wash the pot together, said Mr Cunningham.

A thought seemed to strike him. He turned suddenly to the invalid and said:

—Do you know what, Tom, has just occurred to me? You might join in and we'd have a four-handed reel.

—Good idea, said Mr Power. The four of us together.

Mr Kernan was silent. The proposal conveyed very little meaning to his mind but, understanding that some spiritual agencies were about to concern themselves on his behalf, he thought he owed it to his dignity to show a stiff neck. He took no part in the conversation for a long while but listened, with an air of calm enmity, while his friends discussed the Jesuits.

—I haven't such a bad opinion of the Jesuits, he said, intervening at length. They're an educated order. I believe they mean well too.

—They're the grandest order in the Church, Tom, said Mr Cunningham, with enthusiasm. The General of the Jesuits stands next to the Pope.

—There's no mistake about it, said Mr M'Coy, if you want a thing well done and no flies about it you go to a Jesuit. They're the boyos have influence. I'll tell you a case in point. . . .

—The Jesuits are a fine body of men, said Mr Power.

—It's a curious thing, said Mr Cunningham, about the Jesuit Order. Every other order of the Church had to be reformed at some time or other but the Jesuit Order was never once reformed. It never fell away.

—Is that so? asked Mr M'Coy.

—That's a fact, said Mr Cunningham. That's history.

—Look at their church, too, said Mr Power. Look at the congregation they have.

—The Jesuits cater for the upper classes, said Mr M'Coy.

—Of course, said Mr Power.

—Yes, said Mr Kernan. That's why I have a feeling for them. It's some of those secular priests, ignorant, bumptious—

—They're all good men, said Mr Cunningham, each in his own way. The Irish priesthood is honoured all the world over.

—O yes, said Mr Power.

—Not like some of the other priesthoods on the continent, said Mr M'Coy, unworthy of the name.

—Perhaps you're right, said Mr Kernan, relenting.

—Of course I'm right, said Mr Cunningham. I haven't been in the world all this time and seen most sides of it without being a judge of character.

The gentlemen drank again, one following another's example. Mr Kernan seemed to be weighing something in his mind. He was impressed. He had a high opinion of Mr Cunningham as a judge of character and as a reader of faces. He asked for particulars.

—O, it's just a retreat, you know, said Mr Cunningham. Father Purdon is giving it. It's for business men, you know.

—He won't be too hard on us, Tom, said Mr Power persuasively.

—Father Purdon? Father Purdon? said the invalid.

—O, you must know him, Tom, said Mr Cunningham, stoutly. Fine jolly fellow! He's a man of the world like ourselves.

—Ah, . . . yes. I think I know him. Rather red face; tall.

—That's the man.

—And tell me, Martin. . . . Is he a good preacher?

—Mmmno. . . . It's not exactly a sermon, you know. It's just a kind of a friendly talk, you know, in a common-sense way.

Mr Kernan deliberated. Mr M'Coy said:

—Father Tom Burke, that was the boy!

—O, Father Tom Burke, said Mr Cunningham, that was a born orator. Did you ever hear him, Tom?

—Did I ever hear him! said the invalid, nettled. Rather! I heard him. . . .

—And yet they say he wasn't much of a theologian, said Mr Cunningham.

—Is that so? said Mr M'Coy.

—O, of course, nothing wrong, you know. Only sometimes, they say, he didn't preach what was quite orthodox.

—Ah! . . . he was a splendid man, said Mr M'Coy.

—I heard him once, Mr Kernan continued. I forget
the subject of his discourse now. Crofton and I were
in the back of the . . . pit, you know . . . the—

—The body, said Mr Cunningham.

—Yes, in the back near the door. I forget now what.
. . . O yes, it was on the Pope, the late Pope. I remember it well. Upon my word it was magnificent, the style
of the oratory. And his voice! God! hadn't he a voice!
The Prisoner of the Vatican, he called him. I remember Crofton saying to me when we came out—

—But he's an Orangeman, Crofton, isn't he? said Mr
Power.

—'Course he is, said Mr Kernan, and a damned decent
Orangeman too. We went into Butler's in Moore Street
—faith, I was genuinely moved, tell you the God's truth
—and I remember well his very words. *Kernan,* he said,
we worship at different altars, he said, *but our belief is
the same.* Struck me as very well put.

—There's a good deal in that, said Mr Power. There
used always be crowds of Protestants in the chapel
when Father Tom was preaching.

—There's not much difference between us, said Mr
M'Coy. We both believe in—

He hesitated for a moment.

—. . . in the Redeemer. Only they don't believe in
the Pope and in the mother of God.

—But, of course, said Mr Cunningham quietly and
effectively, our religion is *the* religion, the old, original
faith.

—Not a doubt of it, said Mr Kernan warmly.

Mrs Kernan came to the door of the bedroom and announced:

—Here's a visitor for you!

—Who is it?

—Mr Fogarty.

—O, come in! come in!

A pale oval face came forward into the light. The arch of its fair trailing moustache was repeated in the fair eyebrows looped above pleasantly astonished eyes. Mr Fogarty was a modest grocer. He had failed in business in a licensed house in the city because his financial condition had constrained him to tie himself to second-class distillers and brewers. He had opened a small shop on Glasnevin Road where, he flattered himself, his manners would ingratiate him with the housewives of the district. He bore himself with a certain grace, complimented little children and spoke with a neat enunciation. He was not without culture.

Mr Fogarty brought a gift with him, a half-pint of special whisky. He inquired politely for Mr Kernan, placed his gift on the table and sat down with the company on equal terms. Mr Kernan appreciated the gift all the more since he was aware that there was a small account for groceries unsettled between him and Mr Fogarty. He said:

—I wouldn't doubt you, old man. Open that, Jack, will you?

Mr Power again officiated. Glasses were rinsed and five small measures of whisky were poured out. This new influence enlivened the conversation. Mr Fogarty, sitting on a small area of the chair, was specially interested.

—Pope Leo XIII., said Mr Cunningham, was one of the lights of the age. His great idea, you know, was the union of the Latin and Greek Churches. That was the aim of his life.

—I often heard he was one of the most intellectual men in Europe, said Mr Power. I mean apart from his being Pope.

—So he was, said Mr Cunningham, if not *the* most so. His motto, you know, as Pope, was *Lux upon Lux—Light upon Light.*

—No, no, said Mr Fogarty eagerly. I think you're wrong there. It was *Lux in Tenebris,* I think—*Light in Darkness.*

—O, yes, said Mr M'Coy, *Tenebrae.*

—Allow me, said Mr Cunningham positively, it was *Lux upon Lux.* And Pius IX. his predecessor's motto was *Crux upon Crux*—that is, *Cross upon Cross*—to show the difference between their two pontificates.

The inference was allowed. Mr Cunningham continued.

—Pope Leo, you know, was a great scholar and a poet.

—He had a strong face, said Mr Kernan.

—Yes, said Mr Cunningham. He wrote Latin poetry.

—Is that so? said Mr Fogarty.

Mr M'Coy tasted his whisky contentedly and shook his head with a double intention, saying:

—That's no joke, I can tell you.

—We didn't learn that, Tom, said Mr Power, following Mr M'Coy's example, when we went to the penny-a-week school.

—There was many a good man went to the penny-a-week school with a sod of turf under his oxter, said Mr Kernan sententiously. The old system was the best: plain honest education. None of your modern trumpery. . . .

—Quite right, said Mr Power.

—No superfluities, said Mr Fogarty.

He enunciated the word and then drank gravely.

—I remember reading, said Mr Cunningham, that one of Pope Leo's poems was on the invention of the photograph—in Latin, of course.

—On the photograph! exclaimed Mr Kernan.

—Yes, said Mr Cunningham.

He also drank from his glass.

—Well, you know, said Mr M'Coy, isn't the photograph wonderful when you come to think of it?

—O, of course, said Mr Power, great minds can see things.

—As the poet says: *Great minds are very near to madness,* said Mr Fogarty.

Mr Kernan seemed to be troubled in mind. He made an effort to recall the Protestant theology on some thorny points and in the end addressed Mr Cunningham.

—Tell me, Martin, he said. Weren't some of the Popes —of course, not our present man, or his predecessor, but some of the old Popes—not exactly . . . you know . . . up to the knocker?

There was a silence. Mr Cunningham said:

—O, of course, there were some bad lots. . . . But the astonishing thing is this. Not one of them, not the biggest drunkard, not the most . . . out-and-out ruffian, not one of them ever preached *ex cathedra* a word of false doctrine. Now isn't that an astonishing thing?

—That is, said Mr Kernan.

—Yes, because when the Pope speaks *ex cathedra,* Mr Fogarty explained, he is infallible.

—Yes, said Mr Cunningham.

—O, I know about the infallibility of the Pope. I remember I was younger then. . . . Or was it that—?

Mr Fogarty interrupted. He took up the bottle and helped the others to a little more. Mr M'Coy, seeing that there was not enough to go round, pleaded that he had not finished his first measure. The others accepted under protest. The light music of whisky falling into glasses made an agreeable interlude.

—What's that you were saying, Tom? asked Mr M'Coy.

—Papal infallibility, said Mr Cunningham, that was the greatest scene in the whole history of the Church.

—How was that, Martin? asked Mr Power.

Mr Cunningham held up two thick fingers.

—In the sacred college, you know, of cardinals and archbishops and bishops there were two men who held out against it while the others were all for it. The whole conclave except these two was unanimous. No! They wouldn't have it!

—Ha! said Mr M'Coy.

—And they were a German cardinal by the name of Dolling . . . or Dowling . . . or—

—Dowling was no German, and that's a sure five, said Mr Power, laughing.

—Well, this great German cardinal, whatever his name was, was one; and the other was John MacHale.

—What? cried Mr Kernan. Is it John of Tuam?

—Are you sure of that now? asked Mr Fogarty dubiously. I thought it was some Italian or American.

—John of Tuam, repeated Mr Cunningham, was the man.

He drank and the other gentlemen followed his lead. Then he resumed:

—There they were at it, all the cardinals and bishops and archbishops from all the ends of the earth and these two fighting dog and devil until at last the Pope himself stood up and declared infallibility a dogma of the Church *ex cathedra*. On the very moment John Mac-Hale, who had been arguing and arguing against it, stood up and shouted out with the voice of a lion: *Credo!*

—*I believe!* said Mr Fogarty.

—*Credo!* said Mr Cunningham. That showed the faith he had. He submitted the moment the Pope spoke.

—And what about Dowling? asked Mr M'Coy.

—The German cardinal wouldn't submit. He left the Church.

Mr Cunningham's words had built up the vast image of the Church in the minds of his hearers. His deep raucous voice had thrilled them as it uttered the word of belief and submission. When Mrs Kernan came into the room drying her hands she came into a solemn company. She did not disturb the silence, but leaned over the rail at the foot of the bed.

—I once saw John MacHale, said Mr Kernan, and I'll never forget it as long as I live.

He turned towards his wife to be confirmed.

—I often told you that?

Mrs Kernan nodded.

—It was at the unveiling of Sir John Gray's statue. Edmund Dwyer Gray was speaking, blathering away, and here was this old fellow, crabbed-looking old chap, looking at him from under his bushy eyebrows.

Mr Kernan knitted his brows and, lowering his head like an angry bull, glared at his wife.

—God! he exclaimed, resuming his natural face, I never saw such an eye in a man's head. It was as much as to say: *I have you properly taped, my lad.* He had an eye like a hawk.

—None of the Grays was any good, said Mr Power.

There was a pause again. Mr Power turned to Mrs Kernan and said with abrupt joviality:

—Well, Mrs Kernan, we're going to make your man here a good holy pious and God-fearing Roman Catholic.

He swept his arm round the company inclusively.

—We're all going to make a retreat together and confess our sins—and God knows we want it badly.

—I don't mind, said Mr Kernan, smiling a little nervously.

Mrs Kernan thought it would be wiser to conceal her satisfaction. So she said:

—I pity the poor priest that has to listen to your tale.

Mr Kernan's expression changed.

—If he doesn't like it, he said bluntly, he can . . . do the other thing. I'll just tell him my little tale of woe. I'm not such a bad fellow—

Mr Cunningham intervened promptly.

—We'll all renounce the devil, he said, together, not forgetting his works and pomps.

—Get behind me, Satan! said Mr Fogarty, laughing and looking at the others.

Mr Power said nothing. He felt completely outgeneralled. But a pleased expression flickered across his face.

—All we have to do, said Mr Cunningham, is to stand up with lighted candles in our hands and renew our baptismal vows.

—O, don't forget the candle, Tom, said Mr M'Coy, whatever you do.

—What? said Mr Kernan. Must I have a candle?

—O yes, said Mr Cunningham.

—No, damn it all, said Mr Kernan sensibly, I draw the line there. I'll do the job right enough. I'll do the

retreat business and confession, and . . . all that business. But . . . no candles! No, damn it all, I bar the
candles!

He shook his head with farcical gravity.

—Listen to that! said his wife.

—I bar the candles, said Mr Kernan, conscious of
having created an effect on his audience and continuing
to shake his head to and fro. I bar the magic-lantern
business.

Everyone laughed heartily.

—There's a nice Catholic for you! said his wife.

—No candles! repeated Mr Kernan obdurately. That's
off!

.   .   .   .

The transept of the Jesuit Church in Gardiner Street
was almost full; and still at every moment gentlemen
entered from the side-door and, directed by the lay-
brother, walked on tiptoe along the aisles until they
found seating accommodation. The gentlemen were all
well dressed and orderly. The light of the lamps of the
church fell upon an assembly of black clothes and white
collars, relieved here and there by tweeds, on dark
mottled pillars of green marble and on lugubrious can-
vasses. The gentlemen sat in the benches, having hitched
their trousers slightly above their knees and laid their
hats in security. They sat well back and gazed formally
at the distant speck of red light which was suspended
before the high altar.

In one of the benches near the pulpit sat Mr Cunningham and Mr Kernan. In the bench behind sat Mr
M'Coy alone: and in the bench behind him sat Mr
Power and Mr Fogarty. Mr M'Coy had tried unsuccessfully to find a place in the bench with the others and,
when the party had settled down in the form of a
quincunx, he had tried unsuccessfully to make comic

remarks. As these had not been well received he had desisted. Even he was sensible of the decorous atmosphere and even he began to respond to the religious stimulus. In a whisper Mr Cunningham drew Mr Kernan's attention to Mr Harford, the moneylender, who sat some distance off, and to Mr Fanning, the registration agent and mayor maker of the city, who was sitting immediately under the pulpit beside one of the newly elected councillors of the ward. To the right sat old Michael Grimes, the owner of three pawnbroker's shops, and Dan Hogan's nephew, who was up for the job in the Town Clerk's office. Farther in front sat Mr Hendrick, the chief reporter of *The Freeman's Journal*, and poor O'Carroll, an old friend of Mr Kernan's, who had been at one time a considerable commercial figure. Gradually, as he recognised familiar faces, Mr Kernan began to feel more at home. His hat, which had been rehabilitated by his wife, rested upon his knees. Once or twice he pulled down his cuffs with one hand while he held the brim of his hat lightly, but firmly, with the other hand.

A powerful-looking figure, the upper part of which was draped with a white surplice, was observed to be struggling up into the pulpit. Simultaneously the congregation unsettled, produced handkerchiefs and knelt upon them with care. Mr Kernan followed the general example. The priest's figure now stood upright in the pulpit, two-thirds of its bulk, crowned by a massive red face, appearing above the balustrade.

Father Purdon knelt down, turned towards the red speck of light and, covering his face with his hands, prayed. After an interval he uncovered his face and rose. The congregation rose also and settled again on its benches. Mr Kernan restored his hat to its original position on his knee and presented an attentive face to

the preacher. The preacher turned back each wide
sleeve of his surplice with an elaborate large gesture
and slowly surveyed the array of faces. Then he said:

> *For the children of this world are wiser in their gen-*
> *eration than the children of light. Wherefore make unto*
> *yourselves friends out of the mammon of iniquity so*
> *that when you die they may receive you into everlasting*
> *dwellings.*

Father Purdon developed the text with resonant as-
surance. It was one of the most difficult texts in all the
Scriptures, he said, to interpret properly. It was a text
which might seem to the casual observer at variance
with the lofty morality elsewhere preached by Jesus
Christ. But, he told his hearers, the text had seemed
to him specially adapted for the guidance of those
whose lot it was to lead the life of the world and who
yet wished to lead that life not in the manner of worldlings. It was a text for business men and professional
men. Jesus Christ, with His divine understanding of
every cranny of our human nature, understood that all
men were not called to the religious life, that by far the
vast majority were forced to live in the world and, to a
certain extent, for the world: and in this sentence He
designed to give them a word of counsel, setting before
them as exemplars in the religious life those very worshippers of Mammon who were of all men the least
solicitous in matters religious.

He told his hearers that he was there that evening
for no terrifying, no extravagant purpose; but as a
man of the world speaking to his fellow-men. He came
to speak to business men and he would speak to them
in a businesslike way. If he might use the metaphor, he
said, he was their spiritual accountant; and he wished

each and every one of his hearers to open his books, the books of his spiritual life, and see if they tallied accurately with conscience.

Jesus Christ was not a hard taskmaster. He understood our little failings, understood the weakness of our poor fallen nature, understood the temptations of this life. We might have had, we all had from time to time, our temptations: we might have, we all had, our failings. But one thing only, he said, he would ask of his hearers. And that was: to be straight and manly with God. If their accounts tallied in every point to say:

—Well, I have verified my accounts. I find all well.

But if, as might happen, there were some discrepancies, to admit the truth, to be frank and say like a man:

—Well, I have looked into my accounts. I find this wrong and this wrong. But, with God's grace, I will rectify this and this. I will set right my accounts.

The Dead

LILY, the caretaker's daughter, was literally run off her feet. Hardly had she brought one gentleman into the little pantry behind the office on the ground floor and helped him off with his overcoat than the wheezy hall-door bell clanged again and she had to scamper along the bare hallway to let in another guest. It was well for her she had not to attend to the ladies also. But Miss Kate and Miss Julia had thought of that and had converted the bathroom upstairs into a ladies' dressing-room. Miss Kate and Miss Julia were there, gossiping and laughing and fussing, walking after each other to the head of the stairs, peering down over the banisters and calling down to Lily to ask her who had come.

It was always a great affair, the Misses Morkan's annual dance. Everybody who knew them came to it, members of the family, old friends of the family, the members of Julia's choir, any of Kate's pupils that were grown up enough and even some of Mary Jane's pupils too. Never once had it fallen flat. For years and years it had gone off in splendid style as long as anyone could remember; ever since Kate and Julia, after the death of their brother Pat, had left the house in Stoney Batter and take Mary Jane, their only niece, to live with them in the dark gaunt house on Usher's Island, the upper part of which they had rented from Mr Fulham, the corn-factor on the ground floor. That was a good thirty years ago if it was a day. Mary Jane, who was then a little girl in short clothes, was now the main prop of the household for she had the organ in Haddington Road. She had been through the Academy and gave a pupils' concert every year in the upper room of the Antient Concert Rooms. Many of her pupils belonged to better-class families on the Kingstown and Dalkey line. Old as they were, her aunts also did their share. Julia, though she was quite grey, was still the leading soprano in Adam and Eve's, and Kate, being too feeble to go about much, gave music lessons to beginners on the old square piano in the back room. Lily, the caretaker's daughter, did housemaid's work for them. Though their life was modest they believed in eating well; the best of everything: diamond-bone sirloins, three-shilling tea and the best bottled stout. But Lily seldom made a mistake in the orders so that she got on well with her three mistresses. They were fussy, that was all. But the only thing they would not stand was back answers.

Of course they had good reason to be fussy on such a night. And then it was long after ten o'clock and yet there was no sign of Gabriel and his wife. Besides they were dreadfully afraid that Freddy Malins might turn up screwed. They would not wish for worlds that any of Mary Jane's pupils should see him under the influence; and when he was like that it was sometimes very hard to manage him. Freddy Malins always came late but they wondered what could be keeping Gabriel: and that was what brought them every two minutes to the banisters to ask Lily had Gabriel or Freddy come.

—O, Mr Conroy, said Lily to Gabriel when she opened the door for him, Miss Kate and Miss Julia thought you were never coming. Good-night, Mrs Conroy.

—I'll engage they did, said Gabriel, but they forget that my wife here takes three mortal hours to dress herself.

He stood on the mat, scraping the snow from his goloshes, while Lily led his wife to the foot of the stairs and called out:

—Miss Kate, here's Mrs Conroy.

Kate and Julia came toddling down the dark stairs at once. Both of them kissed Gabriel's wife, said she must be perished alive and asked was Gabriel with her.

—Here I am as right as the mail, Aunt Kate! Go on up. I'll follow, called out Gabriel from the dark.

He continued scraping his feet vigorously while the three women went upstairs, laughing, to the ladies' dressing-room. A light fringe of snow lay like a cape on the shoulders of his overcoat and like toecaps on the toes of his goloshes; and, as the buttons of his overcoat slipped with a squeaking noise through the snow-stiffened frieze, a cold fragrant air from out-of-doors escaped from crevices and folds.

—Is it snowing again, Mr Conroy? asked Lily.

She had preceded him into the pantry to help him off with his overcoat. Gabriel smiled at the three syllables she had given his surname and glanced at her. She was a slim, growing girl, pale in complexion and with hay-coloured hair. The gas in the pantry made her look still paler. Gabriel had known her when she was a child and used to sit on the lowest step nursing a rag doll.

—Yes, Lily, he answered, and I think we're in for a night of it.

He looked up at the pantry ceiling, which was shaking with the stamping and shuffling of feet on the floor above, listened for a moment to the piano and then glanced at the girl, who was folding his overcoat carefully at the end of a shelf.

—Tell me, Lily, he said in a friendly tone, do you still go to school?

—O no, sir, she answered. I'm done schooling this year and more.

—O, then, said Gabriel gaily, I suppose we'll be going to your wedding one of these fine days with your young man, eh?

The girl glanced back at him over her shoulder and said with great bitterness:

—The men that is now is only all palaver and what they can get out of you.

Gabriel coloured as if he felt he had made a mistake and, without looking at her, kicked off his goloshes and flicked actively with his muffler at his patent-leather shoes.

He was a stout tallish young man. The high colour

of his cheeks pushed upwards even to his forehead where it scattered itself in a few formless patches of pale red; and on his hairless face there scintillated restlessly the polished lenses and the bright gilt rims of the glasses which screened his delicate and restless eyes. His glossy black hair was parted in the middle and brushed in a long curve behind his ears where it curled slightly beneath the groove left by his hat.

When he had flicked lustre into his shoes he stood up and pulled his waistcoat down more tightly on his plump body. Then he took a coin rapidly from his pocket.

—O Lily, he said, thrusting it into her hands, it's Christmastime, isn't it? Just . . . here's a little. . . .

He walked rapidly towards the door.

—O no, sir! cried the girl, following him. Really, sir, I wouldn't take it.

—Christmas-time! Christmas-time! said Gabriel, almost trotting to the stairs and waving his hand to her in deprecation.

The girl, seeing that he had gained the stairs, called out after him:

—Well, thank you, sir.

He waited outside the drawing-room door until the waltz should finish, listening to the skirts that swept against it and to the shuffling of feet. He was still discomposed by the girl's bitter and sudden retort. It had cast a gloom over him which he tried to dispel by arranging his cuffs and the bows of his tie. Then he took from his waistcoat pocket a little paper and glanced at the headings he had made for his speech. He was undecided about the lines from Robert Browning for he feared they would be above the heads of his hearers. Some quotation that they could recognise from Shakespeare or from the Melodies would be better. The in-

delicate clacking of the men's heels and the shuffling of
their soles reminded him that their grade of culture
differed from his. He would only make himself ridiculous
by quoting poetry to them which they could not understand. They would think that he was airing his superior
education. He would fail with them just as he had failed
with the girl in the pantry. He had taken up a wrong
tone. His whole speech was a mistake from first to last,
an utter failure.

Just then his aunts and his wife came out of the
ladies' dressing-room. His aunts were two small plainly
dressed old women. Aunt Julia was an inch or so the
taller. Her hair, drawn low over the tops of her ears,
was grey; and grey also, with darker shadows, was her
large flaccid face. Though she was stout in build and
stood erect her slow eyes and parted lips gave her the
appearance of a woman who did not know where she
was or where she was going. Aunt Kate was more
vivacious. Her face, healthier than her sister's, was all
puckers and creases, like a shrivelled red apple, and her
hair, braided in the same old-fashioned way, had not
lost its ripe nut colour.

They both kissed Gabriel frankly. He was their favourite nephew, the son of their dead elder sister, Ellen,
who had married T. J. Conroy of the Port and Docks.

—Gretta tells me you're not going to take a cab back
to Monkstown to-night, Gabriel, said Aunt Kate.

—No, said Gabriel, turning to his wife, we had quite
enough of that last year, hadn't we? Don't you remember, Aunt Kate, what a cold Gretta got out of it? Cab
windows rattling all the way, and the east wind blowing
in after we passed Merrion. Very jolly it was. Gretta
caught a dreadful cold.

Aunt Kate frowned severely and nodded her head at
every word.

—Quite right, Gabriel, quite right, she said. You can't be too careful.

—But as for Gretta there, said Gabriel, she'd walk home in the snow if she were let.

Mrs Conroy laughed.

—Don't mind him, Aunt Kate, she said. He's really an awful bother, what with green shades for Tom's eyes at night and making him do the dumb-bells, and forcing Eva to eat the stirabout. The poor child! And she simply hates the sight of it! . . . O, but you'll never guess what he makes me wear now!

She broke out into a peal of laughter and glanced at her husband, whose admiring and happy eyes had been wandering from her dress to her face and hair. The two aunts laughed heartily too, for Gabriel's solicitude was a standing joke with them.

—Goloshes! said Mrs Conroy. That's the latest. Whenever it's wet underfoot I must put on my goloshes. To-night even he wanted me to put them on, but I wouldn't. The next thing he'll buy me will be a diving suit.

Gabriel laughed nervously and patted his tie reassuringly while Aunt Kate nearly doubled herself, so heartily did she enjoy the joke. The smile soon faded from Aunt Julia's face and her mirthless eyes were directed towards her nephew's face. After a pause she asked:

—And what are goloshes, Gabriel?

—Goloshes, Julia! exclaimed her sister. Goodness me, don't you know what goloshes are? You wear them over your . . . over your boots, Gretta, isn't it?

—Yes, said Mrs Conroy. Guttapercha things. We both have a pair now. Gabriel says everyone wears them on the continent.

—O, on the continent, murmured Aunt Julia, nodding her head slowly.

Gabriel knitted his brows and said, as if he were slightly angered:

—It's nothing very wonderful but Gretta thinks it very funny because she says the word reminds her of Christy Minstrels.

—But tell me, Gabriel, said Aunt Kate, with brisk tact. Of course, you've seen about the room. Gretta was saying . . .

—O, the room is all right, replied Gabriel. I've taken one in the Gresham.

—To be sure, said Aunt Kate, by far the best thing to do. And the children, Gretta, you're not anxious about them?

—O, for one night, said Mrs Conroy. Besides, Bessie will look after them.

—To be sure, said Aunt Kate again. What a comfort it is to have a girl like that, one you can depend on! There's that Lily, I'm sure I don't know what has come over her lately. She's not the girl she was at all.

Gabriel was about to ask his aunt some questions on this point but she broke off suddenly to gaze after her sister who had wandered down the stairs and was craning her neck over the banisters.

—Now, I ask you, she said, almost testily, where is Julia going? Julia! Julia! Where are you going?

Julia, who had gone halfway down one flight, came back and announced blandly:

—Here's Freddy.

At the same moment a clapping of hands and a final flourish of the pianist told that the waltz had ended. The drawing-room door was opened from within and some couples came out. Aunt Kate drew Gabriel aside hurriedly and whispered into his ear:

—Slip down, Gabriel, like a good fellow and see if he's all right, and don't let him up if he's screwed. I'm sure he's screwed. I'm sure he is.

Gabriel went to the stairs and listened over the banisters. He could hear two persons talking in the pantry. Then he recognised Freddy Malins' laugh. He went down the stairs noisily.

—It's such a relief, said Aunt Kate to Mrs Conroy, that Gabriel is here. I always feel easier in my mind when he's here. . . . Julia, there's Miss Daly and Miss Power will take some refreshment. Thanks for your beautiful waltz, Miss Daly. It made lovely time.

A tall wizen-faced man, with a stiff grizzled moustache and swarthy skin, who was passing out with his partner said:

—And may we have some refreshment, too, Miss Morkan?

—Julia, said Aunt Kate summarily, and here's Mr Browne and Miss Furlong. Take them in, Julia, with Miss Daly and Miss Power.

—I'm the man for the ladies, said Mr Browne, pursing his lips until his moustache bristled and smiling in all his wrinkles. You know, Miss Morkan, the reason they are so fond of me is—

He did not finish his sentence, but, seeing that Aunt Kate was out of earshot, at once led the three young ladies into the back room. The middle of the room was occupied by two square tables placed end to end, and on these Aunt Julia and the caretaker were straightening and smoothing a large cloth. On the sideboard were arrayed dishes and plates, and glasses and bundles of knives and forks and spoons. The top of the closed square piano served also as a sideboard for viands and sweets. At a smaller sideboard in one corner two young men were standing, drinking hop-bitters.

Mr Browne led his charges thither and invited them all, in jest, to some ladies' punch, hot, strong and sweet. As they said they never took anything strong he opened three bottles of lemonade for them. Then he asked one of the young men to move aside, and, taking hold of the decanter, filled out for himself a goodly measure of whisky. The young men eyed him respectfully while he took a trial sip.

—God help me, he said, smiling, it's the doctor's orders.

His wizened face broke into a broader smile, and the three young ladies laughed in musical echo to his pleasantry, swaying their bodies to and fro, with nervous jerks of their shoulders. The boldest said:

—O, now, Mr Browne, I'm sure the doctor never ordered anything of the kind.

Mr Browne took another sip of his whisky and said, with sidling mimicry:

—Well, you see, I'm like the famous Mrs Cassidy, who is reported to have said: *Now, Mary Grimes, if I don't take it, make me take it, for I feel I want it.*

His hot face had leaned forward a little too confidentially and he had assumed a very low Dublin accent so that the young ladies, with one instinct, received his speech in silence. Miss Furlong, who was one of Mary Jane's pupils, asked Miss Daly what was the name of the pretty waltz she had played; and Mr Browne, seeing that he was ignored, turned promptly to the two young men who were more appreciative.

A red-faced young woman, dressed in pansy, came into the room, excitedly clapping her hands and crying:

—Quadrilles! Quadrilles!

Close on her heels came Aunt Kate, crying:

—Two gentlemen and three ladies, Mary Jane!

—O, here's Mr Bergin and Mr Kerrigan, said Mary

Jane. Mr. Kerrigan, will you take Miss Power? Miss Furlong, may I get you a partner, Mr Bergin. O, that'll just
do now.

—Three ladies, Mary Jane, said Aunt Kate.

The two young gentlemen asked the ladies if they
might have the pleasure, and Mary Jane turned to Miss
Daly.

—O, Miss Daly, you're really awfully good, after playing for the last two dances, but really we're so short of
ladies to-night.

—I don't mind in the least, Miss Morkan.

—But I've a nice partner for you, Mr Bartell D'Arcy,
the tenor. I'll get him to sing later on. All Dublin is
raving about him.

—Lovely voice, lovely voice! said Aunt Kate.

As the piano had twice begun the prelude to the first
figure Mary Jane led her recruits quickly from the room.
They had hardly gone when Aunt Julia wandered slowly
into the room, looking behind her at something.

—What is the matter, Julia? asked Aunt Kate anxiously. Who is it?

Julia, who was carrying in a column of table-napkins,
turned to her sister and said, simply, as if the question
had surprised her:

—It's only Freddy, Kate, and Gabriel with him.

In fact right behind her Gabriel could be seen pilot-
ing Freddy Malins across the landing. The latter, a
young man of about forty, was of Gabriel's size and
build, with very round shoulders. His face was fleshy
and pallid, touched with colour only at the thick hanging lobes of his ears and at the wide wings of his nose.
He had coarse features, a blunt nose, a convex and receding brow, tumid and protruded lips. His heavy-
lidded eyes and the disorder of his scanty hair made him
look sleepy. He was laughing heartily in a high key at a

story which he had been telling Gabriel on the stairs and at the same time rubbing the knuckles of his left fist backwards and forwards into his left eye.

—Good-evening, Freddy, said Aunt Julia.

Freddy Malins bade the Misses Morkan good-evening in what seemed an offhand fashion by reason of the habitual catch in his voice and then, seeing that Mr Browne was grinning at him from the sideboard, crossed the room on rather shaky legs and began to repeat in an undertone the story he had just told to Gabriel.

—He's not so bad, is he? said Aunt Kate to Gabriel.

Gabriel's brows were dark but he raised them quickly and answered:

—O no, hardly noticeable.

—Now, isn't he a terrible fellow! she said. And his poor mother made him take the pledge on New Year's Eve. But come on, Gabriel, into the drawing-room.

Before leaving the room with Gabriel she signalled to Mr Browne by frowning and shaking her forefinger in warning to and fro. Mr Browne nodded in answer and, when she had gone, said to Freddy Malins:

—Now, then, Teddy, I'm going to fill you out a good glass of lemonade just to buck you up.

Freddy Malins, who was nearing the climax of his story, waved the offer aside impatiently but Mr Browne, having first called Freddy Malins' attention to a disarray in his dress, filled out and handed him a full glass of lemonade. Freddy Malins' left hand accepted the glass mechanically, his right hand being engaged in the mechanical readjustment of his dress. Mr Browne, whose face was once more wrinkling with mirth, poured out for himself a glass of whisky while Freddy Malins exploded, before he had well reached the climax of his story, in a kink of high-pitched bronchitic laughter and, setting down his untasted and overflowing glass, began

to rub the knuckles of his left fist backwards and forwards into his left eye, repeating words of his last phrase
as well as his fit of laughter would allow him.

.   .   .   .

Gabriel could not listen while Mary Jane was playing
her Academy piece, full of runs and difficult passages,
to the hushed drawing-room. He liked music but the
piece she was playing had no melody for him and he
doubted whether it had any melody for the other listeners, though they had begged Mary Jane to play something. Four young men, who had come from the refreshment-room to stand in the doorway at the sound of the
piano, had gone away quietly in couples after a few
minutes. The only persons who seemed to follow the
music were Mary Jane herself, her hands racing along
the key-board or lifted from it at the pauses like those
of a priestess in momentary imprecation, and Aunt Kate
standing at her elbow to turn the page.

Gabriel's eyes, irritated by the floor, which glittered
with beeswax under the heavy chandelier, wandered to
the wall above the piano. A picture of the balcony scene
in *Romeo and Juliet* hung there and beside it was a
picture of the two murdered princes in the Tower which
Aunt Julia had worked in red, blue and brown wools
when she was a girl. Probably in the school they had
gone to as girls that kind of work had been taught, for
one year his mother had worked for him as a birthday
present a waistcoat of purple tabinet, with little foxes'
heads upon it, lined with brown satin and having round
mulberry buttons. It was strange that his mother had
had no musical talent though Aunt Kate used to call
her the brains carrier of the Morkan family. Both she
and Julia had always seemed a little proud of their
serious and matronly sister. Her photograph stood before the pierglass. She held an open book on her knees

and was pointing out something in it to Constantine who, dressed in a man-o'-war suit, lay at her feet. It was she who had chosen the names for her sons for she was very sensible of the dignity of family life. Thanks to her, Constantine was now senior curate in Balbriggan and, thanks to her, Gabriel himself had taken his degree in the Royal University. A shadow passed over his face as he remembered her sullen opposition to his marriage. Some slighting phrases she had used still rankled in his memory; she had once spoken of Gretta as being country cute and that was not true of Gretta at all. It was Gretta who had nursed her during all her last long illness in their house at Monkstown.

He knew that Mary Jane must be near the end of her piece for she was playing again the opening melody with runs of scales after every bar and while he waited for the end the resentment died down in his heart. The piece ended with a trill of octaves in the treble and a final deep octave in the bass. Great applause greeted Mary Jane as, blushing and rolling up her music nervously, she escaped from the room. The most vigorous clapping came from the four young men in the doorway who had gone away to the refreshment-room at the beginning of the piece but had come back when the piano had stopped.

Lancers were arranged. Gabriel found himself partnered with Miss Ivors. She was a frank-mannered talkative young lady, with a freckled face and prominent brown eyes. She did not wear a low-cut bodice and the large brooch which was fixed in the front of her collar bore on it an Irish device.

When they had taken their places she said abruptly:

—I have a crow to pluck with you.

—With me? said Gabriel.

She nodded her head gravely.

—What is it? asked Gabriel, smiling at her solemn manner.

—Who is G. C.? answered Miss Ivors, turning her eyes upon him.

Gabriel coloured and was about to knit his brows, as if he did not understand, when she said bluntly:

—O, innocent Amy! I have found out that you write for *The Daily Express*. Now, aren't you ashamed of yourself?

—Why should I be ashamed of myself? asked Gabriel, blinking his eyes and trying to smile.

—Well, I'm ashamed of you, said Miss Ivors frankly. To say you'd write for a rag like that. I didn't think you were a West Briton.

A look of perplexity appeared on Gabriel's face. It was true that he wrote a literary column every Wednesday in *The Daily Express,* for which he was paid fifteen shillings. But that did not make him a West Briton surely. The books he received for review were almost more welcome than the paltry cheque. He loved to feel the covers and turn over the pages of newly printed books. Nearly every day when his teaching in the college was ended he used to wander down the quays to the second-hand booksellers, to Hickey's on Bachelor's Walk, to Webb's or Massey's on Aston's Quay, or to O'Clohissey's in the by-street. He did not know how to meet her charge. He wanted to say that literature was above politics. But they were friends of many years' standing and their careers had been parallel, first at the University and then as teachers: he could not risk a grandiose phrase with her. He continued blinking his eyes and trying to smile and murmured lamely that he saw nothing political in writing reviews of books.

When their turn to cross had come he was still perplexed and inattentive. Miss Ivors promptly took his hand in a warm grasp and said in a soft friendly tone:

—Of course, I was only joking. Come, we cross now.

When they were together again she spoke of the University question and Gabriel felt more at ease. A friend of hers had shown her his review of Browning's poems. That was how she had found out the secret: but she liked the review immensely. Then she said suddenly:

—O, Mr Conroy, will you come for an excursion to the Aran Isles this summer? We're going to stay there a whole month. It will be splendid out in the Atlantic. You ought to come. Mr. Clancy is coming, and Mr Kilkelly and Kathleen Kearney. It would be splendid for Gretta too if she'd come. She's from Connacht, isn't she?

—Her people are, said Gabriel shortly.

—But you will come, won't you? said Miss Ivors, laying her warm hand eagerly on his arm.

—The fact is, said Gabriel, I have already arranged to go—

—Go where? asked Miss Ivors.

—Well, you know, every year I go for a cycling tour with some fellows and so—

—But where? asked Miss Ivors.

—Well, we usually go to France or Belgium or perhaps Germany, said Gabriel awkwardly.

—And why do you go to France and Belgium, said Miss Ivors, instead of visiting your own land?

—Well, said Gabriel, it's partly to keep in touch with the languages and partly for a change.

—And haven't you your own language to keep in touch with—Irish? asked Miss Ivors.

—Well, said Gabriel, if it comes to that, you know, Irish is not my language.

Their neighbours had turned to listen to the cross-examination. Gabriel glanced right and left nervously and tried to keep his good humour under the ordeal which was making a blush invade his forehead.

—And haven't you your own land to visit, continued Miss Ivors, that you know nothing of, your own people, and your own country?

—O, to tell you the truth, retorted Gabriel suddenly, I'm sick of my own country, sick of it!

—Why? asked Miss Ivors.

Gabriel did not answer for his retort had heated him.

—Why? repeated Miss Ivors.

They had to go visiting together and, as he had not answered her, Miss Ivors said warmly:

—Of course, you've no answer.

Gabriel tried to cover his agitation by taking part in the dance with great energy. He avoided her eyes for he had seen a sour expression on her face. But when they met in the long chain he was surprised to feel his hand firmly pressed. She looked at him from under her brows for a moment quizzically until he smiled. Then, just as the chain was about to start again, she stood on tiptoe and whispered into his ear:

—West Briton!

When the lancers were over Gabriel went away to a remote corner of the room where Freddy Malins' mother was sitting. She was a stout feeble old woman with white hair. Her voice had a catch in it like her son's and she stuttered slightly. She had been told that Freddy had come and that he was nearly all right. Gabriel asked her whether she had had a good crossing. She lived with her married daughter in Glasgow and came to Dublin on a visit once a year. She answered placidly that she had had a beautiful crossing and that the captain had been most attentive to her. She spoke also of the beautiful house her daughter kept in Glasgow, and of all the nice friends they had there. While her tongue rambled on Gabriel tried to banish from his mind all memory of the unpleasant incident with Miss Ivors. Of course the girl or woman, or whatever she was, was an enthusiast but there was a time for all things. Perhaps he ought not to have answered her like that. But she had no right to call him a West Briton before people, even in joke. She had tried to make him ridiculous before people, heckling him and staring at him with her rabbit's eyes.

He saw his wife making her way towards him through the waltzing couples. When she reached him she said into his ear:

—Gabriel, Aunt Kate wants to know won't you carve the goose as usual. Miss Daly will carve the ham and I'll do the pudding.

—All right, said Gabriel.

—She's sending in the younger ones first as soon as this waltz is over so that we'll have the table to ourselves.

—Were you dancing? asked Gabriel.

—Of course I was. Didn't you see me? What words had you with Molly Ivors?

—No words. Why? Did she say so?

—Something like that. I'm trying to get that Mr D'Arcy to sing. He's full of conceit, I think.

—There were no words, said Gabriel moodily, only she wanted me to go for a trip to the west of Ireland and I said I wouldn't.

His wife clasped her hands excitedly and gave a little jump.

—O, do go, Gabriel, she cried. I'd love to see Galway again.

—You can go if you like, said Gabriel coldly.

She looked at him for a moment, then turned to Mrs Malins and said:

—There's a nice husband for you, Mrs Malins.

While she was threading her way back across the room Mrs Malins, without adverting to the interruption, went on to tell Gabriel what beautiful places there were in Scotland and beautiful scenery. Her son-in-law brought them every year to the lakes and they used to go fishing. Her son-in-law was a splendid fisher. One day he caught a fish, a beautiful big big fish, and the man in the hotel boiled it for their dinner.

Gabriel hardly heard what she said. Now that supper was coming near he began to think again about his speech and about the quotation. When he saw Freddy Malins coming across the room to visit his mother Gabriel left the chair free for him and retired into the embrasure of the window. The room had already cleared and from the back room came the clatter of plates and knives. Those who still remained in the drawing-room seemed tired of dancing and were conversing quietly in little groups. Gabriel's warm trembling fingers tapped the cold pane of the window. How cool it must be outside! How pleasant it would be to walk out alone, first along by the river and then through the park! The snow would be lying on the branches of the trees and forming a bright cap on the top of the Wellington Monument. How much more pleasant it would be there than at the supper-table!

He ran over the headings of his speech: Irish hospitality, sad memories, the Three Graces, Paris, the quotation from Browning. He repeated to himself a phrase he had written in his review: *One feels that one is listening to a thought-tormented music.* Miss Ivors had praised the review. Was she sincere? Had she really any life of

her own behind all her propagandism? There had never
been any ill-feeling between them until that night. It unnerved him to think that she would be at the supper-
table, looking up at him while he spoke with her critical
quizzing eyes. Perhaps she would not be sorry to see him
fail in his speech. An idea came into his mind and gave
him courage. He would say, alluding to Aunt Kate and
Aunt Julia: *Ladies and Gentlemen, the generation which
is now on the wane among us may have had its faults
but for my part I think it had certain qualities of hospitality, of humour, of humanity, which the new and
very serious and hypereducated generation that is growing up around us seems to me to lack*. Very good: that
was one for Miss Ivors. What did he care that his aunts
were only two ignorant old women?

A murmur in the room attracted his attention. Mr
Browne was advancing from the door, gallantly escorting Aunt Julia, who leaned upon his arm, smiling and
hanging her head. An irregular musketry of applause
escorted her also as far as the piano and then, as Mary
Jane seated herself on the stool, and Aunt Julia, no
longer smiling, half turned so as to pitch her voice fairly
into the room, gradually ceased. Gabriel recognised the
prelude. It was that of an old song of Aunt Julia's—
Arrayed for the Bridal. Her voice, strong and clear in
tone, attacked with great spirit the runs which embellish
the air and though she sang very rapidly she did not
miss even the smallest of the grace notes. To follow the
voice, without looking at the singer's face, was to feel
and share the excitement of swift and secure flight.
Gabriel applauded loudly with all the others at the close
of the song and loud applause was borne in from the
invisible supper-table. It sounded so genuine that a little
colour struggled into Aunt Julia's face as she bent to
replace in the music-stand the old leather-bound song-

book that had her initials on the cover. Freddy Malins, who had listened with his head perched sideways to hear her better, was still applauding when everyone else had ceased and talking animatedly to his mother who nodded her head gravely and slowly in acquiescence. At last, when he could clap no more, he stood up suddenly and hurried across the room to Aunt Julia whose hand he seized and held in both his hands, shaking it when words failed him or the catch in his voice proved too much for him.

—I was just telling my mother, he said, I never heard you sing so well, never. No, I never heard your voice so good as it is to-night. Now! Would you believe that now? That's the truth. Upon my word and honour that's the truth. I never heard your voice sound so fresh and so . . . so clear and fresh, never.

Aunt Julia smiled broadly and murmured something about compliments as she released her hand from his grasp. Mr Browne extended his open hand towards her and said to those who were near him in the manner of a showman introducing a prodigy to an audience:

—Miss Julia Morkan, my latest discovery!

He was laughing very heartily at this himself when Freddy Malins turned to him and said:

—Well, Browne, if you're serious you might make a worse discovery. All I can say is I never heard her sing half so well as long as I am coming here. And that's the honest truth.

—Neither did I, said Mr Browne. I think her voice has greatly improved.

Aunt Julia shrugged her shoulders and said with meek pride:

—Thirty years ago I hadn't a bad voice as voices go.

—I often told Julia, said Aunt Kate emphatically, that

she was simply thrown away in that choir. But she never
would be said by me.

She turned as if to appeal to the good sense of the
others against a refractory child while Aunt Julia gazed
in front of her, a vague smile of reminiscence playing
on her face.

—No, continued Aunt Kate, she wouldn't be said or
led by anyone, slaving there in that choir night and day,
night and day. Six o'clock on Christmas morning! And
all for what?

—Well, isn't it for the honour of God, Aunt Kate?
asked Mary Jane, twisting round on the piano-stool and
smiling.

Aunt Kate turned fiercely on her niece and said:

—I know all about the honour of God, Mary Jane, but
I think it's not at all honourable for the pope to turn out
the women out of the choirs that have slaved there all
their lives and put little whipper-snappers of boys over
their heads. I suppose it is for the good of the Church
if the pope does it. But it's not just, Mary Jane, and
it's not right.

She had worked herself into a passion and would have
continued in defence of her sister for it was a sore subject with her but Mary Jane, seeing that all the dancers
had come back, intervened pacifically:

—Now, Aunt Kate, you're giving scandal to Mr
Browne who is of the other persuasion.

Aunt Kate turned to Mr Browne, who was grinning
at this allusion to his religion, and said hastily:

—O, I don't question the pope's being right. I'm only
a stupid old woman and I wouldn't presume to do such
a thing. But there's such a thing as common everyday
politeness and gratitude. And if I were in Julia's place
I'd tell that Father Healy straight up to his face . . .

—And besides, Aunt Kate, said Mary Jane, we really are all hungry and when we are hungry we are all very quarrelsome.

—And when we are thirsty we are also quarrelsome, added Mr Browne.

—So that we had better go to supper, said Mary Jane, and finish the discussion afterwards.

On the landing outside the drawing-room Gabriel found his wife and Mary Jane trying to persuade Miss Ivors to stay for supper. But Miss Ivors, who had put on her hat and was buttoning her cloak, would not stay. She did not feel in the least hungry and she had already overstayed her time.

—But only for ten minutes, Molly, said Mrs Conroy. That won't delay you.

—To take a pick itself, said Mary Jane, after all your dancing.

—I really couldn't, said Miss Ivors.

—I am afraid you didn't enjoy yourself at all, said Mary Jane hopelessly.

—Ever so much, I assure you, said Miss Ivors, but you really must let me run off now.

—But how can you get home? asked Mrs Conroy.

—O, it's only two steps up the quay.

Gabriel hesitated a moment and said:

—If you will allow me, Miss Ivors, I'll see you home if you really are obliged to go.

But Miss Ivors broke away from them.

—I won't hear of it, she cried. For goodness sake go in to your suppers and don't mind me. I'm quite well able to take care of myself.

—Well, you're the comical girl, Molly, said Mrs Conroy frankly.

—*Beannacht libh*, cried Miss Ivors, with a laugh, as she ran down the staircase.

Mary Jane gazed after her, a moody puzzled expression on her face, while Mrs Conroy leaned over the banisters to listen for the hall-door. Gabriel asked himself was he the cause of her abrupt departure. But she did not seem to be in ill humour: she had gone away laughing. He stared blankly down the staircase.

At that moment Aunt Kate came toddling out of the supper-room, almost wringing her hands in despair.

—Where is Gabriel? she cried. Where on earth is Gabriel? There's everyone waiting in there, stage to let, and nobody to carve the goose!

—Here I am, Aunt Kate! cried Gabriel, with sudden animation, ready to carve a flock of geese, if necessary.

A fat brown goose lay at one end of the table and at the other end, on a bed of creased paper strewn with sprigs of parsley, lay a great ham, stripped of its outer skin and peppered over with crust crumbs, a neat paper frill round its shin and beside this was a round of spiced beef. Between these rival ends ran parallel lines of side-dishes: two little minsters of jelly, red and yellow; a shallow dish full of blocks of blancmange and red jam, a large green leaf-shaped dish with a stalk-shaped handle, on which lay bunches of purple raisins and peeled almonds, a companion dish on which lay a solid rectangle of Smyrna figs, a dish of custard topped with grated nutmeg, a small bowl full of chocolates and sweets wrapped in gold and silver papers and a glass vase in which stood some tall celery stalks. In the centre of the table there stood, as sentries to a fruit-stand which upheld a pyramid of oranges and American apples, two squat old-fashioned decanters of cut glass, one containing port and the other dark sherry. On the closed square piano a pudding in a huge yellow dish lay in waiting and behind it were three squads of bottles of stout and

ale and minerals, drawn up according to the colours of
their uniforms, the first two black, with brown and red
labels, the third and smallest squad white, with trans-
verse green sashes.

Gabriel took his seat boldly at the head of the table
and, having looked to the edge of the carver, plunged
his fork firmly into the goose. He felt quite at ease now
for he was an expert carver and liked nothing better
than to find himself at the head of a well-laden table.

—Miss Furlong, what shall I send you? he asked. A
wing or a slice of the breast?

—Just a small slice of the breast.

—Miss Higgins, what for you?

—O, anything at all, Mr Conroy.

While Gabriel and Miss Daly exchanged plates of
goose and plates of ham and spiced beef Lily went from
guest to guest with a dish of hot floury potatoes wrapped
in a white napkin. This was Mary Jane's idea and she
had also suggested apple sauce for the goose but Aunt
Kate had said that plain roast goose without apple sauce
had always been good enough for her and she hoped
she might never eat worse. Mary Jane waited on her
pupils and saw that they got the best slices and Aunt
Kate and Aunt Julia opened and carried across from the
piano bottles of stout and ale for the gentlemen and
bottles of minerals for the ladies. There was a great deal
of confusion and laughter and noise, the noise of orders
and counter-orders, of knives and forks, of corks and
glass-stoppers. Gabriel began to carve second helpings
as soon as he had finished the first round without serving
himself. Everyone protested loudly so that he compro-
mised by taking a long draught of stout for he had found
the carving hot work. Mary Jane settled down quietly to
her supper but Aunt Kate and Aunt Julia were still
toddling round the table, walking on each other's heels,

getting in each other's way and giving each other un-heeded orders. Mr Browne begged of them to sit down and eat their suppers and so did Gabriel but they said there was time enough so that, at last, Freddy Malins stood up and, capturing Aunt Kate, plumped her down on her chair amid general laughter.

When everyone had been well served Gabriel said, smiling:

—Now, if anyone wants a little more of what vulgar people call stuffing let him or her speak.

A chorus of voices invited him to begin his own supper and Lily came forward with three potatoes which she had reserved for him.

—Very well, said Gabriel amiably, as he took another preparatory draught, kindly forget my existence, ladies and gentlemen, for a few minutes.

He set to his supper and took no part in the conversation with which the table covered Lily's removal of the plates. The subject of talk was the opera company which was then at the Theatre Royal. Mr Bartell D'Arcy, the tenor, a dark-complexioned young man with a smart moustache, praised very highly the leading contralto of the company but Miss Furlong thought she had a rather vulgar style of production. Freddy Malins said there was a negro chieftain singing in the second part of the Gaiety pantomime who had one of the finest tenor voices he had ever heard.

—Have you heard him? he asked Mr Bartell D'Arcy across the table.

—No, answered Mr Bartell D'Arcy carelessly.

—Because, Freddy Malins explained, now I'd be curious to hear your opinion of him. I think he has a grand voice.

—It takes Teddy to find out the really good things, said Mr Browne familiarly to the table.

—And why couldn't he have a voice too? asked Freddy Malins sharply. Is it because he's only a black?

Nobody answered this question and Mary Jane led the table back to the legitimate opera. One of her pupils had given her a pass for *Mignon.* Of course it was very fine, she said, but it made her think of poor Georgina Burns. Mr Browne could go back farther still, to the old Italian companies that used to come to Dublin—Tietjens, Ilma de Murzka, Campanini, the great Trebelli, Giuglini, Ravelli, Aramburo. Those were the days, he said, when there was something like singing to be heard in Dublin. He told too of how the top gallery of the old Royal used to be packed night after night, of how one night an Italian tenor had sung five encores to *Let Me Like a Soldier Fall,* introducing a high C every time, and of how the gallery boys would sometimes in their enthusiasm unyoke the horses from the carriage of some great *prima donna* and pull her themselves through the streets to her hotel. Why did they never play the grand old operas now, he asked, *Dinorah, Lucrezia Borgia?* Because they could not get the voices to sing them: that was why.

—O, well, said Mr Bartell D'Arcy, I presume there are as good singers to-day as there were then.

—Where are they? asked Mr Browne defiantly.

—In London, Paris, Milan, said Mr Bartell D'Arcy warmly. I suppose Caruso, for example, is quite as good, if not better than any of the men you have mentioned.

—Maybe so, said Mr Browne. But I may tell you I doubt it strongly.

—O, I'd give anything to hear Caruso sing, said Mary Jane.

—For me, said Aunt Kate, who had been picking a

bone, there was only one tenor. To please me, I mean. But I suppose none of you ever heard of him.

—Who was he, Miss Morkan? asked Mr Bartell D'Arcy politely.

—His name, said Aunt Kate, was Parkinson. I heard him when he was in his prime and I think he had then the purest tenor voice that was ever put into a man's throat.

—Strange, said Mr Bartell D'Arcy. I never even heard of him.

—Yes, yes, Miss Morkan is right, said Mr Browne. I remember hearing of old Parkinson but he's too far back for me.

—A beautiful pure sweet mellow English tenor, said Aunt Kate with enthusiasm.

Gabriel having finished, the huge pudding was transferred to the table. The clatter of forks and spoons began again. Gabriel's wife served out spoonfuls of the pudding and passed the plates down the table. Midway down they were held up by Mary Jane, who replenished them with raspberry or orange jelly or with blancmange and jam. The pudding was of Aunt Julia's making and she received praises for it from all quarters. She herself said that it was not quite brown enough.

—Well, I hope, Miss Morkan, said Mr Browne, that I'm brown enough for you because, you know, I'm all brown.

All the gentlemen, except Gabriel, ate some of the pudding out of compliment to Aunt Julia. As Gabriel never ate sweets the celery had been left for him. Freddy Malins also took a stalk of celery and ate it with his pudding. He had been told that celery was a capital thing for the blood and he was just then under doctor's care. Mrs Malins, who had been silent all through the supper, said that her son was going down to Mount Melleray in a week or so. The table then spoke of Mount Melleray, how bracing the air was down there, how hospitable the monks were and how they never asked for a penny-piece from their guests.

—And do you mean to say, asked Mr Browne incredulously, that a chap can go down there and put up there as if it were a hotel and live on the fat of the land and then come away without paying a farthing?

—O, most people give some donation to the monastery when they leave, said Mary Jane.

—I wish we had an institution like that in our Church, said Mr Browne candidly.

He was astonished to hear that the monks never spoke, got up at two in the morning and slept in their coffins. He asked what they did it for.

—That's the rule of the order, said Aunt Kate firmly.

—Yes, but why? asked Mr Browne.

Aunt Kate repeated that it was the rule, that was all. Mr Browne still seemed not to understand. Freddy Malins explained to him, as best he could, that the monks were trying to make up for the sins committed by all the sinners in the outside world. The explanation was not very clear for Mr Browne grinned and said:

—I like that idea very much but wouldn't a comfortable spring bed do them as well as a coffin?

—The coffin, said Mary Jane, is to remind them of their last end.

As the subject had grown lugubrious it was buried in a silence of the table during which Mrs Malins could be heard saying to her neighbour in an indistinct undertone:

—They are very good men, the monks, very pious men.

The raisins and almonds and figs and apples and

oranges and chocolates and sweets were now passed
about the table and Aunt Julia invited all the guests to
have either port or sherry. At first Mr Bartell D'Arcy
refused to take either but one of his neighbours nudged
him and whispered something to him upon which he
allowed his glass to be filled. Gradually as the last glasses
were being filled the conversation ceased. A pause followed, broken only by the noise of the wine and by un-
settlings of chairs. The Misses Morkan, all three, looked
down at the tablecloth. Someone coughed once or twice
and then a few gentlemen patted the table gently as a
signal for silence. The silence came and Gabriel pushed
back his chair and stood up.

The patting at once grew louder in encouragement
and then ceased altogether. Gabriel leaned his ten trembling fingers on the tablecloth and smiled nervously at
the company. Meeting a row of upturned faces he raised
his eyes to the chandelier. The piano was playing a
waltz tune and he could hear the skirts sweeping against
the drawing-room door. People, perhaps, were standing
in the snow on the quay outside, gazing up at the
lighted windows and listening to the waltz music. The
air was pure there. In the distance lay the park where
the trees were weighted with snow. The Wellington
Monument wore a gleaming cap of snow that flashed
westward over the white field of Fifteen Acres.

He began:

—Ladies and Gentlemen.

—It has fallen to my lot this evening, as in years past,
to perform a very pleasing task but a task for which I
am afraid my poor powers as a speaker are all too in-
adequate.

—No, no! said Mr Browne.

—But, however that may be, I can only ask you to-
night to take the will for the deed and to lend me

your attention for a few moments while I endeavour to express to you in words what my feelings are on this occasion.

—Ladies and Gentlemen. It is not the first time that we have gathered together under this hospitable roof, around this hospitable board. It is not the first time that we have been the recipients—or perhaps, I had better say, the victims—of the hospitality of certain good ladies.

He made a circle in the air with his arm and paused. Everyone laughed or smiled at Aunt Kate and Aunt Julia and Mary Jane who all turned crimson with pleasure. Gabriel went on more boldly:

—I feel more strongly with every recurring year that our country has no tradition which does it so much honour and which it should guard so jealously as that of its hospitality. It is a tradition that is unique as far as my experience goes (and I have visited not a few places abroad) among the modern nations. Some would say, perhaps, that with us it is rather a failing than anything to be boasted of. But granted even that, it is, to my mind, a princely failing, and one that I trust will long be cultivated among us. Of one thing, at least, I am sure. As long as this one roof shelters the good ladies aforesaid—and I wish from my heart it may do so for many and many a long year to come—the tradition of genuine warm-hearted courteous Irish hospitality, which our forefathers have handed down to us and which we in turn must hand down to our descendants, is still alive among us.

A hearty murmur of assent ran round the table. It shot through Gabriel's mind that Miss Ivors was not there and that she had gone away discourteously: and he said with confidence in himself:

—Ladies and Gentlemen.

—A new generation is growing up in our midst, a generation actuated by new ideas and new principles. It is serious and enthusiastic for these new ideas and its enthusiasm, even when it is misdirected, is, I believe, in the main sincere. But we are living in a sceptical and, if I may use the phrase, a thought-tormented age: and sometimes I fear that this new generation, educated or hypereducated as it is, will lack those qualities of humanity, of hospitality, of kindly humour which belonged to an older day. Listening to-night to the names of all those great singers of the past it seemed to me, I must confess, that we were living in a less spacious age. Those days might, without exaggeration, be called spacious days: and if they are gone beyond recall let us hope, at least, that in gatherings such as this we shall still speak of them with pride and affection, still cherish in our hearts the memory of those dead and gone great ones whose fame the world will not willingly let die.

—Hear, hear! said Mr Browne loudly.

—But yet, continued Gabriel, his voice falling into a softer inflection, there are always in gatherings such as this sadder thoughts that will recur to our minds: thoughts of the past, of youth, of changes, of absent faces that we miss here to-night. Our path through life is strewn with many such sad memories: and were we to brood upon them always we could not find the heart to go on bravely with our work among the living. We have all of us living duties and living affections which claim, and rightly claim, our strenuous endeavours.

—Therefore, I will not linger on the past. I will not let any gloomy moralising intrude upon us here to-night. Here we are gathered together for a brief moment from the bustle and rush of our everyday routine. We are met here as friends, in the spirit of good-fellowship, as colleagues also to a certain extent, in the true spirit of *camaraderie,* and as the guests of—what shall I call them?—the Three Graces of the Dublin musical world.

The table burst into applause and laughter at this sally. Aunt Julia vainly asked each of her neighbours in turn to tell her what Gabriel had said.

—He says we are the Three Graces, Aunt Julia, said Mary Jane.

Aunt Julia did not understand but she looked up, smiling, at Gabriel, who continued in the same vein:

—Ladies and Gentlemen.

—I will not attempt to play to-night the part that Paris played on another occasion. I will not attempt to choose between them. The task would be an invidious one and one beyond my poor powers. For when I view them in turn, whether it be our chief hostess herself, whose good heart, whose too good heart, has become a byword with all who know her, or her sister, who seems to be gifted with perennial youth and whose singing must have been a surprise and a revelation to us all to-night, or, last but not least, when I consider our youngest hostess, talented, cheerful, hard-working and the best of nieces, I confess, Ladies and Gentlemen, that I do not know to which of them I should award the prize.

Gabriel glanced down at his aunts and, seeing the large smile on Aunt Julia's face and the tears which had risen to Aunt Kate's eyes, hastened to his close. He raised his glass of port gallantly, while every member of the company fingered a glass expectantly, and said loudly:

—Let us toast them all three together. Let us drink to their health, wealth, long life, happiness and prosperity and may they long continue to hold the proud and self-won position which they hold in their profession and the position of honour and affection which they hold in our hearts.

All the guests stood up, glass in hand, and, turning towards the three seated ladies, sang in unison, with Mr Browne as leader:

> *For they are jolly gay fellows,*
> *For they are jolly gay fellows,*
> *For they are jolly gay fellows,*
> *Which nobody can deny.*

Aunt Kate was making frank use of her handkerchief and even Aunt Julia seemed moved. Freddy Malins beat time with his pudding-fork and the singers turned towards one another, as if in melodious conference, while they sang, with emphasis:

> *Unless he tells a lie,*
> *Unless he tells a lie.*

Then, turning once more towards their hostesses, they sang:

> *For they are jolly gay fellows,*
> *For they are jolly gay fellows,*
> *For they are jolly gay fellows,*
> *Which nobody can deny.*

The acclamation which followed was taken up beyond the door of the supper-room by many of the other guests and renewed time after time, Freddy Malins acting as officer with his fork on high.

.   .   .   .

The piercing morning air came into the hall where they were standing so that Aunt Kate said:

—Close the door, somebody. Mrs Malins will get her death of cold.

—Browne is out there, Aunt Kate, said Mary Jane.

—Browne is everywhere, said Aunt Kate, lowering her voice.

Mary Jane laughed at her tone.

—Really, she said archly, he is very attentive.

—He has been laid on here like the gas, said Aunt Kate in the same tone, all during the Christmas.

She laughed herself this time good-humouredly and then added quickly:

—But tell him to come in, Mary Jane, and close the door. I hope to goodness he didn't hear me.

At that moment the hall-door was opened and Mr Browne came in from the doorstep, laughing as if his heart would break. He was dressed in a long green overcoat with mock astrakhan cuffs and collar and wore on his head an oval fur cap. He pointed down the snow-covered quay from where the sound of shrill prolonged whistling was borne in.

—Teddy will have all the cabs in Dublin out, he said.

Gabriel advanced from the little pantry behind the office, struggling into his overcoat and, looking round the hall, said:

—Gretta not down yet?

—She's getting on her things, Gabriel, said Aunt Kate.

—Who's playing up there? asked Gabriel.

—Nobody. They're all gone.

—O no, Aunt Kate, said Mary Jane. Bartell D'Arcy and Miss O'Callaghan aren't gone yet.

—Someone is strumming at the piano, anyhow, said Gabriel.

Mary Jane glanced at Gabriel and Mr Browne and said with a shiver:

—It makes me feel cold to look at you two gentlemen muffled up like that. I wouldn't like to face your journey home at this hour.

—I'd like nothing better this minute, said Mr Browne stoutly, than a rattling fine walk in the country or a fast drive with a good spanking goer between the shafts.

—We used to have a very good horse and trap at home, said Aunt Julia sadly.

—The never-to-be-forgotten Johnny, said Mary Jane, laughing.

Aunt Kate and Gabriel laughed too.

—Why, what was wonderful about Johnny? asked Mr Browne.

—The late lamented Patrick Morkan, our grandfather, that is, explained Gabriel, commonly known in his later years as the old gentleman, was a glue-boiler.

—O, now, Gabriel, said Aunt Kate, laughing, he had a starch mill.

—Well, glue or starch, said Gabriel, the old gentleman had a horse by the name of Johnny. And Johnny used to work in the old gentleman's mill, walking round and round in order to drive the mill. That was all very well; but now comes the tragic part about Johnny. One fine day the old gentleman thought he'd like to drive out with the quality to a military review in the park.

—The Lord have mercy on his soul, said Aunt Kate compassionately.

—Amen, said Gabriel. So the old gentleman, as I said, harnessed Johnny and put on his very best tall hat and his very best stock collar and drove out in grand style from his ancestral mansion somewhere near Back Lane, I think.

Everyone laughed, even Mrs Malins, at Gabriel's manner and Aunt Kate said:

—O now, Gabriel, he didn't live in Back Lane, really. Only the mill was there.

—Out from the mansion of his forefathers, continued Gabriel, he drove with Johnny. And everything went on beautifully until Johnny came in sight of King Billy's statue: and whether he fell in love with the horse King

Billy sits on or whether he thought he was back again in the mill, anyhow he began to walk round the statue.

Gabriel paced in a circle round the hall in his goloshes amid the laughter of the others.

—Round and round he went, said Gabriel, and the old gentleman, who was a very pompous old gentleman, was highly indignant. *Go on, sir! What do you mean, sir? Johnny! Johnny! Most extraordinary conduct! Can't understand the horse!*

The peals of laughter which followed Gabriel's imitation of the incident were interrupted by a resounding knock at the hall-door. Mary Jane ran to open it and let in Freddy Malins. Freddy Malins, with his hat well back on his head and his shoulders humped with cold, was puffing and steaming after his exertions.

—I could only get one cab, he said.

—O, we'll find another along the quay, said Gabriel.

—Yes, said Aunt Kate. Better not keep Mrs Malins standing in the draught.

Mrs Malins was helped down the front steps by her son and Mr Browne and, after many manœuvres, hoisted into the cab. Freddy Malins clambered in after her and spent a long time settling her on the seat, Mr Browne helping him with advice. At last she was settled comfortably and Freddy Malins invited Mr Browne into the cab. There was a good deal of confused talk, and then Mr Browne got into the cab. The cabman settled his rug over his knees, and bent down for the address. The confusion grew greater and the cabman was directed differently by Freddy Malins and Mr Browne, each of whom had his head out through a window of the cab. The difficulty was to know where to drop Mr Browne along the route and Aunt Kate, Aunt Julia and Mary Jane helped the discussion from the doorstep with cross-directions and contradictions and abundance of laughter.

As for Freddy Malins he was speechless with laughter. He popped his head in and out of the window every moment, to the great danger of his hat, and told his mother how the discussion was progressing till at last Mr Browne shouted to the bewildered cabman above the din of everybody's laughter:

—Do you know Trinity College?

—Yes, sir, said the cabman.

—Well, drive bang up against Trinity College gates, said Mr Browne, and then we'll tell you where to go. You understand now?

—Yes, sir, said the cabman.

—Make like a bird for Trinity College.

—Right, sir, cried the cabman.

The horse was whipped up and the cab rattled off along the quay amid a chorus of laughter and adieus.

Gabriel had not gone to the door with the others. He was in a dark part of the hall gazing up the staircase. A woman was standing near the top of the first flight, in the shadow also. He could not see her face but he could see the terracotta and salmonpink panels of her skirt which the shadow made appear black and white. It was his wife. She was leaning on the banisters, listening to something. Gabriel was surprised at her stillness and strained his ear to listen also. But he could hear little save the noise of laughter and dispute on the front steps, a few chords struck on the piano and a few notes of a man's voice singing.

He stood still in the gloom of the hall, trying to catch the air that the voice was singing and gazing up at his wife. There was grace and mystery in her attitude as if she were a symbol of something. He asked himself what is a woman standing on the stairs in the shadow, listening to distant music, a symbol of. If he were a painter he would paint her in that attitude. Her blue felt hat

would show off the bronze of her hair against the darkness and the dark panels of her skirt would show off the
light ones. *Distant Music* he would call the picture if he
were a painter.

The hall-door was closed; and Aunt Kate, Aunt Julia
and Mary Jane came down the hall, still laughing.

—Well, isn't Freddy terrible? said Mary Jane. He's
really terrible.

Gabriel said nothing but pointed up the stairs towards
where his wife was standing. Now that the hall-door was
closed the voice and the piano could be heard more
clearly. Gabriel held up his hand for them to be silent.
The song seemed to be in the old Irish tonality and the
singer seemed uncertain both of his words and of his
voice. The voice, made plaintive by distance and by the
singer's hoarseness, faintly illuminated the cadence of
the air with words expressing grief:

> *O, the rain falls on my heavy locks*
> *And the dew wets my skin,*
> *My babe lies cold . . .*

—O, exclaimed Mary Jane. It's Bartell D'Arcy singing
and he wouldn't sing all the night. O, I'll get him to
sing a song before he goes.

—O do, Mary Jane, said Aunt Kate.

Mary Jane brushed past the others and ran to the
staircase but before she reached it the singing stopped
and the piano was closed abruptly.

—O, what a pity! she cried. Is he coming down,
Gretta?

Gabriel heard his wife answer yes and saw her come
down towards them. A few steps behind her were Mr
Bartell D'Arcy and Miss O'Callaghan.

—O, Mr D'Arcy, cried Mary Jane, it's downright

mean of you to break off like that when we were all in raptures listening to you.

—I have been at him all the evening, said Miss O'Callaghan, and Mrs Conroy too and he told us he had a dreadful cold and couldn't sing.

—O, Mr D'Arcy, said Aunt Kate, now that was a great fib to tell.

—Can't you see that I'm as hoarse as a crow? said Mr D'Arcy roughly.

He went into the pantry hastily and put on his overcoat. The others, taken aback by his rude speech, could find nothing to say. Aunt Kate wrinkled her brows and made signs to the others to drop the subject. Mr D'Arcy stood swathing his neck carefully and frowning.

—It's the weather, said Aunt Julia, after a pause.

—Yes, everybody has colds, said Aunt Kate readily, everybody.

—They say, said Mary Jane, we haven't had snow like it for thirty years; and I read this morning in the newspapers that the snow is general all over Ireland.

—I love the look of snow, said Aunt Julia sadly.

—So do I, said Miss O'Callaghan. I think Christmas is never really Christmas unless we have the snow on the ground.

—But poor Mr D'Arcy doesn't like the snow, said Aunt Kate, smiling.

Mr D'Arcy came from the pantry, fully swathed and buttoned, and in a repentant tone told them the history of his cold. Everyone gave him advice and said it was a great pity and urged him to be very careful of his throat in the night air. Gabriel watched his wife who did not join in the conversation. She was standing right under the dusty fanlight and the flame of the gas lit up the rich bronze of her hair which he had seen her dry-

ing at the fire a few days before. She was in the same
attitude and seemed unaware of the talk about her. At
last she turned towards them and Gabriel saw that there
was colour on her cheeks and that her eyes were shining.
A sudden tide of joy went leaping out of his heart.

—Mr D'Arcy, she said, what is the name of that song
you were singing?

—It's called *The Lass of Aughrim*, said Mr D'Arcy,
but I couldn't remember it properly. Why? Do you
know it?

—*The Lass of Aughrim*, she repeated. I couldn't think
of the name.

—It's a very nice air, said Mary Jane. I'm sorry you
were not in voice to-night.

—Now, Mary Jane, said Aunt Kate, don't annoy Mr
D'Arcy. I won't have him annoyed.

Seeing that all were ready to start she shepherded
them to the door where good-night was said:

—Well, good-night, Aunt Kate, and thanks for the
pleasant evening.

—Good-night, Gabriel. Good-night, Gretta!

—Good-night, Aunt Kate, and thanks ever so much.
Good-night, Aunt Julia.

—O, good-night, Gretta, I didn't see you.

—Good-night, Mr D'Arcy. Good-night, Miss O'Callaghan.

—Good-night, Miss Morkan.

—Good-night, again.

—Good-night, all. Safe home.

—Good-night. Good-night.

The morning was still dark. A dull yellow light
brooded over the houses and the river; and the sky
seemed to be descending. It was slushy underfoot; and
only streaks and patches of snow lay on the roofs, on the
parapets of the quay and on the area railings. The lamps

were still burning redly in the murky air and, across the
river, the palace of the Four Courts stood out men-
acingly against the heavy sky.

She was walking on before him with Mr Bartell
D'Arcy, her shoes in a brown parcel tucked under one
arm and her hands holding her skirt up from the slush.
She had no longer any grace of attitude but Gabriel's
eyes were still bright with happiness. The blood went
bounding along his veins; and the thoughts went rioting
through his brain, proud, joyful, tender, valorous.

She was walking on before him so lightly and so erect
that he longed to run after her noiselessly, catch her by
the shoulders and say something foolish and affectionate
into her ear. She seemed to him so frail that he longed
to defend her against something and then to be alone
with her. Moments of their secret life together burst like
stars upon his memory. A heliotrope envelope was lying
beside his breakfast-cup and he was caressing it with his
hand. Birds were twittering in the ivy and the sunny
web of the curtain was shimmering along the floor: he
could not eat for happiness. They were standing on the
crowded platform and he was placing a ticket inside the
warm palm of her glove. He was standing with her in
the cold, looking in through a grated window at a man
making bottles in a roaring furnace. It was very cold.
Her face, fragrant in the cold air, was quite close to
his; and suddenly she called out to the man at the furnace:

—Is the fire hot, sir?

But the man could not hear her with the noise of the
furnace. It was just as well. He might have answered
rudely.

A wave of yet more tender joy escaped from his heart
and went coursing in warm flood along his arteries. Like
the tender fires of stars moments of their life together,

that no one knew of or would ever know of, broke upon and illumined his memory. He longed to recall to her those moments, to make her forget the years of their dull existence together and remember only their moments of ecstasy. For the years, he felt, had not quenched his soul or hers. Their children, his writing, her household cares had not quenched all their souls' tender fire. In one letter that he had written to her then he had said: *Why is it that words like these seem to me so dull and cold? Is it because there is no word tender enough to be your name?*

Like distant music these words that he had written years before were borne towards him from the past. He longed to be alone with her. When the others had gone away, when he and she were in their room in the hotel, then they would be alone together. He would call her softly:

—Gretta!

Perhaps she would not hear at once: she would be undressing. Then something in his voice would strike her. She would turn and look at him. . . .

At the corner of Winetavern Street they met a cab. He was glad of its rattling noise as it saved him from conversation. She was looking out of the window and seemed tired. The others spoke only a few words, pointing out some building or street. The horse galloped along wearily under the murky morning sky, dragging his old rattling box after his heels, and Gabriel was again in a cab with her, galloping to catch the boat, galloping to their honeymoon.

As the cab drove across O'Connell Bridge Miss O'Callaghan said:

—They say you never cross O'Connell Bridge without seeing a white horse.

—I see a white man this time, said Gabriel.

—Where? asked Mr Bartell D'Arcy.

Gabriel pointed to the statue, on which lay patches of snow. Then he nodded familiarly to it and waved his hand.

—Good-night, Dan, he said gaily.

When the cab drew up before the hotel Gabriel jumped out and, in spite of Mr Bartell D'Arcy's protest, paid the driver. He gave the man a shilling over his fare. The man saluted and said:

—A prosperous New Year to you, sir.

—The same to you, said Gabriel cordially.

She leaned for a moment on his arm in getting out of the cab and while standing at the curbstone, bidding the others good-night. She leaned lightly on his arm, as lightly as when she had danced with him a few hours before. He had felt proud and happy then, happy that she was his, proud of her grace and wifely carriage. But now, after the kindling again of so many memories, the first touch of her body, musical and strange and perfumed, sent through him a keen pang of lust. Under cover of her silence he pressed her arm closely to his side; and, as they stood at the hotel door, he felt that they had escaped from their lives and duties, escaped from home and friends and run away together with wild and radiant hearts to a new adventure.

An old man was dozing in a great hooded chair in the hall. He lit a candle in the office and went before them to the stairs. They followed him in silence, their feet falling in soft thuds on the thickly carpeted stairs. She mounted the stairs behind the porter, her head bowed in the ascent, her frail shoulders curved as with a burden, her skirt girt tightly about her. He could have flung his arms about her hips and held her still for his arms were trembling with desire to seize her and only the stress of his nails against the palms of his hands held

the wild impulse of his body in check. The porter halted
on the stairs to settle his guttering candle. They halted
too on the steps below him. In the silence Gabriel
could hear the falling of the molten wax into the tray
and the thumping of his own heart against his ribs.

The porter led them along a corridor and opened a
door. Then he set his unstable candle down on a toilet-
table and asked at what hour they were to be called in
the morning.

—Eight, said Gabriel.

The porter pointed to the tap of the electric-light and
began a muttered apology but Gabriel cut him short.

—We don't want any light. We have light enough
from the street. And I say, he added, pointing to the
candle, you might remove that handsome article, like a
good man.

The porter took up his candle again, but slowly for he
was surprised by such a novel idea. Then he mumbled
good-night and went out. Gabriel shot the lock to.

A ghostly light from the street lamp lay in a long shaft
from one window to the door. Gabriel threw his overcoat
and hat on a couch and crossed the room towards the
window. He looked down into the street in order that
his emotion might calm a little. Then he turned and
leaned against a chest of drawers with his back to the
light. She had taken off her hat and cloak and was standing before a large swinging mirror, unhooking her waist.
Gabriel paused for a few moments, watching her, and
then said:

—Gretta!

She turned away from the mirror slowly and walked
along the shaft of light towards him. Her face looked so
serious and weary that the words would not pass Gabriel's lips. No, it was not the moment yet.

—You looked tired, he said.

—I am a little, she answered.

—You don't feel ill or weak?

—No, tired: that's all.

She went on to the window and stood there, looking out. Gabriel waited again and then, fearing that diffidence was about to conquer him, he said abruptly:

—By the way, Gretta!

—What is it?

—You know that poor fellow Malins? he said quickly.

—Yes. What about him?

—Well, poor fellow, he's a decent sort of chap after all, continued Gabriel in a false voice. He gave me back that sovereign I lent him and I didn't expect it really. It's a pity he wouldn't keep away from that Browne, because he's not a bad fellow at heart.

He was trembling now with annoyance. Why did she seem so abstracted? He did not know how he could begin. Was she annoyed, too, about something? If she would only turn to him or come to him of her own accord! To take her as she was would be brutal. No, he must see some ardour in her eyes first. He longed to be master of her strange mood.

—When did you lend him the pound? she asked, after a pause.

Gabriel strove to restrain himself from breaking out into brutal language about the sottish Malins and his pound. He longed to cry to her from his soul, to crush her body against his, to overmaster her. But he said:

—O, at Christmas, when he opened that little Christmas-card shop in Henry Street.

He was in such a fever of rage and desire that he did not hear her come from the window. She stood before him for an instant, looking at him strangely. Then, suddenly raising herself on tiptoe and resting her hands lightly on his shoulders, she kissed him.

—You are a very generous person, Gabriel, she said.

Gabriel, trembling with delight at her sudden kiss and at the quaintness of her phrase, put his hands on her hair and began smoothing it back, scarcely touching it with his fingers. The washing had made it fine and brilliant. His heart was brimming over with happiness. Just when he was wishing for it she had come to him of her own accord. Perhaps her thoughts had been running with his. Perhaps she had felt the impetuous desire that was in him and then the yielding mood had come upon her. Now that she had fallen to him so easily he wondered why he had been so diffident.

He stood, holding her head between his hands. Then, slipping one arm swiftly about her body and drawing her towards him, he said softly:

—Gretta dear, what are you thinking about?

She did not answer nor yield wholly to his arm. He said again, softly:

—Tell me what it is, Gretta. I think I know what is the matter. Do I know?

She did not answer at once. Then she said in an outburst of tears:

—O, I am thinking about that song, *The Lass of Aughrim.*

She broke loose from him and ran to the bed and, throwing her arms across the bed-rail, hid her face. Gabriel stood stock-still for a moment in astonishment and then followed her. As he passed in the way of the cheval-glass he caught sight of himself in full length, his broad, well-filled shirt-front, the face whose expression always puzzled him when he saw it in a mirror and his glimmering gilt-rimmed eyeglasses. He halted a few paces from her and said:

—What about the song? Why does that make you cry?

She raised her head from her arms and dried her eyes

with the back of her hand like a child. A kinder note
than he had intended went into his voice.

—Why, Gretta? he asked.

—I am thinking about a person long ago who used to
sing that song.

—And who was the person long ago? asked Gabriel,
smiling.

—It was a person I used to know in Galway when I
was living with my grandmother, she said.

The smile passed away from Gabriel's face. A dull
anger began to gather again at the back of his mind and
the dull fires of his lust began to glow angrily in his
veins.

—Someone you were in love with? he asked ironically.

—It was a young boy I used to know, she answered,
named Michael Furey. He used to sing that song, *The
Lass of Aughrim*. He was very delicate.

Gabriel was silent. He did not wish her to think that
he was interested in this delicate boy.

—I can see him so plainly, she said after a moment.
Such eyes as he had: big dark eyes! And such an expression in them—an expression!

—O then, you were in love with him? said Gabriel.

—I used to go out walking with him, she said, when I
was in Galway.

A thought flew across Gabriel's mind.

—Perhaps that was why you wanted to go to Galway
with that Ivors girl? he said coldly.

She looked at him and asked in surprise:

—What for?

Her eyes made Gabriel feel awkward. He shrugged
his shoulders and said:

—How do I know? To see him perhaps.

She looked away from him along the shaft of light
towards the window in silence.

—He is dead, she said at length. He died when he was only seventeen. Isn't it a terrible thing to die so young as that?

—What was he? asked Gabriel, still ironically.

—He was in the gasworks, she said.

Gabriel felt humiliated by the failure of his irony and by the evocation of this figure from the dead, a boy in the gasworks. While he had been full of memories of their secret life together, full of tenderness and joy and desire, she had been comparing him in her mind with another. A shameful consciousness of his own person assailed him. He saw himself as a ludicrous figure, acting as a pennyboy for his aunts, a nervous well-meaning sentimentalist, orating to vulgarians and idealising his own clownish lusts, the pitiable fatuous fellow he had caught a glimpse of in the mirror. Instinctively he turned his back more to the light lest she might see the shame that burned upon his forehead.

He tried to keep up his tone of cold interrogation but his voice when he spoke was humble and indifferent.

—I suppose you were in love with this Michael Furey, Gretta, he said.

—I was great with him at that time, she said.

Her voice was veiled and sad. Gabriel, feeling now how vain it would be to try to lead her whither he had purposed, caressed one of her hands and said, also sadly:

—And what did he die of so young, Gretta? Consumption, was it?

—I think he died for me, she answered.

A vague terror seized Gabriel at this answer as if, at that hour when he had hoped to triumph, some impalpable and vindictive being was coming against him, gathering forces against him in its vague world. But he shook himself free of it with an effort of reason and continued to caress her hand. He did not question her again for he felt that she would tell him of herself. Her hand was warm and moist: it did not respond to his touch but he continued to caress it just as he had caressed her first letter to him that spring morning.

—It was in the winter, she said, about the beginning of the winter when I was going to leave my grandmother's and come up here to the convent. And he was ill at the time in his lodgings in Galway and wouldn't be let out and his people in Oughterard were written to. He was in decline, they said, or something like that. I never knew rightly.

She paused for a moment and sighed.

—Poor fellow, she said. He was very fond of me and he was such a gentle boy. We used to go out together, walking, you know, Gabriel, like the way they do in the country. He was going to study singing only for his health. He had a very good voice, poor Michael Furey.

—Well; and then? asked Gabriel.

—And then when it came to the time for me to leave Galway and come up to the convent he was much worse and I wouldn't be let see him so I wrote a letter saying I was going up to Dublin and would be back in the summer and hoping he would be better then.

She paused for a moment to get her voice under control and then went on:

—Then the night before I left I was in my grandmother's house in Nuns' Island, packing up, and I heard gravel thrown up against the window. The window was so wet I couldn't see so I ran downstairs as I was and slipped out the back into the garden and there was the poor fellow at the end of the garden, shivering.

—And did you not tell him to go back? asked Gabriel.

—I implored of him to go home at once and told him he would get his death in the rain. But he said he did

not want to live. I can see his eyes as well as well! He
was standing at the end of the wall where there was a
tree.

—And did he go home? asked Gabriel.

—Yes, he went home. And when I was only a week in
the convent he died and he was buried in Oughterard
where his people came from. O, the day I heard that,
that he was dead!

She stopped, choking with sobs, and, overcome by
emotion, flung herself face downward on the bed, sobbing in the quilt. Gabriel held her hand for a moment
longer, irresolutely, and then, shy of intruding on her
grief, let it fall gently and walked quietly to the window.

She was fast asleep.

Gabriel, leaning on his elbow, looked for a few moments unresentfully on her tangled hair and half-open
mouth, listening to her deep-drawn breath. So she had
had that romance in her life: a man had died for her
sake. It hardly pained him now to think how poor a
part he, her husband, had played in her life. He watched
her while she slept as though he and she had never lived
together as man and wife. His curious eyes rested long
upon her face and on her hair: and, as he thought of
what she must have been then, in that time of her first
girlish beauty, a strange friendly pity for her entered
his soul. He did not like to say even to himself that her
face was no longer beautiful but he knew that it was
no longer the face for which Michael Furey had braved
death.

Perhaps she had not told him all the story. His eyes
moved to the chair over which she had thrown some of
her clothes. A petticoat string dangled to the floor. One
boot stood upright, its limp upper fallen down: the fel-

low of it lay upon its side. He wondered at his riot of
emotions of an hour before. From what had it proceeded? From his aunt's supper, from his own foolish
speech, from the wine and dancing, the merry-making
when saying good-night in the hall, the pleasure of the
walk along the river in the snow. Poor Aunt Julia! She
too, would soon be a shade with the shade of Patrick
Morkan and his horse. He had caught that haggard look
upon her face for a moment when she was singing
Arrayed for the Bridal. Soon, perhaps, he would be sitting in that same drawing-room, dressed in black, his
silk hat on his knees. The blinds would be drawn down
and Aunt Kate would be sitting beside him, crying and
blowing her nose and telling him how Julia had died. He
would cast about in his mind for some words that might
console her, and would find only lame and useless ones.
Yes, yes: that would happen very soon.

The air of the room chilled his shoulders. He stretched
himself cautiously along under the sheets and lay down
beside his wife. One by one they were all becoming
shades. Better pass boldly into that other world, in the
full glory of some passion, than fade and wither dis-
mally with age. He thought of how she who lay beside
him had locked in her heart for so many years that
image of her lover's eyes when he had told her that he
did not wish to live.

Generous tears filled Gabriel's eyes. He had never felt
like that himself towards any woman but he knew that
such a feeling must be love. The tears gathered more
thickly in his eyes and in the partial darkness he imagined he saw the form of a young man standing under
a dripping tree. Other forms were near. His soul had approached that region where dwell the vast hosts of the
dead. He was conscious of, but could not apprehend, their wayward and flickering existence. His own

identity was fading out into a grey impalpable world: the solid world itself which these dead had one time reared and lived in was dissolving and dwindling.

A few light taps upon the pane made him turn to the window. It had begun to snow again. He watched sleepily the flakes, silver and dark, falling obliquely against the lamplight. The time had come for him to set out on his journey westward. Yes, the newspapers were right: snow was general all over Ireland. It was falling on every part of the dark central plain, on the treeless hills, falling softly upon the Bog of Allen and, farther westward, softly falling into the dark mutinous Shannon waves. It was falling, too, upon every part of the lonely churchyard on the hill where Michael Furey lay buried. It lay thickly drifted on the crooked crosses and head-stones, on the spears of the little gate, on the barren thorns. His soul swooned slowly as he heard the snow falling faintly through the universe and faintly falling, like the descent of their last end, upon all the living and the dead.

A Portrait of the Artist as a Young Man

"Et ignotas animum dimittit in artes."
Ovid, *Metamorphoses*, VIII, 188.

The Definitive Text
corrected from the Dublin holograph

EDITOR'S PREFACE

THE English edition having encountered the usual
obstacles, *A Portrait of the Artist as a Young Man*
was first brought out in 1916 by a New York publisher,
B. W. Huebsch (now The Viking Press). The dates and
places of composition, ten years spent mainly in Trieste,
are indicated on the last page. The present version is
the end-product of a series of revisions and reconsider-
ations which seems to have started from journals and
notebooks kept during college. That period, which coin-
cides with the final chapter of the *Portrait,* is much more
amply covered by the surviving fragment of an earlier
version, *Stephen Hero,* which has recently been edited
by Professor Theodore Spencer. It is well worth reading
for its vivid presentation of figures and episodes which
have faded into the background of the completed book:
the poignant death of Stephen's sister, Isabel; his boyish
infatuation with Emma Clery, the belle of his Gaelic
class; the stormy reception accorded by classmates and
teachers to his essay on drama and life; the circumstan-
tial details of his family's social decline and his mother's
distressed piety. Comparison of the two books will show,
however, that what was lost in color was gained in
clarity of outline and firmness of style. By concentrat-
ing upon his protagonist, Joyce intensified his leading

themes. To speak of impersonality, in so egocentric a connection, may sound far-fetched; but the *Portrait* is rather a credo than an autobiography; it is charged throughout with a fervent intellectuality, from which more worldly claims are mere distractions. Between its intellectual preoccupations (philosophy, theology, esthetics) and its everyday occupations (city, church, family) exists a gap which only language can span. The poet, through his command of words, is a mediator between the world of ideas and the world of reality. The very name of Joyce's hero designates his symbolic role, since Dedalus is the classical prototype of the artist, while Stephen's Green is the square where University College stands. As the record of a developing mind—perhaps the finest English example of the pedagogical novel—the *Portrait* conforms to an educational pattern. Thus in the first chapter Stephen is the youngest boy at Clongowes Wood School, a reconditioned castle haunted by the ghosts of Irish rebels; here the living shadow of Parnell falls across his awakening consciousness. In the next three chapters, still under the tutelage of the Jesuits, Stephen attends a day school in Dublin; his extracurricular experiments with sex, accentuated by the terrors of a retreat, bring on a religious crisis. The concluding scenes are set at that institution for which Newman propounded his *Idea of a University;* here Stephen responds to his vocation, completes his education, and makes a clean break. Henceforth art will mean not only his way of life, but a criticism of the life he has heretofore known. Retrospectively *Ulysses* picks up the story of his first exile in Paris and hasty return to Ireland. And *Dubliners* fills out this unique self-portrait with delineations of Stephen's more typical fellow-citizens.

I

ONCE upon a time and a very good time it was there was a moocow coming down along the road and this moocow that was coming down the road met a nicens little boy named baby tuckoo. . . .

His father told him that story: his father looked at him through a glass: he had a hairy face.

He was baby tuckoo. The moocow came down the road where Betty Byrne lived: she sold lemon platt.

> O, the wild rose blossoms
> On the little green place.

He sang that song. That was his song.

> O, the green wothe botheth.

When you wet the bed first it is warm then it gets cold. His mother put on the oilsheet. That had the queer smell.

His mother had a nicer smell than his father. She played on the piano the sailor's hornpipe for him to dance. He danced:

> Tralala lala
> Tralala tralaladdy
> Tralala lala
> Tralala lala.

Uncle Charles and Dante clapped. They were older than his father and mother but uncle Charles was older than Dante.

Dante had two brushes in her press. The brush with the maroon velvet back was for Michael Davitt and the brush with the green velvet back was for Parnell. Dante gave him a cachou every time he brought her a piece of tissue paper.

The Vances lived in number seven. They had a different father and mother. They were Eileen's father and mother. When they were grown up he was going to marry Eileen. He hid under the table. His mother said:

—O, Stephen will apologise.

Dante said:

—O, if not, the eagles will come and pull out his eyes.

> *Pull out his eyes,*
> *Apologise,*
> *Apologise,*
> *Pull out his eyes,*
>
> *Apologise,*
> *Pull out his eyes,*
> *Pull out his eyes,*
> *Apologise*

*   *   *

The wide playgrounds were swarming with boys. All were shouting and the prefects urged them on with strong cries. The evening air was pale and chilly and after every charge and thud of the footballers the greasy leather orb flew like a heavy bird through the grey light. He kept on the fringe of his line, out of sight of his prefect, out of the reach of the rude feet, feigning to run now and then. He felt his body small and weak amid the throng of players and his eyes were weak and watery. Rody Kickham was not like that: he would be captain of the third line all the fellows said.

Rody Kickham was a decent fellow but Nasty Roche

was a stink. Rody Kickham had greaves in his number and a hamper in the refectory. Nasty Roche had big hands. He called the Friday pudding dog-in-the-blanket. And one day he had asked:

—What is your name?

Stephen had answered:

—Stephen Dedalus.

Then Nasty Roche had said:

—What kind of a name is that?

And when Stephen had not been able to answer Nasty Roche had asked:

—What is your father?

Stephen had answered:

—A gentleman.

Then Nasty Roche had asked:

—Is he a magistrate?

He crept about from point to point on the fringe of his line, making little runs now and then. But his hands were bluish with cold. He kept his hands in the side-pockets of his belted grey suit. That was a belt round his pocket. And belt was also to give a fellow a belt. One day a fellow had said to Cantwell:

—I'd give you such a belt in a second.

Cantwell had answered:

—Go and fight your match. Give Cecil Thunder a belt. I'd like to see you. He'd give you a toe in the rump for yourself.

That was not a nice expression. His mother had told him not to speak with the rough boys in the college. Nice mother! The first day in the hall of the castle when she had said goodbye she had put up her veil double to her nose to kiss him: and her nose and eyes were red. But he had pretended not to see that she was going to cry. She was a nice mother but she was not so nice when she cried. And his father had given him two fiveshilling pieces for pocket money. And his father had told him if he wanted anything to write home to him and, whatever he did, never to peach on a fellow. Then at the door of the castle the rector had shaken hands with his father and mother, his soutane fluttering in the breeze, and the car had driven off with his father and mother on it. They had cried to him from the car, waving their hands:

—Goodbye, Stephen, goodbye!
—Goodbye, Stephen, goodbye!

He was caught in the whirl of a scrimmage and, fearful of the flashing eyes and muddy boots, bent down to look through the legs. The fellows were struggling and groaning and their legs were rubbing and kicking and stamping. Then Jack Lawton's yellow boots dodged out the ball and all the other boots and legs ran after. He ran after them a little way and then stopped. It was useless to run on. Soon they would be going home for the holidays. After supper in the studyhall he would exchange the number pasted up inside his desk from seventyseven to seventysix.

It would be better to be in the studyhall than out there in the cold. The sky was pale and cold but there were lights in the castle. He wondered from which window Hamilton Rowan had thrown his hat on the haha and had there been flowerbeds at that time under the windows One day when he had been called to the castle the butler had shown him the marks of the soldiers' slugs in the wood of the door and had given him a piece of shortbread that the community ate. It was nice and warm to see the lights in the castle. It was like something in a book. Perhaps Leicester Abbey was like that. And there were nice sentences in Doctor Cornwell's Spelling Book. They were like poetry but they were only sentences to learn the spelling from.

Wolsey died in Leicester Abbey
Where the abbots buried him.
Canker is a disease of plants,
Cancer one of animals.

It would be nice to lie on the hearthrug before the
fire, leaning his head upon his hands, and think on
those sentences. He shivered as if he had cold slimy
water next his skin. That was mean of Wells to shoulder him into the square ditch because he would not
swop his little snuffbox for Wells's seasoned hacking
chestnut, the conqueror of forty. How cold and slimy
the water had been! A fellow had once seen a big rat
jump into the scum. Mother was sitting at the fire with
Dante waiting for Brigid to bring in the tea. She had
her feet on the fender and her jewelly slippers were so
hot and they had such a lovely warm smell! Dante
knew a lot of things. She had taught him where the
Mozambique Channel was and what was the longest
river in America and what was the name of the highest
mountain in the moon. Father Arnall knew more than
Dante because he was a priest but both his father and
uncle Charles said that Dante was a clever woman and
a wollread woman. And when Dante made that noise
after dinner and then put up her hand to her mouth:
that was heartburn.

A voice cried far out on the playground:

—All in!

Then other voices cried from the lower and third
lines:

—All in! All in!

The players closed around, flushed and muddy, and
he went among them, glad to go in. Rody Kickham
held the ball by its greasy lace. A fellow asked him to
give it one last: but he walked on without even answer-

ing the fellow. Simon Moonan told him not to because the prefect was looking. The fellow turned to Simon Moonan and said:

—We all know why you speak. You are McGlade's suck.

Suck was a queer word. The fellow called Simon Moonan that name because Simon Moonan used to tie the prefect's false sleeves behind his back and the prefect used to let on to be angry. But the sound was ugly. Once he had washed his hands in the lavatory of the Wicklow Hotel and his father pulled the stopper up by the chain after and the dirty water went down through the hole in the basin. And when it had all gone down slowly the hole in the basin had made a sound like that: suck. Only louder.

To remember that and the white look of the lavatory made him feel cold and then hot. There were two cocks that you turned and water came out: cold and hot. He felt cold and then a little hot: and he could see the names printed on the cocks. That was a very queer thing.

And the air in the corridor chilled him too. It was queer and wettish. But soon the gas would be lit and in burning it made a light noise like a little song. Always the same: and when the fellows stopped talking in the playroom you could hear it.

It was the hour for sums. Father Arnall wrote a hard sum on the board and then said:

—Now then, who will win? Go ahead, York! Go ahead, Lancaster!

Stephen tried his best but the sum was too hard and he felt confused. The little silk badge with the white rose on it that was pinned on the breast of his jacket began to flutter. He was no good at sums but he tried his best so that York might not lose. Father Arnall's

face looked very black but he was not in a wax: he was
laughing. Then Jack Lawton cracked his fingers and
Father Arnall looked at his copybook and said:

—Right. Bravo Lancaster! The red rose wins. Come
on now, York! Forge ahead!

Jack Lawton looked over from his side. The little silk
badge with the red rose on it looked very rich because
he had a blue sailor top on. Stephen felt his own face
red too, thinking of all the bets about who would get
first place in elements, Jack Lawton or he. Some weeks
Jack Lawton got the card for first and some weeks
he got the card for first. His white silk badge fluttered
and fluttered as he worked at the next sum and heard
Father Arnall's voice. Then all his eagerness passed
away and he felt his face quite cool. He thought his
face must be white because it felt so cool. He could not
get out the answer for the sum but it did not matter.
White roses and red roses: those were beautiful colours
to think of. And the cards for first place and second
place and third place were beautiful colours too: pink
and cream and lavender. Lavender and cream and pink
roses were beautiful to think of. Perhaps a wild rose
might be like those colours and he remembered the
song about the wild rose blossoms on the little green
place. But you could not have a green rose. But perhaps somewhere in the world you could.

The bell rang and then the classes began to file out
of the rooms and along the corridors towards the refectory. He sat looking at the two prints of butter on his
plate but could not eat the damp bread. The tablecloth
was damp and limp. But he drank off the hot weak tea
which the clumsy scullion, girt with a white apron,
poured into his cup. He wondered whether the scullion's apron was damp too or whether all white things
were cold and damp. Nasty Roche and Saurin drank

cocoa that their people sent them in tins. They said
they could not drink the tea; that it was hogwash. Their
fathers were magistrates, the fellows said.

All the boys seemed to him very strange. They had
all fathers and mothers and different clothes and
voices. He longed to be at home and lay his head on his
mother's lap. But he could not: and so he longed for
the play and study and prayers to be over and to be in
bed.

He drank another cup of hot tea and Fleming
said:

—What's up? Have you a pain or what's up with you?

—I don't know, Stephen said.

—Sick in your breadbasket, Fleming said, because
your face looks white. It will go away.

—O yes, Stephen said.

But he was not sick there. He thought that he was
sick in his heart if you could be sick in that place. Fleming was very decent to ask him. He wanted to cry. He
leaned his elbows on the table and shut and opened the
flaps of his ears. Then he heard the noise of the refectory every time he opened the flaps of his ears. It made
a roar like a train at night. And when he closed the
flaps the roar was shut off like a train going into a
tunnel. That night at Dalkey the train had roared like
that and then, when it went into the tunnel, the roar
stopped. He closed his eyes and the train went on,
roaring and then stopping; roaring again, stopping. It
was nice to hear it roar and stop and then roar out of
the tunnel again and then stop.

Then the higher line fellows began to come down
along the matting in the middle of the refectory, Paddy
Rath and Jimmy Magee and the Spaniard who was
allowed to smoke cigars and the little Portuguese who
wore the woolly cap. And then the lower line tables

and the tables of the third line. And every single fellow had a different way of walking.

He sat in a corner of the playroom pretending to watch a game of dominos and once or twice he was able to hear for an instant the little song of the gas. The prefect was at the door with some boys and Simon Moonan was knotting his false sleeves. He was telling them something about Tullabeg.

Then he went away from the door and Wells came over to Stephen and said:

—Tell us, Dedalus, do you kiss your mother before you go to bed?

Stephen answered:

—I do.

Wells turned to the other fellows and said:

—O, I say, here's a fellow says he kisses his mother every night before he goes to bed.

The other fellows stopped their game and turned round, laughing. Stephen blushed under their eyes and said:

—I do not.

Wells said:

—O, I say, here's a fellow says he doesn't kiss his mother before he goes to bed.

They all laughed again. Stephen tried to laugh with them. He felt his whole body hot and confused in a moment. What was the right answer to the question? He had given two and still Wells laughed. But Wells must know the right answer for he was in third of grammar. He tried to think of Wells's mother but he did not dare to raise his eyes to Wells's face. He did not like Wells's face. It was Wells who had shouldered him into the square ditch the day before because he would not swop his little snuffbox for Wells's seasoned hacking chestnut, the conqueror of forty. It was a mean

thing to do; all the fellows said it was. And how cold
and slimy the water had been! And a fellow had once
seen a big rat jump plop into the scum.

The cold slime of the ditch covered his whole body;
and, when the bell rang for study and the lines filed out
of the playrooms, he felt the cold air of the corridor
and staircase inside his clothes. He still tried to think
what was the right answer. Was it right to kiss his
mother or wrong to kiss his mother? What did that
mean, to kiss? You put your face up like that to say
goodnight and then his mother put her face down. That
was to kiss. His mother put her lips on his cheek; her
lips were soft and they wetted his cheek; and they made
a tiny little noise: kiss. Why did people do that with
their two faces?

Sitting in the studyhall he opened the lid of his desk
and changed the number pasted up inside from
seventyseven to seventysix. But the Christmas vacation
was very far away: but one time it would come because
the earth moved round always.

There was a big picture of the earth on the first page
of his geography: a big ball in the middle of clouds.
Fleming had a box of crayons and one night during
free study he had coloured the earth green and the
clouds maroon. That was like the two brushes in
Dante's press, the brush with the green velvet back for
Parnell and the brush with the maroon velvet back
for Michael Davitt. But he had not told Fleming to
colour them those colours. Fleming had done it himself.

He opened the geography to study the lesson; but he
could not learn the names of places in America. Still
they were all different places that had those different
names. They were all in different countries and the

countries were in continents and the continents were in the world and the world was in the universe.

He turned to the flyleaf of the geography and read what he had written there: himself, his name and where he was.

Stephen Dedalus
Class of Elements
Clongowes Wood College
Sallins
County Kildare
Ireland
Europe
The World
The Universe

That was in his writing: and Fleming one night for a cod had written on the opposite page:

Stephen Dedalus is my name,
Ireland is my nation.
Clongowes is my dwellingplace
And heaven my expectation.

He read the verses backwards but then they were not poetry. Then he read the flyleaf from the bottom to the top till he came to his own name. That was he: and he read down the page again. What was after the universe? Nothing. But was there anything round the universe to show where it stopped before the nothing place began? It could not be a wall but there could be a thin thin line there all round everything. It was very big to think about everything and everywhere. Only God could do that. He tried to think what a big thought that must be but he could think only of God. God was God's name just as his name was Stephen. *Dieu* was the French for

God and that was God's name too; and when anyone prayed to God and said *Dieu* then God knew at once that it was a French person that was praying. But though there were different names for God in all the different languages in the world and God understood what all the people who prayed said in their different languages still God remained always the same God and God's real name was God.

It made him very tired to think that way. It made him feel his head very big. He turned over the flyleaf and looked wearily at the green round earth in the middle of the maroon clouds. He wondered which was right, to be for the green or for the maroon, because Dante had ripped the green velvet back off the brush that was for Parnell one day with her scissors and had told him that Parnell was a bad man. He wondered if they were arguing at home about that. That was called politics. There were two sides in it: Dante was on one side and his father and Mr Casey were on the other side but his mother and Uncle Charles were on no side. Every day there was something in the paper about it.

It pained him that he did not know well what politics meant and that he did not know where the universe ended. He felt small and weak. When would he be like the fellows in poetry and rhetoric? They had big voices and big boots and they studied trigonometry. That was very far away. First came the vacation and then the next term and then vacation again and then again another term and then again the vacation. It was like a train going in and out of tunnels and that was like the noise of the boys eating in the refectory when you opened and closed the flaps of the ears. Term, vacation; tunnel, out; noise, stop. How far away it was! It was better to go to bed to sleep. Only prayers in the chapel and then bed. He shivered and yawned. It would be lovely in bed after the sheets got a bit hot. First they were so cold to get into. He shivered to think how cold they were first. But then they got hot and then he could sleep. It was lovely to be tired. He yawned again. Night prayers and then bed: he shivered and wanted to yawn. It would be lovely in a few minutes. He felt a warm glow creeping up from the cold shivering sheets, warmer and warmer till he felt warm all over, ever so warm; ever so warm and yet he shivered a little and still wanted to yawn.

The bell rang for night prayers and he filed out of the studyhall after the others and down the staircase and along the corridors to the chapel. The corridors were darkly lit and the chapel was darkly lit. Soon all would be dark and sleeping. There was cold night air in the chapel and the marbles were the colour the sea was at night. The sea was cold day and night: but it was colder at night. It was cold and dark under the seawall beside his father's house. But the kettle would be on the hob to make punch.

The prefect of the chapel prayed above his head and his memory knew the responses:

> O Lord, open our lips
> And our mouth shall announce Thy praise.
> Incline unto our aid, O God!
> O Lord, make haste to help us!

There was a cold night smell in the chapel. But it was a holy smell. It was not like the smell of the old peasants who knelt at the back of the chapel at Sunday mass. That was a smell of air and rain and turf and corduroy. But they were very holy peasants. They breathed behind him on his neck and sighed as they prayed. They lived in Clane, a fellow said: there were little cottages there and he had seen a woman standing at the halfdoor of a cottage with a child in her arms, as the cars had come past from Sallins. It would be lovely to sleep for one night in that cottage before the fire of smoking turf, in the dark lit by the fire, in the warm dark, breathing the smell of the peasants, air and rain and turf and corduroy. But, O, the road there between the trees was dark! You would be lost in the dark. It made him afraid to think of how it was.

He heard the voice of the prefect of the chapel saying the last prayer. He prayed it too against the dark outside under the trees.

> *Visit, we beseech Thee, O Lord, this habitation and drive away from it all the snares of the enemy. May Thy holy angels dwell herein to preserve us in peace and may Thy blessing be always upon us through Christ, Our Lord. Amen.*

His fingers trembled as he undressed himself in the dormitory. He told his fingers to hurry up. He had to undress and then kneel and say his own prayers and be in bed before the gas was lowered so that he might not go to hell when he died. He rolled his stockings off and put on his nightshirt quickly and knelt trembling at his bedside and repeated his prayers quickly quickly, fearing that the gas would go down. He felt his shoulders shaking as he murmured:

> *God bless my father and my mother and spare them to me!*
> *God bless my little brothers and sisters and spare them to me!*
> *God bless Dante and uncle Charles and spare them to me!*

He blessed himself and climbed quickly into bed and, tucking the end of the nightshirt under his feet, curled

himself together under the cold white sheets, shaking
and trembling. But he would not go to hell when he
died; and the shaking would stop. A voice bade the
boys in the dormitory goodnight. He peered out for an
instant over the coverlet and saw the yellow curtains
round and before his bed that shut him off on all sides.
The light was lowered quietly.

The prefect's shoes went away. Where? Down the
staircase and along the corridors or to his room at the
end? He saw the dark. Was it true about the black dog
that walked there at night with eyes as big as carriagelamps? They said it was the ghost of a murderer. A
long shiver of fear flowed over his body. He saw the
dark entrance hall of the castle. Old servants in old
dress were in the ironingroom above the staircase. It
was long ago. The old servants were quiet. There was a
fire there but the hall was still dark. A figure came up
the staircase from the hall. He wore the white cloak of a
marshal; his face was pale and strange; he held his
hand pressed to his side. He looked out of strange eyes
at the old servants. They looked at him and saw their
master's face and cloak and knew that he had received
his deathwound. But only the dark was where they
looked: only dark silent air. Their master had received
his deathwound on the battlefield of Prague far away
over the sea. He was standing on the field; his hand was
pressed to his side; his face was pale and strange and he
wore the white cloak of a marshal.

O how cold and strange it was to think of that! All
the dark was cold and strange. There were pale strange
faces there, great eyes like carriagelamps. They were
the ghosts of murderers, the figures of marshals who
had received their deathwound on battlefields far away
over the sea. What did they wish to say that their faces
were so strange?

Visit, we beseech Thee, O Lord, this habitation and drive away from it all . . .

Going home for the holidays! That would be lovely: the fellows had told him. Getting up on the cars in the early wintry morning outside the door of the castle. The cars were rolling on the gravel. Cheers for the rector!

Hurray! Hurray! Hurray!

The cars drove past the chapel and all caps were raised. They drove merrily along the country roads. The drivers pointed with their whips to Bodenstown. The fellows cheered. They passed the farmhouse of the Jolly Farmer. Cheer after cheer after cheer. Through Clane they drove, cheering and cheered. The peasant women stood at the halfdoors, the men stood here and there. The lovely smell there was in the wintry air: the smell of Clane: rain and wintry air and turf smouldering and corduroy.

The train was full of fellows: a long long chocolate train with cream facings. The guards went to and fro opening, closing, locking, unlocking the doors. They were men in dark blue and silver; they had silvery whistles and their keys made a quick music: click, click: click, click.

And the train raced on over the flat lands and past the Hill of Allen. The telegraphpoles were passing, passing. The train went on and on. It knew. There were coloured lanterns in the hall of his father's house and ropes of green branches. There were holly and ivy round the pierglass and holly and ivy, green and red, twined round the chandeliers. There were red holly and green ivy round the old portraits on the walls. Holly and ivy for him and for Christmas.

Lovely . . .

All the people. Welcome home, Stephen! Noises of welcome. His mother kissed him. Was that right? His father was a marshal now: higher than a magistrate. Welcome home, Stephen!

Noises . . .

There was a noise of curtainrings running back along the rods, of water being splashed in the basins. There was a noise of rising and dressing and washing in the dormitory: a noise of clapping of hands as the prefect went up and down telling the fellows to look sharp. A pale sunlight showed the yellow curtains drawn back, the tossed beds. His bed was very hot and his face and body were very hot.

He got up and sat on the side of his bed. He was weak. He tried to pull on his stocking. It had a horrid rough feel. The sunlight was queer and cold.

Fleming said:

—Are you not well?

He did not know; and Fleming said:

—Get back into bed. I'll tell McGlade you're not well.

—He's sick.

—Who is?

—Tell McGlade.

—Get back into bed.

—Is he sick?

A fellow held his arms while he loosened the stocking clinging to his foot and climbed back into the hot bed.

He crouched down between the sheets, glad of their tepid glow. He heard the fellows talk among themselves about him as they dressed for mass. It was a mean thing to do, to shoulder him into the square ditch, they were saying.

Then their voices ceased; they had gone. A voice at his bed said:

—Dedalus, don't spy on us, sure you won't?

Wells's face was there. He looked at it and saw that Wells was afraid.

—I didn't mean to. Sure you won't?

His father had told him, whatever he did, never to peach on a fellow. He shook his head and answered no and felt glad. Wells said:

—I didn't mean to, honour bright. It was only for cod. I'm sorry.

The face and the voice went away. Sorry because he was afraid. Afraid that it was some disease. Canker was a disease of plants and cancer one of animals; or another different. That was a long time ago then out on the playgrounds in the evening light, creeping from point to point on the fringe of his line, a heavy bird flying low through the grey light. Leicester Abbey lit up. Wolsey died there. The abbots buried him themselves.

It was not Wells's face, it was the prefect's. He was not foxing. No, no: he was sick really. He was not foxing. And he felt the prefect's hand on his forehead; and he felt his forehead warm and damp against the prefect's cold damp hand. That was the way a rat felt, slimy and damp and cold. Every rat had two eyes to look out of. Sleek slimy coats, little little feet tucked up to jump, black shiny eyes to look out of. They could understand how to jump. But the minds of rats could not understand trigonometry. When they were dead they lay on their sides. Their coats dried then. They were only dead things.

The prefect was there again and it was his voice that was saying that he was to get up, that Father Minister had said he was to get up and dress and go to the infirmary. And while he was dressing himself as quickly as he could the prefect said:

—We must pack off to Brother Michael because we have the collywobbles! Terrible thing to have the colly-wobbles! How we wobble when we have the colly-wobbles!

He was very decent to say that. That was all to make him laugh. But he could not laugh because his cheeks and lips were all shivery: and then the prefect had to laugh by himself.

The prefect cried:

—Quick march! Hayfoot! Strawfoot!

They went together down the staircase and along the corridor and past the bath. As he passed the door he remembered with a vague fear the warm turfcoloured bogwater, the warm moist air, the noise of plunges, the smell of the towels, like medicine.

Brother Michael was standing at the door of the infirmary and from the door of the dark cabinet on his right came a smell like medicine. That came from the bottles on the shelves. The prefect spoke to Brother Michael and Brother Michael answered and called the prefect sir. He had reddish hair mixed with grey and a queer look. It was queer that he would always be a brother. It was queer too that you could not call him sir because he was a brother and had a different kind of look. Was he not holy enough or why could he not catch up on the others?

There were two beds in the room and in one bed there was a fellow: and when they went in he called out:

—Hello! It's young Dedalus! What's up?

—The sky is up, Brother Michael said.

He was a fellow out of the third of grammar and, while Stephen was undressing, he asked Brother Michael to bring him a round of buttered toast.

—Ah, do! he said.

—Butter you up! said Brother Michael. You'll get your walking papers in the morning when the doctor comes.

—Will I? the fellow said. I'm not well yet.

Brother Michael repeated:

—You'll get your walking papers, I tell you.

He bent down to rake the fire. He had a long back like the long back of a tramhorse. He shook the poker gravely and nodded his head at the fellow out of third of grammar.

Then Brother Michael went away and after a while the fellow out of third of grammar turned in towards the wall and fell asleep.

That was the infirmary. He was sick then. Had they written home to tell his mother and father? But it would be quicker for one of the priests to go himself to tell them. Or he would write a letter for the priest to bring.

Dear Mother

I am sick. I want to go home. Please come and take me home. I am in the infirmary.

Your fond son,
Stephen

How far away they were! There was cold sunlight outside the window. He wondered if he would die. You could die just the same on a sunny day. He might die before his mother came. Then he would have a dead mass in the chapel like the way the fellows had told him it was when Little had died. All the fellows would be at the mass, dressed in black, all with sad faces. Wells too would be there but no fellow would look at him. The rector would be there in a cope of black and gold and there would be tall yellow candles on the altar and round the catafalque. And they would carry the coffin out of the chapel slowly and he would be buried in the little graveyard of the community off the main avenue of limes. And Wells would be sorry then for what he had done. And the bell would toll slowly.

He could hear the tolling. He said over to himself the song that Brigid had taught him.

> *Dingdong! The castle bell!*
> *Farewell, my mother!*
> *Bury me in the old churchyard*
> *Beside my eldest brother.*
> *My coffin shall be black,*
> *Six angels at my back,*
> *Two to sing and two to pray*
> *And two to carry my soul away.*

How beautiful and sad that was! How beautiful the words were where they said *Bury me in the old churchyard!* A tremor passed over his body. How sad and how beautiful! He wanted to cry quietly but not for himself: for the words, so beautiful and sad, like music. The bell! The bell! Farewell! O farewell!

The cold sunlight was weaker and Brother Michael was standing at his bedside with a bowl of beeftea. He was glad for his mouth was hot and dry. He could hear them playing on the playgrounds. And the day was going on in the college just as if he were there.

Then Brother Michael was going away and the fellow out of third of grammar told him to be sure and come back and tell him all the news in the paper. He told Stephen that his name was Athy and that his father kept a lot of racehorses that were spiffing jumpers and that his father would give a good tip to Brother Michael any time he wanted it because Brother Michael was very decent and always told him the news out of the paper they got every day up in the castle.

There was every kind of news in the paper: accidents, shipwrecks, sports and politics.

—Now it is all about politics in the paper, he said. Do your people talk about that too?

—Yes, Stephen said.

—Mine too, he said.

Then he thought for a moment and said:

—You have a queer name, Dedalus, and I have a queer name too, Athy. My name is the name of a town. Your name is like Latin.

Then he asked:

—Are you good at riddles?

Stephen answered:

—Not very good.

Then he said:

—Can you answer me this one? Why is the county Kildare like the leg of a fellow's breeches?

Stephen thought what could be the answer and then said:

—I give it up.

—Because there is a thigh in it, he said. Do you see the joke? Athy is the town in the county Kildare and a thigh is the other thigh.

—O, I see, Stephen said.

—That's an old riddle, he said.

After a moment he said:

—I say!

—What? asked Stephen.

—You know, he said, you can ask that riddle another way?

—Can you? said Stephen.

—The same riddle, he said. Do you know the other way to ask it?

—No, said Stephen.

—Can you not think of the other way? he said.

He looked at Stephen over the bedclothes as he spoke. Then he lay back on the pillow and said:

—There is another way but I won't tell you what it is.

Why did he not tell it? His father, who kept the racehorses, must be a magistrate too like Saurin's father and Nasty Roche's father. He thought of his own father, of how he sang songs while his mother played and of how he always gave him a shilling when he asked for sixpence and he felt sorry for him that he was not a magistrate like the other boys' fathers. Then why was he sent to that place with them? But his father had told him that he would be no stranger there because his granduncle had presented an address to the liberator there fifty years before. You could know the people of that time by their old dress. It seemed to him a solemn time: and he wondered if that was the time when the fellows in Clongowes wore blue coats with brass buttons and yellow waistcoats and caps of rabbit-skin and drank beer like grownup people and kept greyhounds of their own to course the hares with.

He looked at the window and saw that the daylight had grown weaker. There would be cloudy grey light over the playgrounds. There was no noise on the playgrounds. The class must be doing the themes or perhaps Father Arnall was reading a legend out of the book.

It was queer that they had not given him any medicine. Perhaps Brother Michael would bring it back when he came. They said you got stinking stuff to drink when you were in the infirmary. But he felt better now than before. It would be nice getting better slowly. You could get a book then. There was a book in the library about Holland. There were lovely foreign names in it and pictures of strangelooking cities and ships. It made you feel so happy.

How pale the light was at the window! But that was nice. The fire rose and fell on the wall. It was like waves. Someone had put coal on and he heard voices. They were talking. It was the noise of the waves. Or the waves were talking among themselves as they rose and fell.

He saw the sea of waves, long dark waves rising and falling, dark under the moonless night. A tiny light twinkled at the pierhead where the ship was entering: and he saw a multitude of people gathered by the waters' edge to see the ship that was entering their harbour. A tall man stood on the deck, looking out towards the flat dark land: and by the light at the pierhead he saw his face, the sorrowful face of Brother Michael.

He saw him lift his hand towards the people and heard him say in a loud voice of sorrow over the waters:

—He is dead. We saw him lying upon the catafalque.

A wail of sorrow went up from the people.

—Parnell! Parnell! He is dead!

They fell upon their knees, moaning in sorrow.

And he saw Dante in a maroon velvet dress and with a green velvet mantle hanging from her shoulders walking proudly and silently past the people who knelt by the waters' edge.

*   *   *

A great fire, banked high and red, flamed in the grate and under the ivytwined branches of the chandelier the Christmas table was spread. They had come home a little late and still dinner was not ready: but it would be ready in a jiffy, his mother had said. They were waiting for the door to open and for the servants to come in, holding the big dishes covered with their heavy metal covers.

All were waiting: uncle Charles, who sat far away in the shadow of the window, Dante and Mr Casey, who sat in the easychairs at either side of the hearth, Stephen, seated on a chair between them, his feet resting on the toasted boss. Mr Dedalus looked at himself in the pierglass above the mantelpiece, waxed out his moustache-ends and then, parting his coattails, stood with his back to the glowing fire: and still, from time to time, he withdrew a hand from his coattail to wax out one of his moustache-ends. Mr Casey leaned his head to one side and, smiling, tapped the gland of his neck with his fingers. And Stephen smiled too for he knew now that it was not true that Mr Casey had a purse of silver in his throat. He smiled to think how the silvery noise which Mr Casey used to make had deceived him. And when he had tried to open Mr Casey's hand to see if the purse of silver was hidden there he had seen that the fingers could not be straightened out: and Mr Casey had told him that he had got those three cramped fingers making a birthday present for Queen Victoria.

Mr Casey tapped the gland of his neck and smiled at Stephen with sleepy eyes: and Mr Dedalus said to him:

—Yes. Well now, that's all right. O, we had a good walk, hadn't we, John? Yes . . . I wonder if there's any likelihood of dinner this evening. Yes. . . . O, well now, we got a good breath of ozone round the Head today. Ay, bedad.

He turned to Dante and said:

—You didn't stir out at all, Mrs Riordan?

Dante frowned and said shortly:

—No.

Mr Dedalus dropped his coattails and went over to the sideboard. He brought forth a great stone jar of whisky from the locker and filled the decanter slowly, bending now and then to see how much he had poured in. Then replacing the jar in the locker he poured a little of the whisky into two glasses, added a little water and came back with them to the fireplace.

—A thimbleful, John, he said, just to whet your appetite.

Mr Casey took the glass, drank, and placed it near him on the mantelpiece. Then he said:

—Well, I can't help thinking of our friend Christopher manufacturing . . .

He broke into a fit of laughter and coughing and added:

—. . . manufacturing that champagne for those fellows.

Mr Dedalus laughed loudly.

—Is it Christy? he said. There's more cunning in one of those warts on his bald head than in a pack of jack foxes.

He inclined his head, closed his eyes, and, licking his lips profusely, began to speak with the voice of the hotelkeeper.

—And he has such a soft mouth when he's speaking to you, don't you know. He's very moist and watery about the dewlaps, God bless him.

Mr Casey was still struggling through his fit of coughing and laughter. Stephen, seeing and hearing the hotelkeeper through his father's face and voice, laughed.

Mr Dedalus put up his eyeglass and, staring down at him, said quietly and kindly:

—What are you laughing at, you little puppy, you?

The servants entered and placed the dishes on the

table. Mrs Dedalus followed and the places were arranged.

—Sit over, she said.

Mr Dedalus went to the end of the table and said:

—Now, Mrs Riordan, sit over. John, sit you down, my hearty.

He looked round to where uncle Charles sat and said:

—Now then, sir, there's a bird here waiting for you.

When all had taken their seats he laid his hand on the cover and then said quickly, withdrawing it:

—Now, Stephen.

Stephen stood up in his place to say the grace before meals:

Bless us, O Lord, and these Thy gifts which through Thy bounty we are about to receive through Christ Our Lord. Amen.

All blessed themselves and Mr Dedalus with a sigh of pleasure lifted from the dish the heavy cover pearled around the edge with glistening drops.

Stephen looked at the plump turkey which had lain, trussed and skewered, on the kitchen table. He knew that his father had paid a guinea for it in Dunn's of D'Olier Street and that the man had prodded it often at the breastbone to show how good it was: and he remembered the man's voice when he had said:

—Take that one, sir. That's the real Ally Daly.

Why did Mr Barrett in Clongowes call his pandybat a turkey? But Clongowes was far away: and the warm heavy smell of turkey and ham and celery rose from the plates and dishes and the great fire was banked high and red in the grate and the green ivy and red holly made you feel so happy and when dinner was ended the big plumpudding would be carried in, studded with peeled almonds and sprigs of holly, with bluish fire running around it and a little green flag flying from the top.

It was his first Christmas dinner and he thought of his little brothers and sisters who were waiting in the nursery, as he had often waited, till the pudding came. The deep low collar and the Eton jacket made him feel queer and oldish: and that morning when his mother had brought him down to the parlour, dressed for mass, his father had cried. That was because he was thinking of his own father. And uncle Charles had said so too.

Mr Dedalus covered the dish and began to eat hungrily. Then he said:

—Poor old Christy, he's nearly lopsided now with roguery.

—Simon, said Mrs Dedalus, you haven't given Mrs Riordan any sauce.

Mr Dedalus seized the sauceboat.

—Haven't I? he cried. Mrs Riordan, pity the poor blind.

Dante covered her plate with her hands and said:

—No, thanks.

Mr Dedalus turned to uncle Charles.

—How are you off, sir?

—Right as the mail, Simon.

—You, John?

—I'm all right. Go on yourself.

—Mary? Here, Stephen, here's something to make your hair curl.

He poured sauce freely over Stephen's plate and set the boat again on the table. Then he asked uncle Charles was it tender. Uncle Charles could not speak because his mouth was full but he nodded that it was.

—That was a good answer our friend made to the canon. What? said Mr Dedalus.

—I didn't think he had that much in him, said Mr Casey.

—*I'll pay you your dues, father, when you cease turning the house of God into a pollingbooth.*

—A nice answer, said Dante, for any man calling himself a catholic to give to his priest.

—They have only themselves to blame, said Mr Dedalus suavely. If they took a fool's advice they would confine their attention to religion.

—It is religion, Dante said. They are doing their duty in warning the people.

—We go to the house of God, Mr Casey said, in all humility to pray to our Maker and not to hear election addresses.

—It is religion, Dante said again. They are right. They must direct their flocks.

—And preach politics from the altar, is it? asked Mr Dedalus.

—Certainly, said Dante. It is a question of public morality. A priest would not be a priest if he did not tell his flock what is right and what is wrong.

Mrs Dedalus laid down her knife and fork, saying:

—For pity's sake and for pity sake let us have no political discussion on this day of all days in the year.

—Quite right, ma'am, said uncle Charles. Now, Simon, that's quite enough now. Not another word now.

—Yes, yes, said Mr Dedalus quickly.

He uncovered the dish boldly and said:

—Now then, who's for more turkey?

Nobody answered. Dante said:

—Nice language for any catholic to use!

—Mrs Riordan, I appeal to you, said Mrs Dedalus, to let the matter drop now.

Dante turned on her and said:

—And am I to sit here and listen to the pastors of my church being flouted?

—Nobody is saying a word against them, said Mr Dedalus, so long as they don't meddle in politics.

—The bishops and priests of Ireland have spoken, said Dante, and they must be obeyed.

—Let them leave politics alone, said Mr Casey, or the people may leave their church alone.

—You hear? said Dante turning to Mrs Dedalus.

—Mr Casey! Simon! said Mrs Dedalus. Let it end now.

—Too bad! Too bad! said uncle Charles.

—What? cried Mr Dedalus. Were we to desert him at the bidding of the English people?

—He was no longer worthy to lead, said Dante. He was a public sinner.

—We are all sinners and black sinners, said Mr Casey coldly.

—*Woe be to the man by whom the scandal cometh!* said Mrs Riordan. *It would be better for him that a millstone were tied about his neck and that he were cast into the depth of the sea rather than that he should scandalise one of these, my least little ones.* That is the language of the Holy Ghost.

—And very bad language if you ask me, said Mr Dedalus coolly.

—Simon! Simon! said uncle Charles. The boy.

—Yes, yes, said Mr Dedalus. I meant about the . . . I was thinking about the bad language of that railway porter. Well now, that's all right. Here, Stephen, show me your plate, old chap. Eat away now. Here.

He heaped up the food on Stephen's plate and served uncle Charles and Mr Casey to large pieces of turkey and splashes of sauce. Mrs Dedalus was eating little and Dante sat with her hands in her lap. She was red in the face. Mr Dedalus rooted with the carvers at the end of the dish and said:

—There's a tasty bit here we call the pope's nose. If any lady or gentleman . . .

He held a piece of fowl up on the prong of the carvingfork. Nobody spoke. He put it on his own plate, saying:

—Well, you can't say but you were asked. I think I had better eat it myself because I'm not well in my health lately.

He winked at Stephen and, replacing the dishcover, began to eat again.

There was a silence while he ate. Then he said:

—Well now, the day kept up fine after all. There were plenty of strangers down too.

Nobody spoke. He said again:

—I think there were more strangers down than last Christmas.

He looked round at the others whose faces were bent towards their plates and, receiving no reply, waited for a moment and said bitterly:

—Well, my Christmas dinner has been spoiled anyhow.

There could be neither luck nor grace, Dante said, in a house where there is no respect for the pastors of the church.

Mr Dedalus threw his knife and fork noisily on his plate.

—Respect! he said. Is it for Billy with the lip or for the tub of guts up in Armagh? Respect!

—Princes of the church, said Mr Casey with slow scorn.

—Lord Leitrim's coachman, yes, said Mr Dedalus.

—They are the Lord's anointed, Dante said. They are an honour to their country.

—Tub of guts, said Mr Dedalus coarsely. He has a handsome face, mind you, in repose. You should see that fellow lapping up his bacon and cabbage of a cold winter's day. O Johnny!

He twisted his features into a grimace of heavy bestiality and made a lapping noise with his lips.

—Really, Simon, said Mrs Dedalus, you should not speak that way before Stephen. It's not right.

—O, he'll remember all this when he grows up, said Dante hotly—the language he heard against God and religion and priests in his own home.

—Let him remember too, cried Mr Casey to her from across the table, the language with which the priests and the priest's pawns broke Parnell's heart and hounded him into his grave. Let him remember that too when he grows up.

—Sons of bitches! cried Mr Dedalus. When he was down they turned on him to betray him and rend him like rats in a sewer. Lowlived dogs! And they look it! By Christ, they look it!

—They behaved rightly, cried Dante. They obeyed their bishops and their priests. Honour to them!

—Well, it is perfectly dreadful to say that not even for one day in the year, said Mrs Dedalus, can we be free from these dreadful disputes!

Uncle Charles raised his hands mildly and said:

—Come now, come now, come now! Can we not have our opinions whatever they are without this bad temper and this bad language? It is too bad surely.

Mrs Dedalus spoke to Dante in a low voice but Dante said loudly:

—I will not say nothing. I will defend my church and my religion when it is insulted and spit on by renegade catholics.

Mr Casey pushed his plate rudely into the middle of

the table and, resting his elbows before him, said in a hoarse voice to his host:

—Tell me, did I tell you that story about a very famous spit?

—You did not, John, said Mr Dedalus.

—Why then, said Mr Casey, it is a most instructive story. It happened not long ago in the county Wicklow where we are now.

He broke off and, turning towards Dante, said with quiet indignation:

—And I may tell you, ma'am, that I, if you mean me, am no renegade catholic. I am a catholic as my father was and his father before him and his father before him again when we gave up our lives rather than sell our faith.

—The more shame to you now, Dante said, to speak as you do.

—The story, John, said Mr Dedalus smiling. Let us have the story anyhow.

—Catholic indeed! repeated Dante ironically. The blackest protestant in the land would not speak the language I have heard this evening.

Mr Dedalus began to sway his head to and fro, crooning like a country singer.

—I am no protestant, I tell you again, said Mr Casey flushing.

Mr Dedalus, still crooning and swaying his head, began to sing in a grunting nasal tone:

> *O, come all you Roman catholics*
> *That never went to mass.*

He took up his knife and fork again in good humour and set to eating, saying to Mr Casey:

—Let us have the story, John. It will help us to digest.

Stephen looked with affection at Mr Casey's face which stared across the table over his joined hands. He liked to sit near him at the fire, looking up at his dark fierce face. But his dark eyes were never fierce and his slow voice was good to listen to. But why was he then against the priests? Because Dante must be right then. But he had heard his father say that she was a spoiled nun and that she had come out of the convent in the Alleghanies when her brother had got the money from the savages for the trinkets and the chainies. Perhaps that made her severe against Parnell. And she did not like him to play with Eileen because Eileen was a protestant and when she was young she knew children that used to play with protestants and the protestants used to make fun of the litany of the Blessed Virgin. *Tower of Ivory,* they used to say, *House of Gold!* How could a woman be a tower of ivory or a house of gold? Who was right then? And he remembered the evening in the infirmary in Clongowes, the dark waters, the light at the pierhead and the moan of sorrow from the people when they had heard.

Eileen had long white hands. One evening when playing tig she had put her hands over his eyes: long and white and thin and cold and soft. That was ivory: a cold white thing. That was the meaning of *Tower of Ivory.*

—The story is very short and sweet, Mr Casey said. It was one day down in Arklow, a cold bitter day, not long before the chief died. May God have mercy on him!

He closed his eyes wearily and paused. Mr Dedalus took a bone from his plate and tore some meat from it with his teeth, saying:

—Before he was killed, you mean.

Mr Casey opened his eyes, sighed and went on:

—It was down in Arklow one day. We were down there at a meeting and after the meeting was over we had to make our way to the railway station through the crowd. Such booing and baaing, man, you never heard. They called us all the names in the world. Well there was one old lady, and a drunken old harridan she was surely, that paid all her attention to me. She kept dancing along beside me in the mud bawling and screaming into my face: *Priesthunter! The Paris Funds! Mr Fox! Kitty O'Shea!*

—And what did you do, John? asked Mr Dedalus.

—I let her bawl away, said Mr Casey. It was a cold day and to keep up my heart I had (saving your presence, ma'am) a quid of Tullamore in my mouth and sure I couldn't say a word in any case because my mouth was full of tobacco juice.

—Well, John?

—Well. I let her bawl away, to her heart's content, *Kitty O'Shea* and the rest of it till at last she called that lady a name that I won't sully this Christmas board nor your ears, ma'am, nor my own lips by repeating.

He paused. Mr Dedalus, lifting his head from the bone, asked:

—And what did you do, John?

—Do! said Mr Casey. She stuck her ugly old face up at me when she said it and I had my mouth full of tobacco juice. I bent down to her and *Phth!* says I to her like that.

He turned aside and made the act of spitting.

—*Phth!* says I to her like that, right into her eye.

He clapped a hand to his eye and gave a hoarse scream of pain.

—*O Jesus, Mary and Joseph!* says she. *I'm blinded! I'm blinded and drownded!*

He stopped in a fit of coughing and laughter, repeating:

—*I'm blinded entirely.*

Mr Dedalus laughed loudly and lay back in his chair while uncle Charles swayed his head to and fro.

Dante looked terribly angry and repeated while they laughed:

—Very nice! Ha! Very nice!

It was not nice about the spit in the woman's eye. But what was the name the woman had called Kitty O'Shea that Mr Casey would not repeat? He thought of Mr Casey walking through the crowds of people and making speeches from a wagonette. That was what he had been in prison for and he remembered that one night Sergeant O'Neill had come to the house and had stood in the hall, talking in a low voice with his father and chewing nervously at the chinstrap of his cap. And that night Mr Casey had not gone to Dublin by train but a car had come to the door and he had heard his father say something about the Cabinteely road.

He was for Ireland and Parnell and so was his father: and so was Dante too for one night at the band on the esplanade she had hit a gentleman on the head with her umbrella because he had taken off his hat when the band played *God save the Queen* at the end.

Mr Dedalus gave a snort of contempt.

—Ah, John, he said. It is true for them. We are an unfortunate priestridden race and always were and always will be till the end of the chapter.

Uncle Charles shook his head, saying:

—A bad business! A bad business!

Mr Dedalus repeated:

—A priestridden Godforsaken race!

He pointed to the portrait of his grandfather on the wall to his right.

—Do you see that old chap up there, John? he said.
He was a good Irishman when there was no money in
the job. He was condemned to death as a whiteboy. But
he had a saying about our clerical friends, that he
would never let one of them put his two feet under his
mahogany.

Dante broke in angrily:

—If we are a priestridden race we ought to be proud
of it! They are the apple of God's eye. *Touch them not,*
says Christ, *for they are the apple of My eye.*

—And can we not love our country then? asked Mr
Casey. Are we not to follow the man that was born to
lead us?

—A traitor to his country! replied Dante. A traitor,
an adulterer! The priests were right to abandon him.
The priests were always the true friends of Ireland.

—Were they, faith? said Mr Casey.

He threw his fist on the table and, frowning angrily,
protruded one finger after another.

—Didn't the bishops of Ireland betray us in the time
of the union when bishop Lanigan presented an address
of loyalty to the Marquess Cornwallis? Didn't the bishops and priests sell the aspirations of their country in
1829 in return for catholic emancipation? Didn't they
denounce the fenian movement from the pulpit and in
the confessionbox? And didn't they dishonour the ashes
of Terence Bellew MacManus?

His face was glowing with anger and Stephen felt the
glow rise to his own cheek as the spoken words thrilled
him. Mr Dedalus uttered a guffaw of coarse scorn.

—O, by God, he cried, I forgot little old Paul Cullen! Another apple of God's eye!

Dante bent across the table and cried to Mr Casey:

—Right! Right! They were always right! God and
morality and religion come first.

Mrs Dedalus, seeing her excitement, said to her:

—Mrs Riordan, don't excite yourself answering them.

—God and religion before everything! Dante cried. God and religion before the world!

Mr Casey raised his clenched fist and brought it down on the table with a crash.

—Very well, then, he shouted hoarsely, if it comes to that, no God for Ireland!

—John! John! cried Mr Dedalus, seizing his guest by the coatsleeve.

Dante stared across the table, her cheeks shaking. Mr Casey struggled up from his chair and bent across the table towards her, scraping the air from before his eyes with one hand as though he were tearing aside a cobweb.

—No God for Ireland! he cried. We have had too much God in Ireland. Away with God!

—Blasphemer! Devil! screamed Dante, starting to her feet and almost spitting in his face.

Uncle Charles and Mr Dedalus pulled Mr Casey back into his chair again, talking to him from both sides reasonably. He stared before him out of his dark flaming eyes, repeating:

—Away with God, I say!

Dante shoved her chair violently aside and left the table, upsetting her napkinring which rolled slowly along the carpet and came to rest against the foot of an easychair. Mrs Dedalus rose quickly and followed her towards the door. At the door Dante turned round violently and shouted down the room, her cheeks flushed and quivering with rage:

—Devil out of hell! We won! We crushed him to death! Fiend!

The door slammed behind her.

Mr Casey, freeing his arms from his holders, suddenly bowed his head on his hands with a sob of pain.

—Poor Parnell! he cried loudly. My dead king!

He sobbed loudly and bitterly.

Stephen, raising his terrorstricken face, saw that his father's eyes were full of tears.

*   *   *

The fellows talked together in little groups.

One fellow said:

—They were caught near the Hill of Lyons.

—Who caught them?

—Mr Gleeson and the minister. They were on a car.

The same fellow added:

—A fellow in the higher line told me.

Fleming asked:

—But why did they run away, tell us?

—I know why, Cecil Thunder said. Because they had fecked cash out of the rector's room.

—Who fecked it?

—Kickham's brother. And they all went shares in it. But that was stealing. How could they have done that?

—A fat lot you know about it, Thunder! Wells said. I know why they scut.

—Tell us why.

—I was told not to, Wells said.

—O, go on, Wells, all said. You might tell us. We won't let it out.

Stephen bent forward his ear to hear. Wells looked round to see if anyone was coming. Then he said secretly:

—You know the altar wine they keep in the press in the sacristy?

—Yes.

—Well, they drank that and it was found out who did it by the smell. And that's why they ran away, if you want to know.

And the fellow who had spoken first said:

—Yes, that's what I heard too from the fellow in the higher line.

The fellows were all silent. Stephen stood among them, afraid to speak, listening. A faint sickness of awe made him feel weak. How could they have done that? He thought of the dark silent sacristy. There were dark wooden presses there where the crimped surplices lay quietly folded. It was not the chapel but still you had to speak under your breath. It was a holy place. He remembered the summer evening he had been there to be dressed as a boatbearer, the evening of the procession to the little altar in the wood. A strange and holy place. The boy that held the censer had swung it gently to and fro near the door with the silvery cap lifted by the middle chain to keep the coals lighting. That was called charcoal: and it had burned quietly as the fellow had swung it gently and had given off a weak sour smell. And then when all were vested he had stood holding out the boat to the rector and the rector had put a spoonful of incense in it and it had hissed on the red coals.

The fellows were talking together in little groups here and there on the playground. The fellows seemed to him to have grown smaller: that was because a sprinter had knocked him down the day before, a fellow out of second of grammar. He had been thrown by the fellow's machine lightly on the cinderpath and his spectacles had been broken in three pieces and some of the grit of the cinders had gone into his mouth.

That was why the fellows seemed to him smaller and

farther away and the goalposts so thin and far and the soft grey sky so high up. But there was no play on the football grounds for cricket was coming: and some said that Barnes would be the prof and some said it would be Flowers. And all over the playgrounds they were playing rounders and bowling twisters and lobs. And from here and from there came the sounds of the cricketbats through the soft grey air. They said: pick, pack, pock, puck: like drops of water in a fountain slowly falling in the brimming bowl.

Athy, who had been silent, said quietly:

—You are all wrong.

All turned towards him eagerly.

—Why?

—Do you know?

—Who told you?

—Tell us, Athy.

Athy pointed across the playground to where Simon Moonan was walking by himself kicking a stone before him.

—Ask him, he said.

The fellows looked there and then said:

—Why him?

—Is he in it?

—Tell us, Athy. Go on. You might if you know.

Athy lowered his voice and said:

—Do you know why those fellows scut? I will tell you but you must not let on you know.

He paused for a moment and then said mysteriously:

—They were caught with Simon Moonan and Tusker Boyle in the square one night.

The fellows looked at him and asked:

—Caught?

—What doing?

Athy said:

—Smugging.

All the fellows were silent: and Athy said:

—And that's why.

Stephen looked at the faces of the fellows but they were all looking across the playground. He wanted to ask somebody about it. What did that mean about the smugging in the square?

Why did the five fellows out of the higher line run away for that? It was a joke, he thought. Simon Moonan had nice clothes and one night he had shown him a ball of creamy sweets that the fellows of the football fifteen had rolled down to him along the carpet in the middle of the refectory when he was at the door. It was the night of the match against the Bective Rangers and the ball was made just like a red and green apple only it opened and it was full of the creamy sweets. And one day Boyle had said that an elephant had two tuskers instead of two tusks and that was why he was called Tusker Boyle but some fellows called him Lady Boyle because he was always at his nails, paring them.

Eileen had long thin cool white hands too because she was a girl. They were like ivory; only soft. That was the meaning of *Tower of Ivory* but protestants could not understand it and made fun of it. One day he had stood beside her looking into the hotel grounds. A waiter was running up a trail of bunting on the flagstaff and a fox terrier was scampering to and fro on the sunny lawn. She had put her hand into his pocket where his hand was and he had felt how cool and thin and soft her hand was. She had said that pockets were funny things to have: and then all of a sudden she had broken away and had run laughing down the sloping curve of the path. Her fair hair had streamed out behind her like gold in the sun. *Tower of Ivory. House of*

Gold. By thinking of things you could understand them.

But why in the square? You went there when you wanted to do something. It was all thick slabs of slate and water trickled all day out of tiny pinholes and there was a queer smell of stale water there. And behind the door of one of the closets there was a drawing in red pencil of a bearded man in a Roman dress with a brick in each hand and underneath was the name of the drawing:

Balbus was building a wall.

Some fellows had drawn it there for a cod. It had a funny face but it was very like a man with a beard. And on the wall of another closet there was written in backhand in beautiful writing:

Julius Cæsar wrote The Calico Belly.

Perhaps that was why they were there because it was a place where some fellows wrote things for cod. But all the same it was queer what Athy said and the way he said it. It was not a cod because they had run away. He looked with the others in silence across the playground and began to feel afraid.

At last Fleming said:

—And we are all to be punished for what other fellows did?

—I won't come back, see if I do, Cecil Thunder said. Three days' silence in the refectory and sending us up for six and eight every minute.

—Yes, said Wells. And old Barrett has a new way of twisting the note so that you can't open it and fold it again to see how many ferulæ you are to get. I won't come back too.

—Yes, said Cecil Thunder, and the prefect of studies was in second of grammar this morning.

—Let us get up a rebellion, Fleming said. Will we?

All the fellows were silent. The air was very silent

and you could hear the cricketbats but more slowly than before: pick, pock.

Wells asked:

—What is going to be done to them?

—Simon Moonan and Tusker are going to be flogged, Athy said, and the fellows in the higher line got their choice of flogging or being expelled.

And which are they taking? asked the fellow who had spoken first.

—All are taking expulsion except Corrigan, Athy answered. He's going to be flogged by Mr Gleeson.

—Is it Corrigan that big fellow? said Fleming. Why, he'd be able for two of Gleeson!

—I know why, Cecil Thunder said. He is right and the other fellows are wrong because a flogging wears off after a bit but a fellow that has been expelled from college is known all his life on account of it. Besides Gleeson won't flog him hard.

—It's best of his play not to, Fleming said.

—I wouldn't like to be Simon Moonan and Tusker, Cecil Thunder said. But I don't believe they will be flogged. Perhaps they will be sent up for twice nine.

—No, no, said Athy. They'll both get it on the vital spot.

Wells rubbed himself and said in a crying voice:

—Please, sir, let me off!

Athy grinned and turned up the sleeves of his jacket, saying:

> It can't be helped;
> It must be done.
> So down with your breeches
> And out with your bum.

The fellows laughed; but he felt that they were a little afraid. In the silence of the soft grey air he heard the cricketbats from here and from there: pock. That was a sound to hear but if you were hit then you would feel a pain. The pandybat made a sound too but not like that. The fellows said it was made of whalebone and leather with lead inside: and he wondered what was the pain like. There were different kinds of pains for all the different kinds of sounds. A long thin cane would have a high whistling sound and he wondered what was that pain like. It made him shivery to think of it and cold: and what Athy said too. But what was there to laugh at in it? It made him shivery: but that was because you always felt like a shiver when you let down your trousers. It was the same in the bath when you undressed yourself. He wondered who had to let them down, the master or the boy himself. O how could they laugh about it that way?

He looked at Athy's rolledup sleeves and knuckly inky hands. He had rolled up his sleeves to show how Mr Gleeson would roll up his sleeves. But Mr Gleeson had round shiny cuffs and clean white wrists and fattish white hands and the nails of them were long and pointed. Perhaps he pared them too like Lady Boyle. But they were terribly long and pointed nails. So long and cruel they were though the white fattish hands were not cruel but gentle. And though he trembled with cold and fright to think of the cruel long nails and of the high whistling sound of the cane and of the chill you felt at the end of your shirt when you undressed yourself yet he felt a feeling of queer quiet pleasure inside him to think of the white fattish hands, clean and strong and gentle. And he thought of what Cecil Thunder had said; that Mr Gleeson would not flog Corrigan hard. And Fleming had said he would not because it was best of his play not to. But that was not why.

A voice from far out on the playground cried:

—All in!

And other voices cried:

—All in! All in!

During the writing lesson he sat with his arms folded, listening to the slow scraping of the pens. Mr Harford went to and fro making little signs in red pencil and sometimes sitting beside the boy to show him how to hold the pen. He had tried to spell out the headline for himself though he knew already what it was for it was the last of the book. *Zeal without prudence is like a ship adrift.* But the lines of the letters were like fine invisible threads and it was only by closing his right eye tight tight and staring out of the left eye that he could make out the full curves of the capital.

But Mr Harford was very decent and never got into a wax. All the other masters got into dreadful waxes. But why were they to suffer for what fellows in the higher line did? Wells had said that they had drunk some of the altar wine out of the press in the sacristy and that it had been found out who had done it by the smell. Perhaps they had stolen a monstrance to run away with it and sell it somewhere. That must have been a terrible sin, to go in there quietly at night, to open the dark press and steal the flashing gold thing into which God was put on the altar in the middle of flowers and candles at benediction while the incense went up in clouds at both sides as the fellow swung the censer and Dominic Kelly sang the first part by himself in the choir. But God was not in it of course when they stole it. But still it was a strange and a great sin even to touch it. He thought of it with deep awe; a terrible and strange sin: it thrilled him to think of it in the silence when the pens scraped lightly. But to drink the altar wine out of the press and be found out by the smell was a sin too: but it was not terrible and strange. It only

made you feel a little sickish on account of the smell of
the wine. Because on the day when he had made his
first holy communion in the chapel he had shut his eyes
and opened his mouth and put out his tongue a little:
and when the rector had stooped down to give him the
holy communion he had smelt a faint winy smell off
the rector's breath after the wine of the mass. The word
was beautiful: wine. It made you think of dark purple
because the grapes were dark purple that grew in
Greece outside houses like white temples. But the faint
smell off the rector's breath had made him feel a sick
feeling on the morning of his first communion. The day
of your first communion was the happiest day of your
life. And once a lot of generals had asked Napoleon
what was the happiest day of his life. They thought he
would say the day he won some great battle or the day
he was made an emperor. But he said:

—Gentlemen, the happiest day of my life was the
day on which I made my first holy communion.

Father Arnall came in and the Latin lesson began
and he remained still, leaning on the desk with his arms
folded. Father Arnall gave out the themebooks and he
said that they were scandalous and that they were all to
be written out again with the corrections at once. But
the worst of all was Fleming's theme because the pages
were stuck together by a blot: and Father Arnall held it
up by a corner and said it was an insult to any master
to send him up such a theme. Then he asked Jack
Lawton to decline the noun *mare* and Jack Lawton
stopped at the ablative singular and could not go on
with the plural.

—You should be ashamed of yourself, said Father
Arnall sternly. You, the leader of the class!

Then he asked the next boy and the next and the
next. Nobody knew. Father Arnall became very quiet,

more and more quiet as each boy tried to answer and could not. But his face was blacklooking and his eyes were staring though his voice was so quiet. Then he asked Fleming and Fleming said that that word had no plural. Father Arnall suddenly shut the book and shouted at him:

—Kneel out there in the middle of the class. You are one of the idlest boys I ever met. Copy out your themes again the rest of you.

Fleming moved heavily out of his place and knelt between the two last benches. The other boys bent over their themebooks and began to write. A silence filled the classroom and Stephen, glancing timidly at Father Arnall's dark face, saw that it was a little red from the wax he was in.

Was that a sin for Father Arnall to be in a wax or was he allowed to get into a wax when the boys were idle because that made them study better or was he only letting on to be in a wax? It was because he was allowed because a priest would know what a sin was and would not do it. But if he did it one time by mistake what would he do to go to confession? Perhaps he would go to confession to the minister. And if the minister did it he would go to the rector: and the rector to the provincial: and the provincial to the general of the jesuits. That was called the order: and he had heard his father say that they were all clever men. They could all have become highup people in the world if they had not become jesuits. And he wondered what Father Arnall and Paddy Barrett would have become and what Mr McGlade and Mr Gleeson would have become if they had not become jesuits. It was hard to think what because you would have to think of them in a different way with different coloured coats and trousers and with beards and moustaches and different kinds of hats.

The door opened quietly and closed. A quick whisper ran through the class: the prefect of studies. There was an instant of dead silence and then the loud crack of a pandybat on the last desk. Stephen's heart leapt up in fear.

—Any boys want flogging here, Father Arnall? cried the prefect of studies. Any lazy idle loafers that want flogging in this class?

He came to the middle of the class and saw Fleming on his knees.

—Hoho! he cried. Who is this boy? Why is he on his knees? What is your name, boy?

—Fleming, sir.

—Hoho, Fleming! An idler of course. I can see it in your eye. Why is he on his knees, Father Arnall?

—He wrote a bad Latin theme, Father Arnall said, and he missed all the questions in grammar.

—Of course he did! cried the prefect of studies. Of course he did! A born idler! I can see it in the corner of his eye.

He banged his pandybat down on the desk and cried:

—Up, Fleming! Up, my boy!

Fleming stood up slowly.

—Hold out! cried the prefect of studies.

Fleming held out his hand. The pandybat came down on it with a loud smacking sound: one, two, three, four, five, six.

—Other hand!

The pandybat came down again in six loud quick smacks.

—Kneel down! cried the prefect of studies.

Fleming knelt down squeezing his hands under his armpits, his face contorted with pain, but Stephen knew how hard his hands were because Fleming was always rubbing rosin into them. But perhaps he was in great pain for the noise of the pandies was terrible. Stephen's heart was beating and fluttering.

—At your work, all of you! shouted the prefect of studies. We want no lazy idle loafers here, lazy idle little schemers. At your work, I tell you. Father Dolan will be in to see you every day. Father Dolan will be in tomorrow.

He poked one of the boys in the side with the pandy-bat, saying:

—You, boy! When will Father Dolan be in again?

—Tomorrow, sir, said Tom Furlong's voice.

—Tomorrow and tomorrow and tomorrow, said the prefect of studies. Make up your minds for that. Every day Father Dolan. Write away. You, boy, who are you?

Stephen's heart jumped suddenly.

—Dedalus, sir.

—Why are you not writing like the others?

—I . . . my . . .

He could not speak with fright.

—Why is he not writing. Father Arnall?

—He broke his glasses, said Father Arnall, and I exempted him from work.

—Broke? What is this I hear? What is this your name is? said the prefect of studies.

—Dedalus, sir.

—Out here, Dedalus. Lazy little schemer. I see schemer in your face. Where did you break your glasses?

Stephen stumbled into the middle of the class, blinded by fear and haste.

—Where did you break your glasses? repeated the prefect of studies.

—The cinderpath, sir.

—Hoho! The cinderpath! cried the prefect of studies.
I know that trick.

Stephen lifted his eyes in wonder and saw for a
moment Father Dolan's whitegrey not young face, his
baldy whitegrey head with fluff at the sides of it, the
steel rims of his spectacles and his nocoloured eyes
looking through the glasses. Why did he say he knew
that trick?

—Lazy idle little loafer! cried the prefect of studies.
Broke my glasses! An old schoolboy trick! Out with
your hand this moment!

Stephen closed his eyes and held out in the air his
trembling hand with the palm upwards. He felt the
prefect of studies touch it for a moment at the fingers
to straighten it and then the swish of the sleeve of the
soutane as the pandybat was lifted to strike. A hot
burning stinging tingling blow like the loud crack of a
broken stick made his trembling hand crumple together
like a leaf in the fire: and at the sound and the pain
scalding tears were driven into his eyes. His whole body
was shaking with fright, his arm was shaking and his
crumpled burning livid hand shook like a loose leaf in
the air. A cry sprang to his lips, a prayer to be let off.
But though the tears scalded his eyes and his limbs
quivered with pain and fright he held back the hot tears
and the cry that scalded his throat.

—Other hand! shouted the prefect of studies.

Stephen drew back his maimed and quivering right
arm and held out his left hand. The soutane sleeve
swished again as the pandybat was lifted and a loud
crashing sound and a fierce maddening tingling burning
pain made his hand shrink together with the palms and
fingers in a livid quivering mass. The scalding water
burst forth from his eyes and, burning with shame and
agony and fear, he drew back his shaking arm in terror

and burst out into a whine of pain. His body shook with a palsy of fright and in shame and rage he felt the scalding cry come from his throat and the scalding tears falling out of his eyes and down his flaming cheeks.

—Kneel down! cried the prefect of studies.

Stephen knelt down quickly pressing his beaten hands to his sides. To think of them beaten and swollen with pain all in a moment made him feel so sorry for them as if they were not his own but someone else's that he felt sorry for. And as he knelt, calming the last sobs in his throat and feeling the burning tingling pain pressed in to his sides, he thought of the hands which he had held out in the air with the palms up and of the firm touch of the prefect of studies when he had steadied the shaking fingers and of the beaten swollen reddened mass of palm and fingers that shook helplessly in the air.

—Get at your work, all of you, cried the prefect of studies from the door. Father Dolan will be in every day to see if any boy, any lazy idle little loafer wants flogging. Every day. Every day.

The door closed behind him.

The hushed class continued to copy out the themes. Father Arnall rose from his seat and went among them, helping the boys with gentle words and telling them the mistakes they had made. His voice was very gentle and soft. Then he returned to his seat and said to Fleming and Stephen:

—You may return to your places, you two.

Fleming and Stephen rose and, walking to their seats, sat down. Stephen, scarlet with shame, opened a book quickly with one weak hand and bent down upon it, his face close to the page.

It was unfair and cruel because the doctor had told

him not to read without glasses and he had written home to his father that morning to send him a new pair. And Father Arnall had said that he need not study till the new glasses came. Then to be called a schemer before the class and to be pandied when he always got the card for first or second and was the leader of the Yorkists! How could the prefect of studies know that it was a trick? He felt the touch of the prefect's fingers as they had steadied his hand and at first he had thought he was going to shake hands with him because the fingers were soft and firm: but then in an instant he had heard the swish of the soutane sleeve and the crash. It was cruel and unfair to make him kneel in the middle of the class then: and Father Arnall had told them both that they might return to their places without making any difference between them. He listened to Father Arnall's low and gentle voice as he corrected the themes. Perhaps he was sorry now and wanted to be decent. But it was unfair and cruel. The prefect of studies was a priest but that was cruel and unfair. And his whitegrey face and the no-coloured eyes behind the steelrimmed spectacles were cruel looking because he had steadied the hand first with his firm soft fingers and that was to hit it better and louder.

—It's a stinking mean thing, that's what it is, said Fleming in the corridor as the classes were passing out in file to the refectory, to pandy a fellow for what is not his fault.

—You really broke your glasses by accident, didn't you? Nasty Roche asked.

Stephen felt his heart filled by Fleming's words and did not answer.

—Of course he did! said Fleming. I wouldn't stand it. I'd go up and tell the rector on him.

—Yes, said Cecil Thunder eagerly, and I saw him lift the pandybat over his shoulder and he's not allowed to do that.

—Did they hurt much? Nasty Roche asked.

—Very much, Stephen said.

—I wouldn't stand it, Fleming repeated, from Baldyhead or any other Baldyhead. It's a stinking mean low trick, that's what it is. I'd go straight up to the rector and tell him about it after dinner.

—Yes, do. Yes, do, said Cecil Thunder.

—Yes, do. Yes, go up and tell the rector on him, Dedalus, said Nasty Roche, because he said that he'd come in tomorrow again to pandy you.

—Yes, yes. Tell the rector, all said.

And there were some fellows out of second of grammar listening and one of them said:

—The senate and the Roman people declared that Dedalus had been wrongly punished.

It was wrong; it was unfair and cruel: and, as he sat in the refectory, he suffered time after time in memory the same humiliation until he began to wonder whether it might not really be that there was something in his face which made him look like a schemer and he wished he had a little mirror to see. But there could not be; and it was unjust and cruel and unfair.

He could not eat the blackish fish fritters they got on Wednesdays in Lent and one of his potatoes had the mark of the spade in it. Yes, he would do what the fellows had told him. He would go up and tell the rector that he had been wrongly punished. A thing like that had been done before by somebody in history, by some great person whose head was in the books of history. And the rector would declare that he had been wrongly punished because the senate and the Roman people always declared that the men who did that had been wrongly punished. Those were the great men whose names were in Richmal Magnall's Questions. History was all about those men and what they did and that was what Peter Parley's Tales about Greece and Rome were all about. Peter Parley himself was on the first page in a picture. There was a road over a heath with grass at the side and little bushes: and Peter Parley had a broad hat like a protestant minister and a big stick and he was walking fast along the road to Greece and Rome.

It was easy what he had to do. All he had to do was when the dinner was over and he came out in his turn to go on walking but not out to the corridor but up the staircase on the right that led to the castle. He had nothing to do but that: to turn to the right and walk fast up the staircase and in half a minute he would be in the low dark narrow corridor that led through the castle to the rector's room. And every fellow had said that it was unfair, even the fellow out of second of grammar who had said that about the senate and the Roman people.

What would happen? He heard the fellows of the higher line stand up at the top of the refectory and heard their steps as they came down the matting: Paddy Rath and Jimmy Magee and the Spaniard and the Portuguese and the fifth was big Corrigan who was going to be flogged by Mr Gleeson. That was why the prefect of studies had called him a schemer and pandied him for nothing: and, straining his weak eyes, tired with the tears, he watched big Corrigan's broad shoulders and big hanging black head passing in the file. But he had done something and besides Mr Gleeson would not flog him hard: and he remembered how big Corrigan looked in the bath. He had skin the same colour as the turfcoloured bogwater in the shallow end of the bath and when he walked along the side his feet slapped loudly on the wet tiles and at every step his thighs shook a little because he was fat.

The refectory was half empty and the fellows were still passing out in file. He could go up the staircase because there was never a priest or a prefect outside the refectory door. But he could not go. The rector would side with the prefect of studies and think it was a schoolboy trick and then the prefect of studies would come in every day the same only it would be worse because he would be dreadfully waxy at any fellow going up to the rector about him. The fellows had told him to go but they would not go themselves. They had forgotten all about it. No, it was best to forget all about it and perhaps the prefect of studies had only said he would come in. No, it was best to hide out of the way because when you were small and young you could often escape that way.

The fellows at his table stood up. He stood up and passed out among them in the file. He had to decide. He was coming near the door. If he went on with the fellows he could never go up to the rector because he could not leave the playground for that. And if he went and was pandied all the same all the fellows would make fun and talk about young Dedalus going up to the rector to tell on the prefect of studies.

He was walking down along the matting and he saw the door before him. It was impossible: he could not. He thought of the baldy head of the prefect of studies with the cruel nocoloured eyes looking at him and he heard the voice of the prefect of studies asking him twice what his name was. Why could he not remember the name when he was told the first time? Was he not listening the first time or was it to make fun out of the name? The great men in the history had names like that and nobody made fun of them. It was his own name that he should have made fun of if he wanted to make fun. Dolan: it was like the name of a woman that washed clothes.

He had reached the door and, turning quickly up to the right, walked up the stairs and, before he could make up his mind to come back, he had entered the low dark narrow corridor that led to the castle. And as he crossed the threshold of the door of the corridor he saw, without turning his head to look, that all the fellows were looking after him as they went filing by.

He passed along the narrow dark corridor, passing little doors that were the doors of the rooms of the community. He peered in front of him and right and left through the gloom and thought that those must be portraits. It was dark and silent and his eyes were weak and tired with tears so that he could not see. But he thought they were the portraits of the saints and great men of the order who were looking down on him silently as he passed: saint Ignatius Loyola holding an open book and pointing to the words *Ad Majorem Dei Gloriam* in it, saint Francis Xavier pointing to his chest, Lorenzo Ricci with his berretta on his head like one of the prefects of the lines, the three patrons of holy youth, saint Stanislaus Kostka, saint Aloysius Gonzaga and blessed John Berchmans, all with young faces because they died when they were young, and Father Peter Kenny sitting in a chair wrapped in a big cloak.

He came out on the landing above the entrance hall and looked about him. That was where Hamilton Rowan had passed and the marks of the soldiers' slugs were there. And it was there that the old servants had seen the ghost in the white cloak of a marshal.

An old servant was sweeping at the end of the landing. He asked him where was the rector's room and the old servant pointed to the door at the far end and looked after him as he went on to it and knocked.

There was no answer. He knocked again more loudly and his heart jumped when he heard a muffled voice say:

—Come in!

He turned the handle and opened the door and fumbled for the handle of the green baize door inside. He found it and pushed it open and went in.

He saw the rector sitting at a desk writing. There was a skull on the desk and a strange solemn smell in the room like the old leather of chairs.

His heart was beating fast on account of the solemn place he was in and the silence of the room: and he looked at the skull and at the rector's kindlooking face.

—Well, my little man, said the rector, what is it?

Stephen swallowed down the thing in his throat and said:

—I broke my glasses, sir.

The rector opened his mouth and said:

—O!

Then he smiled and said:

—Well, if we broke our glasses we must write home for a new pair.

—I wrote home, sir, said Stephen, and Father Arnall said I am not to study till they come.

—Quite right! said the rector.

Stephen swallowed down the thing again and tried to keep his legs and his voice from shaking.

—But, sir . . .

—Yes?

—Father Dolan came in today and pandied me because I was not writing my theme.

The rector looked at him in silence and he could feel the blood rising to his face and the tears about to rise to his eyes.

The rector said:

—Your name is Dedalus, isn't it?

—Yes, sir.

—And where did you break your glasses?

—On the cinderpath, sir. A fellow was coming out of the bicycle house and I fell and they got broken. I don't know the fellow's name.

The rector looked at him again in silence. Then he smiled and said:

—O, well, it was a mistake; I am sure Father Dolan did not know.

—But I told him I broke them, sir, and he pandied me.

—Did you tell him that you had written home for a new pair? the rector asked.

—No, sir.

—O well then, said the rector, Father Dolan did not understand. You can say that I excuse you from your lessons for a few days.

Stephen said quickly for fear his trembling would prevent him:

—Yes, sir, but Father Dolan said he will come in tomorrow to pandy me again for it.

—Very well, the rector said, it is a mistake and I shall speak to Father Dolan myself. Will that do now?

Stephen felt the tears wetting his eyes and murmured:

—O yes sir, thanks.

The rector held his hand across the side of the desk where the skull was and Stephen, placing his hand in it for a moment, felt a cool moist palm.

—Good day now, said the rector, withdrawing his hand and bowing.

—Good day, sir, said Stephen.

He bowed and walked quietly out of the room, closing the doors carefully and slowly.

But when he had passed the old servant on the landing and was again in the low narrow dark corridor he began to walk faster and faster. Faster and faster he hurried on through the gloom excitedly. He bumped his elbow against the door at the end and, hurrying down the staircase, walked quickly through the two corridors and out into the air.

He could hear the cries of the fellows on the playgrounds. He broke into a run and, running quicker and quicker, ran across the cinderpath and reached the third line playground, panting.

The fellows had seen him running. They closed round him in a ring, pushing one against another to hear.

—Tell us! Tell us!

—What did he say?

—Did you go in?

—What did he say?

—Tell us! Tell us!

He told them what he had said and what the rector had said and, when he had told them, all the fellows flung their caps spinning up into the air and cried:

—Hurroo!

They caught their caps and sent them up again spinning skyhigh and cried again:

—Hurroo! Hurroo!

They made a cradle of their locked hands and hoisted him up among them and carried him along till he struggled to get free. And when he had escaped from them they broke away in all directions, flinging

their caps again into the air and whistling as they went
spinning up and crying:

—Hurroo!

And they gave three groans for Baldyhead Dolan
and three cheers for Conmee and they said he was the
decentest rector that was ever in Clongowes.

The cheers died away in the soft grey air. He was
alone. He was happy and free: but he would not be
anyway proud with Father Dolan. He would be very
quiet and obedient: and he wished that he could do
something kind for him to show him that he was not
proud.

The air was soft and grey and mild and evening was
coming. There was the smell of evening in the air, the
smell of the fields in the country where they digged up
turnips to peel them and eat them when they went out
for a walk to Major Barton's, the smell there was in the
little wood beyond the pavilion where the gallnuts were.

The fellows were practising long shies and bowing
lobs and slow twisters. In the soft grey silence he could
hear the bump of the balls: and from here and from
there through the quiet air the sound of the cricket
bats: pick, pack, pock, puck: like drops of water in a
fountain falling softly in the brimming bowl.

II

UNCLE CHARLES smoked such black twist
that at last his nephew suggested to him to enjoy his morning smoke in a little outhouse at the end of
the garden.

—Very good, Simon. All serene, Simon, said the old
man tranquilly. Anywhere you like. The outhouse will
do me nicely: it will be more salubrious.

—Damn me, said Mr Dedalus frankly, if I know how you can smoke such villainous awful tobacco. It's like gunpowder, by God.

—It's very nice, Simon, replied the old man. Very cool and mollifying.

Every morning, therefore, uncle Charles repaired to his outhouse but not before he had creased and brushed scrupulously his back hair and brushed and put on his tall hat. While he smoked the brim of his tall hat and the bowl of his pipe were just visible beyond the jambs of the outhouse door. His arbour, as he called the reeking outhouse which he shared with the cat and the garden tools, served him also as a soundingbox: and every morning he hummed contentedly one of his favourite songs: *O, twine me a bower* or *Blue eyes and golden hair* or *The Groves of Blarney* while the grey and blue coils of smoke rose slowly from his pipe and vanished in the pure air.

During the first part of the summer in Blackrock uncle Charles was Stephen's constant companion. Uncle Charles was a hale old man with a welltanned skin, rugged features and white side whiskers. On week days he did messages between the house in Carysfort Avenue and those shops in the main street of the town with which the family dealt. Stephen was glad to go with him on these errands for uncle Charles helped him very liberally to handfuls of whatever was exposed in open boxes and barrels outside the counter. He would seize a handful of grapes and sawdust or three or four American apples and thrust them generously into his grandnephew's hand while the shopman smiled uneasily; and, on Stephen's feigning reluctance to take them, he would frown and say:

—Take them, sir. Do you hear me, sir? They're good for your bowels.

When the order list had been booked the two would go on to the park where an old friend of Stephen's father, Mike Flynn, would be found seated on a bench, waiting for them. Then would begin Stephen's run round the park. Mike Flynn would stand at the gate near the railway station, watch in hand, while Stephen ran round the track in the style Mike Flynn favoured, his head high lifted, his knees well lifted and his hands held straight down by his sides. When the morning practice was over the trainer would make his comments and sometimes illustrate them by shuffling along for a yard or so comically in an old pair of blue canvas shoes. A small ring of wonderstruck children and nursemaids would gather to watch him and linger even when he and uncle Charles had sat down again and were talking athletics and politics. Though he had heard his father say that Mike Flynn had put some of the best runners of modern times through his hands Stephen often glanced with mistrust at his trainer's flabby stubblecovered face, as it bent over the long stained fingers through which he rolled his cigarette, and with pity at the mild lustreless blue eyes which would look up suddenly from the task and gaze vaguely into the blue distance while the long swollen fingers ceased their rolling and grains and fibres of tobacco fell back into the pouch.

On the way home uncle Charles would often pay a visit to the chapel and, as the font was above Stephen's reach, the old man would dip his hand and then sprinkle the water briskly about Stephen's clothes and on the floor of the porch. While he prayed he knelt on his red hankerchief and read above his breath from a thumbblackened prayerbook wherein catchwords were printed at the foot of every page. Stephen knelt at his side respecting, though he did not share, his piety. He often wondered what his granduncle prayed for so seriously. Perhaps he prayed for the souls in purgatory or for the grace of a happy death or perhaps he prayed that God might send him back a part of the big fortune he had squandered in Cork.

On Sundays Stephen with his father and his granduncle took their constitutional. The old man was a nimble walker in spite of his corns and often ten or twelve miles of the road were covered. The little village of Stillorgan was the parting of the ways. Either they went to the left towards the Dublin mountains or along the Goatstown road and thence into Dundrum, coming home by Sandyford. Trudging along the road or standing in some grimy wayside publichouse his elders spoke constantly of the subjects nearer their hearts, of Irish politics, of Munster and of the legends of their own family, to all of which Stephen lent an avid ear. Words which he did not understand he said over and over to himself till he had learned them by heart: and through them he had glimpses of the real world about him. The hour when he too would take part in the life of that world seemed drawing near and in secret he began to make ready for the great part which he felt awaited him the nature of which he only dimly apprehended.

His evenings were his own; and he pored over a ragged translation of *The Count of Monte Cristo*. The figure of that dark avenger stood forth in his mind for whatever he had heard or divined in childhood of the strange and terrible. At night he built up on the parlour table an image of the wonderful island cave out of transfers and paper flowers and coloured tissue paper and strips of the silver and golden paper in which chocolate is wrapped. When he had broken up this scenery, weary of its tinsel, there would come to his mind the

bright picture of Marseilles, of sunny trellisses and of
Mercedes. Outside Blackrock, on the road that led to
the mountains, stood a small whitewashed house in the
garden of which grew many rosebushes: and in this
house, he told himself, another Mercedes lived. Both
on the outward and on the homeward journey he
measured distance by this landmark: and in his imagination he lived through a long train of adventures,
marvellous as those in the book itself, towards the close
of which there appeared an image of himself, grown
older and sadder, standing in a moonlit garden with
Mercedes who had so many years before slighted his
love, and with a sadly proud gesture of refusal, saying:

—Madam, I never eat muscatel grapes.

He became the ally of a boy named Aubrey Mills
and founded with him a gang of adventurers in the
avenue. Aubrey carried a whistle dangling from his
buttonhole and a bicycle lamp attached to his belt
while the others had short sticks thrust daggerwise
through theirs. Stephen, who had read of Napoleon's
plain style of dress, chose to remain unadorned and
thereby heightened for himself the pleasure of taking
counsel with his lieutenant before giving orders. The
gang made forays into the gardens of old maids or went
down to the castle and fought a battle on the shaggy
weedgrown rocks, coming home after it weary strag-
glers with the stale odours of the foreshore in their
nostrils and the rank oils of the seawrack upon their
hands and in their hair.

Aubrey and Stephen had a common milkman and
often they drove out in the milkcar to Carrickmines
where the cows were at grass. While the men were
milking the boys would take turns in riding the tract-
able mare round the field. But when autumn came the
cows were driven home from the grass: and the first

sight of the filthy cowyard at Stradbrook with its foul green puddles and clots of liquid dung and steaming brantroughs sickened Stephen's heart. The cattle which had seemed so beautiful in the country on sunny days revolted him and he could not even look at the milk they yielded.

The coming of September did not trouble him this year for he was not to be sent back to Clongowes. The practice in the park came to an end when Mike Flynn went into hospital. Aubrey was at school and had only an hour or two free in the evening. The gang fell asunder and there were no more nightly forays or battles on the rocks. Stephen sometimes went round with the car which delivered the evening milk: and these chilly drives blew away his memory of the filth of the cowyard and he felt no repugnance at seeing the cowhairs and hayseeds on the milkman's coat. Whenever the car drew up before a house he waited to catch a glimpse of a wellscrubbed kitchen or of a softlylighted hall and to see how the servant would hold the jug and how she would close the door. He thought it should be a pleasant life enough, driving along the roads every evening to deliver milk, if he had warm gloves and a fat bag of gingernuts in his pocket to eat from. But the same foreknowledge which had sickened his heart and made his legs sag suddenly as he raced round the park, the same intuition which had made him glance with mistrust at his trainer's flabby stubblecovered face as it bent heavily over his long stained fingers, dissipated any vision of the future. In a vague way he understood that his father was in trouble and that this was the reason why he himself had not been sent back to Clongowes. For some time he had felt the slight changes in his house; and these changes in what he had deemed unchangeable were so many slight shocks to his boyish conception of the world. The ambition which he felt astir at times in the darkness of his soul sought no outlet. A dusk like that of the outer world obscured his mind as he heard the mare's hoofs clattering along the tramtrack on the Rock Road and the great can swaying and rattling behind him.

He returned to Mercedes and, as he brooded upon her image, a strange unrest crept into his blood. Sometimes a fever gathered within him and led him to rove alone in the evening along the quiet avenue. The peace of the gardens and the kindly lights in the windows poured a tender influence into his restless heart. The noise of children at play annoyed him and their silly voices made him feel, even more keenly than he had felt at Clongowes, that he was different from others. He did not want to play. He wanted to meet in the real world the unsubstantial image which his soul so constantly beheld. He did not know where to seek it or how: but a premonition which led him on told him that this image would, without any overt act of his, encounter him. They would meet quietly as if they had known each other and had made their tryst, perhaps at one of the gates or in some more secret place. They would be alone, surrounded by darkness and silence: and in that moment of supreme tenderness he would be transfigured. He would fade into something impalpable under her eyes and then in a moment, he would be transfigured. Weakness and timidity and inexperience would fall from him in that magic moment.

*   *   *

Two great yellow caravans had halted one morning before the door and men had come tramping into the house to dismantle it. The furniture had been hustled out through the front garden which was strewn with

wisps of straw and rope ends and into the huge vans at
the gate. When all had been safely stowed the vans
had set off noisily down the avenue: and from the
window of the railway carriage, in which he had sat
with his redeyed mother, Stephen had seen them lum-
bering heavily along the Merrion Road.

The parlour fire would not draw that evening and Mr
Dedalus rested the poker against the bars of the grate
to attract the flame. Uncle Charles dozed in a corner of
the half furnished uncarpeted room and near him the
family portraits leaned against the wall. The lamp on
the table shed a weak light over the boarded floor,
muddied by the feet of the vanmen. Stephen sat on a
footstool beside his father listening to a long and incoherent monologue. He understood little or nothing of it
at first but he became slowly aware that his father had
enemies and that some fight was going to take place.
He felt too that he was being enlisted for the fight, that
some duty was being laid upon his shoulders. The sudden flight from the comfort and revery of Blackrock,
the passage through the gloomy foggy city, the thought
of the bare cheerless house in which they were now to
live made his heart heavy: and again an intuition or
foreknowledge of the future came to him. He understood also why the servants had often whispered together in the hall and why his father had often stood
on the hearthrug, with his back to the fire, talking
loudly to uncle Charles who urged him to sit down and
eat his dinner.

—There's a crack of the whip left in me yet, Stephen, old chap, said Mr Dedalus, poking at the dull fire
with fierce energy. We're not dead yet, sonny. No, by
the Lord Jesus (God forgive me) nor half dead.

Dublin was a new and complex sensation. Uncle
Charles had grown so witless that he could no longer

be sent out on errands and the disorder in settling in
the new house left Stephen freer than he had been in
Blackrock. In the beginning he contented himself with
circling timidly round the neighbouring square or, at
most, going half way down one of the side streets: but
when he had made a skeleton map of the city in his
mind he followed boldly one of its central lines until he
reached the customhouse. He passed unchallenged
among the docks and along the quays wondering at the
multitude of corks that lay bobbing on the surface of
the water in a thick yellow scum, at the crowds of quay
porters and the rumbling carts and the illdressed
bearded policeman. The vastness and strangeness of the
life suggested to him by the bales of merchandise
stocked along the walls or swung aloft out of the holds
of steamers wakened again in him the unrest which had
sent him wandering in the evening from garden to
garden in search of Mercedes. And amid this new
bustling life he might have fancied himself in another
Marseilles but that he missed the bright sky and the
sunwarmed trellisses of the wineshops. A vague dissat-
isfaction grew up within him as he looked on the quays
and on the river and on the lowering skies and yet he
continued to wander up and down day after day as if
he really sought someone that eluded him.

He went once or twice with his mother to visit their
relatives: and, though they passed a jovial array of
shops lit up and adorned for Christmas, his mood of
embittered silence did not leave him. The causes of his
embitterment were many, remote and near. He was
angry with himself for being young and the prey of
restless foolish impulses, angry also with the change of
fortune which was reshaping the world about him into
a vision of squalor and insincerity. Yet his anger lent
nothing to the vision. He chronicled with patience what

he saw, detaching himself from it and testing its morti-
fying flavour in secret.

He was sitting on the backless chair in his aunt's
kitchen. A lamp with a reflector hung on the japanned
wall of the fireplace and by its light his aunt was reading the evening paper that lay on her knees. She looked
a long time at a smiling picture that was set in it and
said musingly:

—The beautiful Mabel Hunter!

A ringletted girl stood on tiptoe to peer at the picture
and said softly:

—What is she in, mud?

—In the pantomime, love.

The child leaned her ringletted head against her
mother's sleeve, gazing on the picture, and murmured
as if fascinated:

—The beautiful Mabel Hunter!

As if fascinated, her eyes rested long upon those
demurely taunting eyes and she murmured again de-
votedly:

—Isn't she an exquisite creature?

And the boy who came in from the street, stamping
crookedly under his stone of coal, heard her words. He
dropped his load promptly on the floor and hurried to
her side to see. But she did not raise her easeful head to
let him see. He mauled the edges of the paper with his
reddened and blackened hands, shouldering her aside
and complaining that he could not see.

He was sitting in the narrow breakfast room high up
in the old darkwindowed house. The firelight flickered
on the wall and beyond the window a spectral dusk was
gathering upon the river. Before the fire an old woman
was busy making tea and, as she bustled at her task,
she told in a low voice of what the priest and the
doctor had said. She told too of certain changes she

had seen in her of late and of her odd ways and sayings. He sat listening to the words and following the
ways of adventure that lay open in the coals, arches
and vaults and winding galleries and jagged caverns.

Suddenly he became aware of something in the
doorway. A skull appeared suspended in the gloom of
the doorway. A feeble creature like a monkey was
there, drawn thither by the sound of voices at the fire.
A whining voice came from the door, asking:

—Is that Josephine?

The old bustling woman answered cheerily from the
fireplace:

—No, Ellen. It's Stephen.

—O . . . O, good evening, Stephen.

He answered the greeting and saw a silly smile break
over the face in the doorway.

—Do you want anything, Ellen? asked the old
woman at the fire.

But she did not answer the question and said:

—I thought it was Josephine. I thought you were
Josephine, Stephen.

And, repeating this several times, she fell to laughing
feebly.

He was sitting in the midst of a children's party at
Harold's Cross. His silent watchful manner had grown
upon him and he took little part in the games. The
children, wearing the spoils of their crackers, danced
and romped noisily and, though he tried to share their
merriment, he felt himself a gloomy figure amid the
gay cocked hats and sunbonnets.

But when he had sung his song and withdrawn into a
snug corner of the room he began to taste the joy of his
loneliness. The mirth, which in the beginning of the
evening had seemed to him false and trivial, was like a
soothing air to him, passing gaily by his senses, hiding

from other eyes the feverish agitation of his blood while through the circling of the dancers and amid the music and laughter her glance travelled to his corner, flattering, taunting, searching, exciting his heart.

In the hall the children who had stayed latest were putting on their things: the party was over. She had thrown a shawl about her and, as they went together towards the tram, sprays of her fresh warm breath flew gaily above her cowled head and her shoes tapped blithely on the glassy road.

It was the last tram. The lank brown horses knew it and shook their bells to the clear night in admonition. The conductor talked with the driver, both nodding often in the green light of the lamp. On the empty seats of the tram were scattered a few coloured tickets. No sound of footsteps came up or down the road. No sound broke the peace of the night save when the lank brown horses rubbed their noses together and shook their bells.

They seemed to listen, he on the upper step and she on the lower. She came up to his step many times and went down to hers again between their phrases and once or twice stood close beside him for some moments on the upper step, forgetting to go down, and then went down. His heart danced upon her movements like a cork upon a tide. He heard what her eyes said to him from beneath their cowl and knew that in some dim past, whether in life or in revery, he had heard their tale before. He saw her urge her vanities, her fine dress and sash and long black stockings, and knew that he had yielded to them a thousand times. Yet a voice within him spoke above the noise of his dancing heart, asking him would he take her gift to which he had only to stretch out his hand. And he remembered the day when he and Eileen had stood looking into the hotel grounds, watching the waiters running up a trail of bunting on the flagstaff and the fox terrier scampering to and fro on the sunny lawn, and how, all of a sudden, she had broken out into a peal of laughter and had run down the sloping curve of the path. Now, as then, he stood listlessly in his place, seemingly a tranquil watcher of the scene before him.

—She too wants me to catch hold of her, he thought. That's why she came with me to the tram. I could easily catch hold of her when she comes up to my step: nobody is looking. I could hold her and kiss her.

But he did neither: and, when he was sitting alone in the deserted tram, he tore his ticket into shreds and stared gloomily at the corrugated footboard.

The next day he sat at his table in the bare upper room for many hours. Before him lay a new pen, a new bottle of ink and a new emerald exercise. From force of habit he had written at the top of the first page the initial letters of the jesuit motto: A.M.D.G. On the first line of the page appeared the title of the verses he was trying to write: To E— C—. He knew it was right to begin so for he had seen similar titles in the collected poems of Lord Byron. When he had written this title and drawn an ornamental line underneath he fell into a daydream and began to draw diagrams on the cover of the book. He saw himself sitting at his table in Bray the morning after the discussion at the Christmas dinner-table, trying to write a poem about Parnell on the back of one of his father's second moiety notices. But his brain had then refused to grapple with the theme and, desisting, he had covered the page with the names and addresses of certain of his classmates:

Roderick Kickham
John Lawton
Anthony MacSwiney
Simon Moonan

Now it seemed as if he would fail again but, by dint of brooding on the incident, he thought himself into confidence. During this process all these elements which he deemed common and insignificant fell out of the scene. There remained no trace of the tram itself nor of the trammen nor of the horses: nor did he and she appear vividly. The verses told only of the night and the balmy breeze and the maiden lustre of the moon. Some undefined sorrow was hidden in the hearts of the protagonists as they stood in silence beneath the leafless trees and when the moment of farewell had come the kiss, which had been withheld by one, was given by both. After this the letters L.D.S. were written at the foot of the page and, having hidden the book, he went into his mother's bedroom and gazed at his face for a long time in the mirror of her dressingtable.

But his long spell of leisure and liberty was drawing to its end. One evening his father came home full of news which kept his tongue busy all through dinner. Stephen had been awaiting his father's return for there had been mutton hash that day and he knew that his father would make him dip his bread in the gravy. But he did not relish the hash for the mention of Clongowes had coated his palate with a scum of disgust.

—I walked bang into him, said Mr Dedalus for the fourth time, just at the corner of the square.

—Then I suppose, said Mrs Dedalus, he will be able to arrange it. I mean about Belvedere.

—Of course he will, said Mr Dedalus. Don't I tell you he's provincial of the order now?

—I never liked the idea of sending him to the christian brothers myself, said Mrs Dedalus.

—Christian brothers be damned! said Mr Dedalus. Is it with Paddy Stink and Mickey Mud? No, let him stick to the jesuits in God's name since he began with them. They'll be of service to him in after years. Those are the fellows that can get you a position.

—And they're a very rich order, aren't they, Simon?

—Rather. They live well, I tell you. You saw their table at Clongowes. Fed up, by God, like gamecocks.

Mr Dedalus pushed his plate over to Stephen and bade him finish what was on it.

—Now then, Stephen, he said, you must put your shoulder to the wheel, old chap. You've had a fine long holiday.

—O, I'm sure he'll work very hard now, said Mrs Dedalus, especially when he has Maurice with him.

—O, Holy Paul, I forgot about Maurice, said Mr Dedalus. Here, Maurice! Come here, you thickheaded ruffian! Do you know I'm going to send you to a college where they'll teach you to spell c.a.t. cat. And I'll buy you a nice little penny handkerchief to keep your nose dry. Won't that be grand fun?

Maurice grinned at his father and then at his brother. Mr Dedalus screwed his glass into his eye and stared hard at both his sons. Stephen mumbled his bread without answering his father's gaze.

—By the bye, said Mr Dedalus at length, the rector, or provincial, rather, was telling me that story about you and Father Dolan. You're an impudent thief, he said.

—O, he didn't, Simon!

—Not he! said Mr Dedalus. But he gave me a great account of the whole affair. We were chatting, you know, and one word borrowed another. And, by the way, who do you think he told me will get that job in the corporation? But I'll tell you that after. Well, as I was saying, we were chatting away quite friendly and he asked me did our friend here wear glasses still and then he told me the whole story.

—And was he annoyed, Simon?

—Annoyed! Not he! *Manly little chap!* he said.

Mr Dedalus imitated the mincing nasal tone of the provincial.

—Father Dolan and I, when I told them all at dinner about it, Father Dolan and I had a great laugh over it. *You better mind yourself, Father Dolan,* said I, *or young Dedalus will send you up for twice nine.* We had a famous laugh together over it. Ha! Ha! Ha!

Mr Dedalus turned to his wife and interjected in his natural voice:

—Shows you the spirit in which they take the boys there. O, a jesuit for your life, for diplomacy!

He reassumed the provincial's voice and repeated:

—*I told them all at dinner about it and Father Dolan and I and all of us we had a hearty laugh together over it. Ha! Ha! Ha!*

* * *

The night of the Whitsuntide play had come and Stephen from the window of the dressingroom looked out on the small grassplot across which lines of Chinese lanterns were stretched. He watched the visitors come down the steps from the house and pass into the theatre. Stewards in evening dress, old Belvedereans, loitered in groups about the entrance to the theatre and ushered in the visitors with ceremony. Under the sudden glow of a lantern he could recognise the smiling face of a priest.

The Blessed Sacrament had been removed from the

tabernacle and the first benches had been driven so as to leave the dais of the altar and the space before it free. Against the walls stood companies of barbells and Indian clubs; the dumbbells were piled in one corner: and in the midst of countless hillocks of gymnasium shoes and sweaters and singlets in untidy brown parcels there stood the stout leatherjacketed vaulting horse waiting its turn to be carried up on the stage. A large bronze shield, tipped with silver, leaned against the panel of the altar also waiting its turn to be carried up on the stage and set in the middle of the winning team at the end of the gymnastic display.

Stephen, though in deference to his reputation for essaywriting he had been elected secretary to the gymnasium, had had no part in the first section of the programme but in the play which formed the second section he had the chief part, that of a farcical pedagogue. He had been cast for it on account of his stature and grave manners for he was now at the end of his second year at Belvedere and in number two.

A score of the younger boys in white knickers and singlets came pattering down from the stage, through the vestry and into the chapel. The vestry and chapel were peopled with eager masters and boys. The plump bald sergeantmajor was testing with his foot the springboard of the vaulting horse. The lean young man in a long overcoat, who was to give a special display of intricate club swinging, stood near watching with interest, his silvercoated clubs peeping out of his deep sidepockets. The hollow rattle of the wooden dumbbells was heard as another team made ready to go up on the stage: and in another moment the excited prefect was hustling the boys through the vestry like a flock of geese, flapping the wings of his soutane nervously and crying to the laggards to make haste. A little troop of

Neapolitan peasants were practising their steps at the end of the chapel, some circling their arms above their heads, some swaying their baskets of paper violets and curtseying. In a dark corner of the chapel at the gospel side of the altar a stout old lady knelt amid her copious black skirts. When she stood up a pinkdressed figure, wearing a curly golden wig and an oldfashioned straw sunbonnet, with black pencilled eyebrows and cheeks delicately rouged and powdered, was discovered. A low murmur of curiosity ran round the chapel at the discovery of this girlish figure. One of the prefects, smiling and nodding his head, approached the dark corner and, having bowed to the stout old lady, said pleasantly:

—Is this a beautiful young lady or a doll that you have here, Mrs Tallon?

Then, bending down to peer at the smiling painted face under the leaf of the bonnet, he exclaimed:

—No! Upon my word I believe it's little Bertie Tallon after all!

Stephen at his post by the window heard the old lady and the priest laugh together and heard the boys' murmur of admiration behind him as they passed forward to see the little boy who had to dance the sunbonnet dance by himself. A movement of impatience escaped him. He let the edge of the blind fall and, stepping down from the bench on which he had been standing, walked out of the chapel.

He passed out of the schoolhouse and halted under the shed that flanked the garden. From the theatre opposite came the muffled noise of the audience and sudden brazen clashes of the soldiers' band. The light spread upwards from the glass roof making the theatre seem a festive ark, anchored among the hulks of houses, her frail cables of lanterns looping her to her moorings. A sidedoor of the theatre opened suddenly and a shaft of light flew across the grassplots. A sudden burst of music issued from the ark, the prelude of a waltz: and when the sidedoor closed again the listener could hear the faint rhythm of the music. The sentiment of the opening bars, their languor and supple movement, evoked the incommunicable emotion which had been the cause of all his day's unrest and of his impatient movement of a moment before. His unrest issued from him like a wave of sound: and on the tide of flowing music the ark was journeying, trailing her cables of lanterns in her wake. Then a noise like dwarf artillery broke the movement. It was the clapping that greeted the entry of the dumbbell team on the stage.

At the far end of the shed near the street a speck of pink light showed in the darkness and as he walked towards it he became aware of a faint aromatic odour. Two boys were standing in the shelter of a doorway, smoking, and before he reached them he had recognised Heron by his voice.

—Here comes the noble Dedalus! cried a high throaty voice. Welcome to our trusty friend!

This welcome ended in a soft peal of mirthless laughter as Heron salaamed and then began to poke the ground with his cane.

—Here I am, said Stephen, halting and glancing from Heron to his friend.

The latter was a stranger to him but in the darkness, by the aid of the glowing cigarettetips, he could make out a pale dandyish face, over which a smile was travelling slowly, a tall overcoated figure and a hard hat. Heron did not trouble himself about an introduction but said instead:

—I was just telling my friend Wallis what a lark it would be tonight if you took off the rector in the part of the schoolmaster. It would be a ripping good joke.

Heron made a poor attempt to imitate for his friend Wallis the rector's pedantic bass and then, laughing at his failure, asked Stephen to do it.

—Go on, Dedalus, he urged, you can take him off rippingly. *He that will not hear the churcha let him be to theea as the heathena and the publicana.*

The imitation was prevented by a mild expression of anger from Wallis in whose mouthpiece the cigarette had become too tightly wedged.

—Damn this blankety blank holder, he said, taking it from his mouth and smiling and frowning upon it tolerantly. It's always getting stuck like that. Do you use a holder?

—I don't smoke, answered Stephen.

—No, said Heron, Dedalus is a model youth. He doesn't smoke and he doesn't go to bazaars and he doesn't flirt and he doesn't damn anything or damn all.

Stephen shook his head and smiled in his rival's flushed and mobile face, beaked like a bird's. He had often thought it strange the Vincent Heron had a bird's face as well as a bird's name. A shock of pale hair lay on the forehead like a ruffled crest: the forehead was narrow and bony and a thin hooked nose stood out between the closeset prominent eyes which were light and inexpressive. The rivals were school friends. They sat together in class, knelt together in the chapel, talked together after beads over their lunches. As the fellows in number one were undistinguished dullards Stephen and Heron had been during the year the virtual heads of the school. It was they who went up to the rector together to ask for a free day or to get a fellow off.

—O by the way, said Heron suddenly, I saw your governor going in.

The smile waned on Stephen's face. Any allusion

made to his father by a fellow or by a master put his
calm to rout in a moment. He waited in timorous silence to hear what Heron might say next. Heron, however, nudged him expressively with his elbow and said:

—You're a sly dog, Dedalus!

—Why so? said Stephen.

—You'd think butter wouldn't melt in your mouth,
said Heron. But I'm afraid you're a sly dog.

—Might I ask you what you are talking about? said
Stephen urbanely.

—Indeed you might, answered Heron. We saw her,
Wallis, didn't we? And deucedly pretty she is too. And
so inquisitive! *And what part does Stephen take, Mr
Dedalus? And will Stephen not sing, Mr Dedalus?*
Your governor was staring at her through that eyeglass
of his for all he was worth so that I think the old man
has found you out too. I wouldn't care a bit, by Jove.
She's ripping, isn't she, Wallis?

—Not half bad, answered Wallis quietly as he placed
his holder once more in the corner of his mouth.

A shaft of momentary anger flew through Stephen's
mind at these indelicate allusions in the hearing of a
stranger. For him there was nothing amusing in a girl's
interest and regard. All day he had thought of nothing
but their leavetaking on the steps of the tram at Harold's Cross, the stream of moody emotions it had made
to course through him, and the poem he had written
about it. All day he had imagined a new meeting with
her for he knew that she was to come to the play. The
old restless moodiness had again filled his breast as it
had done on the night of the party but had not found
an outlet in verse. The growth and knowledge of two
years of boyhood stood between then and now, forbidding such an outlet: and all day the stream of gloomy
tenderness within him had started forth and returned

upon itself in dark courses and eddies, wearying him in the end until the pleasantry of the prefect and the painted little boy had drawn from him a movement of impatience.

—So you may as well admit, Heron went on, that we've fairly found you out this time. You can't play the saint on me any more, that's one sure five.

A soft peal of mirthless laughter escaped from his lips and, bending down as before, he struck Stephen lightly across the calf of the leg with his cane, as if in jesting reproof.

Stephen's movement of anger had already passed. He was neither flattered nor confused but simply wished the banter to end. He scarcely resented what had seemed to him at first a silly indelicateness for he knew that the adventure in his mind stood in no danger from their words: and his face mirrored his rival's false smile.

—Admit! repeated Heron, striking him again with his cane across the calf of the leg.

The stroke was playful but not so lightly given as the first one had been. Stephen felt the skin tingle and glow slightly and almost painlessly; and bowing submissively, as if to meet his companion's jesting mood, began to recite the *Confiteor*. The episode ended well for both Heron and Wallis laughed indulgently at the irreverence.

The confession came only from Stephen's lips and, while they spoke the words, a sudden memory had carried him to another scene called up, as if by magic, at the moment when he had noted the faint cruel dimples at the corners of Heron's smiling lips and had felt the familiar stroke of the cane against his calf and had heard the familiar word of admonition:

—Admit.

It was towards the close of his first term in the college when he was in number six. His sensitive nature was still smarting under the lashes of an undivined and squalid way of life. His soul was still disquieted and cast down by the dull phenomenon of Dublin. He had emerged from a two years' spell of revery to find himself in the midst of a new scene, every event and figure of which affected him intimately, disheartened him or allured and, whether alluring or disheartening, filled him always with unrest and bitter thoughts. All the leisure which his school life left him was passed in the company of subversive writers whose gibes and violence of speech set up a ferment in his brain before they passed out of it into his crude writings.

The essay was for him the chief labour of his week and every Tuesday, as he marched from home to the school, he read his fate in the incidents of the way, pitting himself against some figure ahead of him and quickening his pace to outstrip it before a certain goal was reached or planting his steps scrupulously in the spaces of the patchwork of the footpath and telling himself that he would be first and not first in the weekly essay.

On a certain Tuesday the course of his triumphs was rudely broken. Mr Tate, the English master, pointed his finger at him and said bluntly:

—This fellow has heresy in his essay.

A hush fell on the class. Mr Tate did not break it but dug with his hand between his crossed thighs while his heavily starched linen creaked about his neck and wrists. Stephen did not look up. It was a raw spring morning and his eyes were still smarting and weak. He was conscious of failure and of detection, of the squalor of his own mind and home, and felt against his neck the raw edge of his turned and jagged collar.

A short loud laugh from Mr Tate set the class more at ease.

—Perhaps you didn't know that, he said.

—Where? asked Stephen.

Mr Tate withdrew his delving hand and spread out the essay.

—Here. It's about the Creator and the soul. Rrm . . . rrm . . . rrm. . . . Ah! *without a possibility of ever approaching nearer*. That's heresy.

Stephen murmured:

—I meant *without a possibility of ever reaching*.

It was a submission and Mr Tate, appeased, folded up the essay and passed it across to him, saying:

—O . . . Ah! *ever reaching*. That's another story.

But the class was not so soon appeased. Though nobody spoke to him of the affair after class he could feel about him a vague general malignant joy.

A few nights after this public chiding he was walking with a letter along the Drumcondra Road when he heard a voice cry:

—Halt!

He turned and saw three boys of his own class coming towards him in the dusk. It was Heron who had called out and, as he marched forward between his two attendants, he cleft the air before him with a thin cane, in time to their steps. Boland, his friend, marched beside him, a large grin on his face, while Nash came on a few steps behind, blowing from the pace and wagging his great red head.

As soon as the boys had turned into Clonliffe Road together they began to speak about books and writers, saying what books they were reading and how many books there were in their fathers' bookcases at home. Stephen listened to them in some wonderment for Boland was the dunce and Nash the idler of the class.

In fact after some talk about their favourite writers
Nash declared for Captain Marryat who, he said, was
the greatest writer.

—Fudge! said Heron. Ask Dedalus. Who is the
greatest writer, Dedalus?

Stephen noted the mockery in the question and
said:

—Of prose do you mean?

—Yes.

—Newman, I think.

—Is it Cardinal Newman? asked Boland.

—Yes, answered Stephen.

The grin broadened on Nash's freckled face as he
turned to Stephen and said:

—And do you like Cardinal Newman, Dedalus?

—O, many say that Newman has the best prose
sytle, Heron said to the other two in explanation. Of
course he's not a poet.

—And who is the best poet, Heron? asked Boland.

—Lord Tennyson, of course, answered Heron.

—O, yes, Lord Tennyson, said Nash. We have all his
poetry at home in a book.

At this Stephen forgot the silent vows he had been
making and burst out:

—Tennyson a poet! Why, he's only a rhymester!

—O, get out! said Heron. Everyone knows that
Tennyson is the greatest poet.

—And who do you think is the greatest poet? asked
Boland, nudging his neighbour.

—Byron, of course, answered Stephen.

Heron gave the lead and all three joined in a scorn-
ful laugh.

—What are you laughing at? asked Stephen.

—You, said Heron. Byron the greatest poet! He's
only a poet for uneducated people.

—He must be a fine poet! said Boland.

—You may keep your mouth shut, said Stephen, turning on him boldly. All you know about poetry is what you wrote up on the slates in the yard and were going to be sent to the loft for.

Boland, in fact, was said to have written on the slates in the yard a couplet about a classmate of his who often rode home from the college on a pony:

> As Tyson was riding into Jerusalem
> He fell and hurt his Alec Kafoozelum.

This thrust put the two lieutenants to silence but Heron went on:

—In any case Byron was a heretic and immoral too.

—I don't care what he was, cried Stephen hotly.

—You don't care whether he was a heretic or not? said Nash.

—What do you know about it? shouted Stephen. You never read a line of anything in your life except a trans or Boland either.

—I know that Byron was a bad man, said Boland.

—Here, catch hold of this heretic, Heron called out.

In a moment Stephen was a prisoner.

—Tate made you buck up the other day, Heron went on, about the heresy in your essay.

—I'll tell him tomorrow, said Boland.

—Will you? said Stephen. You'd be afraid to open your lips.

—Afraid?

—Ay. Afraid of your life.

—Behave yourself! cried Heron, cutting at Stephen's legs with his cane.

It was the signal for their onset. Nash pinioned his

arms behind while Boland seized a long cabbage stump which was lying in the gutter. Struggling and kicking under the cuts of the cane and the blows of the knotty stump Stephen was borne back against a barbed wire fence.

—Admit that Byron was no good.

—No.

—Admit.

—No.

—Admit.

—No. No.

At last after a fury of plunges he wrenched himself free. His tormentors set off towards Jones's Road, laughing and jeering at him, while he, torn and flushed and panting, stumbled after them half blinded with tears, clenching his fists madly and sobbing.

While he was still repeating the *Confiteor* amid the indulgent laughter of his hearers and while the scenes of that malignant episode were still passing sharply and swiftly before his mind he wondered why he bore no malice now to those who had tormented him. He had not forgotten a whit of their cowardice and cruelty but the memory of it called forth no anger from him. All the descriptions of fierce love and hatred which he had met in books had seemed to him therefore unreal. Even that night as he stumbled homewards along Jones's Road he had felt that some power was divesting him of that suddenwoven anger as easily as a fruit is divested of its soft ripe peel.

He remained standing with his two companions at the end of the shed, listening idly to their talk or to the bursts of applause in the theatre. She was sitting there among the others perhaps waiting for him to appear. He tried to recall her appearance but could not. He could remember only that she had worn a shawl about her head like a cowl and that her dark eyes had invited and unnerved him. He wondered had he been in her thoughts as she had been in his. Then in the dark and unseen by the other two he rested the tips of the fingers of one hand upon the palm of the other hand, scarcely touching it and yet pressing upon it lightly. But the pressure of her fingers had been lighter and steadier: and suddenly the memory of their touch traversed his brain and body like an invisible warm wave.

A boy came towards them, running along under the shed. He was excited and breathless.

—O, Dedalus, he cried, Doyle is in a great bake about you. You're to go in at once and get dressed for the play. Hurry up, you better.

—He's coming now, said Heron to the messenger with a haughty drawl, when he wants to.

The boy turned to Heron and repeated:

—But Doyle is in an awful bake.

—Will you tell Doyle with my best compliments that I damned his eyes? answered Heron.

—Well, I must go now, said Stephen, who cared little for such points of honour.

—I wouldn't, said Heron, damn me if I would. That's no way to send for one of the senior boys. In a bake, indeed! I think it's quite enough that you're taking a part in his bally old play.

This spirit of quarrelsome comradeship which he had observed lately in his rival had not seduced Stephen from his habits of quiet obedience. He mistrusted the turbulence and doubted the sincerity of such comradeship which seemed to him a sorry anticipation of manhood. The question of honour here raised was, like all such questions, trivial to him. While his mind had been pursuing its intangible phantoms and turning in irresolution from such pursuit he had heard about him the constant voices of his father and of his masters, urging him to be a gentleman above all things and urging him to be a good catholic above all things. These voices had now come to be hollowsounding in his ears. When the gymnasium had been opened he had heard another voice urging him to be strong and manly and healthy and when the movement towards national revival had begun to be felt in the college yet another voice had bidden him be true to his country and help to raise up her fallen language and tradition. In the profane world, as he foresaw, a worldly voice would bid him raise up his father's fallen state by his labours and, meanwhile, the voice of his school comrades urged him to be a decent fellow, to shield others from blame or to beg them off and to do his best to get free days for the school. And it was the din of all these hollowsounding voices that made him halt irresolutely in the pursuit of phantoms. He gave them ear only for a time but he was happy only when he was far from them, beyond their call, alone or in the company of phantasmal comrades.

In the vestry a plump freshfaced jesuit and an elderly man, in shabby blue clothes, were dabbling in a case of paints and chalks. The boys who had been painted walked about or stood still awkwardly, touching their faces in a gingerly fashion with their furtive fingertips. In the middle of the vestry a young jesuit, who was then on a visit to the college, stood rocking himself rhythmically from the tips of his toes to his heels and back again, his hands thrust well forward into his sidepockets. His small head set off with glossy red curls and his newly shaven face agreed well with the spotless decency of his soutane and with his spotless shoes.

As he watched this swaying form and tried to read for himself the legend of the priest's mocking smile there came into Stephen's memory a saying which he had heard from his father before he had been sent to Clongowes, that you could always tell a jesuit by the style of his clothes. At the same moment he thought he saw a likeness between his father's mind and that of this smiling welldressed priest: and he was aware of some desecration of the priest's office or of the vestry itself, whose silence was now routed by loud talk and joking and its air pungent with the smells of the gasjets and the grease.

While his forehead was being wrinkled and his jaws painted black and blue by the elderly man he listened distractedly to the voice of the plump young jesuit which bade him speak up and make his points clearly. He could hear the band playing *The Lily of Killarney* and knew that in a few moments the curtain would go up. He felt no stage fright but the thought of the part he had to play humiliated him. A remembrance of some of his lines made a sudden flush rise to his painted cheeks. He saw her serious alluring eyes watching him from among the audience and their image at once swept away his scruples, leaving his will compact. Another nature seemed to have been lent him: the infection of the excitement and youth about him entered into and transformed his moody mistrustfulness. For one rare moment he seemed to be clothed in the real apparel of boyhood: and, as he stood in the wings among the other players, he shared the common mirth amid which the drop scene was hauled upwards by two ablebodied priests with violent jerks and all awry.

A few moments after he found himself on the stage amid the garish gas and the dim scenery, acting before the innumerable faces of the void. It surprised him to see that the play which he had known at rehearsals for a disjointed lifeless thing had suddenly assumed a life of its own. It seemed now to play itself, he and his fellow actors aiding it with their parts. When the curtain fell on the last scene he heard the void filled with applause and, through a rift in the side scene, saw the simple body before which he had acted magically deformed, the void of faces breaking at all points and falling asunder into busy groups.

He left the stage quickly and rid himself of his mummery and passed out through the chapel into the college garden. Now that the play was over his nerves cried for some further adventure. He hurried onwards as if to overtake it. The doors of the theatre were all open and the audience had emptied out. On the lines which he had fancied the moorings of an ark a few lanterns swung in the night breeze, flickering cheerlessly. He mounted the steps from the garden in haste, eager that some prey should not elude him, and forced his way through the crowd in the hall and past the two jesuits who stood watching the exodus and bowing and shaking hands with the visitors. He pushed onward nervously, feigning a still greater haste and faintly conscious of the smiles and stares and nudges which his powdered head left in its wake.

When he came out on the steps he saw his family waiting for him at the first lamp. In a glance he noted that every figure of the group was familiar and ran down the steps angrily.

—I have to leave a message down in George's Street, he said to his father quickly. I'll be home after you.

Without waiting for his father's questions he ran across the road and began to walk at breakneck speed down the hill. He hardly knew where he was walking. Pride and hope and desire like crushed herbs in his heart sent up vapours of maddening incense before the eyes of his mind. He strode down the hill amid the tumult of suddenrisen vapours of wounded pride and fallen hope and baffled desire. They steamed upwards before his anguished eyes in dense and maddening fumes and passed away above him till at last the air was clear and cold again.

A film still veiled his eyes but they burned no longer. A power, akin to that which had often made anger or resentment fall from him, brought his steps to rest. He stood still and gazed up at the sombre porch of the morgue and from that to the dark cobbled laneway at its side. He saw the word *Lotts* on the wall of the lane and breathed slowly the rank heavy air.

—That is horse piss and rotted straw, he thought. It is a good odour to breathe. It will calm my heart. My heart is quite calm now. I will go back.

*   *   *

Stephen was once again seated beside his father in the corner of a railway carriage at Kingsbridge. He was travelling with his father by the night mail to Cork. As the train steamed out of the station he recalled his childish wonder of years before and every event of his first day at Clongowes. But he felt no wonder now. He saw the darkening lands slipping past him, the silent telegraphpoles passing his window swiftly every four seconds, the little glimmering stations, manned by a few silent sentries, flung by the mail behind her and twinkling for a moment in the darkness like fiery grains flung backwards by a runner.

He listened without sympathy to his father's evocation of Cork and of scenes of his youth, a tale broken by sighs or draughts from his pocketflask whenever the image of some dead friend appeared in it or whenever the evoker remembered suddenly the purpose of his actual visit. Stephen heard but could feel no pity. The images of the dead were all strange to him save that of uncle Charles, an image which had lately been fading out of memory. He knew, however, that his father's property was going to be sold by auction and in the manner of his own dispossession he felt the world give the lie rudely to his phantasy.

At Maryborough he fell asleep. When he awoke the train had passed out of Mallow and his father was stretched asleep on the other seat. The cold light of the dawn lay over the country, over the unpeopled fields and the closed cottages. The terror of sleep fascinated his mind as he watched the silent country or heard from time to time his father's deep breath or sudden sleepy movement. The neighbourhood of unseen sleepers filled him with strange dread as though they could harm him; and he prayed that the day might come quickly. His prayer, addressed neither to God nor saint, began with a shiver, as the chilly morning breeze crept through the chink of the carriage door to his feet, and ended in a trail of foolish words which he made to fit the insistent rhythm of the train; and silently, at intervals of four seconds, the telegraphpoles held the galloping notes of the music between punctual bars. This furious music allayed his dread and, leaning against the windowledge, he let his eyelids close again.

They drove in a jingle across Cork while it was still early morning and Stephen finished his sleep in a bedroom of the Victoria Hotel. The bright warm sunlight was streaming through the window and he could hear the din of traffic. His father was standing before the dressingtable, examining his hair and face and moustache with great care, craning his neck across the waterjug and drawing it back sideways to see the better. While he did so he sang softly to himself with quaint accent and phrasing:

'Tis youth and folly
Makes young men marry,
So here, my love, I'll
   No longer stay.
What can't be cured, sure,
Must be injured, sure,
   So I'll go to
   Amerikay.

My love she's handsome,
My love she's bonny:
She's like good whisky
   When it is new;
But when 'tis old
And growing cold
It fades and dies like
   The mountain dew.

The consciousness of the warm sunny city outside his window and the tender tremors with which his father's voice festooned the strange sad happy air, drove off all the mists of the night's ill humour from Stephen's brain. He got up quickly to dress and, when the song had ended, said:

—That's much prettier than any of your other *come-all-yous.*

—Do you think so? asked Mr Dedalus.

—I like it, said Stephen.

—It's a pretty old air, said Mr Dedalus, twirling the points of his moustache. Ah, but you should have heard Mick Lacy sing it! Poor Mick Lacy! He had little turns for it, grace notes he used to put in that I haven't got. That was the boy who could sing a *come-all-you,* if you like.

Mr Dedalus had ordered drisheens for breakfast and during the meal he crossexamined the waiter for local

news. For the most part they spoke at crosspurposes
when a name was mentioned, the waiter having in
mind the present holder and Mr Dedalus his father or
perhaps his grandfather.

—Well, I hope they haven't moved the Queen's College anyhow, said Mr Dedalus, for I want to show it to
this youngster of mine.

Along the Mardyke the trees were in bloom. They
entered the grounds of the college and were led by the
garrulous porter across the quadrangle. But their
progress across the gravel was brought to a halt after
every dozen or so paces by some reply of the porter's.

—Ah, do you tell me so? And is poor Pottlebelly
dead?

—Yes, sir. Dead, sir.

During these halts Stephen stood awkwardly behind
the two men, weary of the subject and waiting restlessly
for the slow march to begin again. By the time they
had crossed the quadrangle his restlessness had risen to
fever. He wondered how his father, whom he knew for
a shrewd suspicious man, could be duped by the servile
manners of the porter; and the lively southern speech
which had entertained him all the morning now irritated his ears.

They passed into the anatomy theatre where Mr
Dedalus, the porter aiding him, searched the desks for
his initials. Stephen remained in the background, de-
pressed more than ever by the darkness and silence of
the theatre and by the air it wore of jaded and formal
study. On the desk before him he read the word *Fœtus*
cut several times in the dark stained wood. The sudden
legend startled his blood: he seemed to feel the absent
students of the college about him and to shrink from
their company. A vision of their life, which his father's
words had been powerless to evoke, sprang up before

him out of the word cut in the desk. A broadshouldered student with a moustache was cutting in the letters with a jackknife, seriously. Other students stood or sat near him laughing at his handiwork. One jogged his elbow. The big student turned on him, frowning. He was dressed in loose grey clothes and had tan boots.

Stephen's name was called. He hurried down the steps of the theatre so as to be as far away from the vision as he could be and, peering closely at his father's initials, hid his flushed face.

But the word and the vision capered before his eyes as he walked back across the quadrangle and towards the college gate. It shocked him to find in the outer world a trace of what he had deemed till then a brutish and individual malady of his own mind. His recent monstrous reveries came thronging into his memory. They too had sprung up before him, suddenly and furiously, out of mere words. He had soon given in to them and allowed them to sweep across and abase his intellect, wondering always where they came from, from what den of monstrous images, and always weak and humble towards others, restless and sickened of himself when they had swept over him.

—Ay, bedad! And there's the Groceries sure enough! cried Mr Dedalus. You often heard me speak of the Groceries, didn't you, Stephen. Many's the time we went down there when our names had been marked, a crowd of us, Harry Peard and little Jack Mountain and Bob Dyas and Maurice Moriarty, the Frenchman, and Tom O'Grady and Mick Lacy that I told you of this morning and Joey Corbet and poor little good hearted Johnny Keevers of the Tantiles.

The leaves of the trees along the Mardyke were astir and whispering in the sunlight. A team of cricketers passed, agile young men in flannels and blazers, one of them carrying the long green wicketbag. In a quiet bystreet a German band of five players in faded uniforms and with battered brass instruments was playing to an audience of street arabs and leisurely messenger boys. A maid in a white cap and apron was watering a box of plants on a sill which shone like a slab of limestone in the warm glare. From another window open to the air came the sound of a piano, scale after scale rising into the treble.

Stephen walked on at his father's side, listening to stories he had heard before, hearing again the names of the scattered and dead revellers who had been the companions of his father's youth. And a faint sickness sighed in his heart. He recalled his own equivocal position in Belvedere, a free boy, a leader afraid of his own authority, proud and sensitive and suspicious, battling against the squalor of his life and against the riot of his mind. The letters cut in the stained wood of the desk stared upon him, mocking his bodily weakness and futile enthusiasms and making him loathe himself for his own mad and filthy orgies. The spittle in his throat grew bitter and foul to swallow and the faint sickness climbed to his brain so that for a moment he closed his eyes and walked on in darkness.

He could still hear his father's voice.

—When you kick out for yourself, Stephen—as I daresay you will one of those days—remember, whatever you do, to mix with gentlemen. When I was a young fellow I tell you I enjoyed myself. I mixed with fine decent fellows. Everyone of us could do something. One fellow had a good voice, another fellow was a good actor, another could sing a good comic song, another was a good oarsman or a good racketplayer, another could tell a good story and so on. We kept the ball rolling anyhow and enjoyed ourselves and saw a bit of life and we were none the worse of it either. But we were all gentlemen, Stephen—at least I hope we were—and bloody good honest Irishmen too. That's the kind of fellows I want you to associate with, fellows of the right kidney. I'm talking to you as a friend, Stephen. I don't believe in playing the stern father. I don't believe a son should be afraid of his father. No, I treat you as your grandfather treated me when I was a young chap. We were more like brothers than father and son. I'll never forget the first day he caught me smoking. I was standing at the end of the South Terrace one day with some maneens like myself and sure we thought we were grand fellows because we had pipes stuck in the corners of our mouths. Suddenly the governor passed. He didn't say a word, or stop even. But the next day, Sunday, we were out for a walk together and when we were coming home he took out his cigar case and said: *By the bye, Simon, I didn't know you smoked:* or something like that. Of course I tried to carry it off as best I could. *If you want a good smoke,* he said, *try one of these cigars. An American captain made me a present of them last night in Queenstown.*

Stephen heard his father's voice break into a laugh which was almost a sob.

—He was the handsomest man in Cork at that time, by God he was! The women used to stand to look after him in the street.

He heard the sob passing loudly down his father's throat and opened his eyes with a nervous impulse. The sunlight breaking suddenly on his sight turned the sky and clouds into a fantastic world of sombre masses with lakelike spaces of dark rosy light. His very brain was sick and powerless. He could scarcely interpret the letters of the signboards of the shops. By his monstrous

way of life he seemed to have put himself beyond the
limits of reality. Nothing moved him or spoke to him
from the real world unless he heard in it an echo of the
infuriated cries within him. He could respond to no
earthly or human appeal, dumb and insensible to the
call of summer and gladness and companionship,
wearied and dejected by his father's voice. He could
scarcely recognise as his his own thoughts, and repeated slowly to himself:

—I am Stephen Dedalus. I am walking beside my
father whose name is Simon Dedalus. We are in Cork,
in Ireland. Cork is a city. Our room is in the Victoria
Hotel. Victoria and Stephen and Simon. Simon and
Stephen and Victoria. Names.

The memory of his childhood suddenly grew dim.
He tried to call forth some of its vivid moments but
could not. He recalled only names: Dante, Parnell,
Clane, Clongowes. A little boy had been taught geography by an old woman who kept two brushes in her
wardrobe. Then he had been sent away from home to a
college. In the college he had made his first communion
and eaten slim jim out of his cricketcap and watched
the firelight leaping and dancing on the wall of a little
bedroom in the infirmary and dreamed of being dead,
of mass being said for him by the rector in a black and
gold cope, of being buried then in the little graveyard
of the community off the main avenue of limes. But he
had not died then. Parnell had died. There had been no
mass for the dead in the chapel and no procession. He
had not died but he had faded out like a film in the
sun. He had been lost or had wandered out of existence
for he no longer existed. How strange to think of him
passing out of existence in such a way, not by death
but by fading out in the sun or by being lost and
forgotten somewhere in the universe! It was strange to

see his small body appear again for a moment: a little boy in a grey belted suit. His hands were in his side-pockets and his trousers were tucked in at the knees by elastic bands.

On the evening of the day on which the property was sold Stephen followed his father meekly about the city from bar to bar. To the sellers in the market, to the barmen and barmaids, to the beggars who importuned him for a lob Mr Dedalus told the same tale, that he was an old Corkonian, that he had been trying for thirty years to get rid of his Cork accent up in Dublin and that Peter Pickackafax beside him was his eldest son but that he was only a Dublin jackeen.

They had set out early in the morning from New-combe's coffeehouse where Mr Dedalus' cup had rattled noisily against its saucer, and Stephen had tried to cover that shameful sign of his father's drinkingbout of the night before by moving his chair and coughing. One humiliation had succeeded another: the false smiles of the market sellers, the curvettings and oglings of the barmaids with whom his father flirted, the compliments and encouraging words of his father's friends. They had told him that he had a great look of his grandfather and Mr Dedalus had agreed that he was an ugly likeness. They had unearthed traces of a Cork accent in his speech and made him admit that the Lee was a much finer river than the Liffey. One of them in order to put his Latin to the proof had made him translate short passages from Dilectus and asked him whether it was correct to say: *Tempora mutantur nos et mutamur in illis* or *Tempora mutantur et nos mutamur in illis*. Another, a brisk old man, whom Mr Dedalus called Johnny Cashman, had covered him with confusion by asking him to say which were prettier, the Dublin girls or the Cork girls.

—He's not that way built, said Mr Dedalus. Leave him alone. He's a levelheaded thinking boy who doesn't bother his head about that kind of nonsense.

—Then he's not his father's son, said the little old man.

—I don't know, I'm sure, said Mr Dedalus, smiling complacently.

—Your father, said the little old man to Stephen, was the boldest flirt in the city of Cork in his day. Do you know that?

Stephen looked down and studied the tiled floor of the bar into which they had drifted.

—Now don't be putting ideas into his head, said Mr Dedalus. Leave him to his Maker.

—Yerra, sure I wouldn't put any ideas into his head. I'm old enough to be his grandfather. And I am a grandfather, said the little old man to Stephen. Do you know that?

—Are you? asked Stephen.

—Bedad I am, said the little old man. I have two bouncing grandchildren out at Sunday's Well. Now then! What age do you think I am? And I remember seeing your grandfather in his red coat riding out to hounds. That was before you were born.

—Ay, or thought of, said Mr Dedalus.

—Bedad I did, repeated the little old man. And, more than that, I can remember even your greatgrandfather, old John Stephen Dedalus, and a fierce old fireeater he was. Now then! There's a memory for you!

—That's three generations—four generations, said another of the company. Why, Johnny Cashman, you must be nearing the century.

—Well, I'll tell you the truth, said the little old man. I'm just twentyseven years of age.

—We're as old as we feel, Johnny, said Mr Dedalus.

And just finish what you have there, and we'll have another. Here, Tim or Tom or whatever your name is, give us the same again here. By God, I don't feel more than eighteen myself. There's that son of mine there not half my age and I'm a better man than he is any day of the week.

—Draw it mild now, Dedalus. I think it's time for you to take a back seat, said the gentleman who had spoken before.

—No, by God! asserted Mr Dedalus. I'll sing a tenor song against him or I'll vault a fivebarred gate against him or I'll run with him after the hounds across the country as I did thirty years ago along with the Kerry Boy and the best man for it.

—But he'll beat you here, said the little old man, tapping his forehead and raising his glass to drain it.

—Well, I hope he'll be as good a man as his father. That's all I can say, said Mr Dedalus.

—If he is, he'll do, said the little old man.

—And thanks be to God, Johnny, said Mr Dedalus, that we lived so long and did so little harm.

—But did so much good, Simon, said the little old man gravely. Thanks be to God we lived so long and did so much good.

Stephen watched the three glasses being raised from the counter as his father and his two cronies drank to the memory of their past. An abyss of fortune or of temperament sundered him from them. His mind seemed older than theirs: it shone coldly on their strifes and happiness and regrets like a moon upon a younger earth. No life or youth stirred in him as it had stirred in them. He had known neither the pleasure of companionship with others nor the vigour of rude male health nor filial piety. Nothing stirred within his soul but a cold and cruel and loveless lust. His childhood was dead or lost and with it his soul capable of simple joys, and he was drifting amid life like the barren shell of the moon.

> Art thou pale for weariness
> Of climbing heaven and gazing on the earth,
> Wandering companionless . . . ?

He repeated to himself the lines of Shelley's fragment. Its alternation of sad human ineffectualness with vast inhuman cycles of activity chilled him, and he forgot his own human and ineffectual grieving.

※　　※　　※

Stephen's mother and his brother and one of his cousins waited at the corner of quiet Foster Place while he and his father went up the steps and along the colonnade where the highland sentry was parading. When they had passed into the great hall and stood at the counter Stephen drew forth his orders on the governor of the bank of Ireland for thirty and three pounds; and these sums, the moneys of his exhibition and essay prize, were paid over to him rapidly by the teller in notes and in coin respectively. He bestowed them in his pockets and feigned composure and suffered the friendly teller, to whom his father chatted, to take his hand across the broad counter and wish him a brilliant career in after life. He was impatient of their voices and could not keep his feet at rest. But the teller still deferred the serving of others to say he was living in changed times and that there was nothing like giving a boy the best education that money could buy. Mr Dedalus lingered in the hall gazing about him and up at the roof and telling Stephen, who urged him to come out, that they were standing in the house of commons of the old Irish parliament.

—God help us! he said piously, to think of the men of those times, Stephen, Hely Hutchison and Flood and Henry Grattan and Charles Kendal Bushe, and the noblemen we have now, leaders of the Irish people at home and abroad. Why, by God, they wouldn't be seen dead in a tenacre field with them. No, Stephen, old chap, I'm sorry to say that they are only as I roved out one fine May morning in the merry month of sweet July.

A keen October wind was blowing round the bank. The three figures standing at the edge of the muddy path had pinched cheeks and watery eyes. Stephen looked at his thinly clad mother and remembered that a few days before he had seen a mantle priced at twenty guineas in the windows of Barnardo's.

—Well that's done, said Mr Dedalus.

—We had better go to dinner, said Stephen. Where?

—Dinner? said Mr Dedalus. Well, I suppose we had better, what?

—Some place that's not too dear, said Mrs Dedalus.

—Underdone's?

—Yes. Some quiet place.

—Come along, said Stephen quickly. It doesn't matter about the dearness.

He walked on before them with short nervous steps, smiling. They tried to keep up with him, smiling also at his eagerness.

—Take it easy like a good young fellow, said his father. We're not out for the half mile, are we?

For a swift season of merrymaking the money of his prizes ran through Stephen's fingers. Great parcels of groceries and delicacies and dried fruits arrived from the city. Every day he drew up a bill of fare for the family and every night led a party of three or four to the theatre to see *Ingomar* or *The Lady of Lyons*. In his coat pockets he carried squares of Vienna chocolate for his guests while his trousers' pockets bulged with masses of silver and copper coins. He bought presents for everyone, overhauled his room, wrote out resolutions, marshalled his books up and down their shelves, pored upon all kinds of price lists, drew up a form of commonwealth for the household by which every member of it held some office, opened a loan bank for his family and pressed loans on willing borrowers so that he might have the pleasure of making out receipts and reckoning the interests on the sums lent. When he could do no more he drove up and down the city in trams. Then the season of pleasure came to an end. The pot of pink enamel paint gave out and the wainscot of his bedroom remained with its unfinished and illplastered coat.

His household returned to its usual way of life. His mother had no further occasion to upbraid him for squandering his money. He too returned to his old life at school and all his novel enterprises fell to pieces. The commonwealth fell, the loan bank closed its coffers and its books on a sensible loss, the rules of life which he had drawn about himself fell into desuetude.

How foolish his aim had been! He had tried to build a breakwater of order and elegance against the sordid tide of life without him and to dam up, by rules of conduct and active interests and new filial relations, the powerful recurrence of the tides within him. Useless. From without as from within the water had flowed over his barriers: their tides began once more to jostle fiercely above the crumbled mole.

He saw clearly too his own futile isolation. He had not gone one step nearer the lives he had sought to approach nor bridged the restless shame and rancour that divided him from mother and brother and sister.

He felt that he was hardly of the one blood with them but stood to them rather in the mystical kinship of fosterage, fosterchild and fosterbrother.

He burned to appease the fierce longings of his heart before which everything else was idle and alien. He cared little that he was in mortal sin, that his life had grown to be a tissue of subterfuge and falsehood. Beside the savage desire within him to realise the enormities which he brooded on nothing was sacred. He bore cynically with the shameful details of his secret riots in which he exulted to defile with patience whatever image had attracted his eyes. By day and by night he moved among distorted images of the outer world. A figure that had seemed to him by day demure and innocent came towards him by night through the winding darkness of sleep, her face transfigured by a lecherous cunning, her eyes bright with brutish joy. Only the morning pained him with its dim memory of dark orgiastic riot, its keen and humiliating sense of transgression.

He returned to his wanderings. The veiled autumnal evenings led him from street to street as they had led him years before along the quiet avenues of Blackrock. But no vision of trim front gardens or of kindly lights in the windows poured a tender influence upon him now. Only at times, in the pauses of his desire, when the luxury that was wasting him gave room to a softer languor, the image of Mercedes traversed the background of his memory. He saw again the small white house and the garden of rosebushes on the road that led to the mountains and he remembered the sadly proud gesture of refusal which he was to make there, standing with her in the moonlit garden after years of estrangement and adventure. At those moments the soft speeches of Claude Melnotte rose to his lips and eased his unrest. A tender premonition touched him of the tryst he had then looked forward to and, in spite of the horrible reality which lay between his hope of then and now, of the holy encounter he had then imagined at which weakness and timidity and inexperience were to fall from him.

Such moments passed and the wasting fires of lust sprang up again. The verses passed from his lips and the inarticulate cries and the unspoken brutal words rushed forth from his brain to force a passage. His blood was in revolt. He wandered up and down the dark slimy streets peering into the gloom of lanes and doorways, listening eagerly for any sound. He moaned to himself like some baffled prowling beast. He wanted to sin with another of his kind, to force another being to sin with him and to exult with her in sin. He felt some dark presence moving irresistibly upon him from the darkness, a presence subtle and murmurous as a flood filling him wholly with itself. Its murmur besieged his ears like the murmur of some multitude in sleep; its subtle streams penetrated his being. His hands clenched convulsively and his teeth set together as he suffered the agony of its penetration. He stretched out his arms in the street to hold fast the frail swooning form that eluded him and incited him: and the cry that he had strangled for so long in his throat issued from his lips. It broke from him like a wail of despair from a hell of sufferers and died in a wail of furious entreaty, a cry for an iniquitous abandonment, a cry which was but the echo of an obscene scrawl which he had read on the oozing wall of a urinal.

He had wandered into a maze of narrow and dirty streets. From the foul laneways he heard bursts of hoarse riot and wrangling and the drawling of drunken singers. He walked onward, undismayed, wondering whether he had strayed into the quarter of the jews.

Women and girls dressed in long vivid gowns traversed the street from house to house. They were leisurely and perfumed. A trembling seized him and his eyes grew dim. The yellow gasflames arose before his troubled vision against the vapoury sky, burning as if before an altar. Before the doors and in the lighted halls groups were gathered arrayed as for some rite. He was in another world: he had awakened from a slumber of centuries.

He stood still in the middle of the roadway, his heart clamouring against his bosom in a tumult. A young woman dressed in a long pink gown laid her hand on his arm to detain him and gazed into his face. She said gaily:

—Good night, Willie dear!

Her room was warm and lightsome. A huge doll sat with her legs apart in the copious easychair beside the bed. He tried to bid his tongue speak that he might seem at ease, watching her as she undid her gown, noting the proud conscious movements of her perfumed head.

As he stood silent in the middle of the room she came over to him and embraced him gaily and gravely. Her round arms held him firmly to her and he, seeing her face lifted to him in serious calm and feeling the warm calm rise and fall of her breast, all but burst into hysterical weeping. Tears of joy and relief shone in his delighted eyes and his lips parted though they would not speak.

She passed her tinkling hand through his hair, calling him a little rascal.

—Give me a kiss, she said.

His lips would not bend to kiss her. He wanted to be held firmly in her arms, to be caressed slowly, slowly, slowly. In her arms he felt that he had suddenly become strong and fearless and sure of himself. But his lips would not bend to kiss her.

With a sudden movement she bowed his head and joined her lips to his and he read the meaning of her movements in her frank uplifted eyes. It was too much for him. He closed his eyes, surrendering himself to her, body and mind, conscious of nothing in the world but the dark pressure of her softly parting lips. They pressed upon his brain as upon his lips as though they were the vehicle of a vague speech; and between them he felt an unknown and timid pressure, darker than the swoon of sin, softer than sound or odour.

III

THE swift December dusk had come tumbling clownishly after its full day and, as he stared through the dull square of the window of the school-room, he felt his belly crave for its food. He hoped there would be stew for dinner, turnips and carrots and bruised potatoes and fat mutton pieces to be ladled out in thick peppered flourfattened sauce. Stuff it into you, his belly counselled him.

It would be a gloomy secret night. After early night-fall the yellow lamps would light up, here and there, the squalid quarter of the brothels. He would follow a devious course up and down the streets, circling always nearer and nearer in a tremor of fear and joy, until his feet led him suddenly round a dark corner. The whores would be just coming out of their houses making ready for the night, yawning lazily after their sleep and settling the hairpins in their clusters of hair. He would pass by them calmly waiting for a sudden movement of his own will or a sudden call to his sinloving soul from their soft perfumed flesh. Yet as he prowled in quest of that call, his senses, stultified only by his desire, would note keenly all that wounded or shamed them; his eyes, a ring of porter froth on a clothless table or a photograph of two soldiers standing to attention or a gaudy playbill; his ears, the drawling jargon of greeting:

—Hello, Bertie, any good in your mind?

—Is that you, pigeon?

—Number ten. Fresh Nelly is waiting on you.

—Goodnight, husband! Coming in to have a short time?

The equation on the page of his scribbler began to spread out a widening tail, eyed and starred like a peacock's; and, when the eyes and stars of its indices had been eliminated, began slowly to fold itself together again. The indices appearing and disappearing were eyes opening and closing; the eyes opening and closing were stars being born and being quenched. The vast cycle of starry life bore his weary mind outward to its verge and inward to its centre, a distant music accompanying him outward and inward. What music? The music came nearer and he recalled the words, the words of Shelley's fragment upon the moon wandering companionless, pale for weariness. The stars began to crumble and a cloud of fine stardust fell through space.

The dull light fell more faintly upon the page whereon another equation began to unfold itself slowly and to spread abroad its widening tail. It was his own soul going forth to experience, unfolding itself sin by sin, spreading abroad the balefire of its burning stars and folding back upon itself, fading slowly, quenching its own lights and fires. They were quenched: and the cold darkness filled chaos.

A cold lucid indifference reigned in his soul. At his

first violent sin he had felt a wave of vitality pass out of him and had feared to find his body or his soul maimed by the excess. Instead the vital wave had carried him on its bosom out of himself and back again when it receded: and no part of body or soul had been maimed but a dark peace had been established between them. The chaos in which his ardour extinguished itself was a cold indifferent knowledge of himself. He had sinned mortally not once but many times and he knew that, while he stood in danger of eternal damnation for the first sin alone, by every succeeding sin he multiplied his guilt and his punishment. His days and works and thoughts could make no atonement for him, the fountains of sanctifying grace having ceased to refresh his soul. At most, by an alms given to a beggar whose blessing he fled from, he might hope wearily to win for himself some measure of actual grace. Devotion had gone by the board. What did it avail to pray when he knew that his soul lusted after its own destruction? A certain pride, a certain awe, withheld him from offering to God even one prayer at night though he knew it was in God's power to take away his life while he slept and hurl his soul hellward ere he could beg for mercy. His pride in his own sin, his loveless awe of God, told him that his offence was too grievous to be atoned for in whole or in part by a false homage to the Allseeing and Allknowing.

—Well now, Ennis, I declare you have a head and so has my stick! Do you mean to say that you are not able to tell me what a surd is?

The blundering answer stirred the embers of his contempt of his fellows. Towards others he felt neither shame nor fear. On Sunday mornings as he passed the churchdoor he glanced coldly at the worshippers who stood bareheaded, four deep, outside the church, morally present at the mass which they could neither see nor hear. Their dull piety and the sickly smell of the cheap hairoil with which they had anointed their heads repelled him from the altar they prayed at. He stooped to the evil of hypocrisy with others, sceptical of their innocence which he could cajole so easily.

On the wall of his bedroom hung an illuminated scroll, the certificate of his prefecture in the college of the sodality of the Blessed Virgin Mary. On Saturday mornings when the sodality met in the chapel to recite the little office his place was a cushioned kneelingdesk at the right of the altar from which he led his wing of boys through the responses. The falsehood of his position did not pain him. If at moments he felt an impulse to rise from his post of honour and, confessing before them all his unworthiness, to leave the chapel, a glance at their faces restrained him. The imagery of the psalms of prophecy soothed his barren pride. The glories of Mary held his soul captive: spikenard and myrrh and frankincense, symbolising the preciousness of God's gifts to her soul, rich garments, symbolising her royal lineage, her emblems, the lateflowering plant and lateblossoming tree, symbolising the agelong gradual growth of her cultus among men. When it fell to him to read the lesson towards the close of the office he read it in a veiled voice, lulling his conscience to its music.

Quasi cedrus exaltata sum in Libanon et quasi cupressus in monte Sion. Quasi palma exaltata sum in Gades et quasi plantatio rosae in Jericho. Quasi uliva speciosa in campis et quasi platanus exaltata sum juxta aquam in plateis. Sicut cinnamomum et balsamum aromatizans odorem dedi et quasi myrrha electa dedi suavitatem odoris.

His sin, which had covered him from the sight of God, had led him nearer to the refuge of sinners. Her eyes seemed to regard him with mild pity; her holiness, a strange light glowing faintly upon her frail flesh, did not humiliate the sinner who approached her. If ever he was impelled to cast sin from him and to repent the impulse that moved him was the wish to be her knight. If ever his soul, reentering her dwelling shyly after the frenzy of his body's lust had spent itself, was turned towards her whose emblem is the morning star, *bright and musical, telling of heaven and infusing peace*, it was when her names were murmured softly by lips whereon there still lingered foul and shameful words, the savour itself of a lewd kiss.

That was strange. He tried to think how it could be but the dusk, deepening in the schoolroom, covered over his thoughts. The bell rang. The master marked the sums and cuts to be done for the next lesson and went out. Heron, beside Stephen, began to hum tunelessly.

My excellent friend Bombados.

Ennis, who had gone to the yard, came back, saying:

—The boy from the house is coming up for the rector.

A tall boy behind Stephen rubbed his hands and said:

—That's game ball. We can scut the whole hour. He won't be in till after half two. Then you can ask him questions on the catechism, Dedalus.

Stephen, leaning back and drawing idly on his scribbler, listened to the talk about him which Heron checked from time to time by saying:

—Shut up, will you. Don't make such a bally racket!

It was strange too that he found an arid pleasure in

following up to the end the rigid lines of the doctrines of the church and penetrating into obscure silences only to hear and feel the more deeply his own condemnation. The sentence of saint James which says that he who offends against one commandment becomes guilty of all had seemed to him first a swollen phrase until he had begun to grope in the darkness of his own state. From the evil seed of lust all other deadly sins had sprung forth: pride in himself and contempt of others, covetousness in using money for the purchase of unlawful pleasure, envy of those whose vices he could not reach to and calumnious murmuring against the pious, gluttonous enjoyment of food, the dull glowering anger amid which he brooded upon his longing, the swamp of spiritual and bodily sloth in which his whole being had sunk.

As he sat in his bench gazing calmly at the rector's shrewd harsh face his mind wound itself in and out of the curious questions proposed to it. If a man had stolen a pound in his youth and had used that pound to amass a huge fortune how much was he obliged to give back, the pound he had stolen only or the pound together with the compound interest accruing upon it or all his huge fortune? If a layman in giving baptism pour the water before saying the words is the child baptised? Is baptism with a mineral water valid? How comes it that while the first beatitude promises the kingdom of heaven to the poor of heart the second beatitude promises also to the meek that they shall possess the land? Why was the sacrament of the eucharist instituted under the two species of bread and wine if Jesus Christ be present body and blood, soul and divinity, in the bread alone and in the wine alone? Does a tiny particle of the consecrated bread contain all the body and blood of Jesus Christ or a part only of the body and blood? If the wine change into vinegar and the host crumble into corruption after they have been consecrated is Jesus Christ still present under their species as God and as man?

—Here he is! Here he is!

A boy from his post at the window had seen the rector come from the house. All the catechisms were opened and all heads bent upon them silently. The rector entered and took his seat on the dais. A gentle kick from the tall boy in the bench behind urged Stephen to ask a difficult question.

The rector did not ask for a catechism to hear the lesson from. He clasped his hands on the desk and said:

—The retreat will begin on Wednesday afternoon in honour of saint Francis Xavier whose feast day is Saturday. The retreat will go on from Wednesday to Friday. On Friday confession will be heard all the afternoon after beads. If any boys have special confessors perhaps it will be better for them not to change. Mass will be on Saturday morning at nine o'clock and general communion for the whole college. Saturday will be a free day. Sunday of course. But Saturday and Sunday being free days some boys might be inclined to think that Monday is a free day also. Beware of making that mistake. I think you, Lawless, are likely to make that mistake.

—I, sir? Why, sir?

A little wave of quiet mirth broke forth over the class of boys from the rector's grim smile. Stephen's heart began slowly to fold and fade with fear like a withering flower.

The rector went on gravely:

—You are all familiar with the story of the life of saint Francis Xavier, I suppose, the patron of your college. He came of an old and illustrious Spanish family and you remember that he was one of the first followers of saint Ignatius. They met in Paris where Francis Xavier was professor of philosophy at the university. This young and brilliant nobleman and man of letters entered heart and soul into the ideas of our glorious founder, and you know that he, at his own desire, was sent by saint Ignatius to preach to the Indians He is called, as you know, the apostle of the Indies. He went from country to country in the east, from Africa to India, from India to Japan, baptising the people. He is said to have baptised as many as ten thousand idolaters in one month. It is said that his right arm had grown powerless from having been raised so often over the heads of those whom he baptised. He wished then to go to China to win still more souls for God but he died of fever on the island of Sancian. A great saint, saint Francis Xavier! A great soldier of God!

The rector paused and then, shaking his clasped hands before him, went on:

—He had the faith in him that moves mountains. Ten thousand souls won for God in a single month! That is a true conqueror, true to the motto of our order: *ad majorem Dei gloriam!* A saint who has great power in heaven, remember: power to intercede for us in our grief, power to obtain whatever we pray for if it be for the good of our souls, power above all to obtain for us the grace to repent if we be in sin. A great saint, saint Francis Xavier! A great fisher of souls!

He ceased to shake his clasped hands and, resting them against his forehead, looked right and left of them keenly at his listeners out of his dark stern eyes.

In the silence their dark fire kindled the dusk into a tawny glow. Stephen's heart had withered up like a flower of the desert that feels the simoom coming from afar.

*   *   *

*—Remember only thy last things and thou shalt not sin for ever—*words taken, my dear little brothers in Christ, from the book of Ecclesiastes, seventh chapter, fortieth verse. In the name of the Father and of the Son and of the Holy Ghost. Amen.

Stephen sat in the front bench of the chapel. Father Arnall sat at the table to the left of the altar. He wore about his shoulders a heavy cloak; his pale face was drawn and his voice broken with rheum. The figure of his old master, so strangely rearisen, brought back to Stephen's mind his life at Clongowes: the wide playgrounds, swarming with boys, the square ditch, the little cemetery off the main avenue of limes where he had dreamed of being buried, the firelight on the wall of the infirmary where he lay sick, the sorrowful face of Brother Michael. His soul, as these memories came back to him, became again a child's soul.

—We are assembled here today, my dear little brothers in Christ, for one brief moment far away from the busy bustle of the outer world to celebrate and to honour one of the greatest of saints, the apostle of the Indies, the patron saint also of your college, saint Francis Xavier. Year after year for much longer than any of you, my dear little boys, can remember or than I can remember the boys of this college have met in this very chapel to make their annual retreat before the feast day of their partron saint. Time has gone on and brought with it its changes. Even in the last few years what changes can most of you not remember? Many of the boys who sat in those front benches a few years ago are perhaps now in distant lands, in the burning tropics or immersed in professional duties or in seminaries or voyaging over the vast expanse of the deep or, it may be, already called by the great God to another life and to the rendering up of their stewardship. And still as the years roll by, bringing with them changes for good and bad, the memory of the great saint is honoured by the boys of his college who make every year their annual retreat on the days preceding the feast day set apart by our holy mother the church to transmit to all the ages the name and fame of one of the greatest sons of catholic Spain.

—Now what is the meaning of this word *retreat* and why is it allowed on all hands to be a most salutary practice for all who desire to lead before God and in the eyes of men a truly christian life? A retreat, my dear boys, signifies a withdrawal for a while from the cares of our life, the cares of this workaday world, in order to examine the state of our conscience, to reflect on the mysteries of holy religion and to understand better why we are here in this world. During these few days I intend to put before you some thoughts concerning the four last things. They are, as you know from your catechism, death, judgment, hell and heaven. We shall try to understand them fully during these few days so that we may derive from the understanding of them a lasting benefit to our souls. And remember, my dear boys, that we have been sent into this world for one thing and for one thing alone: to do God's holy will and to save our immortal souls. All else is worthless. One thing alone is needful, the salvation of one's soul. What doth it profit a man to gain the whole world if he suffer the loss of his immortal soul? Ah, my dear boys, believe me there is nothing in this wretched world that can make up for such a loss.

—I will ask you therefore, my dear boys, to put away

from your minds during these few days all worldly thoughts, whether of study or pleasure or ambition, and to give all your attention to the state of your souls. I need hardly remind you that during the days of the retreat all boys are expected to preserve a quiet and pious demeanour and to shun all loud unseemly pleasure. The elder boys, of course, will see that this custom is not infringed and I look especially to the prefects and officers of the sodality of Our Blessed Lady and of the sodality of the holy angels to set a good example to their fellowstudents.

—Let us try therefore to make this retreat in honour of saint Francis with our whole heart and our whole mind. God's blessing will then be upon all your year's studies. But, above and beyond all, let this retreat be one to which you can look back in after years when maybe you are far from this college and among very different surroundings, to which you can look back with joy and thankfulness and give thanks to God for having granted you this occasion of laying the first foundation of a pious honourable zealous christian life. And if, as may so happen, there be at this moment in these benches any poor soul who has had the unutterable misfortune to lose God's holy grace and to fall into grievous sin I feverently trust and pray that this retreat may be the turningpoint in the life of that soul. I pray to God through the merits of its zealous servant Francis Xavier that such a soul may be led to sincere repentance and that the holy communion on saint Francis' day of this year may be a lasting covenant between God and that soul. For just and unjust, for saint and sinner alike, may this retreat be a memorable one.

—Help me, my dear little brothers in Christ. Help me by your pious attention, by your own devotion, by

your outward demeanour. Banish from your minds all
worldly thoughts and think only of the last things,
death, judgment, hell and heaven. He who remembers
these things, says Ecclesiastes, shall not sin for ever. He
who remembers the last things will act and think with
them always before his eyes. He will live a good life
and die a good death, believing and knowing that, if he
has sacrificed much in this earthly life, it will be given
to him a hundredfold and a thousandfold more in the
life to come, in the kingdom without end—a blessing,
my dear boys, which I wish you from my heart, one
and all, in the name of the Father and of the Son and
of the Holy Ghost. Amen.

As he walked home with silent companions a thick
fog seemed to compass his mind. He waited in stupor
of mind till it should lift and reveal what it had hidden.
He ate his dinner with surly appetite and, when the
meal was over and the greasestrewn plates lay abandoned on the table, he rose and went to the window,
clearing the thick scum from his mouth with his tongue
and licking it from his lips. So he had sunk to the state
of a beast that licks his chaps after meat. This was the
end; and a faint glimmer of fear began to pierce the fog
of his mind. He pressed his face against the pane of the
window and gazed out into the darkening street. Forms
passed this way and that through the dull light. And
that was life. The letters of the name of Dublin lay
heavily upon his mind, pushing one another surlily
hither and thither with slow boorish insistence. His soul
was fattening and congealing into a gross grease, plunging ever deeper in its dull fear into a sombre threatening dusk, while the body that was his stood, listless and
dishonoured, gazing out of darkened eyes, helpless, perturbed and human for a bovine god to stare upon.

The next day brought death and judgment, stirring

his soul slowly from its listless despair. The faint glimmer of fear became a terror of spirit as the hoarse voice of the preacher blew death into his soul. He suffered its agony. He felt the deathchill touch the extremities and creep onward towards the heart, the film of death veiling the eyes, the bright centres of the brain extinguished one by one like lamps, the last sweat oozing upon the skin, the powerlessness of the dying limbs, the speech thickening and wandering and failing, the heart throbbing faintly and more faintly, all but vanquished, the breath, the poor breath, the poor helpless human spirit, sobbing and sighing, gurgling and rattling in the throat. No help! No help! He, he himself, his body to which he had yielded was dying. Into the grave with it! Nail it down into a wooden box, the corpse. Carry it out of the house on the shoulders of hirelings. Thrust it out of men's sight into a long hole in the ground, into the grave, to rot, to feed the mass of its creeping worms and to be devoured by scuttling plumpbellied rats.

And while the friends were still standing in tears by the bedside the soul of the sinner was judged. At the last moment of consciousness the whole earthly life passed before the vision of the soul and, ere it had time to reflect, the body had died and the soul stood terrified before the judgmentseat. God, who had long been merciful, would then be just. He had long been patient, pleading with the sinful soul, giving it time to repent, sparing it yet awhile. But that time had gone. Time was to sin and to enjoy, time was to scoff at God and at the warnings of His holy church, time was to defy His majesty, to disobey His commands, to hoodwink one's fellow men, to commit sin after sin and sin after sin and to hide one's corruption from the sight of men. But that time was over. Now it was God's turn: and He was not to be hoodwinked or deceived. Every sin would then come forth from its lurkingplace, the most rebellious against the divine will and the most degrading to our poor corrupt nature, the tiniest imperfection and the most heinous atrocity. What did it avail then to have been a great emperor, a great general, a marvellous inventor, the most learned of the learned? All were as one before the judgmentseat of God. He would reward the good and punish the wicked. One single instant was enough for the trial of a man's soul. One single instant after the body's death, the soul had been weighed in the balance. The particular judgment was over and the soul had passed to the abode of bliss or to the prision of purgatory or had been hurled howling into hell.

Nor was that all. God's justice had still to be vindicated before men: after the particular there still remained the general judgment. The last day had come. Doomsday was at hand. The stars of heaven were falling upon the earth like the figs cast by the figtree which the wind had shaken. The sun, the great luminary of the universe, had become as sackcloth of hair. The moon was bloodred. The firmament was as a scroll rolled away. The archangel Michael, the prince of the heavenly host, appeared glorious and terrible against the sky. With one foot on the sea and one foot on the land he blew from the archangelical trumpet the brazen death of time. The three blasts of the angel filled all the universe. Time is, time was but time shall be no more. At the last blast the souls of universal humanity throng towards the valley of Jehoshaphat, rich and poor, gentle and simple, wise and foolish, good and wicked. The soul of every human being that has ever existed, the souls of all those who shall yet be born, all the sons and daughters of Adam, all are assembled on that su-

preme day. And lo the supreme judge is coming! No
longer the lowly Lamb of God, no longer the meek
Jesus of Nazareth, no longer the Man of Sorrows, no
longer the Good Shepherd, He is seen now coming
upon clouds, in great power and majesty, attended by
nine choirs of angels, angels and archangels, principali-
ties, powers and virtues, thrones and dominations,
cherubim and seraphim, God Omnipotent, God Everlasting. He speaks: and His voice is heard even at the
farthest limits of space, even in the bottomless abyss.
Supreme Judge, from His sentence there will be and
can be no appeal. He calls the just to His side, bidding
them enter into the kingdom, the eternity of bliss, prepared for them. The unjust He casts from Him, crying
in His offended majesty: *Depart from me, ye cursed,
into everlasting fire which was prepared for the devil
and his angels.* O what agony then for the miserable
sinners! Friend is torn apart from friend, children are
torn from their parents, husbands from their wives.
The poor sinner holds out his arms to those who were
dear to him in this earthly world, to those whose simple
piety perhaps he made a mock of, to those who counselled him and tried to lead him on the right path, to a
kind brother, to a loving sister, to the mother and father who loved him so dearly. But it is too late: the just
turn away from the wretched damned souls which now
appear before the eyes of all in their hideous and evil
character. O you hypocrites, O you whited sepulchres,
O you who present a smooth smiling face to the world
while your soul within is a foul swamp of sin, how
will it fare with you in that terrible day?

And this day will come, shall come, must come; the
day of death and the day of judgment. It is appointed
unto man to die and after death the judgment. Death is
certain. The time and manner are uncertain, whether

from long disease or from some unexpected accident; the Son of God cometh at an hour when you little expect Him. Be therefore ready every moment, seeing that you may die at any moment. Death is the end of us all. Death and judgment, brought into the world by the sin of our first parents, are the dark portals that close our earthly existence, the portals that open into the unknown and the unseen, portals through which every soul must pass, alone, unaided save by its good works, without friend or brother or parent or master to help it, alone and trembling. Let that thought be ever before our minds and then we cannot sin. Death, a cause of terror to the sinner, is a blessed moment for him who has walked in the right path, fulfilling the duties of his station in life, attending to his morning and evening prayers, approaching the holy sacrament frequently and performing good and merciful works. For the pious and believing catholic, for the just man, death is no cause of terror. Was it not Addison, the great English writer, who, when on his deathbed, sent for the wicked young earl of Warwick to let him see how a christian can meet his end. He it is and he alone, the pious and believing christian, who can say in his heart:

> O grave, where is thy victory?
> O death, where is thy sting?

Every word of it was for him. Against his sin, foul and secret, the whole wrath of God was aimed. The preacher's knife had probed deeply into his diseased conscience and he felt now that his soul was festering in sin. Yes, the preacher was right. God's turn had come. Like a beast in its lair his soul had lain down in its own filth but the blasts of the angel's trumpet had driven him forth from the darkness of sin

into the light. The words of doom cried by the angel
shattered in an instant his presumptuous peace. The
wind of the last day blew through his mind; his sins,
the jeweleyed harlots of his imagination, fled before the
hurricane, squeaking like mice in their terror and huddled under a mane of hair.

As he crossed the square, walking homeward, the
light laughter of a girl reached his burning ear. The
frail gay sound smote his heart more strongly than a
trumpetblast, and, not daring to lift his eyes, he turned
aside and gazed, as he walked, into the shadow of the
tangled shrubs. Shame rose from his smitten heart and
flooded his whole being. The image of Emma appeared
before him and, under her eyes, the flood of shame
rushed forth anew from his heart. If she knew to what
his mind had subjected her or how his brutelike lust
had torn and trampled upon her innocence! Was that
boyish love? Was that chivalry? Was that poetry? The
sordid details of his orgies stank under his very nostrils: the sootcoated packet of pictures which he had
hidden in the flue of the fireplace and in the presence
of whose shameless or bashful wantonness he lay for
hours sinning in thought and deed; his monstrous
dreams, peopled by apelike creatures and by harlots
with gleaming jewel eyes; the foul long letters he had
written in the joy of guilty confession and carried secretly for days and days only to throw them under
cover of night among the grass in the corner of a field
or beneath some hingeless door or in some niche in the
hedges where a girl might come upon them as she
walked by and read them secretly. Mad! Mad! Was it
possible he had done these things? A cold sweat broke
out upon his forehead as the foul memories condensed
within his brain.

When the agony of shame had passed from him he

tried to raise his soul from its abject powerlessness. God and the Blessed Virgin were too far from him: God was too great and stern and the Blessed Virgin too pure and holy. But he imagined that he stood near Emma in a wide land and, humbly and in tears, bent and kissed the elbow of her sleeve.

In the wide land under a tender lucid evening sky, a cloud drifting westward amid a pale green sea of heaven, they stood together, children that had erred. Their error had offended deeply God's majesty though it was the error of two children, but it had not offended her whose beauty *is not like earthly beauty, dangerous to look upon, but like the morning star which is its emblem, bright and musical.* The eyes were not offended which she turned upon them nor reproachful. She placed their hands together, hand in hand, and said, speaking to their hearts:

—Take hands, Stephen and Emma. It is a beautiful evening now in heaven. You have erred but you are always my children. It is one heart that loves another heart. Take hands together, my dear children, and you will be happy together and your hearts will love each other.

The chapel was flooded by the dull scarlet light that filtered through the lowered blinds; and through the fissure between the last blind and the sash a shaft of wan light entered like a spear and touched the embossed brasses of the candlesticks upon the altar that gleamed like the battleworn mail armour of angels.

Rain was falling on the chapel, on the garden, on the college. It would rain for ever, noiselessly. The water would rise inch by inch, covering the grass and shrubs, covering the trees and houses, covering the monuments and the mountain tops. All life would be choked off, noiselessly: birds, men, elephants, pigs, children: noiselessly floating corpses amid the litter of the wreckage of the world. Forty days and forty nights the rain would fall till the waters covered the face of the earth.

It might be. Why not?

—*Hell has enlarged its soul and opened its mouth without any limits*—words taken, my dear little brothers in Christ Jesus, from the book of Isaias, fifth chapter, fourteenth verse. In the name of the Father and of the Son and of the Holy Ghost. Amen.

The preacher took a chainless watch from a pocket within his soutane and, having considered its dial for a moment in silence, placed it silently before him on the table.

He began to speak in a quiet tone.

—Adam and Eve, my dear boys, were, as you know, our first parents and you will remember that they were created by God in order that the seats in heaven left vacant by the fall of Lucifer and his rebellious angels might be filled again. Lucifer, we are told, was a son of the morning, a radiant and mighty angel; yet he fell: he fell and there fell with him a third part of the host of heaven: he fell and was hurled with his rebellious angels into hell. What his sin was we cannot say. Theologians consider that it was the sin of pride, the sinful thought conceived in an instant: *non serviam: I will not serve*. That instant was his ruin. He offended the majesty of God by the sinful thought of one instant and God cast him out of heaven into hell for ever.

—Adam and Eve were then created by God and placed in Eden, in the plain of Damascus, that lovely garden resplendent with sunlight and colour, teeming with luxuriant vegetation. The fruitful earth gave them her bounty: beasts and birds were their willing servants: they knew not the ills our flesh is heir to, disease and poverty and death: all that a great and generous

God could do for them was done. But there was one condition imposed on them by God: obedience to His word. They were not to eat of the fruit of the forbidden tree.

—Alas, my dear little boys, they too fell. The devil, once a shining angel, a son of the morning, now a foul fiend, came in the shape of a serpent, the subtlest of all the beasts of the field. He envied them. He, the fallen great one, could not bear to think that man, a being of clay, should possess the inheritance which he by his sin had forfeited for ever. He came to the woman, the weaker vessel, and poured the poison of his eloquence into her ear, promising her—O, the blasphemy of that promise!—that if she and Adam ate of the forbidden fruit they would become as gods, nay as God Himself. Eve yielded to the wiles of the archtempter. She ate the apple and gave it also to Adam who had not the moral courage to resist her. The poison tongue of Satan had done its work. They fell.

—And then the voice of God was heard in that garden, calling His creature man to account: and Michael, prince of the heavenly host, with a sword of flame in his hand appeared before the guilty pair and drove them forth from Eden into the world, the world of sickness and striving, of cruelty and disappointment, of labour and hardship, to earn their bread in the sweat of their brow. But even then how merciful was God! He took pity on our poor degraded parents and promised that in the fulness of time He would send down from heaven One who would redeem them, make them once more children of God and heirs to the kingdom of heaven: and that One, that Redeemer of fallen man, was to be God's onlybegotten Son, the Second Person of the Most Blessed Trinity, the Eternal Word.

—He came. He was born of a virgin pure, Mary the

virgin mother. He was born in a poor cowhouse in Judea and lived as a humble carpenter for thirty years until the hour of His mission had come. And then, filled with love for men, He went forth and called to men to hear the new gospel.

—Did they listen? Yes, they listened but would not hear. He was seized and bound like a common criminal, mocked at as a fool, set aside to give place to a public robber, scourged with five thousand lashes, crowned with a crown of thorns, hustled through the streets by the jewish rabble and the Roman soldiery, stripped of His garments and hanged upon a gibbet and His side was pierced with a lance and from the wounded body of Our Lord water and blood issued continually.

—Yet even then, in that hour of supreme agony, Our Merciful Redeemer had pity for mankind. Yet even there, on the hill of Calvary, He founded the holy catholic church against which, it is promised, the gates of hell shall not prevail. He founded it upon the rock of ages and endowed it with His grace, with sacraments and sacrifice, and promised that if men would obey the word of His church they would still enter into eternal life but if, after all that had been done for them, they still persisted in their wickedness there remained for them an eternity of torment: hell.

The preacher's voice sank. He paused, joined his palms for an instant, parted them. Then he resumed:

—Now let us try for a moment to realise, as far as we can, the nature of that abode of the damned which the justice of an offended God has called into existence for the eternal punishment of sinners. Hell is a strait and dark and foulsmelling prison, an abode of demons and lost souls, filled with fire and smoke. The straitness of this prisonhouse is expressly designed by God to punish those who refused to be bound by His laws. In earthly prisons the poor captive has at least some liberty of movement, were it only within the four walls of his cell or in the gloomy yard of his prison. Not so in hell. There, by reason of the great number of the damned, the prisoners are heaped together in their awful prison, the walls of which are said to be four thousand miles thick: and the damned are so utterly bound and helpless that, as a blessed saint, saint Anselm, writes in his book on similitudes, they are not even able to remove from the eye a worm that gnaws it.

—They lie in exterior darkness. For, remember, the fire of hell gives forth no light. As, at the command of God, the fire of the Babylonian furnace lost its heat but not its light so, at the command of God, the fire of hell, while retaining the intensity of its heat, burns eternally in darkness. It is a neverending storm of darkness, dark flames and dark smoke of burning brimstone, amid which the bodies are heaped one upon another without even a glimpse of air. Of all the plagues with which the land of the Pharaohs was smitten one plague alone, that of darkness, was called horrible. What name, then, shall we give to the darkness of hell which is to last not for three days alone but for all eternity?

—The horror of this strait and dark prison is increased by its awful stench. All the filth of the world, all the offal and scum of the world, we are told, shall run there as to a vast reeking sewer when the terrible conflagration of the last day has purged the world. The brimstone too which burns there in such prodigious quantity fills all hell with its intolerable stench; and the bodies of the damned themselves exhale such a pestilential odour that as saint Bonaventure says, one of them alone would suffice to infect the whole world. The very air of this world, that pure element, becomes foul and unbreathable when it has been long enclosed. Consider then what must be the foulness of the air of hell. Imagine some foul and putrid corpse that has lain rotting and decomposing in the grave, a jellylike mass of liquid corruption. Imagine such a corpse a prey to flames, devoured by the fire of burning brimstone and giving off dense choking fumes of nauseous loathsome decomposition. And then imagine this sickening stench, multiplied a millionfold and a millionfold again from the millions upon millions of fetid carcasses massed together in the reeking darkness, a huge and rotting human fungus. Imagine all this and you will have some idea of the horror of the stench of hell.

—But this stench is not, horrible though it is, the greatest physical torment to which the damned are subjected. The torment of fire is the greatest torment to which the tyrant has ever subjected his fellowcreatures. Place your finger for a moment in the flame of a candle and you will feel the pain of fire. But our earthly fire was created by God for the benefit of man, to maintain in him the spark of life and to help him in the useful arts whereas the fire of hell is of another quality and was created by God to torture and punish the unrepentant sinner. Our earthly fire also consumes more or less rapidly according as the object which it attacks is more or less combustible so that human ingenuity has even succeeded in inventing chemical preparations to check or frustrate its action. But the sulphurous brimstone which burns in hell is a substance which is specially designed to burn for ever and for ever with unspeakable fury. Moreover our earthly fire destroys at the same time as it burns so that the more intense it is the shorter is its duration: but the fire of hell has this property that it preserves that which it burns and though it rages with incredible intensity it rages for ever.

—Our earthly fire again, no matter how fierce or widespread it may be, is always of a limited extent: but the lake of fire in hell is boundless, shoreless and bottomless. It is on record that the devil himself, when asked the question by a certain soldier, was obliged to confess that if a whole mountain were thrown into the burning ocean of hell it would be burned up in an instant like a piece of wax. And this terrible fire will not afflict the bodies of the damned only from without but each lost soul will be a hell unto itself, the boundless fire raging in its very vitals. O, how terrible is the lot of those wretched beings! The blood seethes and boils in the veins, the brains are boiling in the skull, the heart in the breast glowing and bursting, the bowels a redhot mass of burning pulp, the tender eyes flaming like molten balls.

—And yet what I have said as to the strength and quality and boundlessness of this fire is as nothing when compared to its intensity, an intensity which it has as being the instrument chosen by divine design for the punishment of soul and body alike. It is a fire which proceeds directly from the ire of God, working not of its own activity but as an instrument of divine vengeance. As the waters of baptism cleanse the soul with the body so do the fires of punishment torture the spirit with the flesh. Every sense of the flesh is tortured and every faculty of the soul therewith: the eyes with impenetrable utter darkness, the nose with noisome odours, the ears with yells and howls and execrations, the taste with foul matter, leprous corruption, nameless suffocating filth, the touch with redhot goads and spikes, with cruel tongues of flame. And through the several torments of the senses the immortal soul is tortured eternally in its very essence amid the leagues upon leagues of glowing fires kindled in the abyss by the offended majesty of the Omnipotent God and fanned into everlasting and ever increasing fury by the breath of the anger of the Godhead.

—Consider finally that the torment of this infernal prison is increased by the company of the damned themselves. Evil company on earth is so noxious that even the plants, as if by instinct, withdraw from the company of whatsoever is deadly or hurtful to them. In hell all laws are overturned: there is no thought of family or country, of ties, of relationships. The damned howl and scream at one another, their torture and rage intensified by the presence of beings tortured and raging like themselves. All sense of humanity is forgotten. The yells of the suffering sinners fill the remotest corners of the vast abyss. The mouths of the damned are full of blasphemies against God and of hatred for their fellowsufferers and of curses against those souls which were their accomplices in sin. In olden times it was the custom to punish the parricide, the man who had raised his murderous hand against his father, by casting him into the depths of the sea in a sack in which were placed a cock, a monkey and a serpent. The intention of those lawgivers who framed such a law, which seems cruel in our times, was to punish the criminal by the company of hateful and hurtful beasts. But what is the fury of those dumb beasts compared with the fury of execration which bursts from the parched lips and aching throats of the damned in hell when they behold in their companions in misery those who aided and abetted them in sin, those whose words sowed the first seeds of evil thinking and evil living in their minds, those whose immodest suggestions led them on to sin, those whose eyes tempted and allured them from the path of virtue. They turn upon those accomplices and upbraid them and curse them. But they are helpless and hopeless: it is too late now for repentance.

—Last of all consider the frightful torment to those damned souls, tempters and tempted alike, of the company of the devils. These devils will afflict the damned in two ways, by their presence and by their reproaches. We can have no idea of how horrible these devils are. Saint Catherine of Siena once saw a devil and she has written that, rather than look again for one single instant on such a frightful monster, she would prefer to walk until the end of her life along a track of red coals. These devils, who were once beautiful angels, have become as hideous and ugly as they once were beautiful. They mock and jeer at the lost souls whom they dragged down to ruin. It is they, the foul demons, who are made in hell the voices of conscience. Why did you sin? Why did you lend an ear to the temptings of fiends? Why did you turn aside from your pious practices and good works? Why did you not shun the occasions of sin? Why did you not leave that evil companion? Why did you not give up that lewd habit, that impure habit? Why did you not listen to the counsels of your confessor? Why did you not, even after you had fallen the first or the second or the third or the fourth or the hundredth time, repent of your evil ways and turn to God who only waited for your repentance to absolve you of your sins? Now the time for repentance has gone by. Time is, time was, but time shall be no more! Time was to sin in secrecy, to indulge in that sloth and pride, to covet the unlawful, to yield to the promptings of your lower nature, to live like the beasts of the field, nay worse than the beasts of the field for they, at least, are but brutes and have not reason to

guide them: time was but time shall be no more. God
spoke to you by so many voices but you would not
hear. You would not crush out that pride and anger in
your heart, you would not restore those illgotten goods,
you would not obey the precepts of your holy church
nor attend to your religious duties, you would not
abandon those wicked companions, you would not
avoid those dangerous temptations. Such is the language of those fiendish tormentors, words of taunting
and of reproach, of hatred and of disgust. Of disgust,
yes! For even they, the very devils, when they sinned
sinned by such a sin as alone was compatible with such
angelical natures, a rebellion of the intellect: and they,
even they, the foul devils must turn away, revolted and
disgusted, from the contemplation of those unspeakable
sins by which degraded man outrages and defiles the
temple of the Holy Ghost, defiles and pollutes himself.

—O, my dear little brothers in Christ, may it never
be our lot to hear that language! May it never be our
lot, I say! In the last day of terrible reckoning I pray
fervently to God that not a single soul of those who are
in this chapel today may be found among those miserable beings whom the Great Judge shall command to
depart for ever from His sight, that not one of us may
ever hear ringing in his ears the awful sentence of
rejection: *Depart from me, ye cursed, into everlasting
fire which was prepared for the devil and his angels!*

He came down the aisle of the chapel, his legs shaking and the scalp of his head trembling as though it had
been touched by ghostly fingers. He passed up the
staircase and into the corridor along the walls of which
the overcoats and waterproofs hung like gibbeted male-
factors, headless and dripping and shapeless. And at
every step he feared that he had already died, that his

soul had been wrenched forth of the sheath of his body, that he was plunging headlong through space.

He could not grip the floor with his feet and sat heavily at his desk, opening one of his books at random and poring over it. Every word for him! It was true. God was almighty. God could call him now, call him as he sat at his desk, before he had time to be conscious of the summons. God had called him. Yes? What? Yes? His flesh shrank together as it felt the approach of the ravenous tongues of flames, dried up as it felt about it the swirl of stifling air. He had died. Yes. He was judged. A wave of fire swept through his body: the first. Again a wave. His brain began to glow. Another. His brain was simmering and bubbling within the cracking tenement of the skull. Flames burst forth from his skull like a corolla, shrieking like voices:

—Hell! Hell! Hell! Hell! Hell!

Voices spoke near him:

—On hell.

—I suppose he rubbed it into you well.

—You bet he did. He put us all into a blue funk.

—That's what you fellows want: and plenty of it to make you work.

He leaned back weakly in his desk. He had not died. God had spared him still. He was still in the familiar world of the school. Mr Tate and Vincent Heron stood at the window, talking, jesting, gazing out at the bleak rain, moving their heads.

—I wish it would clear up. I had arranged to go for a spin on the bike with some fellows out by Malahide. But the roads must be kneedeep.

—It might clear up, sir.

The voices that he knew so well, the common words, the quiet of the classroom when the voices paused and the silence was filled by the sound of softly browsing cattle as the other boys munched their lunches tranquilly, lulled his aching soul.

There was still time. O Mary, refuge of sinners, intercede for him! O Virgin Undefiled, save him from the gulf of death!

The English lesson began with the hearing of the history. Royal persons, favourites, intriguers, bishops, passed like mute phantoms behind their veil of names. All had died: all had been judged. What did it profit a man to gain the whole world if he lost his soul? At last he had understood: and human life lay around him, a plain of peace whereon antlike men laboured in brotherhood, their dead sleeping under quiet mounds. The elbow of his companion touched him and his heart was touched: and when he spoke to answer a question of his master he heard his own voice full of the quietude of humility and contrition.

His soul sank back deeper into depths of contrite peace, no longer able to suffer the pain of dread, and sending forth, as she sank, a faint prayer. Ah yes, he would still be spared; he would repent in his heart and be forgiven; and then those above, those in heaven, would see what he would do to make up for the past: a whole life, every hour of life. Only wait.

—All, God! All, all!

A messenger came to the door to say that confessions were being heard in the chapel. Four boys left the room; and he heard others passing down the corridor. A tremulous chill blew round his heart, no stronger than a little wind, and yet, listening and suffering silently, he seemed to have laid an ear against the muscle of his own heart, feeling it close and quail, listening to the flutter of its ventricles.

No escape. He had to confess, to speak out in words what he had done and thought, sin after sin. How? How?

—Father, I . . .

The thought slid like a cold shining rapier into his tender flesh: confession. But not there in the chapel of the college. He would confess all, every sin of deed and thought, sincerely: but not there among his school companions. Far away from there in some dark place he would murmur out his own shame: and he besought God humbly not to be offended with him if he did not dare to confess in the college chapel: and in utter abjection of spirit he craved forgiveness mutely of the boyish hearts about him.

Time passed.

He sat again in the front bench of the chapel. The daylight without was already failing and, as it fell slowly through the dull red blinds, it seemed that the sun of the last day was going down and that all souls were being gathered for the judgment.

—*I am cast away from the sight of Thine eyes:* words taken, my dear little brothers in Christ, from the Book of Psalms, thirtieth chapter, twentythird verse. In the name of the Father and of the Son and of the Holy Ghost. Amen.

The preacher began to speak in a quiet friendly tone. His face was kind and he joined gently the fingers of each hand, forming a frail cage by the union of their tips.

—This morning we endeavoured, in our reflection upon hell, to make what our holy founder calls in his book of spiritual exercises, the composition of place. We endeavoured, that is, to imagine with the senses of the mind, in our imagination, the material character of that awful place and of the physical torments which all

who are in hell endure. This evening we shall consider
for a few moments the nature of the spiritual torments
of hell.

—Sin, remember, is a twofold enormity. It is a base
consent to the promptings of our corrupt nature to the
lower instincts, to that which is gross and beastlike; and
it is also a turning away from the counsel of our higher
nature, from all that is pure and holy, from the Holy
God Himself. For this reason mortal sin is punished in
hell by two different forms of punishment, physical and
spiritual.

—Now of all these spiritual pains by far the greatest
is the pain of loss, so great, in fact, that in itself it is a
torment greater than all the others. Saint Thomas, the
greatest doctor of the church, the angelic doctor, as he
is called, says that the worst damnation consists in this
that the understanding of man is totally deprived of
divine light and his affection obstinately turned away
from the goodness of God. God, remember, is a being
infinitely good and therefore the loss of such a being
must be a loss infinitely painful. In this life we have not
a very clear idea of what such a loss must be but the
damned in hell, for their greater torment, have a full
understanding of that which they have lost and understand that they have lost it through their own sins and
have lost it for ever. At the very instant of death the
bonds of the flesh are broken asunder and the soul at
once flies towards God. The soul tends towards God as
towards the centre of her existence. Remember, my
dear little boys, our souls long to be with God. We
come from God, we live by God, we belong to God:
we are His, inalienably His. God loves with a divine
love every human soul and every human soul lives in
that love. How could it be otherwise? Every breath that
we draw, every thought of our brain, every instant of

life proceed from God's inexhaustible goodness. And if it be pain for a mother to be parted from her child, for a man to be exiled from hearth and home, for friend to be sundered from friend, O think what pain, what anguish, it must be for the poor soul to be spurned from the presence of the supremely good and loving Creator Who has called that soul into existence from nothingness and sustained it in life and loved it with an immeasurable love. This, then, to be separated for ever from its greatest good, from God, and to feel the anguish of that separation, knowing full well that it is unchangeable, this is the greatest torment which the created soul is capable of bearing, *pœna damni*, the pain of loss.

—The second pain which will afflict the souls of the damned in hell is the pain of conscience. Just as in dead bodies worms are engendered by putrefaction so in the souls of the lost there arises a perpetual remorse from the putrefaction of sin, the sting of conscience, the worm, as Pope Innocent the Third calls it, of the triple sting. The first sting inflicted by this cruel worm will be the memory of past pleasures. O what a dreadful memory will that be! In the lake of alldevouring flame the proud king will remember the pomps of his court, the wise but wicked man his libraries and instruments of research, the lover of artistic pleasures his marbles and pictures and other art treasures, he who delighted in the pleasures of the table his gorgeous feasts, his dishes prepared with such delicacy, his choice wines; the miser will remember his hoard of gold, the robber his illgotten wealth, the angry and revengeful and merciless murderers their deeds of blood and violence in which they revelled, the impure and adulterous the unspeakable and filthy pleasures in

which they delighted. They will remember all this and
loathe themselves and their sins. For how miserable
will all those pleasures seem to the soul condemned to
suffer in hellfire for ages and ages. How they will rage
and fume to think that they have lost the bliss of
heaven for the dross of earth, for a few pieces of metal,
for vain honours, for bodily comforts, for a tingling of
the nerves. They will repent indeed: and this is the
second sting of the worm of conscience, a late and
fruitless sorrow for sins committed. Divine justice insists that the understanding of those miserable wretches
be fixed continually on the sins of which they were
guilty and moreover, as saint Augustine points out,
God will impart to them His own knowledge of sin so
that sin will appear to them in all its hideous malice as
it appears to the eyes of God Himself. They will behold
their sins in all their foulness and repent but it will be
too late and then they will bewail the good occasions
which they neglected. This is the last and deepest and
most cruel sting of the worm of conscience. The conscience will say: You had time and opportunity to
repent and would not. You were brought up religiously
by your parents. You had the sacraments and graces
and indulgences of the church to aid you. You had the
minister of God to preach to you, to call you back
when you had strayed, to forgive you your sins, no
matter how many, how abominable, if only you had
confessed and repented. No. You would not. You
flouted the ministers of holy religion, you turned your
back on the confessional, you wallowed deeper and
deeper in the mire of sin. God appealed to you, threatened you, entreated you to return to Him. O what
shame, what misery! The Ruler of the universe entreated you, a creature of clay, to love Him Who made

you and to keep His law. No. You would not. And now, though you were to flood all hell with your tears if you could still weep, all that sea of repentance would not gain for you what a single tear of true repentance shed during your mortal life would have gained for you. You implore now a moment of earthly life wherein to repent: in vain. That time is gone: gone for ever.

—Such is the threefold sting of conscience, the viper which gnaws the very heart's core of the wretches in hell so that filled with hellish fury they curse themselves for their folly and curse the evil companions who have brought them to such ruin and curse the devils who tempted them in life and now mock them and torture them in eternity and even revile and curse the Supreme Being Whose goodness and patience they scorned and slighted but Whose justice and power they cannot evade.

—The next spiritual pain to which the damned are subjected is the pain of extension. Man, in this earthly life, though he be capable of many evils, is not capable of them all at once inasmuch as one evil corrects and counteracts another just as one poison frequently corrects another. In hell on the contrary one torment, instead of counteracting another, lends it still greater force: and moreover as the internal faculties are more perfect than the external senses, so are they more capable of suffering. Just as every sense is afflicted with a fitting torment so is every spiritual faculty; the fancy with horrible images, the sensitive faculty with alternate longing and rage, the mind and understanding with an interior darkness more terrible even than the exterior darkness which reigns in that dreadful prison. The malice, impotent though it be, which possesses these demon souls is an evil of boundless extension, of limitless duration, a frightful state of wickedness which we can scarcely realise unless we bear in mind the enormity of sin and the hatred God bears to it.

—Opposed to this pain of extension and yet coexistent with it we have the pain of intensity. Hell is the centre of evils and, as you know, things are more intense at their centres than at their remotest points. There are no contraries or admixtures of any kind to temper or soften in the least the pains of hell. Nay, things which are good in themselves become evil in hell. Company, elsewhere a source of comfort to the afflicted, will be there a continual torment: knowledge, so much longed for as the chief good of the intellect, will there be hated worse than ignorance: light, so much coveted by all creatures from the lord of creation down to the humblest plant in the forest, will be loathed intensely. In this life our sorrows are either not very long or not very great because nature either overcomes them by habits or puts an end to them by sinking under their weight. But in hell the torments cannot be overcome by habit. For while they are of terrible intensity they are at the same time of continual variety, each pain, so to speak, taking fire from another and reendowing that which has enkindled it with a still fiercer flame. Nor can nature escape from these intense and various tortures by succumbing to them for the soul is sustained and maintained in evil so that its suffering may be the greater. Boundless extension of torment, incredible intensity of suffering, unceasing variety of torture—this is what the divine majesty, so outraged by sinners, demands, this is what the holiness of heaven, slighted and set aside for the lustful and low pleasures of the corrupt flesh, requires, this is what the

blood of the innocent Lamb of God, shed for the redemption of sinners, trampled upon by the vilest of the
vile, insists upon.

—Last and crowning torture of all the tortures of
that awful place is the eternity of hell. Eternity! O,
dread and dire word. Eternity! What mind of man can
understand it? And, remember, it is an eternity of pain.
Even though the pains of hell were not so terrible as
they are yet they would become infinite as they are
destined to last for ever. But while they are everlasting
they are at the same time, as you know, intolerably
intense, unbearably extensive. To bear even the sting of
an insect for all eternity would be a dreadful torment.
What must it be, then, to bear the manifold tortures of
hell for ever? For ever! For all eternity! Not for a year
or for an age but for ever. Try to imagine the awful
meaning of this. You have often seen the sand on the
seashore. How fine are its tiny grains! And how many
of those tiny little grains go to make up the small
handful which a child grasps in its play. Now imagine a
mountain of that sand, a million miles high, reaching
from the earth to the farthest heavens, and a million
miles broad, extending to remotest space, and a million
miles in thickness: and imagine such an enormous
mass of countless particles of sand multiplied as often
as there are leaves in the forest, drops of water in the
mighty ocean, feathers on birds, scales on fish, hairs on
animals, atoms in the vast expanse of the air: and
imagine that at the end of every million years a little
bird came to that mountain and carried away in its
beak a tiny grain of that sand. How many millions
upon millions of centuries would pass before that bird
had carried away even a square foot of that mountain,
how many eons upon eons of ages before it had carried
away all. Yet at the end of that immense stretch of

time not even one instant of eternity could be said to have ended. At the end of all those billions and trillions of years eternity would have scarcely begun. And if that mountain rose again after it had been all carried away and if the bird came again and carried it all away again grain by grain: and if it so rose and sank as many times as there are stars in the sky, atoms in the air, drops of water in the sea, leaves on the trees, feathers upon birds, scales upon fish, hairs upon animals, at the end of all those innumerable risings and sinkings of that immeasurably vast mountain not one single instant of eternity could be said to have ended; even then, at the end of such a period, after that eon of time the mere thought of which makes our very brain reel dizzily, eternity would have scarcely begun.

—A holy saint (one of our own fathers I believe it was) was once vouchsafed a vision of hell. It seemed to him that he stood in the midst of a great hall, dark and silent save for the ticking of a great clock. The ticking went on unceasingly; and it seemed to this saint that the sound of the ticking was the ceaseless repetition of the words: ever, never; ever, never. Ever to be in hell, never to be in heaven; ever to be shut off from the presence of God, never to enjoy the beatific vision; ever to be eaten with flames, gnawed by vermin, goaded with burning spikes, never to be free from those pains; ever to have the conscience upbraid one, the memory enrage, the mind filled with darkness and despair, never to escape; ever to curse and revile the foul demons who gloat fiendishly over the misery of their dupes, never to behold the shining raiment of the blessed spirits; ever to cry out of the abyss of fire to God for an instant, a single instant, of respite from such awful agony, never to receive, even for an instant, God's pardon; ever to suffer, never to enjoy; ever to be damned, never to be saved; ever, never; ever, never. O what a dreadful pun-ishment! An eternity of endless agony, of endless bod-ily and spiritual torment, without one ray of hope, without one moment of cessation, of agony limitless in extent, limitless in intensity, of torment infinitely last-ing, infinitely varied, of torture that sustains eternally that which it eternally devours, of anguish that ever-lastingly preys upon the spirit while it racks the flesh, an eternity, every instant of which is itself an eternity, and that eternity an eternity of woe. Such is the terrible punishment decreed for those who die in mortal sin by an almighty and a just God.

—Yes, a just God! Men, reasoning always as men, are astonished that God should mete out an everlasting and infinite punishment in the fires of hell for a single grievous sin. They reason thus because, blinded by the gross illusion of the flesh and the darkness of human understanding, they are unable to comprehend the hideous malice of mortal sin. They reason thus because they are unable to comprehend that even venial sin is of such a foul and hideous nature that even if the omnipotent Creator could end all the evil and misery in the world, the wars, the diseases, the robberies, the crimes, the deaths, the murders, on condition that He allowed a single venial sin to pass unpunished, a single venial sin, a lie, an angry look, a moment of wilful sloth, He, the great omnipotent God, could not do so because sin, be it in thought or deed, is a transgression of His law and God would not be God if He did not punish the transgressor.

—A sin, an instant of rebellious pride of the intel-lect, made Lucifer and a third part of the cohorts of angels fall from their glory. A sin, an instant of folly and weakness, drove Adam and Eve out of Eden and brought death and suffering into the world. To retrieve the consequences of that sin the Only Begotten Son of God came down to earth, lived and suffered and died a most painful death, hanging for three hours on the cross.

—O, my dear little brethren in Christ Jesus, will we then offend that good Redeemer and provoke His anger? Will we trample again upon that torn and mangled corpse? Will we spit upon that face so full of sorrow and love? Will we too, like the cruel jews and the brutal soldiers, mock that gentle and compassionate Saviour Who trod alone for our sake the awful winepress of sorrow? Every word of sin is a wound in His tender side. Every sinful act is a thorn piercing His head. Every impure thought deliberately yielded to, is a keen lance transfixing that sacred and loving heart. No, no. It is impossible for any human being to do that which offends so deeply the divine majesty, that which is punished by an eternity of agony, that which crucifies again the Son of God and makes a mockery of Him.

—I pray to God that my poor words may have availed today to confirm in holiness those who are in a state of grace, to strengthen the wavering, to lead back to the state of grace the poor soul that has strayed if any such be among you. I pray to God, and do you pray with me, that we may repent of our sins. I will ask you now, all of you, to repeat after me the act of contrition, kneeling here in this humble chapel in the presence of God. He is there in the tabernacle burning with love for mankind, ready to comfort the afflicted. Be not afraid. No matter how many or how foul the sins if only you repent of them they will be forgiven you. Let no worldly shame hold you back. God is still the merciful Lord Who wishes not the eternal death of the sinner but rather that he be converted and live.

—He calls you to Him. You are His. He made you

out of nothing. He loved you as only a God can love. His arms are open to receive you even though you have sinned against Him. Come to Him, poor sinner, poor vain and erring sinner. Now is the acceptable time. Now is the hour.

The priest rose and, turning towards the altar, knelt upon the step before the tabernacle in the fallen gloom. He waited till all in the chapel had knelt and every least noise was still. Then, raising his head, he repeated the act of contrition, phrase by phrase, with fervour. The boys answered him phrase by phrase. Stephen, his tongue cleaving to his palate, bowed his head, praying with his heart.

—O my God!—
—O my God!—
—I am heartily sorry—
—I am heartily sorry—
—for having offended Thee—
—for having offended Thee—
—and I detest my sins—
—and I detest my sins—
—above every other evil—
—above every other evil—
—because they displease Thee, my God—
—because they displease Thee, my God—
—Who art so deserving—
—Who art so deserving—
—of all my love—
—of all my love—
—and I firmly purpose—
—and I firmly purpose—
—by Thy holy grace—
—by Thy holy grace—

—never more to offend Thee—
—never more to offend Thee—
—and to amend my life—
—and to amend my life—

❖   ❖   ❖

He went up to his room after dinner in order to be alone with his soul: and at every step his soul seemed to sigh: at every step his soul mounted with his feet, sighing in the ascent, through a region of viscid gloom.

He halted on the landing before the door and then, grasping the porcelain knob, opened the door quickly. He waited in fear, his soul pining within him, praying silently that death might not touch his brow as he passed over the threshold, that the fiends that inhabit darkness might not be given power over him. He waited still at the threshold as at the entrance to some dark cave. Faces were there; eyes: they waited and watched.

—We knew perfectly well of course that although it was bound to come to the light he would find considerable difficulty in endeavouring to try to induce himself to try to endeavour to ascertain the spiritual plenipotentiary and so we knew of course perfectly well—

Murmuring faces waited and watched; murmurous voices filled the dark shell of the cave. He feared intensely in spirit and in flesh but, raising his head bravely, he strode into the room firmly. A doorway, a room, the same room, same window. He told himself calmly that those words had absolutely no sense which had seemed to rise murmurously from the dark. He told himself that it was simply his room with the door open.

He closed the door and, walking swiftly to the bed, knelt beside it and covered his face with his hands. His hands were cold and damp and his limbs ached with chill. Bodily unrest and chill and weariness beset him, routing his thoughts. Why was he kneeling there like a child saying his evening prayers? To be alone with his soul, to examine his conscience, to meet his sins face to face, to recall their times and manners and circumstances, to weep over them. He could not weep. He could not summon them to his memory. He felt only an ache of soul and body, his whole being, memory, will, understanding, flesh, benumbed and weary.

That was the work of devils, to scatter his thoughts and overcloud his conscience, assailing him at the gates of the cowardly and sincorrupted flesh: and, praying God timidly to forgive him his weakness, he crawled up on to the bed and, wrapping the blankets closely about him, covered his face again with his hands. He had sinned. He had sinned so deeply against heaven and before God that he was not worthy to be called God's child.

Could it be that he, Stephen Dedalus, had done those things? His conscience sighed in answer. Yes, he had done them, secretly, filthily, time after time, and, hardened in sinful impenitence, he had dared to wear the mask of holiness before the tabernacle itself while his soul within was a living mass of corruption. How came it that God had not struck him dead? The leprous company of his sins closed about him, breathing upon him, bending over him from all sides. He strove to forget them in an act of prayer, huddling his limbs closer together and binding down his eyelids: but the senses of his soul would not be bound and, though his eyes were shut fast, he saw the places where he had sinned and, though his ears were tightly covered, he heard. He desired with all his will not to hear or see.

He desired till his frame shook under the strain of his desire and until the senses of his soul closed. They closed for an instant and then opened. He saw.

A field of stiff weeds and thistles and tufted nettle-bunches. Thick among the tufts of rank stiff growth lay battered canisters and clots and coils of solid excrement. A faint marshlight struggled upwards from all the ordure through the bristling greygreen weeds. An evil smell, faint and foul as the light, curled upwards sluggishly out of the canisters and from the stale crusted dung.

Creatures were in the field; one, three, six: creatures were moving in the field, hither and thither. Goatish creatures with human faces, hornybrowed, lightly bearded and grey as indiarubber. The malice of evil glittered in their hard eyes, as they moved hither and thither, trailing their long tails behind them. A rictus of cruel malignity lit up greyly their old bony faces. One was clasping about his ribs a torn flannel waistcoat, another complained monotonously as his beard stuck in the tufted weeds. Soft language issued from their spittleless lips as they swished in slow circles round and round the field, winding hither and thither through the weeds, dragging their long tails amid the rattling canisters. They moved in slow circles, circling closer and closer to enclose, to enclose, soft language issuing from their lips, their long swishing tails besmeared with stale shite, thrusting upwards their terrific faces . . .

Help!

He flung the blankets from him madly to free his face and neck. That was his hell. God had allowed him to see the hell reserved for his sins: stinking, bestial, malignant, a hell of lecherous goatish fiends. For him! For him!

He sprang from the bed, the reeking odour pouring down his throat, clogging and revolting his entrails. Air! The air of heaven! He stumbled towards the window, groaning and almost fainting with sickness. At the washstand a convulsion seized him within; and, clasping his cold forehead wildly, he vomited profusely in agony.

When the fit had spent itself he walked weakly to the window and, lifting the sash, sat in a corner of the embrasure and leaned his elbow upon the sill. The rain had drawn off; and amid the moving vapours from point to point of light the city was spinning about herself a soft cocoon of yellowish haze. Heaven was still and faintly luminous and the air sweet to breathe, as in a thicket drenched with showers: and amid peace and shimmering lights and quiet fragrance he made a covenant with his heart.

He prayed:

—He once had meant to come on earth in heavenly glory but we sinned: and then He could not safely visit us but with a shrouded majesty and a bedimmed radiance for He was God. So He came Himself in weakness not in power and He sent thee, a creature in His stead, with a creature's comeliness and lustre suited to our state. And now thy very face and form, dear mother, speak to us of the Eternal; not like earthly beauty, dangerous to look upon, but like the morning star which is thy emblem, bright and musical, breathing purity, telling of heaven and infusing peace. O harbinger of day! O light of the pilgrim! Lead us still as thou hast led. In the dark night, across the bleak wilderness guide us on to our Lord Jesus, guide us home.

His eyes were dimmed with tears and, looking humbly up to heaven, he wept for the innocence he had lost.

When evening had fallen he left the house and the first touch of the damp dark air and the noise of the door as it closed behind him made ache again his conscience, lulled by prayer and tears. Confess! Confess! It was not enough to lull the conscience with a tear and a prayer. He had to kneel before the minister of the Holy Ghost and tell over his hidden sins truly and repentantly. Before he heard again the footboard of the housedoor trail over the threshold as it opened to let him in, before he saw again the table in the kitchen set for supper he would have knelt and confessed. It was quite simple.

The ache of conscience ceased and he walked onward swiftly through the dark streets. There were so many flagstones on the footpath of that street and so many streets in that city and so many cities in the world. Yet eternity had no end. He was in mortal sin. Even once was a mortal sin. It could happen in an instant. But how so quickly? By seeing or by thinking of seeing. The eyes see the thing, without having wished first to see. Then in an instant it happens. But does that part of the body understand or what? The serpent, the most subtle beast of the field. It must understand when it desires in one instant and then prolongs its own desire instant after instant, sinfully. It feels and understands and desires. What a horrible thing! Who made it to be like that, a bestial part of the body able to understand bestially and desire bestially? Was that then he or an inhuman thing moved by a lower soul than his soul? His soul sickened at the thought of a torpid snaky life feeding itself out of the

tender marrow of his life and fattening upon the slime
of lust. O why was that so? O why?

He cowered in the shadow of the thought, abasing
himself in the awe of God Who had made all things
and all men. Madness. Who could think such a
thought? And, cowering in darkness and abject, he
prayed mutely to his angel guardian to drive away with
his sword the demon that was whispering to his brain.

The whisper ceased and he knew then clearly that his
own soul had sinned in thought and word and deed
wilfully through his own body. Confess! He had to
confess every sin. How could he utter in words to the
priest what he had done? Must, must. Or how could he
explain without dying of shame? Or how could he have
done such things without shame? A madman, a loathsome madman! Confess! O he would indeed to be free
and sinless again! Perhaps the priest would know. O
dear God!

He walked on and on through illlit streets, fearing to
stand still for a moment lest it might seem that he held
back from what awaited him, fearing to arrive at that
towards which he still turned with longing. How beautiful must be a soul in the state of grace when God
looked upon it with love!

Frowsy girls sat along the curbstones before their
baskets. Their dank hair hung trailed over their brows.
They were not beautiful to see as they crouched in the
mire. But their souls were seen by God; and if their
souls were in a state of grace they were radiant to see:
and God loved them, seeing them.

A wasting breath of humiliation blew bleakly over
his soul to think of how he had fallen, to feel that those
souls were dearer to God than his. The wind blew over
him and passed on to the myriads and myriads of other
souls on whom God's favour shone now more and now

less, stars now brighter and now dimmer, sustained and failing. And the glimmering souls passed away, sustained and failing, merged in a moving breath. One soul was lost; a tiny soul: his. It flickered once and went out, forgotten, lost. The end: black cold void waste.

Consciousness of place came ebbing back to him slowly over a vast tract of time unlit, unfelt unlived. The squalid scene composed itself around him; the common accents, the burning gasjets in the shops, odours of fish and spirits and wet sawdust, moving men and women. An old woman was about to cross the street, an oilcan in her hand. He bent down and asked her was there a chapel near.

—A chapel, sir? Yes, sir. Church Street chapel.

—Church?

She shifted the can to her other hand and directed him: and, as she held out her reeking withered right hand under its fringe of shawl, he bent lower towards her, saddened and soothed by her voice.

—Thank you.

—You are quite welcome, sir.

The candles on the high altar had been extinguished but the fragrance of incense still floated down the dim nave. Bearded workmen with pious faces were guiding a canopy out through a sidedoor, the sacristan aiding them with quiet gestures and words. A few of the faithful still lingered, praying before one of the sidealtars or kneeling in the benches near the confessionals. He approached timidly and knelt at the last bench in the body, thankful for the peace and silence and fragrant shadow of the church. The board on which he knelt was narrow and worn and those who knelt near him were humble followers of Jesus. Jesus too had been born in poverty and had worked in the shop of a carpenter, cutting boards and planing them, and had first spoken of the kingdom of God to poor fishermen, teaching all men to be meek and humble of heart.

He bowed his head upon his hands, bidding his heart be meek and humble that he might be like those who knelt beside him and his prayer as acceptable as theirs. He prayed beside them but it was hard. His soul was foul with sin and he dared not ask forgiveness with the simple trust of those whom Jesus, in the mysterious ways of God, had called first to His side, the carpenters, the fishermen, poor and simple people following a lowly trade, handling and shaping the wood of trees, mending their nets with patience.

A tall figure came down the aisle and the penitents stirred: and at the last moment, glancing up swiftly, he saw a long grey beard and the brown habit of a capuchin. The priest entered the box and was hidden. Two penitents rose and entered the confessional at either side. The wooden slide was drawn back and the faint murmur of a voice troubled the silence.

His blood began to murmur in his veins, murmuring like a sinful city summoned from its sleep to hear its doom. Little flakes of fire fell and powdery ashes fell softly, alighting on the houses of men. They stirred, waking from sleep, troubled by the heated air.

The slide was shot back. The penitent emerged from the side of the box. The farther slide was drawn. A woman entered quietly and deftly where the first penitent had knelt. The faint murmur began again.

He could still leave the chapel. He could stand up, put one foot before the other and walk out softly and then run, run, run swiftly through the dark streets. He could still escape from the shame. Had it been any terrible crime but that one sin! Had it been murder! Little fiery flakes fell and touched him at all points, shameful thoughts, shameful words, shameful acts. Shame covered him wholly like fine glowing ashes falling continually. To say it in words! His soul, stifling and helpless, would cease to be.

The slide was shot back. A penitent emerged from the farther side of the box. The near slide was drawn. A penitent entered where the other penitent had come out. A soft whispering noise floated in vaporous cloudlets out of the box. It was the woman: soft whispering cloudlets, soft whispering vapour, whispering and vanishing.

He beat his breast with his fist humbly, secretly under cover of the wooden armrest. He would be at one with others and with God. He would love his neighbour. He would love God Who had made and loved him. He would kneel and pray with others and be happy. God would look down on him and on them and would love them all.

It was easy to be good. God's yoke was sweet and light. It was better never to have sinned, to have remained always a child, for God loved little children and suffered them to come to Him. It was a terrible and a sad thing to sin. But God was merciful to poor sinners who were truly sorry. How true that was! That was indeed goodness.

The slide was shot to suddenly. The penitent came out. He was next. He stood up in terror and walked blindly into the box.

At last it had come. He knelt in the silent gloom and raised his eyes to the white crucifix suspended above him. God could see that he was sorry. He would tell all his sins. His confession would be long, long. Everybody in the chapel would know then what a sinner he had been. Let them know. It was true. But God had promised to forgive him if he was sorry. He was sorry. He clasped his hands and raised them towards the white form, praying with his darkened eyes, praying with all his trembling body, swaying his head to and fro like a lost creature, praying with whimpering lips.

—Sorry! Sorry! O sorry!

The slide clicked back and his heart bounded in his breast. The face of an old priest was at the grating, averted from him, leaning upon a hand. He made the sign of the cross and prayed of the priest to bless him for he had sinned. Then, bowing his head, he repeated the *Confiteor* in fright. At the words *my most grievous fault* he ceased, breathless.

—How long is it since your last confession, my child?

—A long time, father.

—A month, my child?

—Longer, father.

—Three months, my child?

—Longer, father.

—Six months?

—Eight months, father.

He had begun. The priest asked:

—And what do you remember since that time?

He began to confess his sins: masses missed, prayers not said, lies.

—Anything else, my child?

Sins of anger, envy of others, gluttony, vanity, disobedience.

—Anything else, my child?

—Sloth.

—Anything else, my child?

There was no help. He murmured:

—I . . . committed sins of impurity, father.

The priest did not turn his head.

—With yourself, my child?

—And . . . with others.

—With women, my child?

—Yes, father.

—Were they married women, my child?

He did not know. His sins trickled from his lips, one by one, trickled in shameful drops from his soul festering and oozing like a sore, a squalid stream of vice. The last sins oozed forth, sluggish, filthy. There was no more to tell. He bowed his head, overcome.

The priest was silent. Then he asked:

—How old are you, my child?

—Sixteen, father.

The priest passed his hand several times over his face. Then, resting his forehead against his hand, he leaned towards the grating and, with eyes still averted, spoke slowly. His voice was weary and old.

—You are very young, my child, he said, and let me implore of you to give up that sin. It is a terrible sin. It kills the body and it kills the soul. It is the cause of many crimes and misfortunes. Give it up, my child, for God's sake. It is dishonourable and unmanly. You cannot know where that wretched habit will lead you or where it will come against you. As long as you commit that sin, my poor child, you will never be worth one farthing to God. Pray to our mother Mary to help you. She will help you, my child. Pray to Our Blessed Lady when that sin comes into your mind. I am sure you will do that, will you not? You repent of all those sins. I am sure you do. And you will promise God now that by His holy grace you will never offend Him any more by that wicked sin. You will make that solemn promise to God, will you not?

—Yes, father.

The old and weary voice fell like sweet rain upon his quaking parching heart. How sweet and sad!

—Do so, my poor child. The devil has led you astray. Drive him back to hell when he tempts you to dishonour your body in that way—the foul spirit who hates Our Lord. Promise God now that you will give up that sin, that wretched wretched sin.

Blinded by his tears and by the light of God's mercifulness he bent his head and heard the grave words of absolution spoken and saw the priest's hand raised above him in token of forgiveness.

—God bless you, my child. Pray for me.

He knelt to say his penance, praying in a corner of the dark nave: and his prayers ascended to heaven from his purified heart like perfume streaming upwards from a heart of white rose.

The muddy streets were gay. He strode homeward, conscious of an invisible grace pervading and making light his limbs. In spite of all he had done it. He had confessed and God had pardoned him. His soul was made fair and holy once more, holy and happy.

It would be beautiful to die if God so willed. It was beautiful to live if God so willed, to live in grace a life of peace and virtue and forbearance with others.

He sat by the fire in the kitchen, not daring to speak for happiness. Till that moment he had not known how beautiful and peaceful life could be. The green square of paper pinned round the lamp cast down a tender shade. On the dresser was a plate of sausages and white pudding and on the shelf there were eggs. They would be for the breakfast in the morning after the communion in the college chapel. White pudding and eggs and sausages and cups of tea. How simple and beautiful was life after all! And life lay all before him.

In a dream he fell asleep. In a dream he rose and saw that it was morning. In a waking dream he went through the quiet morning towards the college.

The boys were all there, kneeling in their places. He knelt among them, happy and shy. The altar was heaped with fragrant masses of white flowers: and in the morning light the pale flames of the candles among the white flowers were clear and silent as his own soul.

He knelt before the altar with his classmates, holding the altar cloth with them over a living rail of hands. His hands were trembling, and his soul trembled as he heard the priest pass with the ciborium from communicant to communicant.

—*Corpus Domini nostri.*

Could it be? He knelt there sinless and timid: and he would hold upon his tongue the host and God would enter his purified body.

—*In vitam eternam. Amen.*

Another life! A life of grace and virtue and happiness! It was true. It was not a dream from which he would wake. The past was past.

—*Corpus Domini nostri.*

The ciborium had come to him.

IV

SUNDAY was dedicated to the mystery of the Holy Trinity, Monday to the Holy Ghost, Tuesday to the Guardian Angels, Wednesday to Saint Joseph, Thursday to the Most Blessed Sacrament of the Altar, Friday to the Suffering Jesus, Saturday to the Blessed Virgin Mary.

Every morning he hallowed himself anew in the presence of some holy image or mystery. His day began with an heroic offering of its every moment of thought or action for the intentions of the sovereign pontiff and with an early mass. The raw morning air whetted his resolute piety; and often as he knelt among the few

worshippers at the sidealtar, following with his inter-
leaved prayerbook the murmur of the priest, he glanced
up for an instant towards the vested figure standing in
the gloom between the two candles which were the old
and the new testaments and imagined that he was
kneeling at mass in the catacombs.

His daily life was laid out in devotional areas. By
means of ejaculations and prayers he stored up un-
grudgingly for the souls in purgatory centuries of days
and quarantines and years; yet the spiritual triumph
which he felt in achieving with ease so many fabulous
ages of canonical penances did not wholly reward his
zeal of prayer since he could never know how much
temporal punishment he had remitted by way of
suffrage for the agonising souls: and, fearful lest in
the midst of the purgatorial fire, which differed from
the infernal only in that it was not everlasting, his
penance might avail no more than a drop of moisture,
he drove his soul daily through an increasing circle of
works of supererogation.

Every part of his day, divided by what he regarded
now as the duties of his station in life, circled about its
own centre of spiritual energy. His life seemed to have
drawn near to eternity; every thought, word and deed,
every instance of consciousness could be made to
revibrate radiantly in heaven: and at times his sense of
such immediate repercussion was so lively that he
seemed to feel his soul in devotion pressing like fingers
the keyboard of a great cash register and to see the
amount of his purchase start forth immediately in
heaven, not as a number but as a frail column of incense or as a slender flower.

The rosaries too which he said constantly—for he
carried his beads loose in his trousers' pockets that he
might tell them as he walked the streets—transformed

themselves into coronals of flowers of such vague unearthly texture that they seemed to him as hueless and
odourless as they were nameless. He offered up each of
his three daily chaplets that his soul might grow strong
in each of the three theological virtues, in faith in the
Father, Who had created him, in hope in the Son Who
had redeemed him, and in love of the Holy Ghost Who
had sanctified him, and this thrice triple prayer he
offered to the Three persons through Mary in the name
of her joyful and sorrowful and glorious mysteries.

On each of the seven days of the week he further
prayed that one of the seven gifts of the Holy Ghost
might descend upon his soul and drive out of it day by
day the seven deadly sins which had defiled it in the
past; and he prayed for each gift on its appointed day,
confident that it would descend upon him, though it
seemed strange to him at times that wisdom and understanding and knowledge were so distinct in their nature
that each should be prayed for apart from the others.
Yet he believed that at some future stage of his spiritual progress this difficulty would be removed when his
sinful soul had been raised up from its weakness and
enlightened by the Third Person of the Most Blessed
Trinity. He believed this all the more, and with trepidation, because of the divine gloom and silence wherein
dwelt the unseen Paraclete, Whose symbols were a
dove and a mighty wind, to sin against Whom was a
sin beyond forgiveness, the eternal, mysterious secret
Being to Whom, as God, the priests offered up mass
once a 'year, robed in the scarlet of the tongues of
fire.

The imagery through which the nature and kinship
of the Three Persons of the Trinity were darkly shadowed forth in the books of devotion which he read—
the Father contemplating from all eternity as in a mir-

ror His Divine Perfections and thereby begetting eternally the Eternal Son and the Holy Spirit proceeding out of Father and Son from all eternity—were easier of acceptance by his mind by reason of their august incomprehensibility than was the simple fact that God had loved his soul from all eternity, for ages before he had been born into the world, for ages before the world itself had existed.

He had heard the names of the passions of love and hate pronounced solemnly on the stage and in the pulpit, had found them set forth solemnly in books, and had wondered why his soul was unable to harbour them for any time or to force his lips to utter their names with conviction. A brief anger had often invested him but he had never been able to make it an abiding passion and had always felt himself passing out of it as if his very body were being divested with ease of some outer skin or peel. He had felt a subtle, dark and murmurous presence penetrate his being and fire him with a brief iniquitous lust: it too had slipped beyond his grasp leaving his mind lucid and indifferent. This, it seemed, was the only love and that the only hate his soul would harbour.

But he could no longer disbelieve in the reality of love since God Himself had loved his individual soul with divine love from all eternity. Gradually, as his soul was enriched with spiritual knowledge, he saw the whole world forming one vast symmetrical expression of God's power and love. Life became a divine gift for every moment and sensation of which, were it even the sight of a single leaf hanging on the twig of a tree, his soul should praise and thank the Giver. The world for all its solid substance and complexity no longer existed for his soul save as a theorem of divine power and love and universality. So entire and unquestionable was this sense of the divine meaning in all nature granted to his soul that he could scarcely understand why it was in any way necessary that he should continue to live. Yet that was part of the divine purpose and he dared not question its use, he above all others who had sinned so deeply and so foully against the divine purpose. Meek and abased by this consciousness of the one eternal omnipresent perfect reality his soul took up again her burden of pieties, masses and prayers and sacraments and mortifications, and only then for the first time since he had brooded on the great mystery of love did he feel within him a warm movement like that of some newly born life or virtue of the soul itself. The attitude of rapture in sacred art, the raised and parted hands, the parted lips and eyes as of one about to swoon, became for him an image of the soul in prayer, humiliated and faint before her Creator.

But he had been forewarned of the dangers of spiritual exaltation and did not allow himself to desist from even the least or lowliest devotion, striving also by constant mortification to undo the sinful past rather than to achieve a saintliness fraught with peril. Each of his senses was brought under a rigorous discipline. In order to mortify the sense of sight he made it his rule to walk in the street with downcast eyes, glancing neither to right nor left and never behind him. His eyes shunned every encounter with the eyes of women. From time to time also he balked them by a sudden effort of the will, as by lifting them suddenly in the middle of an unfinished sentence and closing the book. To mortify his hearing he exerted no control over his voice which was then breaking, neither sang nor whistled and made no attempt to flee from noises which caused him painful nervous irritation such as the sharpening of knives on the knifeboard, the gathering of cinders on the fireshovel and the twigging of the carpet. To mortify his smell was more difficult as he found in himself no instinctive repugnance to bad odours, whether they were the odours of the outdoor world such as those of dung and tar or the odours of his own person among which he had made many curious comparisons and experiments. He found in the end that the only odour against which his sense of smell revolted was a certain stale fishy stink like that of long-standing urine: and whenever it was possible he subjected himself to this unpleasant odour. To mortify the taste he practised strict habits at table, observed to the letter all the fasts of the church and sought by distraction to divert his mind from the savours of different foods. But it was to the mortification of touch that he brought the most assiduous ingenuity of inventiveness. He never consciously changed his position in bed, sat in the most uncomfortable positions, suffered patiently every itch and pain, kept away from the fire, remained on his knees all through the mass except at the gospels, left parts of his neck and face undried so that air might sting them and, whenever he was not saying his beads, carried his arms stiffly at his sides like a runner and never in his pockets or clasped behind him.

He had no temptations to sin mortally. It surprised him however to find that at the end of his course of intricate piety and selfrestraint he was so easily at the mercy of childish and unworthy imperfections. His prayers and fasts availed him little for the suppression of anger at hearing his mother sneeze or at being disturbed in his devotions. It needed an immense effort of his will to master the impulse which urged him to give outlet to such irritation. Images of the outbursts of trivial anger which he had often noted among his masters, their twitching mouths, closeshut lips and flushed cheeks, recurred to his memory, discouraging him, for all his practice of humility, by the comparison. To merge his life in the common tide of other lives was harder for him than any fasting or prayer, and it was his constant failure to do this to his own satisfaction which caused in his soul at last a sensation of spiritual dryness together with a growth of doubts and scruples. His soul traversed a period of desolation in which the sacraments themselves seemed to have turned into dried up sources. His confession became a channel for the escape of scrupulous and unrepented imperfections. His actual reception of the eucharist did not bring him the same dissolving moments of virginal selfsurrender as did those spiritual communions made by him sometimes at the close of some visit to the Blessed Sacrament. The book which he used for these visits was an old neglected book written by saint Alphonsus Liguori, with fading characters and sere foxpapered leaves. A faded world of fervent love and virginal responses seemed to be evoked for his soul by the reading of its pages in which the imagery of the canticles was interwoven with the communicant's prayers. An inaudible voice seemed to caress the soul, telling her names and glories, bidding her arise as for espousal and come away, bidding her look forth, a spouse, from Amana and from the mountains of the leopards; and the soul seemed to answer with the same inaudible voice, surrendering herself: *Inter ubera mea commorabitur.*

This idea of surrender had a perilous attraction for his mind now that he felt his soul beset once again by the insistent voices of the flesh which began to murmur to him again during his prayers and meditations. It gave him an intense sense of power to know that he could by a single act of consent, in a moment of thought, undo all that he had done. He seemed to feel a flood slowly advancing towards his naked feet and to be waiting for the first faint timid noiseless wavelet to touch his fevered skin. Then, almost at the instant of that touch, almost at the verge of sinful consent, he found himself standing far away from the flood upon a dry shore, saved by a sudden act of the will or a sudden ejaculation: and, seeing the silver line of the flood far away and beginning again its slow advance towards his feet, a new thrill of power and satisfaction shook his soul to know that he had not yielded nor undone all.

When he had eluded the flood of temptation many times in this way he grew troubled and wondered whether the grace which he had refused to lose was not being filched from him little by little. The clear certitude of his own immunity grew dim and to it succeeded a vague fear that his soul had really fallen unawares. It was with difficulty that he won back his old consciousness of his state of grace by telling himself that he had prayed to God at every temptation and that the grace which he had prayed for must have been given to him inasmuch as God was obliged to give it. The very frequency and violence of temptations showed him at last the truth of what he had heard about the trials of the saints. Frequent and violent temptations were a proof that the citadel of the soul had not fallen and that the devil raged to make it fall.

Often when he had confessed his doubts and scruples, some momentary inattention at prayer, a movement of trivial anger in his soul or a subtle wilfulness in speech or act, he was bidden by his confessor to name some sin of his past life before absolution was given him. He named it with humility and shame and repented of it once more. It humiliated and shamed him to think that he would never be freed from it wholly, however holily he might live or whatever virtues or perfections he might attain. A restless feeling of guilt would always be present with him: he would confess and repent and be absolved, confess and repent again and be absolved again, fruitlessly. Perhaps that first hasty confession wrung from him by the fear of hell had not been good? Perhaps, concerned only for his imminent doom, he had not had sincere sorrow for his sin? But the surest sign that his confession had been good and that he had had sincere sorrow for his sin was, he knew, the amendment of his life.

—I have amended my life, have I not? he asked himself.

*   *   *

The director stood in the embrasure of the window, his back to the light, leaning an elbow on the brown crossblind and, as he spoke and smiled, slowly dangling and looping the cord of the other blind. Stephen stood before him, following for a moment with his eyes the waning of the long summer daylight above the roofs or the slow deft movements of the priestly fingers. The priest's face was in total shadow but the waning daylight from behind him touched the deeply grooved temples and the curves of the skull. Stephen followed also with his ears the accents and intervals of the priest's voice as he spoke gravely and cordially of indifferent themes, the vacation which had just ended, the colleges of the order abroad, the transference of masters. The grave and cordial voice went on easily with its tale, and in the pauses Stephen felt bound to set it on again with respectful questions. He knew that the tale was a prelude and his mind waited for the sequel. Ever since the message of summons had come for him from the director his mind had struggled to find the meaning of the message; and during the long restless time he had sat in the college parlour waiting for the director to come in his eyes had wandered from one sober picture to another around the walls and his mind wandered from one guess to another until the meaning of the summons had almost become clear. Then, just as he was wishing that some unforeseen cause might prevent the director from coming, he had heard the handle of the door turning and the swish of a soutane.

The director had begun to speak of the dominican and franciscan orders and of the friendship between saint Thomas and saint Bonaventure. The capuchin dress, he thought, was rather too . . .

Stephen's face gave back the priest's indulgent smile and, not being anxious to give an opinion, he made a slight dubitative movement with his lips.

—I believe, continued the director, that there is some talk now among the capuchins themselves of doing away with it and following the example of the other franciscans.

—I suppose they would retain it in the cloister, said Stephen.

—O, certainly, said the director. For the cloister it is all right but for the street I really think it would be better to do away with, don't you?

—It must be troublesome, I imagine?

—Of course it is, of course. Just imagine when I was in Belgium I used to see them out cycling in all kinds of weather with this thing up about their knees! It was really ridiculous. *Les jupes,* they call them in Belgium.

The vowel was so modified as to be indistinct.

—What do they call them?

—*Les jupes.*

—O.

Stephen smiled again in answer to the smile which he

could not see on the priest's shadowed face, its image
or spectre only passing rapidly across his mind as the
low discreet accent fell upon his ear. He gazed calmly
before him at the waning sky, glad of the cool of the
evening and the faint yellow glow which hid the tiny
flame kindling upon his cheek.

The names of articles of dress worn by women or of
certain soft and delicate stuffs used in their making
brought always to his mind a delicate and sinful perfume. As a boy he had imagined the reins by which
horses are driven as slender silken bands and it shocked
him to feel at Stradbrook the greasy leather of harness.
It had shocked him too when he had felt for the first
time beneath his tremulous fingers the brittle texture of
a woman's stocking for, retaining nothing of all he read
save that which seemed to him an echo or a prophecy
of his own state, it was only amid softworded phrases
or within rosesoft stuffs that he dared to conceive of
the soul or body of a woman moving with tender
life.

But the phrase on the priest's lips was disingenuous
for he knew that a priest should not speak lightly on
that theme. The phrase had been spoken lightly with
design and he felt that his face was being searched by
the eyes in the shadow. Whatever he had heard or read
of the craft of jesuits he had put aside frankly as not
borne out by his own experience. His masters, even
when they had not attracted him, had seemed to him
always intelligent and serious priests, athletic and high-
spirited prefects. He thought of them as men who
washed their bodies briskly with cold water and wore
clean cold linen. During all the years he had lived
among them in Clongowes and in Belvedere he had
received only two pandies and, though these had been
dealt him in the wrong, he knew that he had often

escaped punishment. During all those years he had never heard from any of his masters a flippant word: it was they who had taught him christian doctrine and urged him to live a good life and, when he had fallen into grievous sin, it was they who had led him back to grace. Their presence had made him diffident of himself when he was a muff in Clongowes and it had made him diffident of himself also while he had held his equivocal position in Belvedere. A constant sense of this had remained with him up to the last year of his school life. He had never once disobeyed or allowed turbulent companions to seduce him from his habit of quiet obedience: and, even when he doubted some statement of a master, he had never presumed to doubt openly. Lately some of their judgments had sounded a little childish in his ears and had made him feel a regret and pity as though he were slowly passing out of an accustomed world and were hearing its language for the last time. One day when some boys had gathered round a priest under the shed near the chapel, he had heard the priest say:

—I believe that Lord Macaulay was a man who probably never committed a mortal sin in his life, that is to say, a deliberate mortal sin.

Some of the boys had then asked the priest if Victor Hugo were not the greatest French writer. The priest had answered that Victor Hugo had never written half so well when he had turned against the church as he had written when he was a catholic.

—But there are many eminent French critics, said the priest, who consider that even Victor Hugo, great as he certainly was, had not so pure a French style as Louis Veuillot.

The tiny flame which the priest's allusion had kindled upon Stephen's cheek had sunk down again and his eyes were still fixed calmly on the colorless sky. But an unresting doubt flew hither and thither before his mind. Masked memories passed quickly before him: he recognised scenes and persons yet he was conscious that he had failed to perceive some vital circumstance in them. He saw himself walking about the grounds watching the sports in Clongowes and eating slim jim out of his cricketcap. Some jesuits were walking round the cycletrack in the company of ladies. The echoes of certain expressions used in Clongowes sounded in remote caves of his mind.

His ears were listening to these distant echoes amid the silence of the parlour when he became aware that the priest was addressing him in a different voice.

—I sent for you today, Stephen, because I wished to speak to you on a very important subject.

—Yes, sir.

—Have you ever felt that you had a vocation?

Stephen parted his lips to answer yes and then withheld the word suddenly. The priest waited for the answer and added:

—I mean have you ever felt within yourself, in your soul, a desire to join the order. Think.

—I have sometimes thought of it, said Stephen.

The priest let the blindcord fall to one side and, uniting his hands, leaned his chin gravely upon them, communing with himself.

—In a college like this, he said at length, there is one boy or perhaps two or three boys whom God calls to the religious life. Such a boy is marked off from his companions by his piety, by the good example he shows to others. He is looked up to by them; he is chosen perhaps as prefect by his fellow sodalists. And you, Stephen, have been such a boy in this college, prefect of Our Blessed Lady's sodality. Perhaps you are the boy in this college whom God designs to call to Himself.

A strong note of pride reinforcing the gravity of the priest's voice made Stephen's heart quicken in response.

—To receive that call, Stephen, said the priest, is the greatest honour that the Almighty God can bestow upon a man. No king or emperor on this earth has the power of the priest of God. No angel or archangel in heaven, no saint, not even the Blessed Virgin herself has the power of a priest of God: the power of the keys, the power to bind and to loose from sin, the power of exorcism, the power to cast out from the creatures of God the evil spirits that have power over them, the power, the authority, to make the great God of Heaven come down upon the altar and take the form of bread and wine. What an awful power, Stephen!

A flame began to flutter again on Stephen's cheek as he heard in this proud address an echo of his own proud musings. How often had he seen himself as a priest wielding calmly and humbly the awful power of which angels and saints stood in reverence! His soul had loved to muse in secret on this desire. He had seen himself, a young and silentmannered priest, entering a confessional swiftly, ascending the altarsteps, incensing, genuflecting, accomplishing the vague acts of the priesthood which pleased him by reason of their semblance of reality and of their distance from it. In that dim life which he had lived through in his musings he had assumed the voices and gestures which he had noted with various priests. He had bent his knee sideways like such a one, he had shaken the thurible only slightly like such a one, his chasuble had swung open like that of such another as he had turned to the altar again after having blessed the people. And above all it had pleased him to fill the second place in those dim scenes of his imagining. He shrank from the dignity of celebrant because it displeased him to imagine that all the vague pomp should end in his own person or that the ritual should assign to him so clear and final an office. He longed for the minor sacred offices, to be vested with the tunicle of subdeacon at high mass, to stand aloof from the altar, forgotten by the people, his shoulders covered with a humeral veil, holding the paten within its folds, or, when the sacrifice had been accomplished, to stand as deacon in a dalmatic of cloth of gold on the step below the celebrant, his hands joined and his face towards the people, and sing the chant *Ite, missa est*. If ever he had seen himself celebrant it was as in the pictures of the mass in his child's massbook, in a church without worshippers, save for the angel of the sacrifice, at a bare altar and served by an acolyte scarcely more boyish than himself. In vague sacrificial or sacramental acts alone his will seemed drawn to go forth to encounter reality: and it was partly the absence of an appointed rite which had always constrained him to inaction whether he had allowed silence to cover his anger or pride or had suffered only an embrace he longed to give.

He listened in reverent silence now to the priest's appeal and through the words he heard even more distinctly a voice bidding him approach, offering him secret knowledge and secret power. He would know then what was the sin of Simon Magus and what the sin against the Holy Ghost for which there was no forgiveness. He would know obscure things, hidden from others, from those who were conceived and born children of wrath. He would know the sins, the sinful longings and sinful thoughts and sinful acts, of others, hearing them murmured into his ears in the confes-

sional under the shame of a darkened chapel by the lips
of women and of girls: but rendered immune mysteriously at his ordination by the imposition of hands his
soul would pass again uncontaminated to the white
peace of the altar. No touch of sin would linger upon
the hands with which he would elevate and break the
host; no touch of sin would linger on his lips in prayer
to make him eat and drink damnation to himself, not
discerning the body of the Lord. He would hold his
secret knowledge and secret power, being as sinless as
the innocent: and he would be a priest for ever according to the order of Melchisedec.

—I will offer up my mass tomorrow morning, said
the director, that Almighty God may reveal to you His
holy will. And let you, Stephen, make a novena to your
holy patron saint, the first martyr, who is very powerful
with God, that God may enlighten your mind. But you
must be quite sure, Stephen, that you have a vocation
because it would be terrible if you found afterwards
that you had none. Once a priest always a priest, remember. Your catechism tells you that the sacrament
of Holy Orders is one of those which can be received
only once because it imprints on the soul an indelible
spiritual mark which can never be effaced. It is before
you must weigh well, not after. It is a solemn question,
Stephen, because on it may depend the salvation of
your eternal soul. But we will pray to God together.

He held open the heavy hall door and gave his hand
as if already to a companion in the spiritual life.
Stephen passed out on to the wide platform above the
steps and was conscious of the caress of mild evening
air. Towards Findlater's church a quartet of young men
were striding along with linked arms, swaying their
heads and stepping to the agile melody of their leader's
concertina. The music passed in an instant, as the first

bars of sudden music always did, over the fantastic fabrics of his mind, dissolving them painlessly and noiselessly as a sudden wave dissolves the sandbuilt turrets of children. Smiling at the trivial air he raised his eyes to the priest's face and, seeing in it a mirthless reflection of the sunken day, detached his hand slowly which had acquiesced faintly in that companionship.

As he descended the steps the impression which effaced his troubled selfcommunion was that of a mirthless mask reflecting a sunken day from the threshold of the college. The shadow, then, of the life of the college passed gravely over his consciousness. It was a grave and ordered and passionless life that awaited him, a life without material cares. He wondered how he would pass the first night in the novitiate and with what dismay he would wake the first morning in the dormitory. The troubling odour of the long corridors of Clongowes came back to him and he heard the discreet murmur of the burning gasflames. At once from every part of his being unrest began to irradiate. A feverish quickening of his pulses followed and a din of meaningless words drove his reasoned thoughts hither and thither confusedly. His lungs dilated and sank as if he were inhaling a warm moist unsustaining air and he smelt again the warm moist air which hung in the bath in Clongowes above the sluggish turfcoloured water.

Some instinct, waking at these memories, stronger than education or piety, quickened within him at every near approach to that life, an instinct subtle and hostile, and armed him against acquiescence. The chill and order of the life repelled him. He saw himself rising in the cold of the morning and filing down with the others to early mass and trying vainly to struggle with his prayers against the fainting sickness of his stomach. He saw himself sitting at dinner with the community of a college. What, then, had become of that deeprooted shyness of his which had made him loth to eat or drink under a strange roof? What had come of the pride of his spirit which had always made him conceive himself as a being apart in every order?

The Reverend Stephen Dedalus, S.J.

His name in that new life leaped into characters before his eyes and to it there followed a mental sensation of an undefined face or colour of a face. The colour faded and became strong like a changing glow of pallid brick red. Was it the raw reddish glow he had so often seen on wintry mornings on the shaven gills of the priests? The face was eyeless and sourfavoured and devout, shot with pink tinges of suffocated anger. Was it not a mental spectre of the face of one of the jesuits whom some of the boys called Lantern Jaws and others Foxy Campbell?

He was passing at that moment before the jesuit house in Gardiner Street, and wondered vaguely which window would be his if he ever joined the order. Then he wondered at the vagueness of his wonder, at the remoteness of his soul from what he had hitherto imagined her sanctuary, at the frail hold which so many years of order and obedience had of him when once a definite and irrevocable act of his threatened to end for ever, in time and in eternity, his freedom. The voice of the director urging upon him the proud claims of the church and the mystery and power of the priestly office repeated itself idly in his memory. His soul was not there to hear and greet it and he knew now that the exhortation he had listened to had already fallen into an idle formal tale. He would never swing the thurible before the tabernacle as priest. His destiny was to be elusive of social or religious orders. The wisdom of the priest's appeal did not touch him to the quick. He was destined to learn his own wisdom apart from others or to learn the wisdom of others himself wandering among the snares of the world.

The snares of the world were its ways of sin. He would fall. He had not yet fallen but he would fall silently, in an instant. Not to fall was too hard, too hard: and he felt the silent lapse of his soul, as it would be at some instant to come, falling, falling but not yet fallen, still unfallen but about to fall.

He crossed the bridge over the stream of the Tolka and turned his eyes coldly for an instant towards the faded blue shrine of the Blessed Virgin which stood fowlwise on a pole in the middle of a hamshaped encampment of poor cottages. Then, bending to the left, he followed the lane which led up to his house. The faint sour stink of rotted cabbages came towards him from the kitchengardens on the rising ground above the river. He smiled to think that it was this disorder, the misrule and confusion of his father's house and the stagnation of vegetable life, which was to win the day in his soul. Then a short laugh broke from his lips as he thought of that solitary farmhand in the kitchengardens behind their house whom they had nicknamed the man with the hat. A second laugh, taking rise from the first after a pause, broke from him involuntarily as he thought of how the man with the hat worked, considering in turn the four points of the sky and then regretfully plunging his spade in the earth.

He pushed open the latchless door of the porch and passed through the naked hallway into the kitchen. A group of his brothers and sisters was sitting round the table. Tea was nearly over and only the last of the second watered tea remained in the bottoms of the small glassjars and jampots which did service for teacups. Discarded crusts and lumps of sugared bread, turned brown by the tea which had been poured over them, lay scattered on the table. Little wells of tea lay here and there on the board and a knife with a broken ivory handle was stuck through the pith of a ravaged turnover.

The sad quiet greyblue glow of the dying day came through the window and the open door, covering over and allaying quietly a sudden instinct of remorse in Stephen's heart. All that had been denied them had been freely given to him, the eldest: but the quiet glow of evening showed him in their faces no sign of rancour.

He sat near them at the table and asked where his father and mother were. One answered:

—Goneboro toboro lookboro atboro aboro houseboro.

Still another removal! A boy named Fallon in Belvedere had often asked him with a silly laugh why they moved so often. A frown of scorn darkened quickly his forehead as he heard again the silly laugh of the questioner.

He asked:

—Why are we on the move again, if it's a fair question?

The same sister answered:

—Becauseboro theboro landboro lordboro willboro putboro usboro outboro.

The voice of his youngest brother from the farther side of the fireplace began to sing the air *Oft in the Stilly Night*. One by one the others took up the air until a full choir of voices was singing. They would sing so for hours, melody after melody, glee after glee, till the last pale light died down on the horizon, till the first dark nightclouds came forth and night fell.

He waited for some moments, listening, before he

too took up the air with them. He was listening with pain of spirit to the overtone of weariness behind their frail fresh innocent voices. Even before they set out on life's journey they seemed weary already of the way.

He heard the choir of voices in the kitchen echoed and multiplied through an endless reverberation of the choirs of endless generations of children: and heard in all the echoes an echo also of the recurring note of weariness and pain. All seemed weary of life even before entering upon it. And he remembered that Newman had heard this note also in the broken lines of Virgil *giving utterance, like the voice of Nature herself, to that pain and weariness yet hope of better things which has been the experience of her children in every time.*

       ✿   ✿   ✿

He could wait no longer.

From the door of Byron's publichouse to the gate of Clontarf Chapel, from the gate of Clontarf Chapel to the door of Byron's publichouse and then back again to the chapel and then back again to the publichouse he had paced slowly at first, planting his steps scrupulously in the spaces of the patchwork of the footpath, then timing their fall to the fall of verses. A full hour had passed since his father had gone in with Dan Crosby, the tutor, to find out for him something about the university. For a full hour he had paced up and down, waiting: but he could wait no longer.

He set off abruptly for the Bull, walking rapidly lest his father's shrill whistle might call him back; and in a few moments he had rounded the curve at the police barrack and was safe.

Yes, his mother was hostile to the idea, as he had read from her listless silence. Yet her mistrust pricked him more keenly than his father's pride and he thought coldly how he had watched the faith which was fading down in his soul aging and strengthening in her eyes. A dim antagonism gathered force within him and darkened his mind as a cloud against her disloyalty: and when it passed, cloudlike, leaving his mind serene and dutiful towards her again, he was made aware dimly and without regret of a first noiseless sundering of their lives.

The university! So he had passed beyond the challenge of the sentries who had stood as guardians of his boyhood and had sought to keep him among them that he might be subject to them and serve their ends. Pride after satisfaction uplifted him like long slow waves. The end he had been born to serve yet did not see had led him to escape by an unseen path: and now it beckoned to him once more and a new adventure was about to be opened to him. It seemed to him that he heard notes of fitful music leaping upwards a tone and downwards a diminished fourth, upwards a tone and downwards a major third, like triplebranching flames leaping fitfully, flame after flame, out of a midnight wood. It was an elfin prelude, endless and formless; and, as it grew wilder and faster, the flames leaping out of time, he seemed to hear from under the boughs and grasses wild creatures racing, their feet pattering like rain upon the leaves. Their feet passed in pattering tumult over his mind, the feet of hares and rabbits, the feet of harts and hinds and antelopes, until he heard them no more and remembered only a proud cadence from Newman: *Whose feet are as the feet of harts and underneath the everlasting arms.*

The pride of that dim image brought back to his mind the dignity of the office he had refused. All through his boyhood he had mused upon that which he had so often thought to be his destiny and when the moment had come for him to obey the call he had turned aside, obeying a wayward instinct. Now time lay between: the oils of ordination would never anoint his body. He had refused. Why?

He turned seaward from the road at Dollymount and as he passed on to the thin wooden bridge he felt the planks shaking with the tramp of heavily shod feet. A squad of christian brothers was on its way back from the Bull and had begun to pass, two by two, across the bridge. Soon the whole bridge was trembling and resounding. The uncouth faces passed him two by two, stained yellow or red or livid by the sea, and as he strove to look at them with ease and indifference, a faint stain of personal shame and commiseration rose to his own face. Angry with himself he tried to hide his face from their eyes by gazing down sideways into the shallow swirling water under the bridge but he still saw a reflection therein of their topheavy silk hats, and humble tapelike collars and loosely hanging clerical clothes.

—Brother Hickey.

Brother Quaid.

Brother MacArdle.

Brother Keogh.

Their piety would be like their names, like their faces, like their clothes, and it was idle for him to tell himself that their humble and contrite hearts, it might be, paid a far richer tribute of devotion than his had ever been, a gift tenfold more acceptable than his elaborate adoration. It was idle for him to move himself to be generous towards them, to tell himself that if he ever came to their gates, stripped of his pride, beaten and in beggar's weeds, that they would be generous towards him, loving him as themselves. Idle and embittering, finally, to argue, against his own dispassionate certitude, that the commandment of love bade us not to love our neighbour as ourselves with the same amount and intensity of love but to love him as ourselves with the same kind of love.

He drew forth a phrase from his treasure and spoke it softly to himself:

—A day of dappled seaborne clouds.

The phrase and the day and the scene harmonised in a chord. Words. Was it their colours? He allowed them to glow and fade, hue after hue: sunrise gold, the russet and green of apple orchards, azure of waves, the grey-fringed fleece of clouds. No, it was not their colours: it was the poise and balance of the period itself. Did he then love the rhythmic rise and fall of words better than their associations of legend and colour? Or was it that, being as weak of sight as he was shy of mind, he drew less pleasure from the reflection of the glowing sensible world through the prism of a language many-coloured and richly storied than from the contemplation of an inner world of individual emotions mirrored perfectly in a lucid supple periodic prose?

He passed from the trembling bridge on to firm land again. At that instant, as it seemed to him, the air was chilled and looking askance towards the water he saw a flying squall darkening and crisping suddenly the tide. A faint click at his heart, a faint throb in his throat told him once more of how his flesh dreaded the cold infrahuman odour of the sea: yet he did not strike across the downs on his left but held straight on along the spine of rocks that pointed against the river's mouth.

A veiled sunlight lit up faintly the grey sheet of water where the river was embayed. In the distance along the course of the slowflowing Liffey slender masts flecked the sky and, more distant still, the dim fabric of the city lay prone in haze. Like a scene on some vague arras, old as man's weariness, the image of the seventh city of christendom was visible to him across the timeless air, no older nor more weary nor less patient of subjection than in the days of the thingmote.

Disheartened, he raised his eyes towards the slow-drifting clouds, dappled and seaborne. They were voyaging across the deserts of the sky, a host of no-mads on the march, voyaging high over Ireland, west-ward bound. The Europe they had come from lay out there beyond the Irish Sea, Europe of strange tongues and valleyed and woodbegirt and citadelled and of entrenched and marshalled races. He heard a confused music within him as of memories and names which he was almost conscious of but could not capture even for an instant; then the music seemed to recede, to recede, to recede: and from each receding trail of nebulous music there fell always one longdrawn calling note, piercing like a star the dusk of silence. Again! Again! Again! A voice from beyond the world was calling.

—Hello, Stephanos!

—Here comes The Dedalus!

—Ao! . . . Eh, give it over, Dwyer, I'm telling you or I'll give you a stuff in the kisser for yourself. . . . Ao!

—Good man, Towser! Duck him!

—Come along, Dedalus! Bous Stephanoumenos! Bous Stephaneforos!

—Duck him! Guzzle him now, Towser!

—Help! Help! . . . Ao!

He recognised their speech collectively before he dis-tinguished their faces. The mere sight of that medley of wet nakedness chilled him to the bone. Their bodies, corpsewhite or suffused with a pallid golden light or rawly tanned by the suns, gleamed with the wet of the sea. Their divingstone, poised on its rude supports and rocking under their plunges, and the roughhewn stones of the sloping breakwater over which they scrambled in their horseplay, gleamed with cold wet lustre. The towels with which they smacked their bodies were heavy with cold seawater: and drenched with cold brine was their matted hair.

He stood still in deference to their calls and parried their banter with easy words. How characterless they looked: Shuley without his deep unbuttoned collar, Ennis without his scarlet belt with the snaky clasp, and Connolly without his Norfolk coat with the flapless sidepockets! It was a pain to see them and a swordlike pain to see the signs of adolescence that made repellent their pitiable nakedness. Perhaps they had taken refuge in number and noise from the secret dread in their souls. But he, apart from them and in silence, remembered in what dread he stood of the mystery of his own body.

—Stephanos Dedalos! Bous Stephanoumenos! Bous Stephaneforos!

Their banter was not new to him and now it flattered his mild proud sovereignty. Now, as never before, his strange name seemed to him a prophecy. So timeless seemed the grey warm air, so fluid and impersonal his own mood, that all ages were as one to him. A moment before the ghost of the ancient kingdom of the Danes had looked forth through the vesture of the haze-wrapped city. Now, at the name of the fabulous artificer, he seemed to hear the noise of dim waves and to see a winged form flying above the waves and slowly climbing the air. What did it mean? Was it a quaint device opening a page of some medieval book of prophecies and symbols, a hawklike man flying sunward above the sea, a prophecy of the end he had been born to serve and had been following through the mists of childhood and boyhood, a symbol of the artist forging anew in his workshop out of the sluggish matter of the earth a new soaring impalpable imperishable being?

His heart trembled; his breath came faster and a wild spirit passed over his limbs as though he were soaring sunward. His heart trembled in an ecstasy of fear and his soul was in flight. His soul was soaring in an air beyond the world and the body he knew was purified in a breath and delivered of incertitude and made radiant and commingled with the element of the spirit. An ecstasy of flight made radiant his eyes and wild his breath and tremulous and wild and radiant his windswept limbs.

—One! Two! . . . Look out!

—O, cripes, I'm drowneded!

—One! Two! Three and away!

—Me next! Me next!

—One! . . . Uk!

—Stephaneforos!

His throat ached with a desire to cry aloud, the cry of a hawk or eagle on high, to cry piercingly of his deliverance to the winds. This was the call of life to his soul not the dull gross voice of the world of duties and despair, not the inhuman voice that had called him to the pale service of the altar. An instant of wild flight had delivered him and the cry of triumph which his lips withheld cleft his brain.

—Stephaneforos!

What were they now but cerements shaken from the body of death—the fear he had walked in night and day, the incertitude that had ringed him round, the shame that had abased him within and without—cerements, the linens of the grave?

His soul had arisen from the grave of boyhood,

spurning her graveclothes. Yes! Yes! Yes! He would create proudly out of the freedom and power of his soul, as the great artificer whose name he bore, a living thing, new and soaring and beautiful, impalpable, imperishable.

He started up nervously from the stoneblock for he could no longer quench the flame in his blood. He felt his cheeks aflame and his throat throbbing with song. There was a lust of wandering in his feet that burned to set out for the ends of the earth. On! On! his heart seemed to cry. Evening would deepen above the sea, night fall upon the plains, dawn glimmer before the wanderer and show him strange fields and hills and faces. Where?

He looked northward towards Howth. The sea had fallen below the line of seawrack on the shallow side of the breakwater and already the tide was running out fast along the foreshore. Already one long oval bank of sand lay warm and dry amid the wavelets. Here and there warm isles of sand gleamed above the shallow tide, and about the isles and around the long bank and amid the shallow currents of the beach were light-clad gayclad figures, wading and delving.

In a few moments he was barefoot, his stockings folded in his pockets and his canvas shoes dangling by their knotted laces over his shoulders: and, picking a pointed salteaten stick out of the jetsam among the rocks, he clambered down the slope of the breakwater.

There was a long rivulet in the strand: and, as he waded slowly up its course, he wondered at the endless drift of seaweed. Emerald and black and russet and olive, it moved beneath the current, swaying and turning. The water of the rivulet was dark with endless drift and mirrored the highdrifting clouds. The clouds were drifting above him silently and silently the seatangle was drifting below him; and the grey warm air was still: and a new wild life was singing in his veins.

Where was his boyhood now? Where was the soul that had hung back from her destiny, to brood alone upon the shame of her wounds and in her house of squalor and subterfuge to queen it in faded cerements and in wreaths that withered at the touch? Or where was he?

He was alone. He was unheeded, happy and near to the wild heart of life. He was alone and young and wilful and wildhearted, alone amid a waste of wild air and brackish waters and the seaharvest of shells and tangle and veiled grey sunlight and gayclad lightclad figures, of children and girls and voices childish and girlish in the air.

A girl stood before him in midstream, alone and still, gazing out to sea. She seemed like one whom magic had changed into the likeness of a strange and beautiful seabird. Her long slender bare legs were delicate as a crane's and pure save where an emerald trail of sea-weed had fashioned itself as a sign upon the flesh. Her thighs, fuller and softhued as ivory, were bared almost to the hips where the white fringes of her drawers were like featherings of soft white down. Her slateblue skirts were kilted boldly about her waist and dovetailed behind her. Her bosom was as a bird's soft and slight, slight and soft as the breast of some darkplumaged dove. But her long fair hair was girlish: and girlish, and touched with the wonder of mortal beauty, her face.

She was alone and still, gazing out to sea; and when she felt his presence and the worship of his eyes her eyes turned to him in quiet sufferance of his gaze, without shame or wantonness. Long, long she suffered his gaze and then quietly withdrew her eyes from his and bent them towards the stream, gently stirring the water with her foot hither and thither. The first faint noise of gently moving water broke the silence, low and faint and whispering, faint as the bells of sleep; hither and thither, hither and thither: and a faint flame trembled on her cheek.

—Heavenly God! cried Stephen's soul, in an outburst of profane joy.

He turned away from her suddenly and set off across the strand. His cheeks were aflame; his body was aglow; his limbs were trembling. On and on and on and on he strode, far out over the sands, singing wildly to the sea, crying to greet the advent of the life that had cried to him.

Her image had passed into his soul for ever and no word had broken the holy silence of his ecstasy. Her eyes had called him and his soul had leaped at the call. To live, to err, to fall, to triumph, to recreate life out of life! A wild angel had appeared to him, the angel of mortal youth and beauty, an envoy from the fair courts of life, to throw open before him in an instant of ecstasy the gates of all the ways of error and glory. On and on and on and on!

He halted suddenly and heard his heart in the silence. How far had he walked? What hour was it?

There was no human figure near him nor any sound borne to him over the air. But the tide was near the turn and already the day was on the wane. He turned landward and ran towards the shore and, running up the sloping beach, reckless of the sharp shingle, found a sandy nook amid a ring of tufted sandknolls and lay down there that the peace and silence of the evening might still the riot of his blood.

He felt above him the vast indifferent dome and the calm processes of the heavenly bodies; and the earth beneath him, the earth that had borne him, had taken him to her breast.

He closed his eyes in the languor of sleep. His eyelids trembled as if they felt the vast cyclic movement of the earth and her watchers, trembled as if they felt the strange light of some new world. His soul was swooning into some new world, fantastic, dim, uncertain as under sea, traversed by cloudy shapes and beings. A world, a glimmer, or a flower? Glimmering and trembling, trembling and unfolding, a breaking light, an opening flower, it spread in endless succession to itself, breaking in full crimson and unfolding and fading to palest rose, leaf by leaf and wave of light by wave of light, flooding all the heavens with its soft flushes, every flush deeper than other.

Evening had fallen when he woke and the sand and arid grasses of his bed glowed no longer. He rose slowly and, recalling the rapture of his sleep, sighed at its joy.

He climbed to the crest of the sandhill and gazed about him. Evening had fallen. A rim of the young moon cleft the pale waste of sky like the rim of a silver hoop embedded in grey sand; and the tide was flowing in fast to the land with a low whisper of her waves, islanding a few last figures in distant pools.

V

HE DRAINED his third cup of watery tea to the dregs and set to chewing the crusts of fried bread that were scattered near him, staring into the dark pool of the jar. The yellow dripping had been scooped out like a boghole and the pool under it brought back to his memory the dark turfcoloured water of the bath in

Clongowes. The box of pawntickets at his elbow had just been rifled and he took up idly one after another in his greasy fingers the blue and white dockets, scrawled and sanded and creased and bearing the name of the pledger as Daly or MacEvoy.

1 Pair Buskins.

1 D. Coat.

3 Articles and White.

1 Man's Pants.

Then he put them aside and gazed thoughtfully at the lid of the box, speckled with lousemarks, and asked vaguely:

—How much is the clock fast now?

His mother straightened the battered alarmclock that was lying on its side in the middle of the kitchen mantelpiece until its dial showed a quarter to twelve and then laid it once more on its side.

—An hour and twentyfive minutes, she said. The right time now is twenty past ten. The dear knows you might try to be in time for your lectures.

—Fill out the place for me to wash, said Stephen.

—Katey, fill out the place for Stephen to wash.

—Boody, fill out the place for Stephen to wash.

—I can't, I'm going for blue. Fill it out, you, Maggie.

When the enamelled basin had been fitted into the well of the sink and the old washingglove flung on the side of it he allowed his mother to scrub his neck and root into the folds of his ears and into the interstices at the wings of his nose.

—Well, it's a poor case, she said, when a university student is so dirty that his mother has to wash him.

—But it gives you pleasure, said Stephen calmly.

An earsplitting whistle was heard from upstairs and his mother thrust a damp overall into his hands, saying:

—Dry yourself and hurry out for the love of goodness.

A second shrill whistle, prolonged angrily, brought one of the girls to the foot of the staircase.

—Yes, father?

—Is your lazy bitch of a brother gone out yet?

—Yes, father.

—Sure?

—Yes, father.

—Hm!

The girl came back making signs to him to be quick and go out quietly by the back. Stephen laughed and said:

—He has a curious idea of genders if he thinks a bitch is masculine.

—Ah, it's a scandalous shame for you, Stephen, said his mother, and you'll live to rue the day you set your foot in that place. I know how it has changed you.

—Good morning, everybody, said Stephen, smiling and kissing the tips of his fingers in adieu.

The lane behind the terrace was waterlogged and as he went down it slowly, choosing his steps amid heaps of wet rubbish, he heard a mad nun screeching in the nuns' madhouse beyond the wall.

—Jesus! O Jesus! Jesus!

He shook the sound out of his ears by an angry toss of his head and hurried on, stumbling through the mouldering offal, his heart already bitten by an ache of loathing and bitterness. His father's whistle, his mother's mutterings, the screech of an unseen maniac were to him now so many voices offending and threatening to humble the pride of his youth. He drove their echoes even out of his heart with an execration: but, as he walked down the avenue and felt the grey morning light falling about him through the dripping trees and smelt the strange wild smell of the wet leaves and bark, his soul was loosed of her miseries.

The rainladen trees of the avenue evoked in him, as always, memories of the girls and women in the plays of Gerhart Hauptmann; and the memory of their pale sorrows and the fragrance falling from the wet branches mingled in a mood of quiet joy. His morning walk across the city had begun, and he foreknew that as he passed the sloblands of Fairview he would think of the cloistral silverveined prose of Newman, that as he walked along the North Strand Road, glancing idly at the windows of the provision shops, he would recall the dark humour of Guido Cavalcanti and smile, that as he went by Baird's stonecutting works in Talbot Place the spirit of Ibsen would blow through him like a keen wind, a spirit of wayward boyish beauty, and that passing a grimy marinedealer's shop beyond the Liffey he would repeat the song by Ben Jonson which begins:

I was not wearier where I lay.

His mind, when wearied of its search for the essence of beauty amid the spectral words of Aristotle or Aquinas, turned often for its pleasure to the dainty songs of the Elizabethans. His mind, in the vesture of a doubting monk, stood often in shadow under the windows of that age, to hear the grave and mocking music of the lutenists or the frank laughter of waistcoateers until a laugh too low, a phrase, tarnished by time, of chambering and false honour, stung his monkish pride and drove him on from his lurkingplace.

The lore which he was believed to pass his days brooding upon so that it had rapt him from the companionships of youth was only a garner of slender sentences from Aristotle's poetics and psychology and a *Synopsis Philosophiæ Scholasticæ ad mentem divi*

Thomæ. His thinking was a dusk of doubt and selfmis-
trust lit up at moments by the lightnings of intuition,
but lightnings of so clear a splendour that in those
moments the world perished about his feet as if it had
been fireconsumed: and thereafter his tongue grew
heavy and he met the eyes of others with unanswering
eyes for he felt that the spirit of beauty had folded him
round like a mantle and that in revery at least he had
been acquainted with nobility. But, when this brief
pride of silence upheld him no longer, he was glad to
find himself still in the midst of common lives, passing
on his way amid the squalor and noise and sloth of the
city fearlessly and with a light heart.

Near the hoardings on the canal he met the consumptive man with the doll's face and the brimless hat
coming towards him down the slope of the bridge with
little steps, tightly buttoned into his chocolate overcoat,
and holding his furled umbrella a span or two from
him like a diviningrod. It must be eleven, he thought,
and peered into a dairy to see the time. The clock in
the dairy told him that it was five minutes to five but,
as he turned away, he heard a clock somewhere near
him, but unseen, beating eleven strokes in swift precision. He laughed as he heard it for it made him think
of MacCann and he saw him a squat figure in a shooting jacket and breeches and with a fair goatee, standing
in the wind at Hopkins' corner, and heard him say:

—Dedalus, you're an antisocial being, wrapped up in
yourself. I'm not. I'm a democrat: and I'll work and
act for social liberty and equality among all classes and
sexes in the United States of the Europe of the future.

Eleven! Then he was late for that lecture too. What
day of the week was it? He stopped at a newsagent's to
read the headline of a placard. Thursday. Ten to
eleven, English; eleven to twelve, French; twelve to

one, physics. He fancied to himself the English lecture and felt, even at that distance, restless and helpless. He saw the heads of his classmates meekly bent as they wrote in their notebooks the points they were bidden to note, nominal definitions, essential definitions and examples or dates of birth or death, chief works, a favourable and an unfavourable criticism side by side. His own head was unbent for his thoughts wandered abroad and whether he looked around the little class of students or out of the window across the desolate gardens of the green an odour assailed him of cheerless cellardamp and decay. Another head than his, right before him in the first benches, was poised squarely above its bending fellows like the head of a priest appealing without humility to the tabernacle for the humble worshippers about him. Why was it that when he thought of Cranly he could never raise before his mind the entire image of his body but only the image of the head and face? Even now against the grey curtain of the morning he saw it before him like the phantom of a dream, the face of a severed head or deathmask, crowned on the brows by its stiff black upright hair as by an iron crown. It was a priestlike face, priestlike in its pallor, in the widewinged nose, in the shadowings below the eyes and along the jaws, priestlike in the lips that were long and bloodless and faintly smiling: and Stephen, remembering swiftly how he had told Cranly of all the tumults and unrest and longings in his soul, day after day and night by night, only to be answered by his friend's listening silence, would have told himself that it was the face of a guilty priest who heard confessions of those whom he had not power to absolve but that he felt again in memory the gaze of its dark womanish eyes.

Through this image he had a glimpse of a strange

dark cavern of speculation but at once turned away from it, feeling that it was not yet the hour to enter it. But the nightshade of his friend's listlessness seemed to be diffusing in the air around him a tenuous and deadly exhalation and he found himself glancing from one casual word to another on his right or left in stolid wonder that they had been so silently emptied of instantaneous sense until every mean shop legend bound his mind like the words of a spell and his soul shrivelled up, sighing with age as he walked on in a lane among heaps of dead language. His own consciousness of language was ebbing from his brain and trickling into the very words themselves which set to band and disband themselves in wayward rhythms:

> *The ivy whines upon the wall*
> *And whines and twines upon the wall*
> *The ivy whines upon the wall*
> *The yellow ivy on the wall*
> *Ivy, ivy up the wall.*

Did any one ever hear such drivel? Lord Almighty! Who ever heard of ivy whining on a wall? Yellow ivy: that was all right. Yellow ivory also. And what about ivory ivy?

The word now shone in his brain, clearer and brighter than any ivory sawn from the mottled tusks of elephants. *Ivory, ivoire, avorio, ebur.* One of the first examples that he had learnt in Latin had run: *India mittit ebur*; and he recalled the shrewd northern face of the rector who had taught him to construe the Metamorphoses of Ovid in a courtly English, made whimsical by the mention of porkers and potsherds and chines of bacon. He had learnt what little he knew of the laws of Latin verse from a ragged book written by a Portuguese priest.

Contrahit orator, variant in carmine vates.

The crises and victories and secessions in Roman history were handed on to him in the trite words *in tanto discrimine* and he had tried to peer into the social life of the city of cities through the words *implere ollam denariorum* which the rector had rendered sonorously as the filling of a pot with denaries. The pages of his timeworn Horace never felt cold to the touch even when his own fingers were cold: they were human pages: and fifty years before they had been turned by the human fingers of John Duncan Inverarity and by his brother, William Malcolm Inverarity. Yes, those were noble names on the dusky flyleaf and, even for so poor a Latinist as he, the dusky verses were as fragrant as though they had lain all those years in myrtle and lavender and vervain; but yet it wounded him to think that he would never be but a shy guest at the feast of the world's culture and that the monkish learning, in terms of which he was striving to forge out an esthetic philosophy, was held no higher by the age he lived in than the subtle and curious jargons of heraldry and falconry.

The grey block of Trinity on his left, set heavily in the city's ignorance like a great dull stone set in a cumbrous ring, pulled his mind downward; and while he was striving this way and that to free his feet from the fetters of the reformed conscience he came upon the droll statue of the national poet of Ireland.

He looked at it without anger: for, though sloth of the body and of the soul crept over it like unseen vermin, over the shuffling feet and up the folds of the cloak and around the servile head, it seemed humbly conscious of its indignity. It was a Firbolg in the borrowed cloak of a Milesian; and he thought of his friend

Davin, the peasant student. It was a jesting name between them but the young peasant bore with it lightly saying:

—Go on, Stevie, I have a hard head, you tell me. Call me what you will.

The homely version of his christian name on the lips of his friend had touched Stephen pleasantly when first heard for he was as formal in speech with others as they were with him. Often, as he sat in Davin's rooms in Grantham Street, wondering at his friend's wellmade boots that flanked the wall pair by pair and repeating for his friend's simple ear the verses and cadences of others which were the veils of his own longing and dejection, the rude Firbolg mind of his listener had drawn his mind towards it and flung it back again, drawing it by a quiet inbred courtesy of attention or by a quaint turn of old English speech or by the force of its delight in rude bodily skill—for Davin had sat at the feet of Michael Cusack, the Gael—repelling swiftly and suddenly by a grossness of intelligence or by a bluntness of feeling or by a dull stare of terror in the eyes, the terror of soul of a starving Irish village in which the curfew was still a nightly fear.

Side by side with his memory of the deeds of prowess of his uncle Mat Davin, the athlete, the young peasant worshipped the sorrowful legend of Ireland. The gossip of his fellowstudents which strove to render the flat life of the college significant at any cost loved to think of him as a young fenian. His nurse had taught him Irish and shaped his rude imagination by the broken lights of Irish myth. He stood towards this myth upon which no individual mind had ever drawn out a line of beauty and to its unwieldy tales that divided themselves as they moved down the cycles in the same attitude as towards the Roman catholic religion, the attitude of a dullwitted loyal serf. Whatsoever of thought or of feeling came to him from England or by way of English culture his mind stood armed against in obedience to a password: and of the world that lay beyond England he knew only the foreign legion of France in which he spoke of serving.

Coupling this ambition with the young man's humour Stephen had often called him one of the tame geese: and there was even a point of irritation in the name pointed against that very reluctance of speech and deed in his friend which seemed so often to stand between Stephen's mind, eager of speculation, and the hidden ways of Irish life.

One night the young peasant, his spirit stung by the violent or luxurious language in which Stephen escaped from the cold silence of intellectual revolt, had called up before Stephen's mind a strange vision. The two were walking slowly towards Davin's room through the dark narrow streets of the poorer jews.

—A thing happened to myself, Stevie, last autumn, coming on winter, and I never told it to a living soul and you are the first person now I ever told it to. I disremember if it was October or November. It was October because it was before I came up here to join the matriculation class.

Stephen had turned his smiling eyes towards his friend's face, flattered by his confidence and won over to sympathy by the speaker's simple accent.

—I was away all that day from my own place over in Buttevant—I don't know if you know where that is—at a hurling match between the Croke's Own Boys and the Fearless Thurles and by God, Stevie, that was the hard fight. My first cousin, Fonsy Davin, was stripped to his buff that day minding cool for the Limericks but he was up with the forwards half the time and shouting like mad. I never will forget that day. One of the Crokes made a woeful wipe at him one time with his camaun and I declare to God he was within an aim's ace of getting it at the side of the temple. O, honest to God, if the crook of it caught him that time he was done for.

—I am glad he escaped, Stephen had said with a laugh, but surely that's not the strange thing that happened you?

—Well, I suppose that doesn't interest you but leastways there was such noise after the match that I missed the train home and I couldn't get any kind of a yoke to give me a lift for, as luck would have it, there was a mass meeting that same day over in Castletownroche and all the cars in the country were there. So there was nothing for it only to stay the night or to foot it out. Well, I started to walk and on I went and it was coming on night when I got into the Ballyhoura hills; that's better than ten miles from Kilmallock and there's a long lonely road after that. You wouldn't see the sign of a christian house along the road or hear a sound. It was pitch dark almost. Once or twice I stopped by the way under a bush to redden my pipe and only for the dew was thick I'd have stretched out there and slept. At last, after a bend of the road, I spied a little cottage with a light in the window. I went up and knocked at the door. A voice asked who was there and I answered I was over at the match in Buttevant and was walking back and that I'd be thankful for a glass of water. After a while a young woman opened the door and brought me out a big mug of milk. She was half undressed as if she was going to bed when I knocked and she had her hair hanging; and I thought by her figure and by something in the look of her eyes that she must be carrying a child. She kept me in talk a long while at the door and I thought it strange because her breast and her shoulders were bare. She asked me was I tired and would I like to stop the night there. She said she was all alone in the house and that her husband had gone that morning to Queenstown with his sister to see her off. And all the time she was talking, Stevie, she had her eyes fixed on my face and she stood so close to me I could hear her breathing. When I handed her back the mug at last she took my hand to draw me in over the threshold and said: *Come in and stay the night here. You've no call to be frightened. There's no-one in it but ourselves*. . . . I didn't go in, Stevie. I thanked her and went on my way again, all in a fever. At the first bend of the road I looked back and she was standing at the door.

The last words of Davin's story sang in his memory and the figure of the woman in the story stood forth, reflected in other figures of the peasant women whom he had seen standing in the doorways at Clane as the college cars drove by, as a type of her race and his own, a batlike soul waking to the consciousness of itself in darkness and secrecy and loneliness and, through the eyes and voice and gesture of a woman without guile, calling the stranger to her bed.

A hand was laid on his arm and a young voice cried:

—Ah, gentleman, your own girl, sir! The first handsel today, gentleman. Buy that lovely bunch. Will you, gentleman?

The blue flowers which she lifted towards him and her young blue eyes seemed to him at that instant images of guilelessness; and he halted till the image had vanished and he saw only her ragged dress and damp coarse hair and hoydenish face.

—Do, gentleman! Don't forget your own girl, sir!

—I have no money, said Stephen.

—Buy them lovely ones, will you, sir? Only a penny.

—Did you hear what I said? asked Stephen, bending towards her. I told you I had no money. I tell you again now.

—Well, sure, you will some day, sir, please God, the girl answered after an instant.

—Possibly, said Stephen, but I don't think it likely.

He left her quickly, fearing that her intimacy might turn to gibing and wishing to be out of the way before she offered her ware to another, a tourist from England or a student of Trinity. Grafton Street, along which he walked, prolonged that moment of discouraged poverty. In the roadway at the head of the street a slab was set to the memory of Wolfe Tone and he remembered having been present with his father at its laying. He remembered with bitterness that scene of tawdry tribute. There were four French delegates in a brake and one, a plump smiling young man, held, wedged on a stick, a card on which were printed the words: *Vive l'Irlande!*

But the trees in Stephen's Green were fragrant of rain and the rainsodden earth gave forth its mortal odour, a faint incense rising upward through the mould from many hearts. The soul of the gallant venal city which his elders had told him of had shrunk with time to a faint mortal odour rising from the earth and he knew that in a moment when he entered the sombre college he would be conscious of a corruption other than that of Buck Egan and Burnchapel Whaley.

It was too late to go upstairs to the French class. He crossed the hall and took the corridor to the left which led to the physics theatre. The corridor was dark and silent but not unwatchful. Why did he feel that it was not unwatchful? Was it because he had heard that in Buck Whaley's time there was a secret staircase there?

Or was the jesuit house extraterritorial and was he walking among aliens? The Ireland of Tone and of Parnell seemed to have receded in space.

He opened the door of the theatre and halted in the chilly grey light that struggled through the dusty windows. A figure was crouching before the large grate and by its leanness and greyness he knew that it was the dean of studies lighting the fire. Stephen closed the door quietly and approached the fireplace.

—Good morning, sir! Can I help you?

The priest looked up quickly and said:

—One moment now, Mr Dedalus, and you will see. There is an art in lighting a fire. We have the liberal arts and we have the useful arts. This is one of the useful arts.

—I will try to learn it, said Stephen.

—Not too much coal, said the dean, working briskly at his task, that is one of the secrets.

He produced four candlebutts from the sidepockets of his soutane and placed them deftly among the coals and twisted papers. Stephen watched him in silence. Kneeling thus on the flagstone to kindle the fire and busied with the disposition of his wisps of paper and candlebutts he seemed more than ever a humble server making ready the place of sacrifice in an empty temple, a levite of the Lord. Like a levite's robe of plain linen the faded worn soutane draped the kneeling figure of one whom the canonicals or the bellbordered ephod would irk and trouble. His very body had waxed old in lowly service of the Lord—in tending the fire upon the altar, in bearing tidings secretly, in waiting upon worldlings, in striking swiftly when bidden—and yet had remained ungraced by aught of saintly or of prelatic beauty. Nay, his very soul had waxed old in that service without growing towards light and beauty or spreading abroad a sweet odour of her sanctity—a mortified will no more responsive to the thrill of its obedience than was to the thrill of love or combat his aging body, spare and sinewy, greyed with a silver-pointed down.

The dean rested back on his hunkers and watched the sticks catch. Stephen, to fill the silence, said:

—I am sure I could not light a fire.

—You are an artist, are you not, Mr Dedalus? said the dean, glancing up and blinking his pale eyes. The object of the artist is the creation of the beautiful. What the beautiful is is another question.

He rubbed his hands slowly and drily over the difficulty.

—Can you solve that question now? he asked.

—Aquinas, answered Stephen, says *Pulcra sunt quæ visa placent.*

—This fire before us, said the dean, will be pleasing to the eye. Will it therefore be beautiful?

—In so far as it is apprehended by the sight, which I suppose means here esthetic intellection, it will be beautiful. But Aquinas also says *Bonum est in quod tendit appetitus.* In so far as it satisfies the animal craving for warmth fire is a good. In hell however it is an evil.

—Quite so, said the dean, you have certainly hit the nail on the head.

He rose nimbly and went towards the door, set it ajar and said:

—A draught is said to be a help in these matters.

As he came back to the hearth, limping slightly but with a brisk step, Stephen saw the silent soul of a jesuit look out at him from the pale loveless eyes. Like Ignatius he was lame but in his eyes burned no spark of Ignatius' enthusiasm. Even the legendary craft of the

company, a craft subtler and more secret than its
fabled books of secret subtle wisdom, had not fired his
soul with the energy of apostleship. It seemed as if he
used the shifts and lore and cunning of the world, as
bidden to do, for the greater glory of God, without joy
in their handling or hatred of that in them which was
evil but turning them, with a firm gesture of obedience,
back upon themselves: and for all this silent service it
seemed as if he loved not at all the master and little, if
at all, the ends he served. *Similiter atque senis baculus,*
he was, as the founder would have had him, like a staff
in an old man's hand, to be left in a corner, to be
leaned on in the road at nightfall or in stress of
weather, to lie with a lady's nosegay on a garden seat,
to be raised in menace.

The dean returned to the hearth and began to stroke
his chin.

—When may we expect to have something from you
on the esthetic question? he asked.

—From me! said Stephen in astonishment. I stumble
on an idea once a fortnight if I am lucky.

—These questions are very profound, Mr Dedalus,
said the dean. It is like looking down from the cliffs of
Moher into the depths. Many go down into the depths
and never come up. Only the trained diver can go down
into those depths and explore them and come to the
surface again.

—If you mean speculation, sir, said Stephen, I also
am sure that there is no such thing as free thinking
inasmuch as all thinking must be bound by its own
laws.

—Ha!

—For my purpose I can work on at present by the
light of one or two ideas of Aristotle and Aquinas.

—I see. I quite see your point.

—I need them only for my own use and guidance until I have done something for myself by their light. If the lamp smokes or smells I shall try to trim it. If it does not give light enough I shall sell it and buy another.

—Epictetus also had a lamp, said the dean, which was sold for a fancy price after his death. It was the lamp he wrote his philosophical dissertations by. You know Epictetus?

—An old gentleman, said Stephen coarsely, who said that the soul is very like a bucketful of water.

—He tells us in his homely way, the dean went on, that he put an iron lamp before a statue of one of the gods and that a thief stole the lamp. What did the philosopher do? He reflected that it was in the character of a thief to steal and determined to buy an earthen lamp next day instead of the iron lamp.

A smell of molten tallow came up from the dean's candlebutts and fused itself in Stephen's consciousness with the jingle of the words, bucket and lamp and lamp and bucket. The priest's voice too had a hard jingling tone. Stephen's mind halted by instinct, checked by the strange tone and the imagery and by the priest's face which seemed like an unlit lamp or a reflector hung in a false focus. What lay behind it or within it? A dull torpor of the soul or the dullness of the thundercloud, charged with intellection and capable of the gloom of God?

—I meant a different kind of lamp, sir, said Stephen.

—Undoubtedly, said the dean.

—One difficulty, said Stephen, in esthetic discussion is to know whether words are being used according to the literary tradition or according to the tradition of the marketplace. I remember a sentence of Newman's in which he says of the Blessed Virgin that she was detained in the full company of the saints. The use of the word in the marketplace is quite different. *I hope I am not detaining you.*

—Not in the least, said the dean politely.

—No, no, said Stephen, smiling, I mean . . .

—Yes, yes: I see, said the dean quickly, I quite catch the point: *detain.*

He thrust forward his under jaw and uttered a dry short cough.

—To return to the lamp, he said, the feeding of it is also a nice problem. You must choose the pure oil and you must be careful when you pour it in not to overflow it, not to pour in more than the funnel can hold.

—What funnel? asked Stephen.

—The funnel through which you pour the oil into your lamp.

—That? said Stephen. Is that called a funnel? Is it not a tundish?

—What is a tundish?

—That. The . . . the funnel.

—Is that called a tundish in Ireland? asked the dean. I never heard the word in my life.

—It is called a tundish in Lower Drumcondra, said Stephen laughing, where they speak the best English.

—A tundish, said the dean reflectively. That is a most interesting word. I must look that word up. Upon my word I must.

His courtesy of manner rang a little false, and Stephen looked at the English convert with the same eyes as the elder brother in the parable may have turned on the prodigal. A humble follower in the wake of clamorous conversions, a poor Englishman in Ireland, he seemed to have entered on the stage of jesuit history when that strange play of intrigue and suffering and envy and struggle and indignity had been all but given through—a late comer, a tardy spirit. From what had he set out? Perhaps he had been born and bred among serious dissenters, seeing salvation in Jesus only and abhorring the vain pomps of the establishment. Had he felt the need of an implicit faith amid the welter of sectarianism and the jargon of its turbulent schisms, six principle men, peculiar people, seed and snake baptists, supralapsarian dogmatists? Had he found the true church all of a sudden in winding up to the end like a reel of cotton some finespun line of reasoning upon insufflation or the imposition of hands or the procession of the Holy Ghost? Or had Lord Christ touched him and bidden him follow, like that disciple who had sat at the receipt of custom, as he sat by the door of some zincroofed chapel, yawning and telling over his church pence?

The dean repeated the word yet again.

—Tundish! Well now, that is interesting!

—The question you asked me a moment ago seems to me more interesting. What is that beauty which the artist struggles to express from lumps of earth, said Stephen coldly.

The little word seemed to have turned a rapier point of his sensitiveness against this courteous and vigilant foe. He felt with a smart of dejection that the man to whom he was speaking was a countryman of Ben Jonson. He thought:

—The language in which we are speaking is his before it is mine. How different are the words *home*, *Christ, ale, master,* on his lips and on mine! I cannot speak or write these words without unrest of spirit. His language, so familiar and so foreign, will always be for me an acquired speech. I have not made or accepted its words. My voice holds them at bay. My soul frets in the shadow of his language.

—And to distinguish between the beautiful and the sublime, the dean added. To distinguish between moral beauty and material beauty. And to inquire what kind of beauty is proper to each of the various arts. These are some interesting points we might take up.

Stephen, disheartened suddenly by the dean's firm dry tone, was silent. The dean also was silent: and through the silence a distant noise of many boots and confused voices came up the staircase.

—In pursuing these speculations, said the dean conclusively, there is however the danger of perishing of inanition. First you must take your degree. Set that before you as your first aim. Then little by little, you will see your way. I mean in every sense, your way in life and in thinking. It may be uphill pedalling at first. Take Mr Moonan. He was a long time before he got to the top. But he got there.

—I may not have his talent, said Stephen quietly.

—You never know, said the dean brightly. We never can say what is in us. I most certainly should not be despondent. *Per aspera ad astra.*

He left the hearth quickly and went towards the landing to oversee the arrival of the first arts' class.

Leaning against the fireplace Stephen heard him greet briskly and impartially every student of the class and could almost see the frank smiles of the coarser students. A desolating pity began to fall like a dew upon his easily embittered heart for this faithful servingman of the knightly Loyola, for this halfbrother of the clergy, more venal than they in speech, more steadfast of soul than they, one whom he would never call his ghostly father: and he thought how this man and his companions had earned the name of worldlings at the hands not of the unworldly only but of the worldly also for having pleaded, during all their history, at the bar of God's justice for the souls of the lax and the lukewarm and the prudent.

The entry of the professor was signalled by a few rounds of Kentish fire from the heavy boots of those students who sat on the highest tier of the gloomy theatre under the grey cobwebbed windows. The calling of the roll began and the responses to the names were given out in all tones until the name of Peter Byrne was reached.

—Here!

A deep base note in response came from the upper tier, followed by coughs of protest along the other benches.

The professor paused in his reading and called the next name:

—Cranly!

No answer.

—Mr Cranly!

A smile flew across Stephen's face as he thought of his friend's studies.

—Try Leopardstown! said a voice from the bench behind.

Stephen glanced up quickly but Moynihan's snoutish face, outlined on the grey light, was impassive. A formula was given out. Amid the rustling of the note-books Stephen turned back again and said:

—Give me some paper for God's sake.

—Are you as bad as that? asked Moynihan with a broad grin.

He tore a sheet from his scribbler and passed it down, whispering:

—In case of necessity any layman or woman can do it.

The formula which he wrote obediently on the sheet of paper, the coiling and uncoiling calculations of the professor, the spectrelike symbols of force and velocity fascinated and jaded Stephen's mind. He had heard some say that the old professor was an atheist free-mason. O the grey dull day! It seemed a limbo of painless patient consciousness through which souls of mathematicians might wander, projecting long slender fabrics from plane to plane of ever rarer and paler twilight, radiating swift eddies to the last verges of a universe ever vaster, farther and more impalpable.

—So we must distinguish between elliptical and ellipsoidal. Perhaps some of you gentlemen may be familiar with the works of Mr W. S. Gilbert. In one of his songs he speaks of the billiard sharp who is condemned to play:

> On a cloth untrue
> With a twisted cue
> And elliptical billiard balls.

—He means a ball having the form of the ellipsoid of the principal axes of which I spoke a moment ago.

Moynihan leaned down towards Stephen's ear and murmured:

—What price ellipsoidal balls! Chase me, ladies, I'm in the cavalry!

His fellowstudent's rude humour ran like a gust through the cloister of Stephen's mind, shaking into gay life limp priestly vestments that hung upon the walls, setting them to sway and caper in a sabbath of misrule. The forms of the community emerged from the gustblown vestments, the dean of studies, the portly florid bursar with his cap of grey hair, the president, the little priest with feathery hair who wrote devout verses, the squat peasant form of the professor of economics, the tall form of the young professor of mental science discussing on the landing a case of conscience

with his class like a giraffe cropping high leafage
among a herd of antelopes, the grave troubled prefect of the sodality, the plump roundheaded professor
of Italian with his rogue's eyes. They came ambling
and stumbling, tumbling and capering, kilting their
gowns for leap frog, holding one another back, shaken
with deep fast laughter, smacking one another behind
and laughing at their rude malice, calling to one another by familiar nicknames, protesting with sudden
dignity at some rough usage, whispering two and two
behind their hands.

The professor had gone to the glass cases on the
sidewall from a shelf of which he took down a set of
coils, blew away the dust from many points and, bearing it carefully to the table, held a finger on it while he
proceeded with his lecture. He explained that the wires
in modern coils were of a compound called platinoid
lately discovered by F. W. Martino.

He spoke clearly the initials and surname of the
discoverer. Moynihan whispered from behind:

—Good old Fresh Water Martin!

—Ask him, Stephen whispered back with weary
humour, if he wants a subject for electrocution. He can
have me.

Moynihan, seeing the professor bend over the coils,
rose in his bench and, clacking noiselessly the fingers of
his right hand, began to call with the voice of a
slobbering urchin:

—Please, teacher! Please, teacher! This boy is after
saying a bad word, teacher.

—Platinoid, the professor said solemnly, is preferred
to German silver because it has a lower coefficient
of resistance variation by changes of temperature.
The platinoid wire is insulated and the covering of silk
that insulates it is wound on the ebonite bobbins just

where my finger is. If it were wound single an extra current would be induced in the coils. The bobbins are saturated in hot paraffin wax . . .

A sharp Ulster voice said from the bench below Stephen:

—Are we likely to be asked questions on applied science?

The professor began to juggle gravely with the terms pure science and applied science. A heavybuilt student wearing gold spectacles stared with some wonder at the questioner. Moynihan murmured from behind in his natural voice:

—Isn't MacAlister a devil for his pound of flesh?

Stephen looked down coldly on the oblong skull beneath him overgrown with tangled twinecoloured hair. The voice, the accent, the mind of the questioner offended him and he allowed the offence to carry him towards wilful unkindness, bidding his mind think that the student's father would have done better had he sent his son to Belfast to study and have saved something on the train fare by so doing.

The oblong skull beneath did not turn to meet this shaft of thought and yet the shaft came back to its bowstring: for he saw in a moment the student's wheypale face.

—That thought is not mine, he said to himself quickly. It came from the comic Irishman in the bench behind. Patience. Can you say with certitude by whom the soul of your race was bartered and its elect betrayed—by the questioner or by the mocker? Patience. Remember Epictetus. It is probably in his character to ask such a question at such a moment in such a tone and to pronounce the word *science* as a monosyllable.

The droning voice of the professor continued to wind itself slowly round and round the coils it spoke of, doubling, trebling, quadrupling its somnolent energy as the coil multiplied its ohms of resistance.

Moynihan's voice called from behind in echo to a distant bell:

—Closing time, gents!

The entrance hall was crowded and loud with talk. On a table near the door were two photographs in frames and between them a long roll of paper bearing an irregular tail of signatures. MacCann went briskly to and fro among the students, talking rapidly, answering rebuffs and leading one after another to the table. In the inner hall the dean of studies stood talking to a young professor, stroking his chin gravely and nodding his head.

Stephen, checked by the crowd at the door, halted irresolutely. From under the wide falling leaf of a soft hat Cranly's dark eyes were watching him.

—Have you signed? Stephen asked.

Cranly closed his long thinlipped mouth, communed with himself an instant and answered:

—*Ego habeo.*

—What is it for?

—*Quod?*

—What is it for?

Cranly turned his pale face to Stephen and said blandly and bitterly:

—*Per pax universalis.*

Stephen pointed to the Csar's photograph and said:

—He has the face of a besotted Christ.

The scorn and anger in his voice brought Cranly's eyes back from a calm survey of the walls of the hall.

—Are you annoyed? he asked.

—No, answered Stephen.

—Are you in bad humour?

—No.

—*Credo ut vos sanguinarius mendax estis,* said Cranly, *quia facies vostra monstrat ut vos in damno malo humore estis.*

Moynihan, on his way to the table, said in Stephen's ear:

—MacCann is in tiptop form. Ready to shed the last drop. Brandnew world. No stimulants and votes for the bitches.

Stephen smiled at the manner of this confidence and, when Moynihan had passed, turned again to meet Cranly's eyes.

—Perhaps you can tell me, he said, why he pours his soul so freely into my ear. Can you?

A dull scowl appeared on Cranly's forehead. He stared at the table where Moynihan had bent to write his name on the roll, and then said flatly:

—A sugar!

—*Quis est in malo humore,* said Stephen, *ego aut vos?*

Cranly did not take up the taunt. He brooded sourly on his judgment and repeated with the same flat force:

—A flaming bloody sugar, that's what he is!

It was his epitaph for all dead friendships and Stephen wondered whether it would ever be spoken in the same tone over his memory. The heavy lumpish phrase sank slowly out of hearing like a stone through a quagmire. Stephen saw it sink as he had seen many another, feeling its heaviness depress his heart. Cranly's speech, unlike that of Davin, had neither rare phrases of Elizabethan English nor quaintly turned versions of Irish idioms. Its drawl was an echo of the quays of Dublin given back by a bleak decaying seaport, its energy an echo of the sacred eloquence of Dublin given back flatly by a Wicklow pulpit.

The heavy scowl faded from Cranly's face as Mac-

Cann marched briskly towards them from the other side of the hall.

—Here you are! said MacCann cheerily.

—Here I am! said Stephen.

—Late as usual. Can you not combine the progressive tendency with a respect for punctuality?

—That question is out of order, said Stephen. Next business.

His smiling eyes were fixed on a silverwrapped tablet of milk chocolate which peeped out of the propagandist's breastpocket. A lean student with olive skin and lank black hair thrust his face between the two, glancing from one to the other at each phrase and seeming to try to catch each flying phrase in his open moist mouth. Cranly took a small grey handball from his pocket and began to examine it closely, turning it over and over.

—Next business? said MacCann. Hom!

He gave a loud cough of laughter, smiled broadly and tugged twice at the strawcoloured goatee which hung from his blunt chin.

—The next business is to sign the testimonial.

—Will you pay me anything if I sign? asked Stephen.

—I thought you were an idealist, said MacCann.

The gipsylike student looked about him and addressed the onlookers in an indistinct bleating voice.

—By hell, that's a queer notion. I consider that notion to be a mercenary notion.

His voice faded into silence. No heed was paid to his words. He turned his olive face, equine in expression, towards Stephen, inviting him to speak again.

MacCann began to speak with fluent energy of the Csar's rescript, of Stead, of general disarmament, arbitration in cases of international disputes, of the signs of the times, of the new humanity and the new gospel of life which would make it the business of the community to secure as cheaply as possible the greatest possible happiness of the greatest possible number.

The gipsy student responded to the close of the period by crying:

—Three cheers for universal brotherhood!

—Go on, Temple, said a stout ruddy student near him. I'll stand you a pint after.

—I'm a believer in universal brotherhood, said Temple, glancing about him out of his dark, oval eyes. Marx is only a bloody cod.

Cranly gripped his arm tightly to check his tongue, smiling uneasily, and repeated:

—Easy, easy, easy!

Temple struggled to free his arm but continued, his mouth flecked by a thin foam:

—Socialism was founded by an Irishman and the first man in Europe who preached the freedom of thought was Collins. Two hundred years ago. He denounced priestcraft, the philosopher of Middlesex. Three cheers for John Anthony Collins!

A thin voice from the verge of the ring replied:

—Pip! pip!

Moynihan murmured beside Stephen's ear:

—And what about John Anthony's poor little sister:

> *Lottie Collins lost her drawers;*
> *Won't you kindly lend her yours?*

Stephen laughed and Moynihan, pleased with the result, murmured again:

—We'll have five bob each way on John Anthony Collins.

—I am waiting for your answer, said MacCann briefly.

—The affair doesn't interest me in the least, said Stephen wearily. You know that well. Why do you make a scene about it?

—Good! said MacCann, smacking his lips. You are a reactionary then?

—Do you think you impress me, Stephen asked, when you flourish your wooden sword?

—Metaphors! said MacCann bluntly. Come to facts.

Stephen blushed and turned aside. MacCann stood his ground and said with hostile humour:

—Minor poets, I suppose, are above such trivial questions as the question of universal peace.

Cranly raised his head and held the handball between the two students by way of a peaceoffering, saying:

—*Pax super totum sanguinarium globum.*

Stephen, moving away the bystanders, jerked his shoulder angrily in the direction of the Csar's image, saying:

—Keep your icon. If we must have a Jesus, let us have a legitimate Jesus.

—By hell, that's a good one! said the gipsy student to those about him. That's a fine expression. I like that expression immensely.

He gulped down the spittle in his throat as if he were gulping down the phrase and, fumbling at the peak of his tweed cap, turned to Stephen, saying:

Excuse me, sir, what do you mean by that expression you uttered just now?

Feeling himself jostled by the students near him, he said to them:

—I am curious to know now what he meant by that expression.

He turned again to Stephen and said in a whisper:

—Do you believe in Jesus? I believe in man. Of course, I don't know if you believe in man. I admire you, sir. I admire the mind of man independent of all religions. Is that your opinion about the mind of Jesus?

—Go on, Temple, said the stout ruddy student, returning, as was his wont, to his first idea, that pint is waiting for you.

—He thinks I'm an imbecile, Temple explained to Stephen, because I'm a believer in the power of mind.

Cranly linked his arms into those of Stephen and his admirer and said:

—*Nos ad manum ballum jocabimus.*

Stephen, in the act of being led away, caught sight of MacCann's flushed bluntfeatured face.

—My signature is of no account, he said politely. You are right to go your way. Leave me to go mine.

—Dedalus, said MacCann crisply, I believe you're a good fellow but you have yet to learn the dignity of altruism and the responsibility of the human individual.

A voice said:

—Intellectual crankery is better out of this movement than in it.

Stephen, recognising the harsh tone of MacAlister's voice, did not turn in the direction of the voice. Cranly pushed solemnly through the throng of students, linking Stephen and Temple like a celebrant attended by his ministers on his way to the altar.

Temple bent eagerly across Cranly's breast and said:

—Did you hear MacAlister what he said? That youth is jealous of you. Did you see that? I bet Cranly didn't see that. By hell, I saw that at once.

As they crossed the inner hall the dean of studies was in the act of escaping from the student with whom he had been conversing. He stood at the foot of the staircase, a foot on the lowest step, his threadbare

soutane gathered about him for the ascent with womanish care, nodding his head often and repeating:

—Not a doubt of it, Mr Hackett! Very fine! Not a
doubt of it!

In the middle of the hall the prefect of the college
sodality was speaking earnestly, in a soft querulous
voice, with a boarder. As he spoke he wrinkled a little
his freckled brow and bit, between his phrases, at a tiny
bone pencil.

—I hope the matric men will all come. The first arts
men are pretty sure. Second arts too. We must make
sure of the newcomers.

Temple bent again across Cranly, as they were passing through the doorway, and said in a swift whisper:

—Do you know that he is a married man? He was a
married man before they converted him. He has a wife
and children somewhere. By hell, I think that's the
queerest notion I ever heard! Eh?

His whisper trailed off into sly cackling laughter.
The moment they were through the doorway Cranly
seized him rudely by the neck and shook him, saying:

—You flaming floundering fool! I'll take my dying
bible there isn't a bigger bloody ape, do you know, than
you in the whole flaming bloody world!

Temple wriggled in his grip, laughing still with sly
content, while Cranly repeated flatly at every rude
shake:

—A flaming flaring bloody idiot!

They crossed the weedy garden together. The president, wrapped in a heavy loose cloak, was coming towards them along one of the walks, reading his office.
At the end of the walk he halted before turning and
raised his eyes. The students saluted, Temple fumbling
as before at the peak of his cap. They walked forward
in silence. As they neared the alley Stephen could hear

the thuds of the players' hands and the wet smacks of the ball and Davin's voice crying out excitedly at each stroke.

The three students halted round the box on which Davin sat to follow the game. Temple, after a few moments, sidled across to Stephen and said:

—Excuse me, I wanted to ask you do you believe that Jean Jacques Rousseau was a sincere man?

Stephen laughed outright. Cranly, picking up the broken stave of a cask from the grass at his foot, turned swiftly and said sternly:

—Temple, I declare to the living God if you say another word, do you know, to anybody on any subject I'll kill you *super spottum*.

—He was like you, I fancy, said Stephen, an emotional man.

—Blast him, curse him! said Cranly broadly. Don't talk to him at all. Sure, you might as well be talking, do you know, to a flaming chamberpot as talking to Temple. Go home, Temple. For God's sake, go home.

—I don't care a damn about you, Cranly, answered Temple, moving out of reach of the uplifted stave and pointing at Stephen. He's the only man I see in this institution that has an individual mind.

—Institution! Individual! cried Cranly. Go home, blast you, for you're a hopeless bloody man.

—I'm an emotional man, said Temple. That's quite rightly expressed. And I'm proud that I'm an emotionalist.

He sidled out of the alley, smiling slily. Cranly watched him with a blank expressionless face.

—Look at him! he said. Did you ever see such a go-by-the-wall?

His phrase was greeted by a strange laugh from a student who lounged against the wall, his peaked cap down on his eyes. The laugh, pitched in a high key and coming from a so muscular frame, seemed like the whinny of an elephant. The student's body shook all over and, to ease his mirth, he rubbed both his hands delightedly, over his groins.

—Lynch is awake, said Cranly.

Lynch, for answer, straightened himself and thrust forward his chest.

—Lynch puts out his chest, said Stephen, as a criticism of life.

Lynch smote himself sonorously on the chest and said:

—Who has anything to say about my girth?

Cranly took him at the word and the two began to tussle. When their faces had flushed with the struggle they drew apart, panting. Stephen bent down towards Davin who, intent on the game, had paid no heed to the talk of the others.

—And how is my little tame goose? he asked. Did he sign too?

Davin nodded and said:

—And you, Stevie?

Stephen shook his head.

—You're a terrible man, Stevie, said Davin, taking the short pipe from his mouth. Always alone.

—Now that you have signed the petition for universal peace, said Stephen, I suppose you will burn that little copybook I saw in your room.

As Davin did not answer Stephen began to quote:

—Long pace, fianna! Right incline, fianna! Fianna, by numbers, salute, one, two!

—That's a different question, said Davin. I'm an Irish nationalist, first and foremost. But that's you all out. You're a born sneerer, Stevie.

—When you make the next rebellion with hurleysticks, said Stephen, and want the indispensable informer, tell me. I can find you a few in this college.

—I can't understand you, said Davin. One time I hear you talk against English literature. Now you talk against the Irish informers. What with your name and your ideas . . . Are you Irish at all?

—Come with me now to the office of arms and I will show you the tree of my family, said Stephen.

—Then be one of us, said Davin. Why don't you learn Irish? Why did you drop out of the league class after the first lesson?

—You know one reason why, answered Stephen.

Davin tossed his head and laughed.

—O, come now, he said. Is it on account of that certain young lady and Father Moran? But that's all in your own mind, Stevie. They were only talking and laughing.

Stephen paused and laid a friendly hand upon Davin's shoulder.

—Do you remember, he said, when we knew each other first? The first morning we met you asked me to show you the way to the matriculation class, putting a very strong stress on the first syllable. You remember? Then you used to address the jesuits as father, you remember? I ask myself about you: *Is he as innocent as his speech?*

—I'm a simple person, said Davin. You know that. When you told me that night in Harcourt Street those things about your private life, honest to God, Stevie, I was not able to eat my dinner. I was quite bad. I was awake a long time that night. Why did you tell me those things?

—Thanks, said Stephen. You mean I am a monster.

—No, said Davin, but I wish you had not told me.

A tide began to surge beneath the calm surface of Stephen's friendliness.

—This race and this country and this life produced me, he said. I shall express myself as I am.

—Try to be one of us, repeated Davin. In your heart you are an Irishman but your pride is too powerful.

—My ancestors threw off their language and took another, Stephen said. They allowed a handful of foreigners to subject them. Do you fancy I am going to pay in my own life and person debts they made? What for?

—For our freedom, said Davin.

—No honourable and sincere man, said Stephen, has given up to you his life and his youth and his affections from the days of Tone to those of Parnell but you sold him to the enemy or failed him in need or reviled him and left him for another. And you invite me to be one of you. I'd see you damned first.

—They died for their ideals, Stevie, said Davin. Our day will come yet, believe me.

Stephen, following his own thought, was silent for an instant.

—The soul is born, he said vaguely, first in those moments I told you of. It has a slow and dark birth, more mysterious than the birth of the body. When the soul of a man is born in this country there are nets flung at it to hold it back from flight. You talk to me of nationality, language, religion. I shall try to fly by those nets.

Davin knocked the ashes from his pipe.

—Too deep for me, Stevie, he said. But a man's country comes first. Ireland first, Stevie. You can be a poet or mystic after.

—Do you know what Ireland is? asked Stephen with

cold violence. Ireland is the old sow that eats her farrow.

Davin rose from his box and went towards the players, shaking his head sadly. But in a moment his sadness left him and he was hotly disputing with Cranly and the two players who had finished their game. A match of four was arranged, Cranly insisting, however, that his ball should be used. He let it rebound twice or thrice to his hand and struck it strongly and swiftly towards the base of the alley, exclaiming in answer to its thud:

—Your soul!

Stephen stood with Lynch till the score began to rise. Then he plucked him by the sleeve to come away. Lynch obeyed, saying:

—Let us eke go, as Cranly has it.

Stephen smiled at this sidethrust. They passed back through the garden and out through the hall where the doddering porter was pinning up a notice in the frame. At the foot of the steps they halted and Stephen took a packet of cigarettes from his pocket and offered it to his companion.

—I know you are poor, he said.

—Damn your yellow insolence, answered Lynch.

This second proof of Lynch's culture made Stephen smile again.

—It was a great day for European culture, he said, when you made up your mind to swear in yellow.

They lit their cigarettes and turned to the right. After a pause Stephen began:

—Aristotle has not defined pity and terror. I have. I say . . .

Lynch halted and said bluntly:

—Stop! I won't listen! I am sick. I was out last night on a yellow drunk with Horan and Goggins.

Stephen went on:

—Pity is the feeling which arrests the mind in the presence of whatsoever is grave and constant in human sufferings and unites it with the human sufferer. Terror is the feeling which arrests the mind in the presence of whatsoever is grave and constant in human sufferings and unites it with the secret cause.

—Repeat, said Lynch.

Stephen repeated the definitions slowly.

—A girl got into a hansom a few days ago, he went on, in London. She was on her way to meet her mother whom she had not seen for many years. At the corner of a street the shaft of a lorry shivered the window of the hansom in the shape of a star. A long fine needle of the shivered glass pierced her heart. She died on the instant. The reporter called it a tragic death. It is not. It is remote from terror and pity according to the terms of my definitions.

—The tragic emotion, in fact, is a face looking two ways, towards terror and towards pity, both of which arc phases of it. You see I use the word *arrest*. I mean that the tragic emotion is static. Or rather the dramatic emotion is. The feelings excited by improper art are kinetic, desire or loathing. Desire urges us to possess, to go to something; loathing urges us to abandon, to go from something. These are kinetic emotions. The arts which excite them, pornographical or didactic, are therefore improper arts. The esthetic emotion (I use the general term) is therefore static. The mind is arrested and raised above desire and loathing.

—You say that art must not excite desire, said Lynch. I told you that one day I wrote my name in pencil on the backside of the Venus of Praxiteles in the Museum. Was that not desire?

—I speak of normal natures, said Stephen. You also

told me that when you were a boy in that charming carmelite school you ate pieces of dried cowdung.

Lynch broke again into a whinny of laughter and again rubbed both his hands over his groins but without taking them from his pockets.

—O I did! I did! he cried.

Stephen turned towards his companion and looked at him for a moment boldly in the eyes. Lynch, recovering from his laughter, answered his look from his humbled eyes. The long slender flattened skull beneath the long pointed cap brought before Stephen's mind the image of a hooded reptile. The eyes, too, were reptilelike in glint and gaze. Yet at that instant, humbled and alert in their look, they were lit by one tiny human point, the window of a shrivelled soul, poignant and selfembittered.

—As for that, Stephen said in polite parenthesis, we are all animals. I also am an animal.

—You are, said Lynch.

—But we are just now in a mental world, Stephen continued. The desire and loathing excited by improper esthetic means are really unesthetic emotions not only because they are kinetic in character but also because they are not more than physical. Our flesh shrinks from what it dreads and responds to the stimulus of what it desires by a purely reflex action of the nervous system. Our eyelid closes before we are aware that the fly is about to enter our eye.

—Not always, said Lynch critically.

—In the same way, said Stephen, your flesh responded to the stimulus of a naked statue but it was, I say, simply a reflex action of the nerves. Beauty expressed by the artist cannot awaken in us an emotion which is kinetic or a sensation which is purely physical. It awakens, or ought to awaken, or induces, or ought to induce, an esthetic stasis, an ideal pity or an ideal terror, a stasis called forth, prolonged and at last dissolved by what I call the rhythm of beauty.

—What is that exactly? asked Lynch.

—Rhythm, said Stephen, is the first formal esthetic relation of part to part in any esthetic whole or of an esthetic whole to its part or parts or of any part to the esthetic whole of which it is a part.

—If that is rhythm, said Lynch, let me hear what you call beauty: and, please remember, though I did eat a cake of cowdung once, that I admire only beauty.

Stephen raised his cap as if in greeting. Then, blushing slightly, he laid his hand on Lynch's thick tweed sleeve.

—We are right, he said, and the others are wrong. To speak of these things and to try to understand their nature and, having understood it, to try slowly and humbly and constantly to express, to press out again, from the gross earth or what it brings forth, from sound and shape and colour which are the prison gates of our soul, an image of the beauty we have come to understand—that is art.

They had reached the canal bridge and, turning from their course, went on by the trees. A crude grey light, mirrored in the sluggish water, and a smell of wet branches over their heads seemed to war against the course of Stephen's thought.

—But you have not answered my question, said Lynch. What is art? What is the beauty it expresses?

—That was the first definition I gave you, you sleepyheaded wretch, said Stephen, when I began to try to think out the matter for myself. Do you remember the night? Cranly lost his temper and began to talk about Wicklow bacon.

—I remember, said Lynch. He told us about them flaming fat devils of pigs.

—Art, said Stephen, is a human disposition of sensible or intelligible matter for an esthetic end. You remember the pigs and forget that. You are a distressing pair, you and Cranly.

Lynch made a grimace at the raw grey sky and said:

—If I am to listen to your esthetic philosophy give me at least another cigarette. I don't care about it. I don't even care about women. Damn you and damn everything. I want a job of five hundred a year. You can't get me one.

Stephen handed him the packet of cigarettes. Lynch took the last one that remained, saying simply:

—Proceed!

—Aquinas, said Stephen, says that is beautiful the apprehension of which pleases.

Lynch nodded.

—I remember that, he said. *Pulcra sunt quæ visa placent.*

—He uses the word *visa,* said Stephen, to cover esthetic apprehensions of all kinds, whether through sight or hearing or through any other avenue of apprehension. This word, though it is vague, is clear enough to keep away good and evil which excite desire and loathing. It means certainly a stasis and not a kinesis. How about the true? It produces also a stasis of the mind. You would not write your name in pencil across the hypothenuse of a rightangled triangle.

—No, said Lynch, give me the hypothenuse of the Venus of Praxiteles.

—Static therefore, said Stephen. Plato, I believe, said that beauty is the splendour of truth. I don't think that it has a meaning but the true and the beautiful are akin. Truth is beheld by the intellect which is appeased by the most satisfying relations of the intelligible: beauty is beheld by the imagination which is appeased by the most satisfying relations of the sensible. The first step in the direction of truth is to understand the frame and scope of the intellect itself, to comprehend the act itself of intellection. Aristotle's entire system of philosophy rests upon his book of psychology and that, I think, rests on his statement that the same attribute cannot at the same time and in the same connection belong to and not belong to the same subject. The first step in the direction of beauty is to understand the frame and scope of the imagination, to comprehend the act itself of esthetic apprehension. Is that clear?

—But what is beauty? asked Lynch impatiently. Out with another definition. Something we see and like! Is that the best you and Aquinas can do?

—Let us take woman, said Stephen.

—Let us take her! said Lynch fervently.

—The Greek, the Turk, the Chinese, the Copt, the Hottentot, said Stephen, all admire a different type of female beauty. That seems to be a maze out of which we cannot escape. I see however two ways out. One is this hypothesis: that every physical quality admired by men in women is in direct connection with the manifold functions of women for the propagation of the species. It may be so. The world, it seems, is drearier than even you, Lynch, imagined. For my part I dislike that way out. It leads to eugenics rather than to esthetic. It leads you out of the maze into a new gaudy lectureroom where MacCann, with one hand on *The Origin of Species* and the other hand on the new testament, tells you that you admired the great flanks of Venus because you felt that she would bear you burly offspring and admired her great breasts because you felt that she would give good milk to her children and yours.

—Then MacCann is a sulphuryellow liar, said Lynch energetically.

—There remains another way out, said Stephen, laughing.

—To wit? said Lynch.

—This hypothesis, Stephen began.

A long dray laden with old iron came round the corner of sir Patrick Dun's hospital covering the end of Stephen's speech with the harsh roar of jangled and rattling metal. Lynch closed his ears and gave out oath after oath till the dray had passed. Then he turned on his heel rudely. Stephen turned also and waited for a few moments till his companion's illhumour had had its vent.

—This hypothesis, Stephen repeated, is the other way out: that, though the same object may not seem beautiful to all people, all people who admire a beautiful object find in it certain relations which satisfy and coincide with the stages themselves of all esthetic apprehension. These relations of the sensible, visible to you through one form and to me through another, must be therefore the necessary qualities of beauty. Now, we can return to our old friend saint Thomas for another pennyworth of wisdom.

Lynch laughed.

—It amuses me vastly, he said, to hear you quoting him time after time like a jolly round friar. Are you laughing in your sleeve?

—MacAlister, answered Stephen, would call my esthetic theory applied Aquinas. So far as this side of esthetic philosophy extends Aquinas will carry me all along the line. When we come to the phenomena of artistic conception, artistic gestation and artistic reproduction I require a new terminology and a new personal experience.

—Of course, said Lynch. After all Aquinas, in spite of his intellect, was exactly a good round friar. But you will tell me about the new personal experience and new terminology some other day. Hurry up and finish the first part.

—Who knows? said Stephen, smiling. Perhaps Aquinas would understand me better than you. He was a poet himself. He wrote a hymn for Maundy Thursday. It begins with the words *Pange lingua gloriosi*. They say it is the highest glory of the hymnal. It is an intricate and soothing hymn. I like it: but there is no hymn that can be put beside that mournful and majestic processional song, the *Vexilla Regis* of Venantius Fortunatus.

Lynch began to sing softly and solemnly in a deep bass voice:

> *Impleta sunt quæ concinit*
> *David fideli carmine*
> *Dicendo nationibus*
> *Regnavit a ligno Deus.*

—Thats great! he said, well pleased. Great music!

They turned into Lower Mount Street. A few steps from the corner a fat young man, wearing a silk neckcloth, saluted them and stopped.

—Did you hear the results of the exams? he asked. Griffin was plucked. Halpin and O'Flynn are through the home civil. Moonan got fifth place in the Indian. O'Shaughnessy got fourteenth. The Irish fellows in Clarke's gave them a feed last night. They all ate curry.

His pallid bloated face expressed benevolent malice and, as he had advanced through his tidings of success, his small fatencircled eyes vanished out of sight and his weak wheezing voice out of hearing.

In reply to a question of Stephen's his eyes and his voice came forth again from their lurkingplaces.

—Yes, MacCullagh and I, he said. He's taking pure mathematics and I'm taking constitutional history. There are twenty subjects. I'm taking botany too. You know I'm a member of the field club.

He drew back from the other two in a stately fashion and placed a plump woollengloved hand on his breast, from which muttered wheezing laughter at once broke forth.

—Bring us a few turnips and onions the next time you go out, said Stephen drily, to make a stew.

The fat student laughed indulgently and said:

—We are all highly respectable people in the field club. Last Saturday we went out to Glenmalure, seven of us.

—With women, Donovan? said Lynch.

Donovan again laid his hand on his chest and said:

—Our end is the acquisition of knowledge.

Then he said quickly:

—I hear you are writing some essay about esthetics. Stephen made a vague gesture of denial.

—Goethe and Lessing, said Donovan, have written a lot on that subject, the classical school and the romantic school and all that. The *Laocoon* interested me very much when I read it. Of course it is idealistic, German, ultraprofound.

Neither of the others spoke. Donovan took leave of them urbanely.

—I must go, he said softly and benevolently. I have a strong suspicion, amounting almost to a conviction, that my sister intended to make pancakes today for the dinner of the Donovan family.

—Goodbye, Stephen said in his wake. Don't forget the turnips for me and my mate.

Lynch gazed after him, his lip curling in slow scorn till his face resembled a devil's mask:

—To think that that yellow pancakeeating excrement can get a good job, he said at length, and I have to smoke cheap cigarettes!

They turned their faces towards Merrion Square and went on for a little in silence.

—To finish what I was saying about beauty, said Stephen, the most satisfying relations of the sensible must therefore correspond to the necessary phases of artistic apprehension. Find these and you find the qualities of universal beauty. Aquinas says: *ad pulcritudinem tria requiruntur, integritas, consonantia, claritas.* I translate it so: *Three things are needed for beauty, wholeness, harmony and radiance.* Do these correspond to the phases of apprehension? Are you following?

—Of course, I am, said Lynch. If you think I have an excrementitious intelligence run after Donovan and ask him to listen to you.

Stephen pointed to a basket which a butcher's boy had slung inverted on his head.

—Look at that basket, he said.

—I see it, said Lynch.

—In order to see that basket, said Stephen, your mind first of all separates the basket from the rest of the visible universe which is not the basket. The first phase of apprehension is a bounding line drawn about the object to be apprehended. An esthetic image is presented to us either in space or in time. What is audible is presented in time, what is visible is presented in space. But, temporal or spatial, the esthetic image is first luminously apprehended as selfbounded and selfcontained upon the immeasurable background of space or time which is not it. You apprehend it as *one* thing. You see it as one whole. You apprehend its wholeness. That is *integritas*.

—Bull's eye! said Lynch, laughing. Go on.

—Then, said Stephen, you pass from point to point, led by its formal lines; you apprehend it as balanced part against part within its limits; you feel the rhythm of its structure. In other words the synthesis of immediate perception is followed by the analysis of apprehension. Having first felt that it is *one* thing you feel now that it is a *thing*. You apprehend it as complex, multiple, divisible, separable, made up of its parts, the result of its parts and their sum, harmonious. That is *consonantia*.

—Bull's eye again! said Lynch wittily. Tell me now what is *claritas* and you win the cigar.

—The connotation of the word, Stephen said, is rather vague. Aquinas uses a term which seems to be inexact. It baffled me for a long time. It would lead you to believe that he had in mind symbolism or idealism, the supreme quality of beauty being a light from some other world, the idea of which the matter is but the shadow, the reality of which it is but the symbol. I thought he might mean that *claritas* is the artistic discovery and representation of the divine purpose in anything or a force of generalisation which would make the esthetic image a universal one, make it outshine its proper conditions. But that is literary talk. I understand it so. When you have apprehended that basket as one thing and have then analysed it according to its form and apprehended it as a thing you make the only synthesis which is logically and esthetically permissible. You see that it is that thing which it is and no other thing. The radiance of which he speaks is the scholastic *quidditas*, the *whatness* of a thing. This supreme quality is felt by the artist when the esthetic image is first conceived in his imagination. The mind in that mysterious instant Shelley likened beautifully to a fading coal. The instant wherein that supreme quality of beauty, the clear radiance of the esthetic image, is apprehended luminously by the mind which has been arrested by its wholeness and fascinated by its harmony is the luminous silent stasis of esthetic pleasure, a spiritual state very like to that cardiac condition which the Italian physiologist Luigi Galvani, using a phrase almost as beautiful as Shelley's, called the enchantment of the heart.

Stephen paused and, though his companion did not speak, felt that his words had called up around them a thoughtenchanted silence.

—What I have said, he began again, refers to beauty in the wider sense of the word, in the sense which the word has in the literary tradition. In the marketplace it has another sense. When we speak of beauty in the second sense of the term our judgment is influenced in the first place by the art itself and by the form of that art. The image, it is clear, must be set between the mind or senses of the artist himself and the mind or senses of others. If you bear this in memory you will see that art necessarily divides itself into three forms progressing from one to the next. These forms are: the lyrical form, the form wherein the artist presents his image in immediate relation to himself; the epical form, the form wherein he presents his image in mediate relation to himself and to others; the dramatic form, the form wherein he presents his image in immediate relation to others.

—That you told me a few nights ago, said Lynch, and we began the famous discussion.

—I have a book at home, said Stephen, in which I

have written down questions which are more amusing than yours were. In finding the answers to them I found the theory of esthetic which I am trying to explain. Here are some questions I set myself: *Is a chair finely made tragic or comic? Is the portrait of Mona Lisa good if I desire to see it? Is the bust of Sir Philip Crampton lyrical, epical or dramatic? Can excrement or a child or a louse be a work of art? If not, why not?*

—Why not, indeed? said Lynch, laughing.

—*If a man hacking in fury at a block of wood,* Stephen continued, *make there an image of a cow, is that image a work of art? If not, why not?*

—That's a lovely one, said Lynch, laughing again. That has the true scholastic stink.

—Lessing, said Stephen, should not have taken a group of statues to write of. The art, being inferior, does not present the forms I spoke of distinguished clearly one from another. Even in literature, the highest and most spiritual art, the forms are often confused. The lyrical form is in fact the simplest verbal vesture of an instant of emotion, a rhythmical cry such as ages ago cheered on the man who pulled at the oar or dragged stones up a slope. He who utters it is more conscious of the instant of emotion than of himself as feeling emotion. The simplest epical form is seen emerging out of lyrical literature when the artist prolongs and broods upon himself as the centre of an epical event and this form progresses till the centre of emotional gravity is equidistant from the artist himself and from others. The narrative is no longer purely personal. The personality of the artist passes into the narration itself, flowing round and round the persons and the action like a vital sea. This progress you will see easily in that old English ballad *Turpin Hero* which begins in the first person and ends in the third person. The dramatic form is reached when the vitality which has flowed and eddied round each person fills every person with such vital force that he or she assumes a proper and intangible esthetic life. The personality of the artist, at first a cry or a cadence or a mood and then a fluid and lambent narrative, finally refines itself out of existence, impersonalises itself, so to speak. The esthetic image in the dramatic form is life purified in and reprojected from the human imagination. The mystery of esthetic like that of material creation is accomplished. The artist, like the God of the creation, remains within or behind or beyond or above his handiwork, invisible, refined out of existence, indifferent, paring his fingernails.

—Trying to refine them also out of existence, said Lynch.

A fine rain began to fall from the high veiled sky and they turned into the duke's lawn, to reach the national library before the shower came.

—What do you mean, Lynch asked surlily, by prating about beauty and the imagination in this miserable Godforsaken island? No wonder the artist retired within or behind his handiwork after having perpetrated this country.

The rain fell faster. When they passed through the passage beside the royal Irish academy they found many students sheltering under the arcade of the library. Cranly, leaning against the pillar, was picking his teeth with a sharpened match, listening to some companions. Some girls stood near the entrance door. Lynch whispered to Stephen:

—Your beloved is here.

Stephen took his place silently on the step below the group of students, heedless of the rain which fell fast, turning his eyes towards her from time to time. She too stood silently among her companions. She has no priest to flirt with, he thought with conscious bitterness, remembering how he had seen her last. Lynch was right. His mind, emptied of theory and courage, lapsed back into a listless peace.

He heard the students talking among themselves. They spoke of two friends who had passed the final medical examination, of the chances of getting places on ocean liners, of poor and rich practices.

—That's all a bubble. An Irish country practice is better.

—Hynes was two years in Liverpool and he says the same. A frightful hole he said it was. Nothing but midwifery cases. Half a crown cases.

—Do you mean to say it is better to have a job here in the country than in a rich city like that? I know a fellow . . .

—Hynes has no brains. He got through by stewing, pure stewing.

—Don't mind him. There's plenty of money to be made in a big commercial city.

—Depends on the practice.

—*Ego credo ut vita pauperum est simpliciter atrox, simpliciter sanguinarius atrox, in Liverpoolio.*

Their voices reached his ears as if from a distance in interrupted pulsation. She was preparing to go away with her companions.

The quick light shower had drawn off, tarrying in clusters of diamonds among the shrubs of the quadrangle where an exhalation was breathed forth by the blackened earth. Their trim boots prattled as they stood on the steps of the colonnade, talking quietly and gaily, glancing at the clouds, holding their umbrellas at cunning angles against the few last raindrops, closing them again, holding their skirts demurely.

And if he had judged her harshly? If her life were a simple rosary of hours, her life simple and strange as a bird's life, gay in the morning, restless all day, tired at sundown? Her heart simple and wilful as a bird's heart?

*   *   *

Towards dawn he awoke. O what sweet music! His soul was all dewy wet. Over his limbs in sleep pale cool waves of light had passed. He lay still, as if his soul lay amid cool waters, conscious of faint sweet music. His mind was waking slowly to a tremulous morning knowledge, a morning inspiration. A spirit filled him, pure as the purest water, sweet as dew, moving as music. But how faintly it was inbreathed, how passionlessly, as if the seraphim themselves were breathing upon him! His soul was waking slowly, fearing to awake wholly. It was that windless hour of dawn when madness wakes and strange plants open to the light and the moth flies forth silently.

An enchantment of the heart! The night had been enchanted. In a dream or vision he had known the ecstasy of seraphic life. Was it an instant of enchantment only or long hours and days and years and ages?

The instant of inspiration seemed now to be reflected from all sides at once from a multitude of cloudy circumstance of what had happened or of what might have happened. The instant flashed forth like a point of light and now from cloud on cloud of vague circumstance confused form was veiling softly its afterglow. O! In the virgin womb of the imagination the word was made flesh. Gabriel the seraph had come to the virgin's chamber. An afterglow deepened within his spirit, whence the white flame had passed, deepening to a rose and ardent light. That rose and ardent light was her strange wilful heart, strange that no man had known or would know, wilful from before the beginning of the world: and lured by that ardent roselike glow the choirs of the seraphim were falling from heaven.

> *Are you not weary of ardent ways,*
> *Lure of the fallen seraphim?*
> *Tell no more of enchanted days.*

The verses passed from his mind to his lips and, murmuring them over, he felt the rhythmic movement of a villanelle pass through them. The roselike glow sent forth its rays of rhyme; ways, days, blaze, praise, raise. Its rays burned up the world, consumed the hearts of men and angels: the rays from the rose that was her wilful heart.

> *Your eyes have set man's heart ablaze*
> *And you have had your will of him.*
> *Are you not weary of ardent ways?*

And then? The rhythm died away, ceased, began again to move and beat. And then? Smoke, incense ascending from the altar of the world.

> *Above the flame the smoke of praise*
> *Goes up from ocean rim to rim.*
> *Tell no more of enchanted days.*

Smoke went up from the whole earth, from the vapoury oceans, smoke of her praise. The earth was like a swinging smoking swaying censer, a ball of incense, an ellipsoidal ball. The rhythm died out at once; the cry of his heart was broken. His lips began to murmur the first verses over and over; then went on stumbling through half verses, stammering and baffled; then stopped. The heart's cry was broken.

The veiled windless hour had passed and behind the panes of the naked window the morning light was gathering. A bell beat faintly very far away. A bird twittered; two birds, three. The bell and the bird ceased: and the dull white light spread itself east and west, covering the world, covering the roselight in his heart.

Fearing to lose all, he raised himself suddenly on his elbow to look for paper and pencil. There was neither on the table; only the soupplate he had eaten the rice from for supper and the candlestick with its tendrils of tallow and its paper socket, singed by the last flame. He stretched his arm wearily towards the foot of the bed, groping with his hand in the pockets of the coat that hung there. His fingers found a pencil and then a cigarette packet. He lay back and, tearing open the packet, placed the last cigarette on the windowledge and began to write out the stanzas of the villanelle in small neat letters on the rough cardboard surface.

Having written them out he lay back on the lumpy pillow, murmuring them again. The lumps of knotted flock under his head reminded him of the lumps of knotted horsehair in the sofa of her parlour on which he used to sit, smiling or serious, asking himself why he had come, displeased with her and with himself, confounded by the print of the Sacred Heart above the untenanted sideboard. He saw her approach him in a lull of the talk and beg him to sing one of his curious songs. Then he saw himself sitting at the old piano, striking chords softly from its speckled keys and singing, amid the talk which had risen again in the room, to her who leaned beside the mantelpiece a dainty song of the Elizabethans, a sad and sweet loth to depart, the victory chant of Agincourt, the happy air of Greensleeves. While he sang and she listened, or feigned to listen, his heart was at rest but when the quaint old songs had ended and he heard again the voices in the room he remembered his own sarcasm: the house

where young men are called by their christian names a
little too soon.

At certain instants her eyes seemed about to trust
him but he had waited in vain. She passed now dancing
lightly across his memory as she had been that night at
the carnival ball, her white dress a little lifted, a white
spray nodding in her hair. She danced lightly in the
round. She was dancing towards him and, as she came,
her eyes were a little averted and a faint glow was on
her cheek. At the pause in the chain of hands her hand
had lain in his an instant, a soft merchandise.

—You are a great stranger now.

—Yes. I was born to be a monk.

—I am afraid you are a heretic.

—Are you much afraid?

For answer she had danced away from him along the
chain of hands, dancing lightly and discreetly, giving
herself to none. The white spray nodded to her dancing
and when she was in shadow the glow was deeper on
her cheek.

A monk! His own image started forth a profaner of
the cloister, a heretic franciscan, willing and willing
not to serve, spinning like Gherardino da Borgo San
Donnino, a lithe web of sophistry and whispering in
her ear.

No, it was not his image. It was like the image of the
young priest in whose company he had seen her last,
looking at him out of dove's eyes, toying with the pages
of her Irish phrasebook.

—Yes, yes, the ladies are coming round to us. I can
see it every day. The ladies are with us. The best helpers the language has.

—And the church, Father Moran?

—The church too. Coming round too. The work is
going ahead there too. Don't fret about the church.

Bah! he had done well to leave the room in disdain. He had done well not to salute her on the steps of the library. He had done well to leave her to flirt with her priest, to toy with a church which was the scullerymaid of christendom.

Rude brutal anger routed the last lingering instant of ecstasy from his soul. It broke up violently her fair image and flung the fragments on all sides. On all sides distorted reflections of her image started from his memory: the flowergirl in the ragged dress with damp coarse hair and a hoyden's face who had called herself his own girl and begged his handsel, the kitchengirl in the next house who sang over the clatter of her plates with the drawl of a country singer the first bars of *By Killarney's Lakes and Fells,* a girl who had laughed gaily to see him stumble when the iron grating in the footpath near Cork Hill had caught the broken sole of his shoe, a girl he had glanced at, attracted by her small ripe mouth as she passed out of Jacob's biscuit factory, who had cried to him over her shoulder:

—Do you like what you seen of me, straight hair and curly eyebrows?

And yet he felt that, however he might revile and mock her image, his anger was also a form of homage. He had left the classroom in disdain that was not wholly sincere, feeling that perhaps the secret of her race lay behind those dark eyes upon which her long lashes flung a quick shadow. He had told himself bitterly as he walked through the streets that she was a figure of the womanhood of her country, a batlike soul waking to the consciousness of itself in darkness and secrecy and loneliness, tarrying awhile, loveless and sinless, with her mild lover and leaving him to whisper of innocent transgressions in the latticed ear of a priest. His anger against her found vent in coarse railing at her paramour, whose name and voice and features offended his baffled pride: a priested peasant, with a brother a policeman in Dublin and a brother a potboy in Moycullen. To him she would unveil her soul's shy nakedness, to one who was but schooled in the discharging of a formal rite rather than to him, a priest of eternal imagination, transmuting the daily bread of experience into the radiant body of everliving life.

The radiant image of the eucharist united again in an instant his bitter and despairing thoughts, their cries arising unbroken in a hymn of thanksgiving.

> *Our broken cries and mournful lays*
> *Rise in one eucharistic hymn.*
> *Are you not weary of ardent ways?*
>
> *While sacrificing hands upraise*
> *The chalice flowing to the brim,*
> *Tell no more of enchanted days.*

He spoke the verses aloud from the first lines till the music and rhythm suffused his mind, turning it to quiet indulgence; then copied them painfully to feel them the better by seeing them; then lay back on his bolster.

The full morning light had come. No sound was to be heard: but he knew that all around him life was about to awaken in common noises, hoarse voices, sleepy prayers. Shrinking from that life he turned towards the wall, making a cowl of the blanket and staring at the great overblown scarlet flowers of the tattered wallpaper. He tried to warm his perishing joy in their scarlet glow, imagining a roseway from where he lay upwards to heaven all strewn with scarlet flowers. Weary! Weary! He too was weary of ardent ways.

A gradual warmth, a languorous weariness passed over him, descending along his spine from his closely cowled head. He felt it descend and, seeing himself as he lay, smiled. Soon he would sleep.

He had written verses for her again after ten years. Ten years before she had worn her shawl cowlwise about her head, sending sprays of her warm breath into the night air, tapping her foot upon the glassy road. It was the last tram; the lank brown horses knew it and shook their bells to the clear night in admonition. The conductor talked with the driver, both nodding often in the green light of the lamp. They stood on the steps of the tram, he on the upper, she on the lower. She came up to his step many times between their phrases and went down again and once or twice remained beside him forgetting to go down and then went down. Let be! Let be!

Ten years from that wisdom of children to his folly. If he sent her the verses? They would be read out at breakfast amid the tapping of eggshells. Folly indeed! The brothers would laugh and try to wrest the page from each other with their strong hard fingers. The suave priest, her uncle, seated in his armchair, would hold the page at arm's length, read it smiling and approve of the literary form.

No, no: that was folly. Even if he sent her the verses she would not show them to others. No, no: she could not.

He began to feel that he had wronged her. A sense of her innocence moved him almost to pity her, an innocence he had never understood till he had come to the knowledge of it through sin, an innocence which she too had not understood while she was innocent or before the strange humiliation of her nature had first come upon her. Then first her soul had begun to live as his soul had when he had first sinned: and a tender compassion filled his heart as he remembered her frail pallor and her eyes, humbled and saddened by the dark shame of womanhood.

While his soul had passed from ecstasy to languor where had she been? Might it be, in the mysterious ways of spiritual life, that her soul at those same moments had been conscious of his homage? It might be.

A glow of desire kindled again his soul and fired and fulfilled all his body. Conscious of his desire she was waking from odorous sleep, the temptress of his villanelle. Her eyes, dark and with a look of languor, were opening to his eyes. Her nakedness yielded to him, radiant, warm, odorous and lavishlimbed, enfolded him like a shining cloud, enfolded him like water with a liquid life: and like a cloud of vapour or like waters circumfluent in space the liquid letters of speech, symbols of the element of mystery, flowed forth over his brain.

Are you not weary of ardent ways,
Lure of the fallen seraphim?
Tell no more of enchanted days.

Your eyes have set man's heart ablaze
And you have had your will of him.
Are you not weary of ardent ways?

Above the flame the smoke of praise
Goes up from ocean rim to rim.
Tell no more of enchanted days.

Our broken cries and mournful lays
Rise in one eucharistic hymn.
Are you not weary of ardent ways?

While sacrificing hands upraise
The chalice flowing to the brim,
Tell no more of enchanted days.

And still you hold our longing gaze
With languorous look and lavish limb!
Are you not weary of ardent ways?
Tell no more of enchanted days.

* * *

What birds were they? He stood on the steps of the library to look at them, leaning wearily on his ashplant. They flew round and round the jutting shoulder of a house in Molesworth Street. The air of the late March evening made clear their flight, their dark darting quivering bodies flying clearly against the sky as against a limphung cloth of smoky tenuous blue.

He watched their flight; bird after bird: a dark flash, a swerve, a flash again, a dart aside, a curve, a flutter of wings. He tried to count them before all their darting quivering bodies passed: six, ten, eleven: and wondered were they odd or even in number. Twelve, thirteen: for two came wheeling down from the upper sky. They were flying high and low but ever round and round in straight and curving lines and ever flying from left to right, circling about a temple of air.

He listened to the cries: like the squeak of mice behind the wainscot: a shrill twofold note. But the notes were long and shrill and whirring, unlike the cry of vermin, falling a third or a fourth and trilled as the flying beaks clove the air. Their cry was shrill and clear and fine and falling like threads of silken light unwound from whirring spools.

The inhuman clamour soothed his ears in which his mother's sobs and reproaches murmured insistently and the dark frail quivering bodies wheeling and fluttering and swerving round an airy temple of the tenuous sky soothed his eyes which still saw the image of his mother's face.

Why was he gazing upwards from the steps of the porch, hearing their shrill twofold cry, watching their flight? For an augury of good or evil? A phrase of Cornelius Agrippa flew through his mind and then there flew hither and thither shapeless thoughts from Swedenborg on the correspondence of birds to things of the intellect and of how the creatures of the air have their knowledge and know their times and seasons because they, unlike man, are in the order of their life and have not perverted that order by reason.

And for ages men had gazed upward as he was gazing at birds in flight. The colonnade above him made him think vaguely of an ancient temple and the ashplant on which he leaned wearily of the curved stick of an augur. A sense of fear of the unknown moved in the heart of his weariness, a fear of symbols and portents, of the hawklike man whose name he bore soaring out of his captivity on osierwoven wings, of Thoth, the god of writers, writing with a reed upon a tablet and bearing on his narrow ibis head the cusped moon.

He smiled as he thought of the god's image for it made him think of a bottlenosed judge in a wig, putting commas into a document which he held at arm's length and he knew that he would not have remembered the god's name but that it was like an Irish oath. It was folly. But was it for this folly that he was about to leave for ever the house of prayer and prudence into which he had been born and the order of life out of which he had come?

They came back with shrill cries over the jutting shoulder of the house, flying darkly against the fading air. What birds were they? He thought that they must be swallows who had come back from the south. Then he was to go away for they were birds ever going and coming, building ever an unlasting home under the eaves of men's houses and ever leaving the homes they had built to wander.

> *Bend down your faces, Oona and Aleel,*
> *I gaze upon them as the swallow gazes*
> *Upon the nest under the eave before*
> *He wander the loud waters.*

A soft liquid joy like the noise of many waters flowed over his memory and he felt in his heart the soft peace of silent spaces of fading tenuous sky above the waters, of oceanic silence, of swallows flying through the seadusk over the flowing waters.

A soft liquid joy flowed through the words where the soft long vowels hurtled noiselessly and fell away, lapping and flowing back and ever shaking the white bells of their waves in mute chime and mute peal and soft low swooning cry; and he felt that the augury he had sought in the wheeling darting birds and in the pale space of sky above him had come forth from his heart like a bird from a turret quietly and swiftly.

Symbol of departure or of loneliness? The verses crooned in the ear of his memory composed slowly before his remembering eyes the scene of the hall on the night of the opening of the national theatre. He was alone at the side of the balcony, looking out of jaded eyes at the culture of Dublin in the stalls and at the tawdry scenecloths and human dolls framed by the garish lamps of the stage. A burly policeman sweated behind him and seemed at every moment about to act. The catcalls and hisses and mocking cries ran in rude gusts round the hall from his scattered fellowstudents.

—A libel on Ireland!

—Made in Germany!

—Blasphemy!

—We never sold our faith!

—No Irish woman ever did it!

—We want no amateur atheists.

—We want no budding buddhists.

A sudden swift hiss fell from the windows above him and he knew that the electric lamps had been switched on in the reader's room. He turned into the pillared hall, now calmly lit, went up the staircase and passed in through the clicking turnstile.

Cranly was sitting over near the dictionaries. A thick book, opened at the frontispiece, lay before him on the wooden rest. He leaned back in his chair, inclining his ear like that of a confessor to the face of the medical student who was reading to him a problem from the chess page of a journal. Stephen sat down at his right and the priest at the other side of the table closed his copy of *The Tablet* with an angry snap and stood up.

Cranly gazed after him blandly and vaguely. The medical student went on in a softer voice:

—Pawn to king's fourth.

—We had better go, Dixon, said Stephen in warning. He has gone to complain.

Dixon folded the journal and rose with dignity, saying:

—Our men retired in good order.

—With guns and cattle, added Stephen, pointing to the titlepage of Cranly's book on which was printed *Diseases of the Ox*.

As they passed through a lane of the tables Stephen said:

—Cranly, I want to speak to you.

Cranly did not answer or turn. He laid his book on the counter and passed out, his wellshod feet sounding flatly on the floor. On the staircase he paused and gazing absently at Dixon repeated:

—Pawn to king's bloody fourth.

—Put it that way if you like, Dixon said.

He had a quiet toneless voice and urbane manners and on a finger of his plump clean hand he displayed at moments a signet ring.

As they crossed the hall a man of dwarfish stature came towards them. Under the dome of his tiny hat his unshaven face began to smile with pleasure and he was heard to murmur. The eyes were melancholy as those of a monkey.

—Good evening, captain, said Cranly, halting.

—Good evening, gentlemen, said the stubblegrown monkeyish face.

—Warm weather for March, said Cranly. They have the windows open upstairs.

Dixon smiled and turned his ring. The blackish monkeypuckered face pursed its human mouth with gentle pleasure: and its voice purred:

—Delightful weather for March. Simply delightful.

—There are two nice young ladies upstairs, captain, tired of waiting, Dixon said.

Cranly smiled and said kindly:

—The captain has only one love: sir Walter Scott. Isn't that so, captain?

—What are you reading now, captain? Dixon asked. *The Bride of Lammermoor?*

—I love old Scott, the flexible lips said. I think he writes something lovely. There is no writer can touch sir Walter Scott.

He moved a thin shrunken brown hand gently in the air in time to his praise and his thin quick eyelids beat often over his sad eyes.

Sadder to Stephen's ear was his speech: a genteel accent, low and moist, marred by errors: and listening to it he wondered was the story true and was the thin blood that flowed in his shrunken frame noble and come of an incestuous love?

The park trees were heavy with rain and rain fell still

and ever in the lake, lying grey like a shield. A game of swans flew there and the water and the shore beneath were fouled with their greenwhite slime. They embraced softly, impelled by the grey rainy light, the wet silent trees, the shieldlike witnessing lake, the swans. They embraced without joy or passion, his arm about his sister's neck. A grey woolen cloak was wrapped athwart her from her shoulder to her waist: and her fair head was bent in willing shame. He had loose redbrown hair and tender shapely strong freckled hands. Face. There was no face seen. The brother's face was bent upon her fair rainfragrant hair. The hand freckled and strong and shapely and caressing was Davin's hand.

He frowned angrily upon his thought and on the shrivelled mannikin who had called it forth. His father's gibes at the Bantry gang leaped out of his memory. He held them at a distance and brooded uneasily on his own thought again. Why were they not Cranly's hands? Had Davin's simplicity and innocence stung him more secretly?

He walked on across the hall with Dixon, leaving Cranly to take leave elaborately of the dwarf.

Under the colonnade Temple was standing in the midst of a little group of students. One of them cried:

—Dixon, come over till you hear. Temple is in grand form.

Temple turned on him his dark gipsy eyes.

—You're a hypocrite, O'Keeffe, he said, and Dixon's a smiler. By hell, I think that's a good literary expression.

He laughed slily, looking in Stephen's face, repeating:

—By hell, I'm delighted with that name. A smiler.

A stout student who stood below them on the steps said:

—Come back to the mistress, Temple. We want to
hear about that.

—He had, faith, Temple said. And he was a married
man too. And all the priests used to be dining there. By
hell, I think they all had a touch.

—We shall call it riding a hack to spare the hunter,
said Dixon.

—Tell us, Temple, O'Keeffe said, how many quarts
of porter have you in you?

—All your intellectual soul is in that phrase, O'Keeffe,
said Temple with open scorn.

He moved with a shambling gait round the group
and spoke to Stephen.

—Did you know that the Forsters are the kings of
Belgium? he asked.

Cranly came out through the door of the entrance
hall, his hat thrust back on the nape of his neck and
picking his teeth with care.

—And here's the wiseacre, said Temple. Do you
know that about the Forsters?

He paused for an answer. Cranly dislodged a figseed
from his teeth on the point of his rude toothpick and
gazed at it intently.

—The Forster family, Temple said, is descended
from Baldwin the First, king of Flanders. He was called
the Forester. Forester and Forster are the same name.
A descendant of Baldwin the First, captain Francis
Forster, settled in Ireland and married the daughter of
the last chieftain of Clanbrassil. Then there are the
Blake Forsters. That's a different branch.

—From Baldhead, king of Flanders, Cranly repeated, rooting again deliberately at his gleaming uncovered teeth.

—Where did you pick up all that history? O'Keeffe
asked.

—I know all the history of your family too, Temple said, turning to Stephen. Do you know what Giraldus Cambrensis says about your family?

—Is he descended from Baldwin too? asked a tall consumptive student with dark eyes.

—Baldhead, Cranly repeated, sucking at a crevice in his teeth.

—*Pernobilis et pervetusta familia*, Temple said to Stephen.

The stout student who stood below them on the steps farted briefly. Dixon turned towards him saying in a soft voice:

—Did an angel speak?

Cranly turned also and said vehemently but without anger:

—Goggins, you're the flamingest dirty devil I ever met, do you know.

—I had it on my mind to say that, Goggins answered firmly. It did no-one any harm, did it?

—We hope, Dixon said suavely, that it was not of the kind known to science as a *paulo post futurum*.

—Didn't I tell you he was a smiler? said Temple, turning right and left. Didn't I give him that name?

—You did. We're not deaf, said the tall consumptive.

Cranly still frowned at the stout student below him. Then, with a snort of disgust, he shoved him violently down the steps.

—Go away from here, he said rudely. Go away, you stinkpot. And you are a stinkpot.

Goggins skipped down on to the gravel and at once returned to his place with good humour. Temple turned back to Stephen and asked:

—Do you believe in the law of heredity?

—Are you drunk or what are you or what are you trying to say? asked Cranly, facing round on him with an expression of wonder.

—The most profound sentence ever written, Temple said with enthusiasm, is the sentence at the end of the zoology. Reproduction is the beginning of death.

He touched Stephen timidly at the elbow and said eagerly:

—Do you feel how profound that is because you are a poet?

Cranly pointed his long forefinger.

—Look at him! he said with scorn to the others. Look at Ireland's hope!

They laughed at his words and gesture. Temple turned on him bravely, saying:

—Cranly, you're always sneering at me. I can see that. But I am as good as you any day. Do you know what I think about you now as compared with myself?

—My dear man, said Cranly urbanely, you are incapable, do you know, absolutely incapable of thinking.

—But do you know, Temple went on, what I think of you and of myself compared together?

—Out with it, Temple! the stout student cried from the steps. Get it out in bits!

Temple turned right and left, making sudden feeble gestures as he spoke.

—I'm a ballocks, he said, shaking his head in despair. I am. And I know I am. And I admit it that I am.

Dixon patted him lightly on the shoulder and said mildly:

—And it does you every credit, Temple.

—But he, Temple said, pointing to Cranly. He is a ballocks too like me. Only he doesn't know it. And that's the only difference I see.

A burst of laughter covered his words. But he turned again to Stephen and said with a sudden eagerness:

—That word is a most interesting word. That's the only English dual number. Did you know?

—Is it? Stephen said vaguely.

He was watching Cranly's firmfeatured suffering face, lit up now by a smile of false patience. The gross name had passed over it like foul water poured over an old stone image, patient of injuries: and, as he watched him, he saw him raise his hat in salute and uncover the black hair that stood up stiffly from his forehead like an iron crown.

She passed out from the porch of the library and bowed across Stephen in reply to Cranly's greeting. He also? Was there not a slight flush on Cranly's cheek? Or had it come forth at Temple's words? The light had waned. He could not see.

Did that explain his friend's listless silence, his harsh comments, the sudden intrusions of rude speech with which he had shattered so often Stephen's ardent wayward confessions? Stephen had forgiven freely for he had found this rudeness also in himself towards himself. And he remembered an evening when he had dismounted from a borrowed creaking bicycle to pray to God in a wood near Malahide. He had lifted up his arms and spoken in ecstasy to the sombre nave of the trees, knowing that he stood on holy ground and in a holy hour. And when two constabularymen had come into sight round a bend in the gloomy road he had broken off his prayer to whistle loudly an air from the last pantomime.

He began to beat the frayed end of his ashplant against the base of a pillar. Had Cranly not heard him? Yet he could wait. The talk about him ceased for a moment: and a soft hiss fell again from a window above. But no other sound was in the air and the swallows whose flight he had followed with idle eyes were sleeping.

She had passed through the dusk. And therefore the air was silent save for one soft hiss that fell. And there-

fore the tongues about him had ceased their babble.
Darkness was falling.

Darkness falls from the air.

A trembling joy, lambent as a faint light, played like
a fairy host around him. But why? Her passage through
the darkening air or the verse with its black vowels and
its opening sound, rich and lutelike?

He walked away slowly towards the deeper shadows
at the end of the colonnade, beating the stone softly
with his stick to hide his revery from the students
whom he had left: and allowed his mind to summon
back to itself the age of Dowland and Byrd and Nash.

Eyes, opening from the darkness of desire, eyes that
dimmed the breaking east. What was their languid
grace but the softness of chambering? And what was
their shimmer but the shimmer of the scum that man-
tled the cesspool of the court of a slobbering Stuart.
And he tasted in the language of memory ambered
wines, dying fallings of sweet airs, the proud pavan:
and saw with the eyes of memory kind gentlewomen in
Covent Garden wooing from their balconies with sucking mouths and the poxfouled wenches of the taverns
and young wives that, gaily yielding to their ravishers,
clipped and clipped again.

The images he had summoned gave him no pleasure.
They were secret and enflaming but her image was not
entangled by them. That was not the way to think of
her. It was not even the way in which he thought of
her. Could his mind then not trust itself? Old phrases,
sweet only with a disinterred sweetness like the figseeds
Cranly rooted out of his gleaming teeth.

It was not thought nor vision though he knew
vaguely that her figure was passing homeward through
the city. Vaguely first and then more sharply he smelt
her body. A conscious unrest seethed in his blood. Yes,

it was her body he smelt: a wild and languid smell: the tepid limbs over which his music had flowed desirously and the secret soft linen upon which her flesh distilled odour and a dew.

A louse crawled over the nape of his neck and, putting his thumb and forefinger deftly beneath his loose collar, he caught it. He rolled its body, tender yet brittle as a grain of rice, between thumb and finger for an instant before he let it fall from him and wondered would it live or die. There came to his mind a curious phrase from Cornelius a Lapide which said that the lice born of human sweat were not created by God with the other animals on the sixth day. But the tickling of the skin of his neck made his mind raw and red. The life of his body, illclad, illfed, louseeaten, made him close his eyelids in a sudden spasm of despair: and in the darkness he saw the brittle bright bodies of lice falling from the air and turning often as they fell. Yes; and it was not darkness that fell from the air. It was brightness.

Brightness falls from the air.

He had not even remembered rightly Nash's line. All the images it had awakened were false. His mind bred vermin. His thoughts were lice born of the sweat of sloth.

He came back quickly along the colonnade towards the group of students. Well then, let her go and be damned to her. She could love some clean athlete who washed himself every morning to the waist and had black hair on his chest. Let her.

Cranly had taken another dried fig from the supply in his pocket and was eating it slowly and noisily. Temple sat on the pediment of a pillar, leaning back, his cap pulled down on his sleepy eyes. A squat young man came out of the porch, a leather portfolio tucked under his armpit. He marched towards the group, striking the flags with the heels of his boots and with the ferule of his heavy umbrella. Then, raising the umbrella in salute, he said to all:

—Good evening, sirs.

He struck the flags again and tittered while his head trembled with a slight nervous movement. The tall consumptive student and Dixon and O'Keeffe were speaking in Irish and did not answer him. Then, turning to Cranly, he said:

—Good evening, particularly to you.

He moved the umbrella in indication and tittered again. Cranly, who was still chewing the fig, answered with loud movements of his jaws.

—Good? Yes. It is a good evening.

The squat student looked at him seriously and shook his umbrella gently and reprovingly.

—I can see, he said, that you are about to make obvious remarks.

—Um, Cranly answered, holding out what remained of the halfchewed fig and jerking it towards the squat student's mouth in sign that he should eat.

The squat student did not eat it but, indulging his special humour, said gravely, still tittering and prodding his phrase with his umbrella:

—Do you intend that . . .

He broke off, pointed bluntly to the munched pulp of the fig and said loudly:

—I allude to that.

—Um, Cranly said as before.

—Do you intend that now, the squat student said, as *ipso facto* or, let us say, as so to speak?

Dixon turned aside from his group, saying:

—Goggins was waiting for you, Glynn. He has gone round to the Adelphi to look for you and Moynihan.

What have you there? he asked, tapping the portfolio under Glynn's arm.

—Examination papers, Glynn answered. I give them monthly examinations to see that they are profiting by my tuition.

He also tapped the portfolio and coughed gently and smiled.

—Tuition! said Cranly rudely. I suppose you mean the barefooted children that are taught by a bloody ape like you. God help them!

He bit off the rest of the fig and flung away the butt.

—I suffer little children to come unto me, Glynn said amiably.

—A bloody ape, Cranly repeated with emphasis, and a blasphemous bloody ape!

Temple stood up and, pushing past Cranly, addressed Glynn:

—That phrase you said now, he said, is from the new testament about suffer the children to come to me.

—Go to sleep again, Temple, said O'Keeffe.

—Very well, then, Temple continued, still addressing Glynn, and if Jesus suffered the children to come why does the church send them all to hell if they die unbaptised? Why is that?

—Were you baptised yourself, Temple? the consumptive student asked.

—But why are they sent to hell if Jesus said they were all to come? Temple said, his eyes searching in Glynn's eyes.

Glynn coughed and said gently, holding back with difficulty the nervous titter in his voice and moving his umbrella at every word:

—And, as you remark, if it is thus I ask emphatically whence comes this thusness.

—Because the church is cruel like all old sinners, Temple said.

—Are you quite orthodox on that point, Temple? Dixon said suavely.

—Saint Augustine says that about unbaptised children going to hell, Temple answered, because he was a cruel old sinner too.

—I bow to you, Dixon said, but I had the impression that limbo existed for such cases.

—Don't argue with him, Dixon, Cranly said brutally. Don't talk to him or look at him. Lead him home with a sugan the way you'd lead a bleating goat.

—Limbo! Temple cried. That's a fine invention too. Like hell.

—But with the unpleasantness left out, Dixon said. He turned smiling to the others and said:

—I think I am voicing the opinions of all present in saying so much.

—You are, Glynn said in a firm tone. On that point Ireland is united.

He struck the ferule of his umbrella on the stone floor of the colonnade.

—Hell, Temple said. I can respect that invention of the grey spouse of Satan. Hell is Roman, like the walls of the Romans, strong and ugly. But what is limbo?

—Put him back into the perambulator, Cranly, O'Keeffe called out.

Cranly made a swift step towards Temple, halted, stamping his foot, crying as if to a fowl:

—Hoosh!

Temple moved away nimbly.

—Do you know what limbo is? he cried. Do you know what we call a notion like that in Roscommon?

—Hoosh! Blast you! Cranly cried, clapping his hands.

—Neither my arse nor my elbow! Temple cried out scornfully. And that's what I call limbo.

—Give us that stick here, Cranly said.

He snatched the ashplant roughly from Stephen's hand and sprang down the steps: but Temple, hearing him move in pursuit, fled through the dusk like a wild creature, nimble and fleetfooted. Cranly's heavy boots were heard loudly charging across the quandrangle and then returning heavily, foiled and spurning the gravel at each step.

His step was angry and with an angry abrupt gesture he thrust the stick back into Stephen's hand. Stephen felt that his anger had another cause but, feigning patience, touched his arm slightly and said quietly:

—Cranly, I told you I wanted to speak to you. Come away.

Cranly looked at him for a few moments and asked:

—Now?

—Yes, now, Stephen said. We can't speak here. Come away.

They crossed the quadrangle together without speaking. The birdcall from *Siegfried* whistled softly followed them from the steps of the porch. Cranly turned: and Dixon, who had whistled, called out:

—Where are you fellows off to? What about that game, Cranly?

They parleyed in shouts across the still air about a game of billiards to be played in the Adelphi hotel. Stephen walked on alone and out into the quiet of Kildare Street. Opposite Maple's hotel he stood to wait, patient again. The name of the hotel, a colourless polished wood, and its colourless quiet front stung him like a glance of polite disdain. He stared angrily back at the softly lit drawingroom of the hotel in which he imagined the sleek lives of the patricians of Ireland housed in calm. They thought of army commissions and land agents: peasants greeted them along the roads in the country: they knew the names of certain French dishes and gave orders to jarvies in highpitched provincial voices which pierced through their skintight accents.

How could he hit their conscience or how cast his shadow over the imaginations of their daughters, before their squires begat upon them, that they might breed a race less ignoble than their own? And under the deepened dusk he felt the thoughts and desires of the race to which he belonged flitting like bats, across the dark country lanes, under trees by the edges of streams and near the poolmottled bogs. A woman had waited in the doorway as Davin had passed by at night and, offering him a cup of milk, had all but wooed him to her bed; for Davin had the mild eyes of one who could be secret. But him no woman's eyes had wooed.

His arm was taken in a strong grip and Cranly's voice said:

—Let us eke go.

They walked southward in silence. Then Cranly said:

—That blithering idiot Temple! I swear to Moses, do you know, that I'll be the death of that fellow one time.

But his voice was no longer angry and Stephen wondered was he thinking of her greeting to him under the porch.

They turned to the left and walked on as before. When they had gone on so for some time Stephen said:

—Cranly, I had an unpleasant quarrel this evening.

—With your people? Cranly asked.

—With my mother.

—About religion?

—Yes, Stephen answered.

After a pause Cranly asked:

—What age is your mother?

—Not old, Stephen said. She wishes me to make my easter duty.

—And will you?

—I will not, Stephen said.

—Why not? Cranly said.

—I will not serve, answered Stephen.

—That remark was made before, Cranly said calmly.

—It is made behind now, said Stephen hotly.

Cranly pressed Stephen's arm, saying:

—Go easy, my dear man. You're an excitable bloody man, do you know.

He laughed nervously as he spoke and, looking up into Stephen's face with moved and friendly eyes, said:

—Do you know that you are an excitable man?

—I daresay I am, said Stephen, laughing also.

Their minds, lately estranged, seemed suddenly to have been drawn closer, one to the other.

—Do you believe in the eucharist? Cranly asked.

—I do not, Stephen said.

—Do you disbelieve then?

—I neither believe in it nor disbelieve in it, Stephen answered.

—Many persons have doubts, even religious persons, yet they overcome them or put them aside, Cranly said. Are your doubts on that point too strong?

—I do not wish to overcome them, Stephen answered.

Cranly, embarrassed for a moment, took another fig from his pocket and was about to eat it when Stephen said:

—Don't, please. You cannot discuss this question with your mouth full of chewed fig.

Cranly examined the fig by the light of a lamp under which he halted. Then he smelt it with both nostrils, bit a tiny piece, spat it out and threw the fig rudely into the gutter. Addressing it as it lay, he said:

—Depart from me, ye cursed, into everlasting fire!

Taking Stephen's arm, he went on again and said:

—Do you not fear that those words may be spoken to you on the day of judgment?

—What is offered me on the other hand? Stephen asked. An eternity of bliss in the company of the dean of studies?

—Remember, Cranly said, that he would be glorified.

—Ay, Stephen said somewhat bitterly, bright, agile, impassible and, above all, subtle.

—It is a curious thing, do you know, Cranly said dispassionately, how your mind is supersaturated with the religion in which you say you disbelieve. Did you believe in it when you were at school? I bet you did.

—I did, Stephen answered.

—And were you happier then? Cranly asked softly. Happier than you are now, for instance?

—Often happy, Stephen said, and often unhappy. I was someone else then.

—How someone else? What do you mean by that statement?

—I mean, said Stephen, that I was not myself as I am now, as I had to become.

—Not as you are now, not as you had to become, Cranly repeated. Let me ask you a question. Do you love your mother?

Stephen shook his head slowly.

—I don't know what your words mean, he said simply.

—Have you never loved anyone? Cranly asked.

—Do you mean women?

—I am not speaking of that, Cranly said in a colder tone. I ask you if you ever felt love towards anyone or anything.

Stephen walked on beside his friend, staring gloomily at the footpath.

—I tried to love God, he said at length. It seems now I failed. It is very difficult. I tried to unite my will with the will of God instant by instant. In that I did not always fail. I could perhaps do that still . . .

Cranly cut him short by asking:

—Has your mother had a happy life?

—How do I know? Stephen said.

—How many children had she?

—Nine or ten, Stephen answered. Some died.

—Was your father. . . . Cranly interrupted himself for an instant: and then said: I don't want to pry into your family affairs. But was your father what is called well-to-do? I mean when you were growing up?

—Yes, Stephen said.

—What was he? Cranly asked after a pause.

Stephen began to enumerate glibly his father's attributes.

—A medical student, an oarsman, a tenor, an amateur actor, a shouting politician, a small landlord, a small investor, a drinker, a good fellow, a storyteller, somebody's secretary, something in a distillery, a tax-gatherer, a bankrupt and at present a praiser of his own past.

Cranly laughed, tightening his grip on Stephen's arm, and said:

—The distillery is damn good.

—Is there anything else you want to know? Stephen asked.

—Are you in good circumstances at present?

—Do I look it? Stephen asked bluntly.

—So then, Cranly went on musingly, you were born in the lap of luxury.

He used the phrase broadly and loudly, as he often used technical expressions as if he wished his hearer to understand that they were used by him without conviction.

—Your mother must have gone through a good deal of suffering, he said then. Would you not try to save her from suffering more even if . . . or would you?

—If I could, Stephen said. That would cost me very little.

—Then do so, Cranly said. Do as she wishes you to do. What is it for you? You disbelieve in it. It is a form: nothing else. And you will set her mind at rest.

He ceased and, as Stephen did not reply, remained silent. Then, as if giving utterance to the process of his own thought, he said:

—Whatever else is unsure in this stinking dunghill of a world a mother's love is not. Your mother brings you into the world, carries you first in her body. What do we know about what she feels? But whatever she feels, it, at least, must be real. It must be. What are our ideas or ambitions? Play. Ideas! Why, that bloody bleating goat Temple has ideas. MacCann has ideas too. Every jackass going the roads thinks he has ideas.

Stephen, who had been listening to the unspoken speech behind the words, said with assumed carelessness:

—Pascal, if I remember rightly, would not suffer his mother to kiss him as he feared the contact of her sex.

—Pascal was a pig, said Cranly.

—Aloysius Gonzaga, I think, was of the same mind, Stephen said.

—And he was another pig then, said Cranly.

—The church calls him a saint, Stephen objected.

—I don't care a flaming damn what anyone calls him, Cranly said rudely and flatly. I call him a pig.

Stephen, preparing the words neatly in his mind, continued:

—Jesus, too, seems to have treated his mother with scant courtesy in public but Suarez, a jesuit theologian and Spanish gentleman, has apologised for him.

—Did the idea ever occur to you, Cranly asked, that Jesus was not what he pretended to be?

—The first person to whom that idea occurred, Stephen answered, was Jesus himself.

—I mean, Cranly said, hardening in his speech, did the idea ever occur to you that he was himself a conscious hypocrite, what he called the jews of his time, a whited sepulchre? Or, to put it more plainly, that he was a blackguard?

—That idea never occurred to me, Stephen answered. But I am curious to know are you trying to make a convert of me or a pervert of yourself?

He turned towards his friend's face and saw there a raw smile which some force of will strove to make finely significant.

Cranly asked suddenly in a plain sensible tone:

—Tell me the truth. Were you at all shocked by what I said?

—Somewhat, Stephen said.

—And why were you shocked, Cranly pressed on in the same tone, if you feel sure that our religion is false and that Jesus was not the son of God?

—I am not at all sure of it, Stephen said. He is more like a son of God than a son of Mary.

—And is that why you will not communicate, Cranly asked, because you are not sure of that too, because you feel that the host too may be the body and blood of the son of God and not a wafer of bread? And because you fear that it may be?

—Yes, Stephen said quietly. I feel that and I also fear it.

—I see, Cranly said.

Stephen, struck by his tone of closure, reopened the discussion at once by saying:

—I fear many things: dogs, horses, firearms, the sea, thunderstorms, machinery, the country roads at night.

—But why do you fear a bit of bread?

—I imagine, Stephen said, that there is a malevolent reality behind those things I say I fear.

—Do you fear then, Cranly asked, that the God of the Roman catholics would strike you dead and damn you if you made a sacrilegious communion?

—The God of the Roman catholics could do that now, Stephen said. I fear more than that the chemical action which would be set up in my soul by a false homage to a symbol behind which are massed twenty centuries of authority and veneration.

—Would you, Cranly asked, in extreme danger commit that particular sacrilege? For instance, if you lived in the penal days?

—I cannot answer for the past, Stephen replied. Possibly not.

—Then, said Cranly, you do not intend to become a protestant?

—I said that I had lost the faith, Stephen answered, but not that I had lost selfrespect. What kind of liberation would that be to forsake an absurdity which is logical and coherent and to embrace one which is illogical and incoherent?

They had walked on towards the township of Pembroke and now, as they went on slowly along the avenues, the trees and the scattered lights in the villas soothed their minds. The air of wealth and repose diffused about them seemed to comfort their neediness. Behind a hedge of laurel a light glimmered in the window of a kitchen and the voice of a servant was heard singing as she sharpened knives. She sang, in short broken bars, *Rosie O'Grady*.

Cranly stopped to listen, saying:

—*Mulier cantat.*

The soft beauty of the Latin word touched with an enchanting touch the dark of the evening, with a touch fainter and more persuading than the touch of music or of a woman's hand. The strife of their minds was quelled. The figure of woman as she appears in the liturgy of the church passed silently through the darkness: a whiterobed figure, small and slender as a boy and with a falling girdle. Her voice, frail and high as a boy's, was heard intoning from a distant choir the first words of a woman which pierce the gloom and clamour of the first chanting of the passion:

—*Et tu cum Jesu Galilæo eras.*

And all hearts were touched and turned to her voice, shining like a young star, shining clearer as the voice intoned the proparoxyton and more faintly as the cadence died.

The singing ceased. They went on together, Cranly repeating in strongly stressed rhythm the end of the refrain:

> *And when we are married,*
> *O, how happy we'll be*
> *For I love sweet Rosie O'Grady*
> *And Rosie O'Grady loves me.*

—There's real poetry for you, he said. There's real love.

He glanced sideways at Stephen with a strange smile and said:

—Do you consider that poetry? Or do you know what the words mean?

—I want to see Rosie first, said Stephen.

—She's easy to find, Cranly said.

His hat had come down on his forehead. He shoved it back: and in the shadow of the trees Stephen saw his pale face, framed by the dark, and his large dark eyes. Yes. His face was handsome: and his body was strong and hard. He had spoken of a mother's love. He felt then the sufferings of women, the weaknesses of their bodies and souls: and would shield them with a strong and resolute arm and bow his mind to them.

Away then: it is time to go. A voice spoke softly to Stephen's lonely heart, bidding him go and telling him that his friendship was coming to an end. Yes; he would go. He could not strive against another. He knew his part.

—Probably I shall go away, he said.

—Where? Cranly asked.

—Where I can, Stephen said.

—Yes, Cranly said. It might be difficult for you to live here now. But is it that that makes you go?

—I have to go, Stephen answered.

—Because, Cranly continued, you need not look upon yourself as driven away if you do not wish to go or as a heretic or an outlaw. There are many good believers who think as you do. Would that surprise you? The church is not the stone building nor even the clergy and their dogmas. It is the whole mass of those born into it. I don't know what you wish to do in life. Is it what you told me the night we were standing outside Harcourt Street station?

—Yes, Stephen said, smiling in spite of himself at Cranly's way of remembering thoughts in connection with places. The night you spent half an hour wrangling with Doherty about the shortest way from Sally-gap to Larras.

—Pothead! Cranly said with calm contempt. What does he know about the way from Sallygap to Larras?

Or what does he know about anything for that matter? And the big slobbering washingpot head of him!

He broke out into a loud long laugh.

—Well? Stephen said. Do you remember the rest?

—What you said, is it? Cranly asked. Yes, I remember it. To discover the mode of life or of art whereby your spirit could express itself in unfettered freedom.

Stephen raised his hat in acknowledgment.

—Freedom! Cranly repeated. But you are not free enough yet to commit a sacrilege. Tell me, would you rob?

—I would beg first, Stephen said.

—And if you got nothing, would you rob?

—You wish me to say, Stephen answered, that the rights of property are provisional and that in certain circumstances it is not unlawful to rob. Everyone would act in that belief. So I will not make you that answer. Apply to the jesuit theologian Juan Mariana de Talavera who will also explain to you in what circumstances you may lawfully kill your king and whether you had better hand him his poison in a goblet or smear it for him upon his robe or his saddlebow. Ask me rather would I suffer others to rob me or, if they did, would I call down upon them what I believe is called the chastisement of the secular arm?

—And would you?

—I think, Stephen said, it would pain me as much to do so as to be robbed.

—I see, Cranly said.

He produced his match and began to clean the crevice between two teeth. Then he said carelessly:

—Tell me, for example, would you deflower a virgin?

—Excuse me, Stephen said politely, is that not the ambition of most young gentlemen?

—What then is your point of view? Cranly asked.

His last phrase, soursmelling as the smoke of charcoal and disheartening, excited Stephen's brain, over which its fumes seemed to brood.

—Look here, Cranly, he said. You have asked me what I would do and what I would not do. I will tell you what I will do and what I will not do. I will not serve that in which I no longer believe whether it call itself my home, my fatherland or my church: and I will try to express myself in some mode of life or art as freely as I can and as wholly as I can, using for my defence the only arms I allow myself to use—silence, exile, and cunning.

Cranly seized his arm and steered him round so as to head back towards Leeson Park. He laughed almost slily and pressed Stephen's arm with an elder's affection.

—Cunning indeed! he said. Is it you? You poor poet, you!

—And you made me confess to you, Stephen said, thrilled by his touch, as I have confessed to you so many other things, have I not?

—Yes, my child, Cranly said, still gaily.

—You made me confess the fears that I have. But I will tell you also what I do not fear. I do not fear to be alone or to be spurned for another or to leave whatever I have to leave. And I am not afraid to make a mistake, even a great mistake, a lifelong mistake and perhaps as long as eternity too.

Cranly, now grave again, slowed his pace and said:

—Alone, quite alone. You have no fear of that. And you know what that word means? Not only to be separate from all others but to have not even one friend.

—I will take the risk, said Stephen.

—And not to have any one person, Cranly said, who would be more than a friend, more even than the noblest and truest friend a man ever had.

His words seemed to have struck some deep chord in his own nature. Had he spoken of himself, of himself as he was or wished to be? Stephen watched his face for some moments in silence. A cold sadness was there. He had spoken of himself, of his own loneliness which he feared.

—Of whom are you speaking? Stephen asked at length.

Cranly did not answer.

*   *   *

20 *March:* Long talk with Cranly on the subject of my revolt. He had his grand manner on. I supple and suave. Attacked me on the score of love for one's mother. Tried to imagine his mother: cannot. Told me once, in a moment of thoughtlessness, his father was sixtyone when he was born. Can see him. Strong farmer type. Pepper and salt suit. Square feet. Unkempt grizzled beard. Probably attends coursing matches. Pays his dues regularly but not plentifully to Father Dwyer of Larras. Sometimes talks to girls after nightfall. But his mother? Very young or very old? Hardly the first. If so, Cranly would not have spoken as he did. Old then. Probably, and neglected. Hence Cranly's despair of soul: the child of exhausted loins.

21 *March, morning:* Thought this in bed last night but was too lazy and free to add it. Free, yes. The exhausted loins are those of Elisabeth and Zachary. Then he is the precursor. Item: he eats chiefly belly bacon and dried figs. Read locusts and wild honey. Also, when thinking of him, saw always a stern severed head or deathmask as if outlined on a grey curtain or veronica. Decollation they call it in the fold. Puzzled for the moment by saint John at the Latin gate. What

do I see? A decollated precursor trying to pick the lock.

21 *March, night:* Free. Soulfree and fancyfree. Let the dead bury the dead. Ay. And let the dead marry the dead.

22 *March:* In company with Lynch followed a sizable hospital nurse. Lynch's idea. Dislike it. Two lean hungry greyhounds walking after a heifer.

23 *March:* Have not seen her since that night. Unwell? Sits at the fire perhaps with mamma's shawl on her shoulders. But not peevish. A nice bowl of gruel? Won't you now?

24 *March:* Began with a discussion with my mother. Subject: B.V.M. Handicapped by my sex and youth. To escape held up relations between Jesus and Papa against those between Mary and her son. Said religion was not a lying-in hospital. Mother indulgent. Said I have a queer mind and have read too much. Not true. Have read little and understood less. Then she said I would come back to faith because I had a restless mind. This means to leave church by backdoor of sin and reenter through the skylight of repentance. Cannot repent. Told her so and asked for sixpence. Got threepence.

Then went to college. Other wrangle with little roundhead rogue'seye Ghezzi. This time about Bruno the Nolan. Began in Italian and ended in pidgin English. He said Bruno was a terrible heretic. I said he was terribly burned. He agreed to this with some sorrow. Then gave me recipe for what he calls *risotto alla bergamasca.* When he pronounces a soft *o* he protrudes his full carnal lips as if he kissed the vowel. Has he? And could he repent? Yes, he could: and cry two round rogue's tears, one from each eye.

Crossing Stephen's, that is, my green, remembered

that his countrymen and not mine had invented what Cranly the other night called our religion. A quartet of them, soldiers of the ninetyseventh infantry regiment, sat at the foot of the cross and tossed up dice for the overcoat of the crucified.

Went to library. Tried to read three reviews. Useless. She is not out yet. Am I alarmed? About what? That she will never be out again.

Blake wrote:

> *I wonder if William Bond will die*
> *For assuredly he is very ill.*

Alas, poor William!

I was once at a diorama in Rotunda. At the end were pictures of big nobs. Among them William Ewart Gladstone, just then dead. Orchestra played *O, Willie, we have missed you.*

A race of clodhoppers!

25 *March, morning:* A troubled night of dreams. Want to get them off my chest.

A long curving gallery. From the floor ascend pillars of dark vapours. It is peopled by the images of fabulous kings, set in stone. Their hands are folded upon their knees in token of weariness and their eyes are darkened for the errors of men go up before them for ever as dark vapours.

Strange figures advance from a cave. They are not as tall as men. One does not seem to stand quite apart from another. Their faces are phosphorescent, with darker streaks. They peer at me and their eyes seem to ask me something. They do not speak.

30 *March:* This evening Cranly was in the porch of the library, proposing a problem to Dixon and her brother. A mother let her child fall into the Nile. Still harping on the mother. A crocodile seized the child.

Mother asked it back. Crocodile said all right if she told him what he was going to do with the child, eat it or not eat it.

This mentality, Lepidus would say, is indeed bred out of your mud by the operation of your sun.

And mine? Is it not too? Then into Nilemud with it!

1 *April:* Disapprove of this last phrase.

2 *April:* Saw her drinking tea and eating cakes in Johnston, Mooney and O'Brien's. Rather, lynxeyed Lynch saw her as we passed. He tells me Cranly was invited there by brother. Did he bring his crocodile? Is he the shining light now? Well, I discovered him. I protest I did. Shining quietly behind a bushel of Wicklow bran.

3 *April:* Met Davin at the cigar shop opposite Findlater's church. He was in a black sweater and had a hurleystick. Asked me was it true I was going away and why. Told him the shortest way to Tara was *via* Holyhead. Just then my father came up. Introduction. Father, polite and observant. Asked Davin if he might offer him some refreshment. Davin could not, was going to a meeting. When we came away father told me he had a good honest eye. Asked me why I did not join a rowingclub. I pretended to think it over. Told me then how he broke Pennyfeather's heart. Wants me to read law. Says I was cut out for that. More mud, more crocodiles.

5 *April:* Wild spring. Scudding clouds. O life! Dark stream of swirling bogwater on which appletrees have cast down their delicate flowers. Eyes of girls among the leaves. Girls demure and romping. All fair or auburn: no dark ones. They blush better. Houp-la!

6 *April:* Certainly she remembers the past. Lynch says all women do. Then she remembers the time of her childhood—and mine if I was ever a child. The

past is consumed in the present and the present is living only because it brings forth the future. Statues of women, if Lynch be right, should always be fully draped, one hand of the woman feeling regretfully her own hinder parts.

6 *April, later:* Michael Robartes remembers forgotten beauty and, when his arms wrap her round, he presses in his arms the loveliness which has long faded from the world. Not this. Not at all. I desire to press in my arms the loveliness which has not yet come into the world.

10 *April:* Faintly, under the heavy night, through the silence of the city which has turned from dreams to dreamless sleep as a weary lover whom no caresses move, the sound of hoofs upon the road. Not so faintly now as they come near the bridge: and in a moment as they pass the darkened windows the silence is cloven by alarm as by an arrow. They are heard now far away, hoofs that shine amid the heavy night as gems, hurrying beyond the sleeping fields to what journey's end— what heart?—bearing what tidings?

11 *April:* Read what I wrote last night. Vague words for a vague emotion. Would she like it? I think so. Then I should have to like it also.

13 *April:* That tundish has been on my mind for a long time. I looked it up and find it English and good old blunt English too. Damn the dean of studies and his funnel! What did he come here for to teach us his own language or to learn it from us? Damn him one way or the other!

14 *April:* John Alphonsus Mulrennan has just returned from the west of Ireland. (European and Asiatic papers please copy.) He told us he met an old man there in a mountain cabin. Old man had red eyes and short pipe. Old man spoke Irish. Mulrennan spoke

Irish. Then old man and Mulrennan spoke English. Mulrennan spoke to him about universe and stars. Old man sat, listened, smoked, spat. Then said:

—Ah, there must be terrible queer creatures at the latter end of the world.

I fear him. I fear his redrimmed horny eyes. It is with him I must struggle all through this night till day come, till he or I lie dead, gripping him by the sinewy throat till . . . Till what? Till he yield to me? No. I mean him no harm.

15 *April:* Met her today pointblank in Grafton Street. The crowd brought us together. We both stopped. She asked me why I never came, said she had heard all sorts of stories about me. This was only to gain time. Asked me, was I writing poems? About whom? I asked her. This confused her more and I felt sorry and mean. Turned off that valve at once and opened the spiritual-heroic refrigerating apparatus, invented and patented in all countries by Dante Alighieri. Talked rapidly of myself and my plans. In the midst of it unluckily I made a sudden gesture of a revolutionary nature. I must have looked like a fellow throwing a handful of peas into the air. People began to look at us. She shook hands a moment after and, in going away, said she hoped I would do what I said.

Now I call that friendly, don't you?

Yes, I liked her today. A little or much? Don't know. I liked her and it seems a new feeling to me. Then, in that case, all the rest, all that I thought I thought and all that I felt I felt, all the rest before now, in fact . . . O, give it up, old chap! Sleep it off!

16 *April:* Away! Away!

The spell of arms and voices: the white arms of roads, their promise of close embraces and the black arms of tall ships that stand against the moon, their tale of distant nations. They are held out to say: We are alone. Come. And the voices say with them: We are your kinsmen. And the air is thick with their company as they call to me, their kinsman, making ready to go, shaking the wings of their exultant and terrible youth.

26 *April:* Mother is putting my new secondhand clothes in order. She prays now, she says, that I may learn in my own life and away from home and friends what the heart is and what it feels. Amen. So be it. Welcome, O life! I go to encounter for the millionth time the reality of experience and to forge in the smithy of my soul the uncreated conscience of my race.

27 *April:* Old father, old artificer, stand me now and ever in good stead.

Dublin 1904
Trieste 1914

Exiles

A Play in Three Acts

JOYCE'S drama, *Exiles,* was written during his most fruitful year, 1914, immediately after completing the *Portrait* and before undertaking *Ulysses.* It was published without much difficulty in 1918, and has on occasion been acted without much success. The artistic impulse, as the *Portrait* describes it, begins in personal emotion and ends with impersonal creation. Its initial expression is therefore lyrical; its ultimate medium is dramatic. The epic represents an intermediate stage, equidistant between the author and his characters, as *Ulysses* is suspended between Stephen and Bloom. It might be added, in Joyce's terms, that all of his writing contains a large residue of lyricism. Whether he ever mastered the objectivity of the true dramatist is a question which might well be put to the reader of this play. Within the subjective sphere, it must be admitted, he went on to develop a remarkable kind of psychological dramaturgy in the *Walpurgisnacht* scene (the Circe episode) of *Ulysses. Exiles,* however, harks back to the lessons Joyce learned from the Continental playwrights. An early dramatic effort, entitled *A Brilliant Career* and dedicated to the youthful playwright's own soul, had won him encouragement from a knowledgeable critic,

William Archer. Joyce's first article had been devoted to Ibsen's last play, *When We Dead Awaken,* which is closely paralleled by the situation of *Exiles:* the alternating relationship of an artist and his wife and another couple. The intellectual hero and his earthy friend, Robert, are paired against the womanly Bertha and the maidenly Beatrice. Indeed, this plot is so neat that, unless it be saved by skillful characterization, it runs the danger of becoming mechanical. It may be felt that Joyce, emotionally identified with his protagonist, is rather far away from his other characters. Richard Rowan is too complex; the others are too simple. The three of them are anxious to understand him; he is less concerned with understanding them; in the end he remains, even to his wife, a stranger. Our conclusion may be, as T. S. Eliot concluded of *Hamlet,* that the writer has not quite found an "objective correlative." Since he has not managed to adapt himself to his form, his problem remains a personal one. But in the armchair, if not in the theater, we can follow it with considerable interest; for Richard's dilemma is a restatement of Stephen's; and, though the play is less autobiographical than the novel, it sketches a self-portrait at a later period. The place is still Dublin, and the year is now 1912—the occasion of Joyce's final visit to Ireland. The issue is framed by familiar circumstances: the mother's death, the son's elopement. Should he settle down at home, accept a professorship of Romance languages at his old university, and attempt to Europeanize Ireland? Or would he there be condemned to a state of spiritual estrangement, as bitter as Swift's? We know Joyce's answer, though *Exiles* does not present it. It does suggest the unwavering domestic loyalty that helped him to bear the discomforts of expatriation and to give himself single-mindedly to his art.

Exiles

RICHARD ROWAN, a writer.

BERTHA.

ARCHIE, their son, aged eight years.

ROBERT HAND, journalist.

BEATRICE JUSTICE, his cousin, music teacher.

BRIGID, an old servant of the Rowan family.

A FISHWOMAN.

At Merrion and Ranelagh, suburbs of Dublin.
Summer of the year 1912.

First Act

*T*HE *drawingroom in Richard Rowan's house at Merrion, a suburb of Dublin. On the right, forward, a fireplace, before which stands a low screen. Over the mantelpiece a giltframed glass. Further back in the right wall, folding doors leading to the parlour and kitchen. In the wall at the back to the right a small door leading to a study. Left of this a sideboard. On the wall above the sideboard a framed crayon drawing of a young man. More to the left double doors with glass panels leading out to the garden. In the wall at the left a window looking out on the road. Forward in the same wall a door leading to the hall and the upper part of the house. Between the window and door a lady's davenport stands against the wall. Near it a*

*wicker chair. In the centre of the room a round table.
Chairs, upholstered in faded green plush, stand round
the table. To the right, forward, a smaller table with a
smoking service on it. Near it an easychair and a lounge.
Cocoanut mats lie before the fireplace, beside the lounge
and before the doors. The floor is of stained planking.
The double doors at the back and the folding doors at
the right have lace curtains, which are drawn halfway.
The lower sash of the window is lifted and the window
is hung with heavy green plush curtains. The blind is
pulled down to the edge of the lifted lower sash. It is a
warm afternoon in June and the room is filled with soft
sunlight which is waning.*

BRIGID *and* BEATRICE JUSTICE *come in by the door on
the left.* BRIGID *is an elderly woman, lowsized, with
irongrey hair.* BEATRICE JUSTICE *is a slender dark young
woman of 27 years. She wears a wellmade navyblue
costume and an elegant simply trimmed black straw
hat, and carries a small portfolioshaped handbag.*

BRIGID: The mistress and Master Archie is at the bath.
They never expected you. Did you send word you were
back, Miss Justice?

BEATRICE: No. I arrived just now.

BRIGID, *points to the easychair:* Sit down and I tell
the Master you are here. Were you long in the train?

BEATRICE, *sitting down:* Since morning.

BRIGID: Master Archie got your postcard with the
views of Youghal. You're tired out, I'm sure.

BEATRICE: O, no. *She coughs rather nervously.* Did
he practise the piano while I was away?

BRIGID, *laughs heartily:* Practice, how are you! Is it
Master Archie? He is mad after the milkman's horse
now. Had you nice weather down there, Miss Justice?

BEATRICE: Rather wet, I think.

BRIGID, *sympathetically:* Look at that now. And there is rain overhead too. *Moving towards the study.* I'll tell him you are here.

BEATRICE: Is Mr. Rowan in?

BRIGID, *points:* He is in his study. He is wearing himself out about something he is writing. Up half the night he does be. *Going.* I'll call him.

BEATRICE: Don't disturb him, Brigid. I can wait here till they come back if they are not long.

BRIGID: And I saw something in the letterbox when I was letting you in. *She crosses to the study door, opens it slightly and calls.* Master Richard, Miss Justice is here for Master Archie's lesson.

RICHARD ROWAN *comes in from the study and advances towards* BEATRICE, *holding out his hand. He is a tall athletic young man of a rather lazy carriage. He has light brown hair and a moustache and wears glasses. He is dressed in loose lightgrey tweed.*

RICHARD: Welcome.

BEATRICE, *rises and shakes hands, blushing slightly:* Good afternoon, Mr. Rowan. I did not want Brigid to disturb you.

RICHARD: Disturb me? My goodness!

BRIGID: There is something in the letterbox, sir.

RICHARD, *takes a small bunch of keys from his pocket and hands them to her:* Here.

BRIGID *goes out by the door at the left and is heard opening and closing the box. A short pause. She enters with two newspapers in her hands.*

RICHARD: Letters?

BRIGID: No, sir. Only them Italian newspapers.

RICHARD: Leave them on my desk, will you?

BRIGID *hands him back the keys, leaves the newspapers in the study, comes out again and goes out by the folding doors on the right.*

RICHARD: Please, sit down. Bertha will be back in a moment.

BEATRICE *sits down again in the easychair.* RICHARD *sits beside the table.*

RICHARD: I had begun to think you would never come back. It is twelve days since you were here.

BEATRICE: I thought of that too. But I have come.

RICHARD: Have you thought over what I told you when you were here last?

BEATRICE: Very much.

RICHARD: You must have known it before. Did you? *She does not answer.* Do you blame me?

BEATRICE: No.

RICHARD: Do you think I have acted towards you— badly? No? Or towards anyone?

BEATRICE, *looks at him with a sad puzzled expression:* I have asked myself that question.

RICHARD: And the answer?

BEATRICE: I could not answer it.

RICHARD: If I were a painter and told you I had a book of sketches of you you would not think it so strange, would you?

BEATRICE: It is not quite the same case, is it?

RICHARD, *smiles slightly:* Not quite. I told you also that I would not show you what I had written unless you asked to see it. Well?

BEATRICE: I will not ask you.

RICHARD, *leans forward, resting his elbows on his knees, his hands joined:* Would you like to see it?

BEATRICE: Very much.

RICHARD: Because it is about yourself?

BEATRICE: Yes. But not only that.

RICHARD: Because it is written by me? Yes? Even if what you would find there is sometimes cruel?

BEATRICE, *shyly:* That is part of your mind, too.

RICHARD: Then it is my mind that attracts you? Is that it?

BEATRICE, *hesitating, glances at him for an instant:* Why do you think I come here?

RICHARD: Why? Many reasons. To give Archie lessons. We have known one another so many years, from childhood, Robert, you and I—haven't we? You have always been interested in me, before I went away and while I was away. Then our letters to each other about my book. Now it is published. I am here again. Perhaps you feel that some new thing is gathering in my brain; perhaps you feel that you should know it. Is that the reason?

BEATRICE: No.

RICHARD: Why, then?

BEATRICE: Otherwise I could not see you.

She looks at him for a moment and then turns aside quickly.

RICHARD, *after a pause repeats uncertainly:* Otherwise you could not see me?

BEATRICE, *suddenly confused:* I had better go. They are not coming back. *Rising.* Mr. Rowan, I must go.

RICHARD, *extending his arms:* But you are running away. Remain. Tell me what your words mean. Are you afraid of me?

BEATRICE, *sinks back again:* Afraid? No.

RICHARD: Have you confidence in me? Do you feel that you know me?

BEATRICE, *again shyly:* It is hard to know anyone but oneself.

RICHARD: Hard to know me? I sent you from Rome the chapters of my book as I wrote them; and letters for nine long years. Well, eight years.

BEATRICE: Yes, it was nearly a year before your first letter came.

RICHARD: It was answered at once by you. And from that on you have watched me in my struggle. *Joins his hands earnestly.* Tell me, Miss Justice, did you feel that what you read was written for your eyes? Or that you inspired me?

BEATRICE, *shakes her head:* I need not answer that question.

RICHARD: What then?

BEATRICE, *is silent for a moment:* I cannot say it. You yourself must ask me, Mr. Rowan.

RICHARD, *with some vehemence:* Then that I expressed in those chapters and letters, and in my character and life as well, something in your soul which you could not—pride or scorn?

BEATRICE: Could not?

RICHARD, *leans towards her:* Could not because you dared not. Is that why?

BEATRICE, *bends her head:* Yes.

RICHARD: On account of others or for want of courage —which?

BEATRICE, *softly:* Courage.

RICHARD, *slowly:* And so you have followed me with pride and scorn also in your heart?

BEATRICE: And loneliness.

She leans her head on her hand, averting her face. RICHARD *rises and walks slowly to the window on the left. He looks out for some moments and then returns towards her, crosses to the lounge and sits down near her.*

RICHARD: Do you love him still?

BEATRICE: I do not even know.

RICHARD: It was that that made me so reserved with you—then—even though I felt your interest in me, even though I felt that I too was something in your life.

BEATRICE: You were.

RICHARD: Yet that separated me from you. I was a third person I felt. Your names were always spoken together, Robert and Beatrice, as long as I can remember. It seemed to me, to everyone . . .

BEATRICE: We are first cousins. It is not strange that we were often together.

RICHARD: He told me of your secret engagement with him. He had no secrets from me; I suppose you know that.

BEATRICE, *uneasily:* What happened—between us— is so long ago. I was a child.

RICHARD, *smiles maliciously:* A child? Are you sure? It was in the garden of his mother's house. No? *He points towards the garden.* Over there. You plighted your troth, as they say, with a kiss. And you gave him your garter. Is it allowed to mention that?

BEATRICE, *with some reserve:* If you think it worthy of mention.

RICHARD: I think you have not forgotten it. *Clasping his hands quietly.* I do not understand it. I thought, too, that after I had gone . . . Did my going make you suffer?

BEATRICE: I always knew you would go some day. I did not suffer; only I was changed.

RICHARD: Towards him?

BEATRICE: Everything was changed. His life, his mind, even, seemed to change after that.

RICHARD, *musing:* Yes. I saw that you had changed when I received your first letter after a year; after your illness, too. You even said so in your letter.

BEATRICE: It brought me near to death. It made me see things differently.

RICHARD: And so a coldness began between you, little by little. Is that it?

BEATRICE, *half closing her eyes:* No. Not at once. I

saw in him a pale reflection of you: then that too faded. Of what good is it to talk now?

RICHARD, *with a repressed energy:* But what is this that seems to hang over you? It cannot be so tragic.

BEATRICE, *calmly:* O, not in the least tragic. I shall become gradually better, they tell me, as I grow older. As I did not die then they tell me I shall probably live. I am given life and health again—when I cannot use them. *Calmly and bitterly.* I am convalescent.

RICHARD, *gently:* Does nothing then in life give you peace? Surely it exists for you somewhere.

BEATRICE: If there were convents in our religion perhaps there. At least, I think so at times.

RICHARD, *shakes his head:* No, Miss Justice, not even there. You could not give yourself freely and wholly.

BEATRICE, *looking at him:* I would try.

RICHARD: You would try, yes. You were drawn to him as your mind was drawn towards mine. You held back from him. From me, too, in a different way. You cannot give yourself freely and wholly.

BEATRICE, *joins her hands softly:* It is a terribly hard thing to do, Mr. Rowan—to give oneself freely and wholly—and be happy.

RICHARD: But do you feel that happiness is the best, the highest that we can know?

BEATRICE, *with fervour:* I wish I could feel it.

RICHARD, *leans back, his hands locked together behind his head:* O, if you knew how I am suffering at this moment! For your case, too. But suffering most of all for my own. *With bitter force.* And how I pray that I may be granted again my dead mother's hardness of heart! For some help, within me or without, I must find. And find it I will.

BEATRICE *rises, looks at him intently, and walks away toward the garden door. She turns with in-*

decision, looks again at him and, coming back, leans over the easychair.

BEATRICE, *quietly:* Did she send for you before she died, Mr. Rowan?

RICHARD, *lost in thought:* Who?

BEATRICE: Your mother.

RICHARD, *recovering himself, looks keenly at her for a moment:* So that, too, was said of me here by my friends —that she sent for me before she died and that I did not go?

BEATRICE: Yes.

RICHARD, *coldly:* She did not. She died alone, not having forgiven me, and fortified by the rites of holy church.

BEATRICE: Mr. Rowan, why did you speak to me in such a way?

RICHARD, *rises and walks nervously to and fro:* And what I suffer at this moment you will say is my punishment.

BEATRICE: Did she write to you? I mean before . . .

RICHARD, *halting:* Yes. A letter of warning, bidding me break with the past, and remember her last words to me.

BEATRICE, *softly:* And does death not move you, Mr. Rowan? It is an end. Everything else is so uncertain.

RICHARD: While she lived she turned aside from me and from mine. That is certain.

BEATRICE: From you and from . . . ?

RICHARD: From Bertha and from me and from our child. And so I waited for the end as you say; and it came.

BEATRICE, *covers her face with her hands:* O, no. Surely no.

RICHARD, *fiercely:* How can my words hurt her poor body that rots in the grave? Do you think I do not pity her cold blighted love for me? I fought against her spirit while she lived to the bitter end. *He presses his hand to his forehead.* It fights against me still—in here.

BEATRICE, *as before:* O, do not speak like that.

RICHARD: She drove me away. On account of her I lived years in exile and poverty too, or near it. I never accepted the doles she sent me through the bank. I waited, too, not for her death but for some understanding of me, her own son, her own flesh and blood; that never came.

BEATRICE: Not even after Archie . . . ?

RICHARD, *rudely:* My son, you think? A child of sin and shame! Are you serious? *She raises her face and looks at him.* There were tongues here ready to tell her all, to embitter her withering mind still more against me and Bertha and our godless nameless child. *Holding out his hands to her.* Can you not hear her mocking me while I speak? You must know the voice, surely, the voice that called you "the black protestant," the pervert's daughter. *With sudden selfcontrol.* In any case a remarkable woman.

BEATRICE, *weakly:* At least you are free now.

RICHARD, *nods:* Yes, she could not alter the terms of my father's will nor live for ever.

BEATRICE, *with joined hands:* They are both gone now, Mr. Rowan. They both loved you, believe me. Their last thoughts were of you.

RICHARD, *approaching, touches her lightly on the shoulder, and points to the crayon drawing on the wall:* Do you see him there, smiling and handsome? His last thoughts! I remember the night he died. *He pauses for an instant and then goes on calmly.* I was a boy of fourteen. He called me to his bedside. He knew I wanted to go to the theatre to hear *Carmen.* He told my mother to give me a shilling. I kissed him and went. When I came home he was dead. Those were his last thoughts as far as I know.

BEATRICE: The hardness of heart you prayed for . . . *She breaks off.*

RICHARD, *unheeding:* That is my last memory of him. Is there not something sweet and noble in it?

BEATRICE: Mr. Rowan, something is on your mind to make you speak like this. Something has changed you since you came back three months ago.

RICHARD, *gazing again at the drawing, calmly, almost gaily:* He will help me, perhaps, my smiling handsome father.

A knock is heard at the hall door on the left.

RICHARD, *suddenly:* No, no. Not the smiler, Miss Justice. The old mother. It is her spirit I need. I am going.

BEATRICE: Someone knocked. They have come back.

RICHARD: No, Bertha has a key. It is he. At least, I am going, whoever it is.

He goes out quickly on the left and comes back at once with his straw hat in his hand.

BEATRICE: He? Who?

RICHARD: O, probably Robert. I am going out through the garden. I cannot see him now. Say I have gone to the post. Goodbye.

BEATRICE, *with growing alarm:* It is Robert you do not wish to see?

RICHARD, *quietly:* For the moment, yes. This talk has upset me. Ask him to wait.

BEATRICE: You will come back?

RICHARD: Please God.

He goes out quickly through the garden. BEATRICE *makes as if to follow him and then stops after a few paces.* BRIGID *enters by the folding doors on the right and goes out on the left. The hall door is heard opening.*

A few seconds after BRIGID *enters with* ROBERT HAND. ROBERT HAND *is a middlesized, rather stout man between thirty and forty. He is cleanshaven, with mobile features. His hair and eyes are dark and his complexion sallow. His gait and speech are rather slow. He wears a dark blue morning suit and carries in his hand a large bunch of red roses wrapped in tissue paper.*

ROBERT, *coming toward her with outstretched hand which she takes:* My dearest coz. Brigid told me you were here. I had no notion. Did you send mother a telegram?

BEATRICE, *gazing at the roses:* No.

ROBERT, *following her gaze:* You are admiring my roses. I brought them to the mistress of the house. *Critically.* I am afraid they are not nice.

BRIGID: O, they are lovely, sir. The mistress will be delighted with them.

ROBERT, *lays the roses carelessly on a chair out of sight:* Is nobody in?

BRIGID: Yes, sir. Sit down, sir. They'll be here now any moment. The master was here.

She looks about her and with a half curtsey goes out on the right.

ROBERT, *after a short silence:* How are you, Beatty? And how are all down in Youghal? As dull as ever?

BEATRICE: They were well when I left.

ROBERT, *politely:* O, but I'm sorry I did not know you were coming. I would have met you at the train. Why did you do it? You have some queer ways about you, Beatty, haven't you?

BEATRICE, *in the same tone:* Thank you, Robert. I am quite used to getting about alone.

ROBERT: Yes, but I mean to say . . . O, well, you have arrived in your own characteristic way.

A noise is heard at the window and a boy's voice is

heard calling, "Mr. Hand!" ROBERT *turns:* By Jove, Archie, too, is arriving in a characteristic way!

ARCHIE *scrambles into the room through the open window on the left and then rises to his feet, flushed and panting.* ARCHIE *is a boy of eight years, dressed in white breeches, jersey and cap. He wears spectacles, has a lively manner and speaks with the slight trace of a foreign accent.*

BEATRICE, *going towards him:* Goodness gracious, Archie! What is the matter?

ARCHIE, *rising, out of breath:* Eh! I ran all the avenue.

ROBERT, *smiles and holds out his hand:* Good evening, Archie. Why did you run?

ARCHIE, *shakes hands:* Good evening. We saw you on the top of the tram, and I shouted *Mr. Hand!* But you did not see me. But we saw you, mamma and I. She will be here in a minute. I ran.

BEATRICE, *holding out her hand:* And poor me!

ARCHIE, *shakes hands somewhat shyly:* Good evening, Miss Justice.

BEATRICE: Were you disappointed that I did not come last Friday for the lesson?

ARCHIE, *glancing at her, smiles:* No.

BEATRICE: Glad?

ARCHIE, *suddenly:* But today it is too late.

BEATRICE: A very short lesson?

ARCHIE, *pleased:* Yes.

BEATRICE: But now you must study, Archie.

ROBERT: Were you at the bath?

ARCHIE: Yes.

ROBERT: Are you a good swimmer now?

ARCHIE, *leans against the davenport:* No. Mamma won't let me into the deep place. Can you swim well, Mr. Hand?

ROBERT: Splendidly. Like a stone.

ARCHIE, *laughs:* Like a stone! *Pointing down.* Down that way?

ROBERT, *pointing:* Yes, down; straight down. How do you say that over in Italy?

ARCHIE: That? *Giù. Pointing down and up.* That is *giù* and this is *sù.* Do you want to speak to my pappie?

ROBERT: Yes. I came to see him.

ARCHIE, *going towards the study:* I will tell him. He is in there, writing.

BEATRICE, *calmly, looking at* ROBERT: No; he is out. He is gone to the post with some letters.

ROBERT, *lightly:* O, never mind. I will wait if he is only gone to the post.

ARCHIE: But mamma is coming. *He glances towards the window:* Here she is!

ARCHIE *runs out by the door on the left.* BEATRICE *walks slowly towards the davenport.* ROBERT *remains standing. A short silence.* ARCHIE *and* BERTHA *come in through the door on the left.* BERTHA *is a young woman of graceful build. She has dark grey eyes, patient in expression, and soft features. Her manner is cordial and selfpossessed. She wears a lavender dress and carries her cream gloves knotted round the handle of her sunshade.*

BERTHA, *shaking hands:* Good evening, Miss Justice. We thought you were still down in Youghal.

BEATRICE, *shaking hands:* Good evening, Mrs. Rowan.

BERTHA, *bows:* Good evening, Mr. Hand.

ROBERT, *bowing:* Good evening, *signora!* Just imagine, I didn't know either she was back till I found her here.

BERTHA, *to both:* Did you not come together?

BEATRICE: No. I came first. Mr. Rowan was going out. He said you would be back any moment.

BERTHA: I'm sorry. If you had written or sent over word by the girl this morning . . .

BEATRICE, *laughs nervously:* I arrived only an hour and a half ago. I thought of sending a telegram but it seemed too tragic.

BERTHA: Ah? Only now you arrived?

ROBERT, *extending his arms, blandly:* I retire from public and private life. Her first cousin and a journalist, I know nothing of her movements.

BEATRICE, *not directly to him:* My movements are not very interesting.

ROBERT, *in the same tone:* A lady's movements are always interesting.

BERTHA: But sit down, won't you? You must be very tired.

BEATRICE, *quickly:* No, not at all. I just came for Archie's lesson.

BERTHA: I wouldn't hear of such a thing, Miss Justice, after your long journey.

ARCHIE, *suddenly to* BEATRICE: And, besides, you didn't bring the music.

BEATRICE, *a little confused:* That I forgot. But we have the old piece.

ROBERT, *pinching* ARCHIE'S *ear:* You little scamp. You want to get off the lesson.

BERTHA: O, never mind the lesson. You must sit down and have a cup of tea now. *Going towards the door on the right.* I'll tell Brigid.

ARCHIE: I will, mamma. *He makes a movement to go.*

BEATRICE: No, please Mrs. Rowan. Archie! I would really prefer . . .

ROBERT, *quietly:* I suggest a compromise. Let it be a half-lesson.

BERTHA: But she must be exhausted.

BEATRICE, *quickly:* Not in the least. I was thinking of the lesson in the train.

ROBERT, *to* BERTHA: You see what it is to have a conscience, Mrs. Rowan.

ARCHIE: Of my lesson, Miss Justice?

BEATRICE, *simply:* It is ten days since I heard the sound of a piano.

BERTHA: O, very well. If that is it . . .

ROBERT, *nervously, gaily:* Let us have the piano by all means. I know what is in Beatty's ears at this moment. *To* BEATRICE. Shall I tell?

BEATRICE: If you know.

ROBERT: The buzz of the harmonium in her father's parlour. *To* BEATRICE. Confess.

BEATRICE, *smiling:* Yes. I can hear it.

ROBERT, *grimly:* So can I. The asthmatic voice of protestantism.

BERTHA: Did you not enjoy yourself down there, Miss Justice?

ROBERT, *intervenes:* She did not, Mrs. Rowan. She goes there on retreat, when the protestant strain in her prevails—gloom, seriousness, righteousness.

BEATRICE: I go to see my father.

ROBERT, *continuing:* But she comes back here to my mother, you see. The piano influence is from our side of the house.

BERTHA, *hesitating:* Well, Miss Justice, if you would like to play something . . . But please don't fatigue yourself with Archie.

ROBERT, *suavely:* Do, Beatty. That is what you want.

BEATRICE: If Archie will come?

ARCHIE, *with a shrug:* To listen.

BEATRICE, *takes his hand:* And a little lesson, too. Very short.

BERTHA: Well, afterwards you must stay to tea.

BEATRICE, *to* ARCHIE: Come.

BEATRICE *and* ARCHIE *go out together by the door on the left.* BERTHA *goes towards the davenport, takes off her hat and lays it with her sunshade on the desk. Then taking a key from a little flowervase, she opens a drawer of the davenport, takes out a slip of paper and closes the drawer again.* RORERT *stands watching her.*

BERTHA, *coming towards him with the paper in her hand:* You put this into my hand last night. What does it mean?

ROBERT: Do you not know?

BERTHA, *reads:* "There is one word which I have never dared to say to you." What is the word?

ROBERT: That I have a deep liking for you.

A short pause. The piano is heard faintly from the upper room.

ROBERT, *takes the bunch of roses from the chair:* I brought these for you. Will you take them from me?

BERTHA, *taking them:* Thank you. *She lays them on the table and unfolds the paper again.* Why did you not dare to say it last night?

ROBERT: I could not speak to you or follow you. There were too many people on the lawn. I wanted you to think over it and so I put it into your hand when you were going away.

BERTHA: Now you have dared to say it.

ROBERT, *moves his hand slowly past his eyes:* You passed. The avenue was dim with dusky light. I could see the dark green masses of the trees. And you passed beyond them. You were like the moon.

BERTHA, *laughs:* Why like the moon?

ROBERT: In that dress, with your slim body, walking with little even steps. I saw the moon passing in the dusk till you passed and left my sight.

BERTHA: Did you think of me last night?

ROBERT, *comes nearer:* I think of you always—as something beautiful and distant—the moon or some deep music.

BERTHA, *smiling:* And last night which was I?

ROBERT: I was awake half the night. I could hear your voice. I could see your face in the dark. Your eyes . . . I want to speak to you. Will you listen to me? May I speak?

BERTHA, *sitting down:* You may.

ROBERT, *sitting beside her:* Are you annoyed with me?

BERTHA: No.

ROBERT: I thought you were. You put away my poor flowers so quickly.

BERTHA, *takes them from the table and holds them close to her face:* Is this what you wish me to do with them?

ROBERT, *watching her:* Your face is a flower too— but more beautiful. A wild flower blowing in a hedge. *Moving his chair closer to her.* Why are you smiling? At my words?

BERTHA, *laying the flowers in her lap:* I am wondering if that is what you say—to the others.

ROBERT, *surprised:* What others?

BERTHA: The other women. I hear you have so many admirers.

ROBERT, *involuntarily:* And that is why you too . . . ?

BERTHA: But you have, haven't you?

ROBERT: Friends, yes.

BERTHA: Do you speak to them in the same way?

ROBERT, *in an offended tone:* How can you ask me such a question? What kind of person do you think I am? Or why do you listen to me? Did you not like me to speak to you in that way?

BERTHA: What you said was very kind. *She looks at him for a moment.* Thank you for saying it—and thinking it.

ROBERT, *leaning forward:* Bertha!

BERTHA: Yes?

ROBERT: I have the right to call you by your name. From old times—nine years ago. We were Bertha—and Robert—then. Can we not be so now, too?

BERTHA, *readily:* O yes. Why should we not?

ROBERT: Bertha, you knew. From the very night you landed on Kingstown pier. It all came back to me then. And you knew it. You saw it.

BERTHA: No. Not that night.

ROBERT: When?

BERTHA: The night we landed I felt very tired and dirty. *Shaking her head.* I did not see it in you that night.

ROBERT, *smiling:* Tell me what did you see that night—your very first impression.

BERTHA, *knitting her brows:* You were standing with your back to the gangway, talking to two ladies.

ROBERT: To two plain middleaged ladies, yes.

BERTHA: I recognized you at once. And I saw that you had got fat.

ROBERT, *takes her hand:* And this poor fat Robert—do you dislike him then so much? Do you disbelieve all he says?

BERTHA: I think men speak like that to all women whom they like or admire. What do you want me to believe?

ROBERT: All men, Bertha?

BERTHA, *with sudden sadness:* I think so.

ROBERT: I too?

BERTHA: Yes, Robert. I think you too.

ROBERT: All then—without exception? Or with one

exception? *In a lower tone.* Or is he too—Richard too—like us all—in that at least? Or different?

BERTHA, *looks into his eyes:* Different.

ROBERT: Are you quite sure, Bertha?

BERTHA, *a little confused, tries to withdraw her hand:* I have answered you.

ROBERT, *suddenly:* Bertha, may I kiss your hand? Let me. May I?

BERTHA: If you wish.

He lifts her hand to his lips slowly. She rises suddenly and listens.

BERTHA: Did you hear the garden gate?

ROBERT, *rising also:* No.

A short pause. The piano can be heard faintly from the upper room.

ROBERT, *pleading:* Do not go away. You must never go away now. Your life is here. I came for that too today—to speak to him—to urge him to accept this position. He must. And you must persuade him to. You have a great influence over him.

BERTHA: You want him to remain here.

ROBERT: Yes.

BERTHA: Why?

ROBERT: For your sake because you are unhappy so far away. For his sake too because he should think of his future.

BERTHA, *laughing:* Do you remember what he said when you spoke to him last night?

ROBERT: About . . . ? *Reflecting.* Yes. He quoted the *Our Father* about our daily bread. He said that to take care for the future is to destroy hope and love in the world.

BERTHA: Do you not think he is strange?

ROBERT: In that, yes.

BERTHA: A little—mad?

ROBERT, *comes closer:* No. He is not. Perhaps we are. Why, do you . . . ?

BERTHA, *laughs:* I ask you because you are intelligent.

ROBERT: You must not go away. I will not let you.

BERTHA, *looks full at him:* You?

ROBERT: Those eyes must not go away. *He takes her hands.* May I kiss your eyes?

BERTHA: Do so.

He kisses her eyes and then passes his hand over her hair.

ROBERT: Little Bertha!

BERTHA, *smiling:* But I am not so little. Why do you call me little?

ROBERT: Little Bertha! One embrace? *He puts his arm around her.* Look into my eyes again.

BERTHA, *looks:* I can see the little gold spots. So many you have.

ROBERT, *delighted:* Your voice! Give me a kiss, a kiss with your mouth.

BERTHA: Take it.

ROBERT: I am afraid. *He kisses her mouth and passes his hand many times over her hair.* At last I hold you in my arms!

BERTHA: And are you satisfied?

ROBERT: Let me feel your lips touch mine.

BERTHA: And then you will be satisfied?

ROBERT, *murmurs:* Your lips, Bertha!

BERTHA, *closes her eyes and kisses him quickly:* There. *Puts her hands on his shoulders.* Why don't you say: thanks?

ROBERT, *sighs:* My life is finished—over.

BERTHA: O, don't speak like that now, Robert.

ROBERT: Over, over. I want to end it and have done with it.

BERTHA, *concerned but lightly:* You silly fellow!

ROBERT, *presses her to him:* To end it all—death. To fall from a great high cliff, down, right down into the sea.

BERTHA: Please, Robert . . .

ROBERT: Listening to music and in the arms of the woman I love—the sea, music and death.

BERTHA, *looks at him for a moment:* The woman you love?

ROBERT, *hurriedly:* I want to speak to you, Bertha— alone—not here. Will you come?

BERTHA, *with downcast eyes:* I too want to speak to you.

ROBERT, *tenderly:* Yes, dear, I know. *He kisses her again.* I will speak to you; tell you all; then. I will kiss you, then, long long kisses—when you come to me— long long sweet kisses.

BERTHA: Where?

ROBERT, *in tone of passion:* Your eyes. Your lips. All your divine body.

BERTHA, *repelling his embrace, confused:* I meant where do you wish me to come.

ROBERT: To my house. Not my mother's over there. I will write the address for you. Will you come?

BERTHA: When?

ROBERT: Tonight. Between eight and nine. Come. I will wait for you tonight. And every night. You will?

He kisses her with passion, holding her head between his hands. After a few instants she breaks from him. He sits down.

BERTHA, *listening:* The gate opened.

ROBERT, *intensely:* I will wait for you.

He takes the slip from the table. BERTHA *moves away from him slowly.* RICHARD *comes in from the garden.*

RICHARD, *advancing, takes off his hat:* Good afternoon.

ROBERT, *rises, with nervous friendliness:* Good afternoon, Richard.

BERTHA, *at the table, taking the roses:* Look what lovely roses Mr. Hand brought me.

ROBERT: I am afraid they are overblown.

RICHARD, *suddenly:* Excuse me for a moment, will you?

He turns and goes into his study quickly. ROBERT *takes a pencil from his pocket and writes a few words on the slip; then hands it quickly to* BERTHA.

ROBERT, *rapidly:* The address. Take the tram at Lansdowne Road and ask to be let down near there.

BERTHA, *takes it:* I promise nothing.

ROBERT: I will wait.

RICHARD *comes back from the study.*

BERTHA, *going:* I must put these roses in water.

RICHARD, *handing her his hat:* Yes, do. And please put my hat on the rack.

BERTHA, *takes it:* So I will leave you to yourselves for your talk. *Looking round.* Do you want anything? Cigarettes?

RICHARD: Thanks. We have them here.

BERTHA: Then I can go?

She goes out on the left with RICHARD's *hat, which she leaves in the hall, and returns at once; she stops for a moment at the davenport, replaces the slip in the drawer, locks it, and replaces the key, and, taking the roses, goes towards the right.* ROBERT *precedes her to open the door for her. She bows and goes out.*

RICHARD, *points to the chair near the little table on the right:* Your place of honour.

ROBERT, *sits down:* Thanks. *Passing his hand over*

his brow. Good Lord, **how** warm it is today! The heat pains me here in the eye. **The** glare.

RICHARD: The room is rather dark, I think, with the blind down but if you wish . . .

ROBERT, *quickly:* Not at all. I know what it is—the result of night work.

RICHARD, *sits on the lounge:* Must you?

ROBERT, *sighs:* Eh, yes. I must see part of the paper through every night. And then my leading articles. We are approaching a difficult moment. And not only here.

RICHARD, *after a slight pause:* Have you any news?

ROBERT, *in a different voice:* Yes. I want to speak to you seriously. Today may be an important day for you —or rather, tonight. I saw the vicechancellor this morning. He has the highest opinion of you, Richard. He has read your book, he said.

RICHARD: Did he buy it or borrow it?

ROBERT: Bought it, I hope.

RICHARD: I shall smoke a cigarette. Thirty-seven copies have now been sold in Dublin.

He takes a cigarette from the box on the table, and lights it.

ROBERT, *suavely, hopelessly:* Well, the matter is closed for the present. You have your iron mask on today.

RICHARD, *smoking:* Let me hear the rest.

ROBERT, *again seriously:* Richard, you are too suspicious. It is a defect in you. He assured me he has the highest possible opinion of you, as everyone has. You are the man for the post, he says. In fact, he told me that, if your name goes forward, he will work might and main for you with the senate and I . . . will do my part, of course, in the press and privately. I regard it as a public duty. The chair of romance literature is yours by right, as a scholar, as a literary personality.

RICHARD: The conditions?

ROBERT: Conditions? You mean about the future?

RICHARD: I mean about the past.

ROBERT, *easily:* That episode in your past is forgotten. An act of impulse. We are all impulsive

RICHARD, *looks fixedly at him:* You called it an act of folly, then—nine years ago. You told me I was hanging a weight about my neck.

ROBERT: I was wrong. *Suavely.* Here is how the matter stands, Richard. Everyone knows that you ran away years ago with a young girl . . . How shall I put it? . . . With a young girl not exactly your equal. *Kindly.* Excuse me, Richard, that is not my opinion nor my language. I am simply using the language of people whose opinions I don't share.

RICHARD: Writing one of your leading articles, in fact.

ROBERT: Put it so. Well, it made a great sensation at the time. A mysterious disappearance. My name was involved too, as best man, let us say, on that famous occasion. Of course, they think I acted from a mistaken sense of friendship. Well, all that is known. *With some hesitation.* But what happened afterwards is not known.

RICHARD: No?

RORERT: Of course, it is your affair, Richard. However, you are not so young now as you were then. The expression is quite in the style of my leading articles, isn't it?

RICHARD: Do you, or do you not, want me to give the lie to my past life?

ROBERT: I am thinking of your future life—here. I understand your pride and your sense of liberty. I understand their point of view also. However, there is a way out; it is simply this. Refrain from contradicting any rumours you may hear concerning what happened

. . . or did not happen after you went away. Leave the rest to me.

RICHARD: You will set these rumours afloat?

ROBERT: I will. God help me.

RICHARD, *observing him:* For the sake of social conventions?

ROBERT: For the sake of something else too—our friendship, our lifelong friendship.

RICHARD: Thanks.

ROBERT, *slightly wounded:* And I will tell you the whole truth.

RICHARD, *smiles and bows:* Yes. Do, please.

ROBERT: Not only for your sake. Also for the sake of —your present partner in life.

RICHARD: I see.

He crushes his cigarette softly on the ashtray and then leans forward, rubbing his hands slowly.

RICHARD: Why for her sake?

ROBERT, *also leans forward, quietly:* Richard, have you been quite fair to her? It was her own free choice, you will say. But was she really free to choose? She was a mere girl. She accepted all that you proposed.

RICHARD, *smiles:* That is your way of saying that she proposed what I would not accept.

ROBERT, *nods:* I remember. And she went away with you. But was it of her own free choice? Answer me frankly.

RICHARD, *turns to him, calmly:* I played for her against all that you say or can say; and I won.

ROBERT, *nodding again:* Yes, you won.

RICHARD, *rises:* Excuse me for forgetting. Will you have some whisky?

ROBERT: All things come to those who wait.

RICHARD *goes to the sideboard and brings a small*

tray with the decanter and glasses to the table where he sets it down.

RICHARD, *sits down again, leaning back on the lounge:* Will you please help yourself?

ROBERT, *does so:* And you? Steadfast? *Richard shakes his head.* Lord, when I think of our wild nights long ago—talks by the hour, plans, carouses, revelry . . .

RICHARD: In our house.

ROBERT: It is mine now. I have kept it ever since though I don't go there often. Whenever you like to come let me know. You must come some night. It will be old times again. *He lifts his glass, and drinks.* Prosit!

RICHARD: It was not only a house of revelry; it was to be the hearth of a new life. *Musing.* And in that name all our sins were committed.

ROBERT: Sins! Drinking and blasphemy (*he points*) by me. And drinking and heresy, much worse (*he points again*) by you—are those the sins you mean?

RICHARD: And some others.

ROBERT, *lightly, uneasily:* You mean the women. I have no remorse of conscience. Maybe you have. We had two keys on those occasions. *Maliciously.* Have you?

RICHARD, *irritated:* For you it was all quite natural?

ROBERT: For me it is quite natural to kiss a woman whom I like. Why not? She is beautiful for me.

RICHARD, *toying with the lounge cushion:* Do you kiss everything that is beautiful for you?

ROBERT: Everything—if it can be kissed. *He takes up a flat stone which lies on the table.* This stone, for instance. It is so cool, so polished, so delicate, like a woman's temple. It is silent, it suffers our passion; and it is beautiful. *He places it against his lips.* And so I kiss it because it is beautiful. And what is a woman? A work of nature, too, like a stone or a flower or a bird. A kiss is an act of homage.

RICHARD: It is an act of union between man and woman. Even if we are often led to desire through the sense of beauty can you say that the beautiful is what we desire?

ROBERT, *pressing the stone to his forehead:* You will give me a headache if you make me think today. I cannot think today. I feel too natural, too common. After all, what is most attractive in even the most beautiful woman?

RICHARD: What?

ROBERT: Not those qualities which she has and other women have not but the qualities which she has in common with them. I mean . . . the commonest. *Turning over the stone, he presses the other side to his forehead.* I mean how her body develops heat when it is pressed, the movement of her blood, how quickly she changes by digestion what she eats into—what shall be nameless. *Laughing.* I am very common today. Perhaps that idea never struck you?

RICHARD, *drily:* Many ideas strike a man who has lived nine years with a woman.

ROBERT: Yes. I suppose they do. . . . This beautiful cool stone does me good. Is it a paperweight or a cure for headache?

RICHARD: Bertha brought it home one day from the strand. She, too, says that it is beautiful.

ROBERT, *lays down the stone quietly:* She is right. *He raises his glass, and drinks. A pause.*

RICHARD: Is that all you wanted to say to me?

ROBERT, *quickly:* There is something else. The vice-chancellor sends you, through me, an invitation for to-night—to dinner at his house. You know where he lives? RICHARD *nods.* I thought you might have forgotten.

Strictly private, of course. He wants to meet you again and sends you a very warm invitation.

RICHARD: For what hour?

ROBERT: Eight. But, like yourself, he is free and easy about time. Now, Richard, you must go there. That is all. I feel tonight will be the turningpoint in your life. You will live here and work here and think here and be honoured here—among our people.

RICHARD, *smiling:* I can almost see two envoys starting for the United States to collect funds for my statue a hundred years hence.

ROBERT, *agreeably:* Once I made a little epigram about statues. All statues are of two kinds. *He folds his arms across his chest.* The statue which says: "How shall I get down?" and the other kind (*he unfolds his arms and extends his right arm, averting his head*) the statue which says: "In my time the dunghill was so high."

RICHARD: The second one for me, please.

ROBERT, *lazily:* Will you give me one of those long cigars of yours?

RICHARD *selects a Virginia cigar from the box on the table and hands it to him with the straw drawn out.*

ROBERT, *lighting it:* These cigars Europeanize me. If Ireland is to become a néw Ireland she must first become European. And that is what you are here for, Richard. Some day we shall have to choose between England and Europe. I am a descendant of the dark foreigners: that is why I like to be here. I may be childish. But where else in Dublin can I get a bandit cigar like this or a cup of black coffee? The man who drinks black coffee is going to conquer Ireland. And now I will take just a half measure of that whisky, Richard, to show you there is no ill feeling.

RICHARD, *points:* Help yourself.

ROBERT, *does so:* Thanks. *He drinks and goes on as*

before. Then you yourself, the way you loll on that lounge: then your boy's voice and also—Bertha herself. Do you allow me to call her that, Richard? I mean as an old friend of both of you.

RICHARD: O, why not?

ROBERT, *with animation:* You have that fierce indignation which lacerated the heart of Swift. You have fallen from a higher world, Richard, and you are filled with fierce indignation, when you find that life is cowardly and ignoble. While I . . . shall I tell you?

RICHARD: By all means.

ROBERT, *archly:* I have come up from a lower world and I am filled with astonishment when I find that people have any redeeming virtue at all.

RICHARD, *sits up suddenly and leans his elbows on the table:* You are my friend, then?

ROBERT, *gravely:* I fought for you all the time you were away. I fought to bring you back. I fought to keep your place for you here. I will fight for you still because I have faith in you, the faith of a disciple in his master. I cannot say more than that. It may seem strange to you . . . Give me a match.

RICHARD, *lights and offers him a match:* There is a faith still stranger than the faith of the disciple in his master.

ROBERT: And that is?

RICHARD: The faith of a master in the disciple who will betray him.

ROBERT: The church lost a theologian in you, Richard. But I think you look too deeply into life. *He rises, pressing* RICHARD's *arm slightly.* Be gay. Life is not worth it.

RICHARD, *without rising:* Are you going?

ROBERT: Must. *He turns and says in a friendly tone.* Then it is all arranged. We meet tonight at the vicechancellor's. I shall look in at about ten. So you can have an hour or so to yourselves first. You will wait till I come?

RICHARD: Good.

ROBERT: One more match and I am happy.

RICHARD *strikes another match, hands it to him and rises also.* ARCHIE *comes in by the door on the left, followed by* BEATRICE.

ROBERT: Congratulate me, Beatty. I have won over Richard.

ARCHIE, *crossing to the door on the right, calls:* Mamma, Miss Justice is going.

BEATRICE: On what are you to be congratulated?

ROBERT: On a victory, of course. *Laying his hand lightly on* RICHARD's *shoulder.* The descendant of Archibald Hamilton Rowan has come home.

RICHARD: I am not a descendant of Hamilton Rowan.

ROBERT: What matter?

BERTHA *comes in from the right with a bowl of roses.*

BEATRICE: Has Mr. Rowan . . . ?

ROBERT, *turning towards* BERTHA: Richard is coming tonight to the vicechancellor's dinner. The fatted calf will be eaten: roast, I hope. And next session will see the descendant of a namesake of etcetera, etcetera in a chair of the university. *He offers his hand.* Good afternoon, Richard. We shall meet tonight.

RICHARD, *touches his hand:* At Philippi.

BEATRICE, *shakes hands also:* Accept my best wishes, Mr. Rowan.

RICHARD: Thanks. But do not believe him.

ROBERT, *vivaciously:* Believe me, believe me. *To* BERTHA. Good afternoon, Mrs. Rowan.

BERTHA, *shaking hands, candidly:* I thank you, too. *To* BEATRICE. You won't stay to tea, Miss Justice?

BEATRICE: No, thank you. *Takes leave of her.* I must go. Good afternoon. Goodbye, Archie (*going*).

ROBERT: *Addio*, Archibald.

ARCHIE: *Addio*.

ROBERT: Wait, Beatty. I shall accompany you.

BEATRICE, *going out on the right with* BERTHA: O, don't trouble.

ROBERT, *following her:* But I insist—as a cousin.

BERTHA, BEATRICE, *and* ROBERT *go out by the door on the left.* RICHARD *stands irresolutely near the table.* ARCHIE *closes the door leading to the hall and, coming over to him, plucks him by the sleeve.*

ARCHIE: I say, pappie!

RICHARD, *absently:* What is it?

ARCHIE: I want to ask you a thing.

RICHARD, *sitting on the end of the lounge, stares in front of him:* What is it?

ARCHIE: Will you ask mamma to let me go out in the morning with the milkman?

RICHARD: With the milkman?

ARCHIE: Yes. In the milkcar. He says he will let me drive when we get on to the roads where there are no people. The horse is a very good beast. Can I go?

RICHARD: Yes.

ARCHIE: Ask mamma now can I go. Will you?

RICHARD, *glances towards the door:* I will.

ARCHIE: He said he will show me the cows he has in the field. Do you know how many cows he has?

RICHARD: How many?

ARCHIE: Eleven. Eight red and three white. But one is sick now. No, not sick. But it fell.

RICHARD: Cows?

ARCHIE, *with a gesture:* Eh! Not bulls. Because bulls give no milk. Eleven cows. They must give a lot of milk. What makes a cow give milk?

RICHARD, *takes his hand:* Who knows? Do you understand what it is to give a thing?

ARCHIE: To give? Yes.

RICHARD: While you have a thing it can be taken from you.

ARCHIE: By robbers? No?

RICHARD: But when you give it, you have given it. No robber can take it from you. *He bends his head and presses his son's hand against his cheek.* It is yours then for ever when you have given it. It will be yours always. That is to give.

ARCHIE: But, pappie?

RICHARD: Yes?

ARCHIE: How could a robber rob a cow? Everyone would see him. In the night, perhaps.

RICHARD: In the night, yes.

ARCHIE: Are there robbers here like in Rome?

RICHARD: There are poor people everywhere.

ARCHIE: Have they revolvers?

RICHARD: No.

ARCHIE: Knives? Have they knives?

RICHARD, *sternly:* Yes, yes. Knives and revolvers.

ARCHIE, *disengages himself:* Ask mamma now. She is coming.

RICHARD, *makes a movement to rise:* I will.

ARCHIE: No, sit there, pappie. You wait and ask her when she comes back. I won't be here. I'll be in the garden.

RICHARD, *sinking back again:* Yes. Go.

ARCHIE, *kisses him swiftly:* Thanks.

He runs out quickly by the door at the back leading into the garden. BERTHA *enters by the door on the left. She approaches the table and stands beside it, fingering the petals of the roses, looking at* RICHARD.

RICHARD, *watching her:* Well?

BERTHA, *absently:* Well. He says he likes me.

RICHARD, *leans his chin in his hand:* You showed him his note?

BERTHA: Yes. I asked him what it meant.

RICHARD: What did he say it meant?

BERTHA: He said I must know. I said I had an idea. Then he told me he liked me very much. That I was beautiful—and all that.

RICHARD: Since when!

BERTHA, *again absently:* Since when—what?

RICHARD: Since when did he say he liked you?

BERTHA: Always, he said. But more since we came back. He said I was like the moon in this lavender dress. *Looking at him.* Had you any words with him—about me?

RICHARD, *blandly:* The usual thing. Not about you.

BERTHA: He was very nervous. You saw that?

RICHARD: Yes. I saw it. What else went on?

BERTHA: He asked me to give him my hand.

RICHARD, *smiling:* In marriage?

BERTHA, *smiling:* No, only to hold.

RICHARD: Did you?

BERTHA: Yes. *Tearing off a few petals.* Then he caressed my hand and asked would I let him kiss it. I let him.

RICHARD: Well?

BERTHA: Then he asked could he embrace me—even once? . . . And then . . .

RICHARD: And then?

BERTHA: He put his arm round me.

RICHARD, *stares at the floor for a moment, then looks at her again:* And then?

BERTHA: He said I had beautiful eyes. And asked could he kiss them. *With a gesture.* I said: "Do so."

RICHARD: And he did?

BERTHA: Yes. First one and then the other. *She breaks off suddenly.* Tell me, Dick, does all this disturb you? Because I told you I don't want that. I think you are only pretending you don't mind. I don't mind.

RICHARD, *quietly:* I know, dear. But I want to find out what he means or feels just as you do.

BERTHA, *points at him:* Remember, you allowed me to go on. I told you the whole thing from the beginning.

RICHARD, *as before:* I know, dear . . . And then?

BERTHA: He asked for a kiss. I said: "Take it."

RICHARD: And then?

BERTHA, *crumpling a handful of petals:* He kissed me.

RICHARD: Your mouth?

BERTHA: Once or twice.

RICHARD: Long kisses?

BERTHA: Fairly long. *Reflects.* Yes, the last time.

RICHARD, *rubs his hands slowly; then:* With his lips? Or . . . the other way?

BERTHA: Yes, the last time.

RICHARD: Did he ask you to kiss him?

BERTHA: He did.

RICHARD: Did you?

BERTHA, *hesitates, then looking straight at him:* I did. I kissed him.

RICHARD: What way?

BERTHA, *with a shrug:* O simply.

RICHARD: Were you excited?

BERTHA: Well, you can imagine. *Frowning suddenly.* Not much. He has not nice lips . . . Still I was excited, of course. But not like with you, Dick.

RICHARD: Was he?

BERTHA: Excited? Yes, I think he was. He sighed. He was dreadfully nervous.

RICHARD, *resting his forehead on his hand:* I see.

BERTHA, *crosses towards the lounge and stands near him:* Are you jealous?

RICHARD, *as before:* No.

BERTHA, *quietly:* You are, Dick.

RICHARD: I am not. Jealous of what?

BERTHA: Because he kissed me.

RICHARD, *looks up:* Is that all?

BERTHA: Yes, that's all. Except that he asked me would I meet him.

RICHARD: Out somewhere?

BERTHA: No. In his house.

RICHARD, *surprised:* Over there with his mother, is it?

BERTHA: No, a house he has. He wrote the address for me.

She goes to the desk, takes the key from the flower vase, unlocks the drawer and returns to him with the slip of paper.

RICHARD, *half to himself:* Our cottage.

BERTHA, *hands him the slip:* Here.

RICHARD, *reads it:* Yes. Our cottage.

BERTHA: Your . . . ?

RICHARD: No, his. I call it ours. *Looking at her.* The cottage I told you about so often—that we had the two keys for, he and I. It is his now. Where we used to hold our wild nights, talking, drinking, planning—at that time. Wild nights; yes. He and I together. *He throws the slip on the couch and rises suddenly.* And sometimes I alone. *Stares at her.* But not quite alone. I told you. You remember?

BERTHA, *shocked:* That place?

RICHARD, *walks away from her a few paces and stands still, thinking, holding his chin:* Yes.

BERTHA, *taking up the slip again:* Where is it?

RICHARD: Do you not know?

BERTHA: He told me to take the tram at Lansdowne

Road and to ask the man to let me down there. Is it . . .
is it a bad place?

RICHARD: O no, cottages. *He returns to the lounge
and sits down.* What answer did you give?

BERTHA: No answer. He said he would wait.

RICHARD: Tonight?

BERTHA: Every night, he said. Between eight and
nine.

RICHARD: And so I am to go tonight to interview—
the professor. About the appointment I am to beg for.
Looking at her. The interview is arranged for tonight
by him—between eight and nine. Curious, isn't it? The
same hour.

BERTHA: Very.

RICHARD: Did he ask you had I any suspicion?

BERTHA: No.

RICHARD: Did he mention my name?

BERTHA: No.

RICHARD: Not once?

BERTHA: Not that I remember.

RICHARD, *bounding to his feet:* O yes! Quite clear!

BERTHA: What?

RICHARD, *striding to and fro:* A liar, a thief, and a
fool! Quite clear! A common thief! What else? *With a
harsh laugh.* My great friend! A patriot too! A thief—
nothing else! *He halts, thrusting his hands into his pockets.* But a fool also!

BERTHA, *looking at him:* What are you going to do?

RICHARD, *shortly:* Follow him. Find him. Tell him.
Calmly. A few words will do. Thief and fool.

BERTHA, *flings the slip on the couch:* I see it all!

RICHARD, *turning:* Eh!

BERTHA, *hotly:* The work of a devil.

RICHARD: He?

BERTHA, *turning on him:* No, you! The work of a

devil to turn him against me as you tried to turn my own child against me. Only you did not succeed.

RICHARD: How? In God's name, how?

BERTHA, *excitedly:* Yes, yes. What I say. Everyone saw it. Whenever I tried to correct him for the least thing you went on with your folly, speaking to him as if he were a grownup man. Ruining the poor child, or trying to. Then, of course, I was the cruel mother and only you loved him. *With growing excitement.* But you did not turn him against me—against his own mother. Because why? Because the child has too much nature in him.

RICHARD: I never tried to do such a thing, Bertha. You know I cannot be severe with a child.

BERTHA: Because you never loved your own mother. A mother is always a mother, no matter what. I never heard of any human being that did not love the mother that brought him into the world, except you.

RICHARD, *approaching her quietly:* Bertha, do not say things you will be sorry for. Are you not glad my son is fond of me?

BERTHA: Who taught him to be? Who taught him to run to meet you? Who told him you would bring him home toys when you were out on your rambles in the rain, forgetting all about him—and me? I did. I taught him to love you.

RICHARD: Yes, dear. I know it was you.

BERTHA, *almost crying:* And then you try to turn everyone against me. All is to be for you. I am to appear false and cruel to everyone except to you. Because you take advantage of my simplicity as you did—the first time.

RICHARD, *violently:* And you have the courage to say that to me?

BERTHA, *facing him:* Yes, I have! Both then and now.

Because I am simple you think you can do what you like with me. *Gesticulating*. Follow him now. Call him names. Make him be humble before you and make him despise me. Follow him!

RICHARD, *controlling himself:* You forget that I have allowed you complete liberty—and allow you it still.

BERTHA, *scornfully:* Liberty!

RICHARD: Yes, complete. But he must know that I know. *More calmly*. I will speak to him quietly. *Appealing*. Bertha, believe me, dear! It is not jealousy. You have complete liberty to do as you wish—you and he. But not in this way. He will not despise you. You don't wish to deceive me or to pretend to deceive me— with him, do you?

BERTHA: No, I do not. *Looking full at him*. Which of us two is the deceiver?

RICHARD: Of us? You and me?

BERTHA, *in a calm decided tone:* I know why you have allowed me what you call complete liberty.

RICHARD: Why?

BERTHA: To have complete liberty with—that girl.

RICHARD, *irritated:* But, good God, you knew about that this long time. I never hid it.

BERTHA: You did. I thought it was a kind of friendship between you—till we came back, and then I saw.

RICHARD: So it is, Bertha.

BERTHA, *shakes her head:* No, no. It is much more; and that is why you give me complete liberty. All those things you sit up at night to write about (*pointing to the study*) in there—about her. You call that friendship?

RICHARD: Believe me, Bertha dear. Believe me as I believe you.

BERTHA, *with an impulsive gesture:* My God, I feel it! I know it! What else is between you but love?

RICHARD, *calmly:* You are trying to put that idea into my head but I warn you that I don't take my ideas from other people.

BERTHA, *hotly:* It is, it is! And that is why you allow him to go on. Of course! It doesn't affect you. You love her.

RICHARD: Love! *Throws out his hands with a sigh and moves away from her.* I cannot argue with you.

BERTHA: You can't because I am right. *Following him a few steps.* What would anyone say?

RICHARD, *turns to her:* Do you think I care?

BERTHA: But I care. What would he say if he knew? You, who talk so much of the high kind of feeling you have for me, expressing yourself in that way to another woman. If he did it, or other men, I could understand because they are all false pretenders. But you, Dick! Why do you not tell him then?

RICHARD: You can if you like.

BERTHA: I will. Certainly I will.

RICHARD, *coolly:* He will explain it to you.

BERTHA: He doesn't say one thing and do another. He is honest in his own way.

RICHARD, *plucks one of the roses and throws it at her feet:* He is, indeed! The soul of honour!

BERTHA: You may make fun of him as much as you like. I understand more than you think about that business. And so will he. Writing those long letters to her for years, and she to you. For years. But since I came back I understand it—well.

RICHARD: You do not. Nor would he.

BERTHA, *laughs scornfully:* Of course. Neither he nor I can understand it. Only she can. Because it is such a deep thing!

RICHARD, *angrily:* Neither he nor you—nor she either! Not one of you!

BERTHA, *with great bitterness:* She will! She will understand it! The diseased woman!

She turns away and walks over to the little table on the right. RICHARD *restrains a sudden gesture. A short pause.*

RICHARD, *gravely:* Bertha, take care of uttering words like that!

BERTHA, *turning, excitedly:* I don't mean any harm! I feel for her more than you can because I am a woman. I do, sincerely. But what I say is true.

RICHARD: Is it generous? Think.

BERTHA, *pointing towards the garden:* It is she who is not generous. Remember now what I say.

RICHARD· What?

BERTHA, *comes nearer; in a calmer tone:* You have given that woman very much, Dick. And she may be worthy of it. And she may understand it all, too. I know she is that kind.

RICHARD: Do you believe that?

BERTHA: I do. But I believe you will get very little from her in return—or from any of her clan. Remember my words, Dick. Because she is not generous and they are not generous. Is it all wrong what I am saying? Is it?

RICHARD, *darkly:* No. Not all.

She stoops and, picking up the rose from the floor, places it in the vase again. He watches her. BRIGID *appears at the folding doors on the right.*

BRIGID: The tea is on the table, ma'am.

BERTHA: Very well.

BRIGID: Is Master Archie in the garden?

BERTHA: Yes. Call him in.

BRIGID *crosses the room and goes out into the garden.* BERTHA *goes towards the doors on the right. At the lounge she stops and takes up the slip.*

BRIGID, *in the garden:* Master Archie! You are to come in to your tea.

BERTHA: Am I to go to this place?

RICHARD: Do you want to go?

BERTHA: I want to find out what he means. Am I to go?

RICHARD: Why do you ask me? Decide yourself.

BERTHA: Do you tell me to go?

RICHARD: No.

BERTHA: Do you forbid me to go?

RICHARD: No.

BRIGID, *from the garden:* Come quickly, Master Archie! Your tea is waiting on you.

BRIGID *crosses the room and goes out through the folding doors.* BERTHA *folds the slip into the waist of her dress and goes slowly towards the right. Near the door she turns and halts.*

BERTHA: Tell me not to go and I will not.

RICHARD, *without looking at her:* Decide youself.

BERTHA: Will you blame me then?

RICHARD, *excitedly:* No, no! I will not blame you. You are free. I cannot blame you.

ARCHIE *appears at the garden door.*

BERTHA: I did not deceive you.

She goes out through the folding doors. RICHARD *remains standing at the table.* ARCHIE, *when his mother has gone, runs down to* RICHARD.

ARCHIE, *quickly:* Well, did you ask her?

RICHARD, *starting:* What?

ARCHIE: Can I go?

RICHARD: Yes.

ARCHIE: In the morning? She said yes?

RICHARD: Yes. In the morning.

He puts his arm round his son's shoulders and looks down at him fondly.

Second Act

A ROOM in Robert Hand's cottage at Ranelagh. On the right, forward, a small black piano, on the rest of which is an open piece of music. Farther back a door leading to the street door. In the wall, at the back, folding doors, draped with dark curtains, leading to a bedroom. Near the piano a large table, on which is a tall oil lamp with a wide yellow shade. Chairs, upholstered, near this table. A small cardtable more forward. Against the back wall a bookcase. In the left wall, back, a window looking out into the garden, and, forward, a door and porch, also leading to the garden. Easychairs here and there. Plants in the porch and near the draped folding doors. On the walls are many framed black and white designs. In the right corner, back, a sideboard; and in the centre of the room, left of the table, a group consisting of a standing Turkish pipe, a low oil stove, which is not lit, and a rocking chair. It is the evening of the same day.

ROBERT HAND, in evening dress, is seated at the piano. The candles are not lit but the lamp on the table is lit. He plays softly in the bass the first bars of Wolfram's song in the last act of "Tannhäuser." Then he breaks off and, resting an elbow on the ledge of the keyboard, meditates. Then he rises and, pulling out a pump from behind the piano, walks here and there in the room ejecting from it into the air sprays of perfume. He inhales the air slowly and then puts the pump back behind the piano. He sits down on a chair near the table and, smoothing his hair carefully, sighs once or twice. Then, thrusting his hands into his trousers pockets, he leans back, stretches out his legs, and waits. A knock is heard at the street door. He rises quickly.

ROBERT, *exclaims:* Bertha!

He hurries out by the door on the right. There is a noise of confused greeting. After a few moments ROBERT *enters, followed by* RICHARD ROWAN, *who is in gray tweeds as before but holds in one hand a dark felt hat and in the other an umbrella.*

ROBERT: First of all let me put these outside.

He takes the hat and umbrella, leaves them in the hall and returns.

ROBERT, *pulling round a chair:* Here you are. You are lucky to find me in. Why didn't you tell me today? You were always a devil for surprises. I suppose my evocation of the past was too much for your wild blood. See how artistic I have become. *He points to the walls.* The piano is an addition since your time. I was just strumming out Wagner when you came. Killing time. You see I am ready for the fray. *Laughs.* I was just wondering how you and the vicechancellor were getting on together. *With exaggerated alarm.* But are you going in that suit? O well, it doesn't make much odds, I suppose. But how goes the time? *He takes out his watch.* Twenty past eight already, I declare!

RICHARD: Have you an appointment?

ROBERT, *laughs nervously:* Suspicious to the last!

RICHARD: Then I may sit down?

ROBERT: Of course, of course. *They both sit down.* For a few minutes, anyhow. Then we can both go on together. We are not bound for time. Between eight and nine, he said, didn't he? What time is it, I wonder? *Is about to look again at his watch; then stops.* Twenty past eight, yes.

RICHARD, *wearily, sadly:* Your appointment also was for the same hour. Here.

ROBERT: What appointment?

RICHARD: With Bertha.

ROBERT, *stares at him:* Are you mad?

RICHARD: Are you?

ROBERT, *after a long pause:* Who told you?

RICHARD: She.

A short silence.

ROBERT, *in a low voice:* Yes. I must have been mad. *Rapidly.* Listen to me, Richard. It is a great relief to me that you have come—the greatest relief. I assure you that ever since this afternoon I have thought and thought how I could break it off without seeming a fool. A great relief! I even intended to send word . . . a letter, a few lines. *Suddenly.* But then it was too late . . . *Passes his hand over his forehead.* Let me speak frankly with you; let me tell you everything.

RICHARD: I know everything. I have known for some time.

ROBERT: Since when?

RICHARD: Since it began between you and her.

ROBERT, *again rapidly:* Yes, I was mad. But it was merely lightheadedness. I admit that to have asked her here this evening was a mistake. I can explain everything to you. And I will. Truly.

RICHARD: Explain to me what is the word you longed and never dared to say to her. If you can or will.

ROBERT, *looks down, then raises his head:* Yes. I will. I admire very much the personality of your . . . of . . . your wife. That is the word. I can say it. It is no secret.

RICHARD: Then why did you wish to keep secret your wooing?

ROBERT: Wooing?

RICHARD: Your advances to her, little by little, day after day, looks, whispers. *With a nervous movement of the hands: Insomma,* wooing.

ROBERT, *bewildered:* But how do you know all this?

RICHARD: She told me.

ROBERT: This afternoon?

RICHARD: No. Time after time, as it happened.

ROBERT: You knew? From her? RICHARD *nods.* You were watching us all the time?

RICHARD, *very coldly:* I was watching you.

ROBERT, *quickly:* I mean, watching me. And you never spoke! You had only to speak a word—to save me from myself. You were trying me. *Passes his hand again over his forehead.* It was a terrible trial: now also. *Desperately.* Well, it is past. It will be a lesson to me for all my life. You hate me now for what I have done and for . . .

RICHARD, *quietly, looking at him:* Have I said that I hate you?

ROBERT: Do you not? You must.

RICHARD: Even if Bertha had not told me I should have known. Did you not see that when I came in this afternoon I went into my study suddenly for a moment?

ROBERT: You did. I remember.

RICHARD: To give you time to recover yourself. It made me sad to see your eyes. And the roses too. I cannot say why. A great mass of overblown roses.

ROBERT: I thought I had to give them. Was that strange? *Looks at* RICHARD *with a tortured expression.* Too many, perhaps? Or too old or common?

RICHARD: That was why I did not hate you. The whole thing made me sad all at once.

ROBERT, *to himself:* And this is real. It is happening —to us.

*He stares before him for some moments in silence, as
if dazed; then, without turning his head, continues.*

ROBERT: And she, too, was trying me; making an
experiment with me for your sake!

RICHARD: You know women better than I do. She
says she felt pity for you.

ROBERT, *brooding:* Pitied me, because I am no longer
. . . an ideal lover. Like my roses. Common, old.

RICHARD: Like all men you have a foolish wandering
heart.

ROBERT, *slowly:* Well, you spoke at last. You chose
the right moment.

RICHARD, *leans forward:* Robert, not like this. For us
two, no. Years, a whole life, of friendship. Think a
moment. Since childhood, boyhood . . . No, no. Not
in such a way—like thieves—at night. *Glancing about
him.* And in such a place. No, Robert, that is not for
people like us.

ROBERT: What a lesson! Richard, I cannot tell you
what a relief it is to me that you have spoken—that the
danger is passed. Yes, yes. *Somewhat diffidently.* Because . . . there was some danger for you, too, if you
think. Was there not?

RICHARD: What danger?

ROBERT, *in the same tone:* I don't know. I mean if
you had not spoken. If you had watched and waited on
until . . .

RICHARD: Until?

ROBERT, *bravely:* Until I had come to like her more
and more (because I can assure you it is only a light-
headed idea of mine), to like her deeply, to love her.
Would you have spoken to me then as you have just
now? RICHARD *is silent.* ROBERT *goes on more boldly.*
It would have been different, would it not? For then

it might have been too late while it is not too late now. What could I have said then? I could have said only: You are my friend, my dear good friend. I am very sorry but I love her. *With a sudden fervent gesture.* I love her and I will take her from you, however I can, because I love her.

They look at each other for some moments in silence.

RICHARD, *calmly:* That is the language I have heard often and never believed in. Do you mean by stealth or by violence? Steal you could not in my house because ⁺the doors were open: nor take by violence if there were no resistance.

ROBERT: You forget that the kingdom of heaven suffers violence: and the kingdom of heaven is like a woman.

RICHARD, *smiling:* Go on.

ROBERT, *diffidently, but bravely:* Do you think you have rights over her—over her heart?

RICHARD: None.

ROBERT: For what you have done for her? So much! You claim nothing?

RICHARD: Nothing.

ROBERT, *after a pause strikes his forehead with his hand.* What am I saying? Or what am I thinking? I wish you would upbraid me, curse me, hate me as I deserve. You love this woman. I remember all you told me long ago. She is yours, your work. *Suddenly.* And that is why I, too, was drawn to her. You are so strong that you attract me even through her.

RICHARD: I am weak.

ROBERT, *with enthusiasm:* You, Richard! You are the incarnation of strength.

RICHARD, *holds out his hands:* Feel those hands.

ROBERT, *taking his hands:* Yes. Mine are stronger. But I meant strength of another kind.

RICHARD, *gloomily:* I think you would try to take her by violence.

He withdraws his hands slowly.

ROBERT, *rapidly:* Those are moments of sheer madness when we feel an intense passion for a woman. We see nothing. We think of nothing. Only to possess her. Call it brutal, bestial, what you will.

RICHARD, *a little timidly:* I am afraid that that longing to possess a woman is not love.

ROBERT, *impatiently:* No man ever yet lived on this earth who did not long to possess—I mean to possess in the flesh—the woman whom he loves. It is nature's law.

RICHARD, *contemptuously:* What is that to me? Did I vote it?

ROBERT: But if you love . . . What else is it?

RICHARD, *hesitatingly:* To wish her well.

ROBERT, *warmly:* But the passion which burns us night and day to possess her. You feel it as I do. And it is not what you said now.

RICHARD: Have you . . . ? *He stops for an instance.* Have you the luminous certitude that yours is the brain in contact with which she must think and understand and that yours is the body in contact with which her body must feel? Have you this certitude in yourself?

ROBERT: Have you?

RICHARD, *moved:* Once I had it, Robert: a certitude as luminous as that of my own existence—or an illusion as luminous.

ROBERT, *cautiously:* And now?

RICHARD: If you had it and I could feel that you had it—even now . . .

ROBERT: What would you do?

RICHARD, *quietly:* Go away. You, and not I, would be necessary to her. Alone as I was before I met her.

ROBERT, *rubs his hands nervously:* A nice little load on my conscience!

RICHARD, *abstractedly:* You met my son when you came to my house this afternoon. He told me. What did you feel?

ROBERT, *promptly:* Pleasure.

RICHARD: Nothing else?

ROBERT; Nothing else. Unless I thought of two things at the same time. I am like that. If my best friend lay in his coffin and his face had a comic expression I should smile. *With a little gesture of despair.* I am like that. But I should suffer too, deeply.

RICHARD: You spoke of conscience . . . Did he seem to you a child only—or an angel?

ROBERT, *shakes his head:* No. Neither an angel nor an Anglo-Saxon. Two things, by the way, for which I have very little sympathy.

RICHARD: Never then? Never even . . . with her? Tell me. I wish to know.

ROBERT: I feel in my heart something different. I believe that on the last day (if it ever comes), when we are all assembled together, that the Almighty will speak to us like this. We will say that we lived chastely with one other creature . . .

RICHARD, *bitterly:* Lie to Him?

ROBERT: Or that we tried to. And He will say to us: Fools! Who told you that you were to give yourselves to one being only? You were made to give yourselves to many freely. I wrote that law with My finger on your hearts.

RICHARD: On woman's heart, too?

ROBERT: Yes. Can we close our heart against an affection which we feel deeply? Should we close it? Should she?

RICHARD: We are speaking of bodily union.

ROBERT: Affection between man and woman must come to that. We think too much of it because our minds are warped. For us today it is of no more consequence than any other form of contact—than a kiss.

RICHARD: If it is of no consequence why are you dissatisfied till you reach that end? Why were you waiting here tonight?

ROBERT: Passion tends to go as far as it can; but, you may believe me or not, I had not that in my mind—to reach that end.

RICHARD: Reach it if you can. I will use no arm against you that the world puts in my hand. If the law which God's finger has written on our hearts is the law you say I too am God's creature.

He rises and paces to and fro some moments in silence. Then he goes towards the porch and leans against the jamb. ROBERT *watches him.*

ROBERT: I always felt it. In myself and in others.

RICHARD, *absently:* Yes?

ROBERT, *with a vague gesture:* For all. That a woman, too, has the right to try with many men until she finds love. An immoral idea, is it not? I wanted to write a book about it. I began it . . .

RICHARD, *as before:* Yes?

ROBERT: Because I knew a woman who seemed to me to be doing that—carrying out that idea in her own life. She interested me very much.

RICHARD: When was this?

ROBERT: O, not lately. When you were away.

RICHARD *leaves his place rather abruptly and again paces to and fro.*

ROBERT: You see, I am more honest than you thought.

RICHARD: I wish you had not thought of her now— whoever she was, or is.

ROBERT, *easily:* She was and is the wife of a stock-broker.

RICHARD, *turning:* You know him?

ROBERT: Intimately.

RICHARD *sits down again in the same place and leans forward, his head on his hands.*

ROBERT, *moving his chair a little closer:* May I ask you a question?

RICHARD: You may.

ROBERT, *with some hesitation:* Has it never happened to you in these years—I mean when you were away from her, perhaps, or travelling—to . . . betray her with another. Betray her, I mean, not in love. Carnally, I mean . . . Has that never happened?

RICHARD: It has.

ROBERT: And what did you do?

RICHARD, *as before:* I remember the first time. I came home. It was night. My house was silent. My little son was sleeping in his cot. She, too, was asleep. I wakened her from sleep and told her. I cried beside her bed; and I pierced her heart.

ROBERT: O, Richard, why did you do that?

RICHARD: Betray her?

ROBERT: No. But tell her, waken her from sleep to tell her. It was piercing her heart.

RICHARD: She must know me as I am.

ROBERT: But that is not you as you are. A moment of weakness.

·RICHARD, *lost in thought:* And I was feeding the flame of her innocence with my guilt.

ROBERT, *brusquely:* O, don't talk of guilt and innocence. You have made her all that she is. A strange and wonderful personality—in my eyes, at least.

RICHARD, *darkly:* Or I have killed her.

ROBERT: Killed her?

RICHARD: The virginity of her soul.

ROBERT, *impatiently:* Well lost! What would she be without you?

RICHARD: I tried to give her a new life.

ROBERT: And you have. A new and rich life.

RICHARD: Is it worth what I have taken from her— her girlhood, her laughter, her young beauty, the hopes in her young heart?

ROBERT, *firmly:* Yes. Well worth it. *He looks at* RICHARD *for some moments in silence.* If you had neglected her, lived wildly, brought her away so far only to make her suffer . . .

He stops. RICHARD *raises his head, and looks at him.*

RICHARD: If I had?

ROBERT, *slightly confused:* You know there were ru- mours here of your life abroad—a wild life. Some per- sons who knew you or met you or heard of you in Rome. Lying rumours.

RICHARD, *coldly:* Continue.

ROBERT, *laughs a little harshly:* Even I at times thought of her as a victim. *Smoothly.* And of course, Richard, I felt and knew all the time that you were a man of great talent—of something more than talent. And that was your excuse—a valid one in my eyes.

RICHARD: Have you thought that it is perhaps now— at this moment—that I am neglecting her? *He clasps his hands nervously and leans across toward* ROBERT. I may be silent still. And she may yield to you at last— wholly and many times.

ROBERT, *draws back at once:* My dear Richard, my dear friend, I swear to you I could not make you suffer.

RICHARD, *continuing:* You may then know in soul and body, in a hundred forms, and ever restlessly, what some old theologian, Duns Scotus, I think, called a death of the spirit.

ROBERT, *eagerly:* A death. No; its affirmation! A death! The supreme instant of life from which all coming life proceeds, the eternal law of nature herself.

RICHARD: And that other law of nature, as you call it: change. How will it be when you turn against her and against me; when her beauty, or what seems so to you now, wearies you and my affection for you seems false and odious?

ROBERT: That will never be. Never.

RICHARD: And you turn even against yourself for having known me or trafficked with us both?

ROBERT, *gravely:* It will never be like that, Richard. Be sure of that.

RICHARD, *contemptuously:* I care very little whether it is or not because there is something I fear much more.

ROBERT, *shakes his head:* You fear? I disbelieve you, Richard. Since we were boys together I have followed your mind. You do not know what moral fear is.

RICHARD, *lays his hand on his arm:* Listen. She is dead. She lies on my bed. I look at her body which I betrayed—grossly and many times. And loved, too, and wept over. And I know that her body was always my loyal slave. To me, to me only she gave . . . *He breaks off and turns aside, unable to speak.*

ROBERT, *softly:* Do not suffer, Richard. There is no need. She is loyal to you, body and soul. Why do you fear?

RICHARD, *turns towards him, almost fiercely:* Not that fear. But that I will reproach myself then for having taken all for myself because I would not suffer her to give to another what was hers and not mine to give, because I accepted from her her loyalty and made her life poorer in love. That is my fear. That I stand between her and any moments of life that should be hers, between her and you, between her and anyone, between her and anything. I will not do it. I cannot and I will not. I dare not.

He leans back in his chair breathless, with shining eyes. ROBERT *rises quietly, and stands behind his chair.*

ROBERT: Look here, Richard. We have said all there is to be said. Let the past be past.

RICHARD, *quickly and harshly:* Wait. One thing more. For you, too, must know me as I am—now.

ROBERT: More? Is there more?

RICHARD: I told you that when I saw your eyes this afternoon I felt sad. Your humility and confusion, I felt, united you to me in brotherhood. *He turns half round towards him.* At that moment I felt our whole life together in the past, and I longed to put my arm around your neck.

ROBERT, *deeply and suddenly touched:* It is noble of you, Richard, to forgive me like this.

RICHARD, *struggling with himself:* I told you that I wished you not to do anything false and secret against me—against our friendship, against her; not to steal her from me craftily, secretly, meanly—in the dark, in the night—you, Robert, my friend.

ROBERT: I know. And it was noble of you.

RICHARD, *looks up at him with a steady gaze:* No. Not noble. Ignoble.

ROBERT, *makes an involuntary gesture:* How? Why?

RICHARD, *looks away again: in a lower voice:* That is what I must tell you too. Because in the very core of my ignoble heart I longed to be betrayed by you and by her—in the dark, in the night—secretly, meanly, craftily. By you, my best friend, and by her. I longed for that passionately and ignobly, to be dishonoured for ever in love and in lust, to be . . .

ROBERT, *bending down, places his hands over*
RICHARD's *mouth:* Enough. Enough. *He takes his hands
away.* But no. Go on.

RICHARD: To be for ever a shameful creature and to
build up my soul again out of the ruins of its shame.

ROBERT: And that is why you wished that she . . .

RICHARD, *with calm:* She has spoken always of her
innocence, as I have spoken always of my guilt, hum-
bling me.

ROBERT: From pride, then?

RICHARD: From pride and from ignoble longing. And
from a motive deeper still.

ROBERT, *with decisión:* I understand you.

*He returns to his place and begins to speak at once,
drawing his chair closer.*

ROBERT: May it not be that we are here and now in
the presence of a moment which will free us both—me
as well as you—from the last bonds of what is called
morality. My friendship for you has laid bonds on me.

RICHARD: Light bonds, apparently.

ROBERT: I acted in the dark, secretly. I will do so no
longer. Have you the courage to allow me to act freely?

RICHARD: A duel—between us?

ROBERT, *with growing excitement:* A battle of both
our souls, different as they are, against all that is false
in them and in the world. A battle of your soul against
the spectre of fidelity, of mine against the spectre of
friendship. All life is a conquest, the victory of human
passion over the commandments of cowardice. Will you,
Richard? Have you the courage? Even if it shatters to
atoms the friendship between us, even if it breaks up
for ever the last illusion in your own life? There was an
eternity before we were born: another will come after
we are dead. The blinding instant of passion alone—
passion, free, unashamed, irresistible—that is the only

gate by which we can escape from the misery of what slaves call life. Is not this the language of your own youth that I heard so often from you in this very place where we are sitting now? Have you changed?

RICHARD, *passes his hand across his brow:* Yes. It is the language of my youth.

ROBERT, *eagerly, intensely:* Richard, you have driven me up to this point. She and I have only obeyed your will. You yourself have roused these words in my brain. Your own words. Shall we? Freely? Together?

RICHARD, *mastering his emotion:* Together no. Fight your part alone. I will not free you. Leave me to fight mine.

ROBERT, *rises, decided:* You allow me, then?

RICHARD, *rises also, calmly:* Free yourself.

A knock is heard at the hall door.

ROBERT, *in alarm:* What does this mean?

RICHARD, *calmly:* Bertha, evidently. Did you not ask her to come?

ROBERT: Yes, but . . . *Looking about him.* Then I am going, Richard.

RICHARD: No. I am going.

ROBERT, *desperately:* Richard, I appeal to you. Let me go. It is over. She is yours. Keep her and forgive me, both of you.

RICHARD: Because you are generous enough to allow me?

ROBERT, *hotly:* Richard, you will make me angry with you if you say that.

RICHARD: Angry or not, I will not live on your generosity. You have asked her to meet you here tonight and alone. Solve the question between you.

ROBERT, *promptly:* Open the door. I shall wait in the garden. *He goes towards the porch.* Explain to her, Richard, as best you can. I cannot see her now.

Richard: I shall go. I tell you. Wait out there if you wish.

He goes out by the door on the right. Robert *goes out hastily through the porch but comes back the same instant.*

Robert: An umbrella! *With a sudden gesture.* O!

He goes out again through the porch. The hall door is heard to open and close. Richard *enters, followed by* Bertha, *who is dressed in a darkbrown costume, and wears a small dark red hat. She has neither umbrella nor waterproof.*

Richard, *gaily:* Welcome back to old Ireland!

Bertha, *nervously, seriously:* Is this the place?

Richard: Yes, it is. How did you find it?

Bertha: I told the cabman. I didn't like to ask my way. *Looking about her curiously.* Was he not waiting? Has he gone away?

Richard, *points towards the garden.* He is waiting. Out there. He was waiting when I came.

Bertha, *selfpossessed again.* You see, you came after all.

Richard: Did you think I would not?

Bertha: I knew you could not remain away. You see, after all you are like all other men. You had to come. You are jealous like the others.

Richard: You seem annoyed to find me here.

Bertha: What happened between you?

Richard: I told him I knew everything, that I had known for a long time. He asked how. I said from you.

Bertha: Does he hate me?

Richard: I cannot read in his heart.

Bertha, *sits down helplessly:* Yes. He hates me. He believes I made a fool of him—betrayed him. I knew he would.

Richard: I told him you were sincere with him.

BERTHA: He does not believe it. Nobody would believe it. I should have told him first—not you.

RICHARD: I thought he was a common robber, prepared to use even violence against you. I had to protect you from that.

BERTHA: That I could have done myself.

RICHARD: Are you sure?

BERTHA: It would have been enough to have told him that you knew I was here. Now I can find out nothing. He hates me. He is right to hate me. I have treated him badly, shamefully.

RICHARD, *takes her hand:* Bertha, look at me.

BERTHA, *turns to him.* Well?

RICHARD, *gazes into her eyes and then lets her hand fall.* I cannot read in your heart either.

BERTHA, *still looking at him:* You could not remain away. Do you not trust me? You can see I am quite calm. I could have hidden it all from you.

RICHARD: I doubt that.

BERTHA, *with a slight toss of her head:* O, easily if I had wanted to.

RICHARD, *darkly:* Perhaps you are sorry now that you did not.

BERTHA: Perhaps I am.

RICHARD, *unpleasantly:* What a fool you were to tell me! It would have been so nice if you had kept it secret.

BERTHA: As you do, no?

RICHARD: As I do, yes. *He turns to go.* Goodbye for a while.

BERTHA, *alarmed, rises:* Are you going?

RICHARD: Naturally. My part is ended here.

BERTHA: To her, I suppose?

RICHARD, *astonished:* Who?

BERTHA: Her ladyship. I suppose it is all planned so

that you may have a good opportunity to meet her and have an intellectual conversation!

RICHARD, *with an outburst of rude anger:* To meet the devil's father!

BERTHA, *unpins her hat and sits down:* Very well. You can go. Now I know what to do.

RICHARD, *returns, approaches her:* You don't believe a word of what you say.

BERTHA, *calmly:* You can go. Why don't you?

RICHARD: Then you have come here and led him on in this way on account of me. Is that how it is?

BERTHA: There is one person in all this who is not a fool. And that is you. I am though. And he is.

RICHARD, *continuing:* If so you have indeed treated him badly and shamefully.

BERTHA, *points at him:* Yes. But it was your fault. And I will end it now. I am simply a tool for you. You have no respect for me. You never had because I did what I did.

RICHARD: And has he respect?

BERTHA: He has. Of all the persons I met since I came back he is the only one who has. And he knows what they only suspect. And that is why I liked him from the first and like him still. Great respect for me she has! Why did you not ask her to come away with you nine years ago?

RICHARD: You know why, Bertha. Ask yourself.

BERTHA: Yes, I know why. You knew the answer you would get. That is why.

RICHARD: That is not why. I did not even ask you.

BERTHA: Yes. You knew I would go, asked or not. I do things. But if I do one thing I can do two things. As I have the name I can have the gains.

RICHARD, *with increasing excitement:* Bertha, I accept what is to be. I have trusted you. I will trust you still.

BERTHA: To have that against me. To leave me then. *Almost passionately.* Why do you not defend me then against him? Why do you go away from me now without a word? Dick, my God, tell me what you wish me to do?

RICHARD: I cannot, dear. *Struggling with himself.* Your own heart will tell you. *He seizes both her hands.* I have a wild delight in my soul, Bertha, as I look at you. I see you as you are yourself. That I came first in your life or before him then—that may be nothing to you. You may be his more than mine.

BERTHA: I am not. Only I feel for him, too.

RICHARD: And I do too. You may be his and mine. I will trust you, Bertha, and him too. I must. I cannot hate him since his arms have been around you. You have drawn us near together. There is something wiser than wisdom in your heart. Who am I that I should call myself master of your heart or of any woman's? Bertha, love him, be his, give yourself to him if you desire—or if you can.

BERTHA, *dreamily:* I will remain.

RICHARD: Goodbye.

He lets her hand fall and goes out rapidly on the right. BERTHA *remains sitting. Then she rises and goes timidly towards the porch. She stops near it and, after a little hesitation, calls into the garden.*

BERTHA: Is anyone out there?

At the same time she retreats towards the middle of the room. Then she calls again in the same way.

BERTHA: Is anyone there?

ROBERT *appears in the open doorway that leads in from the garden. His coat is buttoned and the collar is turned up. He holds the doorposts with his hands lightly and waits for* BERTHA *to see him.*

BERTHA, *catching sight of him, starts back: then, quickly.* Robert!

ROBERT: Are you alone?

BERTHA. Yes.

ROBERT, *looking towards the door on the right.* Where is he?

BERTHA: Gone. *Nervously.* You startled me. Where did you come from?

ROBERT, *with a movement of his head:* Out there. Did he not tell you I was out there—waiting?

BERTHA, *quickly:* Yes, he told me. But I was afraid here alone. With the door open, waiting. *She comes to the table and rests her hand on the corner.* Why do you stand like that in the doorway?

ROBERT: Why? I am afraid too.

BERTHA: Of what?

ROBERT: Of you.

BERTHA, *looks down:* Do you hate me now?

ROBERT: I fear you. *Clasping his hands at his back, quietly but a little defiantly.* I fear a new torture—a new trap.

BERTHA, *as before:* For what do you blame me?

ROBERT, *comes forward a few steps, halts: then impulsively:* Why did you lead me on? Day after day, more and more. Why did you not stop me? You could have—with a word. But not even a word! I forgot myself and him. You saw it. That I was ruining myself in his eyes, losing his friendship. Did you want me to?

BERTHA, *looking up:* You never asked me.

ROBERT: Asked you what?

BERTHA: If he suspected—or knew.

ROBERT: And would you have told me?

BERTHA: Yes.

ROBERT, *hesitatingly:* Did you tell him—everything?

BERTHA: I did.

ROBERT: I mean—details.

BERTHA: Everything.

ROBERT, *with forced smile:* I see. You were making an experiment for his sake. On me. Well, why not? It seems I was a good subject. Still, it was a little cruel of you.

BERTHA: Try to understand me, Robert. You must try.

ROBERT, *with polite gesture:* Well, I will try.

BERTHA: Why do you stand like that near the door? It makes me nervous to look at you.

ROBERT: I am trying to understand. And then I am afraid.

BERTHA, *holds out her hand:* You need not be afraid.

(ROBERT *comes towards her quickly and takes her hand.*)

Diffidently. Used you to laugh over me—together? *Drawing his hand away.* But now I must be good or you may laugh over me again—tonight.

BERTHA, *distressed, lays her hand on his arm.* Please listen to me, Robert . . . But you are all wet, drenched! *She passes her hands over his coat.* O, you poor fellow! Out there in the rain all that time! I forgot that.

ROBERT, *laughs:* Yes, you forgot the climate.

BERTHA: But you are really drenched. You must change your coat.

ROBERT, *takes her hands:* Tell me, it is pity then that you feel for me, as he—as Richard—says?

BERTHA: Please change your coat, Robert, when I ask you. You might get a very bad cold from that. Do, please.

ROBERT: What would it matter now?

BERTHA, *looking round her:* Where do you keep your clothes here?

ROBERT, *points to the door at the back:* In there. I fancy I have a jacket here. *Maliciously.* In my bedroom.

BERTHA: Well, go in and take that off.

ROBERT: And you?

BERTHA: I will wait here for you.

ROBERT: Do you command me to?

BERTHA, *laughing:* Yes, I command you.

ROBERT, *promptly:* Then I will. *He goes quickly towards the bedroom door; then turns round.* You won't go away?

BERTHA: No, I will wait. But don't be long.

ROBERT: Only a moment.

He goes into the bedroom, leaving the door open. BERTHA *looks curiously about her and then glances in indecision towards the door at the back.*

ROBERT, *from the bedroom:* You have not gone?

BERTHA: No.

ROBERT: I am in the dark here. I must light the lamp.

He is heard striking a match, and putting a glass shade on a lamp. A pink light comes in through the doorway. BERTHA *glances at her watch at her wristlet and then sits at the table.*

ROBERT, *as before:* Do you like the effect of the light?

BERTHA: O, yes.

ROBERT: Can you admire it from where you are?

BERTHA: Yes, quite well.

ROBERT: It was for you.

BERTHA, *confused:* I am not worthy even of that.

ROBERT, *clearly, harshly:* Love's labour lost.

BERTHA, *rising nervously:* Robert!

ROBERT: Yes?

BERTHA: Come here, quickly! Quickly, I say!

ROBERT: I am ready.

He appears in the doorway, wearing a dark green

velvet jacket. Seeing her agitation, he comes quickly towards her.

ROBERT: What is it, Bertha?

BERTHA, *trembling:* I was afraid.

ROBERT: Of being alone?

BERTHA, *catches his hands:* You know what I mean. My nerves are all upset.

ROBERT: That I . . . ?

BERTHA: Promise me, Robert, not to think of such a thing. Never. If you like me at all. I thought that moment . . .

ROBERT: What an idea?

BERTHA: But promise me if you like me.

ROBERT: If I like you, Bertha! I promise. Of course, I promise. You are trembling all over.

BERTHA: Let me sit down somewhere. It will pass in a moment.

ROBERT: My poor Bertha! Sit down. Come.

He leads her towards a chair near the table. She sits down. He stands beside her.

ROBERT, *after a short pause:* Has it passed?

BERTHA: Yes. It was only for a moment. I was very silly. I was afraid that . . . I wanted to see you near me.

ROBERT: That . . . that you made me promise not to think of?

BERTHA: Yes.

ROBERT, *keenly:* Or something else?

BERTHA, *helplessly:* Robert, I feared something. I am not sure what.

ROBERT: And now?

BERTHA: Now you are here. I can see you. Now it has passed.

ROBERT, *with resignation:* Passed. Yes. Love's labour lost.

BERTHA, *looks up at him:* Listen, Robert. I want to explain to you about that. I could not deceive Dick. Never. In nothing. I told him everything—from the first. Then it went on and on; and still you never spoke or asked me. I wanted you to.

ROBERT: Is that the truth, Bertha?

BERTHA: Yes, because it annoyed me that you could think I was like . . . like the other women I suppose you knew that way. I think that Dick is right too. Why should there be secrets?

ROBERT, *softly:* Still, secrets can be very sweet. Can they not?

BERTHA, *smiles:* Yes, I know they can. But, you see, I could not keep things secret from Dick. Besides, what is the good? They always come out in the end. Is it not better for people to know?

ROBERT, *softly and a little shyly:* How could you, Bertha, tell him everything? Did you? Every single thing that passed between us?

BERTHA: Yes. Everything he asked me.

ROBERT: Did he ask you—much?

BERTHA: You know the kind he is. He asks about everything. The ins and outs.

ROBERT: About our kissing, too?

BERTHA: Of course. I told him all.

ROBERT, *shakes his head slowly:* Extraordinary little person! Were you not ashamed?

BERTHA: No.

ROBERT: Not a bit?

BERTHA: No. Why? Is that terrible?

ROBERT: And how did he take it? Tell me. I want to know everything, too.

BERTHA, *laughs:* It excited him. More than usual.

ROBERT: Why? Is he excitable—still?

BERTHA, *archly:* Yes, very. When he is not lost in his philosophy.

ROBERT: More than I?

BERTHA: More than you? *Reflecting.* How could I answer that? You both are, I suppose?

ROBERT *turns aside and gazes towards the porch, passing his hand once or twice thoughtfully over his hair.*

BERTHA, *gently:* Are you angry with me again?

ROBERT, *moodily:* You are with me.

BERTHA: No, Robert. Why should I?

ROBERT: Because I asked you to come to this place. I tried to prepare it for you. *He points vaguely here and there.* A sense of quietness.

BERTHA, *touching his jacket with her fingers:* And this, too. Your nice velvet coat.

ROBERT: Also. I will keep no secrets from you.

BERTHA: You remind me of someone in a picture. I like you in it . . . But you are not angry, are you?

ROBERT, *darkly:* Yes. That was my mistake. To ask you to come here. I felt it when I looked at you from the garden and saw you—you, Bertha—standing here. *Hopelessly.* But what else could I have done?

BERTHA, *quietly:* You mean because others have been here?

ROBERT: Yes.

He walks away from her a few paces. A gust of wind makes the lamp on the table flicker. He lowers the wick slightly.

BERTHA, *following him with her eyes:* But I knew that before I came. I am not angry with you for it.

ROBERT, *shrugs his shoulders:* Why should you be angry with me after all? You are not even angry with him—for the same thing—or worse.

BERTHA: Did he tell you that about himself?

ROBERT: Yes. He told me. We all confess to one another here. Turn about.

BERTHA: I try to forget it.

ROBERT: It does not trouble you?

BERTHA: Not now. Only I dislike to think of it.

ROBERT: It is merely something brutal, you think? of little importance?

BERTHA: It does not trouble me—now.

ROBERT, *looking at her over his shoulder:* But there is something that would trouble you very much and that you would not try to forget?

BERTHA: What?

ROBERT, *turning towards her:* If it were not only something brutal with this person or that—for a few moments. If it were something fine and spiritual—with one person only—with one woman. *Smiles.* And perhaps brutal too. It usually comes to that sooner or later. Would you try to forget and forgive that?

BERTHA, *toying with her wristlet:* In whom?

ROBERT: In anyone. In me.

BERTHA, *calmly:* You mean in Dick.

ROBERT: I said in myself. But would you?

BERTHA: You think I would revenge myself? Is Dick not to be free too?

ROBERT, *points at her:* That is not from your heart, Bertha.

BERTHA, *proudly:* Yes, it is; let him be free too. He leaves me free also.

ROBERT, *insistently:* And you know why? And understand? And you like it? And you want to be? And it makes you happy? And has made you happy? Always? This gift of freedom which he gave you—nine years ago?

BERTHA, *gazing at him with wide open eyes:* But why do you ask me such a lot of questions, Robert?

ROBERT, *stretches out both hands to her:* Because I had another gift to offer you then—a common simple gift—like myself. If you want to know it I will tell you.

BERTHA, *looking at her watch:* Past is past, Robert. And I think I ought to go now. It is nine almost.

ROBERT, *impetuously:* No, no. Not yet. There is one confession more and we have the right to speak.

He crosses before the table rapidly and sits down beside her.

BERTHA, *turning towards him, places her left hand on his shoulder:* Yes, Robert. I know that you like me. You need not tell me. *Kindly.* You need not confess any more tonight.

A gust of wind enters through the porch, with a sound of moving leaves. The lamp flickers quickly.

BERTHA, *pointing over his shoulder:* Look! It is too high.

Without rising, he bends towards the table, and turns down the wick more. The room is half dark. The light comes in more strongly through the doorway of the bedroom.

ROBERT: The wind is rising. I will close that door.

BERTHA, *listening:* No, it is raining still. It was only a gust of wind.

ROBERT, *touches her shoulder:* Tell me if the air is too cold for you. *Half rising.* I will close it.

BERTHA, *detaining him:* No. I am not cold. Besides, I am going now, Robert. I must.

ROBERT, *firmly:* No, no. There is no *must* now. We were left here for this. And you are wrong, Bertha. The past is not past. It is present here now. My feeling for you is the same now as it was then, because then—you slighted it.

BERTHA: No, Robert. I did not.

ROBERT, *continuing:* You did. And I have felt it all these years without knowing it—till now. Even while I lived—the kind of life you know and dislike to think of —the kind of life to which you condemned me.

BERTHA: I?

ROBERT: Yes, when you slighted the common simple gift I had to offer you—and took his gift instead.

BERTHA, *looking at him:* But you never . . .

ROBERT: No. Because you had chosen him. I saw that. I saw it on the first night we met, we three together. Why did you choose him?

BERTHA, *bends her head:* Is that not love?

ROBERT, *continuing:* And every night when we two— he and I—came to that corner to meet you I saw it and felt it. You remember the corner, Bertha?

BERTHA, *as before:* Yes.

ROBERT: And when you and he went away for your walk and I went along the street alone I felt it. And when he spoke to me about you and told me he was going away—then most of all.

BERTHA: Why then most of all?

ROBERT: Because it was then that I was guilty of my first treason towards him.

BERTHA: Robert, what are you saying? Your first treason against Dick?

ROBERT, *nods:* And not my last. He spoke of you and himself. Of how your life would be together—free and all that. Free, yes! He would not even ask you to go with him. *Bitterly.* He did not. And you went all the same.

BERTHA: I wanted to be with him. You know . . . *Raising her head and looking at him.* You know how we were then—Dick and I.

ROBERT, *unheeding:* I advised him to go alone—not

to take you with him——to live alone in order to see if
what he felt for you was a passing thing which might
ruin your happiness and his career.

BERTHA: Well, Robert. It was unkind of you towards
me. But I forgive you because you were thinking of his
happiness and mine.

ROBERT, *bending closer to her*. No, Bertha. I was not.
And that was my treason. I was thinking of myself——
that you might turn from him when he had gone and he
from you. Then I would have offered you my gift. You
know what it was now. The simple common gift that
men offer to women. Not the best perhaps. Best or worst
——it would have been yours.

BERTHA, *turning away from him:* He did not take
your advice.

ROBERT, *as before:* No. And the night you ran away
together——O, how happy I was!

BERTHA, *pressing his hands:* Keep calm, Robert. I
know you liked me always. Why did you not forget
me?

ROBERT, *smiles bitterly:* How happy I felt as I came
back along the quays and saw in the distance the boat
lit up, going down the black river, taking you away
from me! *In a calmer tone.* But why did you choose
him? Did you not like me at all?

BERTHA: Yes. I liked you because you were his friend.
We often spoke about you. Often and often. Every time
you wrote or sent papers or books to Dick. And I like
you still, Robert. *Looking into his eyes.* I never forgot
you.

ROBERT: Nor I you. I knew I would see you again. I
knew it the night you went away——that you would come
back. And that was why I wrote and worked to see you
again——here.

BERTHA: And here I am. You were right.

ROBERT, *slowly:* Nine years. Nine times more beautiful!

BERTHA, *smiling:* But am I? What do you see in me?

ROBERT, *gazing at her:* A strange and beautiful lady.

BERTHA, *almost disgusted:* O, please don't call me such a thing!

ROBERT, *earnestly:* You are more. A young and beautiful queen.

BERTHA, *with a sudden laugh:* O, Robert!

ROBERT, *lowering his voice and bending nearer to her:* But do you not know that you are a beautiful human being? Do you not know that you have a beautiful body? Beautiful and young?

BERTHA, *gravely:* Some day I will be old.

ROBERT, *shakes his head:* I cannot imagine it. Tonight you are young and beautiful. Tonight you have come back to me. *With passion.* Who knows what will be tomorrow? I may never see you again or never see you as I do now.

BERTHA: Would you suffer?

ROBERT, *looks round the room, without answering:* This room and this hour were made for your coming. When you have gone—all is gone.

BERTHA, *anxiously:* But you will see me again, Robert . . . as before.

ROBERT, *looks full at her.* To make him—Richard— suffer.

BERTHA: He does not suffer.

ROBERT, *bowing his head:* Yes, yes. He does.

BERTHA: He knows we like each other. Is there any harm, then?

ROBERT, *raising his head:* No there is no harm. Why should we not? He does not know yet what I feel. He has left us alone here at night, at this hour, because he longs to know it—he longs to be delivered.

BERTHA: From what?

ROBERT, *moves closer to her and presses her arm as he speaks:* From every law, Bertha, from every bond. All his life he has sought to deliver himself. Every chain but one he has broken and that one we are to break. Bertha—you and I.

BERTHA, *almost inaudibly:* Are you sure?

ROBERT, *still more warmly:* I am sure that no law made by man is sacred before the impulse of passion. *Almost fiercely.* Who made us for one only? It is a crime against our own being if we are so. There is no law before impulse. Laws are for slaves. Bertha, say my name! Let me hear your voice say it. Softly!

BERTHA, *softly:* Robert!

ROBERT, *puts his arm about her shoulder:* Only the impulse towards youth and beauty does not die. *He points towards the porch.* Listen!

BERTHA, *in alarm:* What?

ROBERT: The rain falling. Summer rain on the earth. Night rain. The darkness and warmth and flood of passion. Tonight the earth is loved—loved and possessed. Her lover's arms around her; and she is silent. Speak, dearest!

BERTHA, *suddenly leans forward and listens intently:* Hush!

ROBERT, *listening, smiles:* Nothing. Nobody. We are alone.

A gust of wind blows in through the porch, with a sound of shaken leaves. The flame of the lamp leaps.

BERTHA, *pointing to the lamp:* Look!

ROBERT: Only the wind. We have light enough from the other room.

He stretches his hand across the table and puts out the lamp. The light from the doorway of the bedroom crosses the place where they sit. The room is quite dark.

ROBERT: Are you happy? Tell me.

BERTHA: I am going now, Robert. It is very late. Be satisfied.

ROBERT, *caressing her hair:* Not yet, not yet. Tell me, do you love me a little?

BERTHA: I like you, Robert. I think you are good. *Half rising.* Are you satisfied?

ROBERT, *detaining her, kisses her hair:* Do not go, Bertha! There is time still. Do you love me too? I have waited a long time. Do you love us both—him and also me? Do you, Bertha? The truth! Tell me. Tell me with your eyes. Or speak!

She does not answer. In the silence the rain is heard falling.

Third Act

*T*HE *drawingroom of Richard Rowan's house at Merrion. The folding doors at the right are closed and also the double doors leading to the garden. The green plush curtains are drawn across the window on the left. The room is half dark. It is early in the morning of the next day. Bertha sits beside the window looking out between the curtains. She wears a loose saffron dressing gown. Her hair is combed loosely over the ears and knotted at the neck. Her hands are folded in her lap. Her face is pale and drawn.*

BRIGID *comes in through the folding doors on the right with a featherbroom and duster. She is about to cross but, seeing* BERTHA, *she halts suddenly and blesses herself instinctively.*

BRIGID: Merciful hour, ma'am. You put the heart across me. Why did you get up so early?

BERTHA: What time is it?

BRIGID: After seven, ma'am. Are you long up?

BERTHA: Some time.

BRIGID, *approaching her:* Had you a bad dream that woke you?

BERTHA: I didn't sleep all night. So I got up to see the sun rise.

BRIGID, *opens the double doors:* It's a lovely morning now after all the rain we had. *Turns round.* But you must be dead tired, ma'am. What will the master say at your doing a thing like that? *She goes to the door of the study and knocks.* Master Richard!

BERTHA, *looks round:* He is not there. He went out an hour ago.

BRIGID: Out there, on the strand, is it?

BERTHA: Yes.

BRIGID, *comes towards her and leans over the back of a chair:* Are you fretting yourself, ma'am, about anything?

BERTHA: No, Brigid.

BRIGID: Don't be. He was always like that, meandering off ·by himself somewhere. He is a curious bird, Master Richard, and always was. Sure there isn't a turn in him I don't know. Are you fretting now· maybe because he does be in there (*pointing to the study*) half the night at his books? Leave him alone. He'll come back to you again. Sure he·thinks the sun shines out of your face, ma'am.

BERTHA, *sadly:* That time is gone.

BRIGID, *confidentially:* And good cause I have to remember it—that time when he was paying his addresses

to you. *She sits down beside* BERTHA: *in a lower voice.*
Do you know that he used to tell me all about you and
nothing to his mother, God rest her soul? Your letters
and all.

BERTHA: What? My letters to him?

BRIGID, *delighted:* Yes. I can see him sitting on the
kitchen table, swinging his legs and spinning out of him
yards of talk about you and him and Ireland and all
kinds of devilment—to an ignorant old woman like me.
But that was always his way. But if he had to meet a
grand highup person he'd be twice as grand himself.
Suddenly looks at BERTHA. Is it crying you are now?
Ah, sure, don't cry. There's good times coming still.

BERTHA: No, Brigid, that time comes only once in a
lifetime. The rest of life is good for nothing except to
remember that time.

BRIGID, *is silent for a moment: then says kindly:*
Would you like a cup of tea, ma'am? That would make
you all right.

BERTHA: Yes, I would. But the milkman has not come
yet.

BRIGID: No. Master Archie told me to wake him before he came. He's going out for a jaunt in the car. But
I've a cup left overnight. I'll have the kettle boiling in
a jiffy. Would you like a nice egg with it?

BERTHA: No, thanks.

BRIGID: Or a nice bit of toast?

BERTHA: No, Brigid, thanks. Just a cup of tea.

BRIGID, *crossing to the folding doors:* I won't be a moment. *She stops, turns back and goes towards the door
on the left.* But first I must waken Master Archie or
there'll be ructions.

*She goes out by the door on the left. After a few mo-
ments* BERTHA *rises and goes over to the study. She*

opens the door wide and looks in. One can see a small untidy room with many bookshelves and a large writing-table with papers and an extinguished lamp and before it a padded chair. She remains standing for some time in the doorway, then closes the door again without entering the room. She returns to her chair by the window and sits down. ARCHIE, *dressed as before, comes in by the door on the right, followed by* BRIGID.

ARCHIE, *comes to her and, putting up his face to be kissed, says: Buon giorno,* mamma!

BERTHA, *kissing him: Buon giorno,* Archie! *To* BRIGID. Did you put another vest on him under that one?

BRIGID: He wouldn't let me, ma'am.

ARCHIE: I'm not cold, mamma.

BERTHA: I said you were to put it on, didn't I?

ARCHIE: But where is the cold?

BERTHA, *takes a comb from her head and combs his hair back at both sides:* And the sleep is in your eyes still.

BRIGID: He went to bed immediately after you went out last night, ma'am.

ARCHIE: You know he's going to let me drive, mamma.

BERTHA, *replacing the comb in her hair, embraces him suddenly:* O, what a big man to drive a horse!

BRIGID: Well, he's daft on horses, anyhow.

ARCHIE, *releasing himself:* I'll make him go quick. You will see from the window, mamma. With the whip. *He makes the gesture of cracking a whip and shouts at the top of his voice: Avanti!*

BRIGID: Beat the poor horse, is it?

BERTHA: Come here till I clean your mouth. *She takes her handkerchief from the pocket of her gown, wets it with her tongue and cleans his mouth.* You're all smudges or something, dirty little creature you are.

ARCHIE, *repeats, laughing:* Smudges! What is smudges?

The noise is heard of a milkcan rattled on the railings before the window.

BRIGID, *draws aside the curtains and looks out:* Here he is!

ARCHIE, *rapidly:* Wait. I'm ready. Goodbye, mamma! *He kisses her hastily and turns to go.* Is pappie up?

BRIGID, *takes him by the arm:* Come on with you now.

BERTHA: Mind yourself, Archie, and don't be long or I won't let you go any more.

ARCHIE: All right. Look out of the window and you'll see me. Goodbye.

BRIGID *and* ARCHIE *go out by the door on the left.* BERTHA *stands up and, drawing aside the curtains still more, stands in the embrasure of the window looking out. The hall door is heard opening: then a slight noise of voices and cans is heard. The door is closed. After a moment or two* BERTHA *is seen waving her hand gaily in a salute.* BRIGID *enters and stands behind her, looking over her shoulder.*

BRIGID: Look at the sit of him! As serious as you like.

BERTHA, *suddenly withdrawing from her post:* Stand out of the window. I don't want to be seen.

BRIGID: Why, ma'am, what is it?

BERTHA, *crossing towards the folding doors:* Say I'm not up, that I'm not well. I can't see anyone.

BRIGID, *follows her:* Who is it, ma'am?

BERTHA, *halting:* Wait a moment.

She listens. A knock is heard at the hall door.

BERTHA, *stands a moment in doubt, then:* No, say I'm in.

BRIGID, *in doubt:* Here?

BERTHA, *hurriedly:* Yes. Say I have just got up.

BRIGID *goes out on the left.* BERTHA *goes towards the double doors and fingers the curtains nervously, as if settling them. The hall door is heard to open. Then* BEATRICE JUSTICE *enters and, as* BERTHA *does not turn at once, stands in hesitation near the door on the left. She is dressed as before and has a newspaper in her hand.*

BEATRICE, *advances rapidly:* Mrs. Rowan, excuse me for coming at such an hour.

BERTHA, *turns:* Good morning, Miss Justice. *She comes towards her.* Is anything the matter?

BEATRICE, *nervously:* I don't know. That is what I wanted to ask you.

BERTHA, *looks curiously at her:* You are out of breath. Won't you sit down?

BEATRICE, *sitting down:* Thank you.

BERTHA, *sits opposite her, pointing to her paper:* Is there something in the paper?

BEATRICE, *laughs nervously: opens the paper:* Yes.

BERTHA: About Dick?

BEATRICE: Yes. Here it is. A long article, a leading article, by my cousin. All his life is here. Do you wish to see it?

BERTHA, *takes the paper, and opens it:* Where is it?

BEATRICE: In the middle. It is headed: *A Distinguished Irishman.*

BERTHA: Is it . . . for Dick or against him?

BEATRICE, *warmly:* O, for him! You can read what he says about Mr. Rowan. And I know that Robert stayed in town very late last night to write it.

BERTHA, *nervously:* Yes. Are you sure?

BEATRICE: Yes. Very late. I heard him come home. It was long after two.

BERTHA, *watching her:* It alarmed you? I mean to be awakened at that hour of the morning.

BEATRICE: I am a light sleeper. But I knew he had come from the office and then . . . I suspected he had written an article about Mr. Rowan and that was why he came so late.

BERTHA: How quick you were to think of that!

BEATRICE: Well, after what took place here yesterday afternoon—I mean what Robert said, that Mr. Rowan had accepted this position. It was only natural I should think . . .

BERTHA: Ah, yes. Naturally.

BEATRICE, *hastily:* But that is not what alarmed me. But immediately after I heard a noise in my cousin's room.

BERTHA, *crumples together the paper in her hands, breathlessly:* My God! What is it? Tell me.

BEATRICE, *observing her:* Why does that upset you so much?

BERTHA, *sinking back, with a forced laugh:* Yes, of course, it is very foolish of me. My nerves are all upset. I slept very badly, too. That is why I got up so early But tell me what was it then?

BEATRICE: Only the noise of his valise being pulled along the floor. Then I heard him walking about his room, whistling softly. And then locking it and strapping it.

BERTHA: He is going away!

BEATRICE: That was what alarmed me. I feared he had had a quarrel with Mr. Rowan and that his article was an attack.

BERTHA: But why should they quarrel? Have you noticed anything between them?

BEATRICE: I thought I did. A coldness.

BERTHA: Lately?

BEATRICE: For some time past.

BERTHA, *smoothing the paper out:* Do you know the reason?

BEATRICE, *hesitatingly:* No.

BERTHA, *after a pause:* Well, but if this article is for him, as you say, they have not quarrelled. *She reflects a moment.* And written last night, too.

BEATRICE: Yes. I bought the paper at once to see. But why, then, is he going away so suddenly? I feel that there is something wrong. I feel that something has happened between them.

BERTHA: Would you be sorry?

BEATRICE: I would be very sorry. You see, Mrs. Rowan, Robert is my first cousin and it would grieve me very deeply if he were to treat Mr. Rowan badly, now that he has come back, or if they had a serious quarrel especially because . . .

BERTHA, *toying with the paper:* Because?

BEATRICE: Because it was my cousin who urged Mr. Rowan always to come back. I have that on my conscience.

BERTHA: It should be on Mr. Hand's conscience, should it not?

BEATRICE, *uncertainly:* On mine, too. Because—I spoke to my cousin about Mr. Rowan when he was away and, to a certain extent, it was I . . .

BERTHA, *nods slowly:* I see. And that is on your conscience. Only that?

BEATRICE: I think so.

BERTHA, *almost cheerfully:* It looks as if it was you, Miss Justice, who brought my husband back to Ireland.

BEATRICE: I, Mrs. Rowan?

BERTHA: Yes, you. By your letters to him and then by

speaking to your cousin as you said just now. Do you not think that you are the person who brought him back?

BEATRICE, *blushing suddenly:* No. I could not think that.

BERTHA, *watches her for a moment; then turning aside:* You know that my husband is writing very much since he came back.

BEATRICE: Is he?

BERTHA: Did you not know? *She points towards the study.* He passes the greater part of the night in there writing. Night after night.

BEATRICE: In his study?

BERTHA: Study or bedroom. You may call it what you please. He sleeps there, too, on a sofa. He slept there last night. I can show you if you don't believe me.

She rises to go towards the study. BEATRICE *half rises quickly and makes a gesture of refusal.*

BEATRICE: I believe you, of course, Mrs. Rowan, when you tell me.

BERTHA, *sitting down again:* Yes. He is writing. And it must be about something which has come into his life lately—since we came back to Ireland. Some change. Do you know that any change has come into his life? *She looks searchingly at her.* Do you know it or feel it?

BEATRICE, *answers her look steadily:* Mrs. Rowan, that is not a question to ask me. If any change has come into his life since he came back you must know and feel it.

BERTHA: You could know it just as well. You are very intimate in this house.

BEATRICE: I am not the only person who is intimate here.

They both look at each other coldly in silence for

some moments. BERTHA *lays aside the paper and sits down on a chair nearer to* BEATRICE.

BERTHA, *placing her hand on* BEATRICE's *knee:* So you also hate me, Miss Justice?

BEATRICE, *with an effort:* Hate you? I?

BERTHA, *insistently but softly:* Yes. You know what it means to hate a person?

BEATRICE: Why should I hate you? I have never hated anyone.

BERTHA: Have you ever loved anyone? *She puts her hand on* BEATRICE's *wrist.* Tell me. You have?

BEATRICE, *also softly:* Yes. In the past.

BERTHA: Not now?

BEATRICE: No.

BERTHA: Can you say that to me—truly? Look at me.

BEATRICE, *looks at her:* Yes, I can.

A short pause. BERTHA *withdraws her hand, and turns away her head in some embarrassment.*

BERTHA: You said just now that another person is intimate in this house. You meant your cousin . . . Was it he?

BEATRICE: Yes.

BERTHA: Have you not forgotten him?

BEATRICE, *quietly:* I have tried to.

BERTHA, *clasping her hands:* You hate me. You think I am happy. If you only knew how wrong you are!

BEATRICE, *shakes her head:* I do not.

BERTHA: Happy! When I do not understand anything that he writes, when I cannot help him in any way, when I don't even understand half of what he says to me sometimes! You could and you can. *Excitedly.* But I am afraid for him, afraid for both of them. *She stands up suddenly and goes towards the davenport.* He must not go away like that. *She takes a writing pad from the drawer and writes a few lines in great haste.* No, it is impossible! Is he mad to do such a thing? *Turning to* BEATRICE. Is he still at home?

BEATRICE, *watching her in wonder:* Yes. Have you written to him to ask him to come here?

BERTHA, *rises:* I have. I will send Brigid across with it. Brigid!

She goes out by the door on the left rapidly.

BEATRICE, *gazing after her instinctively:* It is true, then!

She glances toward the door of RICHARD's *study and catches her head in her hands. Then, recovering herself, she takes the paper from the little table, opens it, takes a spectacle case from her handbag and, putting on a pair of spectacles, bends down, reading it.* RICHARD ROWAN *enters from the garden. He is dressed as before but wears a soft hat and carries a thin cane.*

RICHARD, *stands in the doorway, observing her for some moments:* There are demons (*he points out towards the strand*) out there. I heard them jabbering since dawn.

BEATRICE, *starts to her feet:* Mr. Rowan!

RICHARD: I assure you. The isle is full of voices. Yours also. *Otherwise I could not see you,* it said. And her voice. But, I assure you, they are all demons. I made the sign of the cross upside down and that silenced them.

BEATRICE, *stammering:* I came here, Mr. Rowan, so early because . . . to show you this . . . Robert wrote it . . . about you . . . last night.

RICHARD, *takes off his hat:* My dear Miss Justice, you told me yesterday, I think, why you came here and I never forget anything. *Advancing towards her, holding out his hand.* Good morning.

BEATRICE, *suddenly takes off her spectacles and*

places the paper in his hands: I came for this. It is an article about you. Robert wrote it last night. Will you read it?

RICHARD, *bows:* Read it now? Certainly.

BEATRICE, *looks at him in despair:* O, Mr. Rowan, it makes me suffer to look at you.

RICHARD, *opens and reads the paper: Death of the Very Reverend Canon Mulhall.* Is that it?

BERTHA *appears at the door on the left and stands to listen.*

RICHARD, *turns over a page:* Yes, here we are! *A Distinguished Irishman. He begins to read in a rather loud hard voice.* Not the least vital of the problems which confront our country is the problem of her attitude towards those of her children who, having left her in her hour of need, have been called back to her now on the eve of her longawaited victory, to her whom in loneliness and exile they have at last learned to love. In exile, we have said, but here we must distinguish. There is an economic and there is a spiritual exile. There are those who left her to seek the bread by which men live and there are others, nay, her most favoured children, who left her to seek in other lands that food of the spirit by which a nation of human beings is sustained in life. Those who recall the intellectual life of Dublin of a decade since will have many memories of Mr. Rowan. Something of that fierce indignation which lacerated the heart . . .

He raises his eyes from the paper and sees BERTHA *standing in the doorway. Then he lays aside the paper and looks at her. A long silence.*

BEATRICE, *with an effort:* You see, Mr. Rowan, your day has dawned at last. Even here. And you see that you have a warm friend in Robert, a friend who understands you.

RICHARD: Did you notice the little phrase at the beginning: "those who left her in her hour of need?"

He looks searchingly at BERTHA, *turns and walks into his study, closing the door behind him.*

BERTHA, *speaking half to herself:* I gave up everything for him, religion, family, my own peace.

She sits down heavily in an armchair. BEATRICE *comes towards her.*

BEATRICE, *weakly:* But do you not feel also that Mr. Rowan's ideas . . .

BERTHA, *bitterly:* Ideas and ideas! But the people in this world have other ideas or pretend to. They have to put up with him in spite of his ideas because he is able to do something. Me, no. I am nothing.

BEATRICE: You stand by his side.

BERTHA, *with increasing bitterness:* Ah, nonsense, Miss Justice! I am only a thing he got entangled with and my son is—the nice name they give those children. Do you think I am a stone? Do you think I don't see it in their eyes and in their manner when they have to meet me?

BEATRICE: Do not let them humble you, Mrs. Rowan.

BERTHA, *haughtily:* Humble me! I am very proud of myself, if you want to know. What have they ever done for him? I made him a man. What are they all in his life? No more than the dirt under his boots! *She stands up and walks excitedly to and fro.* He can despise me, too, like the rest of them—now. And you can despise me. But you will never humble me, any of you.

BEATRICE: Why do you accuse me?

BERTHA, *going to her impulsively:* I am in such suffering. Excuse me if I was rude. I want us to be friends. *She holds out her hands.* Will you?

BEATRICE, *taking her hands:* Gladly.

BERTHA, *looking at her:* What lovely long eyelashes

you have! And your eyes have such a sad expression!

BEATRICE, *smiling:* I see very little with them. They are very weak.

BERTHA, *warmly:* But beautiful.

She embraces her quietly and kisses her. Then withdraws from her a little shyly. BRIGID *comes in from the left.*

BRIGID: I gave it to himself, ma'am.

BERTHA: Did he send a message?

BRIGID: He was just going out, ma'am. He told me to say he'd be here after me.

BERTHA: Thanks.

BRIGID, *going:* Would you like the tea and the toast now, ma'am?

BERTHA: Not now, Brigid. After perhaps. When Mr. Hand comes show him in at once.

BRIGID: Yes, ma'am.

She goes out on the left.

BEATRICE: I will go now, Mrs. Rowan, before he comes.

BERTHA, *somewhat timidly:* Then we are friends?

BEATRICE, *in the same tone:* We will try to be. *Turning.* Do you allow me to go out through the garden? I don't want to meet my cousin now.

BERTHA: Of course. *She takes her hand.* It is so strange that we spoke like this now. But I always wanted to. Did you?

BEATRICE: I think I did, too.

BERTHA, *smiling:* Even in Rome. When I went out for a walk with Archie I used to think about you, what you were like, because I knew about you from Dick. I used to look at different persons, coming out of churches or going by in carriages, and think that perhaps they were like you. Because Dick told me you were dark.

BEATRICE, *again nervously:* Really?

BERTHA, *pressing her hand:* Goodbye then—for the present.

BEATRICE, *disengaging her hand:* Good morning.

BERTHA: I will see you to the gate.

She accompanies her out through the double doors. They go down through the garden. RICHARD ROWAN *comes in from the study. He halts near the doors, looking down the garden. Then he turns away, comes to the little table, takes up the paper and reads.* BERTHA, *after some moments, appears in the doorway and stands watching him till he has finished. He lays down the paper again and turns to go back to his study.*

BERTHA: Dick!

RICHARD, *stopping:* Well?

BERTHA: You have not spoken to me.

RICHARD: I have nothing to say. Have you?

BERTHA: Do you not wish to know—about what happened last night?

RICHARD: That I will never know.

BERTHA: I will tell you if you ask me.

RICHARD: You will tell me. But I will never know. Never in this world.

BERTHA, *moving towards him:* I will tell you the truth, Dick, as I always told you. I never lied to you.

RICHARD, *clenching his hands in the air, passionately:* Yes, yes. The truth! But I will never know, I tell you.

BERTHA: Why, then, did you leave me last night?

RICHARD, *bitterly:* In your hour of need.

BERTHA, *threateningly:* You urged me to it. Not because you love me. If you loved me or if you knew what love was you would not have left me. For your own sake you urged me to it.

RICHARD: I did not make myself. I am what I am.

BERTHA: To have it always to throw against me. To

make me humble before you, as you always did. To be
free yourself. *Pointing towards the garden.* With her!
And that is your love! Every word you say is false.

RICHARD, *controlling himself:* It is useless to ask you
to listen to me.

BERTHA: Listen to you! She is the person for listening. Why would you waste your time with me? Talk to
her.

RICHARD, *nods his head:* I see. You have driven her
away from me now, as you drove everyone else from
my side—every friend I ever had, every human being
that ever tried to approach me. You hate her.

BERTHA, *warmly:* No such thing! I think you have
made her unhappy as you have made me and as
you made your dead mother unhappy and killed her.
Woman-killer! That is your name.

RICHARD, *turns to go: Arrivederci!*

BERTHA, *excitedly:* She is a fine and high character.
I like her. She is everything that I am not—in birth
and education. You tried to ruin her but you could not.
Because she is well able for you—what I am not. And
you know it.

RICHARD, *almost shouting:* What the devil are you
talking about her for?

BERTHA, *clasping her hands:* O, how I wish I had
never met you! How I curse that day!

RICHARD, *bitterly:* I am in the way, is it? You would
like to be free now. You have only to say the word.

BERTHA, *proudly:* Whenever you like I am ready.

RICHARD: So that you could meet your lover—freely?

BERTHA: Yes.

RICHARD: Night after night?

BERTHA, *gazing before her and speaking with intense
passion:* To meet my lover! *Holding out her arms before
her.* My lover! Yes! My lover!

She bursts suddenly into tears and sinks down on a chair, covering her face with her hands. RICHARD *approaches her slowly and touches her on the shoulder.*

RICHARD: Bertha! *She does not answer.* Bertha, you are free.

BERTHA, *pushes his hand aside and starts to her feet:* Don't touch me! You are a stranger to me. You do not understand anything in me—not one thing in my heart or soul. A stranger! I am living with a stranger!

A knock is heard at the hall door. BERTHA *dries her eyes quickly with her handkerchief and settles the front of her gown.* RICHARD *listens for a moment, looks at her keenly and, turning away, walks into his study.* ROBERT HAND *enters from the left. He is dressed in dark brown and carries in his hand a brown Alpine hat.*

ROBERT, *closing the door quietly behind him:* You sent for me.

BERTHA, *rises:* Yes. Are you mad to think of going away like that—without even coming here—without saying anything?

ROBERT, *advancing towards the table on which the paper lies, glances at it:* What I have to say I said here.

BERTHA: When did you write it? Last night—after I went away?

ROBERT, *gracefully:* To be quite accurate, I wrote part of it—in my mind—before you went away. The rest—the worst part—I wrote after. Much later.

BERTHA: And you could write last night!

ROBERT, *shrugs his shoulders:* I am a welltrained animal. *He comes closer to her.* I passed a long wandering night after . . . in my office, at the vicechancellor's house, in a nightclub, in the streets, in my room. Your image was always before my eyes, your hand in my hand. Bertha, I will never forget last night. *He lays his hat on the table and takes her hand.* Why do you not look at me? May I not touch you?

BERTHA, *points to the study:* Dick is in there.

ROBERT, *drops her hand:* In that case children be good.

BERTHA: Where are you going?

ROBERT: To foreign parts. That is, to my cousin, Jack Justice, *alias* Doggy Justice, in Surrey. He has a nice country place there and the air is mild.

BERTHA: Why are you going?

ROBERT, *looks at her in silence:* Can you not guess one reason?

BERTHA: On account of me?

ROBERT: Yes. It is not pleasant for me to remain here just now.

BERTHA, *sits down helplessly:* But this is cruel to you, Robert. Cruel to me and to him also.

ROBERT: Has he asked . . . what happened?

BERTHA, *joining her hands in despair:* No. He refuses to ask me anything. He says he will never know.

ROBERT, *nods gravely:* Richard is right there. He is always right.

BERTHA: But, Robert, you must speak to him.

ROBERT: What am I to say to him?

BERTHA: The truth! Everything!

ROBERT, *reflects:* No, Bertha. I am a man speaking to a man. I cannot tell him everything.

BERTHA: He will believe that you are going away because you are afraid to face him after last night.

ROBERT, *after a pause:* Well, I am not a coward any more than he. I will see him.

BERTHA, *rises:* I will call him.

ROBERT, *catching her hands:* Bertha! What happened last night? What is the truth that I am to tell? *He gazes earnestly into her eyes.* Were you mine in that sacred night of love? Or have I dreamed it?

BERTHA, *smiles faintly:* Remember your dream of me. You dreamed that I was yours last night.

ROBERT: And that is the truth—a dream? That is what I am to tell?

BERTHA: Yes.

ROBERT, *kisses both her hands:* Bertha! *In a softer voice.* In all my life only that dream is real. I forget the rest. *He kisses her hands again.* And now I can tell him the truth. Call him.

BERTHA *goes to the door of* RICHARD's *study and knocks. There is no answer. She knocks again.*

BERTHA: Dick! *There is no answer.* Mr. Hand is here. He wants to speak to you, to say goodbye. He is going away. *There is no answer. She beats her hand loudly on the panel of the door and calls in an alarmed voice.* Dick! Answer me!

RICHARD ROWAN *comes in from the study. He comes at once to* ROBERT *but does not hold out his hand.*

RICHARD, *calmly:* I thank you for your kind article about me. Is it true that you have come to say good-bye?

ROBERT: There is nothing to thank me for, Richard. Now and always I am your friend. Now more than ever before. Do you believe me, Richard?

RICHARD *sits down on a chair and buries his face in his hands.* BERTHA *and* ROBERT *gaze at each other in silence. Then she turns away and goes out quietly on the right.* ROBERT *goes towards* RICHARD *and stands near him, resting his hands on the back of a chair, looking down at him. There is a long silence. A* FISHWOMAN *is heard crying out as she passes along the road outside.*

THE FISHWOMAN: Fresh Dublin bay herrings! Fresh Dublin bay herrings! Dublin bay herrings!

ROBERT, *quietly:* I will tell you the truth, Richard. Are you listening?

RICHARD, *raises his face and leans back to listen:* Yes.

ROBERT *sits on the chair beside him. The* FISHWOMAN *is heard calling out farther away.*

THE FISHWOMAN: Fresh herrings! Dublin bay herrings!

ROBERT: I failed, Richard. That is the truth. Do you believe me?

RICHARD: I am listening.

ROBERT: I failed. She is yours, as she was nine years ago, when you met her first.

RICHARD: When we met her first, you mean.

ROBERT: Yes. *He looks down for some moments.* Shall I go on?

RICHARD: Yes.

ROBERT: She went away. I was left alone—for the second time. I went to the vicechancellor's house and dined. I said you were ill and would come another night. I made epigrams new and old—that one about the statues also. I drank claret cup. I went to my office and wrote my article. Then . . .

RICHARD: Then?

ROBERT: Then I went to a certain nightclub. There were men there—and also women. At least, they looked like women. I danced with one of them. She asked me to see her home. Shall I go on?

RICHARD: Yes.

ROBERT: I saw her home in a cab. She lives near Donnybrook. In the cab took place what the subtle Duns Scotus calls a death of the spirit. Shall I go on?

RICHARD: Yes.

ROBERT: She wept. She told me she was the divorced wife of a barrister. I offered her a sovereign as she told me she was short of money. She would not take it and

wept very much. Then she drank some melissa water
from a little bottle which she had in her satchel. I saw
her enter her house. Then I walked home. In my room
I found that my coat was all stained with the melissa
water. I had no luck even with my coats yesterday: that
was the second one. The idea came to me then to
change my suit and go away by the morning boat. I
packed my valise and went to bed. I am going away by
the next train to my cousin, Jack Justice, in Surrey.
Perhaps for a fortnight. Perhaps longer. Are you disgusted?

RICHARD: Why did you not go by the boat?

ROBERT: I slept it out.

RICHARD: You intended to go without saying goodbye
—without coming here?

ROBERT: Yes.

RICHARD: Why?

ROBERT: My story is not very nice, is it?

RICHARD: But you have come.

ROBERT: Bertha sent me a message to come.

RICHARD: But for that . . . ?

ROBERT: But for that I should not have come.

RICHARD: Did it strike you that if you had gone without coming here I should have understood it—in my
own way?

ROBERT: Yes, it did.

RICHARD: What, then, do you wish me to believe?

ROBERT: I wish you to believe that I failed. That
Bertha is yours now as she was nine years ago, when
you—when we—met her first.

RICHARD: Do you want to know what I did?

ROBERT: No.

RICHARD: I came home at once.

ROBERT: Did you hear Bertha return?

RICHARD: No. I wrote all the night. And thought.

Pointing to the study. In there. Before dawn I went out and walked the strand from end to end.

ROBERT, *shaking his head:* Suffering. Torturing yourself.

RICHARD: Hearing voices about me. The voices of those who say they love me.

ROBERT, *points to the door on the right:* One. And mine?

RICHARD: Another still.

ROBERT, *smiles and touches his forehead with his right forefinger:* True. My interesting but somewhat melancholy cousin. And what did they tell you?

RICHARD: They told me to despair.

ROBERT: A queer way of showing their love, I must say! And will you despair?

RICHARD, *rising:* No.

A noise is heard at the window. ARCHIE's *face is seen flattened against one of the panes. He is heard calling.*

ARCHIE: Open the window! Open the window!

ROBERT, *looks at* RICHARD: Did you hear his voice, too, Richard, with the others—out there on the strand? Your son's voice. *Smiling.* Listen! How full it is of despair!

ARCHIE: Open the window, please, will you?

ROBERT: Perhaps, there, Richard, is the freedom we seek—you in one way, I in another. In him and not in us. Perhaps . . .

RICHARD: Perhaps . . . ?

ROBERT: I said "perhaps." I would say almost surely if . . .

RICHARD: If what?

ROBERT, *with a faint smile:* If he were mine.

He goes to the window and opens it. ARCHIE *scrambles in.*

ROBERT: Like yesterday—eh?

ARCHIE: Good morning, Mr. Hand. *He runs to* RICH-ARD *and kisses him: Buon giorno, babbo.*

RICHARD: *Buon giorno,* Archie.

ROBERT: And where were you, my young gentleman?

ARCHIE: Out with the milkman. I drove the horse. We went to Booterstown. *He takes off his cap and throws it on a chair.* I am very hungry.

ROBERT, *takes his hat from the table:* Richard, good-bye. *Offering his hand.* To our next meeting!

RICHARD, *rises, touches his hand:* Goodbye.

BERTHA *appears at the door on the right.*

ROBERT, *catches sight of her: to* ARCHIE: Get your cap. Come on with me. I'll buy you a cake and I'll tell you a story.

ARCHIE, *to* BERTHA: May I, mamma?

BERTHA: Yes.

ARCHIE, *takes his cap:* I am ready.

ROBERT, *to* RICHARD *and* BERTHA: Goodbye to pappa and mamma. But not a big goodbye.

ARCHIE: Will you tell me a fairy story, Mr Hand?

ROBERT: A fairy story? Why not? I am your fairy godfather.

They go out together through the double doors and down the garden. When they have gone BERTHA *goes to* RICHARD *and puts her arm round his waist.*

BERTHA: Dick, dear, do you believe now that I have been true to you? Last night and always?

RICHARD, *sadly:* Do not ask me, Bertha.

BERTHA, *pressing him more closely:* I have been, dear. Surely you believe me. I gave you myself—all. I gave up all for you. You took me—and you left me.

RICHARD: When did I leave you?

BERTHA: You left me: and I waited for you to come back to me. Dick, dear, come here to me. Sit down. How tired you must be!

She draws him towards the lounge. He sits down, almost reclining, resting on his arm. She sits on the mat before the lounge, holding his hand.

BERTHA: Yes, dear. I waited for you. Heavens, what I suffered then—when we lived in Rome! Do you remember the terrace of our house?

RICHARD: Yes.

BERTHA: I used to sit there, waiting, with the poor child with his toys, waiting till he got sleepy. I could see all the roofs of the city and the river, the *Tevere*. What is its name?

RICHARD: The Tiber.

BERTHA, *caressing her cheek with his hand:* It was lovely, Dick, only I was so sad. I was alone, Dick, forgotten by you and by all. I felt my life was ended.

RICHARD: It had not begun.

BERTHA: And I used to look at the sky, so beautiful, without a cloud and the city you said was so old: and then I used to think of Ireland and about ourselves.

RICHARD: Ourselves?

BERTHA: Yes. Ourselves. Not a day passes that I do not see ourselves, you and me, as we were when we met first. Every day of my life I see that. Was I not true to you all that time?

RICHARD, *sighs deeply:* Yes, Bertha. You were my bride in exile.

BERTHA: Wherever you go, I will follow you. If you wish to go away now I will go with you.

RICHARD: I will remain. It is too soon yet to despair.

BERTHA, *again caressing his hand:* It is not true that I want to drive everyone from you. I wanted to bring you close together—you and him. Speak to me. Speak out all your heart to me. What you feel and what you suffer.

RICHARD: I am wounded, Bertha.

BERTHA: How wounded, dear? Explain to me what you mean. I will try to understand everything you say. In what way are you wounded?

RICHARD, *releases his hand and, taking her head between his hands, bends it back and gazes long into her eyes:* I have a deep, deep wound of doubt in my soul.

BERTHA, *motionless:* Doubt of me?

RICHARD: Yes.

BERTHA: I am yours. *In a whisper.* If I died this moment, I am yours.

RICHARD, *still gazing at her and speaking as if to an absent person:* I have wounded my soul for you—a deep wound of doubt which can never be healed. I can never know, never in this world. I do not wish to know or to believe. I do not care. It is not in the darkness of belief that I desire you. But in restless living wounding doubt. To hold you by no bonds, even of love, to be united with you in body and soul in utter nakedness— for this I longed. And now I am tired for a while, Bertha. My wound tires me.

He stretches himself out wearily along the lounge. BERTHA *holds his hand still, speaking very softly.*

BERTHA: Forget me, Dick. Forget me and love me again as you did the first time. I want my lover. To meet him, to go to him, to give myself to him. You, Dick. O, my strange wild lover, come back to me again!

She closes her eyes.

Collected Poems

EDITOR'S PREFACE

CHAMBER MUSIC (1907), through the good offices of Arthur Symons, was the first of Joyce's books to reach the public. Though it brought no royalties, it was to gain him a place in the *Imagist Anthology.* It was thus to associate him with the Anglo-American group that included Eliot and Pound, who later helped to publicize Joyce's books. With them he possessed more in common than with the poets of Celtic Twilight. The qualities and limitations of these thirty-six poems, as well as their lack of pretentiousness, are implicit in their title. They are slight, elusive, formal, above all musical. Yeats called some of his poems *Words for Music, Perhaps.* There was no "perhaps" about Joyce's intention, as a singer, to write lyrics that could really be sung. His success may be measured by the number of musicians who have provided them with effective settings. The style is dictated by the exigencies of the form: precise diction, open vowels, repetitions, alliterations, assonance and onomatopoeia, a rare polysyllable stemming a monosyllabic flow. The imagery appeals characteristically to the ear; even the dream-vision of "I hear an army" is largely conveyed by sound. Echoes from books, along with images from musical instruments, contribute to Joyce's "elegant and antique phrase." His models are the Elizabethan lyricists, the airs of Dowland and the words of Shakespeare, whose mood is invoked in "Thou leanest to the shell of night." Literary convention, however, does not entirely account for the stress on love. The large amount 'of verse that Joyce seems to have composed in his Dublin days, his brother tells us, was carefully winnowed and sequentially arranged to make up *Chamber Music. Pomes Penyeach* (1927), as the nominal price made clear, included a dozen poems with "Tilly" for extra measure—the incidental poetic output of twenty years given strenuously to prose. The continuity and contrast have reminded some readers of Blake's *Songs of Innocence and Experience.* Moved by nostalgia, as in the homesick refrain of "Watching the Needleboats at San Sabba," Joyce calls up actual scenes and faces more concretely. A freer rhythm and a sharper tone reveal the author of *Ulysses* in "A Memory of the Players in a Mirror at Midnight." The impressive "Nightpiece," with its metamorphosis of nature into a church, is virtually an English equivalent of Baudelaire's *Harmonie du soir.* When Joyce brought his two volumes together in *Collected Poems* (1936), he added a single poem. *"Ecce Puer,"* written in 1932 on the occasion of his grandson's birth and soon after his father's death, is a small example of mature perfection. The present edition likewise adds two longer poems, autobiographical in impulse and satirical in import, printed by Joyce as private broadsides for circulation among his Dublin friends and enemies. "The Holy Office" (1904) is a personal commentary on an ambiguous Aristotelian metaphor. "Gas from a Burner" (1912), the purported monologue of Joyce's Irish publisher, pays a backhanded tribute to the personalities of the Irish Renaissance. Both combine the Swiftian Hudibrastic with the more delicate Joycean touch.

Chamber Music

I

Strings in the earth and air
   Make music sweet;
Strings by the river where
   The willows meet.

There's music along the river
   For Love wanders there,
Pale flowers on his mantle,
   Dark leaves on his hair.

All softly playing,
   With head to the music bent,
And fingers straying
   Upon an instrument.

II

The twilight turns from amethyst
   To deep and deeper blue,
The lamp fills with a pale green glow
   The trees of the avenue.

The old piano plays an air,
   Sedate and slow and gay;

She bends upon the yellow keys,
   Her head inclines this way.

Shy thoughts and grave wide eyes and hands
   That wander as they list—
The twilight turns to darker blue
   With lights of amethyst.

III

At that hour when all things have repose,
   O lonely watcher of the skies,
   Do you hear the night wind and the sighs
Of harps playing unto Love to unclose
   The pale gates of sunrise?

When all things repose do you alone
   Awake to hear the sweet harps play
   To Love before him on his way,
And the night wind answering in antiphon
   Till night is overgone?

Play on, invisible harps, unto Love,
   Whose way in heaven is aglow
   At that hour when soft lights come and go,
Soft sweet music in the air above
   And in the earth below.

IV

When the shy star goes forth in heaven
   All maidenly, disconsolate,

Hear you amid the drowsy even
  One who is singing by your gate.
His song is softer than the dew
  And he is come to visit you.

O bend no more in revery
  When he at eventide is calling,
Nor muse: Who may this singer be
  Whose song about my heart is falling?
Know you by this, the lover's chant,
  'Tis I that am your visitant.

V

Lean out of the window,
  Goldenhair,
I heard you singing
  A merry air.

My book was closed;
  I read no more,
Watching the fire dance
  On the floor.

I have left my book,
  I have left my room,
For I heard you singing
  Through the gloom.

Singing and singing
  A merry air,
Lean out of the window,
  Goldenhair.

VI

I would in that sweet bosom be
   (O sweet it is and fair it is!)
Where no rude wind might visit me.
   Because of sad austerities
I would in that sweet bosom be.

I would be ever in that heart
   (O soft I knock and soft entreat her!)
Where only peace might be my part.
   Austerities were all the sweeter
So I were ever in that heart.

VII

My love is in a light attire
   Among the apple-trees,
Where the gay winds do most desire
   To run in companies.

There, where the gay winds stay to woo
   The young leaves as they pass,
My love goes slowly, bending to
   Her shadow on the grass;

And where the sky's a pale blue cup
   Over the laughing land,
My love goes lightly, holding up
   Her dress with dainty hand.

VIII

Who goes amid the green wood
  With springtide all adorning her?
Who goes amid the merry green wood
  To make it merrier?

Who passes in the sunlight
  By ways that know the light footfall?
Who passes in the sweet sunlight
  With mien so virginal?

The ways of all the woodland
  Gleam with a soft and golden fire—
For whom does all the sunny woodland
  Carry so brave attire?

O, it is for my true love
  The woods their rich apparel wear—
O, it is for my own true love,
  That is so young and fair.

IX

Winds of May, that dance on the sea,
Dancing a ring-around in glee
From furrow to furrow, while overhead
The foam flies up to be garlanded,
In silvery arches spanning the air,
Saw you my true love anywhere?

Welladay! Welladay!
For the winds of May!
Love is unhappy when love is away!

X

Bright cap and streamers,
    He sings in the hollow:
    Come follow, come follow,
        All you that love.
Leave dreams to the dreamers
    That will not after,
    That song and laughter
        Do nothing move.

With ribbons streaming
    He sings the bolder;
    In troop at his shoulder
        The wild bees hum.
And the time of dreaming
    Dreams is over—
    As lover to lover,
        Sweetheart, I come.

XI

Bid adieu, adieu, adieu,
    Bid adieu to girlish days,
Happy Love is come to woo
    Thee and woo thy girlish ways—
The zone that doth become thee fair,
The snood upon thy yellow hair.

When thou hast heard his name upon
    The bugles of the cherubim
Begin thou softly to unzone
    Thy girlish bosom unto him
And softly to undo the snood
That is the sign of maidenhood.

XII

What counsel has the hooded moon
    Put in thy heart, my shyly sweet,
Of Love in ancient plenilune,
    Glory and stars beneath his feet—
A sage that is but kith and kin
With the comedian Capuchin?

Believe me rather that am wise
    In disregard of the divine,
A glory kindles in those eyes
    Trembles to starlight. Mine, O Mine!
No more be tears in moon or mist
For thee, sweet sentimentalist.

XIII

Go seek her out all courteously,
    And say I come,
Wind of spices whose song is ever
    Epithalamium.
O, hurry over the dark lands
    And run upon the sea

For seas and lands shall not divide us
    My love and me.

Now, wind, of your good courtesy
    I pray you go,
And come into her little garden
    And sing at her window;
Singing: The bridal wind is blowing
    For Love is at his noon;
And soon will your true love be with you,
    Soon, O soon.

XIV

My dove, my beautiful one,
    Arise, arise!
    The night-dew lies
Upon my lips and eyes.

The odorous winds are weaving
    A music of sighs:
    Arise, arise,
My dove, my beautiful one!

I wait by the cedar tree,
    My sister, my love.
    White breast of the dove,
My breast shall be your bed.

The pale dew lies
    Like a veil on my head.
    My fair one, my fair dove,
Arise, arise!

XV

From dewy dreams, my soul, arise,
  From love's deep slumber and from death,
For lo! the trees are full of sighs
  Whose leaves the morn admonisheth.

Eastward the gradual dawn prevails
  Where softly-burning fires appear,
Making to tremble all those veils
  Of grey and golden gossamer.

While sweetly, gently, secretly,
  The flowery bells of morn are stirred
And the wise choirs of faery
  Begin (innumerous!) to be heard.

XVI

O cool is the valley now
  And there, love, will we go
For many a choir is singing now
  Where Love did sometime go.
And hear you not the thrushes calling,
  Calling us away?
O cool and pleasant is the valley
  And there, love, will we stay.

XVII

Because your voice was at my side
   I gave him pain,
Because within my hand I held
   Your hand again.

There is no word nor any sign
   Can make amend—
He is a stranger to me now
   Who was my friend.

XVIII

O Sweetheart, hear you
   Your lover's tale;
A man shall have sorrow
   When friends him fail.

For he shall know then
   Friends be untrue
And a little ashes
   Their words come to.

But one unto him
   Will softly move
And softly woo him
   In ways of love.

His hand is under
   Her smooth round breast;

So he who has sorrow
Shall have rest.

XIX

Be not sad because all men
   Prefer a lying clamour before you:
Sweetheart, be at peace again—
   Can they dishonour you?

They are sadder than all tears;
   Their lives ascend as a continual sigh.
Proudly answer to their tears:
   As they deny, deny.

XX

In the dark pine-wood
   I would we lay,
In deep cool shadow
   At noon of day.

How sweet to lie there,
   Sweet to kiss,
Where the great pine-forest
   Enaisled is!

Thy kiss descending
   Sweeter were
With a soft tumult
   Of thy hair.

O, unto the pine-wood
  At noon of day
Come with me now,
  Sweet love, away.

XXI

He who hath glory lost, nor hath
  Found any soul to fellow his,
Among his foes in scorn and wrath
  Holding to ancient nobleness,
That high unconsortable one—
His love is his companion.

XXII

Of that so sweet imprisonment
  My soul, dearest, is fain—
Soft arms that woo me to relent
  And woo me to detain.
Ah, could they ever hold me there
Gladly were I a prisoner!

Dearest, through interwoven arms
  By love made tremulous,
That night allures me where alarms
  Nowise may trouble us;
But sleep to dreamier sleep be wed
Where soul with soul lies prisoned.

XXIII

This heart that flutters near my heart
  My hope and all my riches is,
Unhappy when we draw apart
  And happy between kiss and kiss;
My hope and all my riches—yes!—
And all my happiness.

For there, as in some mossy nest
  The wrens will divers treasures keep,
I laid those treasures I possessed
  Ere that mine eyes had learned to weep.
Shall we not be as wise as they
Though love live but a day?

XXIV

Silently she's combing,
  Combing her long hair,
Silently and graciously,
  With many a pretty air.

The sun is in the willow leaves
  And on the dappled grass,
And still she's combing her long hair
  Before the looking-glass.

I pray you, cease to comb out,
  Comb out your long hair,

For I have heard of witchery
 Under a pretty air,

That makes as one thing to the lover
 Staying and going hence,
All fair, with many a pretty air
 And many a negligence.

XXV

Lightly come or lightly go:
 Though thy heart presage thee woe,
Vales and many a wasted sun,
 Oread let thy laughter run,
Till the irreverent mountain air
Ripple all thy flying hair.

Lightly, lightly—ever so:
 Clouds that wrap the vales below
At the hour of evenstar
 Lowliest attendants are;
Love and laughter song-confessed
When the heart is heaviest.

XXVI

Thou leanest to the shell of night,
 Dear lady, a divining ear.
In that soft choiring of delight
 What sound hath made thy heart to fear?
Seemed it of rivers rushing forth
From the grey deserts of the north?

That mood of thine, O timorous,
Is his, if thou but scan it well,
Who a mad tale bequeaths to us
At ghosting hour conjurable—
And all for some strange name he read
In Purchas or in Holinshed.

XXVII

Though I thy Mithridates were,
Framed to defy the poison-dart,
Yet must thou fold me unaware
To know the rapture of thy heart,
And I but render and confess
The malice of thy tenderness.

For elegant and antique phrase,
Dearest, my lips wax all too wise;
Nor have I known a love whose praise
Our piping poets solemnize,
Neither a love where may not be
Ever so little falsity.

XXVIII

Gentle lady, do not sing
Sad songs about the end of love;
Lay aside sadness and sing
How love that passes is enough.

Sing about the long deep sleep
Of lovers that are dead, and how

In the grave all love shall sleep:
Love is aweary now.

XXIX

Dear heart, why will you use me so?
   Dear eyes that gently me upbraid,
Still are you beautiful—but O,
   How is your beauty raimented!

Through the clear mirror of your eyes,
   Through the soft sigh of kiss to kiss,
Desolate winds assail with cries
   The shadowy garden where love is.

And soon shall love dissolved be
   When over us the wild winds blow—
But you, dear love, too dear to me,
   Alas! why will you use me so?

XXX

Love came to us in time gone by
   When one at twilight shyly played
And one in fear was standing nigh—
   For Love at first is all afraid.

We were grave lovers. Love is past
   That had his sweet hours many a one;
Welcome to us now at the last
   The ways that we shall go upon.

XXXI

O, it was out by Donnycarney
  When the bat flew from tree to tree
My love and I did walk together;
  And sweet were the words she said to me.

Along with us the summer wind
  Went murmuring—O, happily!—
But softer than the breath of summer
  Was the kiss she gave to me.

XXXII

Rain has fallen all the day.
  O come among the laden trees:
The leaves lie thick upon the way
  Of memories.

Staying a little by the way
  Of memories shall we depart.
Come, my beloved, where I may
  Speak to your heart.

XXXIII

Now, O now, in this brown land
  Where Love did so sweet music make

We two shall wander, hand in hand,
   Forbearing for old friendship' sake,
Nor grieve because our love was gay
Which now is ended in this way.

A rogue in red and yellow dress
   Is knocking, knocking at the tree;
And all around our loneliness
   The wind is whistling merrily.
The leaves—they do not sigh at all
When the year takes them in the fall.

Now, O now, we hear no more
   The vilanelle and roundelay!
Yet will we kiss, sweetheart, before
   We take sad leave at close of day.
Grieve not, sweetheart, for anything—
The year, the year is gathering.

XXXIV

Sleep now, O sleep now,
   O you unquiet heart!
A voice crying "Sleep now"
   Is heard in my heart.

The voice of the winter
   Is heard at the door.
O sleep, for the winter
   Is crying "Sleep no more."

My kiss will give peace now
   And quiet to your heart—

Sleep on in peace now,
O you unquiet heart!

XXXV

All day I hear the noise of waters
    Making moan,
Sad as the sea-bird is, when going
    Forth alone,
He hears the winds cry to the waters'
    Monotone.

The grey winds, the cold winds are blowing
    Where I go.
I hear the noise of many waters
    Far below.
All day, all night, I hear them flowing
    To and fro.

XXXVI

I hear an army charging upon the land,
    And the thunder of horses plunging, foam about their
      knees:
Arrogant, in black armour, behind them stand,
    Disdaining the reins, with fluttering whips, the
      charioteers.

They cry unto the night their battle-name:
    I moan in sleep when I hear afar their whirling
      laughter.

They cleave the gloom of dreams, a blinding flame,
  Clanging, clanging upon the heart as upon an anvil.

They come shaking in triumph their long, green hair:
  They come out of the sea and run shouting by the
    shore.
My heart, have you no wisdom thus to despair?
  My love, my love, my love, why have you left me
    alone?

Pomes Penyeach

Tilly

He travels after a winter sun,
Urging the cattle along a cold red road,
Calling to them, a voice they know,
He drives his beasts above Cabra.

The voice tells them home is warm.
They moo and make brute music with their hoofs.
He drives them with a flowering branch before him,
Smoke pluming their foreheads.

Boor, bond of the herd,
Tonight stretch full by the fire!
I bleed by the black stream
For my torn bough!

Watching the Needleboats
at San Sabba

I heard their young hearts crying
Loveward above the glancing oar
And heard the prairie grasses sighing:
No more, return no more!

O hearts, O sighing grasses,
Vainly your loveblown bannerets mourn!
No more will the wild wind that passes
Return, no more return.

A Flower Given to My Daughter

Frail the white rose and frail are
Her hands that gave
Whose soul is sere and paler
Than time's wan wave.

Rosefrail and fair—yet frailest
A wonder wild
In gentle eyes thou veilest,
My blueveined child.

She Weeps Over Rahoon

Rain on Rahoon falls softly, softly falling,
Where my dark lover lies.
Sad is his voice that calls me, sadly calling,
At grey moonrise.

Love, hear thou
How soft, how sad his voice is ever calling,
Ever unanswered and the dark rain falling,
Then as now.

Dark too our hearts, O love, shall lie and cold
As his sad heart has lain
Under the moongrey nettles, the black mould
And muttering rain.

Tutto è Sciolto

A birdless heaven, seadusk, one lone star
Piercing the west,
As thou, fond heart, love's time, so faint, so far,
Rememberest.

The clear young eyes' soft look, the candid brow,
The fragrant hair,
Falling as through the silence falleth now
Dusk of the air.

Why then, remembering those shy
Sweet lures, repine
When the dear love she yielded with a sigh
Was all but thine?

On the Beach at Fontana

Wind whines and whines the shingle,
The crazy pierstakes groan;
A senile sea numbers each single
Slimesilvered stone.

From whining wind and colder
Grey sea I wrap him warm

And touch his trembling fineboned shoulder
And boyish arm.

Around us fear, descending
Darkness of fear above
And in my heart how deep unending
Ache of love!

Simples

O bella bionda,
Sei come l'onda!

Of cool sweet dew and radiance mild
The moon a web of silence weaves
In the still garden where a child
Gathers the simple salad leaves.

A moondew stars her hanging hair
And moonlight kisses her young brow
And, gathering, she sings an air:
Fair as the wave is, fair, art thou!

Be mine, I pray, a waxen ear
To shield me from her childish croon
And mine a shielded heart for her
Who gathers simples of the moon.

Flood

Goldbrown upon the sated flood
The rockvine clusters lift and sway.

Vast wings above the lambent waters brood
Of sullen day.

A waste of waters ruthlessly
Sways and uplifts its weedy mane
Where brooding day stares down upon the sea
In dull disdain.

Uplift and sway, O golden vine,
Your clustered fruits to love's full flood,
Lambent and vast and ruthless as is thine
Incertitude!

Nightpiece

Gaunt in gloom,
The pale stars their torches,
Enshrouded, wave.
Ghostfires from heaven's far verges faint illume,
Arches on soaring arches,
Night's sindark nave.

Seraphim,
The lost hosts awaken
To service till
In moonless gloom each lapses muted, dim,
Raised when she has and shaken
Her thurible.

And long and loud,
To night's nave upsoaring,
A starknell tolls

As the bleak incense surges, cloud on cloud,
Voidward from the adoring
Waste of souls.

Alone

The moon's greygolden meshes make
All night a veil,
The shorelamps in the sleeping lake
Laburnum tendrils trail.

The sly reeds whisper to the night
A name—her name—
And all my soul is a delight,
A swoon of shame.

A Memory of the Players in a Mirror at Midnight

They mouth love's language. Gnash
The thirteen teeth
Your lean jaws grin with. Lash
Your itch and quailing, nude greed of the flesh.
Love's breath in you is stale, worded or sung,
As sour as cat's breath,
Harsh of tongue.

This grey that stares
Lies not, stark skin and bone.
Leave greasy lips their kissing. None

Will choose her what you see to mouth upon.
Dire hunger holds his hour.
Pluck forth your heart, saltblood, a fruit of tears.
Pluck and devour!

Bahnhofstrasse

The eyes that mock me sign the way
Whereto I pass at eve of day,

Grey way whose violet signals are
The trysting and the twining star.

Ah star of evil! star of pain!
Highhearted youth comes not again

Nor old heart's wisdom yet to know
The signs that mock me as I go.

A Prayer

Again!
Come, give, yield all your strength to me!
From far a low word breathes on the breaking brain
Its cruel calm, submission's misery,
Gentling her awe as to a soul predestined.
Cease, silent love! My doom!

Blind me with your dark nearness, O have mercy, be-
    loved enemy of my will!
I dare not withstand the cold touch that I dread.

Draw from me still
My slow life! Bend deeper on me, threatening head,
Proud by my downfall, remembering, pitying
Him who is, him who was!

Again!
Together, folded by the night, they lay on earth. I hear
From far her low word breathe on my breaking brain.
Come! I yield. Bend deeper upon me! I am here.
Subduer, do not leave me! Only joy, only anguish,
Take me, save me, soothe me, O spare me!

Other Poems

The Holy Office

Myself unto myself will give
This name, Katharsis-Purgative.
I, who dishevelled ways forsook
To hold the poets' grammar-book,
Bringing to tavern and to brothel
The mind of witty Aristotle,
Lest bards in the attempt should err
Must here be my interpreter:
Wherefore receive now from my lip
Peripatetic scholarship.
To enter heaven, travel hell,
Be piteous or terrible
One positively needs the ease
Of plenary indulgences.
For every true-born mysticist
A Dante is, unprejudiced,
Who safe at ingle-nook, by proxy,
Hazards extremes of heterodoxy,
Like him who finds a joy at table
Pondering the uncomfortable.
Ruling one's life by common sense
How can one fail to be intense?
But I must not accounted be
One of that mumming company—

With him who hies him to appease
His giddy dames' frivolities
While they console him when he whinges
With gold-embroidered Celtic fringes—
Or him who sober all the day
Mixes a naggin in his play—
Or him whose conduct "seems to own"
His preference for a man of "tone"—
Or him who plays the ragged patch
To millionaires in Hazelpatch
But weeping after holy fast
Confesses all his pagan past—
Or him who will his hat unfix
Neither to malt nor crucifix
But show to all that poor-dressed be
His high Castilian courtesy—
Or him who loves his Master dear—
Or him who drinks his pint in fear—
Or him who once when snug abed
Saw Jesus Christ without his head
And tried so hard to win for us
The long-lost works of Æschylus.
But all these men of whom I speak
Make me the sewer of their clique.
That they may dream their dreamy dreams
I carry off their filthy streams
For I can do those things for them
Through which I lost my diadem,
Those things for which Grandmother Church
Left me severely in the lurch.
Thus I relieve their timid arses,
Perform my office of Katharsis.
My scarlet leaves them white as wool:
Through me they purge a bellyful.
To sister mummers one and all

I act as vicar-general
And for each maiden, shy and nervous,
I do a similar kind service.
For I detect without surprise
That shadowy beauty in her eyes,
The "dare not" of sweet maidenhood
That answers my corruptive "would."
Whenever publicly we meet
She never seems to think of it;
At night when close in bed she lies
And feels my hand between her thighs
My little love in light attire
Knows the soft flame that is desire.
But Mammon places under ban
The uses of Leviathan
And that high spirit ever wars
On Mammon's countless servitors
Nor can they ever be exempt
From his taxation of contempt.
So distantly I turn to view
The shamblings of that motley crew,
Those souls that hate the strength that mine has
Steeled in the school of old Aquinas.
Where they have crouched and crawled and prayed
I stand, the self-doomed, unafraid,
Unfellowed, friendless and alone,
Indifferent as the herring-bone,
Firm as the mountain-ridges where
I flash my antlers on the air.
Let them continue as is meet
To adequate the balance-sheet.
Though they may labour to the grave
My spirit shall they never have
Nor make my soul with theirs as one
Till the Mahamanvantara be done:

And though they spurn me from their door
My soul shall spurn them evermore.

Gas from a Burner

Ladies and gents, you are here assembled
To hear why earth and heaven trembled
Because of the black and sinister arts
Of an Irish writer in foreign parts.
He sent me a book ten years ago:
I read it a hundred times or so,
Backwards and forwards, down and up,
Through both the ends of a telescope.
I printed it all to the very last word
But by the mercy of the Lord
The darkness of my mind was rent
And I saw the writer's foul intent.
But I owe a duty to Ireland:
I hold her honour in my hand,
This lovely land that always sent
Her writers and artists to banishment
And in a spirit of Irish fun
Betrayed her own leaders, one by one.
'Twas Irish humour, wet and dry,
Flung quicklime into Parnell's eye;
'Tis Irish brains that save from doom
The leaky barge of the Bishop of Rome
For everyone knows the Pope can't belch
Without the consent of Billy Walsh.
O Ireland my first and only love
Where Christ and Caesar are hand and glove!
O lovely land where the shamrock grows!
(Allow me, ladies, to blow my nose)

To show you for strictures I don't care a button
I printed the poems of Mountainy Mutton
And a play he wrote (you've read it, I'm sure)
Where they talk of *"bastard," "bugger"* and *"whore,"*
And a play on the Word and Holy Paul
And some woman's legs that I can't recall,
Written by Moore, a genuine gent
That lives on his property's ten per cent:
I printed mystical books in dozens:
I printed the table-book of Cousins
Though (asking your pardon) as for the verse
'Twould give you a heartburn on your arse:
I printed folklore from North and South
By Gregory of the Golden Mouth:
I printed poets, sad, silly and solemn:
I printed Patrick What-do-you-Colm:
I printed the great John Milicent Synge
Who soars above on an angel's wing
In the playboy shift that he pinched as swag
From Maunsel's manager's travelling-bag.
But I draw the line at that bloody fellow
That was over here dressed in Austrian yellow,
Spouting Italian by the hour
To O'Leary Curtis and John Wyse Power
And writing of Dublin, dirty and dear,
In a manner no blackamoor printer could bear.
Shite and onions! Do you think I'll print
The name of the Wellington Monument,
Sydney Parade and Sandymount tram,
Downes's cakeshop and Williams's jam?
I'm damned if I do—I'm damned to blazes!
Talk about *Irish Names of Places!*
It's a wonder to me, upon my soul,
He forgot to mention Curly's Hole.
No, ladies, my press shall have no share in

So gross a libel on Stepmother Erin.
I pity the poor—that's why I took
A red-headed Scotchman to keep my book.
Poor sister Scotland! Her doom is fell;
She cannot find any more Stuarts to sell.
My conscience is fine as Chinese silk:
My heart is as soft as buttermilk.
Colm can tell you I made a rebate
Of one hundred pounds on the estimate
I gave him for his *Irish Review*.
I love my country—by herrings I do!
I wish you could see what tears I weep
When I think of the emigrant train and ship.
That's why I publish far and wide
My quite illegible railway guide.
In the porch of my printing institute
The poor and deserving prostitute
Plays every night at catch-as-catch-can
With her tight-breeched British artilleryman
And the foreigner learns the gift of the gab
From the drunken draggletail Dublin drab.
Who was it said: Resist not evil?
I'll burn that book, so help me devil.
I'll sing a psalm as I watch it burn
And the ashes I'll keep in a one-handled urn.
I'll penance do with farts and groans
Kneeling upon my marrowbones.
This very next lent I will unbare
My penitent buttocks to the air
And sobbing beside my printing press
My awful sin I will confess.
My Irish foreman from Bannockburn
Shall dip his right hand in the urn
And sign crisscross with reverent thumb
Memento homo upon my bum.

Ecce Puer

Of the dark past
A child is born;
With joy and grief
My heart is torn.

Calm in his cradle
The living lies.
May love and mercy
Unclose his eyes!

Young life is breathed
On the glass;
The world that was not
Comes to pass.

A child is sleeping:
An old man gone.
O, father forsaken,
Forgive your son!

Ulysses

COMPOSED over a seven-year period in three
different cities, *Ulysses,* the chronicle of a fourth,
was published at Paris in 1922. It was not until 1933
that Judge John M. Woolsey, in an enlightened and
enlightening opinion of the United States District Court,
made the book legally available in this country. This
was an appropriate climax to the litigation and contro-
versy, as well as the commercial and mechanical difficulties, that had dogged every step of Joyce's way and
surrounded his masterpiece with an odyssey of its own,
unique in the annals of publishing, which Herbert Gorman has fully documented in his biography. It should be
said at once, since today *Ulysses* can easily be obtained,
that nothing can take the place of the book itself. Because of its architectural unity, its thematic continuity,
its intimate identification with personalities, its recurrent association with localities, it does not lend itself
readily to excerption. It is so rich in show-pieces of
literary technique and insights into human nature, however, that a few of them may justifiably be exhibited
here, in apologetic awareness of what is lost with their
context. Perhaps this sampling may invite some readers,
hitherto overwhelmed by the original text, to continue
their explorations. The present abbreviated comment
can scarcely pretend to do more than relate the follow-

ing passages to the scheme of the novel. It presupposes an acquaintance with Stephen Dedalus who, having returned from Paris, must now decide whether to take up his career at home or abroad. His mother's recent death has confirmed his state of spiritual orphanhood; in his restlessness he resembles Telemachus at the beginning of the *Odyssey*. But Leopold Bloom, a Dubliner who has lost his son in infancy, is the real hero of the story, though his daily round is less heroic than the wanderings of Odysseus, and his homecoming is less authoritative. The paths of these two men, the estranged artist and the ineffectual citizen, cross and recross through the day; they finally meet, but only for a leave-taking—"an instant of all but union." Meanwhile we have had, filtered through their respective minds, a series of minute-by-minute impressions of Dublin in all its aspects. Since each chapter not only covers an hour of Bloomsday, but revives an incident from Homer's epic, our selections are designated—in keeping with Joyce's manuscript—by their Homeric prototypes. Thus the modern Nestor, bumbling with advice, is headmaster of the school where Stephen is temporarily employed. Mr. Bloom makes his trip to the underworld, in a carriage with Stephen's father, by attending a funeral at Glasnevin Cemetery. The Wandering Rocks are the hazards of the streets, to which Stephen finds his sister exposed. The Sirens—who are barmaids—listen with Bloom, while a *basso profundo* renders a patriotic ballad and Joyce weaves assorted sounds into musical prose: from the hesitant tap of a blind piano-tuner to the brash jingle of his wife's lover. The closing pages are the nocturnal meditations of Mrs. Marion Tweedy Bloom, a Penelope whose unfaithfulness is redeemed by a feeling for nature and a passionately affirmative view of life.

Nestor

HE STOOD in the porch and watched the laggard hurry towards the scrappy field where sharp voices were in strife. They were sorted in teams and Mr Deasy came stepping over wisps of grass with gaitered feet. When he had reached the schoolhouse voices again contending called to him. He turned his angry white moustache.

—What is it now? he cried continually without listening.

—Cochrane and Halliday are on the same side, sir, Stephen cried.

—Will you wait in my study for a moment, Mr Deasy said, till I restore order here.

And as he stepped fussily back across the field his old man's voice cried sternly:

—What is the matter? What is it now?

Their sharp voices cried about him on all sides: their many forms closed round him, the garish sunshine bleaching the honey of his illdyed head.

Stale smoky air hung in the study with the smell of drab abraded leather of its chairs. As on the first day he bargained with me here. As it was in the beginning, is now. On the sideboard the tray of Stuart coins, base treasure of a bog: and ever shall be. And snug in their spooncase of purple plush, faded, the twelve apostles having preached to all the gentiles: world without end.

A hasty step over the stone porch and in the corridor. Blowing out his rare moustache Mr Deasy halted at the table.

—First, our little financial settlement, he said.

He brought out of his coat a pocketbook bound by a leather thong. It slapped open and he took from it two notes, one of joined halves, and laid them carefully on the table.

—Two, he said, strapping and stowing his pocketbook away.

And now his strongroom for the gold. Stephen's embarrassed hand moved over the shells heaped in the cold stone mortar: whelks and money cowries and leopard shells: and this, whorled as an emir's turban, and this, the scallop of Saint James. An old pilgrim's hoard, dead treasure, hollow shells.

A sovereign fell, bright and new, on the soft pile of the tablecloth.

—Three, Mr Deasy said, turning his little savingsbox about in his hand. These are handy things to have. See. This is for sovereigns. This is for shillings, sixpence, halfcrowns. And here crowns. See.

He shot from it two crowns and two shillings.

—Three twelve, he said. I think you'll find that's right.

—Thank you, sir, Stephen said, gathering the money together with shy haste and putting it all in a pocket of his trousers.

—No thanks at all, Mr Deasy said. You have earned it.

Stephen's hand, free again, went back to the hollow shells. Symbols too of beauty and of power. A lump in my pocket: Symbols soiled by greed and misery.

—Don't carry it like that, Mr Deasy said. You'll pull it out somewhere and lose it. You just buy one of these machines. You'll find them very handy.

Answer something.

—Mine would be often empty, Stephen said.

The same room and hour, the same wisdom: and I the same. Three times now. Three nooses round me here. Well. I can break them in this instant if I will.

—Because you don't save, Mr Deasy said, pointing his finger. You don't know yet what money is. Money is power, when you have lived as long as I have. I know, I know. If youth but knew. But what does Shakespeare say? *Put but money in thy purse.*

—Iago, Stephen murmured.

He lifted his gaze from the idle shells to the old man's stare.

—He knew what money was, Mr Deasy said. He made money. A poet but an Englishman too. Do you know what is the pride of the English? Do you know what is the proudest word you will ever hear from an Englishman's mouth?

The seas' ruler. His seacold eyes looked on the empty bay: history is to blame: on me and on my words, unhating.

—That on his empire, Stephen said, the sun never sets.

—Ba! Mr Deasy cried. That's not English. A French Celt said that.

He tapped his savingsbox against his thumbnail.

—I will tell you, he said solemnly, what is his proudest boast. *I paid my way.*

Good man, good man.

—*I paid my way. I never borrowed a shilling in my life.* Can you feel that? *I owe nothing.* Can you?

Mulligan, nine pounds, three pairs of socks, one pair brogues, ties. Curran, ten guineas. McCann, one guinea. Fred Ryan, two shillings. Temple, two lunches. Russell, one guinea, Cousins, ten shillings, Bob Reynolds, half a guinea, Köhler, three guineas, Mrs McKernan, five week's board. The lump I have is useless.

—For the moment, no, Stephen answered.

Mr Deasy laughed with rich delight, putting back his savingsbox.

—I knew you couldn't, he said joyously. But one day you must feel it. We are a generous people but we must also be just.

—I fear those big words, Stephen said, which make us so unhappy.

Mr Deasy stared sternly for some moments over the mantelpiece at the shapely bulk of a man in tartan fillibegs: Albert Edward, Prince of Wales.

—You think me an old fogey and an old tory, his thoughtful voice said. I saw three generations since O'Connell's time. I remember the famine. Do you know that the orange lodges agitated for repeal of the union twenty years before O'Connell did or before the prelates of your communion denounced him as a demagogue? You fenians forget some things.

Glorious, pious and immortal memory. The lodge of Diamond in Armagh the splendid behung with corpses of papishes. Hoarse, masked and armed, the planters covenant. The black north and true blue bible. Croppies lie down.

Stephen sketched a brief gesture.

—I have rebel blood in me too, Mr Deasy said. On the spindle side. But I am descended from sir John Blackwood who voted for the union. We are all Irish, all kings' sons.

—Alas, Stephen said.

—*Per vias rectas*, Mr Deasy said firmly, was his motto. He voted for it and put on his topboots to ride to Dublin from the Ards of Down to do so.

Lal the ral the ra
The rocky road to Dublin.

A gruff squire on horseback with shiny topboots. Soft day, sir John. Soft day, your honour . . . Day . . . Day . . . Two topboots jog dangling on to Dublin. Lal the ral the ra, lal the ral the raddy.

—That reminds me, Mr Deasy said. You can do me a favour, Mr Dedalus, with some of your literary friends. I have a letter here for the press. Sit down a moment. I have just to copy the end.

He went to the desk near the window, pulled in his chair twice and read off some words from the sheet on the drum of his typewriter.

—Sit down. Excuse me, he said over his shoulder, *the dictates of common sense.* Just a moment.

He peered from under his shaggy brows at the manuscript by his elbow and, muttering, began to prod the stiff buttons of the keyboard slowly, some times blowing as he screwed up the drum to crase an error.

Stephen seated himself noiselessly before the princely presence. Framed around the walls images of vanished horses stood in homage, their meek heads poised in air: lord Hastings' Repulse, the duke of Westminster's Shotover, the duke of Beaufort's Ceylon, *prix de Paris,* 1866. Elfin riders sat them, watchful of a sign. He saw their speeds, backing king's colours, and shouted with the shouts of vanished crowds.

—Full stop, Mr Deasy bade his keys. But prompt ventilation of this important question . . .

Where Cranly led me to get rich quick, hunting his winners among the mudsplashed brakes, amid the bawls of bookies on their pitches and reek of the canteen, over the motley slush. Even money Fair Rebel: ten to one the field. Dicers and thimble riggers we hurried by after the hoofs, the vying caps and jackets and past the meatfaced woman, a butcher's dame, nuzzling thirstily her clove of orange.

Shouts rang shrill from the boy's playfield and a whir-ring whistle.

Again: a goal. I am among them, among their battling bodies in a medley, the joust of life. You mean that knockkneed mother's darling who seems to be slightly crawsick? Jousts. Time shocked rebounds, shock by shock. Jousts, slush and uproar of battles, the frozen deathspew of the slain, a shout of spear spikes baited with men's bloodied guts.

—Now then, Mr Deasy said, rising.

He came to the table, pinning together his sheets. Stephen stood up.

—I have put the matter into a nutshell, Mr Deasy said. It's about the foot and mouth disease. Just look through it. There can be no two opinions on the matter.

May I trespass on your valuable space. That doctrine of *laissez faire* which so often in our history. Our cattle trade. The way of all our old industries. Liverpool ring which jockeyed the Galway harbour scheme. European conflagration. Grain supplies through the narrow waters of the channel. The pluterperfect imperturbability of the department of agriculture. Pardoned a classical al-lusion. Cassandra. By a woman who was no better than she should be. To come to the point at issue.

—I don't mince words, do I? Mr Deasy asked as Stephen read on.

Foot and mouth disease. Known as Koch's prepara-tion. Serum and virus. Percentage of salted horses. Rinderpest. Emperor's horses at Mürzsteg, lower Aus-tria. Veterinary surgeons. Mr Henry Blackwôod Price. Courteous offer a fair trial. Dictates of common sense. Allimportant question. In every sense of the word take the bull by the horns. Thanking you for the hospitality of your columns.

—I want that to be printed and read, Mr Deasy said.

You will see at the next outbreak they will put an em-
bargo on Irish cattle. And it can be cured. It is cured.
My cousin, Blackwood Price, writes to me it is regularly
treated and cured in Austria by cattledoctors there.
They offer to come over here. I am trying to work up
influence with the department. Now I'm going to try
publicity. I'm surrounded by difficulties, by . . . intrigues, by . . . backstairs influence, by. . . .

He raised his forefinger and beat the air oldly before
his voice spoke.

—Mark my words, Mr Dedalus, he said. England is
in the hands of the jews. In all the highest places: her
finance, her press. And they are the signs of a nation's
decay. Wherever they gather they eat up the nation's
vital strength. I have seen it coming these years. As sure
as we are standing here the jew merchants are already
at their work of destruction. Old England is dying.

He stepped swiftly off, his eyes coming to blue life
as they passed a broad sunbeam. He faced about and
back again.

—Dying, he said, if not dead by now.

> The harlot's cry from street to street
> Shall weave old England's winding sheet.

His eyes open wide in vision stared sternly across the
sunbeam in which he halted.

—A merchant, Stephen said, is one who buys cheap
and sells dear, jew or gentile, is he not?

—They sinned against the light, Mr Deasy said
gravely. And you can see the darkness in their eyes. And
that is why they are wanderers on the earth to this day.

On the steps of the Paris Stock Exchange the gold-
skinned men quoting prices on their gemmed fingers.
Gabbles of geese. They swarmed loud, uncouth about
the temple, their heads thickplotting under maladroit

silk hats. Not theirs: these clothes, this speech, these gestures. Their full slow eyes belied the words, the gestures eager and unoffending, but knew the rancours massed about them and knew their zeal was vain. Vain patience to heap and hoard. Time surely would scatter all. A hoard heaped by the roadside: plundered and passing on. Their eyes knew the years of wandering and, patient, knew the dishonours of their flesh.

—Who has not? Stephen said.

—What do you mean? Mr Deasy asked.

He came forward a pace and stood by the table. His underjaw fell sideways open uncertainly. Is this old wisdom? He waits to hear from me.

—History, Stephen said, is a nightmare from which I am trying to awake.

From the playfield the boys raised a shout. A whirring whistle: goal. What if that nightmare gave you a back kick?

—The ways of the Creator are not our ways, Mr Deasy said. All history moves towards one great goal, the manifestation of God.

Stephen jerked his thumb towards the window, saying:

—That is God.

Hooray! Ay! Whrrwhee!

—What? Mr Deasy asked.

—A shout in the street, Stephen answered, shrugging his shoulders.

Mr Deasy looked down and held for a while the wings of his nose tweaked between his fingers. Looking up again he set them free.

—I am happier than you are, he said. We have committed many errors and many sins. A woman brought sin into the world. For a woman who was no better than she should be, Helen, the runaway wife of Menelaus,

ten years the Greeks made war on Troy. A faithless wife
first brought the strangers to our shore here, MacMur-
rough's wife and her leman O'Rourke, prince of Breffni.
A woman too brought Parnell low. Many errors, many
failures but not the one sin. I am a struggler now at the
end of my days. But I will fight for the right till the end.

> *For Ulster will fight*
> *And Ulster will be right.*

Stephen raised the sheets in his hand.

—Well, sir, he began.

—I foresee, Mr Deasy said, that you will not remain
here very long at this work. You were not born to be a
teacher, I think. Perhaps I am wrong.

—A learner rather, Stephen said.

And here what will you learn more?

Mr Deasy shook his head.

—Who knows? he said. To learn one must be humble.
But life is the great teacher.

Stephen rustled the sheets again.

—As regards these, he began.

—Yes, Mr Deasy said. You have two copies there. If
you can have them published at once.

Telegraph, Irish Homestead.

—I will try, Stephen said, and let you know tomorrow. I know two editors slightly.

—That will do, Mr Deasy said briskly. I wrote last
night to Mr Field, M. P. There is a meeting of the
cattletraders' association today at the City Arms Hotel.
I asked him to lay my letter before the meeting. You
see if you can get it into your two papers. What are
they?

—*The Evening Telegraph* . . .

That will do, Mr Deasy said. There is no time to lose.
Now I have to answer that letter from my cousin.

—Good morning, sir, Stephen said, putting the sheets in his pocket. Thank you.

—Not at all, Mr Deasy said as he searched the papers on his desk. I like to break a lance with you, old as I am.

—Good morning, sir, Stephen said again, bowing to his bent back.

He went out by the open porch and down the gravel path under the trees, hearing the cries of voices and crack of sticks from the playfield. The lions couchant on the pillars as he passed out through the gate; toothless terrors. Still I will help him in his fight. Mulligan will dub me a new name; the bullockbefriending bard.

—Mr Dedalus!

Running after me. No more letters, I hope.

—Just one moment.

—Yes, sir, Stephen said, turning back at the gate.

Mr Deasy halted, breathing hard and swallowing his breath.

—I just wanted to say, he said. Ireland, they say, has the honour of being the only country which never persecuted the jews. Do you know that? No. And do you know why?

He frowned sternly on the bright air.

—Why, sir? Stephen asked, beginning to smile.

—Because she never let them in, Mr Deasy said solemnly.

A coughball of laughter leaped from his throat dragging after it a rattling chain of phlegm. He turned back quickly, coughing, laughing, his lifted arms waving to the air.

—She never let them in, he cried again through his laughter as he stamped on gaitered feet over the gravel of the path. That's why.

On his wise shoulders through the checkerwork of leaves the sun flung spangles, dancing coins.

Hades

THE high railings of Prospects rippled past their gaze. Dark poplars, rare white forms. Forms more frequent, white shapes thronged amid the trees, white fôrms and fragments streaming by mutely, sustaining vain gestures on the air.

The felly harshed against the curbstone: stopped. Martin Cunningham put out his arm and, wrenching back the handle, shoved the door open with his knee. He stepped out. Mr Power and Mr Dedalus followed.

Change that soap now. Mr Bloom's hand unbuttoned his hip pocket swiftly and transferred the paperstuck soap to his inner handkerchief pocket. He stepped out of the carriage, replacing the newspaper his other hand still held.

Paltry funeral: coach and three carriages. It's all the same. Pallbearers, gold reins, requiem mass, firing a volley. Pomp of death. Beyond the hind carriage a hawker stood by his barrow of cakes and fruit. Simnel cakes those are, stuck together: cakes for the dead. Dogbiscuits. Who ate them? Mourners coming out.

He followed his companions. Mr Kernan and Ned Lambert followed, Hynes walking after them. Corny Kelleher stood by the opened hearse and took out the two wreaths. He handed one to the boy.

Where is that child's funeral disappeared to?

A team of horses passed from Finglas with toiling plodding tread, dragging through the funereal silence a creaking wagon on which lay a granite block. The waggoner marching at their head saluted.

Coffin now. Got here before us, dead as he is. Horse looking round at it with his plume skeowways. Dull eye: collar tight on his neck, pressing on a bloodvessel or something. Do they know what they cart out here every day? Must be twenty or thirty funerals every day. Then Mount Jerome for the protestants. Funerals all over the world everywhere every minute. Shovelling them under by the cartload doublequick. Thousands every hour. Too many in the world.

Mourners came out through the gates: woman and a girl. Leanjawed harpy, hard woman at a bargain, her bonnet awry. Girl's face stained with dirt and tears, holding the woman's arm looking up at her for a sign to cry. Fish's face, bloodless and livid.

The mutes shouldered the coffin and bore it in through the gates. So much dead weight. Felt heavier myself stepping out of that bath. First the stiff: then the friends of the stiff. Corny Kelleher and the boy followed with their wreaths. Who is that beside them? Ah, the brother-in-law.

All walked after.

Martin Cunningham whispered:

—I was in mortal agony with you talking of suicide before Bloom.

—What? Mr Power whispered. How so?

—His father poisoned himself, Martin Cunningham whispered. Had the Queen's hotel in Ennis. You heard him say he was going to Clare. Anniversary.

—O God! Mr Power whispered. First I heard of it. Poisoned himself!

He glanced behind him to where a face with dark
thinking eyes followed towards the cardinal's mauso-
leum. Speaking.

—Was he insured? Mr Bloom asked.

—I believe so, Mr Kernan answered, but the policy
was heavily mortgaged. Martin is trying to get the
youngster into Artane.

—How many children did he leave?

—Five. Ned Lambert says he'll try to get one of the
girls into Todd's.

—A sad case, Mr Bloom said gently. Five young children.

—A great blow to the poor wife, Mr Kernan added.

—Indeed yes, Mr Bloom agreed.

Has the laugh at him now.

He looked down at the boots he had blacked and
polished. She had outlived him, lost her husband. More
dead for her than for me. One must outlive the other.
Wise men say. There are more women than men in the
world. Condole with her. Your terrible loss. I hope you'll
soon follow him. For Hindu widows only. She would
marry another. Him? No. Yet who knows after? Widow-
hood not the thing since the old queen died. Drawn on
a guncarriage. Victoria and Albert. Frogmore memorial
mourning. But in the end she put a few violets in her
bonnet. Vain in her heart of hearts. All for a shadow.
Consort not even a king. Her son was the substance.
Something new to hope for not like the past she wanted
back, waiting. It never comes. One must go first: alone
under the ground: and lie no more in her warm bed.

—How are you, Simon? Ned Lambert said softly,
clasping hands. Haven't seen you for a month of Sundays.

—Never better. How are all in Cork's own town?

—I was down there for the Cork park races on Easter
Monday, Ned Lambert said. Same old six and eight-
pence. Stopped with Dick Tivy.

—And how is Dick, the solid man?

—Nothing between himself and heaven, Ned Lambert answered.

—By the holy Paul! Mr Dedalus said in subdued
wonder. Dick Tivy bald?

—Martin is going to get up a whip for the youngsters,
Ned Lambert said, pointing ahead. A few bob a skull.
Just to keep them going till the insurance is cleared up.

—Yes, yes, Mr Dedalus said dubiously. Is that the
eldest boy in front?

—Yes, Ned Lambert said, with the wife's brother.
John Henry Menton is behind. He put down his name
for a quid.

—I'll engage he did, Mr Dedalus said. I often told
poor Paddy he ought to mind that job. John Henry is
not the worst in the world.

—How did he lose it? Ned Lambert asked. Liquor,
what?

—Many a good man's fault, Mr Dedalus said with a
sigh.

They halted about the door of the mortuary chapel.
Mr Bloom stood behind the boy with the wreath, looking down at his sleek combed hair and the slender fur-
rowed neck inside his brandnew collar. Poor boy! Was
he there when the father? Both unconscious. Lighten up
at the last moment and recognise for the last time. All
he might have done. I owe three shillings to O'Grady.
Would he understand? The mutes bore the coffin into
the chapel. Which end is his head?

After a moment he followed the others in, blinking in
the screened light. The coffin lay on its bier before the
chancel four tall yellow candles at its corners. Always

in front of us. Corny Kelleher, laying a wreath at each
fore corner, beckoned to the boy to kneel. The mourners
knelt here and there in praying desks. Mr Bloom stood
behind near the font and, when all had knelt dropped
carefully his unfolded newspaper from his pocket and
knelt his right knee upon it. He fitted his black hat
gently on his left knee and, holding its brim, bent over
piously.

A server, bearing a brass bucket with something in it,
came out through a door. The whitesmocked priest
came after him tidying his stole with one hand, balancing with the other a little book against his toad's
belly. Who'll read the book? I, said the rook.

They halted by the bier and the priest began to read
out of his book with a fluent croak.

Father Coffey. I knew his name was like a coffin.
Dominenamine. Bully about the muzzle he looks. Bosses
the show. Muscular christian. Woe betide anyone that
looks crooked at him: priest. Thou art Peter. Burst sideways like a sheep in clover Dedalus says he will. With
a belly on him like a poisoned pup. Most amusing expressions that man finds. Hhhn: burst sideways.

—*Non intres in judicium cum servo tuo, Domine.*

Makes them feel more important to be prayed over
in Latin. Requiem mass. Crape weepers. Blackedged
notepaper. Your name on the altarlist. Chilly place this.
Want to feed well, sitting in there all the morning in the
gloom kicking his heels waiting for the next please. Eyes
of a toad too. What swells him up that way? Molly gets
swelled after cabbage. Air of the place maybe. Looks
full of bad gas. Must be an infernal lot of bad gas round
the place. Butchers for instance: they get like raw beefsteaks. Who was telling me? Mervyn Brown. Down in
the vaults of saint Werburgh's lovely old organ hundred
and fifty they have to bore a hole in the coffins some-

times to let out the bad gas and burn it. Out it rushes: blue. One whiff of that and you're a goner.

My kneecap is hurting me. Ow. That's better.

The priest took a stick with a knob at the end of it out of the boy's bucket and shook it over the coffin. Then he walked to the other end and shook it again. Then he came back and put it back in the bucket. As you were before you rested. It's all written down: he has to do it.

—*Et ne nos inducas in tentationem.*

The server piped the answers in the treble. I often thought it would be better to have boy servants. Up to fifteen or so. After that of course. . .

Holy water that was, I expect. Shaking sleep out of it. He must be fed up with that job, shaking that thing over all the corpses they trot up. What harm if he could see what he was shaking it over. Every mortal day a fresh batch: middleaged men, old women, children, women dead in childbirth, men with beards, baldheaded business men, consumptive girls with little sparrow's breasts. All the year round he prayed the same thing over them all and shook water on top of them: sleep. On Dignam now.

—*In paradisum.*

Said he was going to paradise or is in paradise. Says that over everybody. Tiresome kind of a job. But he has to say something.

The priest closed his book and went off, followed by the server. Corny Kelleher opened the sidedoors and the gravediggers came in, hoisted the coffin again, carried it out and shoved it on their cart. Corny Kelleher gave one wreath to the boy and one to the brother-in-law. All followed them out of the sidedoors into the mild grey air. Mr Bloom came last, folding his paper again into his pocket. He gazed gravely at the ground till the coffin-cart wheeled off to the left. The metal wheels ground the gravel with a sharp grating cry and the pack of blunt boots followed the barrow along a lane of sepulchres.

The ree the ra the ree the ra the roo. Lord. I mustn't lilt here.

—The O'Connell circle, Mr Dedalus said about him.

Mr Power's soft eyes went up to the apex of the lofty cone.

—He's at rest, he said, in the middle of his people, old Dan O'. But his heart is buried in Rome. How many broken hearts are buried here, Simon!

—Her grave is over there, Jack, Mr Dedalus said. I'll soon be stretched beside her. Let Him take me whenever He likes.

Breaking down, he began to weep to himself quietly, stumbling a little in his walk. Mr Power took his arm.

—She's better where she is, he said kindly.

—I suppose so, Mr Dedalus said with a weak gasp. I suppose she is in heaven if there is a heaven.

Corny Kelleher stepped aside from his rank and allowed the mourners to plod by.

—Sad occasions, Mr Kernan began politely.

Mr Bloom closed his eyes and sadly twice bowed his head.

—The others are putting on their hats, Mr Kernan said. I suppose we can do so too. We are the last. This cemetery is a treacherous place.

They covered their heads.

—The reverend gentleman read the service too quickly, don't you think? Mr Kernan said with reproof.

Mr Bloom nodded gravely, looking in the quick bloodshot eyes. Secret eyes, secret searching eyes. Mason, I think: not sure. Beside him again. We are the last. In the same boat. Hope he'll say something else.

Mr Kernan added:

—The service of the Irish church, used in Mount Jerome, is simpler, more impressive, I must say.

Mr Bloom gave prudent assent. The language of course was another thing.

Mr Kernan said with solemnity:

—*I am the resurrection and the life.* That touches a man's inmost heart.

—It does, Mr Bloom said.

Your heart perhaps but what price the fellow in the six feet by two with his toes to the daisies? No touching that. Seat of the affections. Broken heart. A pump after all, pumping thousands of gallons of blood every day. One fine day it gets bunged up and there you are. Lots of them lying around here: lungs, hearts, livers. Old rusty pumps: damn the thing else. The resurrection and the life. Once you are dead you are dead. That last day idea. Knocking them all up out of their graves. Come forth, Lazarus! And he came fifth and lost the job. Get up! Last day! Then every fellow mousing around for his liver and his lights and the rest of his traps. Find damn all of himself that morning. Pennyweight of powder in a skull. Twelve grammes one pennyweight. Troy measure.

Corny Kelleher fell into step at their side.

—Everything went off A 1, he said. What?

He looked on them from his drawling eye. Policeman's shoulders. With your tooraloom tooraloom.

—As it should be, Mr Kernan said.

—What? Eh? Corny Kelleher said.

Mr Kernan assured him.

—Who is that chap behind with Tom Kernan? John Henry Menton asked. I know his face.

Ned Lambert glanced back.

—Bloom, he said, Madam Marion Tweedy that was, is, I mean, the soprano. She's his wife.

—O, to be sure, John Henry Menton said. I haven't seen her for some time. She was a finelooking woman. I danced with her, wait, fifteen seventeen golden years ago, at Mat Dillon's, in Roundtown. And a good armful she was.

He looked behind through the others.

—What is he? he asked. What does he do? Wasn't he in the stationery line? I fell foul of him one evening, I remember, at bowls.

Ned Lambert smiled.

—Yes, he was, he said, in Wisdom Hely's. A traveller for blottingpaper.

—In God's name, John Henry Menton said, what did she marry a coon like that for? She had plenty of game in her then.

—Has still, Ned Lambert said. He does some canvassing for ads.

John Henry Menton's large eyes stared ahead.

The barrow turned into a side lane. A portly man, ambushed among the grasses, raised his hat in homage. The gravediggers touched their caps.

—John O'Connell, Mr Power said, pleased. He never forgets a friend.

Mr O'Connell shook all their hands in silence. Mr Dedalus said:

—I am come to pay you another visit.

—My dear Simon, the caretaker answered in a low voice. I don't want your custom at all.

Saluting Ned Lambert and John Henry Menton he walked on at Martin Cunningham's side, puzzling two keys at his back.

—Did you hear that one, he asked them, about Mulcahy from the Coombe?

—I did not, Martin Cunningham said.

They bent their silk hats in concert and Hynes inclined his ear. The caretaker hung his thumbs in the loops of his gold watch chain and spoke in a discreet tone to their vacant smiles.

—They tell the story, he said, that two drunks came out here one foggy evening to look for the grave of a friend of theirs. They asked for Mulcahy from the Coombe and were told where he was buried. After traipsing about in the fog they found the grave, sure enough. One of the drunks spelt out the name: Terence Mulcahy. The other drunk was blinding up at a statue of our Saviour the widow had got put up.

The caretaker blinked up at one of the sepulchres they passed. He resumed:

—And, after blinking up at the sacred figure, *Not a bloody bit like the man,* says he. *That's not Mulcahy,* says he, *whoever done it.*

Rewarded by smiles he fell back and spoke with Corny Kelleher, accepting the dockets given him, turning them over and scanning them as he walked.

—That's all done with a purpose, Martin Cunningham explained to Hynes.

—I know, Hynes said, I know that.

—To cheer a fellow up, Martin Cunningham said. It's pure goodheartedness: damn the thing else.

Mr Bloom admired the caretaker's prosperous bulk. All want to be on good terms with him. Decent fellow, John O'Connell, real good sort. Keys: like Keyes's ad: no fear of anyone getting out, no passout checks. *Habeas corpus.* I must see about that ad after the funeral. Did I write Ballsbridge on the envelope I took to cover when she disturbed me writing to Martha? Hope it's not chucked in the dead letter office. Be the better of a shave. Grey sprouting beard. That's the first sign when the hairs come out grey and temper getting cross. Silver threads among the grey. Fancy being his wife. Wonder

how he had the gumption to propose to any girl. Come
out and live in the graveyard. Dangle that before her. It
might thrill her first. Courting death . . . Shades of
night hovering here with all the dead stretched about.
The shadows of the tombs when churchyards yawn and
Daniel O'Connell must be a descendant I suppose who
is this used to say he was a queer breedy man great
catholic all the same like a big giant in the dark. Will o'
the wisp. Gas of graves. Want to keep her mind off it to
conceive at all. Women especially are so touchy. Tell
her a ghost story in bed to make her sleep. Have you
ever seen a ghost? Well, I have. It was pitchdark night.
The clock was on the stroke of twelve. Still they'd kiss
all right if properly keyed up. Whores in Turkish grave-
yards. Learn anything if taken young. You might pick
up a young widow here. Men like that. Love among the
tombstones. Romeo. Spice of pleasure. In the midst of
death we are in life. Both ends meet. Tantalising for the
poor dead. Smell of grilled beefsteaks to the starving
gnawing their vitals. Desire to grig people. Molly wanting to do it at the window. Eight children he has anyway.

He has seen a fair share go under in his time, lying
around him field after field. Holy fields. More room if
they buried them standing. Sitting or kneeling you
couldn't. Standing? His head might come up some day
above ground in a landslip with his hand pointing. All
honeycombed the ground must be: oblong cells. And
very neat he keeps it too, trim grass and edgings. His
garden Major Gamble calls Mount Jerome. Well so it is.
Ought to be flowers of sleep. Chinese cemeteries with
giant poppies growing produce the best opium Mastian-
sky told me. The Botanic Gardens are just over there.
It's the blood sinking in the earth gives new life. Same
idea those jews they said killed the christian boy. Every

man his price. Well preserved fat corpse gentlemen,
epicure, invaluable for fruit garden. A bargain. By car-
cass of William Wilkinson, auditor and accountant, lately
deceased, three pounds thirteen and six With thanks.

I daresay the soil would be quite fat with corpse
manure, bones, flesh, nails, charnelhouses. Dreadful.
Turning green and pink, decomposing. Rot quick in
damp earth. The lean old ones tougher. Then a kind of
a tallowy kind of a cheesy. Then begin to get black,
treacle oozing out of them. Then dried up. Deathmoths.
Of course the cells or whatever they are go on living.
Changing about. Live for ever practically. Nothing to
feed on feed on themselves.

But they must breed a devil of a lot of maggots. Soil
must be simply swirling with them. Your head it simply
swurls. Those pretty little seaside gurls. He looks cheerful enough over it. Gives him a sense of power seeing
all the others go under first. Wonder how he looks at
life. Cracking his jokes too: warms the cockles of his
heart. The one about the bulletin. Spurgeon went to
heaven 4 a. m. this morning. 11 p. m. (closing time).
Not arrived yet. Peter. The dead themselves the
men anyhow would like to hear an odd joke or the
women to know what's in fashion. A juicy pear or ladies'
punch, hot, strong and sweet. Keep out of the damp.
You must laugh sometimes so better do it that way.
Gravediggers in *Hamlet*. Shows the profound knowledge of the human heart. Daren't joke about the dead
for two years at least. *De mortuis nil nisi prius.* Go out
of mourning first. Hard to imagine his funeral. Seems a
sort of a joke. Read your own obituary notice they say
you live longer. Gives you second wind. New lease of
life.

—How many have you for tomorrow? the caretaker
asked.

—Two, Corny Kelleher said. Half ten and eleven.

The caretaker put the papers in his pocket. The barrow had ceased to trundle. The mourners split and moved to each side of the hole, stepping with care round the graves. The gravediggers bore the coffin and set its nose on the brink, looping the bands round it.

Burying him. We come to bury Caesar. His ides of March or June. He doesn't know who is here nor care.

Now who is that lankylooking galoot over there in the macintosh? Now who is he I'd like to know? Now, I'd give a trifle to know who he is. Always someone turns up you never dreamt of. A fellow could live on his lonesome all his life. Yes, he could. Still he'd have to get someone to sod him after he died though he could dig his own grave. We all do. Only man buries. No ants too. First thing strikes anybody. Bury the dead. Say Robinson Crusoe was true to life. Well then Friday buried him. Every Friday buries a Thursday if you come to look at it.

> O, poor Robinson Crusoe,
> How could you possibly do so?

Poor Dignam! His last lie on the earth in his box. When you think of them all it does seem a waste of wood. All gnawed through. They could invent a handsome bier with a kind of panel sliding let it down that way. Ay but they might object to be buried out of another fellow's. They're so particular. Lay me in my native earth. Bit of clay from the holy land. Only a mother and deadborn child ever buried in the one coffin. I see what it means. I see. To protect him as long as possible even in the earth. The Irishman's house is his coffin. Embalming in catacombs, mummies, the same idea.

Mr Bloom stood far back, his hat in his hand, counting the bared heads. Twelve. I'm thirteen. No. The chap

in the macintosh is thirteen. Death's number. Where the
deuce did he pop out of? He wasn't in the chapel, that
I'll swear. Silly superstition that about thirteen.

Nice soft tweed Ned Lambert has in that suit. Tinge
of purple. I had one like that when we lived in Lombard
street west. Dressy fellow he was once. Used to change
three suits in the day. Must get that grey suit of mine
turned by Mesias. Hello. It's dyed. His wife I forgot he's
not married or his landlady ought to have picked out
those threads for him.

The coffin dived out of sight, eased down by the men
straddled on the gravetrestles. They struggled up and
out: and all uncovered. Twenty.

Pause.

If we were all suddenly somebody else.

Far away a donkey brayed. Rain. No such ass. Never
see a dead one, they say. Shame of death. They hide.
Also poor papa went away.

Gentle sweet air blew round the bared heads in a
whisper. Whisper. The boy by the gravehead held his
wreath with both hands staring quietly in the black open
space. Mr Bloom moved behind the portly kindly caretaker. Well cut frockcoat. Weighing them up perhaps to
see which will go next. Well it is a long rest. Feel no
more. It's the moment you feel. Must be damned unpleasant. Can't believe it at first. Mistake must be: someone else. Try the house opposite. Wait, I wanted to I
haven't yet. Then darkened deathchamber. Light they
want. Whispering around you. Would you like to see a
priest? Then rambling and wandering. Delirium all you
hid all your life. The death struggle. His sleep is not
natural. Press his lower eyelid. Watching is his nose
pointed is his jaw sinking are the soles of his feet yellow.
Pull the pillow away and finish it off on the floor since

he's doomed. Devil in that picture of sinner's death showing him a woman. Dying to embrace her in his shirt. Last act of *Lucia. Shall I nevermore behold thee?* Bam! expires. Gone at last. People talk about you a bit: forget you. Don't forget to pray for him. Remember him in your prayers. Even Parnell. Ivy day dying out. Then they follow: dropping into a hole one after the other.

We are praying now for the repose of his soul. Hoping you're well and not in hell. Nice change of air. Out of the fryingpan of life into the fire of purgatory.

Does he ever think of the hole waiting for himself? They say you do when you shiver in the sun. Someone walking over it. Callboy's warning. Near you. Mine over there towards Finglas, the plot I bought. Mamma poor mamma, and little Rudy.

The gravediggers took up their spades and flung heavy clods of clay in on the coffin. Mr Bloom turned his face. And if he was alive all the time? Whew! By Jingo, that would be awful! No, no: he is dead, of course. Of course he is dead. Monday he died. They ought to have some law to pierce the heart and make sure or an electric clock or a telephone in the coffin and some kind of a canvas airhole. Flag of distress. Three days. Rather long to keep them in summer. Just as well to get shut of them as soon as you are sure there's no.

The clay fell softer. Begin to be forgotten. Out of sight, out of mind.

The caretaker moved away a few paces and put on his hat. Had enough of it. The mourners took heart of grace, one by one, covering themselves without show. Mr Bloom put on his hat and saw the portly figure make its way deftly through the maze of graves. Quietly, sure of his ground, he traversed the dismal fields.

Hynes jotting down something in his notebook. Ah,

the names. But he knows them all. No: coming to me.

—I am just taking the names, Hynes said below his breath. What is your christian name? I'm not sure.

—L, Mr Bloom said. Leopold. And you might put down M'Coy's name too. He asked me to.

—Charley, Hynes said writing. I know. He was on the *Freeman* once.

So he was before he got the job in the morgue under Louis Byrne. Good idea a postmortem for doctors. Find out what they imagine they know. He died on a Tuesday. Got the run. Levanted with the cash of a few ads. Charley, you're my darling. That was why he asked me to. O well, does no harm. I saw to that, M'Coy. Thanks, old chap: much obliged. Leave him under an obligation: costs nothing.

—And tell us, Hynes said, do you know that fellow in the, fellow was over there in the. . .

He looked around.

—Macintosh. Yes, I saw him, Mr Bloom said. Where is he now?

—Macintosh, Hynes said, scribbling. I don't know who he is. Is that his name?

He moved away, looking about him.

—No, Mr Bloom began, turning and stopping. I say, Hynes!

Didn't hear. What? Where has he disappeared to? Not a sign. Well of all the. Has anybody here seen? Kay ee double ell. Become invisible. Good Lord, what became of him?

A seventh gravedigger came beside Mr Bloom to take up an idle spade.

—O, excuse me!

He stepped aside nimbly.

Clay, brown, damp, began to be seen in the hole. It rose. Nearly over. A mound of damp clods rose more,

rose, and the gravediggers rested their spades. All uncovered again for a few instants. The boy propped his
wreath against a corner: the brother-in-law his on a
lump. The gravediggers put on their caps and carried
their earthy spades towards the barrow. Then knocked
the blades lightly on the turf: clean. One bent to pluck
from the haft a long tuft of grass. One, leaving his
mates, walked slowly on with shouldered weapon, its
blade blueglancing. Silently at the gravehead another
coiled the coffinband. His navelcord. The brother-in-
law, turning away, placed something in his free hand.
Thanks in silence. Sorry, sir: trouble. Headshake. I know
that. For yourselves just.

The mourners moved away slowly, without aim, by
devious paths, staying awhile to read a name on a tomb.

—Let us go round by the chief's grave, Hynes said.
We have time.

—Let us, Mr Power said.

They turned to the right, following their slow
thoughts. With awe Mr Power's blank voice spoke:

—Some say he is not in that grave at all. That the
coffin was filled with stones. That one day he will come
again.

Hynes shook his head.

—Parnell will never come again, he said. He's there, all
that was mortal of him. Peace to his ashes.

Mr Bloom walked unheeded along his grove by saddened angels, crosses, broken pillars, family vaults, stone
hopes praying with upcast eyes, old Ireland's hearts and
hands. More sensible to spend the money on some charity for the living. Pray for the repose of the soul of. Does
anybody really? Plant him and have done with him.
Like down a coalshoot. Then lump them together to
save time. All souls' day. Twentyseventh I'll be at his
grave. Ten shillings for the gardener. He keeps it free

of weeds. Old man himself. Bent down double with his shears clipping. Near death's door. Who passed away. Who departed this life. As if they did it of their own accord. Got the shove, all of them. Who kicked the bucket. More interesting if they told you what they were. So and so, wheelwright. I travelled for cork lino. I paid five shillings in the pound. Or a woman's with her saucepan. I cooked good Irish stew. Eulogy in a country churchyard it ought to be that poem of whose is it Wordsworth or Thomas Campbell. Entered into rest the protestants put it. Old Dr Murren's. The great physician called him home. Well it's God's acre for them. Nice country residence. Newly plastered and painted. Ideal spot to have a quiet smoke and read the *Church Times*. Marriage ads they never try to beautify. Rusty wreaths hung on knobs, garlands of bronzefoil. Better value that for the money. Still, the flowers are more poetical. The other gets rather tiresome, never withering. Expresses nothing. Immortelles.

A bird sat tamely perched on a poplar branch. Like stuffed. Like the wedding present alderman Hooper gave us. Hu! Not a budge out of him. Knows there are no catapults to let fly at him. Dead animal even sadder. Silly-Milly burying the little dead bird in the kitchen matchbox, a daisychain and bits of broken chainies on the grave.

The Sacred Heart that is: showing it. Heart on his sleeve. Ought to be sideways and red it should be painted like a real heart. Ireland was dedicated to it or whatever that. Seems anything but pleased. Why this infliction? Would birds come then and peck like the boy with the basket of fruit but he said no because they ought to have been afraid of the boy. Apollo that was.

How many! All these here once walked round Dublin. Faithful departed. As you are now so once were we.

Besides how could you remember everybody? Eyes, walk, voice. Well, the voice, yes: gramophone. Have a gramophone in every grave or keep it in the house. After dinner on a Sunday. Put on poor old greatgrandfather Kraahraark! Hellohellohello amawfullyglad kraark awfullygladaseeragain hellohello amarawf kopthsth. Remind you of the voice like the photograph reminds you of the face. Otherwise you couldn't remember the face after fifteen years, say. For instance who? For instance some fellow that died when I was in Wisdom Hely's.

Rtststr! A rattle of pebbles. Wait. Stop.

He looked down intently into a stone crypt. Some animal. Wait. There he goes.

An obese grey rat toddled along the side of the crypt, moving the pebbles. An old stager: greatgrandfather: he knows the ropes. The grey alive crushed itself in under the plinth, wriggled itself in under it. Good hidingplace for treasure.

Who lives there? Are laid the remains of Robert Emery. Robert Emmet was buried here by torchlight, wasn't he? Making his rounds.

Tail gone now.

One of those chaps would make short work of a fellow. Pick the bones clean no matter who it was. Ordinary meat for them. A corpse is meat gone bad. Well and what's cheese? Corpse of milk. I read in that *Voyages in China* that the Chinese say a white man smells like a corpse. Cremation better. Priests dead against it. Devilling for the other firm. Wholesale burners and Dutch oven dealers. Time of the plague. Quicklime fever pits to eat them. Lethal chamber. Ashes to ashes. Or bury at sea. Where is that Parsee tower of silence? Eaten by birds. Earth, fire, water. Drowning they say is the pleasantest. See your whole life in a flash. But being brought back to life no. Can't bury in the air however.

Out of a flying machine. Wonder does the news go about whenever a fresh one is let down. Underground communication. We learned that from them. Wouldn't be surprised. Regular square feed for them. Flies come before he's well dead. Got wind of Dignam. They wouldn't care about the smell of it. Saltwhite crumbling mush of corpse: smell, taste like raw white turnips.

The gates glimmered in front: still open. Back to the world again. Enough of this place. Brings you a bit nearer every time. Last time I was here was Mrs Sinico's funeral. Poor papa too. The love that kills. And even scraping up the earth at night with a lantern like that case I read of to get at fresh buried females or even putrefied with running gravesores. Give you the creeps after a bit. I will appear to you after death. You will see my ghost after death. My ghost will haunt you after death. There is another world after death named hell. I do not like that other world she wrote. No more do I. Plenty to see and hear and feel yet. Feel live warm beings near you. Let them sleep in their maggoty beds. They are not going to get me this innings. Warm beds: warm fullblooded life.

The Wandering Rocks

STEPHEN DEDALUS watched through the webbed window the lapidary's fingers prove a timedulled chain. Dust webbed the window and the showtrays. Dust darkened the toiling fingers with their vulture nails. Dust slept on dull coils of bronze and silver, lozenges of cinnabar, on rubies, leprous and winedark stones.

Born all in the dark wormy earth, cold specks of fire,
evil lights shining in the darkness. Where fallen archangels flung the stars of their brows. Muddy swine-
snouts, hands, root and root, gripe and wrest them.

She dances in a foul gloom where gum burns with
garlic. A sailorman, rustbearded, sips from a beaker rum
and eyes her. A long and seafed silent rut. She dances,
capers, wagging her sowish haunches and her hips, on
her gross belly flapping a ruby egg.

Old Russell with a smeared shammy rag burnished
again his gem, turned it and held it at the point of his
Moses' beard. Grandfather ape gloating on a stolen
hoard.

And you who wrest old images from the burial earth!
The brainsick words of sophists: Antisthenes. A lore of
drugs. Orient and immortal wheat standing from everlasting to everlasting.

Two old women fresh from their whiff of the briny
trudged through Irishtown along London bridge road,
one with a sanded umbrella, one with a midwife's bag
in which eleven cockles rolled.

The whirr of flapping leathern bands and hum of
dynamos from the powerhouse urged Stephen to be on.
Beingless beings. Stop! Throb always without you and
the throb always within. Your heart you sing of. I between them. Where? Between two roaring worlds where
they swirl, I. Shatter them, one and both. But stun myself too in the blow. Shatter me you who can. Bawd and
butcher, were the words. I say! Not yet awhile. A look
around.

Yes, quite true. Very large and wonderful and keeps
famous time. You say right, sir. A Monday morning,
'twas so, indeed.

Stephen went down Bedford row, the handle of the
ash clacking against his shoulderblade. In Clohissey's

window a faded 1860 print of Heenan boxing Sayers
held his eye. Staring backers with square hats stood
round the roped prizering. The heavyweights in light
loincloths proposed gently each to other his bulbous fists.
And they are throbbing: heroes' hearts.

He turned and halted by the slanted bookcart.

—Two pence each, the huckster said. Four for sixpence.

Tattered pages. *The Irish Beekeeper. Life and Miracles of the Curé of Ars. Pocket Guide to Killarney.*

I might find here one of my pawned schoolprizes.
Stephano Dedalo, alumno optimo, palmam ferenti.

Father Conmee, having read his little hours, walked
through the hamlet of Donnycarney, murmuring ves-
pers.

Binding too good probably, what is this? Eighth and
ninth book of Moses. Secret of all secrets. Seal of King
David. Thumbed pages: read and read. Who has passed
here before me? How to soften chapped hands. Recipe
for white wine vinegar. How to win a woman's love. For
me this. Say the following talisman three times with
hands folded:

—*Se el yilo nebrakada femininum! Amor me solo!
Sanktus! Amen.*

Who wrote this? Charms and invocations of the most
blessed abbot Peter Salanka to all true believers di-
vulged. As good as any other abbot's charms, as mum-
bling Joachim's. Down, baldynoddle, or we'll wool your
wool.

—What are you doing here, Stephen?

Dilly's high shoulders and shabby dress.

Shut the book quick. Don't let see.

—What are you doing? Stephen said.

A Stuart face of nonesuch Charles, lank locks falling
at its sides. It glowed as she crouched feeding the fire

with broken boots. I told her of Paris. Late lieabed under
a quilt of old overcoats, fingering a pinchbeck bracelet,
Dan Kelly's token. *Nebrakada femininum.*

—What have you there? Stephen asked.

—I bought it from the other cart for a penny, Dilly
said, laughing nervously. Is it any good?

My eyes they say she has. Do others see me so? Quick,
far and daring. Shadow of my mind.

He took the coverless book from her hand. Charde-
nal's French primer.

—What did you buy that for? he asked. To learn
French?

She nodded, reddening and closing tight her lips.

Show no surprise. Quite natural.

—Here, Stephen said. It's all right. Mind Maggy
doesn't pawn it on you. I suppose all my books are gone.

—Some, Dilly said. We had to.

She is drowning. Agenbite. Save her. Agenbite. All
against us. She will drown me with her, eyes and hair.
Lank coils of seaweed hair around me, my heart, my
soul. Salt green death.

We.

Agenbite of inwit. Inwit's agenbite.

Misery! Misery!

The Sirens

TAP.

—*Qui sdegno*, Ben, said Father Cowley.

—No, Ben, Tom Kernan interfered, *The Croppy Boy*.
Our native Doric.

—Ay do, Ben, Mr Dedalus said. Good men and true.

—Do, do, they begged in one.

I'll go. Here, Pat, return. Come. He came, he came, he did not stay. To me. How much?

—What key? Six sharps?

—F sharp major, Ben Dollard said.

Bob Cowley's outstretched talon gripped the black deepsounding chords.

Must go prince Bloom told Richie prince. No, Richie said. Yes, must. Got money somewhere. He's on for a razzle backache spree. Much? He seehears lipspeech. One and nine. Penny for yourself. Here. Give him twopence tip. Deaf, bothered. But perhaps he has wife and family waiting, waiting Patty come home. Hee hee hee hee. Deaf wait while they wait.

But wait. But hear. Chordsdark. Lugugugubrious. Low. In a cave of the dark middle earth. Embedded ore. Lumpmusic.

The voice of dark age, of unlove, earth's fatigue made grave approach, and painful, come from afar, from hoary mountains, called on good men and true. The priest he sought, with him would he speak a word.

Tap.

Ben Dollard's voice barreltone. Doing his level best to say it. Croak of vast manless moonless womoonless marsh. Other comedown. Big ships' chandler's business he did once. Remember: rosiny ropes, ships' lanterns. Failed to the tune of ten thousand pounds. Now in the Iveagh home. Cubicle number so and so. Number one Bass did that for him.

The priest's at home. A false priest's servant bade him welcome. Step in. The holy father. Curlycues of chords.

Ruin them. Wreck their lives. Then build them cubicles to end their days in. Hushaby. Lullaby. Die, dog. Little dog, die.

The voice of warning, solemn warning, told them the youth had entered a lonely hall, told them how solemn fell his footstep there, told them the gloomy chamber, the vested priest sitting to shrive.

Decent soul. Bit addled now. Thinks he'll win in *Answers* poets' picture puzzle. We hand you crisp five pound note. Bird sitting hatching in a nest. Lay of the last minstrel he thought it was. See blank tee what domestic animal? Tee dash ar most courageous mariner. Good voice he has still. No eunuch yet with all his belongings.

Listen. Bloom listened. Richie Goulding listened. And by the door deaf Pat, bald Pat, tipped Pat, listened.

The chords harped slower.

The voice of penance and of grief came slow, embellished tremulous. Ben's contrite beard confessed: *in nomine Domini,* in God's name. He knelt. He beat his hand upon his breast, confessing: *mea culpa.*

Latin again. That holds them like birdlime. Priest with the communion corpus for those women. Chap in the mortuary, coffin or coffey, *corpusnomine.* Wonder where that rat is by now. Scrape.

Tap.

They listened: tankards and Miss Kennedy, George Lidwell eyelid well expressive, fullbusted satin. Kernan, Si.

The sighing voice of sorrow sang. His sins. Since easter he had cursed three times. You bitch's bast. And once at masstime he had gone to play. Once by the churchyard he had passed and for his mother's rest he had not prayed. A boy. A croppy boy.

Bronze, listening by the beerpull, gazed far away. Soulfully. Doesn't half know I'm. Molly great dab at seeing anyone looking.

Bronze gazed far sideways. Mirror there. Is that best side of her face? They always know. Knock at the door. Last tip to titivate.

Cockcarracarra.

What do they think when they hear music? Way to catch rattlesnakes. Night Michael Gunn gave us the box. Tuning up. Shah of Persia liked that best. Remind him of home sweet home. Wiped his nose in curtain too. Custom his country perhaps. That's music too. Not as bad as it sounds. Tootling. Brasses braying asses through uptrunks. Doublebasses, helpless, gashes in their sides. Woodwinds mooing cows. Semigrand open crocodile music hath jaws. Woodwind like Goodwin's name.

She looked fine. Her crocus dress she wore, lowcut, belongings on show. Clove her breath was always in theatre when she bent to ask a question. Told her what Spinoza says in that book of poor papa's. Hypnotised, listening. Eyes like that. She bent. Chap in dresscircle, staring down into her with his operaglass for all he was worth. Beauty of music you must hear twice. Nature woman half a look. God made the country man the tune. Met him pike hoses. Philosophy. O rocks!

All gone. All fallen. At the siege of Ross his father, at Gorey all his brothers fell. To Wexford, we are the boys of Wexford, he would. Last of his name and race.

I too, last my race. Milly young student. Well, my fault perhaps. No son. Rudy. Too late now. Or if not? If not? If still?

He bore no hate.

Hate. Love. Those are names. Rudy. Soon I am old.

Big Ben his voice unfolded. Great voice, Richie Goulding said, a flush struggling in his pale, to Bloom, soon old but when was young.

Ireland comes now. My country above the king. She

listens. Who fears to speak of nineteen four? Time to be shoving. Looked enough.

—*Bless me, father,* Dollard the croppy cried. *Bless me and let me go.*

Tap.

Bloom looked, unblessed to go. Got up to kill: on eighteen bob a week. Fellows shell out the dibs. Want to keep your weathereye open. Those girls, those lovely. By the sad sea waves. Chorusgirl's romance. Letters read out for breach of promise. From Chickabiddy's own Mumpsypum. Laughter in court. Henry. I never signed it. The lovely name you.

Low sank the music, air and words. Then hastened. The false priest rustling soldier from his cassock. A yeoman captain. They know it all by heart. The thrill they itch for. Yeoman cap.

Tap. Tap.

Thrilled, she listened, bending in sympathy to hear.

Blank face. Virgin should say: or fingered only. Write something on it: page. If not what becomes of them? Decline, despair. Keeps them young. Even admire themselves. See. Play on her. Lip blow. Body of white woman, a flute alive. Blow gentle. Loud. Three holes all women. Goddess I didn't see. They want it: not too much polite. That's why he gets them. Gold in your pockets, brass in your face. With look to look: songs without words. Molly that hurdygurdy boy. She knew he meant the monkey was sick. Or because so like the Spanish. Understand animals too that way. Solomon did. Gift of nature.

Ventriloquise. My lips closed. Think in my stom, What?

Will? You? I. Want. You. To.

With hoarse rude fury the yeoman cursed. Swelling in

apoplectic bitch's bastard. A good thought, boy, to come. One hour's your time to live, your last.

Tap. Tap.

Thrill now. Pity they feel. To wipe away a tear for martyrs. For all things dying, want do, dying to, die. For that all things born. Poor Mrs Purefoy. Hope she's over. Because their wombs.

A liquid of womb of woman eyeball gazed under a fence of lashes, calmly, hearing. See real beauty of the eye when she not speaks. On yonder river. At each slow satiny heaving bosom's wave (her heaving embon) red rose rose slowly, sank red rose. Heartbeats her breath: breath that is life. And all the tiny tiny fernfoils trembled of maidenhair.

But look. The bright stars fade. O rose! Castille. The morn. Ha. Lidwell. For him then not for. Infatuated. I like that? See her from here though. Popped corks, splashes of beerfroth, stacks of empties.

On the smooth jutting beerpull laid Lydia hand lightly, plumply, leave it to my hands. All lost in pity for croppy. Fro, to: to, fro: over the polished knob (she knows his eyes, my eyes, her eyes) her thumb and finger passed in pity: passed, repassed and, gently touching, then slid so smoothly, slowly down, a cool firm white enamel baton protruding through their sliding ring.

With a cock with a carra.

Tap. Tap. Tap.

I hold this house. Amen. He gnashed in fury. Traitors swing.

The chords consented. Very sad thing. But had to be. Get out before the end. Thanks, that was heavenly. Where's my hat. Pass by her. Can leave that *Freeman*. Letter I have. Suppose she were the? No. Walk, walk, walk. Like Cashel Boylo Connoro Coylo Tisdall Maurice Tisntdall Farrell. Waaaaaaalk.

Well, I must be. Are you off? Yrfmstbyes. Blmstup.
O'er ryehigh blue. Bloom stood up. Ow. Soap feeling
rather sticky behind. Must have sweated: music. That
lotion, remember. Well, so long. High grade. Card inside, yes.

By deaf Pat in the doorway, straining ear, Bloom
passed.

At Geneva barrack that young man died. At Passage
was his body laid. Dolor! O, he dolores! The voice of
the mournful chanter called to dolorous prayer.

By rose, by satiny bosom, by the fondling hand, by
slops, by empties, by popped corks, greeting in going,
past eyes and maidenhair, bronze and faint gold in
deepseashadow, went Bloom, soft Bloom, I feel so lonely
Bloom.

Tap. Tap. Tap.

Pray for him, prayed the bass of Dollard. You who
hear in peace. Breathe a prayer, drop a tear, good men,
good people. He was the croppy boy.

Scaring eavesdropping boots croppy bootsboy Bloom
in the Ormond hallway heard growls and roars of bravo,
fat backslapping, their boots all treading, boots not
the boots the boy. General chorus off for a swill to wash
it down. Glad I avoided.

—Come on, Ben, Simon Dedalus said. By God, you're
as good as ever you were.

—Better, said Tomgin Kernan. Most trenchant rendi-
tion of that ballad, upon my soul and honour it is.

—Lablache, said Father Cowley.

Ben Dollard bulkily cachuchad towards the bar,
mightily praisefed and all big roseate, on heavyfooted
feet, his gouty fingers nakkering castagnettes in the air.

Big Benaben Dollard. Big Benben. Big Benben.

Penelope

. . . a quarter after what an unearthly hour I suppose theyre just getting up in China now combing out
their pigtails for the day well soon have the nuns ringing the angelus theyve nobody coming in to spoil their
sleep except an odd priest or two for his night office
the alarmclock next door at cockshout clattering the
brains out of itself let me see if I can doze off 1 2 3 4 5
what kind of flowers are those they invented like the
stars the wallpaper in Lombard street was much nicer
the apron he gave me was like that something only I
only wore it twice better lower this lamp and try again
so as I can get up early Ill go to Lambes there beside
Findlaters and get them to send us some flowers to put
about the place in case he brings him home tomorrow
today I mean no no Fridays an unlucky day first I want
to do the place up someway the dust grows in it I think
while Im asleep then we can have music and cigarettes
I can accompany him first I must clean the keys of the
piano with milk whatll I wear shall I wear a white rose
or those fairy cakes in Liptons I love the smell of a rich
big shop at 7½d. a lb or the other ones with the cherries
in them and the pinky sugar 11d a couple of lbs of
course a nice plant for the middle of the table Id get
that cheaper in wait wheres this I saw them not long
ago I love flowers Id love to have the whole place swimming in roses God of heaven theres nothing like nature
the wild mountains then the sea and the waves rushing
then the beautiful country with fields of oats and wheat
and all kinds of things and all the fine cattle going about

that would do your heart good to see rivers and lakes
and flowers all sorts of shapes and smells and colours
springing up even out of the ditches primroses and violets nature it is as for them saying theres no God I
wouldnt give a snap of my two fingers for all their learning why dont they go and create something I often
asked him atheists or whatever they call themselves go
and wash the cobbles off themselves first then they go
howling for the priest and they dying and why why because theyre afraid of hell on account of their bad conscience ah yes I know them well who was the first person in the universe before there was anybody that made
it all who ah that they dont know neither do I so there
you are they might as well try to stop the sun from
rising tomorrow the sun shines for you he said the day
we were lying among the rhododendrons on Howth
head in the grey tweed suit and his straw hat the day I
got him to propose to me yes first I gave him the bit of
seedcake out of my mouth and it was leapyear like now
yes 16 years ago my God after that long kiss I near lost
my breath yes he said I was a flower of the mountain
yes so we are flowers all a womans body yes that was
one true thing he said in his life and the sun shines for
you today yes that was why I liked him because I saw
he understood or felt what a woman is and I knew I
could always get round him and I gave him all the
pleasure I could leading him on till he asked me to say
yes and I wouldnt answer first only looked out over the
sea and the sky I was thinking of so many things he
didnt know of Mulvey and Mr Stanhope and Hester and
father and old captain Groves and the sailors playing all
birds fly and I say stoop and washing up dishes they
called it on the pier and the sentry in front of the gov-
ernors house with the thing round his white helmet poor
devil half roasted and the Spanish girls laughing in their

shawls and their tall combs and the auctions in the
morning the Greeks and the jews and the Arabs and
the devil knows who else from all the ends of Europe
and Duke street and the fowl market all clucking outside Larby Sharons and the poor donkeys slipping half
asleep and the vague fellows in the cloaks asleep in the
shade on the steps and the big wheels of the carts of the
bulls and the old castle thousands of years old yes and
those handsome Moors all in white and turbans like
kings asking you to sit down in their little bit of a shop
and Ronda with the old windows of the posadas glancing eyes a lattice hid for her lover to kiss the iron and
the wineshops half open at night and the castanets and
the night we missed the boat at Algeciras the watchman
going about serene with his lamp and O that awful
deepdown torrent O and the sea the sea crimson sometimes like fire and the glorious sunsets and the figtrees
in the Alameda gardens yes and all the queer little
streets and pink and blue and yellow houses and the
rosegardens and the jessamine and geraniums and cac-
tuses and Gibraltar as a girl where I was a Flower of the
mountain yes when I put the rose in my hair like the
Andalusian girls used or shall I wear a red yes and how
he kissed me under the Moorish wall and I thought well
as well him as another and then I asked him with my
eyes to ask again yes and then he asked me would I yes
to say yes my mountain flower and first I put my arms
around him yes and drew him down to me so he could
feel my breasts all perfume yes and his heart was going
like mad and yes I said yes I will Yes.

Finnegans Wake

EDITOR'S PREFACE

THE literary experiments that Joyce performed, during the seventeen years that followed the publication of *Ulysses,* appeared as "Work in Progress" in the international magazine, *transition.* The definitive work, under the title of *Finnegans Wake,* was given to a world bewildered by other enigmas in 1939. Joyce's death two years later deprived his readers, not only of a contemplated epic on the sea, but of an authorized commentary similar to Stuart Gilbert's on *Ulysses.* The fact that critics have already arrived at rough agreement as to its methods and premises, its characters and situations, is a testimonial to the artistic sincerity and intellectual rigor of Joyce's last book. But it would not be worth the trouble of elucidation if it did not offer the immediate satisfactions of humor and poetry. Its texture is so close, its structure so organic, that it cannot yet be considered readable in the sense of an ordinary novel. Indeed, it begins with the latter part of a sentence, the beginning of which is found on the last page. This circular construction, which carries out Vico's philosophy of history, invites us to plunge in almost anywhere. By printing certain fragments in pamphlet form, however, Joyce seems to have recognized that they were especially attractive and instructive for this purpose. Two of them are reprinted here in their final versions: "Anna Livia Plurabelle" and "Tales Told of Shem and Shaun." The additional selection is made up of three closely related passages from the first chapter, introducing Mr. Humphrey Chimpden Earwicker, whose name alliterates with "Here Comes Everybody" and other phrases on nearly every page. Ultimately he personifies Howth Castle and Environs, the head of the sleeping giant that embodies Dublin. Literally a tavern-keeper, he has many figurative associations: he transforms the Wellington Monument into a museum of the world's great battles; as a Norse invader, he engages in a prehistoric dialogue with a local deafmute. A pirate queen, by kidnaping his children, draws down the hundred-letter thunder-word, which reverberates to the original fall of man as well as the tumble of the bricklayer Finnegan. His tempestuous relations with the heroine, Anna Livia, together with her struggles on his behalf, provoke the gossip of two washer-women on the banks of the Liffey. Joyce has made a memorable phonograph record of the metamorphosis that ends this section. Sooner or later his polymorphous figures resolve themselves into one large family. His father and mother images, a rock and a river, are those of Yeats's "Easter, 1916." His daughter is the leap-year cloud-girl and his sons are the twins, Shem and Shaun. Their eternal opposition, which exemplifies Bruno's metaphysics, is driven home by an edifying pair of fables. The Fox and the Grapes represent the Pope and the Primate of Ireland; the Ant and the Grasshopper speak for space and time, and for the philistine and the artist as well. All this, and an infinite variety of other things, turn out to be merely a dream—but a dream which recapitulates many mythologies, and encompasses the endless vagaries of the human imagination.

Here Comes Everybody

Y ET may we not see still the brontoichthyan form
outlined aslumbered, even in our own nighttime
by the sedge of the troutling stream that Bronto loved
and Brunto has a lean on. *Hic cubat edilis. Apud liber-
tinam parvulam.* Whatif she be in flags or flitters,
reekierags or sundyechosies, with a mint of mines or
beggar a pinnyweight. Arrah, sure, we all love little
Anny Ruiny, or, we mean to say, lovelittle Anna Rayiny,
when unda her brella, mid piddle med puddle, she ninny-
nannygoes nancing by. Yoh! Brontolone slaaps, yoh
snoores. Upon Benn Heather, in Seeple Isout too. The
cranic head on him, caster of his reasons, peer yuthner
in yondmist. Whooth? His clay feet, swarded in verdi-
grass, stick up starck where he last fellonem, by the
mund of the magazine wall, where our maggy seen all,
with her sisterin shawl. While over against this belles'
alliance beyond Ill Sixty, ollollowed ill! bagsides of the
fort, bom, tarabom, tarabom, lurk the ombushes, the
site of the lyffing-in-wait of the upjock and hockums.
Hence when the clouds roll by, jamey, a proudseye view
is enjoyable of our mounding's mass, now Wallinstone
national museum, with, in some greenish distance, the
charmful waterloose country and the two quitewhite
villagettes who hear show of themselves so gigglesomes
minxt the follyages, the prettilees! Penetrators are permitted into the museomound free. Welsh and the Paddy
Patkinses, one shelenk! Redismembers invalids of old
guard find poussepousse pousseypram to sate the sort

711

of their butt. For her passkey supply to the janitrix, the
mistress Kathe. Tip.

This the way to the museyroom. Mind your hats goan
in! Now yiz are in the Willingdone Museyroom. This is
a Prooshious gunn. This is a ffrinch. Tip. This is the flag
of the Prooshious, the Cap and Soracer. This is the bul-
let that byng the flag of the Prooshious. This is the
ffrinch that fire on the Bull that bang the flag of the
Prooshious. Saloos the Crossgunn! Up with your pike
and fork! Tip. (Bullsfoot! Fine!) This is the triplewon
hat of Lipoleum. Tip. Lipoleumhat. This is the Willingdone on his same white harse, the Cokenhape. This is
the big Sraughter Willingdone, grand and magentic in
his goldtin spurs and his ironed dux and his quarterbrass
woodyshoes and his magnate's gharters and his bang-
kok's best and goliar's goloshes and his pulluponeasyan
wartrews. This is his big wide harse. Tip. This is the
three lipoleum boyne grouching down in the living
detch. This is an inimyskilling inglis, this is a scotcher
grey, this is a davy, stooping. This is the bog lipoleum
mordering the lipoleum beg. A Gallawghurs argaumunt.
This is the petty lipoleum boy that was nayther bag nor
bug. Assaye, assaye! Touchole Fitz Tuomush. Dirty
MacDyke. And Hairy O'Hurry. All of them arminus-
varminus. This is Delian alps. This is Mont Tivel, this
is Mont Tipsey, this is the Grand Mons Injun. This is
the crimealine of the alps hooping to sheltershock the
three lipoleums. This is the jinnies with their legahorns
feinting to read in their handmade's book of stralegy
while making their war undisides the Willingdone. The
jinnies is a cooin her hand and the jinnies is a ravin her
hair and the Willingdone git the band up. This is big
Willingdone mormorial tallowscoop Wounderworker
obscides on the flanks of the jinnies. Sexcaliber hross-

power. Tip. This is me Belchum sneaking his phillippy out of his most Awful Grimmest Sunshat Cromwelly. Looted. This is the jinnies' hastings dispatch for to irrigate the Willingdone. Dispatch in thin red lines cross the shortfront of me Belchum. Yaw, yaw, yaw! Leaper Orthor. Fear siecken! Fieldgaze thy tiny frow. Hugacting. Nap. That was the tictacs of the jinnies for to fontannoy the Willingdone. Shee, shee, shee! The jinnies is jillous agincourting all the lipoleums. And the lipoleums is gonn boycottoncrezy onto the one Willingdone. And the Willingdone git the band up. This is bode Belchum, bonnet to busby, breaking his secred word with a ball up his ear to the Willingdone. This is the Willingdone's hurold dispitchback. Dispitch desployed on the regions rare of me Belchum. Salamangra! Ayi, ayi, ayi! Cherry jinnies. Figtreeyou! Damn fairy ann, Voutre. Willingdone. That was the first joke of Willingdone, tic for tac. Hee, hee, hee! This is me Belchum in his twelvemile cowchooks, weet, tweet and stampforth foremost, footing the camp for the jinnies. Drink a sip, drankasup, for he's as sooner buy a guinness than he'd stale store stout. This is Rooshious balls. This is a ttrinch. This is mistletropes. This is Canon Futter with the popynose. After his hundred days' indulgence. This is the blessed. Tarra's widdars! This is jinnies in the bonny bawn blooches. This is lipoleums in the rowdy howses. This is the Willingdone, by the splinters of Cork, order fire. Tonnerre! (Bullsear! Play!) This is camelry, this is floodens, this is the solphereens in action, this is their mobbily, this is panickburns. Almeidagad! Arthiz too loose! This is Willingdone cry. Brum! Brum! Cumbrum! This is jinnies cry. Underwetter! Goat strip Finnlambs! This is jinnies rinning away to their ousterlists dowan a bunkersheels. With a nip nippy nip and a trip trippy

trip so airy. For their heart's right there. Tip. This is me
Belchum's tinkyou tankyou silvoor plate for citchin the
crapes in the cool of his canister. Poor the pay! This is
the bissmark of the marathon merry of the jinnies they
left behind them. This is the Willingdone branlish his
same marmorial tallowscoop Sophy-Key-Po for his royal
divorsion on the rinnaway jinnies. Gambariste della
porca! Dalaveras fimmieras! This is the pettiest of the
lipoleums, Toffeethief, that spy on the Willingdone from
his big white harse, the Capeinhope. Stonewall Willingdone is an old maxy montrumeny. Lipoleums is nice
hung bushellors. This is hiena hinnessy laughing alout
at the Willingdone. This is lipsyg dooley krieging the
funk from the hinnessy. This is the hinndoo Shimar Shin
between the dooley boy and the hinnessy. Tip. This is
the wixy old Willingdone picket up the half of the three-
foiled hat of lipoleums fromoud of the bluddle filth. This
is the hinndoo waxing ranjymad for a bombshoob. This
is the Willingdone hanking the half of the hat of lipoleums up the tail on the buckside of his big white harse.
Tip. That was the last joke of Willingdone. Hit, hit, hit!
This is the same white harse of the Willingdone, Culpen-
help, waggling his tailoscrupp with the half of a hat of
lipoleums to insoult on the hinndoo seeboy. Hney, hney,
hney! (Bullsrag! Foul!) This is the seeboy, madrashat-
taras, upjump and pumpim, cry to the Willingdone: Ap
Pukkaru! Pukka Yurap! This is the Willingdone, born-
stable ghentleman, tinders his maxbotch to the cursigan
Shimar Shin. Basucker youstead! This is the dooforhim
seeboy blow the whole of the half of the hat of lipoleums off of the top of the tail on the back of his big
wide harse. Tip (Bullseye! Game!) How Copenhagen
ended. This way the museyroom. Mind your boots goan
out.

✼   ✼   ✼

In the name of Anem this carl on the kopje in pelted thongs a parth a lone who the joebiggar be he? Forshapen his pigmaid hoagshead, shroonk his plodsfoot. He hath locktoes, this. shortshins, and, Obeold that's pectoral, his mammamuscles most mousterious. It is slaking nuncheon out of some thing's brain pan. Me seemeth a dragon man. He is almonthst on the kiep fief by here, is Comestipple Sacksoun, be it junipery or febrewery, marracks or alebrill or the ramping riots of pouriose and froriose. What a quhare soort of a mahan. It is evident the michindaddy. Lets we overstep his fire defences and these kraals of slitsucked marrogbones. (Cave!) He can prapsposterus the pillory way to Hirculos pillar. Come on, fool porterfull, hosiered women blown monk sewer? Scuse us, chorley guy! You tollerday donsk? N. You tolkatiff scowegian? Nn. You spigotty anglease? Nnn. You phonio saxo? Nnnn. Clear all so! 'Tis a Jute. Let us swop hats and excheck a few strong verbs weak oach eather yapyazzard abast the blooty creeks.

Jute.—Yutah!

Mutt.—Mukk's pleasurad.

Jute.—Are you jeff?

Mutt.—Somehards.

Jute.—But you are not jeffmute?

Mutt.—Noho. Only an utterer.

Jute.—Whoa? Whoat is the mutter with you?

Mutt.—I became a stun a stummer.

Jute.—What a hauhauhauhaudibble thing, to be cause! How, Mutt?

Mutt.—Aput the buttle, surd.

Jute.—Whose poddle? Wherein?

Mutt.—The Inns of Dungtarf where Used awe to be he.

Jute.—You that side your voise are almost inedible
to me. Become a bitskin more wiseable, as if
I were you.

Mutt.—Has? Has at? Hasatency? Urp, Boohooru!
Booru Usurp! I trumple from rath in mine
mines when I rimimirim!

Jute.—One eyegonblack. Bisons is bisons. Let me
fore all your hasitancy cross your qualm with
trink gilt. Here have sylvan coyne, a piece of
oak. Ghinees hies good for you.

Mutt.—Louee, louee! How wooden I not know it,
the intellible greytcloak of Cedric Silkyshag!
Cead mealy faulty rices for one dabblin bar.
Old grilsy growlsy! He was poached on in
that eggtentical spot. Here where the liveries,
Monomark. There where the missers moony,
Minnikin passe.

Jute.—Simply because as Taciturn pretells, our
wrongstoryshortener, he dumptied the whole-
borrow of rubbages on to soil here.

Mutt.—Just how a puddinstone inat the brookcells by
a riverpool.

Jute.—Load Allmarshy! Wid wad for a norse like?

Mutt.—Somular with a bull on a clompturf. Rooks
roarum rex roome! I could snore to him of the
spumy horn, with his woolseley side in, by the
neck I am sutton on, did Brian d' of Linn.

Jute.—Boildoyle and rawhoney on me when I can
beuraly forsstand a weird from sturk to finnic
in such a patwhat as your rutterdamrotter.
Onheard of and umscene! Gut aftermeal! See
you doomed.

Mutt.—Quite agreem. Bussave a sec. Walk a dun
blink roundward this albutisle and you skull
see how olde ye plaine of my Elters, hunfree

and ours, where wone to wail whimbrel to peewee o'er the saltings, where wilby citie by law of isthmon, where by a droit of signory, icefloe was from his Inn the Byggning to whose Finishthere Punct. Let erehim ruhmuhrmuhr. Mearmerge two races, swete and brack. Morthering rue. Hither, craching eastuards, they are in surgence: hence, cool at ebb, they requiesce. Countlessness of livestories have netherfallen by this plage, flick as flowflakes, litters from aloft, like a waast wizzard all of whirlworlds. Now are all tombedto the mound, isges to isges, erde from erde. Pride, O pride, thy prize!

Jute.—°Stench!

Mutt.—Fiatfuit! Hereinunder lyethey. Llarge by the smal an' everynight life olso th'estrange, babylone the greatgrandhotelled with' tit tit tittlehouse, alp on earwig, drukn on ild, likeas equal to anequal in this sound seemetery which iz leebez luv.

Jute.—'Zmorde!

Mutt.—Meldundlcizc! By the fearse wave behoughted. Despond's sung. And thanacestross mound have swollup them all. This ourth of years is not save brickdust and being humus the same roturns. He who runes may rede it on all fours. O'c'stle, n'wc'stle, tr'c'stle, crumbling! Sell me sooth the fare for Humblin! Humblady Fair. But speak it allsosiftly, moulder! Be in your whisht!

Jute.—Whysht?

Mutt.—The gyant Forficules with Amni the fay.

Jute.—Howe?

Mutt.—Here is viceking's graab.

Jute.—Hwaad!

Mutt.—Ore you astoneaged, jute you?

Jute.—Oye am thonthorstrok, thing mud.

*   *   *

It was of a night, late, lang time agone, in an auldstane eld, when Adam was delvin and his madameen spinning watersilts, when mulk mountynotty man was everybully and the first leal ribberrobber that ever had her ainway everybuddy to his lovesaking eyes and everybilly lived alove with everybiddy else, and Jarl van Hoother had his burnt head high up in his lamphouse, laying cold hands on himself. And his two little jiminies, cousins of ourn, Tristopher and Hilary, were kickaheeling their dummy on the oil cloth flure of his homerigh, castle and earthenhouse. And, be dermot, who come to the keep of his inn only the niece-of-his-in-law, the prankquean. And the prankquean pulled a rosy one and made her wit foreninst the dour. And she lit/up and fireland was ablaze. And spoke she to the dour in her petty perusienne: Mark the Wans, why do I am alook alike a poss of porterpease? And that was how the skirtmisshes began. But the dour handworded her grace in dootch nossow: Shut! So her grace o'malice kidsnapped up the jiminy Tristopher and into the shandy westerness she rain, rain, rain. And Jarl van Hoother warlessed after her with soft dovesgall: Stop deef stop come back to my earin stop. But she swaradid to him: Unlikelihud. And there was a brannewail that same sabboath night of falling angles somewhere in Erio. And the prankquean went for her forty years' walk in Tourlemonde and she washed the blessings of the lovespots off the jiminy with soap sulliver suddles and she had her four owlers masters for to tauch him his tickles and she converted him to the onesure allgood and he became a

luderman. So then she started to rain and to rain and,
be redtom, she was back again at Jarl van Hoother's in
a brace of samers and the jiminy with her in her pina-
frond, lace at night, at another time. And where did she
come but to the bar of his bristolry. And Jarl von Hoother had his baretholobruised heels drowned in his cel-
larmalt, shaking warm hands with himself and the
jimminy Hilary and the dummy in their first infancy
were below on the tearsheet, wringing and coughing,
like brodar and histher. And the prankquean nipped a
paly one and lit up again and redcocks flew flackering
from the hillcombs. And she made her witter before the
wicked, saying: Mark the Twy, why do I am alook alike
two poss of porterpease? And: Shut! says the wicked,
handwording her madesty. So her madesty a forethought
set down a jiminy and took up a jiminy and all the lili-
path ways to Woeman's Land she rain, rain, rain. And
Jarl von Hoother bleethered atter her with a loud fine-
gale: Stop domb stop come back with my earring stop.
But the prankquean swaradid: Am liking it. And there
was a wild ole grannewwail that laurency night of star-
shootings somewhere in Erio. And the prankquean went
for her forty years' walk in Turnlemeem and she punched
the curses of cromcruwell with the nail of a top into the
jiminy and she had her four larksical monitrix to touch
him his tears and she provorted him to the onecertain
allsecure and he became a tristian. So then she started
raining, raining, and in a pair of changers, be dom ter,
she was back again at Jarl von Hoother's and the Larry-
hill with her under her abromette. And why would she
halt at all if not by the ward of his mansionhome of
another nice lace for the third charm? And Jarl von
Hoother had his hurricane hips up to his pantrybox,
ruminating in his holdfour stomachs (Dare! O dare!),
and the jiminy Toughertrees and the dummy were be-

love on the watercloth, kissing and spitting, and roguing
and poghuing, like knavepaltry and naivebride and in
their second infancy. And the prankquean picked a
blank and lit out and the valleys lay twinkling. And she
made her wittest in front of the arkway of trihump,
asking: Mark the Tris, why do I am alook alike three
poss of porter pease? But that was how the skirtmishes
endupped. For like the campbells acoming with a fork
lance of lightning, Jarl von Hoother Boanerges himself,
the old terror of the dames, came hip hop handihap out
through the pikeopened arkway of his three shuttoned
castles, in his broadginger hat and his civic chollar and
his allabuff hemmed and his bullbraggin soxangloves
and his ladbroke breeks and his cattegut bandolair and
his furframed panuncular cumbottes like a rudd yellan
gruebleen orangeman in his violet indigonation, to the
whole length of the strength of his bowman's bill. And
he clopped his rude hand to his eacy hitch and he
ordurd and his thick spch spck for her to shut up shop,
dappy. And the duppy shot the shutter clup (Perkod-
huskurunbarggruauyagokgorlayorgromgremmitghund-
hurthrumathunaradidillifaititillibumullunukkunun!) And
they all drank free. For one man in his armour was a fat
match always for any girls under shurts. And that was
the first peace of illiterative porthery in all the flamend
floody flatuous world. How kirssy the tiler made a sweet
unclose to the Narwhealian captol. Saw fore shalt thou
sea. Betoun ye and be. The prankquean was to hold
her dummyship and the jimminies was to keep the
peacewave and van Hoother was to git the wind up.
Thus the hearsomeness of the burger felicitates the
whole of the polis.

Anna Livia Plurabelle

O
tell me all about
Anna Livia! I want to hear all
about Anna Livia. Well, you know Anna Livia? Yes, of
course, we all know Anna Livia. Tell me all. Tell me
now. You'll die when you hear. Well, you know, when
the old cheb went futt and did what you know. Yes,
I know, go on. Wash quit and don't be dabbling. Tuck
up your sleeves and loosen your talktapes. And don't
butt me—hike!—when you bend. Or whatever it was
they threed to make out he thried to two in the Fiendish
park. He's an awful old reppe. Look at the shirt of him!
Look at the dirt of it! He has all my water black on me.
And it steeping and stuping since this time last wik.
How many goes is it I wonder I washed it? I know by
heart the places he likes to saale, duddurty devil! Scorching my hand and starving my famine to make his private
linen public. Wallop it well with your battle and clean
it. My wrists are wrusty rubbing the mouldaw stains.
And the dneepers of wet and the gangres of sin in it!
What was it he did a tail at all on Animal Sendai? And
how long was he under loch and neagh? It was put in
the newses what he did, nicies and priers, the King
fierceas Humphrey, with illysus distilling, exploits and
all. But toms will till. I know he well. Temp untamed
will hist for no man. As you spring so shall you neap.
O, the roughty old rappe! Minxing marrage and making
loof. Reeve Gootch was right and Reeve Drughad was

sinistrous! And the cut of him! And the strut of him!
How he used to hold his head as high as a howeth, the
famous eld duke alien, with a hump of grandeur on him
like a walking wiesel rat. And his derry's own drawl and
his corksown blather and his doubling stutter and his
gullaway swank. Ask Lictor Hackett or Lector Reade
of Garda Growley or the Boy with the Billyclub. How
elster is he a called at all? Qu'appelle? Huges Caput
Earlyfouler. Or where was he born or how was he found?
Urgothland, Tvistown on the Kattekat? New Hunshire,
Concord on the Merrimake? Who blocksmitt her saft
anvil or yelled lep to her pail? Was her banns never
loosened in Adam and Eve's or were him and her but
captain spliced? For mine ether duck I thee drake. And
by my wildgaze I thee gander. Flowey and Mount on
the brink of time makes wishes and fears for a happy
isthmass. She can show all her lines, with love, license
to play. And if they don't remarry that hook and eye
may! O, passmore that and oxus another! Don Dom
Dombdomb and his wee follyo! Was his help inshored
in the Stork and Pelican against bungelars, flu and third
risk parties? I heard he dug good tin with his doll,
delvan first and duvlin after, when he raped her home,
Sabrine asthore, in a parakeet's cage, by dredgerous
lands and devious delts, playing catched and mythed
with the gleam of her shadda, (if a flic had been there
to pop up and pepper him!) past auld min's manse and
Maisons Allfou and the rest of incurables and the last
of immurables, the quaggy waag for stumbling. Who
sold you that jackalantern's tale? Pemmican's pasty pie!
Not a grasshoop to ring her, not an antsgrain of ore.
In a gabbard he barqued it, the boat of life, from the
harbourless Ivernikan Okean, till he spied the loom of
his landfall and he loosed two croakers from under his
tilt, the gran Phenician rover. By the smell of her kelp

they made the pigeonhouse. Like fun they did! But
where was Himself, the timoneer? That marchantman
he suivied their scutties right over the wash, his camel-
eer's burnous breezing up on him, till with his runagate
bowmpriss he roade and borst her bar. Pilcomayo! Such-
caughtawan! And the whale's away with the grayling!
Tune your pipes and fall ahumming, you born ijypt,
and you're nothing short of one! Well, ptellomey soon
and curb your escumo. When they saw him shoot swift
up her sheba sheath, like any gay lord salomon, her bulls
they were ruhring, surfed with spree. Boyarka buah!
Boyana bueh! He erned his lille Bunbath hard, our staly
bred, the trader. He did. Look at here. In this wet of
his prow. Don't you know he was kaldt a bairn of the
brine, Wasserbourne the waterbaby? Havemmarea, so
he was! H.C.E. has a codfisck ee. Shyr she's nearly as
badher as him herself. Who? Anna Livia? Ay, Anna
Livia. Do you know she was calling bakvandets sals
from all around, nyumba noo, chamba choo, to go in
till him, her erring cheef, and tickle the pontiff aisy-oisy?
She was? Gota pot! Yssel that the limmat? As El Negro
winced when he wonced in La Plate. O, tell me all I
want to hear, how loft she was lift a laddery dextro! A
coneywink after the bunting fell. Letting on she didn't
care, sina feza, me absantee, him man in passession, the
proxenete! Proxenete and phwhat is phthat? Emme for
your reussischer Honddu jarkon! Tell us in franca lan-
gua. And call a spate a spate. Did they never sharee
you cbro at skol, you antiabecedarian? It's just the same
as if I was to go par examplum now in conservancy's
cause out of telekinesis and proxenete you. For coxyt
sake and is that what she is? Botlettle I thought she'd
act that loa. Didn't you spot her in her windaug, wub-
bling up on an osiery chair, with a meusic before her all
cunniform letters, pretending to ribble a reedy derg on

a fiddle she bogans without a band on? Sure she can't
fiddan a dee, with bow or abandon! Sure, she can't!
Tista suck. Well, I never now heard the like of that!
Tell me moher. Tell me moatst. Well, old Humber was
as glommen as grampus, with the tares at his thor and
the buboes for ages and neither bowman nor shot abroad
and bales allbrant on the crests of rockies and nera
lamp in kitchen or church and giant's holes in Grafton's
causeway and deathcap mushrooms round Funglus
grave and the great tribune's barrow all darnels oc-
cumule, sittang sambre on his sett, drammen and drom-
men, usking queasy quizzers of his ruful continence,
his childlinen scarf to encourage his obsequies where
he'd check their debths in that mormon's thames, be
questing and handsetl, hop, step and a deepend, with
his berths in their toiling moil, his swallower open from
swolf to fore and the snipes of the gutter pecking his
crocs, hungerstriking all alone and holding doomsdag
over hunselv, dreeing his weird, with his dander up,
and his fringe combed over his eygs and droming on
loft till the sight of the sternes, after zwarthy kowse and
weedy broeks and the tits of buddy and the loits of pest
and to peer was Parish worth thette mess. You'd think
all was dodo belonging to him how he durmed adranse
in durance vaal. He had been belching for severn years.
And there she was, Anna Livia, she darent catch a win-
kle of sleep, purling around like a chit of a child, Wenda-
wanda, a fingerthick, in a Lapsummer skirt and damazon
cheeks, for to ishim bonzour to her dear dubber Dan.
With neuphraties and sault from his maggias. And an
odd time she'd cook him up blooms of fisk and lay to
his heartsfoot her meddery eygs, yayis, and staynish
beacons on toasc and a cupenhave so weeshywashy of
Greenland's tay or a dzoupgan of Kaffue mokau an sable
or Sikiang sukry or his ale of ferns in trueart pewter and

a shinkobread (hamjambo, bana?) for to plaise that
man hog stay his stomicker till her pyrraknees shrunk to
nutmeg graters while her togglejoints shuck with goyt
and as rash as she'd russ with her peakload of vivers up
on her sieve (metauwero rage it swales and rieses) my
hardey Hek he'd kast them frome him, with a stour of
scorn, as much as to say you sow and you sozh, and if he
didn't peg the platteau on her tawe, believe you me,
she was safe enough. And then she'd esk to vistule a
hymn, *The Heart Bowed Down* or *The Rakes of Mallow*
or Chelli Michele's *La Calumnia è un Vermicelli* or a
balfy bit ov *old Jo Robidson.* Sucho fuffing a fifeing
'twould cut you in two! She'd bate the hen that crowed
on the turrace of Babbel. What harm if she knew how
to cockle her mouth! And not a mag out of Him no
more than out of the mangle weight. Is that a faith?
That's the fact. Then riding the ricka and roya ro-
manche, Annona, gebroren aroostokrat Nivia, dochter of
Sense and Art, with Sparks' pirryphlickathims funkling
her fan, anner frostivying tresses dasht with virevlies—
while the prom beauties sreeked nith their bearers' skins!
—in a period gown of changeable jade that would robe
the wood of two cardinals' chairs and crush poor Cullen
and smother MacCabe. O blazerskate! Theirs porpor
patches! And brahming to him down the feedchute,
with her femtyfyx kinds of fondling endings, the poother
rambling off her nose: *Vuggybarney, Wickerymandy!
Hello, ducky, please don't die!* Do you know what she
started cheeping after, with a choicey voicey like water-
glucks or Madame Delba to Romeoreszk? You'll never
guess. Tell me. Tell me. *Phoebe, dearest, tell, O tell me*
and *I loved you better nor you knew.* And letting on
hoon var daft about the warbly sangs from over holmen:
High hellskirt saw ladies hensmoker lilyhung pigger:
and soay and soan and so firth and so forth in a tone

sonora and Oom Bothar below like Bheri-Bheri in his
sandy cloak, so umvolosy, as deaf as a yawn, the stult!
Go away! Poor deef old deary! Yare only teasing! Anna
Liv? As chalk is my judge! And didn't she up in sorgues
and go and trot doon and stand in her douro, puffing
her old dudheen, and every shirvant siligirl or wensum
farmerette walking the pilend roads, Sawy, Fundally,
Daery or Maery, Milucre, Awny or Graw, usedn't she
make her a simp or sign to slip inside by the sullyport?
You don't say, the sillypost? Bedouix but I do! Calling
them in, one by one (To Blockbeddum here! Here the
Shoebenacaddie!) and legging a jig or so on the sihl to
show them how to shake their benders and the dainty
how to bring to mind the gladdest garments out of sight
and all the way of a maid with a man and making a sort of
a cackling noise like two and a penny or half a crown
and holding up a silliver shiner. Lordy, lordy, did she
so? Well, of all the ones ever I heard! Throwing all the
neiss little whores in the world at him! To inny captured
wench you wish of no matter what sex of pleissful ways
two adda tammar a lizzy a lossie to hug and hab haven
in Humpy's apron!

And what was the wyerye rima she made! Odet!
Odet! Tell me the trent of it while I'm lathering hail out
of Denis Florence MacCarthy's combies. Rise it, flut ye,
pian piena! I'm dying down off my iodine feet until I
lerryn Anna Livia's cushingloo, that was writ by one and
rede by two and trouved by a poule in the parco! I can
see that, I see you are. How does it tummel? Listen now.
Are you listening? Yes, yes! Idneed I am! Tarn your ore
ouse! Essonne inne!

*By earth and the cloudy but I badly want a brandnew
bankside, bedamp and I do, and a plumper at that!*

*For the putty affair I have is wore out, so it is, sitting,
yaping and waiting for my old Dane hodder dodderer,*

my life in death companion, my frugal key of our larder, my much-altered camel's hump, my jointspoiler, my maymoon's honey, my fool to the last Decemberer, to wake himself out of his winter's doze and bore me down like he used to.

Is there irwell a lord of the manor or a knight of the shire at strike, I wonder, that'd dip me a dace or two in cash for washing and darning his worshipful socks for him now we're run out of horse-brose and milk?

Only for my short Brittas bed made's as snug as it smells it's out I'd lep and off with me to the slobs della Tolka or the plage au Clontarf to feale the gay aire of my salt troublin bay and the race of the saywint up me ambushure.

Onon! Onon! tell me more. Tell me every tiny teign. I want to know every single ingul. Down to what made the potters fly into jagsthole. And why were the vesles vet. That homa fever's winning me wome. If a mahun of the horse but hard me! We'd be bundukiboi meet askarigal. Well, now comes the hazelhatchery part. After Clondalkin the Kings's Inns. We'll soon be there with the freshet. How many aleveens had she in tool? I can't rightly rede you that. Close only knows. Some say she had three figures to fill and confined herself to a hundred eleven, wan bywan bywan, making mean-acuminamoyas. Olaph lamm et, all that pack? We won't have room in the kirkeyaard. She can't remember half of the cradlenames she smacked on them by the grace of her boxing bishop's infallible slipper, the cane for Kund and abbles for Eyolf and ayther nayther for Yakov Yea. A hundred and how? They did well to re-christien her Pluhurabelle. O lorelcy! What a loddon lodes! Heigh ho! But it's quite on the cards she'll shed more and merrier, twills and trills, sparefours and spoil-fives, nordsihkes and sudsevers and ayes and neins to

a litter. Grandfarthring nap and Messamisery and the
knave of all knaves and the joker. Heehaw! She must
have been a gadabount in her day, so she must, more
than most. Shoal she was, gidgad. She had a flewmen
of her owen. Then a toss nare scared that lass, so aimai
moe, that's agapo! Tell me, tell me, how cam she camlin
through all her fellows, the neckar she was, the diveline?
Casting her perils before our swains from Fonte-in-
Monte to Tidingtown and from Tidingtown tilhavet.
Linking one and knocking the next, tapting a flank and
tipting a jutty and palling in and pietaring out and
clyding by on her eastway. Waiwhou was the first thur-
ever burst? Someone he was, whuebra they were, in a
tactic attack or in single combat. Tinker, tilar, souldrer,
salor, Pieman Peace or Polistaman. That's the thing I'm
elwys on edge to esk. Push up and push vardar and
come to uphill headquarters! Was it waterlows year,
after Grattan or Flood, or when maids were in Arc or
when three stood hosting? Fidaris will find where the
Doubt arises like Nieman from Nirgends found the Nihil.
Worry you sighin foh, Albern, O Anser? Untie the gem-
man's fistiknots, Qvic and Nuancee! She can't put her
hand on him for the moment. Tez thelon langlo, walking weary! Such a loon waybashwards to row! She sid
herself she hardly knows whuon the annals her graveller
was, a dynast of Leinster, a wolf of the sea, or what he
did or how blyth she played or how, when, why, where
and who offon he jumpnad her and how it was gave her
away. She was just a young thin pale soft shy slim slip
of a thing then, sauntering, by silvamoonlake and he was
a heavy trudging lurching lieabroad of a Curraghman,
making his hay for whose sun to shine on, as tough as
the oaktrees (peats be with them!) used to rustle that
time down by the dykes of killing Kildare, for forstfell-
foss with a plash across her. She thought she's sankh

neathe the ground with nymphant shame when he gave
her the tigris eye! O happy fault! Me wish it was he!
You're wrong there, corribly wrong! Tisn't only tonight
you're anacheronistic! It was ages behind that when
nullahs were nowhere, in county Wickenlow, garden of
Erin, before she ever dreamt she'd lave Kilbride and go
foaming under Horsepass bridge, with the great souther-
western windstorming her traces and the midland's
grainwaster asarch for her track, to wend her ways by-
andby, robecca or worse, to spin and to grind, to swab
and to thrash, for all her golden lifey in the barley-
fields and pennylotts of Humphrey's fordofhurdlestown
and lie with a landleaper, wellingtonorsehcr. Alesse, the
lagos of girly days! For the dove of the dunas! Wasut?
Izod? Are you sarthin suir? Not where the Finn fits into
the Mourne, not where the Nore takes lieve of Blœm,
not where the Braye divarts the Farer, not where the
Moy changez her minds twixt Cullin and Conn tween
Cunn and Collin? Or where Neptune sculled and Triton-
ville rowed and leandros three bumped heroines two?
Neya, narev, nen, nonni, nos! Then whereabouts in Ow
and Ovoca? Was it yst with wyst or Lucan Yokan or
where the hand of man has never set foot? Dell me
where, the fairy ferse time! I will if you listen. You know
the dinkel dale of Luggelaw? Well, there once dwelt a
local heremite, Michael Arklow was his riverend name,
(with many a sigh I aspersed his lavabibs!) and one
venersderg in junojuly, oso sweet and so cool and so
limber she looked, Nance the Nixie, Nanon L'Escaut, in
the silence, of the sycomores, all listening, the kindling
curves you simply can't stop feeling, he plunged both
of his newly anointed hands, the core of his cushlas, in
her singimari saffron strumans of hair, parting them and
soothing her and mingling it, that was deep dark and
ample like this red bog at sundown. By that Vale Vow-

close's lucydlac, the reignbeau's heavenarches arronged
orranged her. Afrothdizzying galbs, her enamelled eyes
indergoading him on to the vierge violetian. Wish a
wish! Why a why? Mavro! Letty Lerck's lafing light
throw those laurals now on her daphdaph teasesong
petrock. Maass! But the majik wavus has elfun anon
meshes. And Simba the Slayer of his Oga is slewd. He
cuddle not help himself, thurso that hot on him, he had
to forget the monk in the man so, rubbing her up and
smoothing her down, he baised his lippes in smiling
mood, kiss akiss after kisokushk (as he warned her
niver to, niver to, nevar) on Anna-na-Poghue's of the
freckled forehead. While you'd parse secheressa she
hielt her souff'. But she ruz two feet hire in her aisne
aestumation. And steppes on stilts ever since. That was
kissuahealing with bantur for balm! O, wasn't he the
bold priest? And wasn't she the naughty Livvy? Nautic
Naama's now her navn. Two lads in scoutsch breeches
went through her before that, Barefoot Burn and Wal-
lowme Wade, Lugnaquillia's noblesse pickts, before she
had a hint of a hair at her fanny to hide or a bossom to
tempt a birch canoedler not to mention a bulgic porter-
house barge. And ere that again, leada, laida, all un-
raidy, too faint to buoy the fairiest rider, too frail to
flirt with a cygnet's plume, she was licked by a hound,
Chirripa-Chirruta, while poing her pee, pure and simple,
on the spur of the hill in old Kippure, in birdsong and
shearingtime, but first of all, worst of all, the wiggly
livvly, she sideslipped out by a gap in the Devil's glen
while Sally her nurse was sound asleep in a sloot and,
feefee fiefie, fell over a spillway before she found her
stride and lay and wriggled in all the stagnant black
pools of rainy under a fallow coo and she laughed
innocefree with her limbs aloft and a whole drove of

maiden hawthorns blushing and looking askance upon her.

Drop me the sound of the findhorn's name, Mtu or Mti, somebogger was wisness. And drip me why in the flenders was she frickled. And trickle me through was she marcellewaved or was it weirdly a wig she wore. And whitside did they droop their glows in their florry, aback to wist or affront to sea? In fear to hear the dear so near or longing loth and loathing longing? Are you in the swim or are you out? O go in, go on, go an! I mean about what you know. I know right well what you mean. Rother! You'd like the coifs and guimpes, snouty, and me to do the greasy jub on old Veronica's wipers. What am I rancing now and I'll thank you? Is it a pinny or is it a surplice? Arran, where's your nose? And where's the starch? That's not the vesdre benediction smell. I can tell from here by their *eau de Colo* and the scent of her oder they're Mrs Magrath's. And you ought to have aird them. They've moist come off her. Creases in silk they are, not crampton lawn. Baptiste me, father, for she has sinned! Through her catchment ring she freed them easy, with her hips' hurrahs for her knees' dontelleries. The only parr with frills in old the plain. So they are, I declare! Welland well! If tomorrow keeps fine who'll come tripping to sightsee? How'll? Ask me next what I haven't got! The Belvedarean exhibitioners. In their cruisery caps and oarsclub colours. What hoo, they band! And what hoa, they buck! And here is her nubilee letters too. Ellis on quay in scarlet thread. Linked for the world on a flushcaloured field. Annan exe after to show they're not Laura Keown's. O, may the diabolo twisk your seifety pin! You child of Mammon, Kinsella's Lilith! Now who has been tearing the leg of her drawers on her? Which leg is it? The one with the

bells on it. Rinse them out and aston along with you!
Where did I stop? Never stop! Continuarration! You're
not there yet. I amstel waiting. Garonne, garonne!

Well, after it was put in the Mercy Cordial Mendi-
cants' Sitterdag-Zindeh-Munaday Wakeschrift (for once
they sullied their white kidloves, chewing cuds after
their dinners of cheeckin and beggin, with their show
us it here and their mind out of that and their when
you're quite finished with the reading matarial), even
the snee that snowdon his hoaring hair had a skunner
against him. Thaw, thaw, sava, savuto! Score Her Chuff
Exsquire! Everywhere erriff you went and every bung
you arver dropped into, in cit or suburb or in addled
areas, the Rose and Bottle or Phoenix Tavern or Power's
Inn or Jude's Hotel or wherever you scoured the coun-
tryside from Nannywater to Vartryville or from Porta
Lateen to the lootin quarter you found his ikom etched
tipside down or the cornerboys cammocking his guy
and Morris the Man, with the role of a royss in his turgos
the turrible, (Evropeahahn cheic house, unskimmed
sooit and yahoort, hamman now cheekmee, Ahdahm this
way make, Fatima, half turn!) reeling and railing round
the local as the peihos piped und ubanjees twanged,
with oddfellow's triple tiara busby rotundarinking round
his · scalp. Like Pate-by-the-Neva or Pete-over-Meer.
This is the Hausman all paven and stoned, that cribbed
the Cabin that never was owned that cocked his leg and
hennad his Egg. And the mauldrin rabble around him
in areopage, fracassing a great bingkan cagnan with
their timpan crowders. Mind your Grimmfather! Think
of your Ma! Hing the Hong is his jove's hangnomen!
Lilt a bolero, bulling a law! She swore on croststyx nyne
wyndabouts she's be level with all the snags of them yet.
Par the Vulnerable Virgin's Mary del Dame! So she said
to herself she'd frame a plan to fake a shine, the mischief-

maker, the like of it you niever heard. What plan? Tell
me quick and dongu so crould! What the meurther did
she mague? Well, she bergened a zakbag, a shammy
mailsack, with the lend of a loan of the light of his lam-
pion, off one of her swapsons, Shaun the Post, and then
she went and consulted her chapboucqs, old Mot
Moore, Casey's Euclid and the Fashion Display and
made herself tidal to join in the mascarete. O gig goggle
of gigguels. I can't tell you how! It's too screaming to
rizo, rabbit it all! Minneha, minnehi minaaehe, minneho!
O but you must, you must really! Make my hear it gurgle
gurgle, like the farest gargle gargle in the dusky dirgle
dargle! By the holy well of Mulhuddart I swear I'd
pledge my chanza getting to heaven through Tirry and
Killy's mount of impiety to hear it all, aviary word! O,
leave me my faculties, woman, a while! If you don't like
my story get out of the punt. Well, have it your own
way, so. Here, sit down and do as you're bid. Take my
stroke and bend to your bow. Forward in and pull your
overthepoise! Lisp it slaney and crisp it quiet. Deel me
longsome. Tongue your time now. Breathe thet deep.
Thouat's the fairway. Hurry slow and scheldt you go.
Lynd us your blessed ashes here till I scrub the canon's
underpants. Flow now. Ower more. And pooleypooley.

First she let her hair fal and down it flussed to her
feet its teviots winding coils. Then, mothernaked, she
sampood herself with galawater and fraguant pistania
mud, wupper and lauar, from crown to sole. Next she
greesed the groove of her keel, warthes and wears and
mole and itcher, with antifouling butterscatch and tur-
fentidc and serpenthyme and with leafmould she ushered round prunella isles and eslats dun, quincecunct,
allover her little mary. Peeld gold of waxwork her jelly-
belly and her grains of incense anguille bronze. And
after that she wove a garland for her hair. She pleated

it. She plaited it. Of meadowgrass and riverflags, the
bulrush and waterweed, and of fallen griefs of weeping
willow. Then she made her bracelets and her anklets
and her armlets and a jetty amulet for necklace of clicking cobbles and pattering pebbles and rumbledown
rubble, richmond and rehr, of Irish rhunerhinerstones
and shellmarble bangles. That done, a dawk of smut to
her airy ey, Annushka Lutetiavitch Pufflovah, and the
lellipos cream to her lippeleens and the pick of the
paintbox for her pommettes, from strawbirry reds to
extra violates, and she sendred her boudeloire maids to
His Affluence, Ciliegia Grande and Kirschie Real, the
two chirsines, with respecks from his missus, seepy and
sewery, and a request might she passe of him for a minnikin. A call to pay and light a taper, in Brie-on-Arrosa,
back in a sprizzling. The cock striking mine, the stalls
bridely sign, there's Zambosy waiting for Me! She said
she wouldn't be half her length away. Then, then, as
soon as the lump his back was turned, with her mealie-
bag slang over her shulder, Anna Livia, oysterface, forth
of her bassein came.

Describe her! Hustle along, why can't you? Spitz on
the iern while it's hot. I wouldn't miss her for irthing on
nerthe. Not for the lucre of lomba strait. Oceans of
Gaud, I mosel hear that! Ogowe presta! Leste, before
Julia sees her! Ishekarry and washemeskad, the carishy
caratimaney? Whole lady fair? Duodecimoroon? Bon a
ventura? Malagassy? What had she on, the liddel oud
oddity? How much did she scallop, harness and
weights? Here she is, Amnisty Ann! Call her calamity
electrifies man.

No electress at all but old Moppa Necessity, angin
mother of injons. I'll tell you a test. But you must sit
still. Will you hold your peace and listen well to what

I am going to say now? It might have been ten or twenty
to one of the night of Allclose or the next of April when
the flip of her hoogly igloo flappered and out toetippit a
bushman woman, the dearest little moma ever you saw,
nodding around her, all smiles, with ems of embarras
and aues to awe, between two ages, a judyqueen, not up
to your elb. Quick, look at her cute and saise her quirk
for the bicker she lives the slicker she grows. Save us
and tagus! No more? Werra where in ourthe did you ever
pick a Lambay chop as big as a battering ram? Ay,
you're right. I'm epte to forgetting, Like Liviam Liddle
did Loveme Long. The linth of my hough, I say! She
wore a ploughboy's nailstudded clogs, a pair of plough-
fields in themselves: a sugarloaf hat with a gaudyquiviry
peak and a band of gorse for an arnoment and a hundred streamers dancing off it and a guildcred pin to
pierce it: owlglassy bicycles boggled her eyes: and a fish-
netzeveil for the sun not to spoil the wrinklings of her
hydeaspects: potatorings boucled the loose laubes of her
laudsnarers: her nude cuba stockings were salmospot-
speckled: she sported a galligo shimmy of hazevaipar
tinto that never was fast till it ran in the washing: stout
stays, the rivals, lined her length; her bloodorange buck-
knickers, a two in one garment, showed natural nigger
boggers, fancyfastened, free to undo: her blackstripe
tan joseph was sequansewn and teddybearlined, with
wavy rushgreen epaulettes and a leadown here and
there of royal swansruff: a brace of gaspers stuck in her
hayrope garters: her civvy codroy coat with alpheubett
buttons was boundaried round with a twobar tunnel
belt: a fourpenny bit in each pocketside weighed her
safe from the blowaway windrush; she had a clothespeg
tight astride on her joki's nose and she kep on grinding
a sommething quaint in her fiumy mouth and the rrreke

of the fluve of the tail of the gawan of her snuffdrab
siouler's skirt trailed ffiffty odd Irish miles behind her
lungarhodes.

Hellsbells, I'm sorry I missed her! Sweet gumptyum
and nobody fainted! But in whelk of her mouths? Was
her naze alight? Everyone that saw her said the dowce
little delia looked a bit queer. Lotsy trotsy, mind the
poddle! Missus, be good and don't fol in the say! Fenny
poor hex she must have charred. Kickhams a frumpier
ever you saw! Making mush mullet's eyes at her boys
dobelon. And they crowned her their chariton queen, all
the maids. Of the may? You don't say! Well for her she
couldn't see herself. I recknitz wharfore the darling mur-
rayed her mirror. She did? Mersey me! There was a
koros of drouthdropping surfacemen, boomslanging and
plugchewing, fruiteyeing and flowerfeeding, in contemplation of the fluctuation and the undification of her
filimentation, lolling and leasing on North Lazers' Waal
all eelfare week by the Jukar Yoick's and as soon as they
saw her meander by that marritime way in her grass-
winter's weeds and twigged who was under her arch-
deaconess bonnet, Avondale's fish and Clarence's poison,
sedges an to aneber, Wit-upon-Crutches to Master Bates:
*Between our two southsates and the granite they're
warming, or her face has been lifted or Alp has doped!*
But what was the game in her mixed baggyrhatty?
Just the tembo in her tumbo or pilipili from her pepper-
pot? Saas and taas and specis bizaas. And where in
thunder did she plunder? Fore the battle or efter the
ball? I want to get it frisk from the soorce. I aubette my
bearb it's worth while poaching on! Shake it up, do,
do! That's a good old son of a ditch! I promise I'll make
it worth your while. And I don't mean maybe. Nor yet
with a goodfor. Spey me pruth and I'll tale you true.

Well, arundgirond in a waveney lyne aringarouma

she pattered and swung and sidled, dribbling her
boulder through narrowa mosses, the diliskydrear on
our drier side and the vilde vetchvine agin us, curara
here, careero there, not knowing which medway or
weser to strike 'it, edereider, making chattahoochee all
to her ain chichiu, like Santa Claus at the cree of the
pale and puny, nistling to hear for their tiny hearties,
her arms encircling Isolabella, then running with rec-
onciled Romas and Reims, on like a lech to be off like
a dart, then bathing Dirty Hans' spatters with spittle,
with a Christmas box apiece for aisch and iveryone of
her childer, the birthday gifts they dreamt they gabe
her, the spoiled she fleetly laid at our door! On the matt,
by the pourch and inunder the cellar. The rivulets ran
aflod to see, the glashaboys, the pollynooties. Out of the
paunschaup on to the pyre. And they all about her, ju-
venile leads and ingenuinas, from the slime of their
slums and artesaned wellings, rickets and riots, like the
Smyly boys at their vicereine's levee. Vivi vienne, little
Annchen! Vielo Anna, high life! Sing us a sula, O, su-
suria! Ausone sidulcis! Hasn't she tambre! Chipping her
and raising a bit of a chir or a jary every dive she'd neb
in her culdee sacco of wabbash she raabed and reach
out her maundy meerschaundize, poor souvenir as per
ricorder and all for sore aringarung, stinkers and heelers,
laggards and primelads, her furzeborn sons and dribble-
derry daughters, a thousand and one of them, and
wickerpotluck for each of them. For evil and ever. And
kiks the buch. A tinker's bann and a barrow to boil his
billy for Gipsy Lee; a cartridge of cockaleekie soup
for Chummy the Guardsman; for sulky Pender's acid
nephew deltoïd drops, curiously strong; a cough and a
rattle and wildrose cheeks for poor Piccolina Petite Mac-
Farlanc; a jigsaw puzzle of needles and pins and
blankets and shins between them for Isabel, Jezebel and

Llewelyn Mmarriage; a brazen nose and pigiron mittens for Johnny Walker Beg; a papar flag of the saints
and stripes for Kevineen O'Dea; a puffpuff for Pudge
Craig and a nightmarching hare for Techertim Tombigby; waterleg and gumboots each for Bully Hayes and
Hurricane Hartigan; a prodigal heart and fatted calves
for Buck Jones, the pride of Clonliffe; a loaf of bread and
a father's early aim for Val from Skibereen; a jauntingcar
for Larry Doolin, the Ballyclee jackeen; a seasick trip
on a government ship for Teague O'Flanagan; a louse
and trap for Jerry Coyle; slushmincepies for Andy Mackenzie; a hairclip and clackdish for Penceless Peter; that
twelve sounds look for G. V. Brooke; a drowned doll,
to face downwards for modest Sister Anne Mortimer;
altar falls for.Blanchisse's bed; Wildairs' breechettes for
Magpeg Woppington; to Sue Dot a big eye; to Sam Dash
a false step; snakes in clover, picked and scotched, and
a vaticanned viper catcher's visa for Patsy Presbys; a
reiz every morning for Standfast Dick and a drop every
minute for Stumblestone Davy; scruboak beads for beatified Biddy; two appletweed stools for Eva Mobbely;
for Saara Philpot a jordan vale tearorne; a pretty box
of Pettyfib's Powder for Eileen Aruna to whiten her
teeth and outflash Helen Arhone; a whippingtop for
Eddy Lawless; for Kitty Coleraine of Butterman's Lane
a penny wise for her foolish pitcher; a putty shovel for
Terry the Puckaun; an apotamus mask for Promoter
Dunne; a niester egg with a twicedated shell and a dynamight right for Pavl the Curate; a collera morbous for
Mann in the Cloack; a starr and girton for Draper and
Deane; for Will-of-the-Wisp and Barny-the-Bark two
mangolds noble to sweeden their bitters; for Oliver
Bound a way in his frey; for Seumas, thought little, a
crown he feels big; a tibertine's pile with a Congoswood
cross on the back for Sunny Twimjim; a praises be and

spare me days for Brian the Bravo; penteplenty of pity
with lubilashings of lust for Olona Lena Magdalena;
for Camilla, Dromilla, Ludmilla, Mamilla, a bucket, a
packet, a book and a pillow; for Nancy Shannon a
Tuami brooch; for Dora Riparia Hopeandwater a cool-
ing douche and a warmingpan; a pair of Blarney braggs
for Wally Meagher; a hairpin slatepencil for Elsie Oram
to scratch her toby, doing her best with her volgar frac-
tions; an old age pension for Betty Bellezza; a bag of
the blues for Funny Fitz; a *Missa pro Messa* for Taff de
Taff; Jill, the spoon of a girl, for Jack, the broth of a
boy; a Rogerson Crusoe's Friday fast for Caducus Angelus Rubiconstein; three hundred and sixtysix poplin
tyne for revery warp in the weaver's woof for Victor
Hugonot; a stiff steaded rake and good varians muck for
Kate the Cleaner; a hole in the ballad for Hosty; two
dozen of cradles for J.F.X.P. Coppinger; tenpounten
on the pop for the daulphins born with five spoiled
squibs for Infanta; a letter to last a lifetime for Maggi
beyond by the ashpit; the heftiest frozenmeat woman
from Lusk to Livienbad for Felim the Ferry; spas and
speranza and symposium's syrup for decayed and blind
and gouty Gough; a change of naves and joys of ills for
Armoricus Tristram Amoor Saint Lawrence; a guillotine
shirt for Reuben Redbreast and hempen suspendeats for
Brennan on the Moor; an oakanknee for Conditor
Sawyer and musquodoboits for Great Tropical Scott; a
C₃ peduncle for Karmalite Kane; a sunless map of the
month, including the sword and stamps, for Shemus
O'Shaun the Post; a jackal with hide for Browne but
Nolan; a stonecold shoulder for Donn Joe Vance; all lock
and no stable for Honorbright Merreytrickx; a big drum
for Billy Dunboyne; a guilty goldeny bellows, below me
blow me, for Ida Ida and a hushaby rocker, Elletrouve-
tout, for Who-is-silvier—Where-is-he?; whatever you

like to swilly to swash, Yuinness or Yennessy, Laagen or
Niger, for Festus King and Roaring Peter and Frisky
Shorty and Treacle Tom and O. B. Behan and Sully the
Thug and Master Magrath and Peter Cloran and O'Dela-
warr Rossa and Nerone MacPacem and whoever you
chance to meet knocking around; and a pig's bladder
balloon for Selina Susquehanna Stakelum. But what did
she give to Pruda Ward and Katty Kanel and Peggy
Quilty and Briery Brosna and Teasy Kieran and Ena
Lappin and Muriel Maassy and Zusan Camac and
Melissa Bradogue and Flora Ferns and Fauna Fox-
Goodman and Grettna Greaney and Penelope Inglesante
and Lezba Licking like Leytha Liane and Roxana Rohan
with Simpatica Sohan and Una Bina Laterza and Trina
La Mesme and Philomena O'Farrell and Irmak Elly and
Josephine Foyle and Snakeshead Lily and Fountainoy
Laura and Marie Xavier Agnes Daisy Frances de Sales
Macleay? She gave them ilcka madre's daughter a moon-
flower and a bloodvein: but the grapes that ripe before
reason to them that devide the vinedress. So on Izzy, her
shamemaid, love shone befond her tears as from Shem,
her penmight, life past befoul his prime.

My colonial, wardha bagful! A bakereen's dusind with
tithe tillies to boot. That's what you may call a tale of a
tub! And Hibernonian market! All that and more under
one crinoline envelope if you dare to break the pork-
barrel seal. No wonder they'd run from her pison plague.
Throw us your hudson soap for the honour of Clane!
The wee taste the water left. I'll raft it back, first thing
in the marne. Merced mulde! Ay, and don't forget the
reckitts I lohaned you. You've all the swirls your side
of the current. Well, am I to blame for that if I have?
Who said you're to blame for that if you have? You're
a bit on the sharp side. I'm on the wide. Only snuffers'
cornets drifts my way that the cracka dvine chucks out

of his cassock, with her estheryear's marsh narcissus to make him recant his vanitty fair. Foul strips of his chinook's bible I do be reading, dodwell disgustered but chickled with chuckles at the tittles is drawn on the tattlepage. *Senior ga dito: Faciasi Omo! E omo fu fò.* Ho! Ho! *Senior ga dito: Faciasi Hidamo! Hidamo se ga facessà.* Ha! Ha! And *Die Windermere Dichter* and Lefanu (Sheridan's) old *House by the Coachyard* and Mill (J.) *On Woman* with *Ditto on the Floss*. Ja, a swamp for Altmuehler and a stone for his flossies! I know how racy they move his wheel. My hands are blawcauld between isker and suda like that piece of pattern chayney there, lying below. Or where is it? Lying beside the sedge I saw it. Hoangho, my sorrow, I've lost it! Aimihi! With that turbary water who could see? So near and yet so far! But O, gihon! I lovat a gabber. I could listen to maure and moravar again. Regn onder river. Flies do your float. Thick is the life for mere.

Well, you know or don't you kennet or haven't I told you every telling has a taling and that's the he and the she of it. Look, look, the dusk is growing! My branches lofty are taking root. And my cold cher's gone ashley. Fieluhr? Filou! What age is at? It saon is late. 'Tis endless now senne eye or erewone last saw Waterhouse's clogh. They took it asunder, I hurd thum sigh. When will they reassemble it? O, my back, my back, my bach! I'd want to go to Aches-les-Pains. Pingpong! There's the Belle for Sexaloitez! And Concepta de Send-us-pray! Pang! Wring out the clothes! Wring in the dew! Godavari, vert the showers! And grant thaya grace! Aman. Will we spread them here now? Ay, we will. Flip! Spread on your bank and I'll spread mine on mine. Flep! It's what I'm doing. Spread! It's churning chill. Der went is rising. I'll lay a few stones on the hostel sheets. A man and his bride embraced between them. Else I'd

have sprinkled and folded them only. And I'll tie my
butcher's apron here. It's suety yet. The strollers will
pass it by. Six shifts, ten kerchiefs, nine to hold to the
fire and this for the code, the convent napkins, twelve,
one baby's shawl. Good mother Jossiph knows, she said.
Whose head? Mutter snores? Deataceas! Wharnow are
alle her childer, say? In kingdome gone or power to
come or gloria be to them farther? Allalivial, allalluvial!
Some here, more no more, more again lost alla stranger.
I've heard tell that same brooch of the Shannons was
married into a family in Spain. And all the Dunders de
Dunnes in Markland's Vineland beyond Brendan's her-
ring pool takes number nine in yangsee's hats. And one
of Biddy's beads went bobbing till she rounded up lost
histereve with a marigold and a cobbler's candle in a
side strain of a main drain of a manzinahurries off Bachelor's Walk. But all that's left to the last of the Meaghers
in the loup of the years prefixed and between is one knee-
buckle and two hooks in the front. Do you tell me that
now? I do in troth. Orara por Orbe and poor Las Ani-
mas! Ussa, Ulla, we're umbas all! Mezha, didn't you
hear it a deluge of times, ufer and ufer, respund to
spond? You deed, you deed! I need, I need! It's that
irrawaddyng I've stoke in my aars. It all but husheth
the lethest zswound. Oronoko! What's your trouble? Is
that the great Finnleader himself in his joakimono on his
statue riding the high horse there forehengist? Father of
Otters, it is himself! Yonne there! Isset that? On Falla-
reen Common? You're thinking of Astley's Amphitheay-
ter where the bobby restrained you making sugarstuck
pouts to the ghostwhite horse of the Peppers. Throw the
cobwebs from your eyes, woman, and spread your washing proper! It's well I know your sort of slop. Flap! Ireland sober is Ireland stiff. Lord help you, Maria, full of
grease, the load is with me! Your prayers. I sonht zo!

Madammangut! Were you lifting your elbow, tell us,
glazy cheeks, in Conway's Carrigacurra canteen? Was
I what, hobbledyhips? Flop! Your rere gait's creako-
rheuman bitts your butts disagrees. Amn't I up since the
damp dawn, marthared mary allacook, with Corrigan's
pulse and varicoarse veins, my pramaxle smashed, Alice
Jane in decline and my oneeyed mongrel twice run over,
soaking and bleaching boiler rags, and sweating cold, a
widow like me, for to deck my tennis champion son, the
laundryman with the lavandier flannels? You won your
limpopo limp from the husky hussars when Collars and
Cuffs was heir to the town and your slur gave the stink
to Carlow. Holy Scamander, I sar it again! Near the
golden falls. Icis on us! Seints of light! Zezere! Subdue
your noise, you hamble creature! What is it but a black-
burry growth or the dwyergray ass them four old codg-
ers owns. Are you meanam Tarpey and Lyons and
Gregory? I meyne now, thank all, the four of them, and
the roar of them, that draves that stray in the mist and
old Johnny MacDougal along with them. Is that the
Poolbeg flasher beyant, pharphar, or a fireboat coasting
nyar the Kishtna or a glow I behold within a hedge or
my Garry come back from the Indes? Wait till the honey-
ing of the lune, love! Die eve, little eve, die! We see
that wonder in your eye. We'll meet again, we'll part
once more. The spot I'll seek if the hour you'll find. My
chart shines high where the blue milk's upset. Forgive-
mequick, I'm going! Bubye! And you, pluck your watch,
forgetmenot. Your evenlode. So save to jurna's end! My
sights are swimming thicker on me by the shadows to
this place. I sow home slowly now by own way, moy-
valley way. Towy I too, rathmine.

Ah, but she was the queer old skeowsha anyhow,
Anna Livia, trinkettoes! And sure he was the quare old
buntz too, Dear Dirty Dumpling, foostherfather of fin-

galls and dotthergills. Gammer and gaffer we're all their gangsters. Hadn't he seven dams to wive him? And every dam had her seven crutches. And every crutch had its seven hues. And each hue had a differing cry. Sudds for me and supper for you and the doctor's bill for Joe John. Befor! Bifur! He married his markets, cheap by foul, I know, like any Etrurian Catholic Heathen, in their pinky limony creamy birnies and their turkiss indienne mauves. But at milkidmass who was the spouse? Then all that was was fair. Tys Elvenland! Teems of times and happy returns. The seim anew. Ordovico or viricordo. Anna was, Livia is, Plurabelle's to be. Northmen's thing made southfolk's place but howmulty plurators made eachone in person? Latin me that, my trinity scholard, out of eure sanscreed into oure eryan! *Hircus Civis Eblanensis!* He had buckgoat paps on him, soft ones for orphans. Ho, Lord! Twins of his bosom. Lord save us! And ho! Hey? What all men. Hot? His tittering daughters of. Whawk?

Can't hear with the waters of. The chittering waters of. Flittering bats, fieldmice bawk talk. Ho! Are you not gone ahome? What Thom Malone? Can't hear with bawk of bats, all thim liffeying waters of. Ho, talk save us! My foos won't moos. I feel as old as yonder elm. A tale told of Shaun or Shem? All Livia's daughtersons. Dark hawks hear us. Night! Night! My ho head halls. I feel as heavy as yonder stone. Tell me of John or Shaun? Who were Shem and Shaun the living sons or daughters of? Night now! Tell me, tell me, tell me, elm! Night night! Telmetale of stem or stone. Beside the rivering waters of, hitherandthithering waters of. Night!

Tales Told of Shem and Shaun

GENTES and laitymen, fullstoppers and semicolonials, hybreds and lubberds!

Eins within a space and a wearywide space it wast ere wohned a Mookse. The onesomeness wast alltolonely, archunsitslike, broady oval, and a Mookse he would a walking go (My hood! cries Antony Romeo), so one grandsumer evening, after a great morning and his good supper of gammon and spittish, having flabelled his eyes, pilleoled his nostrils, vacticanated his ears and palliumed his throats, he put on his impermeable, seized his impugnable, harped on his crown and stepped out of his immobile *De Rure Albo* (socolled becauld it was chalkfull of masterplasters and had borgeously letout gardens strown with cascadas, pintacostecas, horthoducts and currycombs) and set off from Ludstown *a spasso* to see how badness was badness in the weirdest of all pensible ways.

As he set off with his father's sword, his *lancia spezzata,* he was girded on, and with that between his legs and his turkeels, our once in only Bragspear, he clanked, to my clinking, from veetoes to threetop, every inch of an immortal.

He had not walked over a pentiadpair of parsecs from his azylium when at the turning of the Shinshone Lanteran near Saint Bowcry's-without-his-Walls he came (secunding to the one one oncth of the propecies, *Amnis Limina Permanent*) upon the most unconsciously boggylooking stream he ever locked his eyes with. Out

of the colliens it took a rise by daubing itself Ninon. It
looked little and it smelt of brown and it thought in nar
rows and it talked showshallow. And as it rinn it dribbled like any lively purliteasy: *My, my, my! Me and me!
Little down dream don't I love thee!*

And, I declare, what was there on the yonder bank
of the stream that would be a river, parched on a limb
of the olum, bolt downright, but the Gripes? And no
doubt he was fit to be dried for why had he not been
having the juice of his times?

His pips had been neatly all drowned on him; his
polps were charging odours every older minute; he was
quickly for getting the dresser's desdaign on the flyleaf
of his frons; and he was quietly for giving the bailiff's
distrain on to the bulkside of his *cul de Pompe.* In all
his specious heavings, as be lived by Optimus Maximus,
the Mookse had never seen his Dubville brooder on-low
so nigh to a pickle.

Adrian (that was the Mookse now's assumptinome)
stuccstill phiz-à-phiz to the Gripes in an accessit of
aurignacian. But Allmookse must to Moodend much as
Allrouts, austereways or wastersways, in roaming run
through Room. Hic sor a stone, singularly illud, and on
hoc stone Seter satt huc sate which it filled quite popos-
terously and by acclammitation to its fullest justotoryum
and whereopum with his unfallable encyclicling upom
his alloilable, diupetriark of the wouest, and the athe-
mystsprinkled pederect he always walked with, *Deus-
dedit,* cheek by jowel with his frisherman's blague,
Bellua Triumphanes, his everyway addedto wallat's col-
lectium, for yea longer he lieved yea broader he be-
taught of it, the fetter, the summe and the haul it cost,
he looked the first and last micahlike laicness of Quartus
the Fifth and Quintus the Sixth and Sixtus the Seventh
giving allnight sitting to Lio the Faultyfindth.

—Good appetite us, sir Mookse! How do you do it? cheeped the Gripes in a wherry whiggy maudelenian woice and the jackasses all within bawl laughed and brayed for his intentions for they knew their sly toad lowry now. I am rarumominum blessed to see you, my dear mouster. Will you not perhopes tell me everything if you are pleased, sanity? All about aulne and lithial and allsall allinall about awn and liseias? Ney?

Think of it! O miserendissimest retempter! A Gripes!

—Rats! bullowed the Mookse most telesphorously, the concionator, and the sissymusses and the zozzymusses in their robenhauses quailed to hear his tardeynois at all for you cannot wake a silken nouse out of a hoarse oar. Blast yourself and your anathomy infairioriboos! No, hang you for an animal rurale! I am superbly in my supremest poncif! Abase you, baldyqueens! Gather behind me, satraps! Rots!

—I am till infinity obliged with you, bowed the Gripes, his whine having gone to his palpruy head. I am still always having a wish on all my extremities. By the watch, what is the time, pace?

Figure it! The pining peever! To a Mookse!

—Ask my index, mund my achilles, swell my obolum, woshup my nase serene, answered the Mookse, rapidly by turning clement, urban, eugenious and celestian in the formose of good grogory humours. Quote awhore? That is quite about what I came on *my* missions with *my* intentions *laudibiliter* to settle with *you*, barbarousse. Let thor be orlog. Let Pauline be Irene. Let you be Beeton. And let me be Los Angeles. Now measure your length. Now estimate my capacity. Well, sour? Is this space of our couple of hours too dimensional for you, temporiser? Will you give you up? *Como? Fuert it?*

Sancta Patientia! You should have heard the voice that answered him! *Culla vosellina.*

—I was just thinkling upon that, swees Mooksey, but,
for all the rimc on my raisins, if I connow make my submission, I cannos give you up, the Gripes whimpered
from nethermost of his wanhope. Ishallassoboundbewil-
sothoutoosezit. My tumble, loudy bullocker, is my own.
My velicity is too fit in one stockend. And my spetial
inexshellsis the belowing things ab ove. But I will never
be abler to tell Your Honoriousness (here he near lost
his limb) though my corked father was bott a pseudo-
waiter, whose o'cloak you ware.

Incredible! Well, hear the inevitable.

—*Your* temple, *sus in cribro!* Semperexcommunicam-
biambisumers. Tugurios-in-Newrobe or Tukurias-in-
Ashies. Novarome, my creature, blievend bleives. My
building space in lyonine city is always to let to leonlike
Men, the Mookse in a most consistorous allocution pom-
pifically with immediate jurisdiction constantinently
concludded (what a crammer for the shapewrucked
Gripes!). And I regret to proclaim that it is out of my
temporal to help you from being killed my inchies,
(what a thrust!), as we first met each other newwhere
so airly. (Poor little sowsieved subsquashed Gripes! I
begin to feel contemption for him!). My side, thank de-
cretals, is as safe as motherour's houses, he continued,
and I can seen from my holeydome what it is to be
wholly sane. Unionjok and be joined to yok! Parysis, *tu
sais,* crucycrooks, belongs to him who parises himself.
And there I must leave you subject for the pressing. I
can prove that against you, weight a momentum, mein
goot enemy! or Cospol's not our star. I bet you this dozen
odd. This foluminous dozen odd. *Quas primas*—but 'tis
bitter to compote my knowledge's fructos of. Tomes.

Elevating, to give peint to his blick, his jewelled pederect to the allmysty cielung, he luckystruck blueild out

of a few shouldbe santillants, a cloister of starabouts over Maples, a lucciolys in Teresa street and a stopsign before Sophy Barratt's, he gaddered togodder the odds docence of his vellumes, gresk, letton and russicruxian, onto the lapse of his prolegs, into umfullth onescuppered, and sat about his widerproof. He proved it well whoonearth dry and drysick times, and *vremiament, tu cesses,* to the extinction of Niklaus altogether (Niklaus Alopysius having been the once Gripes's popwilled nimbum) by Neuclidius and Inexagoras and Mumfsen and Thumpsem, by Orasmus and by Amenius, by Anacletus the Jew and by Malachy the Augurer and by the Cappon's collection and after that, with Cheekee's gelatine and Alldaybrandy's formolon, he reproved it ehrltogether when not in that order sundering in some different order, alter three thirty and a hundred times by the binomial dioram and the penic walls and the ind, the Inklespill legends and the rure, the rule of the hoop and the blessons of expedience and the jus, the jugicants of Pontius Pilax and all the mummyscrips in Sick Bokes' Juncroom and the Chapters for the Cunning of the Chapters of the Conning Fox by Tail.

While that Mooksius with preprocession and with proprecession, duplicitly and diplussedly, was promulgating ipsofacts and sadcontras this raskolly Gripos he had allbust seceded in monophysicking his illsobordunates. But asawfulas he had caught his base semenoyous sarchnaktiers to combuccinate upon the silipses of his aspillouts and the acheporeoozers of his haggyown pneumax to synerethetise with the breadchestviousness of his sweeatovular ducose sofarfully the loggerthuds of his sakellaries were fond at variance with the synodals of his somepooliom and his babskissed nepogreasymost got the hoof from his philioquus.

—Efter thousand yaws, O Gripes con my sheepskins, yow will be belined to the world, enscayed Mookse the pius.

—Ofter thousand yores, amsered Gripes the gregary, be the goat of MacHammud's, yours may be still, O Mookse, more botheared.

—Us shall be chosen as the first of the last by the electress of Vale Hollow, obselved the Mookse nobily, for par the unicum of Elelijiacks, Us am in Our stabulary and that is what Ruby and Roby fall for, blissim.

The Pills, the Nasal Wash (Yardly's), the Army Man Cut, as british as bondstrict and as straightcut as when that brokenarched traveller from Nuzuland . . .

—Wee, cumfused the Gripes limply, shall not even be the last of the first, wee hope, when oust are visitated by the Veiled Horror. And, he added: Mee are relying entirely, see the fortethurd of Elissabed, on the weightiness of mear's breath. Puffut!

Unsightbared embouscher, relentless foe to social and business succes! (Hourihaleine) It might have been a happy evening but . . .

And they viterberated each other, *canis et coluber* with the wildest ever wielded since Tarriestinus lashed Pissasphaltium.

—Unuchorn!

—Ungulant!

—Uvuloid!

—Uskybeak!

And bullfolly answered volleyball.

Nuvoletta in her lightdress, spunn of sisteen shimmers, was looking· down on them, leaning over the bannistars and listening all she childishly could. How she was brightened when Shouldrups in his glaubering hochskied his welkinstuck and how she was overclused when Kneesknobs on his zwivvel was makeacting such

a paulse of himshelp! She was alone. All her nubied
companions were asleeping with the squirrels. Their
mivver, Mrs Moonan, was off in the Fuerst quarter
scrubbing the backsteps of Number 28. Fuvver, that
Skand, he was up in Norwood's sokaparlour, eating
oceans of Voking's Blemish. Nuvoletta listened as she
reflected herself, though the heavenly one with his con-
stellatria and his emanations stood between, and she
tried all she tried to make the Mookse look up at her
(but *he* was fore too adiaptotously farseeing) and to
make the Gripes hear how coy she could be (though he
was much too schystimatically auricular about *his ens*
to heed her) but it was all mild's vapour moist. Not
even her feignt reflection, Nuvoluccia, could they toke
their gnoses off for their minds with intrepifide fate and
bungless curiasity, were conclaved with Heliogobbleus
and Commodus and Enobarbarus and whatever the co-
ordinal dickens they did as their damprauch of papyrs
and buchstubs said. As if that was their spiration! As
if theirs could duiparate her queendim! As if she would
be third perty to search on search proceedings! She
tried all the winsome wonsome ways her four winds had
taught her. She tossed her sfumastelliacinous hair like
la princesse de la Petite Bretagne and she rounded her
mignons arms like Mrs Cornwallis-West and she smiled
over herself like the beauty of the image of the pose of
the daughter of the queen of the Emperour of Irelande
and she sighed after herself as were she born to bride
with Tristis Tristior Tristissimus. But, sweet madonine,
she might fair as well have carried her daisy's worth to
Florida. For the Mookse, a dogmad Accanite, were not
amoosed and the Gripes, a dubliboused Catalick, wis
pinefully obliviscent.

—I see, she sighed. There are menner.

The siss of the whisp of the sigh of the softzing at the

stir of the ver grose O arundo of a long one in midias
reeds: and shades began to glidder along the banks,
greepsing, greepsing, duusk unto duusk, and it was as
glooming as gloaming could be in the waste of all peac-
able worlds. Metamnisia was allsoonome coloroform
brune; citherior spiane an eaulande, innemorous and
unnumerose. The Mookse had a sound eyes right but
he could not all hear. The Gripes had light ears left yet
he could but ill see. He ceased. And he ceased, tung
and trit, and it was neversoever so dusk of both of
them. But still Moo thought on the deeps of the undths
he would profoundth come the morrokse and still Gri
feeled of the scripes he would escipe if by grice he had
luck enoupes.

Oh, how it was duusk! From Vallee Maraia to Grasya-
plaina, dormimust echo! Ah dew! Ah dew! It was so
duusk that the tears of night began to fall, first by ones
and twos, then by threes and fours, at last by fives and
sixes of sevens, for the tired ones were wecking, as we
weep now with them. O! O! O! Par la pluie!

Then there came down to the thither bank a woman
of no appearance (I believe she was a Black with chills
at her feet) and she gathered up his hoariness the
Mookse motamourfully where he was spread and carried him away to her invisible dwelling, thats hights,
Aquila Rapax, for he was the holy sacred solem and
poshup spit of her boshop's apron. So you see the Mookse
he had reason as I knew and you knew and he knew
all along. And there came down to the hither bank a
woman to all important (though they say that she was
comely, spite the cold in her heed) and, for he was as
like it as blow it to a hawker's hank, she plucked down
the Gripes, torn panicky autotone, in angeu from his
limb and cariad away its beotitubes with her to her unseen shieling, it is, *De Rore Coeli*. And so the poor

Gripes got wrong; for that is always how a Gripes is, always was and always will be. And it was never so thoughtful of either of them. And there were left now an only elmtree and but a stone. Polled with pietrous, Sierre but saule. O! Yes! And Nuvoletta, a lass.

Then Nuvoletta reflected for the last time in her little long life and she made up all her myriads of drifting minds in one. She cancelled all her engauzements. She climbed over the bannistars; she gave a childy cloudy cry: *Nuée! Nuée!* A lightdress fluttered. She was gone. And into the river that had been a stream (for a thousand of tears had gone eon her and come on her and she was stout and struck on dancing and her muddied name was Missisliffi) there fell a tear, a singult tear, the loveliest of all tears (I mean for those crylove fables fans who are 'keen' on the prettypretty commonface sort of thing you meet by hopeharrods) for it was a leaptear. But the river tripped on her by and by, lapping as though her heart was brook: *Why, why, why! Weh, O weh! I'se so silly to be flowing but I no canna stay!*

*   *   *

The Gracehoper was always jigging ajog, hoppy on akkant of his joyicity, (he had a partner pair of findlestilts to supplant him), or, if not, he was always making ungraceful overtures to Floh and Luse and Bienie and Vespatilla to play pupa-pupa and pulicy-pulicy and langtennas and pushpygyddyum and to commence insects with him, there mouthparts to his orefice and his gambills to there airy, processes, even if only in chaste, ameng the everlistings, behold a waspering pot. He would of curse melissciously, by his fore feelhers, flexors, contractors, depressors and extensors, lamely, harry me, marry me, bury me, bind me, till she was puce for shame and allso fourmish her in Spinner's housery at the earthsbest schoppinhour so summery as his cottage, which was cald fourmillierly Tingsomingenting, groped up. Or, if he was always striking up funny funereels with Besterfarther Zeuts, the Aged One, with all his wigeared corollas, albedinous and oldbuoyant, inscythe his elytrical wormcasket and Dehlia and Peonia, his druping nymphs, bewheedling him, compound eyes on hornitosehead, and Auld Letty Plussiboots to scratch his cacumen and cackle his tramsitus, diva deborah (seven bolls of sapo, a lick of lime, two spurts of fussfor, three-furts of sulph, a shake o'shouker, doze grains of migniss and a mesfull of midcap pitchies. The whool of the whaal in the wheel of the whorl of the Boubou from Bourneum has thus come to taon!), and with tambarins and cantoridettes soturning around his eggshill rock-coach their dance McCaper in retrophoebia, beck from bulk, like fantastic disossed and jenny aprils, to the ra, the ra, the ra, the ra, langsome heels and langsome toesis, attended to by a mutter and doffer duffmatt bax-ingmotch and a myrmidins of pszozlers pszinging *Satyr's Caudledayed Nice* and *Hombly, Dombly Sod We Awhile* but *Ho, Time Timeagen, Wake!* For if sciencium (what's what) can mute uns nought, 'a thought, abought the Great Sommboddy within the Omniboss, perhops an artsaccord (hoot's hoot) might sing ums tumtim abutt the Little Newbuddies that ring his panch. A high old tide for the barheated publics and the whole day as gratiis! Fudder and lighting for ally looty, any filly in a fog, for O'Cronione lags acrumbling in his sands but his sunsunsuns still tumble on. Erething above ground, as his Book of Breathings bed him, so as everwhy, sham or shunner, zeemliangly to kick time.

Grouscious me and scarab my sahul! What a bagateller it is! Libelulous! Inzanzarity! Pou! Pschla! Ptuh! What a zeit for the goths! vented the Ondt, who, not being a sommerfool, was thothfolly making chilly spaces at his-phex affront of the icinglass of his windhame, which was cold antitopically Nixnixundnix. We shall not come to party at that lopp's, he decided possibly, for he is not on our social list. Nor to Ba's berial nether, thon sloghard, this oldeborre's yaar ablong as there's a khul on a khat. Nefersenless, when he had safely looked up his ovipository, he loftet hails and prayed: May he me no voida water! Seekit Hatup! May no he me tile pig shed on! Suckit Hotup! As broad as Beppy's realm shall flourish my reign shall flourish! As high as Heppy's hevn shall flurrish my haine shall hurrish! Shall grow, shall flourish! Shall hurrish! Hummum.

The Ondt was a weltall fellow, raumybult and abel-boobied, bynear saw altitudinous wee a schelling in kopfers. He was sair sair sullemn and chairmanlooking when he was not making spaces in his psyche, but, laus! when he wore making spaces on his ikey, he ware mouche mothst secred and muravyingly wisechairman-looking. Now whim the sillybilly of a Gracehoper had jingled through a jungle of love and debts and jangled through a jumble of life in doubts afterworse, wetting with the bimblebeaks, drikking with nautonects, bilking with durrydunglecks and horing after ladybirdies (*ich-nehmon diagelegenaitoikon*) he fell joust as sieck as a sexton and tantoo pooveroo quant a churchprince, and wheer the midges to wend hemsylph or vosch to sirch for grub for his corapusse or to find a hospes, alick, he wist gnit! Bruko dry! fuko spint! Sultamont osa bare! And volomundo osi videvide! Nichtsnichtsundnichts! Not one pickopeck of muscowmoncy to bag a tittlebits of beebread! Iomio! Iomio! Crick's corbicule, which a plight! O moy Bog, he contrited with melancholy. Me-blizzered, him sluggered! I am heartily hungry!

He had eaten all the whilepaper, swallowed the lus-

tres, devoured forty flights of styearcases, chewed up all
the mensas and seccles, ronged the records, made mund-
balls of the ephemerids and vorasioused most glutinously
with the very timeplace in the ternitary—not too dusty
a cicada of neutriment for a chittinous chip so mitey.
But when Chrysalmas was on the bare branches, off he
went from Tingsomingenting. He took a round stroll
and he took a stroll round and he took a round stroll-
again till the grillies in his head and the leivnits in his
hair made him thought he had the Tossmania. Had he
twicycled the sees of the deed and trestraversed their
revermer? Was he come to hevre with his engiles or
gone to hull with the poop? The June snows was flock-
ing in thuckflues on the hegelstomes, millipeeds of it
and myriopoods, and a lugly whizzling tournedos, the
Boraborayellers, blohablasting tegolhuts up to tetties
and ruching sleets off the coppeehouses, playing ragno-
wrock rignewreck, with an irritant, penetrant, siphonop-
terous spuk. Graussssssss! Opr! Graussssssss! Opr!

The Gracehoper who, though blind as batflea, yet
knew, not a leetle beetle, his good smetterling of entymol-
ogy asped nissunitimost lous nor liceens but promptly
tossed himself in the vico, phthin and phthir, on top of
his buzzer, tezzily wondering wheer would his aluck
alight or boss of both appease and the next time he
makes the aquinatance of the Ondt after this they have
met themselves, these mouschical unsummables, it shall
be motylucky if he will beheld not a world of differents.
Behailed His Gross the Ondt, prostrandvorous upon his
dhrone, in his Papylonian babooshkees, smolking a spatial brunt of Hosana cigals, with unshrinkables farfall-
ing from his unthinkables, swarming of himself in his
sunnyroom, sated before his comfortumble phullupsuppy
of a plate o'monkynous and a confucion of minthe (for
he was a conformed aceticist and aristotaller), as appi

as a oneysucker or a baskerboy on the Libido, with Floh
biting his leg thigh and Luse lugging his luff leg and
Bieni bussing him under his bonnet and Vespatilla blowing cosy fond tutties up the allabroad length of the large
of his smalls. As entomate as intimate could pinchably
be. Emmet and demmet and be jiltses crazed and be
jadeses whipt! schneezed the Gracehoper, aguepe with
ptchjelasys and at his wittol's indts, what have eyefor-
sight!

The Ondt, that true and perfect host, a spiter aspinne,
was making the greatest spass a body could with his
queens laceswinging for he was spizzing all over him
like thingsumanything in formicolation, boundlessly
blissfilled in an allallahbath of houris. He was ameising
himself hugely at crabround and marypose, chasing
Floh out of charity and tickling Luse, I hope too, and
tackling Bienie, faith, as well, and jucking Vespatilla
jukely by the chimiche. Never did Dorsan from Dun-
shanagan dance it with more devilry! The veripatetic
imago of the impossible Gracehoper on his odderkop in
the myre, after his thrice ephemeral journeeys, sans
mantis ne shooshooe, featherweighed animule, actually
and presumptuably sinctifying chronic's despair, was
sufficiently and probably coocoo much for his chorous
of gravitates. Let him be Artalone the Weeps with his
parisites peeling off him I'll be Highfee the Crackasider.
Flunkey Footle furloughed foul, writing off his phoney,
but Conte Carme makes the melody that mints the
moncy. *Ad majorem l.s.d.! Divi gloriam.* A darkener of
the threshold. Haru? Orimis, capsizer of his antboat,
sekketh rede from Evil-it-is, lord of loaves in Amongded.
Be it! So be it! Thou-who-thou-art, the fleet-as-spind-
hrift, impfang thee of mine wideheight. Haru!

The thing pleased him andt, and andt,

He larved ond he larved on he merd such a nauses
The Gracehoper feared he would mixplace his fauces.
I forgive you, grondt Ondt, said the Gracehoper, weep-
    ing,
For their sukes of the sakes you are safe in whose keep-
    ing.
Teach Floh and Luse polkas, show Bienie where's sweet
And be sure Vespatilla fines fat ones to heat.
As I once played the piper I must now pay the count
So saida to Moyhammlet and marhaba to your Mount!
Let who likes lump above so what flies be a full 'un;
I could not feel moregruggy if this was prompollen.
I pick up your reproof, the horsegift of a friend,
For the prize of your save is the price of my spend.
Can castwhores pulladeftkiss if oldpollocks forsake 'em
Or Culex feel etchy if Pulex don't wake him?
A locus to loue, a term it t'embarass,
These twain are the twins that tick Homo Vulgaris.
Has Aquileone nort winged to go syf
Since the Gwyfyn we were in his farrest drewbryf
And that Accident Man not beseeked where his story
    ends
Since longsephyring sighs sought heartseast for their
    orience?
We are Wastenot with Want, precondamned, two and
    true,
Till Nolans go volants and Bruneyes come blue.
Ere those gidflirts now gadding you quit your mocks for
    my gropes
An extense must impull, an elapse must elopes,
Of my tectucs takestock, tinktact, and ail's weal;
As I view by your farlook hale yourself to my heal.
Partiprise my thinwhins whiles my blink points un-
    broken on

Your whole's whercabroads with Tout's trightyright
    token on.
My in risible universe youdly haud find
Sulch oxtrabeeforeness meat soveal behind.
Your feats end enormous, your volumes immense
(May the Graces I hoped for sing your Ondtship song
    sense!),
Your genus its worldwide, your spacest sublime!
But, Holy Saltmartin, why can't you beat time?

In the name of the former and of the latter and of
their holocaust. Allmen.

Bibliographical Note [1966]

The present text, reprinted from the editions of Joyce's works listed below, has been collated with other editions and revised by the editor in accordance with the author's later corrections, in all cases except that of *A Portrait of the Artist as a Young Man,* which reproduces the Definitive Text prepared by Chester G. Anderson, with Richard Ellmann, for the 1964 Viking Press edition, and that of *Dubliners,* which reproduces the Definitive Text prepared by Robert Scholes, in consultation with Richard Ellmann, for the 1968 Viking Press edition (see the Publisher's Note on page 16). To the *Collected Poems* have been added two broadsides privately printed by the author: *The Holy Office* (Pola, 1904) and *Gas from a Burner* (Flushing, 1912); these were included in Herbert Gorman's *James Joyce* (New York: Rinehart, 1939).

Dubliners, Definitive Text, New York: The Viking Press, 1968.
Dubliners, New York: The Modern Library, 1926.
A Portrait of the Artist as a Young Man, Definitive Text, New York: The Viking Press, 1964.
Exiles, Norfolk, Conn.: New Directions, 1945.
Collected Poems, New York: The Viking Press, 1937.
Ulysses, New York: The Modern Library, 1934.
Finnegans Wake (with author's corrections), New York: The Viking Press, 1945.

With the exception of *Ulysses* (published by Random House), all these books are currently available in editions published by The Viking Press.

For readers who wish to pursue the subject further:

WORKS BY JOYCE

The Critical Writings of James Joyce, edited by Ellsworth Mason and Richard Ellmann, New York, 1959.
Letters of James Joyce, Volume I, edited by Stuart Gilbert, New York, 1957; Volumes II and III, edited by Richard Ellmann, New York, 1966.

Stephen Hero: A Part of the First Draft of "A Portrait of the Artist as a Young Man," Norfolk, Conn., 1944; rev. ed., 1963.

WORKS ABOUT JOYCE: *Biographical*

Frank Budgen, *James Joyce and the Making of "Ulysses,"* Bloomington, Ind., 1960.

Richard Ellmann, *James Joyce,* New York, 1959.

Stanislaus Joyce, *My Brother's Keeper: James Joyce's Early Years,* New York, 1958.

WORKS ABOUT JOYCE: *Critical and Bibliographical*

James S. Atherton, *The Books at the Wake: A Study of Literary Allusions in James Joyce's "Finnegans Wake,"* New York, 1960.

Samuel Beckett and others, *Our Exagmination Round His Factification for Incamination of Work in Progress,* Norfolk, Conn., 1939; rev. ed., 1962.

Joseph Campbell and Henry Morton Robinson, *A Skeleton Key to "Finnegans Wake,"* New York, 1944.

T. S. Eliot (ed.), *Introducing James Joyce,* London, 1942.

Stuart Gilbert, *James Joyce's "Ulysses": A Study,* New York, 1930.

Adaline Glasheen, *A Second Census of "Finnegans Wake,"* Evanston, Ill., 1963.

Miles L. Hanley (comp.), *A Word Index to James Joyce's "Ulysses,"* Madison, Wis., 1937.

Richard M. Kain, *Fabulous Voyager: James Joyce's "Ulysses,"* Chicago, Ill., 1947.

Harry Levin, *James Joyce: A Critical Introduction,* Norfolk, Conn., 1941; rev. ed., 1960.

Joseph Prescott, *Exploring James Joyce,* Carbondale, Ill., 1964.

John J. Slocum and Herbert Cahoon, *A Bibliography of James Joyce, 1882-1941,* New Haven, Conn., 1953.

Edmund Wilson, *Axel's Castle: A Study in the Imaginative Literature of 1870-1930,* New York, 1931.

He looked up with irritation, and Johann saw that he wasn't as old as he'd first thought. He was probably in his late thirties, but his serious and dignified demeanor made him appear much older.

"The lecture has just finished," the doctor said irritably. "If you overslept, ask one of your drunken pals to tell you what they learned today—although I doubt they understood anything at all." He looked Johann up and down. "And wash yourself before you show up next time. You're a disgrace to the whole university!"

"I . . . I'm not a student," replied Johann uncertainly. "Are you Doctor Jodocus Gallus?"

The skinny man nodded impatiently. "Why are you asking?"

"I've got a letter for you." Johann handed him the tattered piece of paper he'd carried next to his heart for so many weeks. Jodocus Gallus studied the seal and gasped with surprise. "A letter from old Archibaldus, after all these years! Is it true? I think I wasn't even a magister yet the last time I saw him."

He broke the seal, unfolded the paper, awkwardly put on his eye glasses, and read the letter. Finally, he looked back up at Johann. This time his expression wasn't irritable but curious. He blinked at Johann from behind his glasses.

"Well, if Archibaldus is to be believed, you're a veritable prodigy. Where did you meet my old friend from our student days?"

"On . . . on a journey to Venice. He was my teacher for a while."

"And? How is he doing?"

"Oh, he sends his regards. He's decided to stay in Venice a while longer—the climate agrees with his old bones, he says." Johann thought he better not tell the doctor about the gruesome death of his friend.

"Ah, beautiful Venice! La Serenissima!" Jodocus Gallus gave a wistful smile. "How I'd love to be there with Archibaldus now instead of here in this stinking Palatinate backwater. They call it a university town, but in reality the so-called scholars do everything to prevent learning from happening. And those lazy students aren't any better. Paris, Rome, Prague—those are modern universities, but Heidelberg? Bah! Even Leipzig has better and more advanced teachers."

Johann decided to say nothing and just give the occasional nod while the doctor grumbled and moaned. Finally, Rector Gallus concluded his litany with a dismissive gesture. "But let's quit lamenting. Archibaldus believes you're a good student. Do you have money to pay for your matriculation? Any references?"

"No," replied Johann. He still had a few coins left, but he knew that it would never be enough for the matriculation fees.

"Hang on—let me get this straight." Jodocus Gallus raised his eyebrows, looking like a bird of prey about to swoop down on a mouse. "You have no money, you don't come from a wealthy or at least honorable family, and you have no references other than this old rag?"

Johann shook his head dejectedly. Suddenly the whole plan seemed ludicrous to him. How could he have believed the university would take him in? Jodocus Gallus gave a roaring laugh.

"Typical Archibaldus!" He grinned. "Did you really think a crumpled letter from my old friend would be enough? I may be the rector, but I can't do as I please. What would the chancellor say if I simply smuggled you in?"

"I . . . I'm sorry for wasting your precious time," said Johann. He gave a shrug and gestured at the blackboard with the formulas from the lecture. "And I thank you for the introduction to Euclid's fifth postulate. I listened to your lecture from outside and thoroughly enjoyed it."

Gallus looked surprised. "You know Euclid's elements?"

"Magister Archibaldus taught me," said Johann in a low voice.

"Hmm. What do you know about the Euclidean algorithm?"

Johann thought for a moment, and then he walked to the blackboard, picked up the chalk, and started to write. "The Euclidean algorithm is a method to determine the greatest common divisor of two natural numbers," he explained. "If CD measures unequal to AB, and the smaller part is removed from the greater in turns from AB and CD, one ends up with a number that equals the previous one without leaving a remainder."

"That is correct." Gallus rubbed his beardless chin pensively. "And what about rhetoric? Do you know Plato's differentiation between sophists and philosophers?"

Johann answered this question and all that followed. The doctor quizzed him on grammar, dialectic, astronomy, and geometry. When he was finished, Gallus clapped his hands and grinned.

"I'll be damned—you know more than my students after the baccalaureate. It would seem Archibaldus was right: you are a prodigy. You've come out of nowhere and made our young dandies from wealthy families look like a bunch of slow-witted peasants." He gave a dry laugh before turning serious again, eyeing

Johann closely. "Hmm, maybe there is a solution for you after all. I'd have to speak with Partschneider . . . Yes, it might just work. If he's got space at the paupers' hostel." He turned to the door. "Wait here."

Johann sat down on a bench by the wall and stared at the formulas of the Euclidean algorithm. One moment the rector was telling him to leave, and now everything had changed again. He couldn't believe the language of mathematics might have helped to steer his life in a new direction.

After a while, Jodocus Gallus returned with two elderly men who also wore long black gowns. The doctor pointed at Johann. "That's him," Gallus told the other men, who eyed the unkempt youth with suspicion. "See for yourself."

They tested his knowledge in the trivium and then in the subjects of the quadrivium. The examination took over an hour. At the end, the three men exchanged a look of agreement.

"He shall have the spot," said the man standing on the right, who was fat and had small, deep-set eyes and saggy red cheeks. "I've rarely examined a novice who already knows so much. Truly astonishing."

"Yes, although he's no longer the youngest, it would seem," said the other man, who had gray hair and bad teeth. He scrutinized Johann closely. "How old are you, lad?"

"Eighteen," replied Johann.

"That's rather old."

"I beg your pardon, Magister Partschneider," said the fat one with a laugh. "There are even older students at your hostel. One could almost think you don't like the look of him."

"It's not his looks. It's something else," replied the magister, his eyes still fixating on Johann. "There's something about him I don't like. But I'll admit he knows a lot and seems very intelligent."

"Well, I think we'll grant him a one-year scholarship," suggested Rector Gallus. "Let's see if he proves himself worthy. Agreed?"

The others nodded, and Jodocus Gallus turned to Johann. "It is agreed. That reminds me—I haven't even asked for your name. What is it, boy?"

Johann's instincts told him it might be better not to use his real name. Heidelberg wasn't that far from Knittlingen, after all. What would happen if someone recognized him?

"My name is Faustus," he said after a brief hesitation. "Johann Faustus, from Simmern."

It was the first place that popped into his head; he'd met someone from Simmern on the road a few days before. Doctor Gallus smiled.

"Faustus, the lucky one? What an unusual name. I hope you will find your luck here in Heidelberg, young Faustus." He stood up and shook Johann's hand. "Welcome to our university," he said. "You will swear your oath to me tonight. Oh, and by the way—now you're under our instruction. And as your rector I'm telling you: go wash yourself and do something about your clothes, or else I'll have you thrown into the *Karzer*, our very own jail for students."

The first few days in Heidelberg were like an additional course of study for Johann.

He could hardly believe his luck—the famous Heidelberg University had accepted him! But this stroke of luck meant a lot of hard work. Everything was new to him, and he had to learn countless small things that were a given for all the other students. At least that way he didn't get a chance to brood over the events in Venice.

The university's campus was a maze of new buildings, former monastery buildings, churches, and squares where lectures and seminars were held according to a fixed schedule. Johann heard that the Jewish ghetto used to be situated on the university grounds, but following the expulsion of the Jews from Heidelberg more than a hundred years ago, the count palatine had all the old houses torn down and built new ones in their place. The synagogue had been turned into the university chapel, which doubled as a lecture hall.

Johann estimated there were more than a hundred students in gowns and berets strutting from lecture to lecture through the narrow lanes of the university quarter. They acted like young doctors, proudly carrying bundles of books that they'd borrowed at one of the three university libraries. Students were permitted to copy from some of the books, while others—the most precious ones—were chained to desks. Borrowing books was a bureaucratic process so difficult that Johann thought it should require its own examination.

All lectures were held in Latin, and the students mostly spoke Latin among each other, too. They wanted to distance themselves from the citizens of Heidelberg, who often considered the rebellious young lads a thorn in their side. The students would roam the streets at night, singing loudly and acting raucously, brawling or frequenting the whorehouse at Grosse Mantelgasse Lane to let off steam. Like at all universities of the empire, women weren't permitted.

Most students lived at hostels, where further classes and exercises were held under the supervision of an older magister. The hostels were noisy until late at night, in spite of the strict rules. Johann, however, was staying at the paupers' hostel, a plain building that housed six poor but gifted students and six equally poor magisters. It was considered particularly strict and was headed by Magister Partschneider, whom Johann had met during his first examination. The suspicious old man had made it clear from the first day that he was keeping an eye on Johann.

"And I still say," he grumbled, "there's something about you I don't like. Sooner or later I'll find out what it is." When Johann walked past him into his sparsely furnished chamber, he could feel Partschneider's eyes. It felt as though the man could see right through him—see who he really was.

Nothing but a juggler and a fraud.

In the first week, Johann had found a friend among the other five poor students, and now they shared a room at the hostel. The student's name was Valentin Brander, and he was a delicate boy with drooping shoulders who always looked as if he was afraid of getting a beating. But his eyes gleamed with intelligence and mischief. Valentin was the son of a plain monastery blacksmith and came from a Dominican monastery in the Palatinate. The abbot himself had recommended him to the university.

Since the wealthy students from good families avoided the inhabitants of the paupers' hostel like the plague, Johann and Valentin spent almost every evening together, playing chess—a game that Valentin had taught Johann. After the first few hours, Johann had become completely entranced by the devilish game. Its complex moves allowed him to become fully immersed and temporarily forget about everything else.

Even Margarethe.

But then a thought of her would suddenly break through again, like a lightning bolt that struck him out of nowhere. He would stare into the distance and wouldn't hear anything else around him.

"What is it now?" whispered Valentin in class one day during a lecture. "You're one of the best first-year students, you seem to know everything, and then you suddenly gawk like a stupid calf. Better watch out Partschneider doesn't catch you dreaming."

Johann shook himself and continued to focus on his studies. Originally, he had planned to start searching for Margarethe right away, but he became so busy with his new surroundings that he hadn't had a chance yet. Saint John's Eve came and went and he barely noticed it. The university was like a giant, all-devouring beast.

For the next few weeks Johann worked hard on the subjects of the trivium: grammar, dialectic, and rhetoric. He had learned much from Archibaldus and also from Tonio already, and yet it felt like he was just beginning. He wrote down everything he heard during the lectures, answered the questions of the doctors, and posed intelligent counterquestions while the other students around him slept off the previous night's excesses. Most of them had been sent by their rich fathers and would leave the university with only a bachelor's degree, which could be obtained in merely two years. Some students quit even sooner. Johann, though, was inquisitive, clever, and highly ambitious, which didn't raise his popularity among his fellow students. Sometimes he wondered why he learned so much faster than everyone else. It was uncanny: he remembered almost instantly anything he read. It was a gift he'd possessed since childhood, but it seemed to him it had grown in the last two years—since his time with Tonio.

But there was another reason why the students tended to avoid Johann. It was as if he was surrounded by something dark and mysterious, like a poisonous cloud that only few people penetrated. Magister Partschneider hadn't been the only one to notice Johann's dark aura.

Whenever Johann woke up bathed in sweat in the morning, he knew that he'd dreamed of Archibaldus again, crucified against the wall.

Of Archibaldus and of Margarethe.

He had been scouring the university's libraries for anything on a certain Gilles de Rais—the mysterious name Archibaldus had left him—but found nothing. Nor did he find anything about the phrase *homo Deus est*, and he didn't want to ask any of his teachers about it. He'd learned from Archibaldus and Signore Barbarese that there was some sort of dark secret surrounding the phrase, that it was even associated with heresy. And so he buried his blackest memories in the depths of his mind, where they sometimes surfaced to torture him in his dreams. He also postponed his search for Margarethe time and time again—partly because he was afraid of what would happen if he found her. Would she even receive him, or would she curse him and have him chased out of town? Johann always remembered the last words Margarethe had spoken to him back in Knittlingen.

You are the devil . . .

Johann barely noticed summer coming to an end. One evening, as he and Valentin once again sat together over a game of chess and Johann took particularly long to decide on his next move, Valentin addressed him with concern.

"What's the matter with you? I mean, you've never been the most talkative guy, but you've barely uttered a word in days. Something's brewing inside you, I can tell. Is it because the students from the Swabian hostel stole your lecture notes the other day?"

"Why would I care about those dimwits?" Johann shook his head and knocked over one of Valentin's knights with his rook. "The Swabians are as thick as newts. There's no point in arguing with them—even though I'd advise them against bumping into me in a dark alley at the moment," he added grimly.

"Better watch out there. Hans Altmayer, their leader, already has it in for you. If a dozen Swabians attack you at once, not even the oh-so-proud Johann Faustus stands a chance."

Valentin wagged his finger with mock severity. Johann hadn't even told his only friend among the students his real name. There had already been a few scuffles between him and other students, and Johann always left his knife at home now to avoid getting into serious trouble. Larger weapons like épées and swords were forbidden on campus. But fists were enough for Johann, and he'd even used them to help Valentin out of tricky situations. Johann was considered an unpleasant opponent who was better avoided. His fellow students respected him, and some envied his intelligence and knowledge, but no one loved him. No one wanted to go out for a beer with him, and he avoided seeking the company of anyone except Valentin.

Unlike his tall, athletic new friend, Valentin was short and scrawny. His hair was thinning even though he was only seventeen years old. Like Johann, he was smart and hungry for knowledge, but he was also highly sensitive and had been the victim of many beatings. The two of them usually sat together during lectures.

"If it isn't Altmayer bothering you, then what is it?" asked Valentin persistently.

Johann sighed and pushed the chessboard aside. Why shouldn't he tell Valentin about his fears? Maybe his friend knew how one went about finding a married girl one hadn't seen in two years and whose last name one didn't even know.

"It's about a girl," he started awkwardly. "Not just any girl, but I fear she's the love of my life. She's been part of my life for as long as I can remember."

Johann told Valentin about Margarethe, about their times together and how he'd left his hometown. He even told Valentin the real name of his birthplace. His friend frowned.

"I thought you were from Simmern."

"There were certain . . . incidents at Knittlingen that I preferred not to mention to the rector," said Johann. "I'll tell you about it another time."

"Faustus, Faustus . . . the mysterious stranger." Valentin gave him a wink. "Whatever the case," he said and placed his queen in front of his king, "now your Margarethe has married some winemaker from around here, and you're looking for her. Are you sure that's such a good idea? Maybe she's happy with her husband and you'd be bringing unwanted memories."

"If she's happy, then at least I want to know—understand?" snapped Johann. "I can't get her out of my head. Her laughter, her merry eyes—she was the sun of my life. Whenever I got too mired in brooding, she shook me awake. She . . . she rescued me more times than I can remember."

"Enough already!" Valentin shook his head and laughed. "I can tell you're incurably in love." He touched his nose. "Hmm. Do you at least know the husband's name?"

Johann shrugged. "I know nothing except that he's a vintner from Heidelberg. For all I know, she might not even live here and the merchant in Venice was talking nonsense."

"A Heidelberg vintner marries a girl from Knittlingen. That shouldn't be too hard to find out." Valentin rubbed his beardless chin. "The folks at the taverns in the Bergheim quarter might know something—that's where most winegrowers live. Could be worth a shot. Only, I don't know what the dear husband will say when his wife's old flame shows up all of a sudden. We'll have to be careful."

He grinned. "But I wouldn't mind a few mugs of Heidelberg white—as long as you're paying."

"You . . . you would help me?"

"Matter of honor among fellow students! We just need to make sure old Partschneider doesn't get wind of anything. Every night he locks this place up like a prison."

"Let that be my concern," replied Johann, smirking. "Disappearing is one of my many talents. You know, I used to be a magician in one of my former lives. And now back to the game." He leaned over the board and made his move. "Bishop beats queen. Checkmate."

Valentin smacked his forehead with one hand. "Damn, you're good for someone who's only just learned the game. I don't get you—one moment you're bemoaning your undying love, and the next you make a move as if you've been thinking about nothing else the whole time. Sometimes I'd really like to know what's going on in that head of yours, Johann Faustus."

It wasn't until the following Saturday that the two students managed to slip away in the evening. Magister Partschneider always locked the door, and the windows were barred, but in an opportune moment Johann stole the key from the hook in the hallway. Using beeswax, he cast a mold of the key and took it to the Heidelberg blacksmith the same day. With their second key, Valentin and Johann were now able to leave their quarters after dark.

The Bergheim neighborhood was in the city's western section, not far from campus. Many craftsmen lived there, but also winegrowers whose vineyards flourished along the slopes of the Neckar River. The taverns were busy on this Saturday night. Numerous students were about, drinking wine and beer from large clay mugs, bawling their filthy Latin songs, and trying to lure the Heidelberg girls into nearby barns and press houses for a quick tryst.

Valentin and Johann had decided to visit all the taverns one after another—not an easy feat in a student city like Heidelberg. To keep Johann from coming under suspicion, Valentin would lead the conversation with the locals while Johann was supposed to remain in the background. Even though they tried to go easy on the wine, Johann felt rather drunk after the fourth tavern—and they still hadn't learned a thing.

When they entered the fifth tavern late at night and with heavy steps, Johann saw immediately that it was full of students from the Swabian hostel. Among the half-drunk students was their leader, Hans Altmayer, who'd played a few dirty tricks on Johann already. Altmayer, the son of a wealthy cloth merchant from Esslingen, was an oaf who used his time at the university mainly to hone his bullying skills. When Johann walked past without acknowledging him, Altmayer doffed his beret mockingly. He was tall and of strong build but not very agile, as Johann had found out during their first run-in. Johann had easily outmaneuvered him in that scuffle.

"Look at that, the beggars from the poorhouse were allowed out tonight," jeered Altmayer, looking around at his friends. "Better keep an eye on your purses now—those paupers like to pickpocket."

His fellow students hooted with laughter, but Johann ignored them, his eyes following Valentin, who sat down at a table with some farmers. Johann leaned against a wall, where a smiling young maid soon brought him a mug of frothing beer. Hans Altmayer and the other Swabian students put their heads together and shot poisonous glances in his direction, but they didn't dare attack him openly inside the tavern.

Johann had taken only a few sips when Valentin returned to his side. His friend seemed very excited.

"I think I found something," Valentin said quietly. "Those farmers know of a winemaker who married less than two years ago. It's his second wife. The first one died of the spotted fever and didn't bear him any children—"

"And the second?"

"Comes from Knittlingen, is flaxen haired, and has freckles."

"That's Margarethe!" exclaimed Johann so loudly that the people standing nearby turned to look at them.

"Shh! Shut up and listen. Something appears to be wrong with the girl. They didn't really want to say anything else on the matter and muttered something about dark forces and witchcraft—"

"What's happened to Margarethe?"

"I don't know! You'd have to ask her husband. His name is Jakob Kohlschreiber, he's quite the boozer, and—"

"And where do I find him?" asked Johann excitedly.

"I'm trying to tell you." Valentin's mouth was close to his ear now. "He's sitting on his own in the corner over there—see him?"

Johann turned his head slowly. In a corner, a little apart from the other tables, was a man with a large jug of wine. His thinning brown hair stuck out at the sides in tufts. His face was bloated from alcohol and his lips fleshy. He might have been a strapping and muscular young man once, but now a potbelly bulged underneath his vest, and his whole body was soft like a wet sponge. His clothes were stained but also showed that he was wealthy enough.

Johann brusquely handed his mug to Valentin.

"What are you doing?" asked his friend.

"I'm going to talk to the fellow," replied Johann. "I didn't travel hundreds of miles just to chicken out now. I want to know how Margarethe is doing."

"Be careful. The man looks dangerous. And drunk."

"So am I." Johann turned away and walked toward the table in the corner.

The man stared into his mug without noticing him. But when Johann sat down opposite him, he looked up with surprise. Then his expression turned sour.

"And who said you could sit with me?" he grumbled. "Go back to your pals. Lazy student riffraff. There's nothing for you here."

"Trust me, I'm just as sick of those good-for-nothings as you are," replied Johann, trying to sound as sober as possible. "My father is a vintner and sent me to college here. But I'd rather learn a proper trade instead of all that useless nonsense. I wouldn't be much good as a merchant, either—something hands-on would suit me, like a smith or carpenter or growing wine."

"Mmh, yes, winemaking is an honest profession," said Jakob Kohlschreiber, looking a little less surly now.

Johann casually dropped a coin onto the table. It was one of the last he'd kept from Venice. It was made of pure silver, and Kohlschreiber eyed it greedily. Johann snapped his fingers at the young maid.

"Is it possible to get something better than this sour swill in here?" he asked haughtily.

When the girl saw the coin, she turned on her heel and returned shortly thereafter with a jug of wine and two fresh mugs. Johann filled them and pushed one mug over to Kohlschreiber.

"Be so kind and share a jug with a young guy who's trying to forget his misery," he said.

He didn't have to ask Kohlschreiber twice. He emptied the mug and filled it again.

"Not bad," the vintner said. "Almost as good as my own wine."

"But what use is the best wine when the wench is no good?" said Johann, taking a long sip and watching Kohlschreiber from the corner of his eye. "My girl ran away with another fellow just the other day—and I haven't stopped drinking since."

Jakob Kohlschreiber gave a bitter laugh. "My woman ran away, too, but not with another man. Her cold body would still lie in my bed, but her mind was somewhere else. Probably on Blocksberg Mountain, where the witches dance. Damned sorcery!"

Johann leaned forward. "How do you mean?"

"Well, the woman is possessed by the devil. I should have known. I met her through my brother-in-law, who sometimes goes to Knittlingen on business. Do you know Knittlingen?"

Johann nodded uncertainly. "A little."

"Well, there was a well-situated girl. The dowry wasn't very big, but she's the daughter of the Knittlingen prefect. I thought it was a good bargain. And she's easy on the eye."

Oh yes, she is, thought Johann. *As beautiful as the sun after a dark night.*

"I was deceived," Kohlschreiber went on angrily. "The devil's inside that woman—but the father never said a word! Apparently, she didn't speak for weeks following an incident in the woods with some young lad. She didn't say much with me in the beginning, either." He burped and wiped his lips. "Not the worst trait for a wife to have, really. I don't like bickering women. But when I tried to perform my marital duty, she stopped talking altogether. The only time she said a word was in her sleep—terrible words . . ." Kohlschreiber lowered his voice. "She spoke about Satan, about missing children, and about a hand reaching for her . . . 'The boogeyman, he is coming to take me, he will take us all,' she muttered in her dreams. Like I said—that woman's possessed by the devil! 'Go away, go away,' she shouted, and the next morning she couldn't remember a thing."

"So . . . so what did you do?" asked Johann.

"What do you think?" Jakob Kohlschreiber leaned back and crossed his fat arms on his chest. "At first I was going to hand her over to the authorities. I mean, who wants a witch in their house? Next thing you know, you fall under suspicion yourself. But then I changed my mind and sent her to Neuburg."

"To Neuburg?"

"The Benedictine nunnery on the Neckar. For all I care, she can spend the rest of her life kneeling before the altar. The Neuburg nuns are particularly strict. I kept the dowry, of course." He gave a malicious laugh. "I'm going to drink it away until I find a new wife. But this time I'm not going to be cheated—not for the third time. The first one couldn't have children, and the next one turned out to be a witch. Damn the useless womenfolk! Hey, where are you going?"

Johann had sprung to his feet. His drunkenness had vanished and he suddenly felt very sober. If he sat here for a moment longer, he would throw his mug at the obnoxious fellow.

"Got to get back to the hostel," he muttered. "Keep the wine."

"Well, I won't say no to that." Kohlschreiber studied Johann with his small eyes. "There's something about you I don't like, boy. You're up to something, aren't you? What is it?"

Instead of replying, Johann walked away, and the winemaker refilled his mug.

Almost blind with grief, Johann headed for the exit. He just wanted to get out of there; he didn't even take the time to look for Valentin. As he was about to go through the door, Hans Altmayer blocked his way.

"And where are you going in such a hurry?" asked Altmayer. "Did you steal something, you—"

He didn't get any further, because Johann thrust his fist into Hans Altmayer's face. All his anger discharged in one single punch. Altmayer went down with a gasp of pain, and his comrades took a step back. Johann's expression told them not to come near. Something eerie and unpredictable flickered in his eyes as if he were a wild animal.

"You will regret this," cried Altmayer, holding his nose while the blood formed a red puddle on the stone floor. "You will regret this, you arrogant bastard!"

But Johann didn't hear him. He had already rushed out into the street. A chilly breeze swept through the night, but it didn't dampen his anger and his grief. Margarethe was so close to him and yet as far as if she were in Venice or Rome—or even farther.

She was at a nunnery.

15

JOHANN STAYED IN BED FOR TWO DAYS. HE REPORTED HIM-
self sick, didn't attend lectures, and spent the days staring at the ceiling of his
room. Not even Valentin got through to him. His friend brought him bread,
soup, and thinned wine, but Johann only drank the wine and left the rest
untouched. When Valentin begged him to tell what had happened, Johann said
nothing.

Johann felt as though night had descended upon him and there was no hope
of daylight returning. Ever since he'd decided in Venice to seek out Margarethe,
this goal had given him the strength to carry on. Now he'd found Margarethe,
but she was unobtainable. He'd never even find out how she was doing. The
Neuburg convent was only about an hour away from Heidelberg, but it was
practically impossible for an outsider to speak with the nuns. The Benedictine
sisters were very withdrawn and hardly ever left the walls of their nunnery—least
of all addled young souls sent there by distraught husbands or fathers. Those
were the only men who might occasionally be granted access, but no one else.

No one else.

An idea flashed through Johann's gloomy thoughts. He sat up in his bed and
reached for the bowl of soup. Suddenly he felt ravenous. His usually bright mind
had been boarded up for the last two days, but finally he saw a way.

A plan was ripening in his mind.

On the morning of the third day, Johann told Magister Partschneider that
he was feeling better. He picked up his satchel with his quill and papers and
went outside as if heading to class. He was careful not to let Valentin see him
leave. His plan was only half-baked, and he was afraid his friend would talk
him out of it. He turned north toward the place where small boats lay moored

near the university chapel. He hired a rowboat from a fisherman and paddled up the Neckar, which was still lazy and calm in early September. To the north and the south rose Heiligenberg and Königstuhl, the two mountains that cradled Heidelberg in their middle. Vineyards stretched on both banks of the river, and sweaty winegrowers carrying packs were hard at work harvesting the first grapes. Margarethe's husband, Jakob Kohlschreiber, was probably among them, unless he was sleeping it off somewhere beneath the vines. Hatred welled up in Johann. He gritted his teeth and rowed faster.

The river went around a gentle bend, and the bridge and the city disappeared out of sight. The Neckar wound its way into the Odenwald Mountains, the wooded ranges at whose foothills Heidelberg was situated. It wasn't long before a monastery-like complex appeared on the slopes above the left bank. It lay on a plateau among meadows above a small village with a mill. A narrow path lined with linden trees led up to the imposing stone building. Johann tied the boat to a dock and walked up the hill, forcing himself not to run. Somewhere up there was Margarethe—so close and yet out of reach. He slowed down and finally arrived at the nunnery, which consisted of a church, several outbuildings, and the abbey. The entire complex was surrounded by a wall, and vineyards rose on the slopes behind it up to the edge of the forest.

Maintaining his distance, Johann circled around the complex, keeping a close eye on any window he saw. He tried to figure out which ones belonged to living quarters. On the east side, the wall ran close to a bulky building, and Johann thought he could make out moving shadows behind the second-story windows. He guessed the room beyond those windows might be the parlatory— the only place where the nuns were permitted to lead longer conversations.

Johann nodded with determination. He'd found the right place. He walked to a crumbling old wall and took the quill, inkwell, and paper from his bag and wrote down the letter he'd composed in his mind on the way. Then he pinched tiny holes with a needle in certain places. He folded the document and sealed it with the wax print of a Venetian coin that showed some kind of old crest. The sisters wouldn't be able to place the coat of arms, but that didn't matter—it was just about making an impression. He patted down his clothes, brushed his fingers through his hair, picked up his sealed letter, and approached the convent gate.

He pulled the bell three times before the small hatch in the door finally opened. The small, wrinkled face of a very old nun appeared. Like all Benedictine nuns, she wore a black bonnet.

"God bless you," she croaked in a bored tone. "What do you want?"

"I'm here to deliver a letter," replied Johann and held up the folded paper for the nun to see.

"A letter, you say? Who for?"

Johann pretended he struggled to remember the name. "Um, I think it was for a certain Margarethe . . ."

"All sisters give up their worldly names in here, you fool," snarled the nun. "Didn't you know that? There is no Sister Margarethe here."

Johann rubbed his nose. "Well, then, I don't know . . ."

"Who sent the letter?"

"Her husband, Jakob Kohlschreiber."

The old nun's face lit up. "Oh! Why didn't you say so right away? And I thought the old miser had forgotten all about his former wife. He's behind with his payments." She held out her hand. "Give it here! I'll take it to Sister Agatha in person."

"Sister Agatha?"

The nun sighed. "That's what Kohlschreiber's wife is called now. Saint Agatha defended her virginity despite being put in a whorehouse and having her breasts cut off by her enemies. And the girl who used to be called Margarethe also pledged her virginity to God, just like all of us here."

I bet it wasn't a difficult decision in your case, thought Johann.

He handed the letter to the old crone. She turned her back to him, but he could tell by the sound that she broke the seal and read the letter. He was glad he'd chosen to use the secret code he and Margarethe had used as children. The nun didn't seem to find anything suspicious. She turned back to him after a while with a look of impatience. "What else do you want?"

"Well, Master Kohlschreiber reckoned you'd give me a kreuzer for my troubles," said Johann.

"Bah, the old penny-pincher can give you a kreuzer himself. Tell him we're waiting for the money he promised. He should count himself lucky we accepted his wife as a novice at all—considering what's happened. And now go with God. Go!"

She slammed the hatch shut in his face, and Johann heard her hurried footsteps moving away. Now all he could do was hope the old woman would deliver his letter.

With quick steps he walked back to the rowboat.

In his excitement, he didn't notice he was being followed.

"You did *what*?"

Valentin gaped at his friend. Johann hadn't lasted through the evening—he was bursting with excitement and needed to share his joy with someone. And so he told Valentin that Margarethe was at the convent with the Benedictine nuns and that he was trying to get in touch with her.

"I wrote her a letter," said Johann. "At first glance, it's just a letter from a husband inquiring about his wife's well-being. But there's a hidden message, and if Margarethe still has some of her wits about her, she'll remember our secret code. I put a few things in the text that only the two of us know about—she'll realize the letter's from me."

Valentin shook his head. "You're insane! If this gets out, you'll be thrown out of the university. A student arranging a liaison with a nun!"

"It's not a liaison," retorted Johann. "And she's not a nun yet—she's a novice, so she hasn't taken her vows. I just need to know how she's doing."

"You said that before. And once you know—then what?" Valentin pointed a finger at him. "Don't fool yourself, Faustus! You won't leave her alone. Do you want to free her from the nunnery by force? Her husband will do anything to keep her there—first and foremost to protect his own reputation."

"Who knows?" Johann pressed his lips together. "Either way—two Sundays from now I'll be standing below that window like I promised in the letter. Then we'll see."

Valentin laughed. "It's madness. But I can tell you've made your decision. Love is blind. But perhaps I can offer some distraction."

"What do you mean?"

Valentin grinned and pulled out some papers full of notes. "Take a look at this. I found it in a book at the library of the college of arts. The notes are by a certain Leonardo da Vinci. Apparently, he's a court painter and scholar in Milan. Have you heard of him?"

"I . . . I might have." Johann's curiosity was immediately kindled. He leafed through the pages with trembling fingers. He saw drawings of a box with a tube coming out of one of its walls and rays of light shining out of the tube. A roaring lion was displayed on a wall—the wall of a room, it would appear. Other drawings showed a lit candle and something that seemed to be a mirror. "What in God's name is that supposed to be?" asked Johann after a while.

"Well, it's something that Leonardo da Vinci calls a *'laterna magica,'* a magic lantern. It's an apparatus that's supposed to make it possible to transfer small images from the inside of the box onto a wall."

"That does indeed sound like magic," whispered Johann.

"And yet it isn't. I read the notes. Da Vinci bases his work on the ideas of someone called Giovanni Fontana, a *medicus* and magician from Venice. Fontana's thoughts make sense to me. If we could get our hands on the materials, we might be able to build the apparatus."

"Images appearing on a wall like magic?" Johann gave a laugh. "That would be so much better than the same old lectures day in, day out. Just imagine if we made pictures appear on the wall of Saint Mary's Chapel while old Spangel drones on. Wouldn't that be a laugh?"

"So—you will help me?" asked Valentin.

Johann winked at him. "Matter of honor among fellow students."

He didn't tell Valentin that he'd already read numerous manuscripts by da Vinci—probably more than were good for him. He had never seen any of the great thinker's notes about this device before, but he knew that there was much of Leonardo da Vinci he hadn't read. Deep down inside, Johann could feel the old fever waking up: the urge to explore, to dig deeper than all the dusty scholars before him. The motto of the uncanny old Signore Barbarese came to his mind.

Aude sapere. Dare to know.

The man may have been a devil worshipper, but the motto held true for Johann, too. And what was so bad about those words? They ought to have been written above the gates of Heidelberg University. But in the few months he'd been here, Johann had realized that even at Heidelberg, only long-established truths were rehashed—nothing new was being discussed, and original thoughts and ideas were frowned upon.

For the first time in days, Johann felt like a human being again. There was the prospect of seeing Margarethe once more, and Valentin had invited him to build this magical apparatus with him. Maybe love and science could be united after all.

The laterna magica helped Johann pass the time until he could see Margarethe again. Every night following their sparse supper, he and Valentin would sit up together in their room and study da Vinci's notes. They also borrowed a book by Giovanni Fontana from the library; it was entitled *Bellicorum Instrumentorum Liber* and was about war machines just like those Leonardo da Vinci had drawn up for the duke of Milan. One image showed a fire-spitting witch with wings— evidently a puppet that moved along tracks, designed to frighten off enemies; another showed in more detail the strange laterna da Vinci had described.

"We need a box that can hold a source of light," said Valentin as he pointed at one of the sketches. "The light is intensified by the mirror and pours out through a hole. If we then place a painted glass plate in front of the hole, the picture appears enlarged on a wall."

"Hmm. We can build the box ourselves," said Johann. "But where do we get the mirror? Something like that is expensive."

"Perhaps Rector Gallus could help us," suggested Valentin. "The old fellow thinks highly of you, and he's got friends up at the castle. They have mirrors there. And I'm sure he'll know someone who can make one of those glass plates for us. It doesn't need to be big. Can you ask him?"

Johann gave a shrug and grinned. "You're right—he seems to like me. But does that mean he'll give me a mirror?"

"Ask him, at least," said Valentin.

Jodocus Gallus had become a kind of mentor to Johann. The rector was much more approachable now than during their first encounter, and several times already he had let Johann have books that other students weren't permitted to borrow. And he asked the stern Magister Partschneider about Johann regularly.

"I can try," said Johann. "But I'd have to tell him something about our doings."

"Just tell him you want to study the sun without spoiling your eyesight," suggested Valentin. "Old Gengen was talking about it in his lecture on astronomy, remember? He uses a camera obscura for his studies, and that's similar to what we're trying to build."

Johann nodded. The camera obscura had been around since the time of Aristotle. If light fell through a tiny hole in a box, an image of the world in front of the box appeared on the inside, but upside down. The camera was accepted at universities as a teaching aid. Astronomers used it so they didn't have to look directly at the sun.

"It might just work," said Johann reluctantly. "That leaves only the painted glass plates. I think getting glass won't be a problem—I've got some savings, and perhaps Gallus will lend me the rest. But who's going to paint the images? If it's an outsider, he's bound to ask questions."

"Um, I could do it," replied Valentin.

"You?" Johann looked at him with surprise. Painting was now considered a trade in its own right, like carpentry, butchery, or masonry. There were entire workshops that produced paintings for churches or wealthy citizens, just like carpenters made tables. Johann had seen many such paintings in Barbarese's house, and he knew how difficult it must be to learn this trade.

"You can paint?" he asked Valentin.

"Not particularly well, but it'll do for our purposes. Look." Valentin shyly pulled out a few tattered pieces of paper from under his bed. They were pages from old books with drawings in their margins. The images showed animals and men with bushy tails or donkey ears, a fat man with a pig's nose, and even a rumpled raven wearing a gown. Johann laughed out loud.

"Why, those are our magisters and doctors! I recognize them all. There is our Partschneider, stern old Gengen, fat Spangel, and scrawny Rentz . . . Ha, and the one with the raven wings is Gallus in his stained gown!"

Valentin grinned. "Exactly right. So you did recognize him?"

"As if he were standing right before me." Johann clapped his hands together. "Valentin, these are great. I had no idea you were so talented."

Valentin shrugged. "Just a few silly sketches. I always hide them under the bed so Partschneider won't find them—I doubt he'd be too pleased."

"Hardly." Johann grinned. "I'm afraid he wouldn't appreciate your talents as they deserve. I do, however." He gave Valentin a pat on the shoulder. "Maybe you should draw a few harmless pictures for our laterna magica to begin with."

Every evening after lectures they worked on their project, studying plans and building the box in the shed next to their hostel. They told Magister

Partschneider they were building an apparatus for their astronomy class that would allow them to watch the heavenly bodies more easily.

After two weeks elapsed, the eagerly anticipated Sunday arrived.

Johann had asked Margarethe in his letter that she show herself in one of the windows at the rear of the nunnery at noon. He hired the boat at the crack of dawn, rowed up the Neckar, and, like last time, moored near the small village by the mill. Then he roamed the nearby vineyards and woods, feeling nervous and impatient. It was the middle of September; on the mowed fields sat rows of dried hay, which the farmers hurled onto their oxcarts with pitchforks. The sky was still blue, but dark thunderclouds had started to pile up in the west. Johann guessed it would rain later that day.

When the sun stood high in the sky, Johann walked down the vineyards toward the monastery wall. The vines reached almost right up to the wall, so Johann was able to remain practically invisible in their shadows. When the bells rang the noon hour, he whistled on two fingers and waited. Nothing stirred.

Johann's heart pounded like mad. Had he come too early? Perhaps the nun hadn't even delivered the letter? Or worse: the sisters had found out about the secret code and questioned Margarethe?

Another thought was so horrible that he pushed it aside instantly: What if Margarethe had read the letter but decided not to show?

Johann whistled again, but still there was nothing. He picked up some small pebbles and threw them against the shutters.

The next few moments felt like an eternity. Then something squeaked, and the right-hand shutter of the outermost window of the second floor opened.

Johann froze. The face of a young woman appeared in the window. She held her hand to her forehead to shield her eyes against the sun, but he had no trouble recognizing her pale, freckled face. A few curly strands of flaxen hair peered out from under the black Benedictine bonnet. Her lips were full and sensual, but her cheeks were hollower than he remembered. Her eyes gleamed with a sadness, an emptiness that was new, and yet she was just as beautiful as on the day he'd left her two years ago.

Up there in the window stood Margarethe.

She looked around searchingly. She hadn't seen him yet, and Johann relished the moment, like a hunter watching a flighty deer in a clearing early in the morning. After a few moments he softly called her name.

"Margarethe, I'm here!"

Only then did she spot him among the vines. Her mouth twisted into a happy smile, but her eyes remained empty.

"Johann!" she whispered. "My God, Johann . . . It . . . it wasn't a dream, then. The letter . . ." Her voice sounded hoarse, rusty.

"I wrote the letter," said Johann, trembling with joy. To see her again after all these years was almost more than he could bear. Memories and images flooded his mind.

"Margarethe," he began. "I . . . I've been searching for you for so long. I . . ." He broke off. The sight of her was too much for him.

"Where have you been?" she asked. "So much time has passed."

Johann realized that Margarethe was talking again. The spell seemed broken, but she was changed. She was a little too far away for him to make out details, but Johann thought he could see wrinkles around her eyes. Could it be true? She was only eighteen, the same as him. He felt like an eternity had gone by since their last encounter.

"Much has happened," he said awkwardly. "I . . . I was forced to leave Knittlingen. My father no longer wanted me in the house, and Martin wasn't found. They blamed me for everything. And you . . . you didn't speak . . ."

"I know." She paused for a long moment and sighed. "Sometimes I remember, but it's just scraps, like wafts of mist. Schillingswald Forest, the boulder with the picture of the devil in the clearing, your naked shoulder in the cave. And then that man . . ."

"What man?" asked Johann.

"The man in the woods . . ." She looked around anxiously, as if someone might sneak up from behind. "Listen, Johann—what's done is done. I've got a new life here. My husband—"

"I know what your so-called husband did," said Johann gruffly.

"Johann, you don't understand. I'm grateful. I feel safe here at the convent."

"Safe from what?" asked Johann.

Margarethe said nothing. The silence tortured Johann. Some pigeons flew up from the roof. Eventually, after what felt like an eternity, Margarethe spoke so quietly that Johann struggled to understand.

"I have dreams, Johann, terrible dreams. In my dreams I see what happened that day in the woods. And I also see what's yet to come. The beast will return! It will rise from the depths and devour the earth. The man told me."

"What beast?"

"We can't see each other again, Johann." Margarethe was crying now. He saw the tears roll down her cheeks. Her words came out like hard lumps. "I'm so terribly afraid . . . Not just for me, but for you, too, and for all of mankind . . . A new age is dawning, the man said. And sometimes I think I'm the only one who knows. That he told only me."

Johann clenched his fists. What was Margarethe talking about? Had she gone crazy after all? Could her drunken husband be right?

"Margarethe, I'm begging you!" he pleaded. "I traveled through so many countries just to see you again. Don't send me away. I want to at least understand what you mean. And I want to tell you what I've been doing for the last couple of years."

Margarethe hesitated, visibly grappling with herself. "On the feast day of Saint Michael the archangel," she said eventually. "I'm scheduled to help with the grape harvest." She gave a sad smile. "Like back in Knittlingen, remember? We used to work in the vineyards together. I'll try to get away from the other sisters so we can meet again. But I beg you, Johann, you must—" She broke off and turned her head. "Someone's coming. I have to go. Go with God!"

She closed the shutters and Johann was alone. Trembling all over, he shut his eyes and saw her face once more, like he'd just seen it in the window. Saw her face and heard the laughter that had saved him twice already.

He had found Margarethe.

And he'd see her again. He would touch her and inhale her scent. And all would be well. What she'd told him of her dreams was nothing but unhappy memories that came back in her sleep—nothing but nightmares like he also suffered from time to time.

Squirming bodies in the trees . . . the forbidden books of Signore Barbarese . . . crucified Archibaldus . . . the writing on the church wall . . .

As he hurried down the fields toward his boat, the heavens suddenly opened. Thunder clapped, and late-summer rain poured down on him. Johann leaned back his head, opened his mouth, and drank the warm drops greedily.

They tasted almost like blood.

~

Below a willow tree by the river stood a figure who watched the young student climb into his boat and row away. Water dripped off the man's hood, soaked his coat, and ran down his boots. But he didn't feel it. A hatred burned inside him that evaporated any cold.

The man waited until the boat disappeared in the rain. Then he walked down to the pier and climbed into his own boat. During the long, wet journey back to Heidelberg, he wondered how he should proceed. He smiled while the rain dripped off his broken nose.

He had time.

~

Boosted by the thought of seeing Margarethe again on the feast day of Saint Michael, Johann blossomed. He worked even harder at his lessons, improved his Greek by translating Aristotle and Plato in his spare time, and badgered his teachers with questions and comments about theological discourse. He avoided Hans Altmayer as much as he could. The leader of the Swabian hostel still bore bruises from Johann's powerful punch, and his nose was crooked and swollen. Johann guessed it would never look the same again, which didn't particularly improve Altmayer's already pockmarked face.

On the few occasions that they passed each other during lectures, Altmayer hissed threats in his direction. "You're dead, Faustus. You just don't know it yet. I'm going to finish you."

"Be my guest," Johann replied coolly. "If you want to lose your teeth as well, you ugly pock-face. But I'm afraid the girls will run away screaming at the sight of you—unless they do so already."

Altmayer clenched his fists. "You'll see where your arrogance gets you," he growled. "Just you wait. You're not untouchable just because you're the rector's pet. I will strike you where you'll expect it the least. Better watch out!"

But neither Altmayer nor his friends ambushed Johann in Heidelberg's dark alleyways on any of the following nights. Evidently, word had gotten around that there was no messing with the strange black-haired student. Besides, he enjoyed the special protection of Rector Gallus.

Johann hadn't yet asked Gallus about the small mirror they needed for the laterna magica. At the end of a lecture on rhetoric, he gathered all his courage and walked up to the lectern.

"So you want to build a camera obscura with young Brander," said Gallus with a smile when Johann had finished. "An excellent tool for observing the sun. But why do you need a mirror?"

"With the mirror, we can transfer the image onto the floor of the box, making it easier for us to copy," Johann explained.

Gallus rocked his head from side to side. "Hmm. I'm not entirely sure that's permissible, but never mind—I'll try to get the mirror for you." He raised a finger. "On one condition!"

"Which is?" asked Johann. He was afraid Gallus would demand to inspect the camera obscura himself.

The rector smiled. "I want you to accompany me to a meeting tomorrow. Up at the castle."

"Up at the castle?" Johann was too puzzled to string a sentence together. "But . . . why . . . ?"

"There are some people I'd like you to meet," said Gallus. "As you've probably come to realize, the university isn't as open to the new spirit of humanism as one would like it to be. It's different at the court of the palatine elector. I belong to a group of scholars who meet there regularly to swap ideas and discuss our views. Our *sodalitas*, as we call this circle of friends, is led by no lesser man than Conrad Celtis. I'm sure you've heard of him before."

Johann nodded with surprise. Not long ago, Conrad Celtis had held a guest lecture in Saint Mary's Chapel, which had been full to the last seat. Celtis was the teacher of the two electoral princes and was considered one of the greatest scholars of the empire—although his modern views didn't always please everyone. But the students admired him all the more. Johann's jaw had dropped while he'd been listening to Celtis's lecture on rhetoric and Aristotle's poetics.

"You . . . you want me to come to the castle with you to meet . . . meet Conrad Celtis?" he stammered.

Doctor Gallus laughed. "If your Latin is as bad as your German just then, I might change my mind. Conrad Celtis himself asked me to bring a few magisters and some promising students to the meeting. The other students all have their baccalaureus, but I think you've earned this visit, as has your friend Valentin

Brander. He might not be quite as clever as you, but he's hardworking—and not as haughty." Gallus closed the book on his lectern. "Well, then, until tomorrow evening by Saint Mary's Chapel, when the bells ring seven o'clock. Be on time or we'll leave without you two." Just before he exited the room, he turned and winked at Johann. "Maybe we'll even find a mirror for your camera obscura there. Though I still don't fully understand what you intend to do with it."

Johann was far too excited that night to sleep. Not only would he see Margarethe again soon, but now he was also invited to Heidelberg Castle! It seemed like all would end well for him after all.

Partschneider gave them a grim nod as Johann and Valentin left for Saint Mary's Chapel the following evening. As they walked through the lanes at dusk, Valentin had a wide grin on his face.

"If only the Swabians could see us now! They'd choke with envy."

"Don't speak too soon," said Johann. "We don't know if Altmayer has been asked to join the group."

"Bah." Valentin waved dismissively. "The only invite he might get is to a drunken bender on Hirschgasse Lane. The Swabians know more about fighting and drinking than rhetoric and poetics."

Several magisters and students were already waiting in the light of a torch by the chapel, and everyone seemed rather excited. To Johann's relief, neither Altmayer nor any of his ruffian friends were among the group. Two night watchmen with lanterns and halberds led the small group up the hill to the castle. Johann still struggled to believe that he, the bastard of a farmer from Knittlingen, was going to visit the electoral court with all these learned men. If only his mother had lived to see it. The other students seemed to share his feelings, nudging and winking at each other while the older magisters and Rector Gallus led the way in a more dignified manner. As a sign of his office, the rector carried a gilded scepter, holding it in front of him like a monstrance.

As if the starry sky had descended upon Heidelberg, dozens of small lights illuminated the windows of the new castle. The path ran first along the castle wall and then across a drawbridge, through the outer ward, and toward a large gate, which opened from the inside with a loud creak. Beyond the gate, the castle courtyard was brightly illuminated by fire baskets. The watchmen escorted the delegation of doctors, magisters, and students into a low room with a vaulted stone ceiling. A long table full of food had been set up inside, and maidservants holding jugs of wine awaited them with smiles. The air was filled with delicious smells of roasted and smoked meats. Johann's stomach growled loudly; in his excitement, he'd hardly eaten anything all day.

Apprehensively, Johann and Valentin sat down together with the other students. No one dared to speak; an awkward silence ensued. Finally, Jodocus Gallus, sitting at the head of the table, clapped his hands.

"How does the saying go?" the rector said with a smile. "*Plenus venter, non studet libenter.* A full stomach doesn't like to study. But neither docs an empty stomach—all the more true for pert young scholars who still have some growing and maturing to do. Help yourselves."

The students attacked the food hungrily. Especially those from poorer families—they hadn't eaten this well in a long time. The feast was in full swing when a side door opened and Conrad Celtis appeared. Johann quickly put down the chicken leg he was eating, and he and the students stood up and bowed respectfully.

Just like during his lecture at the chapel, Conrad Celtis radiated an almost tangible authority. Despite the still summery temperatures, the famous scholar wore a fur-collared gown and a woolen cap. His clothes were embroidered with colorful patterns, giving him the air of a magician. He seemed stern and forbidding at first, but that changed as soon as he spotted Jodocus Gallus among the guests. The two friends and colleagues hugged each other warmly and started a lively conversation in Latin. The other guests took it as a sign to continue their meal; the students also conversed in Latin now.

It wasn't long before passionate discussions started up around the long table, and Johann and Valentin eagerly participated. Johann had rarely felt so at home. His stomach was full, the wine made him talkative, and the conversation touched on subjects from a wide range of fields. They discussed the imperial diet at Worms that had brought about the everlasting public peace the year before; they debated the writings of Petrarch and the globe that a certain Martin Behaim had commissioned in Nuremberg a few years ago, which showed the world more precisely than any other model of the Earth before.

Johann was so engrossed in the conversation that he didn't notice the men approaching behind him. He felt a tap on his shoulder, spun around, and gave a start.

Facing him were Jodocus Gallus and Conrad Celtis.

"Dear colleague, I'd like you to meet an exceptional student," Gallus said to Conrad Celtis. "His name is Johann Faustus."

Celtis smiled. He looked much friendlier up close than behind the lectern of Saint Mary's Chapel. "I see: Faustus the lucky one. A happy-go-lucky, perhaps?" He grinned and gestured at Gallus beside him. "Clearly you've Latinized your name just like our dear Jodocus Gallus here, whose regular name is Rooster. And like me." He winked at Johann. "But Pick doesn't quite have the same ring as Celtis. Although the pick is a useful tool for digging—even for hidden knowledge. Where are you from, my boy?"

"From . . . from Simmern," replied Johann. The lie he'd told Rector Gallus on the day of his matriculation still didn't come easy. "My father worked in the vineyards there."

"Look at that," said Celtis. "Just like me. My father was also a vintner. That's one thing we have in common already. You see, you don't have to be the son of a king to understand the insights of this world. And don't they say *in vino veritas?*" He smiled. "Then this hall must be a true haven of wisdom."

Johann prayed that Celtis wouldn't ask him any more questions about his past, and to his relief, the scholar chose a different topic.

"What is your favorite subject among the seven liberal arts?" asked Celtis.

"Well, there is no easy answer," Johann started awkwardly, feeling his future academic career might depend on his reply. "I believe the seven liberal arts form one unit that prepares us for the higher studies. In the end, they're nothing but the tools we require for the true questions—questions that not even jurisprudence, medicine, or theology know how to answer."

"The true questions?" Celtis looked surprised. "What do you mean?"

Johann swallowed. He sensed he'd ventured out too far. In the chair beside him, Valentin shifted uneasily. Jodocus Gallus shot him a look of warning from behind Celtis. But it was too late to go back.

"I think that if we want to understand the world, we must leave the old knowledge behind and turn to new questions," he continued. "Questions to which the answers may not be found in the subjects we currently study nor in the writs of antiquity."

"Hmm . . ." Celtis considered Johann's words. "But isn't it the essence of humanism to fall back on the wisdom of antiquity?"

"The Greek and Roman scholars thought far indeed, but time hasn't stood still since then," replied Johann with a firmer voice. "We've discovered entire new worlds, so we must ask new questions."

"I think we've heard enough of this foolishness," said Jodocus Gallus, stepping forward to cut off Johann.

Celtis held him back. "Leave him, old friend. Sometimes, a wise thought is hidden at the core of a foolish one. Don't they say that children and fools often speak the truth?" He turned back to Johann. "And what are those new questions supposed to be?" asked Celtis with a smile. He appeared to like the student's nerve.

Johann hesitated. He thought about the books at Barbarese's library, about the drawings by Leonardo da Vinci, the war machines and flying apparatuses, and about the laterna magica he was constructing with Valentin. He thought about the countless questions that had crossed his mind since then, but he didn't dare bother Celtis with them. There was so much he wanted to know—far too much to break down into a few sentences, let alone answer them. That would take weeks, months, years.

Conrad Celtis was still looking at him expectantly, and suddenly Johann knew what he could ask the famous scholar. He still hadn't found in any library a clue about the mysterious name Magister Archibaldus had left for him in his own blood. Perhaps Celtis had heard of it. It was worth a shot.

"I came across a manuscript a while ago," said Johann. "And the author mentioned a certain Gilles de Rais. It sounds like a French name, but I'm not sure. I haven't been able to find anything about him anywhere—it's as if his name has been erased. Could he be a thinker or philosopher I haven't heard of before, someone the church doesn't want us to know about? Someone who might know answers to those new questions?"

"Gilles de Rais?" Celtis froze, and his face turned ashen. "Where did you come across that name?" Now Celtis's voice sounded biting and cold, and as sharp as a sword's cutting edge. "Tell me, how do you know it?"

"I . . . I don't remember exactly," stuttered Johann, feeling extremely uncomfortable all of a sudden. He felt himself blush. "I think it was in the arts library."

"Wherever it was, you need to forget that name again immediately. It brings nothing but evil."

"But—" said Johann.

"Do you believe in evil?" asked Celtis abruptly. "I don't mean the evil of everyday life, like the pickpocket cutting off a purse, the greedy murderer lurking in the dark of night, the counterfeiters, the traitors . . . I mean evil in its purest form as the antagonist to good, like Manichaeism used to teach. Do you believe in such an evil?"

Johann frowned. "I'm afraid I don't understand . . ."

"Well, I haven't fully made up my mind on the matter," continued Celtis. "But if such an evil does exist, it found its perfect vessel in Gilles de Rais. It is for the best that he is forgotten by history. And now I'd like to discuss more-pleasant matters." He gave Johann a sharp look. "Study hard, young Faustus. And before you return to your so-called new questions, find answers to the old ones."

With those words, Celtis turned away and left Johann alone with his thoughts.

16

JOHANN SPENT THE NEXT FEW HOURS IN A TRANCELIKE state. He still took part in conversations, but everything he said and did was mechanical, like a puppet on strings. How could he have been so presumptuous? One of the greatest scholars of the empire—the teacher of the two electoral princes—had spoken to him, and all Johann had asked about was a goddamned name. On top of that, he had bad-mouthed everything that constituted humanism. He had made a complete fool of himself! Even Valentin shook his head again and again.

"You shouldn't have said those things," he whispered to Johann. "Telling Celtis that antiquity isn't the measure of all things and that the current university courses aren't any good?" Then he snickered. "I wouldn't have had the balls."

"Shut up!" snapped Johann. "I know I messed up." He saw from the corner of his eye how the other students stared at him and whispered. Clearly, the news was beginning to make the rounds.

Johann angrily stabbed the slice of roast meat in front of him; it came served on a piece of delicious-smelling white bread. He chewed without tasting anything and kept his eyes down. He thought there was a good chance that the university would expel him following the disastrous conversation. Why should Rector Gallus continue to sponsor him when Johann considered everything he learned at the university to be dated and pointless? For the remainder of dinner, neither Celtis nor Gallus came near his end of the table, and he didn't get the mirror for the laterna magica. It seemed Gallus had chosen to forget about his promise. From one moment to the next, Johann had become persona non grata.

The following days, in every class he attended, Johann was also made to feel that he had gone too far. The whole university seemed to know about his arrogant speech at the castle. Some students smirked when he walked past, while others shoved him or jeered. Hans Altmayer used every opportunity to mock him.

"Make way for Doctor Faustus, our new deacon!" he exclaimed loudly when Johann entered a lecture hall. "I hear he's going to found his own school, where he'll teach the eighth art of snobbery and blathering."

The other students laughed, and Johann quickly sat down at his desk, keeping his head low. He soon found out that the magisters and doctors, too, were ill-disposed toward him. Old Partschneider interrupted his lecture several times to address Johann directly.

"So much for Plato's doctrine of forms," he said coldly and shut his book. "But perhaps young Faustus knows something that goes beyond Plato's idea. Or are the Greek philosophers perhaps not sophisticated enough for him? How about a brief excursus on the matter, dear colleague?"

His fellow students laughed; Johann said nothing, staring at his papers.

Life at the university became hell for him. No matter where he went and what he did, people either avoided him or mocked him. Valentin alone defended him when Altmayer and his companions riled up the other students against Johann. Johann would clench his fists in his pocket, but he never lashed out. He knew it would only make things worse. The building of the laterna magica came to a halt because they didn't have the mirror and a few other materials.

The only thing that cheered up Johann during those days was the thought of seeing Margarethe soon. He counted the days until the feast day of Archangel Michael and wrote short love poems in Greek, which he burned as soon as he finished them. When he lay awake at night, he envisioned a simple life with Margarethe at his side, making wine or farming, with a lively bunch of children around them, somewhere far away from Heidelberg and the university. He fell asleep with those images in his mind.

It was the end of September, only two days before the rendezvous with Margarethe, when Jodocus Gallus called him to the front after a lecture. Johann braced himself for the worst.

The rector looked at him with a serious expression. "I don't think I need to explain what position you got yourself into with your speech up at the castle," he said as he cleaned his glasses. "You'll understand—"

"I will pack my things today," said Johann.

Gallus paused wiping his glasses, astonished. "What are you talking about? Do you think that just because for once the wind is blowing the wrong way you have to abandon ship? Are you that weak? That's not like the Faustus I know."

"So . . . so what do you expect me to do?" asked Johann.

"I don't expect anything." Gallus smiled. "I'm merely delivering an invitation. My friend Conrad Celtis would like to see you again, tonight at the castle. Just you this time. It looks like you're getting a chance to patch things up." He put his glasses back on and studied Johann out of small, reddened eyes. "For whatever reason, Conrad has taken a liking to you. I'd advise you to hold back on the newfangled ideas this time."

"That's . . . I mean . . ." Johann was too confused for words.

"Now you've lost the power of speech for the second time." The rector laughed. "My dear Faustus, I just don't get you. One day you're as smart as three doctors, and the next you're as slow witted as a peasant." He cocked his head and wagged a finger. "Don't put me to shame! If Celtis tells me of any foolishness on your part, I won't be able to keep you here. For a student as young as you, you've made an astonishing number of enemies." Gallus waved his hand impatiently. "Now get out of here before someone sees you with me and draws the wrong conclusions. This place is worse than a bunch of gossiping fishwives."

That evening, Johann walked up to the castle by himself without any watchmen, torches, or fellow students. The guards had been expecting him and led him up a flight of stairs to the rooms of a side wing where Celtis resided during his stays at the castle. The scholar was sitting alone by a big, open fire that cast the plainly furnished room in a dancing red light. Moldy carpets covered the walls, and a rough-hewn chest stood in a corner. Apparently Celtis was no friend of luxury and comforts. When Johann lingered uncertainly in the doorway, the scholar gestured toward a stool by the fire.

"Sit," he commanded coolly.

Johann nodded humbly and took his seat. He had sworn to himself to weigh each word carefully this time.

He began, "Honorable master, I am so—" but Celtis cut him off by placing one finger against his own mouth. For a long moment Celtis just sat and scrutinized Johann while the logs in the fire crackled and crumbled into ashes.

"Do you like poems?" asked Celtis eventually.

Johann nodded, surprised. He hadn't expected this question. "I . . . I write some myself, occasionally. Nothing long, just short, silly lines."

Celtis smiled suddenly, and dimples appeared in his hitherto stony, forbidding face. "So do I, as you probably know. You remind me very much of another stupid young boy who was hell-bent on doing things his own way and exploring new worlds. That was a long time ago." He sighed. "But that's not why I invited you here tonight. It's about that one question you asked me at our last meeting."

"You mean . . . Gilles de Rais?" Johann thought he could feel a cold draft sweep through the room when he spoke the name.

"Yes, Gilles de Rais." Celtis nodded. "May his name be cursed for all eternity. I, too, was once preoccupied with Gilles de Rais, with the dark, the evil in this world. Youth is always fascinated by evil because it goes against order. It is the spirit that denies—much like small children like to say 'no' just to oppose their parents. Evil is the chaos that rails against the established truths and perpetually promises new beginnings. I admit, it's a tempting thought. And I know from personal experience: once a thought has taken root in one's mind, it gnaws and eats and doesn't go away. That is why I decided to tell you about Gilles de Rais. So it stops eating away at you." Celtis paused and stared into the fire, as if the answer to all questions lay in the flames. Then he turned back to Johann.

"Gilles de Rais was no scholar but a French military leader. In fact, he was one of the most famous and bravest knights that country full of noble warriors ever produced. He was a marshal of France and fought alongside the Maid of Orléans, whom the French venerated as a martyr and the English had burned at the stake as a sorceress and heretic. France and England were fighting a war that lasted for over a hundred years and only ended a few decades ago. De Rais was doubtlessly a brave knight, a baron from the lands near the Loire River, and a favorite of the king. He also was a friend of the arts, owned a large library, and tried his hand at acting, bookbinding, and illustrating. But as it often happens, his rapid climb was followed by a dramatic downfall—a fall right down into the depths of hell."

"What happened?" asked Johann in a whisper.

"Gilles de Rais lived the lifestyle of an emperor, holding grand tournaments and feasts. Nothing was good enough for him, and eventually he ran out of money. First he sold and mortgaged his lands. When that no longer sufficed, he turned to alchemy. He hired a throng of alchemists to find the philosopher's stone for him and turn lead to gold. He hoped to pay off his debts that way."

"And? Did he succeed?"

Celtis smiled. "Well, the alchemists, at least, became rich—from his money. De Rais himself sank deeper and deeper into poverty." He paused, and again the only sound came from the crackling logs in the fire. "It must have been around then that he first turned to the devil."

"The . . . the devil?"

Celtis nodded. "He made a pact with him. What exactly this pact entailed we don't know. The interrogation transcripts only tell us what the devil demanded of him—or at least what de Rais believed the devil wanted from him."

"His soul?" guessed Johann.

"No. That was probably too black even for the devil." Celtis shook his head. "De Rais gave him the most innocent thing that exists in the world: children."

One of the burning logs cracked loudly, and Johann shuddered despite the warmth.

Small, twitching bundles in the trees . . .

"De Rais sacrificed children to the devil," Celtis continued. "Not one, not two or three, but hundreds. He slit them open, bathed in their blood, and drank it. Sometimes he watched the children die and violated them at the same time. Others he suspended with ropes from the ceiling of his bedchamber and watched with relish as they danced and squirmed. Allegedly, he'd chant Christian hymns as they died. He also used their blood to write magic formulas to invoke the devil."

Celtis sighed; he seemed to find it hard to tell Johann all this, and yet he went on.

"Some of the children were only four or five years old, and others were older. De Rais lured them into his château by the Loire with sweets and promises, and he kept their heads as mementos. Sometimes he painted the faces and asked his servants which head they thought the prettiest. The commoners knew about it, but no one believed them. They hid their children, but de Rais sent out his henchmen and took them all, one by one. He burned the bodies on large andirons and hid the bones in his castles, where they piled up like in ossuaries. It took decades before he was found out by the authorities. The only reason it came to a trial at all was that the king dropped him."

"And . . . and what happened to him?" asked Johann with a lump in his throat.

"Threatened with torture, Gilles de Rais confessed to his crimes. He was hanged at Nantes, but he lives on in myths and tales. Till this day he is considered the personification of evil, the devil on earth, in some parts of France. But he was just an ordinary man, nothing more. Do you understand?" Conrad Celtis leaned forward. "He was wicked and evil, but he was no demon and certainly not Satan—only the people turned him into that." He breathed out audibly, as if a heavy burden fell away from him. "I told you this story because I don't want you to chase a ghost, young Faustus. No matter what you've read about Gilles de Rais, he is dead, and his bones have long rotted away. He was a person, no more and no less. We men, we don't need the devil, because we are the devil." Celtis slowly shook his head. "I'm rather alone with this opinion, I know. The church can never hear those words. I hope you won't betray me," he added.

"If there is a God, then there must also be a devil," said Johann. "Good can only exist if there is evil, too. The day only bears its name because it differs from the night."

"Yes, that's what the Manichaeans used to teach—they were a sect from the early days of Christianity that has long since perished. Who knows, maybe they were right." Celtis shrugged. "But even if the devil does exist, I'm sure it's not in the shape of a spendthrift French marshal. Still, I admit that the common people need images in order to understand the abstract concepts of good and evil. In this sense—"

"How old would Gilles de Rais be now?" asked Johann abruptly.

"I told you, he is dead. Hanged on the market square of Nantes."

"But if he hadn't been hanged—how old would he be now?" persisted Johann.

Celtis gave another shrug. "I'm guessing around ninety. The war between England and France has been over for a while now." He rose ponderously. "Now let us conclude our conversation for tonight. I'd still like to compose a few lines in Greek. Remember, I only told you all this so you can stop searching for answers that don't exist. Understand? Don't waste the intelligence and ambition you clearly possess on the unimportant. Focus on what's essential."

Johann nodded slowly. "I . . . I think I understand. Thank you."

"Very well. Oh, and . . ." Celtis stopped, turned around, and started rummaging in the chest behind him. "Jodocus asked me to keep an eye out for a mirror for you. I know a glazier here at the castle, and he had this." He held up a piece of mirror about the size of his palm, showing multiple reflections of the flames. "It's just a shard, but at least it's a mirror. Made by the hands of men, the result of intelligence and untiring aspiration—something tangible, not a flight of fancy." Celtis placed the mirror in Johann's hand. "Promise me you'll forget Gilles de Rais for this, all right?"

"I . . . I promise." Johann gratefully accepted the piece of glass. He looked at it and saw a contorted reflection of his face, as if it had been broken into pieces and put back together. He tried to smile, but the result looked strangely twisted.

Almost as if it didn't belong to him, but to Tonio the magician.

Or to a man named Gilles de Rais.

~

When Johann had left, Conrad Celtis remained sitting by the fire, staring into the flames. That accursed cold! He just couldn't get it out of his bones, not even in the middle of summer. It had lodged itself in his core and was eating him up from the inside.

In the same way as hatred and malice can eat a man up until nothing but an empty shell remains, he thought.

Shivering, Celtis rubbed his wrinkled, gouty hands together. He hadn't told the promising young student everything about Gilles de Rais. Some details were so gruesome, so horrendous, that the thought alone could make a man feel sick. It was astonishing—for example—how many different uses there were for the skins of children. Or for their eyes.

Other details sounded too far-fetched. They haunted the tales of the simple people like a poisonous mist that never quite lifted. What was reality? What was merely an old wives' tale? Certain things were so outrageous that they could never become public knowledge. It was impossible to predict how people would react if they found out.

The beast is nigh . . .

Conrad Celtis had been preoccupied with Gilles de Rais for decades. He had found the name in old chronicles and had kept digging. It had become almost an obsession over the years, and Celtis was afraid that this obsession might now be taking hold of a highly inquisitive young student who wasn't ready for such knowledge.

And so Celtis had kept certain pieces of information from Johann. They were all written down in the book where he noted anything he'd ever learned about Gilles de Rais. Celtis had traveled to Paris and Orléans; he had scouted the counties and estates along the Loire and spoken to the old folks. He had found terrible things at the châteaux Champtocé, Machecoul, and Tiffauges. Especially at Tiffauges.

Conrad Celtis closed his eyes and tried to push back the memories into the deepest corner of his consciousness. By and by, the individual pieces had come together in a horrific mosaic. He had written everything down and then locked away the book, as if he could somehow lock away the truth.

And now this young student had come along, this Faustus, and asked about Gilles de Rais. It was as if he'd reawakened the evil with his question.

How did he know the name?

Celtis decided that all his cumulative research was too dangerous to remain in the pages of one book. If it landed in the wrong hands, it could set fire to the world.

He stood up with grim determination and walked over to the chest. He opened it and took out a small, tattered book. The pages were covered with handwriting, and in some places his hand had trembled so badly that the writing was barely legible. Celtis leafed through the pages one last time and shuddered.

This goddamned cold . . .

Then he hurled the book into the flames, which immediately started to devour the pages hungrily. One by one, the pages turned to ashes, and finally the leather book covers burned away, too.

The truth about Gilles de Rais had gone up in smoke for good.

∼

When Johann showed Valentin the shard of mirror the following day, his friend looked at him with surprise.

"Celtis gave this to you, on the request of Rector Gallus?" he asked. "So you aren't as deeply in disgrace as I thought. How was your conversation last night?"

"Oh, I apologized for my rash words and we talked a little about Plato and the Greek tragedies. That was all," replied Johann. "Celtis truly is a learned man."

Valentin scratched his nose. "I still don't understand what your last question was about—you know, up at the castle. About that Gilles de Rais. Who is that guy? Something about it must have angered Celtis very much."

"And now the waves are calm again," replied Johann dismissively.

Celtis's words the day before had unsettled him and stirred up old memories that he'd tried in vain to forget. He hadn't been able to sleep, tortured by those memories: the missing children at Knittlingen and later in the mountains near Innsbruck, the pentagram in the tower, and then the eerie meeting with the man named Poitou—another French name. He and Tonio had conversed in French, of that Johann was sure. But he still didn't know what had really happened in that clearing near Nördlingen.

Small, squirming bundles . . .

Just before dawn, Johann had dug out the knife that had been with him for so long now, and he studied the engraving.

G d R.

What if this knife truly had belonged to Gilles de Rais once upon a time? The blade was razor sharp. What had the knight from the Loire Valley used it for?

Johann shook himself, and Valentin gave him a quizzical look. "What is it?"

"Nothing. Let's speak of something else. What about our laterna magica? Do you think the mirror glass will be enough?"

Valentin turned the shard in his hand thoughtfully. "Hmm. We'll need a glazier to cut it first. The source of light ought to meet the mirror from as many angles as possible to achieve maximum brightness. We can't do anything else until then."

"Then we'll just have to wait a few more days. I have other obligations anyhow."

Valentin grinned. "Let me guess. Something about a girl at a nunnery?" He sighed deeply. "Afterward, don't say I didn't warn you. First the incident with Celtis and now this. If they don't throw you out of school because of arrogance, then they'll do it because you're dallying with a nun."

"Not if you keep your fresh mouth shut," retorted Johann gruffly, and he immediately regretted his words. Why had he allowed his temper to flare up again? He had hoped seeing Margarethe would finally put his mind at rest. Valentin was the only friend he had in Heidelberg—he couldn't lose him, too.

"Forgive me," he said. "Things have been getting the better of me lately. Let's take a look at our laterna magica. I need a distraction."

"There's nothing to forgive." Valentin smiled secretively and gestured toward the door. "Come to the shed. I have a little surprise for you."

Valentin had been busy indeed. The casing was finished and the oil lamp installed; they hoped it would provide a better light than a candle. Valentin shyly pulled a small wooden box from under the table. It contained several glass plates.

"I got the glass from the glazier of the Church of the Holy Spirit," he said. "It's nothing special—just a start. But I think the images might have a nice effect."

Johann picked up the glass plates and held them against the sunlight streaming through the shed's window. He laughed with surprise. Valentin had painted small animal scenes on the glass. Johann made out a wolf, a cat arching its back, and a stag with stately antlers.

"These are fantastic! The stag looks as if he's about to leap off the glass."

"I decided on animals," said Valentin. "They're easier to draw than men, and I can draw them in movement. I botched a little here and there—"

"Don't hide your light under a bushel," said Johann. "Your pictures are excellent. Provided the laterna works, the show is going to be spectacular. Just imagine how much money we could make if we charged admittance."

Valentin crossed his arms on his chest. "I didn't intend to make money out of it. This experiment serves science alone."

"Let's talk about that again another time. It would be such a shame if—"

"I said these pictures aren't for public viewing," said Valentin hotly. "There isn't going to be a spectacle on market squares or at hostels full of drunk students. That's my final word, Johann Faustus! I'm a scholar, not a dishonorable juggler."

The last words hurt Johann to the quick. Valentin had never spoken to him like this before. Clearly, Johann had offended his friend's pride, but he tried not to let anything show.

"All right," Johann said, giving a strained smile. "I heard you. And now show me the sketches one more time to remind me how to insert the glass plates."

～

For the next two days, Johann hardly went to any lectures. He avoided running into others and couldn't wait to see Margarethe again. He told Valentin he needed to prepare for his Greek exams, but the crude letters swam before his eyes, appearing to run away from him like black beetles. What if Margarethe wouldn't be able to steal away from the other nuns? Or worse—what if she regretted her decision and didn't even turn up? Did she still love him?

At the same time, his thoughts kept returning to his conversation with Conrad Celtis and what the scholar had told him about Gilles de Rais. When Archibaldus wrote the name on the church wall in his own blood—what had he been trying to say?

Johann tried to deduce logically like he'd been taught at the university. As Aristotle had done, he started with a hypothesis and supported it with arguments. The only plausible explanation for Archibaldus's death seemed to be some sort of connection to Signore Barbarese. The old magister was murdered just before he was supposed to meet Johann to tell him more about Barbarese. Evidently, the eerie Venetian was indeed a follower of some devil-worshipping sect, and Archibaldus had found out—that was why he'd had to die. But why had Archibaldus written that name on the wall? Perhaps those disciples of Satan invoked Gilles de Rais; perhaps they considered him some sort of master, even if he'd been dead for a long time. That still left the question of what Tonio del Moravia had to do with all this. Archibaldus's last words to Johann had been about Tonio, after all.

It's about your former mentor, Tonio del Moravia. I finally know where I've heard the name before . . .

What was it that Archibaldus had learned about Tonio?

Johann pushed aside his gloomy thoughts and tried to focus on the Greek text before his eyes. Conrad Celtis was right. What did he care about the long-gone Frenchman? He'd try to forget Gilles de Rais. He'd try to forget Archibaldus, the missing children, his little brother Martin, Signore Barbarese, the black potion, and Tonio the sorcerer. All that mattered was the here and now.

And Margarethe.

Finally the feast day of Saint Michael arrived. In the large Church of the Holy Spirit at the market square, the priest read a mass about the victory of the angels over Lucifer and spoke about the eternal damnation awaiting all sinners on Judgment Day. The students were obliged to attend mass, but Johann only listened with one ear. In his thoughts he was already with Margarethe.

After the service he ran down to the quay, hired one of the small boats, and rowed up the Neckar to the nunnery. The vines stretching down to the banks of the river were heavy with grapes. Johann saw the vintners with their crates between the rows; they waved at the boats and laughed as they worked. It had rained in the morning, but now the sun shone warmly and humidity rose in clouds of mist over the hills and forests. Autumn seemed far away, and yet it would be October in just a few days. Johann thought there was a faint smell of cold and wind in the air already.

He docked by the little village with the mill and ran up to the convent vineyards. He looked around nervously but couldn't see any nuns in the hills. Had he arrived early or too late? Had Margarethe changed her mind?

Then he heard giggling and whispering voices. Johann ducked behind the vines and spotted a group of four young nuns in black habits. On their backs they carried crates, which they filled rather halfheartedly. A little farther back walked an older nun, and Johann recognized her as the old hag who had taken his letter at the gate.

"*Silentium!*" she hissed, and the younger sisters flinched as if they'd been struck. Apparently they weren't allowed to speak while picking grapes.

Margarethe wasn't among them. Johann sneaked away as soundlessly as he could and continued to scour the hillside. He didn't dare call out, and so he walked about aimlessly until he finally spotted a lone figure singing softly while she carefully plucked the grapes from the vines. It was an old nursery rhyme, and Johann's heart grew as heavy as a lead weight.

Growing in our garden are parsley and thyme; our Gretchen is the bride, she's looking so fine. Red wine, white wine, tomorrow morn you shall be mine.

He and Margarethe often used to sing this song as children, and to hear it here by the Neckar so many years later almost broke his heart. He remained hidden behind the vines and watched her. Now that she thought she was alone, he could almost see her old smile. Johann drank in the moment before addressing her with a low voice.

Margarethe gave a start, then she turned to him. Her eyes looked both happy and sad at once.

"So you came," she said.

Johann nodded. "I've been longing for this day." He stepped out from between the vines and brought his hand up to her cheek. "Margarethe—"

But she pulled away. "I'm a nun now, Johann. You know what that means."

"Isn't it permitted to touch nuns?" He winked. "Has God forbidden it? Or was it just the grumpy old crone I saw back there?"

"I belong to God now. He protects me and keeps me from harm. He will also ensure that the boogeyman won't come back."

Johann rolled his eyes. "Let's talk about something else. Look what I brought you." He pulled out a deck of playing cards he'd bought off a peddler the day before. "Draw any card."

She hesitated for a while, but then she picked a card, and a smile spread across her face. "Jack of hearts . . . So you're still a magician."

"And a great one at that. After I left Knittlingen, I joined a troupe of jugglers. We crossed the Alps and stayed in Venice after we traveled Italy."

As they meandered through the vines together, Johann told Margarethe all about his adventures with the jugglers; about the gifted fiddle player, Peter Nachtigall; the old drunkard, Archibaldus; about Emilio and strong Mustafa. Only Salome he left out, and neither did he mention his time with Tonio del Moravia. Johann knew Margarethe had never liked the creepy magician, not even as a child. And he was afraid that Tonio would remind her of that fateful afternoon in the clearing in Schillingswald Forest.

"A merchant in Venice told me that you were here in Heidelberg," said Johann at the end of his report. "I left the troupe to find you. I thought . . ." He paused.

"You thought what?" She gave a sad smile. "That I'd drop everything and go with you? You knew I was married."

"But what sort of a marriage is it?" demanded Johann angrily. "Your husband sends you to a nunnery just because you told him of your nightmares!"

"Jakob did right," replied Margarethe. "I feel safe here."

"But do you love him? Have you ever loved him?"

She laughed with despair. "Where do you live, Johann? It was never about love. After the . . . incident in the forest, I was no longer an option for the merchant family from Bretten. There were . . . rumors—involving you, too. And so my father had to marry me off further afield. Jakob Kohlschreiber seemed like a good match to him. Admittedly, he's not the gentlest, and he drinks, but he's a good businessman."

"And a good businessman knows when his wife has become worthless," Johann replied bitterly. "Namely, when she has nightmares and says a few strange things."

"They are no nightmares, Johann," Margarethe said quietly. "It's the truth. The boogeyman will return. He will return and change the world. The final battle between good and evil is near. He told me so himself."

"He? What . . . what are you talking about?" Johann laughed. "If I didn't know better, I'd say you'd gone crazy." He regretted his words instantly, but it was too late. Margarethe's lips became two thin lines.

"Do you know what day it is?" she asked eventually. "It's the day of Archangel Michael. When the angel Lucifer rose against God, it was Michael who stood up to him, together with all the other good angels, the seraphim and cherubim. He threw Lucifer and his followers from the heavens and they fell deeply, right down into hell. But the bringer of light never gave up. He wants to come back—he wants to rule the earth. And very soon the day will come when he shows his evil face again!"

"Margarethe, stop! That's—"

Johann had blurted the request so unexpectedly that he didn't know what to say next. Margarethe gave him a challenging look.

"There's something inside you—I can see it. Something dark, as if the boogeyman already tried to drag you down. Has he? Tell me."

Johann thought of Tonio and the pact they sealed one rainy night in the woods.

You'll fare well with me . . . Shake on it.

He thought about the handshake in Knittlingen and the gruesome death of Margarethe's brother. He thought about the black potion in the woods near Nördlingen, the squirming bodies in the trees, and the fits of temper that had overcome him regularly ever since. But they were nothing but phantoms—ghosts of the past that could no longer touch him.

"No one tried to drag me anywhere," he replied firmly. "I'm a faithful churchgoer, Margarethe." He smiled. "Evil has no power over me."

Johann knew he was lying. He went to mass only on Sundays or when he was forced to, like today. The last time he had prayed properly was at the grave of Peter Nachtigall in Italy. And he didn't think his prayer had reached God's ears.

God was far away.

But now Margarethe was standing in front of him, his angel on earth. If he didn't want to lose her, he had to lie. What else could he do? Her time at the nunnery had left its mark, but he felt certain that he'd find the old Margarethe again if he was given enough time.

"I pray to all the saints to watch over me every day," he said imploringly.

Margarethe nodded. "Pray to Saint Anna, because she helps those who have come close to evil. Will you promise?"

"I . . . I promise," said Johann, remembering that Conrad Celtis had also asked him for a promise a few days ago. He held up a hand. "I swear it upon my mother's soul."

The words had come out before he could think too much about them, but they had a profound effect on Margarethe.

She laughed.

She laughed as merrily as back in the old days, when they'd played in the hay in Knittlingen. Johann's heart leaped with joy.

"I'm so glad, my dear Johann. We're in God's hands." She took a step toward him. "And I'm sure God won't mind you touching me now."

Slowly, he reached out and stroked her cheek. Margarethe closed her eyes and inhaled deeply, as if enjoying the scent of old memories.

"It's so good to feel you," she said softly. "It's like coming home."

He ran his hand through her hair, and Margarethe sighed. Then Johann couldn't wait any longer. He leaned down and kissed her on the mouth. Margarethe winced a little but she didn't pull away.

"God will forgive this, too," he whispered. "What can God say against love? Love is the only weapon we have to fight evil."

She trembled when she squeezed his hand. "Go with God, Johann," she breathed and turned away.

"When can I see you again?" he asked quickly.

"In three or four days, perhaps." Margarethe looked down. "That's when I'll be working in the vineyards next. And now go, before the mother superior catches you. My magician . . ."

She smiled at him one last time before turning around and disappearing between the vines.

"My magician . . . ," whispered Johann, unable to move.

But in fact it was the other way around. Margarethe had cast a spell on him.

17

FOR THE NEXT FEW MONTHS, JOHANN WAS ON A PERMANENT high. He met with Margarethe whenever possible. The nuns often worked out in the fields around Neuburg, and occasionally they even came to the convent's small outpost in Heidelberg. Johann's meetings with Margarethe were always brief and secretive—a few heartfelt words, a touch, a kiss. Johann sensed that Margarethe was opening up to him more and more. Her remarks about the boogeyman and the return of Satan became less frequent, even if she didn't drop them entirely.

Johann tried a few times to get more than a kiss, but Margarethe evaded him each time.

"I'm promised to God," she'd say as they lay together in a field, hidden behind bundles of straw and hay carts. "If the convent wants me to, I will take my vows next year. But even now as a novice, I belong to God."

"I spoke with God in my prayers," said Johann. "He only wants us to be happy."

"Aren't we happy?" asked Margarethe.

And indeed, Johann was happy. Margarethe was nearby, he was studying at the greatest university in the German empire, and his prospects of an academic career were brilliant. Most students had gradually stopped making fun of him or treating him rudely, although, Valentin aside, he still had no real friends at the university—he was too ambitious, haughty, and aloof. But Rector Gallus and several other doctors and magisters were on his side. He also met up regularly with Conrad Celtis at the castle, where they held animated discussions. Among other subjects, they discussed the latest inventions.

"I heard they are planning a clock for the bell tower at Saint Mark's Square in Venice that announces the beginning and the end of our working day," said Johann one evening as they sat in Celtis's dark study. "Until now, men followed the course of the sun—it almost seems like clocks are taking over this task."

Celtis nodded. "And I hear there are apparatuses now that not only measure the hours but the minutes and even seconds. Seconds! No longer than the blink of an eye." He rolled his eyes theatrically. "Time is racing and we race with it. Where is this going to lead?"

"Consider the advantages if everyone went by the same time," said Johann. "Merchants could arrange meetings far more easily, and labor gets a value, measured by the number of hours."

Celtis laughed. "Well, the best time will always be the one that flies along without us even noticing where it's going. I must admit, conversations with you come very close to this feeling. They are, well . . ." He smiled. "Rather refreshing. Johann Faustus certainly has a quick tongue."

They never spoke about Gilles de Rais, and most of the time, Johann managed to forget the name and everything it entailed.

The only major setback during this period involved the laterna magica. It happened during the misty month of November, when the mirror was finally installed and the casing complete. They closed the shutters of the shed and lit the oil lamp inside the box. With trembling hands, Valentin pushed one of the glass plates with the animal pictures into the designated slot. But all that showed on the wall of the shed was an obscure, flickering shadow.

"Damn it," cursed Valentin and fidgeted impatiently with the glass plate. "The light source is far too weak. All the work we put in—and now this!"

"I don't think it's just because of the source of light," Johann said with a frown. "The light is much too diffuse, shining in all directions."

"Well, you can't capture the light like a herd of wild horses," said Valentin mockingly. "As soon as it finds a way out, it goes wherever it wants to. If only I'd never seen those drawings. What a waste of time." He was about to shove the apparatus off the table when Johann held him back.

"We're not giving up yet," he said sternly. "Maybe we'll find a way to focus the light better."

"Sure, sure," jeered Valentin. "Where the great Giovanni Fontana and Leonardo da Vinci failed, the oh-so-famous Doctor Faustus will succeed."

"Who knows, perhaps they'll call me that one day," muttered Johann. A vague idea was buzzing through his mind, but every time he tried to grasp it, it slipped away.

Johann continued to be wary of Hans Altmayer. He got the impression the fellow was hatching something. Whenever they passed each other, Altmayer grinned, placed one finger at his beret, and hinted at a bow.

"Look at that—Herr Faustus, the doctors' pet," he'd say. "Just you wait. The higher you climb, the farther you fall."

"And if you never climb, you remain forever in the stinking gutter," retorted Johann as he walked away.

Johann experienced his personal eureka moment during a lecture by Rector Gallus about Archimedes's principle.

Winter had moved into Heidelberg by now. The snow piled up in the lanes and made it difficult to get around. It was so cold in the lecture halls that the students shivered in their coats and hats. Johann finally understood why the berets had padded earflaps. The small stoves weren't nearly enough to heat the large rooms. Saint Mary's Chapel was the worst, the wind howling through its drafty windows. White clouds came from the mouths of the doctors as they spoke, and thin sheets of ice spread across benches and desks.

It was a bitter cold morning in January, but at least the sun shone weakly through the windows. As usual, the rector wore his strange-looking eye glasses, but the students were accustomed to the sight by now. He took them off only occasionally, when he gazed into the distance. Gallus was talking about the buoyancy of objects when a ray of light fell through the window and directly upon his glasses, which were lying on the lectern in front of him. Johann noticed with amazement how the weak light was bundled in the glasses and appeared on the opposite wall as a bright speck. The speck was brighter than the pale sunlight streaming through the window.

Much brighter.

"Archimedes posits that the upward buoyancy . . . ," Jodocus Gallus was saying when Johann sprang to his feet and rushed out of the hall. Irritated, the rector broke off. "Let us hope it's just the call of nature urging our dear Faustus to leave us thus."

"Or the infallible Herr Faustus already knows everything about Archimedes and is off to invent his own floating object," jeered Altmayer, but no one laughed.

Johann ran over to the low, snow-covered buildings of the school of arts, where Valentin was attending one of Partschneider's classes. Out of breath, he sat down next to Valentin in the last row and leaned over to him.

"I know it now," he whispered.

Valentin turned his head in surprise. "You know what now?"

"I know how we can capture and focus the light inside the laterna magica. We use lenses made of glass! Lenses like they use for eye glasses. Rector Gallus's glasses just gave me the idea."

Johann's voice grew louder, and Magister Partschneider interrupted his lecture irritably. "If the young sirs believe they already know everything, they are welcome to leave the room."

Johann tugged at Valentin's sleeve until his friend gave in and followed him outside.

"Are you crazy?" spat Valentin. "Partschneider will never forgive us!"

"Oh, he'll get over it," replied Johann, grinning. "Much more importantly, we can now complete the laterna magica."

He quickly explained to Valentin what he'd found out. His friend seemed skeptical at first, but then he nodded. "Hmm. I think you're right—it might work with lenses. They bundle the light—I know what you mean about Gallus's glasses. And if we placed several lenses in front of each other—"

"The light would become stronger and the image clearer," added Johann.

He then suddenly remembered the strange tube he'd seen up on the tower by the Alps a long time ago, back when he was still with Tonio. He guessed the tube had also contained several lenses, one behind the other, enabling a person to see farther. He wondered where Tonio had gotten the tube. Johann had never seen anything like it again, not even here at the university.

"I admit, it's a brilliant idea, but unfortunately, we have no lenses nor the money to buy some," said Valentin, interrupting Johann's pondering. "Eye glasses are expensive—perhaps more expensive than mirrors."

"I'll get the lenses," said Johann curtly. "You just worry about fitting them."

Johann had already decided to steal Rector Gallus's glasses—in the name of science. At some distant point in the future he would tell Gallus, and Johann felt certain the man would understand. Besides, he was the rector of Heidelberg

University—surely he could purchase another pair of glasses. And in a few years' time, when Johann had become a highly esteemed doctor himself, they'd laugh about the old story.

Valentin eyed Johann suspiciously. "I don't like you much at the moment, Johann. If you go on like this—"

"Do you want the laterna to work or not?" snarled Johann, cutting him off.

Valentin gave a shrug. "All right, fine. I hope we can talk normally again once we're done with the laterna. Like friends usually talk."

The opportunity for the theft arose a few days later. During a conversation with Rector Gallus following a lecture, Johann saw that the glasses were once again lying on the lectern. It was almost too easy. Johann placed his books on top of them and picked them up together. The rector didn't notice anything.

Johann's heart beat wildly as he walked out of the chapel, but neither Gallus's cutting voice nor any hurried footsteps rang out behind him. In a shady niche between two buildings, he carefully broke the glass lenses from their frames and buried the frames in a pile of snow. A twinge of conscience overcame him; the rector had done so much for him. But then he told himself again that he was acting solely in the name of science, and that Gallus would thank him one day.

When Johann gave the lenses to Valentin, he turned them thoughtfully in his hands. "I'd be glad if they weren't what I think they are," he remarked glumly.

"I have my resources," said Johann. "Best you don't ask."

They formed a tube from a piece of tin and experimented with different distances. Conrad Celtis had also given Johann a metal concave mirror so that the light from the oil lamp was much better bundled. When they felt certain that they were on the right track, they installed the tube into their apparatus, which had grown in size.

It was an evening in February when Valentin finally lit the oil lamp of the laterna magica once more and carefully inserted one of the glass plates into the slot. It was the picture of the cat with the arched back—his favorite. Then he opened the flap at the front.

The result was so overwhelming that they cried out almost simultaneously and took a step back.

From the opposite wall of the shed, a monster stared at them that was as large as a calf and as menacing as a lion on the prowl. The cat's arched back and hissing mouth seemed as lifelike as if it had just walked into the room. The picture was slightly unfocused at the edges and it flickered a little, which added to the ghostly effect. Johann felt as though he had just entered a strange new world.

"That . . . that's incredible!" he gasped.

"It's working!" Valentin grinned from ear to ear. "Do you know what that means? The two of us—two students—have just created an apparatus that not even the great Leonardo da Vinci managed to build. When we show Rector Gallus what—"

"We can't show Rector Gallus," objected Johann.

Valentin's expression darkened. "So it's true."

"It's not just the eye glasses," explained Johann. "We told Gallus we were building a camera obscura. If we turn up with this apparatus instead, he'll know we've been lying to him the whole time."

Johann tried to sound reasonable, but he really was afraid the rector would become angry and accuse him of theft. First and foremost on his mind, however, was a different motivation: the laterna magica was *their* invention, and he didn't want to share it with other scholars. It was their treasure.

And there was another hazy idea taking shape in his head about how he could put the laterna to good use.

"They'll charge us with sorcery," he said, gesturing at the cat staring at them from the wall. "Don't you see how uncanny it looks? Partschneider and some of the other magisters aren't ready for it yet."

"So you're saying we aren't going to show the laterna to anyone at all?" asked Valentin, puzzled.

"Not yet," replied Johann. "One day, perhaps. But it should remain our secret for now."

He gazed at the cat with the arched back, and the vague idea was slowly coming together.

An idea about how he might win over Margarethe after all.

During the cold months, Johann's meetings with Margarethe had been infrequent. There was no more work in the fields, and the nuns mostly stayed indoors. Johann often had to content himself with a long, cold wait beneath one of the convent's windows until Margarethe finally appeared for a few brief moments. To arrange their meetings, they used their secret code in letters that

Johann—bowing and scraping—delivered to the mother superior. Each time, he claimed it was from Margarethe's husband, who in reality never had contacted his wife again. One time Johann even included a short love poem, hoping ardently the mother superior wouldn't notice. The fact that he sometimes felt he was being watched he put down to his fear of getting caught. He couldn't bear to imagine the consequences for him and—more so—for Margarethe if they were discovered.

One night, as he once again waited below a window in the freezing cold, Margarethe had some happy news for him.

"I'm relocating to Heidelberg," she said quietly, trying not to wake the sleeping sisters. "The mother cellarer needs an aide for our outpost there, and I have proven that I'm not only good at writing but also counting. I'll be moving in just a few months."

"But . . . but that's fantastic!" exclaimed Johann. For a brief moment he forgot to keep his voice down. "We'll be able to see much more of each other. You'll have to sell your wares at the market, after all, and—"

"We must be all the more careful, Johann," urged Margarethe. "Sometimes I feel like Mother Superior knows something. She gives me strange looks and didn't want me to go to Heidelberg at first. And then I feel eyes in my back like daggers—"

"Don't start that again," said Johann. "I prayed that the boogeyman won't appear to you again, and so he won't."

"But he will return—I know it. If not now, then later." Margarethe closed her eyes as if she could see an image in her mind's eye. "The devil may have retreated for now, but only because he is preparing for his final, great day. And we must prepare, too!"

"Listen, Margarethe!" Johann came as close to the wall covered in frozen ivy as he could. "You can't say things like that anymore! I've heard at the university that several women have been arrested as witches in the area. Apparently they were dancing on Heiligenberg Mountain, and the bishop himself wrote to the authorities, urging them to be vigilant. Two old women were burned at the stake on Dilsberg Mountain not long ago because they allegedly concocted a pestilence powder from the innards of children. It is dangerous to speak of the devil in times like these."

"And what if these women really were witches?" asked Margarethe. "What if they really murder children, grind up their innards, and celebrate the return of Satan? Have you ever considered that?" She lowered her voice. "The Odenwald Forest is ancient. They say it is named for an evil god who used to rule here."

Johann groaned inwardly. As long as Margarethe was locked up in this nunnery, she'd never get rid of her delusions. He needed to take her out of there—as soon as possible.

"Sometimes I hear voices," whispered Margarethe. "They are the voices of demons who howl and scream and wait for the day of the beast. The day of the beast is coming closer. His followers are waiting for the stars to be favorable. That's what the man said in the forest . . ."

"And what if you heard the voice of an angel?" asked Johann brusquely. "Would you believe him? Would you believe that the devil is just toying with you and that he's not coming back to earth at all? That the boogeyman only exists in your nightmares—that none of it is real?"

Margarethe smiled. "That would be nice, but I'm afraid that'll never happen." She hesitated. "Sometimes I'm not even sure anymore whether I'm not imagining it all. But what I saw back then, and what the boogeyman said to me, it . . . it seemed so real! And then those dreams—those horrible dreams . . ." She sobbed.

Johann winced. When Margarethe cried, his own fear and insecurity returned. What was real and what was imagination? What was true and what was false? He needed Margarethe's laughter like medicine.

The black potion . . .

Back in the forest near Nördlingen it had been the memory of her laughter alone that saved him.

Johann needed her the way she used to be, when her laughter was still like a bulwark against all evil and against his gloomy thoughts and musings.

What he required for Margarethe was no less than a guardian angel.

A guardian angel . . .

Johann said nothing as thoughts raced through his mind. His vague idea was taking shape and turning into a plan, still a little rough around the edges and possibly crazy, but tangible now.

"I'm going to help you," he said eventually. "And soon."

~

Spring arrived so slowly that people almost missed its arrival. Water from icicles began dripping into the lanes, forming puddles at first and then deep mud patches. The magisters lifted their long gowns with disgust and stalked across the worst of the filth. The snow melted, but the cold inside the churches and lecture halls didn't go away.

Johann focused on his studies again. In April, the month of his nineteenth birthday, he passed his baccalaureus, an exam that other students tackled only after two or more years at the university. He graduated as valedictorian, and even old Partschneider nodded approvingly.

"But don't let it go to your head," he said warningly. "Pride comes before a fall."

Johann remembered that Hans Altmayer had once said something similar to him. These days there was a kind of truce between them, but Johann still couldn't shake the feeling that Altmayer was planning something.

He saw much less of Valentin during those weeks. Johann had been very busy with his preparations for the baccalaureus, and he also avoided his friend intentionally. He didn't want Valentin to pester him with questions about Margarethe. Deep down he was hoping that Valentin assumed the liaison was finished for good. Besides, Johann was far too preoccupied with his own plans to have time for friends—plans he didn't want Valentin to know about.

While his friend was attending lectures, Johann often sneaked into the shed and worked on some secret additions to the laterna magica. The changes he made were so minute that he hoped Valentin wouldn't notice. And the additional parts he needed could be inserted and removed as required.

During their few remaining hours together, the two friends locked themselves inside the shed, sat down on stools like two little boys at a puppet show, and admired the fantastic apparitions on the wall: the leaping stag, the cat with the arched back, the wolf with its bared teeth, and all the other animals Valentin had painted onto glass plates. Dust particles danced in the beam of the oil lamp, which was strong and focused now, thanks to the concave mirror and the lenses. The air smelled of whale oil, burned paint, and hot tin. In those moments, Johann and Valentin were as close as brothers. They had created this miracle together, and they couldn't get enough of it.

"It is such a shame we can't show anyone," Valentin said with a sigh and inserted a new plate into the slot. "I mean, it's really just the common people who would consider the laterna to be witchcraft. Why can't we at least show Rector Gallus and perhaps Conrad Celtis? They'd be amazed."

"Let's wait a little longer," replied Johann. "Once I'm a magister I'll be able to present the apparatus as my own invention. That would spare us a lot of awkward questions."

"*Your* invention?" Valentin gave him a confused look. "But we built the laterna together."

"You're right, of course," said Johann. "But I think the degree of magister would elevate the laterna."

Valentin said nothing and stared straight ahead, where the wolf continued to bare his teeth.

Sometimes now, when Johann considered himself to be alone, he hummed high-pitched melodies—not just in his own chamber, but also in the long corridors of the library of arts. When Valentin caught him humming along thus, he laughed out loud.

"Are you wailing about Gretchen the bride again?" he said mockingly. "Just make sure Altmayer doesn't hear you. That would give him something new to bitch about."

Johann cleared his throat. "Spangel asked if I'd join the choir for Easter. Apparently they still need a tenor." He winked at Valentin. "Although I fear I've greased my voice too much with beer and wine."

His humming became like an obsession. Sometimes when they sat together over a game of chess, Valentin would suddenly hear the high-pitched voice from an entirely different corner of the room. He'd spin around with fright each time, but it was only Johann, sitting in front of him with a grin. On one of those occasions he pointed to the ceiling by way of explanation. "I'm merely testing the thesis of Vitruvius about the movement of sound. Conrad Celtis lent me a script by this astonishing Roman architect. Evidently, sounds travel on strange paths. That would be worth a treatise on its own."

Valentin rolled his eyes. "When do you ever *not* think of our studies?"

"Well, art is long, and life is short and fleeting," Johann replied with a shrug and continued to hum.

"Cut it out!" groused Valentin. Then he shook his head. "I'm sorry. My nerves are raw since I'm studying for that accursed baccalaureus." He sighed and pulled a face. "My Greek is a disaster, and I'm no good at dialectic. What am I going to do after the baccalaureus, when they add arithmetic, geometry, music, and astronomy? I've always wondered why you knew so much about all those things from the start. All those star signs and the calculations of the constellations."

"I had a good teacher," said Johann, lost in thought. "He used to show me the stars at night."

"Where was that?" asked Valentin.

"At . . . at a tower. A tower in the woods near the Alps."

Valentin frowned. "I thought you were from Knittlingen in the Kraichgau."

"I traveled for a while," replied Johann vaguely, inwardly cursing himself. He really needed to be more careful about what came out of his mouth. "I journeyed to the Alps once and spent a winter there."

Dark memories rose to the surface of Johann's consciousness—memories he'd been suppressing for a long time.

A blood-red circle . . . A pile of dirty, torn children's clothes . . .

"Are you all right?" asked Valentin with a concerned look. "You're very pale all of a sudden."

Johann shook himself. "It's nothing. I think I just need a little fresh air." He stood up. "Please excuse me. I need to get a few more books to prepare for the next lecture."

Valentin smirked. "Ah, there is the Faustus I know! Never at peace, always searching for something."

You have no idea how right you are, thought Johann.

He forced himself to give his friend a smile, squeezed his hand, and hurried outside, where the fresh breeze swept through his hair.

In May, Margarethe finally came to the Heidelberg house of the Neuburg convent, and now she and Johann saw much more of each other. The nunnery sold its wine, cheese, and vegetables at the market, and Margarethe paid regular visits to their stall and balanced the accounts. On those occasions Johann stood underneath the dark arcades of the Church of the Holy Spirit, waiting for a sign from Margarethe, whereupon they'd both enter the church and sit down as if in prayer, Johann taking the pew behind Margarethe's. He couldn't see her face that way, but at least they could talk.

"I've been praying again," whispered Johann. "And do you know what happened? The very same night an angel appeared in my dreams."

"That's a good sign, Johann," replied Margarethe softly. "He is holding a hand over you so that evil can't reach you."

"He also spoke to me. He said that our love alone can heal us. He holds his hand over us and gives us his blessing."

Margarethe's head was still lowered, but he could tell that she was shaking. "What . . . what do you mean?"

"I think the angel wants you to leave the nunnery. He wants you to go with me, Margarethe, for the two of us to start a new life together in another city. I'm going to be a magister in just two years, and then I'll be able to work at a university or as a teacher in a school, as a clerk, at a library, or—"

"Stop it, Johann! Stop!" Margarethe's voice rose. Several worshippers turned to look at them, and she lowered her head again immediately. "I don't want to hear such things. Nothing but silly daydreams."

"And yet those dreams could become reality, Margarethe. If you wanted them to."

She stood up and rushed out of the church.

Johann clenched his teeth. He had gone too far—too far for the first time. He'd have to proceed more slowly, take it meeting by meeting—but he was so impatient. He wanted to share his life with Margarethe, and sooner rather than later. So he decided to put his plan into action.

There was only one thing left missing.

"You want *what?*" Valentin looked at Johann with wide eyes and put down his stylus. They had met in the common area of their lodging to study up on the Greek philosophers. Valentin wanted to take his baccalaureus in half a year's time, and Johann had promised to help him. There was indeed much room for improvement in Valentin's Greek, and his translations were riddled with mistakes. On top of everything else, Johann's question completely threw him.

"I want you to paint an angel," repeated Johann. "On a glass plate, just like the animals. I'll get you one."

"What in God's name do we need an angel for?"

"Well, I think it wouldn't hurt if there were Christian motifs among our pictures," replied Johann. "If we want to present the laterna to the university scholars one day, we can hardly show them nothing but cats, stags, and wolves. An angel would bring the theologists to our side. The perfect synthesis of faith and science."

"Hmm. Perhaps you're right." Valentin put down the tome about Plutarch's comparative autobiographies of Julius Caesar and Alexander the Great. "I should have time for it after the baccalaureus."

"Why not before?"

Valentin looked surprised. "Before? But—"

"Listen," Johann interrupted. "When I said a while ago that the degree of magister would elevate the laterna—that was a stupid and vain thing to say. I can see that now, and I'm sorry. It was all your idea to begin with, so you should reap the praise for it. What do think about introducing the laterna magica during your exam? Rector Gallus would be best, I think. You could say that we started off building a camera obscura and later decided to take it further."

"And the lenses from his glasses?" asked Valentin skeptically.

"The lenses could have come from anywhere. I'm sure the old man has long forgotten about them. That was months ago, and besides, he's already wearing new ones."

Valentin shook his head. "That wouldn't be right, Johann. You put just as much work into the apparatus."

"I've got my baccalaureus already," replied Johann with a smile. "But I wouldn't mind you mentioning my name in the course of your presentation. What do you say?"

He looked at Valentin expectantly. He tried to appear casual, but inwardly he prayed that Valentin would go for it. It was too important! Important to him, but most of all to Margarethe, because he needed to get her out of that nunnery before her delusions about the devil, boogeymen, and demons consumed her completely.

"All right," said Valentin reluctantly. "Why not? I'll draw an angel. Hmm. A Virgin Mary and a cross wouldn't hurt, either." He started to draw small sketches on the edges of his papers. After just a few moments his enthusiasm seemed kindled. "The angel needs wings and a sword, of course," he said and continued his drawing. "Yes, I think I'll go for an archangel. Archangel Michael, perhaps."

Johann nodded. "I think Archangel Michael is an excellent idea. He symbolizes the fight against evil. The theologists are going to love you."

Valentin smiled and looked up from his sketches. "I never took you for someone so selfless, Johann Faustus." His expression turned more serious. "You told me so little about you and your former life. Sometimes I really don't know who you are. I've been worrying about you and me lately, but clearly for nothing." He smiled again. "You're a true friend."

Johann felt a brief stab of guilt in his chest, but the pain soon passed.

18

"So? Do you like it here?"

Johann lifted the torch, and the flickering flames illuminated the many faded paintings on the cave's vaulted ceiling. Among others, there was a painting in various shades of red of the Virgin Mary with her child. The mother and baby Jesus gazed down kindly on Johann and Margarethe.

"It . . . it's so beautiful," breathed Margarethe. "How do you know this place?"

"Students have plenty of time to go for walks." Johann grinned. "I enjoy roaming Heiligenberg Mountain and being alone with my thoughts. I discovered this cave when I was seeking shelter from a thunderstorm once."

He had found the cave a few weeks earlier, at the foot of Heiligenberg Mountain—one of the last foothills of the Odenwald Mountains, wooded with oak trees and chestnuts. It lay on the other side of the Neckar River, opposite Königstuhl Mountain, and was a popular meeting place for students and young couples trying to keep their loves a secret. It always seemed a little warmer beneath the vast green canopy of the chestnut trees—unlike inside the cave, where it was as cold as winter.

Johann suspected the cave stemmed from a time when Christianity was still new to the area. The paintings were simple, as if drawn by plain peasants, but they bore a grace that many large church paintings lacked. Farther back in the cave stood a crude block of stone that might have served as an altar once.

Margarethe tightened around her shoulders the woolen scarf she wore over her nun's habit. She shivered, and small clouds of steam came from her mouth. "It's cold in here. We shouldn't stay too long. The mother cellarer is expecting me back in Heidelberg. If I stay out too long, she'll grow suspicious—if she isn't already," she said with a sigh.

"Just tell her you were delayed by a storm," said Johann. "Hear for yourself."

And indeed, there was a thunderclap outside, and they could hear the steady rushing of rain. It was the beginning of May and thunderstorms were common, especially in the hills. Since the snow had melted, Margarethe often traveled back and forth between the convent and the house in Heidelberg. The nunnery's produce needed to be transported to town, and the mothers superior and cellarer exchanged messages. The nuns used an oxcart to transport their wares and took the road that ran alongside the Neckar and past Heiligenberg Mountain. Whenever Margarethe traveled by herself, she and Johann took the opportunity for a meeting.

Margarethe's initial shyness had given way to the joy of being together with Johann. They often spoke about their childhood in Knittlingen, their games in the hay loft, playing in the fields, and Johann's little magic tricks, which he still performed for her occasionally. But they never spoke about their last few days together in their hometown. It was as if a thick fog had descended upon that period of time.

Johann's desire for Margarethe had grown continuously over the last few months. To see her without really touching her, to speak to her but not be allowed to embrace her, caused him almost physical pain. At nights he dreamed of her soft skin, the dimples in her cheeks, her deep blue eyes that seemed to absorb all his fears. The best moments were those when she laughed, because then she was back to her old self. And Johann hoped that one day she would fully be back to the way she used to be.

That's what he needed the cave for.

Finding it had been a stroke of luck. It was the one building block he'd been missing. Now everything was ready. He struggled to remain calm and tried not to tremble with excitement. Originally he'd wanted to wait a few more weeks, but when he saw the thunderclouds gathering above Heiligenberg Mountain that morning, he thought the right moment had come.

Like a sign from the heavens, he thought.

But then Johann realized that he hadn't thought of God in a very long time. He had been pretending to pray to God, the saints, and the angels for Margarethe's sake, but he'd always been his own master.

If there was a God he revered, its image was standing well hidden in a dark niche of the cave.

"I really think we ought to leave now," said Margarethe, looking about anxiously. "This place is creepy, despite the beautiful paintings. This whole area is." She lowered her voice and made the sign of the cross. "Didn't you say yourself that there were witches dancing around here? I'm sure they would have done so during Walpurgis Night last week."

"That's what folks were saying," replied Johann with a shrug. "Apparently they saw lights burning on the mountain—but that could have been fires from shepherds."

"Mother Superior says we ought to stay away from Heiligenberg Mountain, even though Saint Michael Monastery is situated on its top. The monastery is dedicated to the archangel and was built on the foundations of a heathen temple—did you know that?" Margarethe shivered as she looked around again. "Allegedly, there is a deep hole somewhere in this forest into which the heathens used to throw people as sacrifices for their gruesome rituals."

For a moment, Johann saw a large fire in his mind's eye; heavy, meaty breasts; and wrinkled hands that groped and touched him everywhere. He thought he could smell soil and something faintly fishy.

O Ostara, hear us . . . O Beltal, hear us . . .

He shook himself and the memory vanished.

"Well, this is definitely not a heathen place," he said quickly. "There is an altar. And look, there are even paintings of angels." Johann led Margarethe deeper into the cave and pointed at some paintings on the ceiling. "They might be archangels. One of them is holding a sword. Perhaps the monks from Saint Michael discovered this cave a long time ago and used it as a chapel and hiding place whenever war raged in the land." He squeezed Margarethe's hand and held the torch so that he could see her face. She squinted against the light. "Margarethe, the . . . the angel spoke to me again, in my dreams. He wants us to be happy together."

"Oh, my dear Johann! Don't make it so hard for me." She returned the squeeze of his hand, and a wave of desire went through Johann. She was so close and yet so far.

"If I were a free woman, believe me, I'd do it," she said with a sad smile. "Yes, I think I'd go away with you. But I've placed my fate into God's hands."

She squeezed his hand again, and tears welled up in her eyes. "I don't know what's right and what's wrong. But I'm sure that what we're doing here is a sin."

"How can it be a sin if we love each other?" asked Johann hotly. "You're a novice, Margarethe. You haven't taken your vows yet. You are free to leave the nunnery anytime you like."

"And then? I'm afraid, Johann. Afraid of what's happening in the world out there. I'm afraid of the boogeyman."

"Do you remember the last time we were in a cave?" whispered Johann. "Back in Schillingswald Forest in Knittlingen. It was the last wonderful moment before our world collapsed. Now we're inside a cave once more—the circle is complete, and all will be well from now on."

He kissed her on the lips, and unlike with the last few attempts, she didn't turn her head away but returned his kiss. Johann shivered. She tasted just as sweet as in his memories, of summer and of juicy grapes. His hand slowly slid up to her bonnet and pushed it back until her flaxen hair came loose.

"Johann, don't," she whispered.

The torch fell to the ground and died.

There was a soft hiss and a faint, almost imperceptible smell of sulfur in the air.

It was pitch black in the cave now. He hugged her tightly and covered her cheeks with kisses.

"No one will find us here, Margarethe! We're inside the womb of Mother Earth, as safe and secure as in the womb of Mother Mary."

"Mother Mary would never condone this—she was a virgin. She—"

Margarethe broke off and stopped fighting him. But instead of returning his kisses, she stepped back and stared at the opposite wall, where the rock altar stood.

"By all the saints!" she exclaimed.

Standing inside the cave, directly behind the altar, was an angel.

He was larger than life, with outstretched wings, and he wore a helmet and cuirass as if ready for the final battle. He carried a sword in his right hand. But his eyes weren't grim like those of a soldier, no—the angel was smiling. His face showed a divine benevolence that was usually found only in depictions of Jesus Christ.

Margarethe stood as if she had turned to stone and become part of the cave—a pillar of dripstone. She didn't say anything.

But then the angel spoke.

"Don't be afraid!" he said in a whispering voice that seemed to come from all directions at once. The sound echoed repeatedly through the vaulted space.

"I've been sent from the heavens to praise your love. What God has joined together, let no church put asunder!"

The angel flickered a little, as if it was about to vanish into thin air and return to the heavens. He was almost translucent—an otherworldly creature. Now he lowered his sword in a blurred movement.

"God's love is great and it shows in the love between men!" he continued. "The devil has no power when love prevails!"

Margarethe woke from her initial shock. She fell to her knees and prayed.

"Holy Michael, our archangel," she whispered. "I thank you, I thank you . . ."

"The devil has no power when love prevails," the angel repeated and raised his sword again. His voice was quieter now, and the apparition grew weaker, twitching and jerking like a candle in the wind.

"Love . . . prevails . . . Love . . . prevails . . ." echoed through the cave.

Then the angel was gone.

Darkness spread through the cave once more, along with a faint smell of lamp oil.

Johann hoped Margarethe wouldn't notice.

"That was the angel from my dreams!" he exclaimed after a few moments. "He is real and he spoke to us!"

Margarethe nodded. She was still on her knees, tears streaming down her cheeks, and she was trembling all over.

"The devil has no power when love prevails," she repeated. "That's what he said. The devil has no power . . ."

Johann knelt down beside her and held her tightly like he used to do when they were children and she felt cold. After a while, he gently lowered her to the ground and kissed her mouth, then her neck. His fingers slid down her black habit.

"When love prevails," he whispered.

~

Archangel Michael appeared to Margarethe and Johann every week now, and sometimes even more often.

Whenever Margarethe took the oxcart from the convent to Heidelberg, Johann waited for her beneath the chestnut trees. Then they would enter the cave and pray. After a while, the angel would appear on the opposite wall and speak to them, preaching about love among men and God's victory over the devil. Sometimes Margarethe spun around in fright because she thought the voice came from right next to her, but the echo in the cave made it seem like the words came from all sides at once, reinforcing the divine effect.

And every time the angel disappeared, they made love.

It wasn't the animalistic ravishing Johann knew from Salome, but more of a tentative discovering. They'd known each other since the days of their childhood and seen each other naked before when swimming in forest lakes or playing in the hay. The last time had been in the cave at Schillingswald Forest, but Johann's memories of that afternoon were hazy. They both enjoyed seeing and feeling how the body of the other had developed, how it had grown and matured. Johann's fingers playfully caressed Margarethe's white breasts and explored between her legs. With tongue and lips he tasted her juices, and Margarethe also became more adventurous with every meeting. The only reason they stopped was because the mother cellarer was waiting—and because it was so cold inside the cave that they both had goose pimples, despite the fires burning inside their bodies.

If Margarethe sometimes cried, it was out of a mixture of shame, fear, and joy.

"Would you really go away with me?" she whispered as she pressed her shivering, naked body against his. They were lying atop an old bearskin and used their coats for blankets. "Away from Heidelberg?"

"I would go to the end of the world with you," replied Johann softly. At the same time he realized that taking Margarethe away wouldn't be as easy as he'd first thought. Her husband would search for her if she left the nunnery, and Johann had started to prepare for his magister degree, which he was determined to complete in Heidelberg. Once he had the magister, he'd be able to take Margarethe to any town he liked and find work as a scribe, teacher, or lecturer. He'd be able to get his doctorate and become a famous scholar—as famous as Conrad Celtis, perhaps. Doctor Faustus, known far and wide!

Maybe I should have waited a little longer with the angel, he sometimes thought. He didn't know how much longer he could keep up the farce. Valentin was growing suspicious, Johann could tell. And it wasn't an easy feat, smuggling the laterna out of the shed each time and reassembling it inside the cave. Sooner or later, Valentin would find out.

"What is it?" asked Margarethe, tracing his lips with her finger. "You're brooding, admit it. Even if I can't see you in this darkness, I can tell when you're brooding."

Johann laughed. "I'm Johann Faustus, remember? I always brood." He sighed theatrically and hoped Margarethe wouldn't notice the uncertainty in his voice.

She sat up, her eyes gleaming like stars in the night. "So you even brood while you're with me?"

Johann greedily kissed her, virtually drinking her in. "The brooding is fading, Margarethe. With every kiss, with every sip. You're my medicine, don't forget. Better than any quack's theriac."

She laughed. "I very much hope so!"

He kissed her again and they made love passionately.

It was the best time in Johann's life, and even though he refused to listen to it, an inkling told him that it wouldn't last forever.

It was mid-June when Conrad Celtis asked him up to the castle once again. It had been a while since they last saw each other. Celtis had been lodging at other courts—Dresden and Mainz—and Johann had focused entirely on his studies. He wanted to gain the degree of magister as fast as possible so he could finally take Margarethe away from Heidelberg.

Celtis received him in the same austere chamber as on previous occasions. The only change was that there now stood a table full of books, parchment scrolls, and documents. Johann had never seen any food or drink in Celtis's room. It was as if the scholar lived solely on literature and iron gall ink.

"So?" asked Celtis once they were both seated by the fire. "How are your studies progressing?"

Johann nodded. "I'm almost done with the works of Plutarch, and I'm well acquainted with Archimedes's mathematical formulas now. Only the Cyrenaics still give me trouble. Aristippus of Cyrene, Arete, Theodorus—"

Celtis waved dismissively. "The Cyrenaics hardly ever feature in the exams, because the doctors don't understand them, either. The sensation of lust appears to be foreign to our learned scholars, even though the Cyrenaics only mean gentle movements by that term." He laughed. "The quality of the teaching staff in Heidelberg is rather below average, as you've probably figured out for yourself by now. With the exception of my old friend Jodocus, of course."

Johann looked at Celtis expectantly. He didn't know what the purpose of this conversation was. Ever since his embarrassing faux pas at Heidelberg Castle, he'd tried not to criticize the magisters and doctors—even if he'd sometimes had to bite his tongue.

"Have you ever considered studying in another city?" asked Celtis abruptly.

Johann straightened up on his stool. He was glad about the question—it would make leaving Heidelberg so much easier. "Indeed, following my magister, I could imagine—"

"I meant sooner. This summer."

Johann's jaw dropped with surprise. He thought he must have misheard. "But . . . but . . . how? I'm in the middle of studying for my magister—"

"Which you can also complete somewhere else. A student of your scope— child's play!" Celtis grinned. "And you would have me as your sponsor."

Johann said nothing for a while. "I'm afraid you'll have to elaborate."

"I will." Celtis leaned forward and lowered his voice. "I'm going to move to Vienna this very summer. The German king, Maximilian himself, has asked me to create a chair for rhetoric and poetics. A great honor! Vienna is the center of the Holy Roman Empire and boasts one of the largest universities."

"I know," whispered Johann. "I . . . I've heard of Vienna." Suddenly he felt like the floor was swaying beneath him, and he clutched his seat tightly.

"I could do with a young assistant by my side. Someone to comb the libraries for old manuscripts for me, archive documents, and separate the wheat from the chaff. Maybe someone who will uncover long-forgotten knowledge."

"And . . . and you thought of me?"

Celtis laughed. "Who else? You may be a little arrogant, and you lack respect for us old folks, but you're smart and ambitious, just like I used to be. And you're by far the best student the university has seen in a long time. Good old Jodocus and I spoke of you just the other day. He told me you pass all your exams summa cum laude."

"You're too kind." Johann lowered his head. Inwardly, he was shaking.

What Celtis had said was true. He was one of the best, and even old Partschneider had to admit it. His intelligence, coupled with everything he'd learned from Tonio and Archibaldus, raised him above the other students. He was predestined to become a great scholar, and with Celtis's offer, there was nothing in the way of this career. Going to Vienna as Celtis's assistant was more than he'd ever hoped for. What would his mother say if she were still alive? Would he get to meet the German king?

But what about Margarethe? He'd always planned on completing his magister here at Heidelberg and then taking her with him. But as an itinerant scholar at the side of Conrad Celtis? How was that going to work?

"You hesitate?" asked Celtis and frowned. "I didn't expect that. If it's about money—"

"It's not about money," said Johann quickly. "It's . . . it's just that there are a few things I still need to see to in Heidelberg."

"Oh, I see!" Celtis winked at him. "A girl. Well, hear this advice from an old rake: love is hot and burns out fast—only art is everlasting. The desire for art—for the sciences, philosophy, literature, and painting—is the only love worth cultivating. Wouldn't you agree?"

Johann said nothing but slowly nodded.

"Your girl will understand," continued Celtis and gave him a pat on the shoulder. "Men like us are meant for greater things, Faustus. Not for child minding and church on Sunday." He stood up. "I expect your answer in two weeks at the latest. I trust you won't disappoint me."

Johann could see in Celtis's eyes that he wouldn't tolerate any objections. But he thought he also saw something else in the man's look. Celtis was studying him closely, as if trying to read his thoughts. Evidently, he wasn't inviting Johann just because he wanted a capable assistant and to support Johann's career.

He wanted to keep an eye on him.

That afternoon, Johann staggered through the lanes of Heidelberg in a daze. What should he do? An offer like this would never come again. The whole world stood open to him, and all he had to do was say yes.

He would have liked to discuss this matter with Valentin. But then he'd have to admit that he was still seeing Margarethe, and Valentin would probably draw the right conclusions. After thinking it over for a long while, Johann finally decided to do what he hadn't done in a long time: get completely and utterly drunk.

In a tavern near the university quarter, he ordered a large jug of wine. There weren't a lot of people drinking at this hour of the afternoon; most students wouldn't arrive until the evening. The sounds of laughter and music wafted in through the door. Preparations for Saint John's Eve were in full swing throughout the city, and Johann realized that he'd been studying at Heidelberg for one whole year now. He had come to find Margarethe, and he had found her. He was happier than ever before in his life, and now he was supposed to leave her again? The more he thought about it, the clearer it became to him that he couldn't do it. He couldn't possibly leave without Margarethe. But he couldn't turn down Celtis's offer, either. So what was he supposed to do?

He emptied the jug in no time. The wine was sour and cheap, but at least it was strong. He ordered another one right away. Johann's mood improved with each sip. There was a solution. He'd have to tell more lies, but he'd lied so many times in the last few years that it hardly mattered. He would take Margarethe with him to Vienna—as his maidservant. It was so easy! Celtis was bound to travel with a large household, and one girl more wouldn't even be noticed. Later, once Johann had his magister and was earning his own money, he would take Margarethe for his wife. Surely Celtis would understand. Until then, Johann would rent a room close to the university for her, and they'd be able to see each other whenever they wanted. All would be well.

Johann took another long sip while his world became simpler by the minute. His plan was genius, really, because Margarethe's husband wouldn't be able to touch them. Who would dare to bother the great Conrad Celtis just because they were looking for some runaway nun? The elector or the bishop, perhaps, but certainly no drunken Heidelberg vintner.

Johann was so thrilled about his plan and so drunk from the two jugs of wine that he didn't notice the man approaching his table.

It was Hans Altmayer.

"Look at that, the great Faustus deigns to have a drink with the common people," jeered Altmayer. His nose, which Johann had broken during their brawl, had long healed, but now it was crooked and made him look even more of a ruffian.

"Better watch out that the alcohol doesn't go to your head," he hissed, glowering at Johann from bloodshot eyes.

Altmayer had been drinking heavily in recent months and had failed his baccalaureus exams. The rector himself had cautioned him and told him that he'd be kicked out of school if he failed another test. The only thing keeping Altmayer at the university right now was the protective hand of his father, who was an influential merchant.

"Pale little students with their noses always in books can't handle anything," Altmayer went on with a smirk. "Real life looks quite different."

Johann rose to his feet. He swayed a little, and his head felt heavy and light as a feather at the same time. More than usual he felt a strong urge to pick a fight with Altmayer. A fury welled up in him like he hadn't felt in years—since his time with the jugglers. Underneath his jerkin, his fingers felt for the knife on his belt. Perhaps he needed to teach Altmayer a proper lesson so he'd finally leave him alone. Johann thought how easily the knife had glided into the eye of the French mercenary back then, as if it were butter. He'd enjoyed the feeling.

"You're right, I lack a lot of practice at drinking," he began quietly. "I'm not as lucky as a drunkard like you—drinking day in, day out, and one day ending up as a red-nosed village teacher in some godforsaken hole, unless you become a traveling student and die in the gutter like a mangy dog. Congratulations!"

Altmayer raised his fist. He, too, was drunk and ready to fight. But suddenly his lips twisted into a strange smile, and he lowered his hand again. "Why should I beat you up, Faustus? Revenge will be much more satisfying."

Then he turned around and walked away. Johann, flushed from the alcohol, staggered after him for a few steps. "Hey, stop, you useless twit, you flat-nosed newt—"

He was about to pounce on Altmayer from behind when someone held him back. He spun around angrily and saw Valentin's worried face.

"So this is where I find you," exclaimed Valentin. "And just in the nick of time, methinks." He grabbed a pitcher from a table and threw cold water into Johann's face. "Wake up before something bad happens!"

"How dare you!" Johann clenched his fist at his side. Then he felt the knife again, and it was as if it slipped into his hand all by itself. The face before him blurred and was replaced by a grinning visage.

Tonio!

Johann raised the knife, ready to strike. Only at the last moment did he realize that it wasn't Tonio standing in front of him but his sole friend. The hallucination vanished, and with it the hatred and anger. Johann dropped his arms. Suddenly he felt awfully tired and empty. What had he done? He'd almost destroyed everything he'd worked so hard for during the last year.

With a groan he collapsed into Valentin's arms.

"I . . . I'm so sorry," he mumbled. "Believe me, I didn't want to do this. Something . . . something came over me."

Johann realized what it was that had made him so angry. He had wanted to stab Tonio del Moravia! Or had it been Tonio who had nearly brought him to stab his friend to death? Would he never be rid of that evil man? The master seemed to stick to him like a curse.

Johann shook himself; his legs felt like they were made of wax. "I want to go . . . home," he slurred. "Sleep."

"No problem." Valentin grinned and caught Johann before he landed on the tavern floor. "The great Faustus, bested by a jug of wine. Finally we've found an adversary you can't outsmart."

The headache the next morning was horrendous, and when it finally subsided, all that was left behind was a feeling of emptiness. That and the realization that Johann had almost stabbed his only friend. He wasn't entirely sure what exactly had happened at the tavern and whether the wine alone was to blame. He decided to cut back on drinking wine and beer from then on. He had never handled alcohol well—it seemed to dissolve the thin wall between his reasonable self and the animal behind it. And every time he got drunk, the nightmares returned.

Small, squirming bundles . . .

Well, at least the alcohol had been good for one thing: he had come to a decision. He would travel to Vienna and take Margarethe with him. How exactly that was going to work, Johann wasn't sure yet. But he felt certain he'd find a solution—he'd always found one so far. But first he had to share the news with Margarethe.

And that meant Saint Michael would have to speak to her one more time.

Johann hadn't intended to make the angel appear anymore. He no longer needed it to, and it was just too dangerous. He wouldn't be able to keep it secret from Valentin for much longer. And he'd lately had the feeling again that he was being watched. He needed the angel just this one final time. Saint Michael would ask Margarethe to follow Johann to Vienna. The angel had to appear one last time, and then Johann would never use such hocus-pocus again. Margarethe was healed. She never spoke of the boogeyman and Satan now.

All would be well. He no longer needed the lies—at least not with Margarethe.

On the day of Saint John's Eve, children ran through the streets, holding sticks adorned with colorful paper ribbons. On the surrounding hills, the young lads were piling up pyres, which they'd set alight after sunset. Fires would also be lit on Heiligenberg Mountain. Margarethe had told Johann that all nuns had to gather at the convent on the feast day of Saint John the Baptist, but not before the late mass. Until then, the sisters enjoyed one of their few days off. And with a hushed voice Margarethe had also told him that the river liked to help itself to an offering on Saint John's night. Many times in the past, dead girls had been fished out of the Neckar the following day.

Carrying the laterna in a pack covered with cloths on his back, dressed like a plain peddler, Johann headed toward their hiding place late in the afternoon. He'd walked this way so many times now that he knew every tree and every bush. The basketlike pack on his back was bulky and heavy, holding not just the laterna but also a long fuse, the oil for the lamp, and another apparatus.

Johann had told Valentin that he was going to the library to study. But instead, he'd waited for Valentin to leave, then gone to the shed to put on his disguise and load his pack. Johann's heart was beating fast, and he kept looking back to check that he wasn't being followed. A few times, as he walked through the woods, he thought he could hear branches snapping behind him, but he guessed his nerves were playing tricks on him. He couldn't wait for all this to be over.

Once Johann arrived at the cave, he lit a torch before setting up the laterna behind the altar, like he'd done so many times before. He took the fuse out of the pack and laid it along the cave wall. The most time-consuming part of the process was setting up the water clock at the laterna. It had taken him a while to figure out how he might change the images in the laterna without having to operate the apparatus himself. Finally he'd found something in old drawings by Hero of Alexandria. The Greek mathematician had constructed machines that used the power of water to move levers. Large levers required a large quantity of water, but for Johann's mechanism, a few gallons sufficed. The water slowly dripped from one container into another, and once it reached a certain weight, the lever was pushed and the image of Saint Michael with his sword raised fell into the slot. After a while, when enough water had dripped back into the first container, the image with the lowered sword appeared. Johann had experimented until the intervals were roughly the same length. The result was a fluid movement that made the archangel appear almost real.

After about two hours, he was finished with his preparations. He covered the apparatus with a gray cloth, making it practically invisible in the dark cave. Then he went outside and waited for Margarethe.

Afternoon had turned to evening, and the first Saint John's fires had been lit on Heiligenberg Mountain. Johann thought he could hear the laughter of young folks from afar. They were probably leaping across the flames, celebrating the shortest night of the year like people had done since time immemorial. Sometimes straw puppets were burned to chase away sickness and demons. Johann had read in old books that they even used to burn real people on that night, and he thought of the alleged witches the bishop had condemned to fire only a few weeks ago—a sacrifice like the heathens used to offer to their dark deities.

A sudden noise made Johann jump, and he breathed a sigh of relief when Margarethe emerged from between the trees. As always, she wore her black nun's habit and a thin woolen scarf around her shoulders. The nights could still be chilly in June, and the cave never warmed up at all. Margarethe shivered and rushed into his arms.

"We can't go on like this for much longer," she whispered. "Living with a lie like this . . . I can't take it anymore. Would you really go away with me?"

"Yes, Margarethe, I would. That's why I traveled all the way from Venice— to be with you." He gently pulled her toward the cave entrance. "Who knows, maybe the angel will appear to us again. Maybe he knows where our path will take us."

Margarethe gave him an intent look, and for a brief moment Johann thought she'd seen right through him.

"I thought about it again last night. Why did the archangel choose us, of all people? Why does he speak to us? There are so many young couples who can't be together despite their love."

"Because you're someone very special, Margarethe. The angel wants to help you—help us—return to the path of love." Johann made a sweeping gesture at the woods around them. "And who knows? Maybe he appears to other couples in the area. This is Heiligenberg Mountain, after all. They built a monastery in the name of Michael the archangel up here. It's his realm."

They entered the cave. The temperature dropped drastically, and small clouds rose from their mouths. Margarethe tightened the scarf around her shoulders.

Johann loved the sudden darkness inside the cave. In here, the world outside, with all its noise and all that striving for glory and knowledge, seemed completely unimportant.

Only the two of them existed.

A torch that Johann had lit earlier burned from a crack in the rock. The light showed them to their bed, which they'd made over the weeks from moss and dead leaves. As they went past, Johann put out the torch, and there was a soft hissing noise that he hoped Margarethe wouldn't hear. Now it was completely dark.

They sank onto their bed and embraced like two children seeking comfort. Johann closed his eyes and inhaled the damp scent of the cave, of soil, fungi, and mossy rocks. But most of all he breathed in Margarethe's smell, which couldn't be compared to anything. He felt so close to her body, it was as if it were his own. In the same moment, he realized that he was happier than ever before.

He could have stayed like this forever.

But he knew he couldn't wait any longer. When he'd put out the torch before, he had also lit the fuse that was burning its way slowly and quietly toward the laterna. By now Johann knew exactly how long it took to get there.

"We should pray," said Johann quietly. "Perhaps the angel will return. I wish he knew the answers to all our questions."

Margarethe nodded and folded her hands in prayer.

"Oh, Saint Michael," she muttered, "I beg you, hear us sinners on earth. Deliver us from evil and show us the path to paradise."

"Deliver us from evil," repeated Johann.

As he'd expected, the fuse reached the oil lamp at that very moment. A bright speck of light appeared on the opposite wall, and inside it was the figure of Archangel Michael with his sword raised. Margarethe gave a small cry. Even though Johann knew the angel was just an image, he shivered. It was as if God was speaking to him through the apparatus.

"He has come down one more time indeed," whispered Margarethe. "Oh gracious Lord!"

"Rejoice and be merry," sounded the strange, unearthly voice of the angel. "For I bring happy tidings!"

As on the other occasions before, Johann turned his head to the side so that his voice was thrown back from the wall. He had seen jugglers use a similar technique for puppets, and for the last several weeks he'd been practicing the trick in the large halls of the library and at the Church of the Holy Spirit. The key was to avoid any sounds that required movement of the lips, or to form them using the tongue and the palate instead of the jaw. It was an ancient technique that had been used by the old Greeks.

"Don't be afraid," whispered the angel. "Loving hearts have nothing to fear. What the dear Lord put together, the world can't tear asunder."

The image changed, and Michael's sword arm pointed downward now. It was just a small movement, but the effect made the figure on the wall seem so much more real.

"Follow the call of love," the angel continued, the voice echoing through the vaulted space. "Follow the call to Vienna . . . Vienna . . . Vienna . . ." The last word echoed several times. Margarethe looked up from her prayers.

"To Vienna? But—"

"I think I know what he means," said Johann in his normal voice. "There is a university in Vienna, too. We could move there, far away from the nunnery, far away from anything preventing us from being together."

"Oh, Johann! Is that really true? Tell me I'm not dreaming!" She threw herself into his arms, and Johann once again inhaled the scent of her hair. Her bonnet slipped backward, and he covered her face with kisses. He thought he could see her cornflower-blue eyes beam in the dark.

He was so happy! There was nothing stopping them now. They would move to Vienna as part of Conrad Celtis's household, he would study, and at some point they'd marry and—

There was a jangling sound followed by the stomping of many boots.

Johann spun around with fright and saw the glow of several torches approaching from the cave entrance. Margarethe screamed. She clung to him, but Johann was paralyzed by shock. He knew right away that this was the end.

A troop of men had entered the cave.

At its front strode Hans Altmayer and Jakob Kohlschreiber, Margarethe's husband.

"Damned witch!" shouted Kohlschreiber, his bloated face glowing red in the light of the torch. "What do you think you're doing? Wallowing in the dirt like a sow with her paramour. But we saw right through you!"

"It's just like I told you," said Hans next to him. He tried to sound calm, but his voice trembled with malicious glee. "I've been watching them for a long time. They always meet in this cave. The devil knows what they're doing in here."

"Look!" cried one of the men behind them. Like the others, he was carrying a short pike and was clad in the garb of a city guard. Evidently Kohlschreiber had gathered support from the Heidelberg city watch before making his way to the cave. With a shaking hand, the guard pointed at the wall behind the altar, where the quivering image of Archangel Michael was still displayed. "By all the saints . . . an angel!"

The others also cried out in surprise. Only Hans remained calm.

"Don't worry, it's not an angel. I'm certain the apparition is somehow connected to the devilish apparatus Faustus always lugs here. He built some sort of thing with Valentin Brander. The image is a deception!"

Hans searched the cave with his torch until he discovered the hidden box beneath the blanket. "Ha! There it is, the devilish machine!"

Hans gave the laterna magica a kick, and with an ugly sound of cracking and shattering, the image of the angel disappeared forever.

Margarethe screamed again. This time the scream was high pitched and mournful, as if it came from a fallen angel.

"What were you up to with that thing, huh?" snarled Jakob Kohlschreiber, stepping toward Johann and Margarethe. "Were you trying to invoke the devil? Is it Lucifer you're praying to in this cave?"

"It . . . it's just an apparatus," replied Johann quietly. Each word came out slowly and with great difficulty, as if he'd forgotten how to speak. "Nothing but an apparatus."

"The Inquisition must learn of this," said Kohlschreiber. Trembling with fury, he pointed at Margarethe, who was covering her face with her hands. Johann wrapped his arms around her and noticed that she was as cold as the cave's rock wall. He didn't know whether she understood what he'd just said.

Nothing but an apparatus . . .

"I never trusted that woman. Cursed be the day her father gave her to me as a wife!" cried Kohlschreiber, nodding grimly. "She's possessed by the devil—he spoke from her mouth every night she lay with me. By God, I tried everything. I found her a place at a nunnery, but clearly, evil can't be driven from her. Only the fire can purge her now."

"And concerning you . . ." Jakob Kohlschreiber glared at Johann, who was still holding Margarethe tightly, as if he could protect her from all evil. "I know you! You sounded me out that time at the tavern. Tried to find out about my wife, you lecherous bastard!"

Hans grinned. "Our rector will be extremely interested to learn what kind of devilish apparatuses his favorite student has been working on—and what kind of a girl he's been dallying with. A nun!" He shook his head in mock sadness. "I believe this is the end of your time at the university, Faustus—at the very least. What did you tell me once? Many an itinerant scholar ends up in the gutter, where he dies like a mangy dog."

"Enough talk," growled Kohlschreiber. "Take them!"

The last words had been addressed to the guards, who stepped toward Johann and Margarethe with lowered pikes. Two of them grabbed Margarethe, who didn't seem to notice what was going on around her. She had started to hum a soft tune. Johann winced when he recognized the melody.

Growing in our garden are parsley and thyme; our Gretchen is the bride, she's looking so fine . . .

It was the song he and Margarethe used to sing as children.

"Take your hands off her!" he screamed. He rushed at the guards and started wrestling with them.

"Don't make it any worse!" shouted Jakob Kohlschreiber. He stepped in and grabbed Johann by the collar like a rabbit. "Or do you want to burn together with the witch? Is that what you want? Burn for this piece of trash?"

He kicked Margarethe, who whimpered and cowered on the ground. Rage swept over Johann like a dark wave. He felt angrier than ever before in his life—angrier even than the time he killed the French mercenary. Reason was blocked out, and an all-consuming hatred burned inside him. Suddenly he was holding his knife in his hand, although he had no idea how it got there. He raised his arm and stabbed wildly into the man in front of him. It felt good, and for a brief moment relief spread through his body, the sweet flavor of revenge trickling down his throat. Johann remembered Tonio's words back when he'd gifted the knife to him.

I'm giving this to you . . . It cuts skin and sinews like butter.

Gasping for breath, Kohlschreiber collapsed in front of him, blood spurting from several wounds in his stomach.

"You . . . you bloody fool," wheezed the vintner, writhing on the floor.

The guards froze with shock when they saw the seriously wounded man. They sensed that the young man with the knife wasn't entirely in control of himself, that something dark had grasped hold of him. For a few moments, the only sound was Kohlschreiber's groaning. Even Hans had taken a step back, but his eyes were flashing deviously.

"Congratulations, Faustus," he spat. "You just dug your own grave."

Johann stared at the bloodied knife in his hand with horror. He suddenly realized what he'd done. His eyes turned to Margarethe, who was holding her arms crossed in front of her chest, rocking back and forth and still humming the children's tune.

Red wine, white wine, tomorrow morn you shall be mine . . .

"Margarethe, I . . . I'm so sorry," he burst out. "I . . . I only wanted us to be happy."

Still none of the other men stirred. They stared with fright at the knife in Johann's hand. Kohlschreiber no longer made any sound, and a pool of blood grew around his plump body. Finally the guards raised their pikes again.

"Take him!" shouted Hans.

And Johann ran.

"Your grave!" rang out Hans's triumphant voice, echoing through the cave. "Your grave!"

Johann ran outside, where night had fallen in the meantime. Saint John's fires were burning on the hills all around, gleaming like eyes behind a dark mask.

"Your grave!" was the last thing Johann heard.

Then the forest swallowed him up.

Johann raced uphill for a long time, panicked like an animal in flight and unable to form a clear thought. It was just like the time he fled from Tonio del Moravia and his companions in the woods near Nördlingen. From one moment to the next he'd lost everything. But this time the shock went much deeper.

He had lost what he loved most.

Margarethe.

He noticed that he'd been running uphill only when the trees ended and he saw the sparkling lights of the Heidelberg watchtowers beneath him, with the castle above the city. He sensed he was looking back on a life he was leaving behind for good.

His life's joy had stayed behind in the cave.

Johann tore at his hair, screamed and raved, cried and whined. Eventually he cowered in a hollow of damp, foul-smelling leaves and repeated the same words over and over.

"I . . . didn't . . . want . . . this . . ."

And at the same time he knew that he alone was to blame. He had played with high stakes and lost everything. It had been his idea to win Margarethe over with the image of the archangel. He should have expected to be followed—he'd always suspected something. Every time he'd returned from the monastery or arrived at the cave, he thought he felt eyes on his back. Sobs racked his body once more.

Margarethe.

He should have stayed with her, defended her with his life. Instead he had run away and left her to the guards. Margarethe's husband had already announced that he'd hand her over to the Inquisition. She wasn't just a nun fooling around with a young student—no, she was suspected of being in league with the devil. And all that just because of the damned laterna magica! He should never have used the apparatus for his own desires. But now it was too late.

So what could he do?

Hans was right—his academic career in Heidelberg was over. And he wouldn't be going to Vienna with Conrad Celtis. Altmayer would make sure the story of Faustus, defiler of nuns and devil worshipper, would make the rounds at the taverns and university. And worse: he had stabbed Jakob Kohlschreiber—probably to death. Not that Johann regretted the man's death, but now he was a murderer and had to flee.

But then he would abandon Margarethe.

Johann swallowed hard. He'd reached a decision.

He would have to go to Heidelberg and hand himself in.

He would explain to the authorities that it was all his fault. He had led Margarethe astray and he had built the laterna magica. No devilish machine, just a simple apparatus. They'd understand, and Margarethe would be saved. At least they wouldn't condemn her as a witch. But he'd need help, and most of all he'd need a witness to confirm his story.

Johann decided to wait until the morning and then find the one person he had left.

Valentin.

He spent the night on the hilltop, gazing down at the Neckar, which wound its way through the valley like a giant black snake. The lights of Heidelberg gleamed beyond, and above them flickered the flames of the Saint John's fires. Johann occasionally thought he could hear screams, presumably from the youth dancing around the fires.

Long before dawn, he went on his way. He entered the city with the first peddlers and farmers carrying their wares to market in their packs. Johann looked like a beggar in his filthy, torn clothes, and the guards didn't recognize him. No one tried to stop him as he slipped through the gate.

He rushed to his residence as fast as he could, climbed across the low wall at the back, and knocked on the window of the room he shared with Valentin—softly at first, but then louder and louder. No one opened. Had his friend already left for the lectures? But it was much too early.

A sense of foreboding overcame Johann.

A damp mist hung in the lanes, and hardly anyone was about. Johann cautiously sneaked over to the western city fortifications. He was headed for one building in particular. The Diebsturm Tower, which served as Heidelberg's prison.

The tower was a bulky construct about ten paces high and built from massive blocks of stone. A few barred windows way up high and a narrow wrought-iron door were the only openings. In front of the tower stood a cart, enveloped in fog. On top of the cart stood a crate about as high as a man, like a mobile prison cell. Two skinny nags were hitched to the wagon.

As Johann approached the tower, the door opened with a squeak, and two guards with halberds emerged. They were followed by two other guards, who were carrying a man in torn clothes. The man's head flopped to one side like that of a ragdoll, and blood was pouring from a wound on his temple.

Johann clasped one hand to his mouth to stop himself from crying out.

The prisoner was Valentin.

Evidently, Hans had made good on his threat and reported Valentin to the authorities. Johann guessed his friend was being accused of helping to build an apparatus that was used to invoke the devil. But why hadn't the university intervened? Why hadn't Rector Gallus been called upon? He would know that the laterna was a scientific invention, not witchcraft. Johann had told the rector all about their plans, and the university had its own jurisdiction.

But then Johann realized that in this case, the city would be responsible. With the accusation of witchcraft, the authorities wasted no time. Johann guessed Valentin was about to be taken to Worms, where the bishop had his seat and where all interrogations of this type took place. Was Margarethe also on her way to Worms?

Had he come too late?

Now the guards opened the door with the barred window at the back of the large crate and shoved the prisoner inside. Johann couldn't tell whether Valentin was conscious or not—or whether he was still alive at all. Still, Johann needed to try to speak with him. Even if he risked being arrested. He waited until the cart began to move, and then he followed it quietly, using the twilight of dawn and the fog to dart from one corner to the next.

His opportunity arrived at the city gate.

The guards driving the wagon stopped to talk to the watchman. Soon the men were hooting with laughter, and it seemed as though a jug of wine was handed around. The street was still relatively empty at this hour, and the fog was thick.

Johann sneaked up to the wagon and tried to catch a glimpse through the barred window. But it was pitch black on the other side, and it smelled of rotten straw and excrement. Then Johann heard a soft groaning.

"Valentin!" he whispered. "Can you hear me? It's me, Johann!"

The groaning stopped abruptly. There was a rustling noise, and a few moments later Valentin's face appeared at the barred window. Johann saw that not only was his friend bleeding from his head, but one of his lips was split open and he was missing a few teeth. And his right eye was swollen shut. His other eye glowered angrily at Johann. There was no trace of warmth or friendship.

"What do you want?" he mumbled.

"Valentin, I . . . ," Johann began desperately. "I . . . I'm so sorry! Please forgive me, I—"

"What is it that you'd like me to forgive? The fact that you lied to me—your only friend—the entire time? That you used the apparatus we built together for your low needs? That you used me just like you use all people? That I'm going to be tried as a sorcerer because of you?" Valentin's good eye gleamed as cold and hard as a diamond. "To you, Faustus, people are nothing but scientific instruments. You use them and then you discard them. How could I be so stupid and not notice sooner? I should have listened to the others, but instead I followed you around like a dumb calf. And now the calf is being led to slaughter."

Johann tried to shake the iron bars; his face was close to Valentin's.

"Valentin . . . you . . . Don't talk like that! I didn't want any of this to happen, believe me! I'm your friend, I—"

Valentin's blood-stained saliva struck his cheek.

"Did you not hear what I said? They're taking me to the Inquisition at Worms! Not even Rector Gallus was able to do anything about it." Valentin laughed hysterically. "They are going to inflict pain on me until I confess to invoking Satan with you. And then they'll burn me alive—while you walk free!"

Johann said nothing. Then he asked the one question he needed to ask, even though he didn't think Valentin would answer it.

"What about Margarethe?"

"Your little nun?" Valentin smiled for the first time, but it was a nasty, twisted smile. "Oh, she was lucky."

Johann's heart beat wildly and he felt wide awake. "Are you saying she . . . she won't be taken to Worms?"

"No, she won't. The worst is behind her. Only God is her judge now."

Johann froze. He struggled to speak because each word was as heavy as a lead weight.

"God . . . is . . . her . . . judge? What . . . what do you mean?"

"Is it so hard to understand? She hanged herself, Faustus! Last night in her cell. I heard the guards cut her down and her dead body drop into the straw. I watched through my window as they carried her away. I guess they nailed her into a barrel and threw her in the river, like they do with all suicides."

The world stopped turning. The universe stood still. The gray morning mist covered Johann's face, but he shed no tears. He was incapable of moving, incapable of speaking.

Reality seemed like the fog wafting past him.

"She is dead, Faustus," Valentin continued. "Did you hear me? And it's your fault. Your greed, your arrogance, your lies killed her." He tilted his head to one side and studied his former friend as if for the last time. "By the way, she confessed to being a witch. I heard it myself. She said the boogeyman would come and get her now. The boogeyman . . ." Valentin's voice was just a whisper now. "Are you the boogeyman, Faustus?"

Suddenly the cart jerked forward. The gate was wide open and the cart rattled onto the bridge. Valentin's face was becoming smaller and smaller.

"Are you the boogeyman, Faustus?" shouted Valentin. "Tell me, are you?"

"Shut up!" yelled Johann. "Shut the hell up!"

Finally he managed to move again. Beside himself with anger and grief, he ran after the wagon onto the bridge. He wanted to smash Valentin's face, grind it like grain under a millstone, and punch it until the man's lips stopped moving. He noticed that he still carried Tonio's knife. He'd put it back in his pocket after he'd stabbed Jakob Kohlschreiber. Now he pulled it back out. He wanted to destroy Valentin, and himself, and the whole world.

"Are you the boogeyman, Faustus?" shouted Valentin once more.

"Shut your goddamned mouth!" Johann had reached the middle of the bridge, the river rushing down below. He was so blinded by rage that he didn't notice the two guards following him. The cart stopped, and two guards with raised halberds approached him from the front as well.

"That's him!" shouted one of them. Johann realized the man was one of the guards from the cave the night before. "The student of the devil who cast a spell on the nun and killed Kohlschreiber. I recognize him!"

The guards were closing in from two sides. Johann stood in the middle of the bridge, knife in hand, and heard Valentin laughing. It was a sad, desperate laugh—the laugh of the only true friend he'd ever had. Now Johann had lost everything. His friend and Margarethe. Everything worth living for.

Are you the boogeyman?

Johann climbed onto the bridge railing. He put the knife back in his pocket, lifted his hands toward the gray sky, and closed his eyes. The moment the guards reached out for him, he jumped.

Margarethe, I'm coming!

The waters of the Neckar swallowed him, but the Lord had no mercy. He made Johann rise to the surface and reach for a tree trunk, coughing and spluttering. Slowly Johann drifted toward the dark forests west of the Odenwald Mountains. The last sound he heard of Heidelberg was Valentin's hysterical laughter.

Though he couldn't be sure that it wasn't Tonio del Moravia's laughter. Or Signore Barbarese's. Or Gilles de Rais's, greeting him from the grave. They were all laughing at him.

Homo Deus est.

The pact was sealed.

Act V

The Awakening of the Beast

19

ON THE MARKET SQUARE, A MAN SCREAMED AS THE PYRE around him caught on fire.

He was tied to a stake with thick ropes, and the guards had stacked the logs knee high around him. The burning wood crackled and smoked while the condemned man begged for mercy—or, at the least, a quick death.

Most of the crowd watched the macabre show in silence, but there were a few who laughed, jeered, or sang dirty rhymes. Over a hundred people had gathered on the Warnheim market square, which was covered in muck and surrounded by crooked half-timbered houses and a decrepit little church. The majority of the spectators were peasants in plain tunics and drawstring shoes. The men came armed with pikes, pitchforks, and cudgels, but there were also women and children among the crowd. Awestruck, they all watched as the man on the pyre screamed. His clothes, skin, and hair were beginning to smolder, and the sweetish smell of fried meat spread across the square.

It reminded Johann of the meal he'd eaten at a tavern the night before—pork with beans and smoked ham.

Wearing his wide-brimmed hat low on his brow and a dirty coat around his shoulders, he was standing in one of the front rows, studying the flames. Blue, yellow, and red, they licked across the wood that had been doused with oil beforehand. The flames reached only to the man's thighs so far, but Johann thought he could see the first blisters forming on the man's face. He leaned forward with interest, his right hand resting on the top of the box-shaped hand-drawn cart he had lugged to the front of the crowd with much difficulty. The blisters were a fascinating phenomenon. He guessed that the heat rose up in waves against the body and increased in strength. Back at Heidelberg University, long ago, he'd read something similar in the writs of Archimedes. Or was it Pythagoras?

Meanwhile, the condemned man's hair had completely caught on fire and his screams turned to inhuman screeching. Until a few moments ago he'd been a handsome lad with soft, almost feminine eyes and long lashes. Now there wasn't much left of that. The burning figure increasingly disappeared behind the acrid black smoke that had now spread across the entire square.

The smoke . . .

With well-practiced movements, Johann removed the lid attached to the front of the box. Unfortunately it had taken too long for the smoke to become thick enough—pity, because otherwise he might have been able to save the life of the young man. But at least the dense smoke his charred body was producing served the second condemned man.

Johann's eyes turned to the second pyre, where another young man stood tied to a stake. His eyes wide with horror, the youth had watched as the first pyre was lit and the fire consumed the man in a gruesome death.

"Holy mother of God!" he pleaded loudly. "Help me!"

An elderly Hegau peasant laughed and spat into the flames, where his saliva vaporized instantly. "Do you really think the Holy Virgin is going to help a sodomite?" he jeered. "No one can help you now, you pederast—not even God himself!"

Perhaps not God, thought Johann, *but someone else can. The Antichrist . . .*

The screams of the first victim had fallen silent by now, and through the dense smoke the onlookers could make out the remains of a blackened body twisted like a doll, the mouth open as if in a final scream. One of the farmers carried a torch to the second pyre.

"Go to hell, sodomite!" he roared, holding the torch to the oil-drenched logs. "And don't forget to kiss the devil's ass!"

At that moment, the devil himself appeared.

He had horns on his head, a goat's foot, and a bushy tail, and his grin was as wide as a skull's. The larger-than-life Satan danced in the smoke of the first fire as if he'd come directly from hell onto the Warnheim market square. Deafening cracks and thunderclaps seemed to prove that the gates of hell stood wide open, and the hellish stink of sulfur spread over the onlookers.

The spectators in the front rows were the first to see the flickering devil in the smoke. They screamed and moved backward, pushing back the people behind them. There were more powerful thunderclaps, and sparks rained down on the market square.

"The devil!" shouted Johann as he hurled another pouch of gunpowder into the flames. "The devil has come upon us! Run, honest folk of Warnheim, run!"

His cries and the gunpowder had the desired effect. Wailing fearfully, the crowd moved back; only a handful of daring young men stayed put, the pikes and forks trembling in their hands.

"Now, Satan," whispered Johann.

He whistled on two fingers, and from the bottom of the cart sprang a large black mastiff. Through the haze of the smoke it looked like the hellhound Cerberus. Growling with its teeth bared, the calf-sized dog stalked toward the peasants, who turned and fled as fast as they could. Chaos broke out across the entire square; people cried, wailed, and ran; some were trampled and couldn't get back up; others threw themselves onto the ground and prayed to God and all the saints. Everyone tried to seek shelter in the lanes around the square or in one of the houses.

Only Johann stayed where he was, calmly inspecting the devil grinning down at him. He hadn't made a bad job of him, even if some strokes of the brush were a tad thick. The devil's horns looked more like those of a cow than a goat, and the cloven foot was a little smudged.

A satanic cow, he thought. *That's all you can do. What a pathetic farce for a professor and doctor, forsooth!*

He whistled Satan back before hurrying over to the second pyre, where the young man tied to the stake still trembled with horror. He was maybe eighteen or twenty years old. His smooth face was blackened by soot, and his trousers and shirt had begun to smolder in places, but other than that he seemed unharmed. Thankfully, only one side of the pile of logs had caught on fire so far.

But it wouldn't be long before the whole pyre would go up in flames.

Johann drew his knife and started to cut the ropes binding the youth to the stake. They were made from several individual strands of hemp rope and soaked in water so they wouldn't catch fire right away.

Shaking and wide eyed, the young man stared at his liberator, who was frantically sawing on the ropes.

"Are . . . are you the devil?" breathed the youth.

"No. But if we don't hurry, you'll meet him soon."

A few moments later, Johann had severed the ropes. He kicked some of the burning logs aside, then he grabbed the young man by the arm and pulled him out of the burning pile. "Quickly now, before the lamp oil in the laterna is used up!"

"The . . . lamp oil? But—"

The fellow didn't resist as Johann dragged him along. Smoke still hovered above the square, but it was growing weaker. The devil gradually dissolved into thin air.

Johann leaned over the box and pulled a few levers, and the devil disappeared as suddenly as it had arrived. A few more quick movements and the glass plate, tube, and laterna were safely stored inside the crate.

The young man gaped with amazement. "That . . . that's sorcery."

"No time for lengthy explanations. Here—put that on and help me pull the cart. Your questions will be answered later."

Johann handed a dark, stained hooded coat to the young man, who quickly put it on. Now the two of them looked like simple peddlers trying to shield their faces from the smoke with their coats. They pushed and pulled the heavy cart across the market square, which was littered with weapons, scraps of clothing, and other hastily dropped bundles. The place was still deserted for now, but already the first curious onlookers peered around the corners and out the doors again.

"The devil has gone!" called out one of them, looking at the burning pyre. "And he's taken the sodomite to hell with him!"

"That's good," he muttered through a thin smile. "Then they won't come looking for us in this world."

Together they dragged the cart through the narrow, dirty lanes away from the square; the large black dog followed them, growling at anyone coming toward them. No one gave them a second look.

Soon the two escapees reached the town gate, which stood wide open. Johann guessed that the watchmen had also rushed to the market square— unless the peasants and the rest of this accursed township had skewered them first. They pressed on without looking back. In a small wooded area not far from Warnheim, they came to a wagon like the ones used by jugglers. Strange-looking symbols, including pentagrams, were painted onto the canvas with red paint. A skinny horse tied to a tree grazed peacefully nearby. When it caught sight of the two men, it whinnied happily and pawed the ground.

The young man hadn't spoken until then, but now he could no longer remain silent.

"What . . . what's the meaning of this?" he began. "Why did you save me from those peasants? Who are you?"

"You'll learn everything in due course," said Johann. "Now help me hitch up the horse and load the laterna magica."

The youth frowned. "The laterna . . . ?"

"For Christ's sake, shut your mouth already, or else I'll feed you to Satan for breakfast!"

The black mastiff growled and bared its teeth, and the young man rushed to help Johann lift the crate off the cart and store it inside the wagon. He caught a glimpse of more crates and chests, and bunches of dried herbs hanging from the ceiling. The inside of the wagon smelled intensely of brandy and resin.

"Hop on the front with me," commanded Johann after he'd finished hitching the horse. "I'll try to answer your questions along the way."

They climbed on the box seat. "Move, old girl!" Johann cracked the reins, and the gray horse started to pull. Screeching and rattling, the wagon left the woods and the small town of Warnheim, where the people still searched for the gateway to hell.

Black columns of smoke rose up behind the walls.

"Now you can speak if you must," said Johann after a while. "But don't even think about thanking God for your life. He had nothing to do with your escape. If anyone did, then the devil."

He could see from the corner of his eye that the young man had been trying to study him furtively for a while. In his eyes lurked both fear and boundless relief. Johann smiled and hoped the boy wouldn't see it underneath the low brim of his hat.

He knew that he appeared creepy to most people. Although he was just in his early thirties, he seemed much older. His face was narrow, almost haggard, and his eyes gleamed black and mysterious. His raven-black hair reached down to his shoulders, and his hat was just as black. His pointed beard was carefully groomed and reinforced with beeswax. The cloak he wore under his old coat was made from black silk and speckled with blue spots, a pattern like stars in the night sky. With a certain amount of satisfaction Johann thought of an image he'd seen of himself not long ago. The beard and the cloak had been very faithfully reproduced. A juggler in Freiburg had sung a few mocking lines about him while holding up a series of painted canvases. Johann had considered hiring the fairground performer as a glass painter, but the man was quite old and didn't seem to be the brightest. He certainly wouldn't know how to play chess.

Johann took off the dirty overcoat and flicked the reins. "Get a move on, you old nag," he grumbled. "Or I'll turn you into a mouse and feed you to Satan. You wouldn't be the first lazy horse to land in the dog's belly."

The young man beside him finally recognized him. His eyebrows shot up and he gasped with surprise.

"You . . . you're the famous Doctor Faustus!" he called out. "The hat, the beard, the cloak—so you are real!"

"And why shouldn't I be?" replied Johann with a shrug as he continued to urge the horse forward. He could never tell how long his tricks would remain undetected. For all they knew, a mob of angry Hegau peasants might be on their way already. The Hegau region wasn't considered particularly safe for travelers—especially not those who led good, honest burghers on a merry chase using sulfur, gunpowder, and magic tricks.

"Well, there are so many rumors about you that it's hard to tell what's true and what's made up." The youth gave a chuckle. "Like the bet in Leipzig, for example."

"What is that about?"

"You straddled a barrel of wine and flew it up the cellar stairs right into the taproom. The innkeeper was forced to give you the barrel, and you emptied it, with the students' help."

"I straddled a barrel?" Johann grinned. "But why didn't I fly out the door rather than share the barrel with a bunch of red-nosed pups? What else have you heard about me?"

"In Cologne, you made a grapevine grow out of a table. And in Erfurt you turned two red roosters and one blade of straw into two oxen and a bale of hay. They say you're an infamous sorcerer and necromancer, and astrologer and alchemist. I don't even know in how many taverns I've heard tales of your adventures." The young man eyed him fearfully. "Some even say you're in league with the devil."

"So? Am I?" Johann gave his new travel companion a piercing look. When the young man gave a little start, Johann laughed. "A man is always that which people want to see in him. Out of everything they say about me, half at the most is true. But I'm not telling you which half." He winked.

It was truly astounding what sort of a reputation he had gained over the last ten years of his travels.

"Your name is Wagner, am I right?"

"Um, yes." The young man nodded, clearly surprised that Johann knew his name. "Wagner. Karl Wagner. I'm a student from Leipzig but have been traveling lately. I don't know how I can ever thank you enough for saving my life! Even if I still don't fully understand how you managed to do it." He cleared his throat and lowered his voice. "Did you use magic? Sorcery?"

Johann waved one hand. "No magic, just science. I'll show you tonight." He bared his teeth, and for a brief moment, his face took on a mocking, almost devilish expression. "And unlike you, I know how you can thank me. Nothing in this life is free, my boy."

Toward evening they came to a dense beech forest, the foliage glowing red and yellow in the fading autumn sun. To the south, the mighty rock face of Hohentwiel Mountain with its castle jutted into the sky; Lake Constance wasn't far from here and pushed fog across the woods. The two men climbed off the wagon and led the horse away from the road until they reached a small meadow lined by moss-covered rocks as tall as a man.

"We should be safe here for now," said Johann, giving the horse some barley from a bag. "Those superstitious peasants avoid this place. They believe it's haunted."

"You've been here before?" asked Karl.

"Let's say I've moved around a fair bit in the last few years. And now quit talking—go find dry wood for a fire. I'm hungry."

While Karl went looking for dry twigs and branches, Johann looked about carefully. He was glad Satan was keeping watch at the edge of the clearing. At the slightest sound, the mastiff would bark and defend its master with teeth and claws. The war in the Hegau region had finished only a few years before. The Swiss confederacy rose against the emperor and Swabia, and since then the word of the emperor didn't carry much weight in this area. The class of knights—for centuries the pillar of the empire—became increasingly impoverished, and to make a living, many knights roamed the lands, thieving and murdering. Here in the Hegau region, too. Not even the everlasting public peace Emperor Maximilian had promised had been able to change this state of affairs. The farmers also suffered, and many had chosen a life in the forests, where they banded together as groups of outlaws. Cities, on the other hand, flourished, and merchants and patricians grew wealthier by the year. The face of the world was changing.

"I think that should be enough wood."

Karl's voice tore Johann from his musings. The student was standing in front of him, his arms laden with dry wood.

"Is everything all right?" asked Karl, frowning.

"Yes, yes." Johann shook himself. "Put the wood down here."

Karl lit a small, flickering fire, and together they prepared a meal of dried meat, carrots, and wild herbs. Satan was given a bone, which it carried under the wagon. Only its glowing red eyes could be seen in the dark.

"Why did you call him Satan?" asked Karl abruptly.

"The dog?" Johann threw the mastiff a rabbit bone, which the large animal ground up noisily. "Like I said—a man is always what people want to see in him. I'm traveling by myself, without hired mercenaries or other protection. When I call Satan, people think I'm truly in league with the devil and leave me alone." He gave a shrug. "Although I must admit—the trick probably wouldn't work if Satan was a cute little poodle."

While they ate, Johann studied Karl Wagner. He was handsome; the girls most likely adored him. And the lad didn't seem stupid—a tad naive, perhaps, but he was still young.

"Can you play chess?" asked Johann brusquely.

Karl looked up from his bowl. "Chess?"

"I play according to the new rules as prescribed by Luis Ramírez Lucena in his book. It contains many interesting openings and moves, the 'smothered mate' among others. Have you heard of it?"

"Um, I'm afraid not. I've played chess a few times, but I fear I'm not very good."

"I will teach you," said Johann, trying not to let his disappointment show. He still hoped he'd chosen the right one.

"You want to know why I saved you?" he asked after a while.

Karl nodded.

"I want to show you something. Wait here." He walked to the back of the wagon and took out the laterna magica. He had installed a few improvements since the first apparatus he'd built with Valentin back in Heidelberg. The casing was now made from copper and had a tube at the front where lenses could be inserted. Another tube at the top allowed the smoke to vent. Also, a larger hollow mirror reflected the light much better.

Johann pointed the front tube toward the canvas of the wagon, opened a flap on the side of the casing, and lit the lamp inside with a burning pine chip. Instantly, a bright, perfectly round circle of light appeared on the side of the wagon.

"Now pay attention," said Johann.

He decided on the image with the white woman. Most of the time it achieved the desired effect. He opened a small container with glass plates, took one out, and inserted it into the slot on the side of the laterna.

Instead of the circle, a white, ghostly woman hovered on the wagon's canvas.

"Dear God," whispered Karl, dropping his plate of food. "What . . . what is that?"

"I don't think I did particularly well with her," said Johann with a shrug. "The white dress looks more like a sheet, and her eyes don't look real. The devil in Warnheim today was a rather sad figure, too. More cattle-beast than lord of the underworld."

"Are . . . are you saying you insert glass plates into this apparatus and then those . . . those images appear?" asked Karl breathlessly. "You deceived those Warnheim peasants?"

Johann waved dismissively. "I'll explain how exactly it works another time. The important thing right now is that you understand that it isn't black magic, just science. The laterna magica is my most important tool. I sell theriac, read palms, cast horoscopes—just like many other traveling artists. But my reputation is all down to my laterna—my wit and knowledge aside." He sighed. "But I'm not happy with the paintings. Let's say my talents lie elsewhere." Johann put out the light and the white woman disappeared. "And that's where you come in. I saw you in Leipzig—or rather, I saw your paintings."

Wagner looked at him with growing amazement. "You . . . you went to the university in Leipzig?"

"I've visited many universities in the last ten years, sometimes as a guest lecturer—if the rector believed my documents—but more frequently as a keen student. There is so much left to learn." Johann wiped his mouth with his hands. "I saw your anatomical sketches in Leipzig, the ones you prepared for the medical lectures of Doctor Joventis. I liked them very much. They . . ." He hesitated. "They reminded me of someone from years ago who also drew well. A good friend. The best and only one I ever had."

"Thank you." Karl stared into the darkness, the logs in the fire crackling quietly. "My father is a well-known surgeon in Leipzig," said the young man after a while. "He wanted me to go to college and study medicine like him. But I really want to become a painter, like Albrecht Dürer or Leonardo da Vinci. Have you heard of them?"

"It's a sin to compare oneself with Leonardo da Vinci," replied Johann gruffly. "A man like him only comes along once every thousand years. And unlike you lazy paint-slinger, he was a genius in all areas. He would easily have gained a doctor's title in medicine or law. You, however, quit your studies."

Wagner's eyes widened once more. "You know? But—"

"I was going to speak with you in Leipzig. But then you up and left. Very annoying."

"I had . . . um . . . trouble at the university that compelled me to leave."

"I think I know what sort of trouble. The same kind of trouble that got you tied to a pyre at Warnheim. It's the kind of trouble with two legs and a proud package in between."

Wagner turned red and looked down. "I . . . don't know what you're talking about."

"You're a sodomite, Karl Wagner. Personally, I couldn't care less, but the law prescribes death by fire. In Leipzig, you got away by the skin of your teeth. But in Warnheim, you found yourself another young lover—"

"It was purely platonic!"

"A term that that uneducated peasant pack doesn't understand." Johann dug a piece of meat from between his teeth. "What a stupid thing to do, letting oneself get caught in the hay with another man in the rebellious Hegau region, of all places. You can count yourself lucky that I followed you. I couldn't save your friend, though."

Wagner hung his head and tears rolled down his cheek. "We'd only known each other for a few hours. Our eyes met at a tavern, and I was overcome by fiery passion. I didn't even know his name. I . . . I know it's against nature, and I tried to fight it for so long. But the devil keeps returning to my body."

"Leave the devil out of it. He's got better things to do than possessing little sodomites. You can forget about your studies, anyhow—for good. Don't think I don't know what that means."

For the first time Johann's eyes were almost sympathetic, but the look vanished as quickly as it had arrived.

"At least I know what you can do instead. Join me on the road and paint glass plates for me. The demand is surprisingly large. Every town has its own patron saint, and in the country there are plenty of natural spirits, gnomes, and other mischievous creatures that can easily be invoked. A few animals wouldn't hurt, either—people like animals, cats in particular. Cats are always good."

Karl Wagner stared at Johann as if he were an apparition of the laterna magica. "You . . . you want me to travel with you and paint pictures on glass?"

"Well, not only that." Johann gave a shrug. "Other things also need to be done. We need to brew theriac, write flyers, announce our shows." He paused to think. "I don't suppose you play an instrument? The bagpipe, for example?"

Wagner shook his head.

"Never mind. I can't stand that instrument anyhow. I pay you one guilder per image, and free food and lodging." Johann held out his hand. "Go on— shake on it."

"I don't know," said Wagner eventually. "When I said I wanted to become a painter, I meant something a little different. I thank you for your offer, but—"

"I'm afraid you don't have a choice." Johann reached into a bag next to him and pulled out a pile of documents. "Do you know what that is?"

Wagner turned pale.

"I found this bundle among the things you had to leave behind at the inn this morning. I must say—touching love letters, even if they're a tad too flowery for me. A memento of your romance in Leipzig, I take it?" When Karl didn't reply, Johann went on. "You can choose whether I send the letters to your father first or to the Leipzig authorities."

"That . . . that's blackmail," said Karl hoarsely.

"Call it what you want." Johann gave him a wink. "In a few weeks' time you'll be glad you have accepted my offer. What could be more exciting than traveling the German lands alongside the most famous magician of the empire?"

He put the bundle of letters away and held out his hand to Wagner again. This time, the student accepted. Johann's grip was so firm that Wagner winced with pain.

"Welcome to the realm of hocus-pocus," said Johann with a grin. "And believe me, you will learn much from me."

It took a long time for Karl Wagner to fall asleep, and even then Johann heard him moan and cry out from time to time. He guessed in the student's dreams he was burning on the pyre next to his paramour. Johann was sorry he hadn't been able to save Karl's lover, but on the other hand, at least he had the young man to himself now. Who knew how Karl would have reacted to his offer otherwise.

Johann struggled to find rest. He was lying on his back, gazing up at the stars, which were the same ones as more than thirty years ago, on the day of his birth. The same stars that once foretold a great future for him.

Born a lucky child, his mother had said. *Born a Faustus.*

Johann gave a silent laugh. The stars, it would seem, played many a nasty trick.

In the thirteen years since his leap into the Neckar he had achieved much, but he hadn't found happiness. He had pulled himself ashore more dead than alive. For two weeks he was held in the firm grip of a fever, and in his dreams Margarethe and Valentin pointed at him with their fingers.

You are the devil, they called out again and again. *You are the devil!*

And they were right. The one true love of his life and his best friend—he was responsible for their deaths. Margarethe had hanged herself because of him, and Valentin had most likely been burned at the stake in Worms. On top of everything else, he had murdered Jakob Kohlschreiber, Margarethe's husband. Johann remembered how much he had enjoyed stabbing the drunken vintner. Who had he been in that moment? Himself? Or a devil in the shape of a man? Either way, he had no trouble understanding why people were afraid of him. He had laden himself with guilt, and it was a guilt that made him wake up screaming at night, a guilt that tortured him like a thousand glowing pairs of pincers, and he still didn't know how he could ever atone for it.

A kindhearted old farmer's wife had nursed him back to health back then. She had prayed for him, not knowing that any prayers for him were wasted. Once he'd recovered from the fever, all that was left of him was an empty shell, the shape of a man but without a goal, without joy, without any reason to carry on.

Then, in a ditch beside the road, he'd found a litter of puppies of which only one was still alive. The dog was as black as his soul, and Johann took it with him. Satan helped him come back to life. Johann doted on the animal so he would never have to dote on another human being again—so that he would never drag anyone down with him again. Man and dog wandered along the Neckar together, toward the Rhine and into the lands beyond. Satan grew, and with it grew Johann's will to live.

Johann.

The name seemed as distant as the stars to him now, even though only thirteen summers had passed since then.

He started with the simple diversions he'd learned from Tonio. Card tricks, juggling balls, coin tricks, the shell game, and even the egg in the blanket returned to his repertoire. Soon he'd saved enough money for a wagon, a horse, and occasionally a night under a warm roof along the imperial road, which carried him through the country like a wide, lazy river. The theriac—cheap liquor infused with herbs and alleged magic powers—caused him to become reasonably well off. He purchased the individual parts he required for the laterna magica and assembled it; he read palms, promised grand futures in his horoscopes, and called himself magister and doctor. Everyone believed him—even the universities. His wit, his gift of public speaking, and his knowledge did the rest.

And so the young Johann Faustus, a Heidelberg student wanted for sorcery and murder, became the infamous Doctor Johann Georg Faustus.

A living legend.

Out of spite and sarcasm he had kept the name he'd used to matriculate at Heidelberg University, the name his mother had lovingly called him. He sometimes went by Faust now—*fist*. No longer a lucky one, but a punch in the face to all the slow-witted, superstitious, and narrow-minded folk out there. Johann smiled. The fact that every little county, bishopric, and duchy worried only about its own affairs had its advantages. No one seemed to make the connection between the murderer from Heidelberg and the famous doctor.

Until now, at least.

Next to him, Karl moaned again, but this time the student was smiling. Johann guessed he was dreaming of happier days with his lover, just like he himself often dreamed of his one true love.

Margarethe.

No day went by that Johann didn't think of her. Of her blue eyes, her flaxen hair, and her laughter, which had saved him in the clearing near Nördlingen all those years ago.

Margarethe.

An owl hooted, and Johann started up from his bed. In the light of the moon he saw wafts of mist floating by the boulders. He suspected that once upon a time this place had been used as a sacrificial site, just like the one near Nördlingen where he had drunk the black potion and escaped from Tonio. He had never heard anything about the magician again. Nor, since leaving Heidelberg, about Gilles de Rais, the insane French marshal who had been dead for almost a hundred years now.

And Johann hoped it would stay that way.

With that thought he finally fell asleep.

The next morning, Johann was up before sunrise. He never slept much; a few hours was enough for him. Sleep was dangerous because it allowed the dreams to return, and so he tried to avoid sleeping at night as much as possiblc. Karl didn't seem to share this problem, as he snored and stretched under his fur blanket. A thin column of smoke still rose from their fire. Dew dripped from the leaves in the trees; fall had arrived with its damp, chilly breeze.

Johann softly whistled for Satan and fed it the remains of last night's dinner. As the mastiff slurped up the scraps, Johann watched the animal with a smile, like a father watching his child at play. He had grown fonder of Satan than of any person he'd met in the last few years. The dog had been his faithful companion on his never-ending journey through the Holy Roman Empire of the German Nation, as the empire was now called. The animal was no longer so young; the fur behind its ears and on its paws was turning gray, and it didn't run as fast as it used to. For a few weeks now it had also been limping. But Satan still provided Johann the respectability and protection he required as a lone traveler. The empire was far from safe; dangers lurked everywhere, not just in the woods. There were no laws outside the cities, and no one to keep order. Everyone had to look out for themselves.

Satan licked its jowls and gazed at its master from bloodshot eyes, evidently hoping for more. Johann stroked the mastiff behind the ears.

"Good dog," he said in a low voice. "You're a good dog." He looked over at Karl. "Let's see how we get on with our new friend. You don't like Karl very much, do you? I guess you're jealous." Satan gave a growl, and Johann laughed.

When he'd seen Karl's drawings in Leipzig, a shiver had run down his spine. The images had immediately reminded him of Valentin in Heidelberg, and so he'd continued to watch the student. The young man's slightly clumsy yet proud demeanor had awakened memories in Johann. He had seen himself as a student in Heidelberg. And then he'd almost lost Karl in the same way he had lost Margarethe and Valentin; he'd arrived just in the nick of time. On the Warnheim market square he'd sworn to himself: never again shall a student burn as a heretic. He would take Karl with him and care for him.

But if he was completely honest with himself, he wasn't doing it because of charitable, Christian feelings or because he merely needed a glass painter for his laterna. He could have hired a painter in one of the larger cities.

No, he did it because he could no longer bear the loneliness.

Despite his fame, despite all his freedom and the knowledge he had gained in recent years, Johann wasn't happy. He had forgotten how to love, because it would seem his love brought misfortune to people. He loved his dog, but the dog didn't know how to play chess. And so he wanted to give it a go with young Karl—in part also to assuage his guilt and atone for Valentin's death.

Johann hoped very much that Karl wouldn't be the next person he led into ruin.

The sound of flapping wings caused him to start from his thoughts. He looked up and saw a crow staring down at him from the branches of a nearby beech tree.

"Beat it, you damned beast!" Johann picked up a rock and threw it at the crow.

With a mocking caw, it flew away just to land on a different branch, where it continued to stare at him. Since his time with Tonio, Johann had hated crows and ravens. Perhaps that was why he always felt like they were watching him. Those birds seemed to be everywhere—in the mountains, lowlands, villages, towns, and cities. They circled above him in the sky and sat on rooftops, on the edges of wells, and on spires.

Sometimes Johann thought it was always the same three birds. Two crows and an old raven with a scuffed, jagged beak.

"Kraa!" called the crow. *"Kraa, kraa!"* Johann threw another stone and missed, and then he gave up with a sigh.

The noise woke Karl. The student rubbed his eyes and looked about. It seemed to take him a while to remember where he was and what had happened the day before. The scrapes and bruises he had suffered during his arrest would heal, but the trauma—Johann wasn't so sure. Karl had come as close to death as a man could.

Johann gave the young man a nod and threw him a piece of bread. "Here, eat," he said. "We must leave soon."

"Why so early?" asked Karl with a yawn. He was pale, and dark shadows lay beneath his eyes; a scabby scratch went right across his forehead. But even in that state, Johann noted, he was handsome.

I'm going to have to look after him, thought Johann. *Better than I looked after Martin, Margarethe, Valentin, and the others.*

"Because this area isn't safe," he replied. "The Warnheim peasants might still be out looking for us. And I won't be able to save you from the fire a second time."

"And where are you headed?" asked Karl.

"North, east, south, west—I'm at home anywhere." Johann shrugged. "But I think we'll head north. There's too much unrest in the south of the empire.

Swabia, Bavaria, the Swiss confederacy . . . war seems to love these climes." He grinned. "And I've never seen the North Sea. The cold ocean beating against the shore."

"The . . . the North Sea?" Karl was suddenly wide awake. "But that's awfully far! It's going to take us many months."

"We have all the time in the world," said Johann. "Remember? You're coming with me, no matter where! Otherwise the next post rider is taking a bundle of letters to Leipzig. Your old life is over." He walked to the wagon. "And now hurry up, you lazybones. You can eat the bread on the way. And I swear I'll teach you Lucena's chess rules before we're out of this goddamned Hegau."

When the horse pulled the wagon back onto the road, the crow was still sitting in the trees. It tilted its head to one side as if listening intently. More flapping of wings came from the low-hanging clouds, and another crow and an old raven with a scuffed beak descended from above. They greeted the first crow with a hoarse croaking that sounded almost human.

When the wagon had rolled out of sight, they spread their wings and took off together.

20

THUS JOHANN AND HIS YOUNG COMPANION HEADED NORTH from Lake Constance. The air became colder, and the autumn wind tore at the wagon's faded canvas. Most of the time, the two very different men sat side by side in silence, Karl occasionally eyeing his eerie companion furtively. Karl still couldn't believe that of all people, the famous Doctor Johann Georg Faustus had saved his life, and that he was now traveling the empire at the man's side. He was torn between admiration and fear. The doctor's black eyes were deep and mysterious, like pools in the woods; dark secrets appeared to lie at their bottom, hidden from regular mortals like him. They seemed to magically draw Karl in as well as frighten him. Even after many days on the road together, Faust remained a mystery to him—not least because the doctor wasn't particularly communicative.

"Is it true that you once found a treasure near Wittenberge by the Elbe?" asked Karl, trying to strike up conversation. They had not long left the city of Ulm.

"What? Is that what they say?" The doctor turned and met Karl's inquisitive gaze. "And? Was it gold ducats, diamonds, or the philosopher's stone? Although according to another rumor, I already found the latter in Krakow." Clearly, the never-ending questions of his new travel companion had begun to annoy Faust, and yet Karl thought he could see a vain side in the itinerant scholar.

"Well, apparently you were digging in an old cellar when you found a worm who guarded a treasure. You chased the worm away with a mirror, and the treasure—"

"Do you really think I would sit on this rickety old wagon and sell cheap swill if I'd found a treasure?"

"It makes for a good story, at least." Karl sighed. "I'm beginning to get the impression that not even half of what they say about you is true."

"You'll have plenty of time to find out what's true and what isn't. Giddyup!"

The doctor flicked the reins and the wagon rattled on, always toward the next rise, the next mountain range on the horizon. Satan stormed ahead, occasionally howling with pleasure, its jowls dripping. Satan was the hellish messenger announcing the famous Doctor Faustus, magician, chiromancer, miracle worker, and astrologer, in the townships along the imperial road. As alternative means of defense, the wagon also carried a sword and a newfangled wheel-lock pistol, but they hadn't needed the weapons so far. The sight of Satan alone made wayside robbers take to their heels.

They usually stopped in larger cities, where Faust and his assistant stayed for several days at a time. In the course of the following weeks they visited Rothenburg ob der Tauber, Würzburg, Mainz, and Frankfurt am Main, a large city of commerce, where they set up shop at the cloth market in front of the city hall and thrilled the crowds. Leipzig aside, Karl hadn't seen much of the empire.

Every city had its own smells. The pungent stench of lime kilns, the delicious smell of baked gingerbread, the numbing scent of hop mash, and the blood odor of freshly slaughtered pigs—but most of all, the stink of the gutter. Dialects changed and so did the people, who gaped at the two travelers as if they were kings from the Orient, and made the sign of the cross once they'd passed. After his initial reservations, Karl began to like this way of traveling. He enjoyed the wide world of the highway, which was so different from the drab routine at the university. His role as the announcer, assistant, and joker was growing on him, even if he'd never become an outstanding juggler.

Faust's reputation preceded him. Even from afar, people recognized the wagon with the strange-looking symbols and the mysterious man on the box seat with the blue-and-black star cloak and the floppy hat. The doctor usually rented a room in one of the better inns and set up on the market square to sell his foul and potent theriac. Faust read palms, cast quick horoscopes, and placed his hand on people's foreheads after previously rubbing his palm with his stinking miracle cure. It was one of Karl's jobs to appear as a blind young soldier who was healed by the famous Doctor Faustus.

But the biggest attraction by far was always the laterna magica.

They'd use the biggest room with shutters at the tavern. People paid two hellers' admittance and had the experience of a lifetime inside the darkened room. They'd never seen anything like it. The spectators trembled with fear as the ghastliest figures appeared on a white sheet stretched at the front of the room: devils, fiends, witches, and ghosts that Faust invoked with a loud voice and then chased away with the help of Latin spells. The cries of the audience could be heard in the streets, and people staggered outside at the end of the show and told others what they'd seen with a mix of fear and delight.

Karl usually worked on the glass paintings at night, in the flickering glow of an oil lamp. For inspiration he used whatever mythical creatures were known in the region where they had stopped: the wild man, evil Trude, the Tatzelworms, werewolves, and malevolent little elves. Occasionally the doctor would watch him at work and mutter strange words.

"Your drawings are different from his," Faust said with a nod, more to himself. "But no less good. Hmm. Not as creative, but more accurate. I think the people like them, and that's the main thing."

Karl never received an answer to the question of who the doctor was talking about.

In the course of weeks, Karl developed a sense for which sort of pictures they just got away with and which would land them at the stake. The church and the cities permitted the game with evil as long as it served their purposes. But still, it was a perpetual balancing act. More than once they had to make a hasty retreat before the town's guards threw them into jail, because some of the images seemed so real that people thought the apocalypse had begun. Karl's wolves had sharp fangs with saliva dripping from the points, and the eyes of the gnomes shone in an eerie light that couldn't stem from this world. Sometimes Karl tried his hand at flowery landscapes or handsome youths, but Faust threw them into the fire every time.

"People must be frightened—that's your job," he'd growl at Karl. "Leave the pretty and angelic to the church."

"But what we're doing here is nothing but cheap trickery!" retorted Karl indignantly. "We could put the laterna to much better use. At universities, for example, to show anatomical—"

"You paint what I tell you to paint and that's the end of it!" snapped Faust grumpily. "I'd rather work on improving your chess skills than watch you waste time on drawing muscular torsos of handsome boys. You're still a lousy player. Now go and sweep the wagon—it's like a pigsty in there."

In moments like those Karl considered leaving the doctor, even though he knew that would turn him into an outlaw. Faust possessed those accursed letters that would forever brand him as a sodomite. If they fell into the wrong hands, he would never be able to return home to Leipzig, nor set foot in any other university towns. He wasn't sure how far-reaching the doctor's influence in the empire was. He seemed to have been everywhere already, which made their travels seem strangely aimless. As far as Karl could tell, Faust's life had been one long, never-ending journey. He wasted all his knowledge, all his wisdom, on dumb peasants and thrill-seeking burghers, as if throwing pearls to the pigs.

When, in fact, the doctor was a walking library. In one of his chests, Faust was keeping books each worth several gold ducats. Karl had leafed through some of them in secret. Lucena's accursed chess book was one of them, but also Gregor Reisch's *Margarita Philosophica*, a precious encyclopedia in twelve volumes, which seemed to contain the collective knowledge of men. Karl also discovered the *Speculum Astronomiae* by Albertus Magnus, who was considered a sorcerer by scholars at Leipzig University and whose name was blacklisted. So was Faust a real magician, too?

Karl sighed deeply and packed away the juggling balls, the garishly colorful costumes, and the bottles of theriac, which reeked of cheap liquor. Then he swept out the wagon before the doctor had one of his infamous tantrums. Faust was like a haunted man, forever on the run, but Karl didn't know what from.

It would be months yet before he'd find out.

~

They took up winter quarters in Erfurt, one of the largest cities of the German empire and roughly in its center.

Johann called Satan back with a shrill whistle as they passed through the wide city gate. The guards, clad in thick woolen coats and fur hats, eyed the strange travelers skeptically at first, but when Johann gave his name and asked Wagner to hand out a few bottles of theriac, the guards allowed them through. Johann had visited the city several times before. The University of Erfurt was considered one of the best in the country, and the rector usually allowed him to hold a few lectures. The students attended in droves and relished the doctor's witty observations and theological discourse, which always bordered closely on heresy. Until a few years ago, Erfurt had been a wealthy city, but the duties the citizens had to pay the Saxon elector and the Mainz bishopric had brought the city to the brink of ruin. When they'd tried to raise the taxes again the year before, the people had rebelled and hanged one of its aldermen.

Erfurt wasn't the only place where the common people had begun to rise against the high and mighty. Johann had seen many rebellions. A few years ago, thousands of farmers had rebelled in the bishopric of Speyer, and their leader, a certain Joß Fritz, had escaped and had been busy riling up people in other regions ever since. The whole country was seething, and Johann waited for the spark that would set off the powder keg.

It couldn't be much longer.

Winter came over Erfurt with icy temperatures and snow, which piled up knee deep in the lanes. Beggars froze beneath bridges, and the poorer households struggled for firewood. The honorable and widely traveled Doctor Faustus and his assistant lodged at one of the better inns on Michaelsgasse Lane, not far from the university. In the evenings, when the musicians struck up a tune and harlots visited the tables with big smiles and low-cut dresses, Johann mostly sat in a corner by himself, while Karl—under the disapproving looks of his master—drank with the younger fellows.

Johann loved his quiet time after the shows and lectures; he despised idle gossip. He enjoyed the fact that while people respected him, they basically feared him and avoided his company—partly, of course, because of the calf-sized dog lying under his table and growling at any unwanted intruder.

Over the years, several women had tried to get close to Doctor Faustus, the mysterious man with raven-black hair and equally black eyes. He had pushed them all away. A few times, when the urge became too strong, he'd visited whores, but the moaning and sighing, the rubbing together of naked bodies, soon repulsed him. When he closed his eyes he saw Margarethe—and then he felt sick. And so he gave up on whores. He lived like a restless monk. Karl's presence didn't change that, even though the young man tried occasionally to encourage Johann to have a little fun.

In Erfurt, Johann decided to be a little nicer to his assistant. The boy was doing a decent job, and even though Karl's endless questions got on his nerves, at least he didn't feel quite as lonely.

One evening, when they sat together at a table at the back—avoided and yet watched by the locals—dining on roast meat and enjoying a jug of wine after a particularly successful show, Johann raised his goblet.

"To your latest paintings," he said to Karl with a smile. "I particularly like the hell-dragon. Three women fainted today. You're doing well!" He threw Satan a bone, which the dog caught in the air and snapped in half with one bite. Johann patted the beast's head lovingly before turning back to Karl. "But we must work on your performance as a blind soldier. People may be dumb, but they are not as stupid as sheep." He shook his head. "No one buys how easily you saunter across the stage as a blind man."

"I'm a student of medicine, not a dishonorable juggler, remember?"

"Don't mock jugglers," replied Johann with sudden coldness in his voice. "They enchant people just like we do."

He emptied his goblet in one gulp and brought it down so hard that several other guests turned their heads and whispered to one another. Karl's remark had woken memories in Johann—memories from his time in Venice, of Salome, Emilio, and Peter the fiddler, whose death he'd foreseen a long time ago. Every now and then this strange gift had befallen him again, but he had learned to handle it. He still struggled when it was young adults and children, but he never told them the truth.

He wondered if he would have foreseen Margarethe's death.

"May I ask you something?" said Karl hesitantly.

Johann forced himself to shake off the memories. When he nodded, Karl cleared his throat. It seemed something had been bothering the young man for a while.

"Why do you do it? I mean, you're a highly educated man. In the last few months, I've heard you speak about Plato and Plutarch. You know about philosophy as well as mechanics. You know Archimedes's formulas by heart as well as those of Pythagoras—even medicine isn't unknown territory to you. You could be a widely respected doctor—rector, even—at any university. Instead—" Karl hesitated.

"Instead what?" asked Johann quietly, pouring himself another glass.

"Instead you travel the lands in a rickety wagon and fool people with those . . . those images, with magic potions, and false horoscopes. They call you a necromancer and a quack. Yes, you're widely known, but you're not respected." Karl sighed. "To be honest, I think your name—and therewith mine—will soon be forgotten again. So tell me, why do you do this to yourself?"

Johann took a sip. He said nothing for a long while, staring into the goblet in front of him, the wine gleaming red as blood. He felt a strong urge to empty the goblet again and hurl it against the wall. But he restrained himself. Instead he leaned back and studied his assistant with amusement.

"Anyone else and I would have thrown the wine at your face for such insolence, but I think it is your right to receive an answer." He leaned forward. "Do you know what I hope? I hope they lock me up one day. I long for that day, even though I know it will never arrive."

"Lock you up?" Karl looked puzzled. "But why? I mean—"

Johann cut him off with a wave of his hand. "Not as a necromancer and sorcerer, silly, but as a fraudster. You know very well that everything we're doing here is fraud. And the people know it, too, but they don't want to see it." He laughed softly. "They want to be spellbound; they want to believe that the devil really exists. Because only if the devil exists does God exist. And so they play along, buy our magic potions, and let themselves be frightened by our glass images. And as long as they do, people like you and me are free to do as we please. It's our task in this world. We act the devil so God can exist."

"Don't you believe in God?" asked Karl with a frown.

Johann hesitated. "Let us imagine there was no God," he said eventually. "Then there'd be nobody to put a stop to our evildoings. After all, our laws are all based on God. There'd be no rules and everything would be allowed. All writings, all thinking . . . a tempting thought. I myself have spent much time on that idea. Too much." Johann stared into the distance for a while before going on. "Chaos would reign, because nothing would make sense any longer. We would be all alone in the universe without any solace, and without hope. That's how I imagine hell. In my darkest hours I sometimes think we're already in hell, only we haven't noticed."

"And if there is a hell, then there is a devil," replied Wagner.

"Oh yes, he exists." Johann took one last, long sip and stared into emptiness. "He exists. He just isn't quite the way we imagine him." He put down his goblet abruptly. "Enough of these gloomy, useless thoughts! It's about time you improved your chess playing. So far it's been rather sad."

Johann reached into his coat pocket and pulled out the square board with the chess pieces. He had carved them himself, during long, sleepless nights, from horn and alabaster. He placed the board on the table and started to sort the pieces like he'd done a thousand times before.

But Karl wasn't looking at the board. Instead he was gazing out the crown-glass window, where thick snowflakes had begun to tumble from the night sky.

"What is it?" asked Johann.

"Oh, nothing. Only . . ." Karl hesitated. "When we spoke of the devil before, I thought I saw someone standing outside the window. A man dressed in black. He seemed to be looking at us—watching us. And his eyes, they . . . they were burning like fire."

"A man dressed in black? And now you think it was the devil?" Johann laughed. "My dear Karl, you've got a greater imagination than I gave you credit for. Most likely it was just a student who wanted to see the great Doctor Faustus up close. Or it was a black cat." With a thin smile, Johann held up the two kings. "Which do you want to be? Black or white? These pieces right here are real, unlike some shadows outside the window."

Johann didn't let it show, but Karl's comment had rattled him more than he cared to admit. Because he, too, had glimpsed a figure in the snow outside.

A man clad in black.

And now you think it was the devil.

Johann cast a furtive glance at the window again. There was a storm brewing outside, and the wind was howling like a lonesome child.

But there was nothing else—nothing but pitch-black night.

The sensation of being watched didn't leave Johann. On the contrary, it was growing stronger by the week. When he walked over to his lectures at the university, he often spun around and looked behind himself. He started carrying his sword on him. Occasionally he thought he saw a particular pair of eyes among the students in the auditorium, and then he would falter in his lecture as he studied the rows of chairs. But all he saw were unfamiliar, guileless faces. He called himself a fool and decided it must be the dark winter's days that made him so nervous and sullen. He had known the feeling of being watched for years—it clung to him like a foul smell. Sometimes the feeling disappeared for a few months and then it returned. But it had never been as strong as here in Erfurt.

And there was something else that bothered him: with his question at the tavern, Karl had touched a sore point.

Why do you do it?

Johann had given Karl a reply, but deep down he didn't know why he was leading this life. Because he didn't know anything else? Or because he was on the run from something—because he was waiting for something to happen? Johann didn't know what that something might be. But the black figure outside the window had awakened something inside him. Something had begun to move. Which direction it would lead, he had no idea.

To improve his mood, he often took Satan on long walks along the river flats of the Gera, outside town. Karl sometimes accompanied him, and they'd discuss medicine. It turned out that the student had learned a fair amount in his time at Leipzig University. He was more intelligent than Johann had first thought, and he possessed a wit and quickness of mind that reminded Johann of Valentin.

"All they went on about in the lectures was Galen," complained Karl. "As if nothing has changed in medicine since antiquity."

"Has anything changed?" asked Johann with a smile. He was reminded of his conversations with Conrad Celtis back in Heidelberg. Back then, he'd also wanted to change the world, just like Karl did now.

"I saw the anatomical sketches of Mondino De' Luzzi," said Karl passionately. "I would love to be able to paint as accurately as he does. Not necessarily the inside of the human body, but still—his brushwork."

"You paint pictures on glass for me, and that's enough," replied Johann gruffly. "For now, at least." He gave the young man a hard look. "And stay away from the Erfurt students! I noticed the looks you were giving them last night. Death by fire is the punishment for sodomy—here in Erfurt, too."

Karl looked abashed. "I know. It's a sin. I pray every night."

"Prayers won't help you on the pyre. The only thing that'll help you there is a pouch full of gunpowder around the neck to bring you a quick death."

Johann whistled for Satan, who came running immediately. When Karl held out his hand to pat it, the animal growled at him.

"I'm afraid he doesn't like me very much. I guess he's jealous."

"She," said Johann, stroking Satan's long back. "Satan is a she."

Karl stared first at Johann and then at the dog. "A *she*? You've got to be joking!"

Johann shook his head. "Check for yourself—although I doubt she'll let you." He gave a shrug. "Unfortunately she doesn't seem able to have pups. I always hoped she'd give me a litter, but now she's too old."

"A she!" Karl shook his head and laughed. "And why not? I always had a hunch that the devil is a woman."

The weeks went by, and in March, when the snow melted on Erfurt's rooftops, Johann decided it was time to head north.

The empire's bigger roads had steadily improved in the last few years; forests had been felled, fords established, bridges built. The brothers Janetto and Francesco de Tasso—descendants of old Lombard nobility—had been instructed by the emperor to develop the German postal network. Between Schongau and Venice alone there were two dozen posthouses now, and messengers on horseback took only six days to get from the Netherlands to Innsbruck.

Post riders dashed past Johann and Wagner in rain, hail, or sunshine. Johann sometimes thought about his youth in Knittlingen and the mail station at the Lion Inn, where everything had started. He remembered how much he'd liked hanging around the Lion as a little boy. The grim-looking post riders, but especially the foreign dialects and tongues, and the strangely clad travelers with their wares from faraway countries had shown him that there was a world beyond the next hill. He had never returned to his hometown, and he didn't know what had become of his stepfather and half brothers, just like he didn't know who his real father was. But he didn't want to know. All those things lay behind him now. He felt that his old life was like Pandora's box: if he opened it, the memories would pour out like swarms of mosquitoes, including the memories of Margarethe, Valentin, Archibaldus, and young Martin . . .

Small, squirming bundles.

In his mind's eye, Johann once again saw the dark figure outside the tavern window in Erfurt. It had been like a harbinger of the past. As if someone had knocked on the window and told him to pick up the scent again. But where? Karl had been closer to the truth than he knew. Johann walked in circles, like old Satan searching for a bone that didn't exist.

Thus they passed through Jena, Halle in Saxony, and Magdeburg, from whence they followed the wide, lazy Elbe River downstream. There were towns Faust had visited before and others he was seeing for the first time, and everywhere they were received enthusiastically. But Faust barely saw his audience, as he was constantly on the lookout for a dark figure—a figure he thought he glimpsed more and more frequently now, behind the crown-glass window of an inn, in alcoves between buildings, in the fog on the fields. At nights he barred the door to his room and studied Albertus Magnus's *Speculum* and other books on astronomy until the morning. In all the years, he still couldn't see in the stars why Tonio had described him as a chosen one. His mother, too, had believed he was born under a lucky star. A traveling scholar, an astronomer from the West, had told her long ago.

Born on the day of the prophet.

What did that mean? And why had Tonio given him the black potion that night near Nördlingen? What had the master planned for him?

The world could lie at your feet—at our feet. You have the power to set the world on fire! Homo Deus est!

As the wagon rattled along the muddy towpaths by the river, Johann racked his brain. Where was this journey leading him? Was his path written in the stars—in the truest sense of the phrase? Was there something in the sky he couldn't see? He'd studied countless books, searched the libraries of every university, but he hadn't found a thing.

Then, one day in August, after so many lost years, three birds showed him the way.

Johann and Karl had passed Wittenberge, where, according to legend, Doctor Faustus had found treasure. The swampy, slightly brackish smell of the Elbe, which flowed toward the North Sea, wafted through the rooms of the plain inn with its crooked walls. As usual, Johann was lying awake in his bed. The nights were light up here in the summer, and he gazed at the few visible stars through the open window. After tossing and turning for a while longer, he got up and walked to the window. He was gazing at the sky, studying the glistening lights, when he realized that the day of his birth had come and gone for another year. The wheel of life kept turning.

At that moment he saw the raven and the two crows.

They were perched in an old oak tree directly opposite the inn and stared at him from small, mean-looking eyes. This time, Johann knew for certain that they were the same birds Tonio used to keep in the cage years ago. At least about the raven he felt certain.

His feathers were the same gray black, and a piece was missing from the bottom of his beak, as if he'd been in a fight. One of his claws was slightly twisted. Johann narrowed his eyes. Could it be possible? He'd heard that ravens could live very long—longer than men. But why should Tonio's birds be here? So much time had passed. Why now, so many years later?

The raven opened its beak and cawed. It sounded almost human.

"Sheel . . . draay . . . ," croaked the raven. *"Sheel . . . draay . . ."* He flapped his wings up and down and stared at Johann intently, as if trying to tell him something.

"Sheel . . . draay . . ."

With one last hoarse croak he spread his wings and flew off to the north. The crows followed.

Johann's gaze followed them for a long time. He could hardly believe it, but he thought he knew what the raven had just said to him.

Sheel . . . draay . . . Gilles de Rais . . .

Once more he stared out into the night. The birds had gone. But now he thought he could see someone standing in the field.

A man dressed in black with glowing red eyes.

Gilles de Rais . . . the devil . . . Tonio del Moravia . . .

Johann rubbed his eyes. When he opened them again, there was nothing but a scarecrow with a tattered coat. But still he knew that evil had returned to his life. He'd tried to run away for fourteen years, but nowhere was safe for him.

Not until he figured out how everything was connected.

The raven and the obscure figure had reminded Johann that there was a dark spot in his life, as black as the soul of the devil. It didn't matter whether he'd imagined everything or whether the birds had indeed been Tonio's—he had to face up to his past, or he'd never find peace. He had to find out why Tonio had called him the chosen one and why he was allegedly born beneath a special star. Everything that had happened since his first encounter with Tonio—the horror in Schillingswald Forest, the eerie events in Venice, the gruesome death of Magister Archibaldus, the stories about Gilles de Rais—they all were stones of a large mosaic that he didn't yet understand.

Johann knew deep down that the day of his birth must be the key to everything. He had to calculate his own nativity, and more accurately than any other horoscope he'd ever drawn up.

Filled with anger and a fierce determination, Johann slammed the shutters closed. Satan shot up from her sleep and looked at her master inquisitively. Johann stroked the dog and muttered some reassuring words.

And then he sat down to think.

By the time dawn broke, he knew what he had to do. Without really knowing why, he had traveled north, as if fate had led his way. And now the birds had shown him where to go next.

Hamburg.

The name of the city flashed through his mind, a tiny scrap of a memory about something Magister Archibaldus had told him many years ago. Yes— maybe he would find what he was looking for in Hamburg. There was one place he hadn't told Karl Wagner about.

A place he should have visited a long time ago.

21

THE THOUGHT OF THE RAVEN AND THE MYSTERIOUS FIGURE in black didn't let go of Johann during the following days and weeks as they made their way toward Hamburg. He couldn't shake the feeling he was being watched. He often looked up at the sky or studied the trees by the wayside, where crows sat in the branches, watching him. He kept his sword and pistol within easy reach behind the box seat now, and sometimes he considered shooting at the crows. But there were too many.

"What's the matter with you?" asked Karl. "It's almost like you're seeing robbers and vagabonds behind every corner."

"More like ghosts of the past," grumbled Johann.

The dark figure, at least, hadn't returned, but crows always seemed to circle above him like birds of prey. A few times Johann thought he could see the raven among them.

Hamburg welcomed them with a ghastly stench. Summer had made a late comeback, and the trash and excrement in the streets reeked to the high heavens. The Hanseatic city was situated between the wide Elbe River and a tributary called Alster, which had been dammed to form a lake. Cadavers and garbage floated in the many canals crisscrossing the city. Like in all other cities of the empire, people dumped their muck directly into the gutter, where it mixed with rotten vegetables and the blood from the butchers and got washed into the city streams and canals. Rats scurried across dark corners and along alleyways; on the squares, market women and peddlers proffered their wares for sale right next to dunghills behind which people relieved themselves. Only down by the Elbe did the air seem a little better, and that was where Johann and Karl parked their wagon, set up a few benches, and welcomed the countless seamen to their shows.

Their spectators were mostly men with angular, weather-beaten faces. They hailed from England, Denmark, Sweden, and other countries that lay even farther away—somewhere to the north and east, beyond the horizon. Foreign-sounding scraps of conversation buzzed through the air, and much of what the eminent and wise Doctor Faustus said no one understood. But seafarers enjoyed jugglery and lighthearted magic tricks no matter where they came from. And they liked the taste of the strong theriac.

From Hamburg, the large sailboats, cogs, hulks, and caravels sailed down the Elbe to the North Sea and from there into the big world. There used to be even more ships arriving and departing from this port, but ever since a Portuguese man named Vasco da Gama had found the sea passage to India about ten years ago, many of the Augsburg and Nuremberg merchants had chosen different routes. Also, pirates occasionally frequented these shores. The heads of those captured were stuck on pikes next to the execution site on Grasbrook, an island in the Elbe.

The shows always took place in the morning, and every afternoon Johann left their camp by the river while Karl and Satan watched the wagon and prepared for the next show.

"Are you perhaps going to a bordello after all?" asked Karl, who was used to his master not telling him where he was going. "The Hamburg whores are famous. It might prove a pleasant distraction for you."

Johann shrugged. "Indeed, I am frequenting a house that brings me pleasure—even if it isn't the kind of pleasure you're imagining. Oh, and by the way, when I return, you'll have brewed two dozen bottles of theriac. Those seamen drink like fish. And remember the glass painting of the pirate. I want it done by tomorrow." With those words, he left and headed into town.

Johann followed the stinking canals until he came to the city hall by the Trostbrücke Bridge. The city hall was a redbrick building multiple stories high, and he'd visited it several times in the last few days. A small side entrance led to a flight of stairs. A little man sat behind a desk on the second floor, nodding happily at Johann.

"Ah, the famous scholar Doctor Faustus," he said and adjusted his monocle. "Yes, yes, always on the hunt for fresh knowledge. And everyone knows that studying the papers leads to a dry throat."

Like every other day, Johann handed the man a bottle of theriac. "I haven't even studied half of your books yet," he grumbled. "If you continue to drink at this pace, I'll soon be out of theriac for my shows."

The bald, scrawny old man in his fur-lined coat and dirty beret grinned with a toothless mouth. "Well, a few drunken spectators less won't hurt. What does it matter—when the door to the world of knowledge is wide open!"

He pulled a long key from his pocket and opened the door behind him. On the other side was a high-ceilinged room with bookshelves reaching from top to bottom. Ladders provided access to the books on the highest shelves. The boards were bending under the weight of the books and parchment scrolls, and the air smelled musty and leathery. To Johann the scent was like violets. The little man made a sweeping gesture. "This library is yours, venerable Doctor—at least until the bells strike six. Then my shift is over." He closed the door behind Johann.

Johann looked around reverently. He still struggled to believe he was the only person in this room, just like the days before. That night near Wittenberge by the Elbe, when he'd seen the dark figure, he'd remembered something from fifteen years ago. Magister Archibaldus came from Hamburg, and on their journey to Venice he'd told Johann about a library. The Hamburg *Ratsbibliothek* was the only public library in the entire German empire. Usually such hoards of knowledge were in private ownership of universities or monasteries whose abbots would never grant entry to the alleged sorcerer and necromancer Doctor Johann Georg Faustus. Here, however, he was free to browse for as long as he liked. The Ratsbibliothek was bigger than the library at the monastery in Maulbronn that he used to visit with Father Antonius, and bigger than that of the creepy Signore Barbarese in Venice. The Hamburg library held many ecclesiastical works but also many secular ones—philosophical treatises as well as Greek dramas and scientific books. Johann had even found some notes by Leonardo da Vinci.

But what he was really after was works on astronomy that would help him with his calculations for the day of his birth. He'd been born on a day when Jupiter and the sun had stood in the same degree of the same zodiac. While that was a little unusual, it wasn't anything extraordinary; many people were born beneath the same constellation because it occurred several times a year. So what was the secret of his birth?

So far he had found several writings by an astronomer named Heinrich von Langenstein, from Vienna, and also a book by Roger Bacon in which the well-known English Franciscan described the construction of a camera obscura for observation of the sun. But none of the books had told him why his date of birth was particularly blessed by the stars. Johann hadn't found any more on Gilles de Rais, either, nor had he found the name Tonio del Moravia in any of the documents.

Johann slowly walked along the rows of books and studied the titles. After a few moments of deliberation, he chose a book he thought sounded promising. It was written by a certain Johannes Müller and, among other topics, discussed the question whether the sun was indeed rotating around the Earth, or whether perhaps the Earth was rotating around the sun. It was a fascinating thought, which Father Bernhard back in Knittlingen had told him about and which was increasingly discussed in scholarly circles these days. Johann carried the book to a desk and started to read. It was very interesting, but it didn't help him in his quest. He was about to put it back on the shelf when he noticed another manuscript on the desk. It had been hidden under some loose pages of parchment, as if someone was in the middle of making a copy. Johann's eyes scanned the title and author.

De Occulta Philosophia by Heinrich Cornelius Agrippa of Nettesheim.

Johann frowned. He had heard of this Agrippa. A clever man who'd apparently studied at the University of Cologne and about whose sharp mind Johann had encountered a few tales. They said he completed his baccalaureus at just fourteen years old, was fluent in eight languages, and despite his young age was already more learned than most doctors in the empire. These days he was lecturing in Cologne whenever he wasn't traveling the country at the invitations of the rich and powerful. Agrippa hadn't made a lot of friends among the clergy with his witty speeches.

Much to his surprise, Johann felt a twinge of jealousy. This Agrippa might actually see eye to eye with him. An equal in a world where true knowledge still struggled in the face of old-fashioned scholasticism and bigotry.

With growing curiosity Johann studied the pages of the manuscript, which had been written in a neat, very small hand. After a few lines he was so engrossed in the work that he forgot everything around him. It was like a miracle! This writ systematically combined all known areas of magic, from chiromancy and astrology to alchemy. Everything that Johann had been taught by Tonio and everything he'd taught himself thereafter was written right here in Latin. How had this Agrippa gained his immense knowledge? A man required decades to learn all this. Johann glanced over the pages and his heart beat faster. This was the best book he'd ever read! It was brilliantly written and blessed with an insight that elevated magic to the same level as faith and science. The astrological observations, too, went further than anything Johann had known until then. He leafed through the manuscript wildly and found to his horror that he was holding only about fifty measly pages.

The book finished before it had properly begun—and the author grandly promised a work of three volumes.

Where on earth?

Johann raced along the other desks and past the rows of shelves. Eventually he picked up the manuscript, opened the door, and waved the pages under the surprised librarian's nose.

"Where is the rest?" he asked curtly.

"The rest of what?" The little man put on his monocle and studied the pages. Then his face lit up. "Oh, that! Interesting, isn't it? A merchant on his way back from England dropped it off yesterday. Apparently Agrippa was in London at the behest of the emperor, and that's where the merchant met him and bought these pages from him. I was going to copy them today. A highly—"

"Where is the rest?" repeated Johann.

The man sighed. "There is no rest. This is all the merchant brought me. He said Agrippa was still working on it."

Johann closed his eyes for a moment. For the first time in a long while he had the feeling he wasn't running in circles.

"I'm buying these pages," he said. "How much?"

"They aren't for sale. I'd have to make a copy—"

"I don't have time for that." Johann placed a gold ducat on the desk. It was the most valuable coin he owned. A fat Erfurt merchant had given it to him for a favorable nativity chart.

The librarian's eyes widened. "You could buy two dozen books for that!"

"I only want this one manuscript. And now excuse me."

Clutching the pages in his hand, Johann hurried outside and ran across the square and through the city gate toward the Elbe.

He was so lost in thought that he didn't notice the figure that entered the Ratsbibliothek the moment he had left it.

At the end of his shift, the librarian had earned three gold ducats: one from that strange Doctor Faustus everyone was talking about, and two more from a man who wanted answers to a few questions and whom the librarian tried to forget as quickly as possible.

By the end of the day all the little man could say about the strange visitor was that his coat—his whole appearance, in fact—had been as black as the night.

Only his eyes seemed to have glowed eerily.

∼

Down by the port, Karl Wagner sat at a wobbly table inside the wagon and painted the beard of a pirate. Not much light came in through the curtain behind the box seat, and the tallow candles smoked terribly, so that Karl was forced to lean closely over the glass plate. He was working with very fine brushes and had to consider each stroke carefully, since the paintings on the glass plates were so small. Karl thought about the famous Nuremberg painter Albrecht Dürer, who probably let his creativity run wild on canvases as tall as a man, while he himself was painting pirate beards the size of a fingernail.

Satan was lying at his feet and growled at every little movement. Karl was increasingly under the impression that the dog wasn't guarding the wagon but him. If he tried to leave the wagon, Satan would probably tear him to pieces. Karl hated the mastiff, but he knew that his master loved her more than anything—and more than anyone. Just then Satan bared her teeth at him again, and Karl gave a strained smile.

"Lousy old mutt," he said and kept smiling. "I guess you love me about as much as I love you. We must get along, though, whether we like it or not. So you better sit like a good dog or there won't be any treats."

He tossed the tip of a sausage to Satan, appeasing the dog for the moment.

Karl tiredly rubbed his eyes and stretched his back. Outside he could hear the sounds of the river: the shouts of the seamen, the ringing of ship bells, the mocking cries of the gulls that had flown inland from the ocean shores.

Karl painted inside the wagon to avoid curious gossips, and for that purpose he'd had a little table made in Wittenberge. He'd grown tired of getting hardly any work done because of all the questions people badgered him with. The pirate he was painting today was Klaus Störtebeker, a bloodthirsty villain who was executed a long time ago. Folks were still telling ghost stories about him. According to legend, after Störtebeker was decapitated he walked past eleven of his men before the hangman tripped him.

Karl sighed and continued his work. Starting tomorrow, the doctor had rented a hall in town where they were going to show the famous Störtebeker with the laterna magica. He hoped he'd manage to capture this accursed pirate on the glass plate by then. He'd spent half the afternoon brewing that stinking theriac. Part of the job was to get up early in the morning and head to Grasbrook Island to pick mint, wormwood, and wild fennel.

Once again doubts crept into Karl's mind as to whether he had chosen the right path. Of course, Doctor Faustus had saved his life, and Karl owed him gratitude. And the man was famous—across the entire empire and beyond. But by now they'd been traveling together for almost a whole year, and the doctor was becoming more frightening by the day. Karl had found many strange books in one of the chests and begun to read them in his lonely hours, even though he didn't fully understand them. The doctor had never told him what he used to do before he took up exploring the empire, but something told Karl that Faust had a dark past, as if he'd been cursed a long time ago. Was that the price he'd had to pay for wealth and fame?

Dabbing his brush very gently, Karl gave the pirate a dashing hat. Störtebeker's gaze was both furious and mysterious at once—as mysterious as that of the doctor, who was on his way to becoming just as legendary as this buccaneer.

Doctor Faustus called himself a fraud, but Karl knew he was much more than that. Faust was the most learned man he'd ever met, blessed with a razor-sharp mind, and open to anything new. Karl worshipped the doctor—probably more than he cared to admit—but he was also afraid of him. Faust sometimes had horrendous fits of rage, and he could be arrogant and awfully sarcastic. And then there were the screams in the night.

The screams at night frightened Karl the most.

They frequently shared a room, and sometimes, when Karl stayed awake for longer than the doctor, he heard him mutter and groan in his sleep. He also cried and sighed in his dreams and repeated the same names over and over again: Margarethe, Martin, Tonio, Gilles de Rais.

The last name, especially, Faust said many times in his sleep.

On top of everything else, the doctor clearly suffered from paranoia, and it was only getting worse. During their trip north he'd often turned around to check the road behind them or stared at the birds in the sky. It was almost as if Faust feared that the birds were watching them. However, Karl had to admit that there had been a few strange occurrences lately. The black figure with the red eyes outside the Erfurt tavern window, for example. And twice more he thought he'd seen the same figure on their journey north, standing among the trees by the wayside. But he hadn't said anything to the doctor for fear of adding to his paranoia.

Karl had learned more from Faust than he ever would have learned at a university. In Leipzig he was nothing but the son of an ambitious father whom he'd never have pleased. Karl had loved his mother very dearly, but she'd passed away years before. Now, on his adventures with the doctor, he was becoming a man. Still, he had made up his mind that he wouldn't travel with the doctor forever. He felt that the heavy melancholy clinging to his master was rubbing off on him. He was going to stay with him for one more winter and then leave in the spring. He no longer cared about those stupid letters—his duty was done.

A movement by the curtain made Karl start from his thoughts. The brush jerked and the awe-inspiring sword he'd been working on turned into a long smudge. Karl swore. Now he'd have to start from the beginning. Below the table, Satan growled and pricked her ears.

"Who's there?" asked Karl harshly. "The doctor is in town. Come back tomorrow."

"Is there going to be another show tomorrow?" asked a high-pitched male voice. "I would so love to see the doctor one more time. And . . . and you, too."

"Me?" Something in the voice piqued Karl's interest. He threw Satan the bone that was supposed to go into the soup for dinner, stood up, and opened the curtain. A handsome boy of about sixteen or seventeen was standing beside the wagon. Karl had noticed him in the last few days—the chap hadn't missed a show. Their eyes had met in a way Karl knew well.

They always knew each other by their eyes.

The youth smiled uncertainly. He was pale and had fine black hair. Judging by his clothes, he was a simple dockworker, although his delicate stature didn't really fit the picture. His eyelashes were as long as a girl's. Karl carefully looked around. It was quiet by the river at the moment. About a stone's throw away, some day laborers were loading crates into a smaller boat that was probably headed for the Alster port, but none of them were looking in their direction. Karl hesitated, but not for long. The doctor wouldn't be back before six—they had enough time.

"Come in," he said and gestured behind himself, winking at the youth. "I want to show you something."

"But . . . but the dog?" the boy asked anxiously and peered through the curtain, where Satan was chewing on the bone.

"It won't hurt you. Not as long as I keep feeding it my dinner, anyhow. Come on in—you have nothing to fear."

The boy did as he was asked. He climbed inside the wagon and looked at everything with curiosity: the dried herbs dangling from the ceiling, and the many crates and chests, some of which stood open, revealing their mysterious contents. When his gaze fell upon the glass plate on the table, he giggled like a girl.

"Oh, that must be Störtebeker. Am I right? You've captured him well!"

"Thank you." Karl was also smiling now. "We're going to show him with our laterna magica."

"With your laterna what?" The youth's eyes grew wide.

"Well, it's an apparatus that allows us to make images appear against a wall," explained Karl patronizingly. "And I paint the pictures. I've even drawn the pope and the emperor. I'm a painter," he added unnecessarily. "Just like Leonardo da Vinci or Albrecht Dürer. Do you know Dürer?"

The youth shook his head.

"I copied his horsemen of the apocalypse," said Karl. "Well, to be honest, I reinterpreted the work. I don't think I've done too badly. Some even say it is better than the original."

The young lad continued to stare at the glass plate. He reverently ran his finger along the edge of the miniature painting. "These must be very valuable."

"What's your name, boy?" asked Karl, trying to change the subject.

The youth took a bow. "Sebastian, sir."

Karl laughed. "You don't need to call me sir—I'm not much older than you. Sebastian is a beautiful name." He winked at him. "And Saint Sebastian was a beautiful man. As handsome as you," he added softly.

By now he felt certain that the boy was here for a particular reason. Karl couldn't say whether it was the boy's own desire or whether he was hoping for money, but at the end of the day it didn't matter. Several times over the last few months he'd met with young men, and while Faust probably had his suspicions, Karl didn't think he noticed anything. Mostly they'd been hasty encounters beneath bridges or in the bushes. There were boys like this one in every town—one only had to find them. They were all connected by their fear of discovery. Good, upright citizens had almost less sympathy for sodomites than they had for heretics, Jews, and well poisoners.

The dainty young man turned away and started to rummage through the chests. "Those are juggling balls, right?" He pulled out one red and one golden leather ball and tried to juggle them. The balls fell to the ground and he laughed.

"Leave it," replied Karl. Suddenly he got the bad feeling that it hadn't been such a good idea to invite the handsome youth into the wagon. His demeanor seemed very experienced—calculated, even. Karl suspected this wasn't the first wagon he had sifted through.

"Leave it, I said!" he repeated more loudly. But the boy didn't listen. He continued to rummage through the chest, lifting out a black hat, red scarves, and a white wooden egg. Then he turned to the chest with the books and carelessly picked up and dropped several volumes.

"Watch out—you're damaging them!" shouted Karl.

Suddenly the youth snorted with surprise. He dropped the books he was holding, bent down, and lifted a knife from the chest. He studied it with awe in his eyes, and Karl also gazed at it with wonder. He had never seen the knife before; it must have been buried underneath all those books. The handle appeared to be carved from some kind of bone and was decorated with black patterns and lines. It looked very old and precious. The boy ran his thumb along the blade with a smile.

"It's so beautiful," he said. "Will you give it to me as a gift?"

Karl cleared his throat. This whole situation was taking a direction he didn't like at all. He gave an awkward laugh. "You're not serious, are you? That knife belongs to the doctor, and he—"

"And now it belongs to me," the boy said decisively. He eyed Karl with a cold stare and pointed the tip of the knife at him. "Or do you want to take it off me?"

Karl nervously glanced at Satan, who was happily chewing on her bone. He couldn't believe it. For once the mutt could have been useful, but she was behaving as gentle as a lamb.

The youth grinned and his eyes flashed wolfishly. "Then we have an understanding. I'm going to take this knife and—"

Suddenly, the curtain was yanked open behind him. To Karl's enormous relief, it was the doctor, arriving back much sooner than anticipated. He was out of breath, and his mouth stood open as if he'd just been about to say something when he happened upon the scene with the boy and the knife.

"What is going on here?" he snapped.

"Um, nothing," said Karl. "We were just talking."

"We?" The doctor looked the youth up and down. Faust seemed to suddenly realize what the boy was holding in his hand. His face turned ashen as if he'd seen a ghost.

"Put that down immediately," said Faust very quietly. "I'm going to count to three, and then Satan will tear you into tiny pieces. Afterward I will feed you to the gulls. One. Two."

The boy dropped the knife and ran past Faust. They could hear his footsteps for a few more moments, and then everything was silent.

"I . . . I'm so—" began Karl, but Faust cut him off with a wave.

"Pack your things. We're leaving."

"But . . . but our show with the laterna," stammered Karl. "Klaus Störtebeker . . ."

"I said we're leaving. And if I catch you with another boy like him, Satan's going to bite off the balls of both of you—understood?"

Karl lowered his eyes and nodded. "Where . . . where are we going?" he asked quietly after a while.

"To Cologne. We're going to visit someone I should have met a long time ago. Years ago. Hitch the horse to the wagon. Now!"

As Karl slunk away, he saw the doctor pick up the knife and gaze at it thoughtfully.

Then he dropped it into the chest as if it had burned his fingers.

22

THE WAGON SLOWLY RATTLED ALONG THE DUSTY ROAD that wound endlessly through the heath. Satan jogged alongside the wagon, panting, and stopped to relieve herself or rest up every now and then. She no longer had the strength for long journeys and tired easily. They had left Hamburg in the early evening and set off in the direction of Lüneburg. The heath glowed purple in the light of the afternoon sun; they had been on the road almost nonstop for three days now, and Johann had barely spoken.

He looked over at Karl, who was sitting next to him with a pinched expression. He probably thought Johann was still angry because of the young lad in Hamburg. And Johann had been angry. It was encounters like those that could cost them both their heads. He didn't care whether Karl lusted after girls, boys, or sheep—as long as he didn't put them both in danger with his escapades. Especially not now that Johann finally had set his sights on a goal and purpose again. He needed to meet Heinrich Agrippa and speak with him about his masterpiece, *De Occulta Philosophia*. If anyone knew about the constellations and prophecies, it would be Agrippa. Maybe Johann would finally learn the mystery of his birth.

And perhaps he'd find out more about Tonio del Moravia and Gilles de Rais.

Had it been coincidence that the young thief in Hamburg found the knife? Johann had kept it for all those years, even though he couldn't tell why. It had brought him nothing but ill luck, but it also served to remind him of the guilt he'd heaped upon himself. He hadn't dared to throw it away—almost as if the act might trigger a curse. The knife had been resting at the very bottom of the chest, and now it had reemerged. When Johann had picked it up from the floor of the wagon, he was reminded of the engraving.

G d R.

Gilles de Rais.

Another murder of crows rose up from the wide-open space of the heath and moved across the sky like a poisonous black cloud. The birds cawed noisily, and suddenly Johann heard the name again.

Sheel draay . . . Gilles de Rais . . . sheel draay . . .

Why couldn't he get that accursed name out of his head? It had been torturing him for years now! As if the name was irrevocably connected to his fate. Like Tonio. Like everything that had happened since those days in Knittlingen.

On this trip, they didn't spend much time on shows, and so they made rapid progress. Large areas of the north of the empire were covered in moors and heath, a desolate, desertlike landscape without any hills to speak of, without valleys, and without lakes. The wind blew up small clouds of any sand the heather shrubs didn't hold down, and several times the wagon wheels got stuck in soft, sandy ruts and they'd have to push the wagon out like from a snowdrift. Once they started to travel along rivers again, the roads became better. Every time they passed through a new county or a new small barony, they had to pay road tolls. The whole empire was like a threadbare carpet sewn from countless tiny scraps and held together only by an emperor who was as far away as the moon.

The closer they came to the Rhine Valley, the lovelier the landscape became. The first vineyards appeared. Finally, twelve exhausting days of travel later, they looked upon the wide ribbon of the Rhine, and they knew it wouldn't be far to Cologne now.

So far, Johann had avoided the city of Cologne, which was one of the largest in the empire. The prior of the Dominican monastery of Cologne was also the papal inquisitor, and he had a reputation for being particularly strict with alleged heretics. Also, the city was a famous pilgrimage destination with countless relics, most notably the remains of the three wise men. Magicians and chiromancers weren't well received in such a place. But the reputation of the legendary Doctor Faustus had even reached Cologne. When Johann loudly declared his name at the city gate, the guards discussed for a while before allowing him in—not without confiscating one or two bottles of theriac. Satan was lying in the back of the wagon. It was difficult enough to gain entrance to the city without the oversized animal, and the dog had been increasingly dragging her right hind leg. Johann was worried about her.

In the northeast, the unfinished spire of the cathedral rose up. The people of Cologne had been working on this architectural masterpiece for more than two hundred and fifty years, and it still wasn't finished. The city was speckled with smaller and larger churches, and almost every single one exhibited some reliquary or other. On their way through the busy streets, they passed many pilgrims with staffs and humble clothing. After Rome and Santiago de Compostela, Cologne was the best-known pilgrimage destination in the Western world. But the city was also a place of learning and boasted one of the largest universities of the empire. The famous Albertus Magnus, whom Johann had venerated since his days at Maulbronn Monastery, had studied theology and been ordained a priest here.

"And where do you propose to find this Agrippa?" asked Karl as they drove the wagon through the narrow, unpaved lanes toward the river. By now Johann had forgiven him for the affair in Hamburg, but he hadn't told Karl what exactly he was hoping to gain from meeting Agrippa. He had merely said he was looking forward to an exchange between learned men.

"Well, Heinrich Agrippa of Nettesheim is no stranger in Cologne," replied Johann. "The bottles of theriac for the guards were a sound investment. They gave me his address. Apparently he lives near the hay market with his sister, who cooks for him. It shouldn't be far now."

They turned onto another narrow lane and neared a two-story half-timbered house that was freshly painted and appeared generally well looked-after. Johann felt himself growing nervous. What if Agrippa refused to receive him? After all, most scholars considered Johann to be nothing but a fraud. Or what if Agrippa couldn't help him? The whole idea—the hasty departure from Hamburg, the hope to learn more about his birth from the famous scholar—suddenly seemed awfully naive. What could he expect? But it was too late to turn back now.

"Wait here," said Johann to Karl. He climbed down from the box seat, walked over to the house, and pulled on the string that operated a bell inside. After a few long moments, a plump young woman wearing a bonnet and an apron opened the door. She gave Johann a friendly albeit reserved look. It seemed she was used to supplicants.

Johann cleared his throat. "My name is Doctor Johann Georg Faustus. I am looking for the eminent scholar Heinrich Cornelius Agrippa of Nettesheim. Can you tell me where to find him?"

"My brother is still at the university," the woman replied curtly. "He'll be home soon. You best wait outside."

Johann was about to make a reply, but Agrippa's sister had already closed the door. With a frown he returned to Karl, who was trying to chase away a bunch of nosy street kids. This wasn't going the way he'd hoped at all.

Soon, a crowd had gathered around the wagon. Johann was wearing his blue-and-black star cloak and the floppy hat, and the strange symbols on the wagon did the rest. Word was spreading fast that a well-known magician was waiting outside Agrippa's house.

"It's the sorcerer Doctor Faustus," whispered an elderly farmer to his wife in a broad Cologne accent. "A necromancer and devil worshipper! I've heard of him. Down at Speyer he made two calves fly to the moon! They're still up there today."

"God protect us," said the old woman, shaking her head. "When two magicians come together, terrible things will happen."

The crowd grumbled, and the first few troublemakers started to pull at the canvas, probably trying to see what sort of devilish things were hidden inside. Karl jumped down and tried to fend off the most daring fellows. But they didn't stop—on the contrary, more and more people came forward, shouting, swearing, and shaking the wagon. The lane was so full of people that they wouldn't be able to get the wagon out. Johann looked about nervously. It wouldn't be long before some city guards turned up, and that wouldn't help his cause at all. He was already considered trouble. Should he set Satan on the mob? But that would only make things worse.

"What's all this about? Off with you, there's nothing to see here!"

Johann turned around and saw a rather short man with a beret and a gown striding through the throng of people. He was probably younger than Johann, but his black university garb and lordly demeanor made him appear older and more dignified. The man had intelligent, alert eyes, a pointed nose, and a thin mouth that seemed set in a permanent sneer. Despite his youth, his hair and thin beard were already turning gray.

"Don't ask *me*—ask the people," replied Johann from the box seat.

"Well, if you are who the people think you are, you are definitely the source of all this trouble." The man smiled and suddenly looked much younger. He spoke with a Cologne accent, which made his stilted way of speaking sound like a cheap farce. "Doctor Faustus, am I right? Considering the sheer number of tales about you, I would have thought you much older."

"Considering the number of your works, Master Agrippa, I thought you, too, were older," replied Johann coolly, still annoyed about the turmoil he had caused. "Or were they written by someone else, perhaps?"

"Touché, dear colleague!" Agrippa laughed and bowed mockingly, the crowd now keeping a respectful distance. "I much prefer an open attack to the backstabbing attempts of all those old scholars who would love nothing more than to see me convicted of heresy. Let us go inside, where we can speak undisturbed." He grinned and gestured toward an alleyway to the left of his house.

"You'll find a gate to the backyard of my humble abode down there. You must forgive my sister, Martha, for not letting you in. We simply get too many supplicants—mostly traveling students hoping for a position. But I wouldn't miss your visit, honorable Doctor. On the way home from the university alone, I heard at least a dozen stories about you."

"Only half of them are true," said Johann with a shrug.

"And he won't tell you which half," said Karl with a sigh.

Agrippa glanced at the young man. "You have an assistant?"

"A talented young man," replied Johann. "Even if his passion runs a little wild at times."

He walked through the crowd at Agrippa's side. The people readily gave way now, and some even took off their hats. But Johann also saw some men and women making the sign of the cross and other gestures to ward off evil. Meanwhile, Karl climbed back onto the box seat and steered the wagon through the crowd toward the alleyway.

The front door was followed by a plainly furnished hallway, with furs and carpets on the walls and fragrant reeds on the floor.

"Follow me into the stove room," said Agrippa as he went up the stairs. "We'll be able to converse undisturbed there. Your assistant may wait in the kitchen and let Martha spoil him. She's made fresh Cologne doughnuts—a veritable delicacy. As for you and me, we will content ourselves with the meager yet equally delicious fare of collegial dispute."

The stove room was dominated by a green tiled stove as high as a man. Such stoves were increasingly the fashion in houses of burghers. Unlike the tidy hallway, this room was very messy. Books and loose pages were strewn across chests and small tables; a brown apple core lay rotting between an inkwell and a quill. Johann smelled parchment, dust, and sweat.

"My realm," said Agrippa with a smile and gestured for Johann to sit on a stool. They both sat down, and Agrippa eyed Johann for a long while.

"Well, well, the famous Doctor Faustus," he said eventually and leaned back. "Someone told me about your lectures at Erfurt. I was impressed by your views on the theological term of God. A little dangerous, though, because it doesn't take much to be called a heretic these days. I know what I'm talking about."

"And you are lecturing here in Cologne?" asked Johann.

"Simple theological discussions without any particular classification—on request of the rector." Agrippa gave a shrug, and Johann wasn't sure whether this show of boredom was an act or real. Agrippa was certainly clever, but he also had something pretentious and loud about him.

Just like me, thought Johann.

"I doubt I'll be staying in Cologne for much longer," continued Agrippa. "I'll probably have to travel to Italy soon. It is my duty to accompany a heavily guarded chest of war as an imperial officer. Earlier this year I helped a friend of mine in Spain to win back his castle. Oh yes, and not long ago I worked in England as an agent. The emperor sent me to develop good trade relations with the new king, Henry VIII. I speak English, you see." He paused and raised one eyebrow. "Do you know the feeling of never being satisfied, always wanting more from life, forever searching and exploring, regardless of the consequences?"

Johann nodded. "Oh yes. I know it well."

Too well.

"I guess that makes us brothers in spirit." Agrippa laughed, and his laugh was soft and melodious, almost like that of a woman. He looked around for a jug of wine, grabbed two dirty cups from a table full of books, and filled them.

"You see, I'm just as restless as you. Today I'm here, tomorrow gone—the *studium generale* includes all parts of life. But you haven't come here just to chat, have you? So why are you here?"

Johann cleared his throat. "While you were in England, you wrote a manuscript. I was fortunate enough to purchase a copy in Hamburg." He nervously pulled out the bundle of pages and smoothed them on the table in front of him. Agrippa shot a glance at them.

"The *Occulta Philosophia*," said the scholar with a nod. "I'm a long way away from finishing it." He sighed. "I should never have let that fat merchant buy a copy. But he paid well, and the emperor is once again in arrears."

"I must congratulate you. It's a masterpiece!" Johann tapped the pages. "No one has ever approached magic as systematically as you have. Astrology, invocations, spells, manticism, potions—"

"Pure theory." Agrippa waved dismissively. "I lack practical experience, and that is where you are the teacher and I am but an eager student. Why are you so interested in it?"

"Well, your work touches questions that"—Johann paused—"that concern me personally."

For the first time Agrippa seemed genuinely interested, and he leaned forward. "What do you mean?"

"Certain things have happened in my life that . . . Well, one could say I am cursed. And I've been wondering for a while now whether those incidents have anything to do with my birth chart. I was born under Jupiter. The sun and Jupiter stood in the same degree of the same zodiac on the day of my birth."

Agrippa nodded. "A strong constellation indeed. Born under the lucky star—hence your name, I guess."

"I haven't found my luck yet," Johann replied bitterly. "Have you ever heard of the expression *born on the day of the prophet*? Apparently it has something to do with my birth."

"No, I'm sorry." Agrippa shook his head. "But I think it's likely that the stars have more to say about your birth than we simple humans can see with our bare eyes." When Johann gave him a quizzical look, Agrippa continued. "I am convinced that there are many more stars out there. Some shine very weakly, as if they were far away. I've always wondered, What lies beyond?"

"Ptolemy wrote that the Earth was surrounded by eight spheres," replied Johann. "And beyond those is nothing."

"And you're content with that explanation?" Agrippa smiled. "You disappoint me, Faustus. Don't you want to find out what lies beyond the eighth sphere?"

"Beyond the eighth sphere." Johann gazed into the distance. "Someone else said those words to me once."

"That someone must have been a wise man." Agrippa emptied his cup in one gulp and refilled both their cups with wine. "But now let us speak of more worldly things. I've got a suggestion for you, Doctor Faustus. You tell me about yourself, and I tell you about the world behind the eighth sphere. If only every second story about you is true, we are going to have a few merry and stimulating weeks."

Agrippa was right. The following weeks were the most stimulating Johann had ever experienced.

Heinrich Cornelius Agrippa of Nettesheim, famous Cologne scholar, was the first person Johann had ever considered an equal. Their conversations were like duels, fought not with the sword but with wit and sharp tongues. The two men came from very different backgrounds. Agrippa was an offspring of Cologne nobility, and his father had been a diplomat in the service of the House of Hapsburg. Agrippa had grown up as a fortunate child, loved by his parents, surrounded by books, and boasting many talents. Johann, on the other hand, was a bastard who'd had to work hard for everything in his life, a juggler, and a fraud.

Even though Agrippa probably knew that most of the stories about Faust weren't true, he was happily entertained by them. A small adventure quickly turned into a scientific discourse, and the two men often sat up late into the night.

"My students told me you can make thunder and lightning," said Agrippa with a smile one evening in the stove room. "So? Can you?"

Johann shrugged. "Let's say I possess enough gunpowder to make the heavens rumble—for the simple folk, at least. The scope of this devilish mixture of sulfur, coal, and saltpeter is truly astonishing. I fear we're far from finished developing and refining this powder, however."

"And how is the real thunder in the sky created?" asked Agrippa, sipping his wine. "In his *Meteorologica*, Aristotle claims that it is the wind colliding with the clouds. What do you think?"

"Do you know Albertus Magnus's rainbow experiment?" replied Johann after some consideration. "An octagonal crystal that is partly placed into the sunlight projects the colors of the rainbow against a wall. Maybe it's a similar story with thunder. Thunder might be created by something we can't see. It is just the consequence, not the cause."

Agrippa rocked his head from side to side. "An interesting thought, dear colleague. I might use it in one of my lectures."

Agrippa mostly spent the mornings at the university, where the students flocked to his lectures to hear the scholar's thoughts, some finding them heretical while others believed they were forward thinking. Johann used the time to browse Agrippa's home library until delicious cooking smells called him to the kitchen. He took lunch with Agrippa's sister and Karl. Satan stayed in the garden by the wagon.

Thus the weeks passed, and soon it was October. The temperatures turned cooler, and rain lashed through the lanes of Cologne. Every now and then Johann still thought he was being watched, but the urge to learn more about the stars on his day of birth and about whatever lay beyond the eighth sphere was so strong that he forgot everything else around him. He and Karl slept at the Golden Crown Inn, one of the city's best taverns. Johann slept deeply and without dreams—better than he had in years. The intellectual exchange with Agrippa made him feel as satisfied as a freshly fed baby. He barely ever thought of Margarethe during that time.

They didn't give any shows with the laterna magica for fear of being accused of heresy. Johann wasn't a particularly popular man in the streets of Cologne; people gossiped about the sorcerer at the house of the controversial scholar, and a few times dung was thrown at him. But he didn't deny himself the pleasure of demonstrating the laterna in the stove room for Agrippa.

"Truly amazing," said his host once the last image—the white woman—had faded and Johann had lit the candles in the room again. "Imagine the possibilities if those images could move like real people."

"And speak," said Johann with a smile. "Who knows—perhaps that day will come, even if you or I won't be there to see it."

Johann gradually learned more about Agrippa's thoughts on the stars. The scholar thought it was possible that there were other suns in the universe—other worlds, even. The universe might be endlessly great, and planet Earth nothing but a speck of dust.

"Consider the comets," Agrippa said to Johann one day. "Where do they come from? From a distant world behind the eighth sphere? How long did it take them to travel here? Since the times of Aristotle people have believed comets are atmospheric evaporations or harbingers of bad news of future events. But I believe they come from much farther away—farther even than the wise astronomer Johannes Müller suspected, but at least he defined them as independent celestial bodies." Agrippa sighed. "It is such a pity our eyes can't see what's beyond the eighth sphere." He gestured at the laterna magica in a corner of the room. "It's a pretty toy, your apparatus. But I wonder if it could also be used differently. Those lenses you used . . ." He hesitated.

"What about them?"

Agrippa picked up the frameless eye glasses he wore occasionally and studied them pensively. "If we look through lenses, we see better. We've known that since the times of Roger Bacon. But what if we could also better see what's in the heavens? If we could see farther, we might understand what makes your birth so special. You speak of a curse—why?"

Johann hesitated.

"Have you ever heard of a Gilles de Rais?" he asked eventually.

Agrippa touched his nose, thinking. Johann thought for the briefest moment he saw a flicker in the scholar's eyes. "I'm afraid I haven't," he replied. "Should I have?"

Johann watched Agrippa closely, but the man's expression remained neutral. If he was lying, he was very good at it.

"It's not important. Please excuse the question." Johann gave a shrug. "Concerning the curse . . . it is as if someone were giving me all the wisdom, all the knowledge in the world, while at the same time placing obstacles in my way. Terrible things have happened all my life, but I was always told that I was blessed with luck. Born on the day of the prophet—how does that fit together with all the awful things that have happened to me? I finally want to know who I am. Do you understand? Only then will my searching come to an end."

"Who you are?" Agrippa couldn't hold back a smile. "Since when do people want to know who they are? An unusual question, don't you think? Somewhat . . . new." He laughed. "But then again, you are an unusual person, Doctor Faustus—almost like a new specimen of our kind."

Johann was so engrossed in his discussions with Agrippa that he sometimes forgot that he had an assistant. Karl did as he pleased in Cologne, and aside from mealtimes, they didn't see each other. Johann didn't look after Karl as he had pledged that he would after they'd first met. His thirst for knowledge was stronger than their friendship.

And so fate—or the curse Johann had spoken about—took its course once again.

~

Karl heard the sounds of music, laughter, and shattering glass as he staggered out of the tavern down by the Rhine and turned his face into the autumn rain. The Black Whale was a disreputable hole, but nevertheless it was frequented by gentlemen of the upper classes. They usually sat in the back, wearing wide-brimmed hats and plain coats to hide their expensive clothing. It wasn't long before a handsome young lad would take a seat beside one such gentleman, and a while later the pair would disappear up a narrow set of stairs.

Karl, too, had been upstairs a few times.

There were days when he cursed himself for what he was doing. Why had God punished him with this vice? He knew it was a cardinal sin punishable with death by fire, but his flesh was weak. Why couldn't he simply love girls like other young men did? It drove him crazy. If what he was doing was a sin, then why had God made him this way? Was it a test, just like the Lord had tested Job? Karl was too afraid even to confess his sins at church now—he feared the priest would disregard the seal of confession. Instead Karl launched himself from one amorous adventure to the next, drowning his guilty conscience with wine and schnapps at the Black Whale.

Suddenly Karl felt nauseated, and he staggered toward the Rhine as quickly as he could, dropped to his knees, and vomited. The lights of the taverns along the port were reflected in the water; they were low, huddled buildings near the docks, warehouses, and fish markets; they lured patrons with whores and other guilty pleasures. Karl retched. If only he could rid himself of his urge this way! Just spew it out like those possessed by the devil sometimes spewed out rusty nails and then they were cured.

For him, it seemed, there was no cure.

He was bound for hell.

What made it all the worse for him was the fact that he loved a man who was unattainable. It had started slowly and stealthily. In the beginning it was merely admiration and respect Karl had felt toward the doctor, but now it was respect coupled with true affection and—Karl quivered with embarrassment—uncouth thoughts. Doctor Faustus was a dozen years older than him, but he was still a good-looking man with soft raven-black hair and a dark, mysterious gaze. Karl thought it was mainly the eyes that attracted him so—gazing at them was like looking into two deep ponds. And he couldn't figure out the mystery that lay at their bottom, no matter how hard he tried.

Karl knew he could never reveal his feelings. The way the doctor ignored him here in Cologne pained him. Yes, they took lunch together and saw each other at the Golden Crown Inn at nights, but Faust was never really with him. His mind was always with that arrogant Agrippa, whose company the doctor found much more stimulating than a conversation with his ignorant assistant. Karl's frustration had edged him from one liaison into the next, even though he hadn't felt good about it. His latest lover in particular seemed a little creepy. He was a pretty lad with hair just as black as the doctor's. But his eyes had something calculating—nasty, even. A few times when they were lying next to each other at night, Karl had sensed the boy's eyes on him. His looks burned like glowing pieces of coal. But as soon as Karl had opened his own eyes, the boy had only smiled at him and covered him in kisses. Just now Karl had been with him again, but this time he'd felt too uncomfortable and had run outside.

Still drunk, Karl got to his feet and wiped his mouth, a bitter flavor on his tongue. He needed this to end! He would go to the doctor and ask to be released. Faust would give him back his letters, and Karl would move on and try to forget the doctor. It would be the best for everyone.

With unsteady steps, Karl walked along the Rhine while rain fell from the sky like cold tears. He had bribed the guards to leave the small gate by the Franken Tower unlocked. The guards made good money with men like him. Only a few years ago it was revealed that more than two hundred respected citizens of Cologne were engaging in sodomy. The whole affair had been swept under the carpet, and until this day honest husbands sneaked through the gate down to the houses of ill repute by the Rhine. Karl looked up at the tower that served as a jail and reminded him of what was in store for him should he be discovered.

Gently, he pushed against the gate. It opened. As soon as he was through he noticed movement in the alcove below the tower. To his relief he realized it was just one of the guards, and the man winked at him conspiratorially. Karl was about to walk past him when the soldier suddenly blocked his way. The man's expression darkened and he drew his sword.

"This is Wagner, the sodomite!" shouted the guard over his shoulder, and Karl saw more men move in the darkness. "Get him!"

Karl heard heavy footsteps, and then men with swords and pikes rushed toward him. The scene had a dreamlike quality to it; everything seemed to move slower than normally. Strangely, Karl felt no fear in that moment. All his senses were entirely focused on survival.

Before the soldiers reached him, he feinted to the right and then dashed past the astonished guard on the left. Even as a small boy Karl had always been one of the quickest. He raced like a hare and swerved left and right while a crossbow bolt whirred past his ear. Behind him the men yelled; Karl stumbled, caught himself, and stormed into a narrow alleyway. He knocked over a barrel, pressed on, and heard angry shouts behind him. He ran aimlessly through the maze of lanes, turning left here and right there until he came to the edge of the larger street that led from the port to the cathedral.

Panicked, gasping for breath, and with a wildly beating heart, Karl looked around. The men had gone. The rain was pouring down and made the moonless night even darker than it already was. It was unlikely that they'd find him now.

At first, a wave of relief washed through him. He had actually managed to shake off the soldiers. But then fear returned, doubly powerful. He was a wanted sodomite—torture and the stake awaited him. The memory of smoke and the smell of burning flesh returned. Karl started to tremble uncontrollably while he feverishly tried to figure out what to do next. Someone must have betrayed him. There was no other explanation for the fact that the fellow at the gate called him by his name.

And if they knew who he was, they'd also know whose assistant he was.

Exhausted and close to tears, Karl leaned against the wall of a house. All was lost! He couldn't return to the inn. Worse still: the doctor himself was in danger of being arrested as a sodomite. Maybe that was the real reason his bribe did no good: they were looking for a reason to arrest the sorcerer and necromancer Doctor Faustus. Karl had to warn him. That was the least he could do.

Still breathing heavily, he sneaked along the dark lane toward the cathedral. The Golden Crown Inn, a freshly whitewashed half-timbered house with crown-glass windows, stood just a stone's throw away. When Karl had a good view of the front door, he cowered in a niche between houses and piles of foul-smelling waste and waited. If he was lucky, Faust was still with Agrippa.

Rats scurried around his feet, and a night watchman walked past very closely without seeing him. After about half an hour, when Karl was soaked to the skin, a man wearing a blue-and-black cloak and a floppy hat approached the inn from the cathedral. Karl breathed a sigh of relief. It was the doctor. With Satan by his side, Faust walked with a spring in his step; Karl guessed the conversation with Agrippa had left the doctor in high spirits. Jealousy flared up in the young assistant, but only for a moment. Then he cautiously stepped out into the street and waved.

Faust took a few moments to recognize him, and even then he approached only reluctantly. When the doctor came closer to Karl, he wrinkled his nose. Satan growled and sniffed at Karl's filthy trousers.

"What happened to you?" asked Faust gruffly. "Did you wallow in the muck?"

"Something . . . something dreadful has happened, Master," burst out Karl. "By God, I . . . I'm so sorry."

Faust immediately turned serious. "What is it? Speak up!"

"May heaven forgive me. I am wanted as a sodomite and I . . . I fear so are you."

As quickly as he could, Karl told the doctor about his visit to the Black Whale, the events at the Franken Tower, and his escape. To his surprise, the doctor remained calm.

"You said they knew your name. That's bad—very bad," he muttered. "You're right. We can't go back to the inn. Nor to Agrippa if we don't want to drag him into this. But where can we go? Where . . . ?" Faust closed his eyes and rubbed his nose.

"Maybe if I hand myself in," whimpered Karl. "If I tell them that you have nothing to do with any of this—"

"Shut up!" barked Faust. "They will try to use it against me one way or another. I should never have—" He broke off and shook his head. "Whatever has happened, we must look ahead now. This running away must come to an end."

"What do you mean?" Karl looked at his master expectantly. "What are you thinking?"

"Listen closely to what I tell you," replied Faust quietly. "We'll only get out of this if we don't make any mistakes now."

"Where . . . where do you want to go?" asked Karl. "The power of the Cologne Inquisition reaches far."

The doctor nodded resolutely as if he'd just made an important decision. The rain was still beating down on them, and small waterfalls ran off Faust's hat.

"I think I know a place where we can stay awhile," said Faust eventually. "I haven't been there in a long time, but it's an ideal place to hide out for a winter—or for as long as it takes until they've forgotten about us again. I should have gone back there much sooner. There is something that might help to answer my questions." His gaze turned into the distance before he spoke again.

"It is a tower."

~

From a window on the second floor of the inn, a man watched as the doctor and his assistant walked away toward the hay market. He could only just make out their outlines through the windows. A liquid as red as blood gleamed in the expensive glass goblet he was holding. The man took a long sip, licked his lips, and smiled.

The end and the beginning were near.

When the doctor had sought out Heinrich Agrippa, the man had been a little concerned. He didn't want Faustus to learn too much—not yet. Even though it most likely wouldn't change his destiny now.

His destiny was written in the stars. Impossible to change.

Still, he'd wanted to avoid those two scholars taking their musings too far. And so he'd intervened. It had been so easy to lure young Karl Wagner in. Everyone had their weak point, their little secret, and it hadn't taken long to find out his.

The man ran his finger along the glass rim of his goblet, creating a humming, almost whining sound. His plan had been for the boy to get caught and tortured, and maybe even executed. It had annoyed him for a while now that Faustus had a companion. The doctor was weakest by himself, and most easily steered. Once his assistant had been arrested, Faust couldn't have stayed in

Cologne any longer, and his conversations with Agrippa would have come to
an end.

The man took another sip of the delicious red drink. Well, now they were
running away together. He'd save Karl for later. The most important thing was
that he didn't lose Faust again like he'd done before. It had taken him a long time
to find him once more. Now that the portentous moment had nearly arrived, he
couldn't lose sight of him. He had watched Faust from a distance for years, had
helped him occasionally, and had even removed obstacles from his path. But for
a few weeks now he had followed him closely, like a sleuth.

The end and the beginning.

Only a few more months.

The man took one last sip, then he carried his goblet over to the cage with
the birds, who greeted him with cawing and flapping.

"Here you go, my little ones," said Tonio del Moravia, pouring the rest of
the red drink from the glass into the bottom of the cage. "Drink! Drink with me
to the day that must come soon. We have waited long enough."

The birds greedily drank up the fresh blood. Standing in the twilight of the
candles in the room, the master looked like he hadn't aged one day.

23

CREAKING AND GROANING, THE WAGON SPED ALONG THE
road by the river. It was still raining when the first glimmer of dawn appeared
above the vineyards in the east.

Johann had been whipping the horse like a madman for almost three hours.
He wanted to get as many miles between them and Cologne as possible before
the guards raised the alarm. Most likely, a delegation of soldiers was already on
its way to catch them. Johann didn't want to begin to imagine what was in store
for them if they got arrested. Two sodomites and heretics dabbling in black
magic! It was just what the Cologne Inquisition had been waiting for, and Karl
had walked straight into their trap.

After Karl had told Johann about his escape, they had rushed to Agrippa's
house. Their wagon was parked there, and Agrippa was the only one who could
help them now. With his connections and a pile of money, they had managed
to get out of the city. A brief hug goodbye had been the only farewell the two
scholars had time for. They had hastily reassured one another that they'd meet
again one day and continue their conversations.

But they'd already had the most important conversation.

Johann knew there was only one place where he might lift the secret surrounding his birth. Agrippa had sparked the idea a few days ago, but only last
night had its meaning become clear to him. They had spoken about lenses,
about eye glasses, and about the laterna magica, and then Agrippa had said
something else.

*But what if we could also better see what's in the heavens? If we could see farther,
we might understand what makes your birth so special.*

Johann knew of an apparatus that might enable him to do just that. But it was hidden at a very dangerous place—a place he hadn't sought out in more than fifteen years. He didn't know if Tonio still visited the place.

Back in the wagon, Satan whined. The old dog wasn't well. She struggled to walk at all now and seemed to be in grave pain, especially after eating. She slept a lot and twitched in her sleep. Johann had given her some theriac to soothe her, but he feared the worst.

I'm going to lose her. Just like I've lost everyone else I ever loved . . .

At least he'd been able to save Karl Wagner. Johann nodded grimly. It had been his fault—he hadn't looked after the boy. The meetings with Agrippa had been more important to him. Just like something had always been more important to him than those he loved. Karl was sitting beside him in silence, only occasionally casting a suffering glance at him that looked much like Satan's.

"Stop looking at me like that," snarled Johann. "What's done is done. I warned you, but I also should have looked after you more."

"I'm so sorry," pleaded Karl. "You and Agrippa—"

"Agrippa and I were reaching the end of our discussions anyhow," said Johann. "I found what I came for. It's time this journey came to an end."

"You said something similar in Cologne," replied Karl. "What do you mean? What journey?"

"The journey of my life."

Johann cracked his whip and shouted at the horse while the wind tore at the wagon's canvas.

They traveled along the Rhine toward Worms, the old imperial city. A stab went through Johann's heart when he thought about the fact that Valentin had been taken to this city to stand trial for heresy. As if the heavens were punishing him, the weather grew worse by the day. It was the coldest fall since anyone could remember, and winter was already making its presence felt at the end of October. An icy wind swept across the plains and bare fields. After about two weeks they crossed the border to Bavaria, where the Alps formed a white chain on the horizon. Johann grew more withdrawn by the day. Every time he looked at that mountain range, the memories returned—memories of Salome and Venice, but also of his time at the tower with Tonio.

The tower.

More than fifteen years ago, Tonio had introduced him to the secrets of the black guild there, but to this day Johann didn't know what the master had really been up to during those cold winter nights. Johann had avoided the area since, almost as if he feared Tonio might be waiting for him there and once again draw him into his dark rituals. But despite his unease about the place, Johann hadn't forgotten what they had buried inside a heavy crate behind the tower upon their departure.

Books and a tube.

A tube that might allow him to see the stars up close. Johann hoped it was still there.

After ten more days they reached the Alps. Meanwhile, winter had fully arrived. The snow wasn't hip deep like the first time Johann had traveled this road, but they still struggled to find the right track between the low-hanging branches. Occasionally they were forced to jump off the wagon and lead the horse through snowdrifts. In the sky above them, crows circled, and Johann tried not to think of them as Tonio's crows. In the last few days, he had frequently heard the cawing of a raven that sounded human, almost like laughter.

Sheel . . . draay . . . sheel . . . draay . . .

Finally, after more than three weeks and a long search, they arrived at the tower.

It still stood atop the hill like a broken tooth, an ancient bulwark at the edge of the Alps. The shed beside it was derelict now, but the entrance to the tower was still barred with the heavy beam, and the windows were still nailed shut the way they'd left it.

Johann breathed a sigh of relief at the sight of the solid black walls. Evidently there hadn't been any unwelcome visitors. Strange, really, because the tower stood in an elevated position and could be spotted from other hills. It was as if it was surrounded by an invisible line that only a few people dared to cross. The black pentagram on the front door probably helped—the drawing looked as clear as on the day of their hasty departure.

Johann jumped off the box seat and rushed to the tower's rear. He swept the snow aside with his feet and saw to his relief that the white stones were still in place. No one had dug around here. Then he walked back to the front and removed the beam from the entrance. He found the large key under the stone plate and turned it in the lock. The door creaked open, and a musty smell like from an ancient crypt engulfed them. It took a few moments for Johann's eyes to adjust to the dim light. At first he thought everything was as they had left it. But then he noticed the changes.

Very unsettling changes.

"This is fantastic!" exclaimed Karl from next to Johann. "I expected a filthy hole—but this looks like a knight's chamber."

Johann said nothing as he studied the furnishings. There was a newly made pinewood shelf, holding about two dozen books. Next to it stood a velvet-covered four-poster bed, a silver-studded chest, and a table with chess pieces made from ivory. Behind a folding screen by the fire stood another bed, and this one was covered in dozens of soft cushions and furs. Johann ran his fingers through the dust that had settled on the pillows.

He was here. But when?

"The complete works of Aristotle are on this shelf," said Karl. The young man had walked into the room and was pulling out books. "Ha! And if I'm not mistaken, this is Avicenna's book on healing. At Leipzig they always told us that it was burned as a work of heresy. Did you furnish this place so nicely and collect all these volumes?"

"A . . . an old friend of mine did," said Johann vaguely. His heart was beating wildly, and once more he felt he was being watched. Tonio had visited the tower in recent years and turned it into a comfortable home. Table, chest, and bed were covered in a thick layer of dust, so he guessed the last visit was a while ago—over a year, perhaps.

But who could tell when the master would return?

Strangely, Tonio hadn't unearthed the crate out back, not as far as Johann could tell, anyhow.

"You're not afraid of black magic, I take it?" said Karl, who was holding up a book with a pentagram on its leather binding.

Johann started when he read the embellished title: *The Sworn Book of Honorius*. It was one of the books he'd read at Signore Barbarese's back in Venice. How on earth had it gotten to the tower? It must have been a different edition. There was no other explanation.

"Put it back," said Johann. "Now. It's not suitable for you. Or for me," he added quietly.

He waited until Karl had placed the book back on the shelf, then he gestured upstairs. "You sleep on the second floor. There's another bed. A bit of fresh straw and some cushions should make it homely enough. The third floor is out of bounds for you, just like the rooftop—you hear me?"

Karl nodded.

"Good," said Johann. "And you'd do well to remember my words. If I ever catch you up there, I'll skin you like a rabbit. Now help me bring Satan inside and light a fire before we freeze to death."

As they got the fire going together, Johann remembered how Tonio had once used almost the exact same words with him. That was a long time ago.

But right at that moment it felt as though no time at all had passed.

They spent the following weeks almost exclusively in the bottommost chamber. Apart from brief trips outside, Satan was always sleeping by the fire. They read a lot and played chess, and Karl's skills improved with each match. Johann still beat him most of the time, but the games were no longer as boring. Sometimes Johann even had to think a little harder. Karl increasingly enjoyed the challenge.

"Ha, you're stumped. Admit it!" he said one time when Johann was taking particularly long to make his move. "I'm making you sweat."

"If anything is making me sweat, it's the damned fire," growled Johann. "You put far too many logs on. It's as hot in here as the pyre you twice narrowly avoided."

Karl's only response was a sheepish look. But there was also something else in his eyes, something Johann couldn't read. He would notice those looks more frequently over the coming weeks but never understand them. Johann was too preoccupied.

On the very first day they'd arrived, Johann had dug up the crate behind the tower and opened it nervously. The tube and books had been wrapped in waxed cloths and were undamaged. Many of the carefully hidden works were about astronomy. Johann found countless rows of tiny numbers and symbols in the margins of the books. It looked as though Tonio had made coded entries, almost like secret messages the master had left for him. Johann thought about the coded messages he and Margarethe had written to each other in Knittlingen. Surely there was a solution to this riddle, too, some kind of key to read the rows of numbers. But try as he might, he couldn't figure it out.

Johann spent many hours trying to solve the mystery, during the day as well as at night. He started with fright every time there was a noise outside—snow falling off the trees, a startled wildcat on the prowl, or the goddamned cawing of the crows. With every sound he thought Tonio had returned.

But the master didn't come. Maybe he had left this place for good?

During clear nights, Johann climbed atop the platform and watched the stars. After a few failed attempts he had finally managed to set up the tube. It wasn't so different from the laterna magica: on the inside were lenses that improved one's eyesight so much that the stars stood clear and bright before him. Everything that usually seemed so far away appeared suddenly within reach. The moon—normally a round yellowish disc with blurred edges—was suddenly covered in craters and lakes of sand, almost like a small version of the Earth. The planets, too, and even the constellations of the eighth sphere were much clearer through the tube.

But Johann still couldn't tell what lay beyond the eighth sphere; he guessed the lenses weren't quite strong enough. And so he hadn't come an inch closer to answering his pressing questions.

He had tried to inspect the lenses closely without taking them out. They appeared to be cut better and more precisely than anything he'd ever seen from glaziers in the empire. They seemed like small miracles to Johann, and not for the first time he asked himself where Tonio had gotten the apparatus. He had never seen anything like it anywhere, not at any courts or at any universities.

As if it stemmed from a foreign world.

Satan enjoyed the warmth and barely ever left the fireplace. Johann always tried to feed her the best cuts of meat, but the dog hardly ate anything. She grew skinnier and skinnier, only lapping up the theriac from time to time. Every time Johann stroked the large animal, she looked at him with loyal eyes. Those eyes nearly broke his heart.

What am I supposed to do when you're no longer with me? he wondered before calling himself a fool for posing such a question to an animal.

On their journey to the tower, they had bought enough provisions so they wouldn't have to go into the village. By now it was snowing so heavily that they couldn't have gone far even if they'd wanted to. The snow piled up outside the door and the windows, so that they had to shovel their way out every time they needed more firewood.

"I feel like we're imprisoned," moaned Karl one afternoon when they once again sat together over a game of chess.

"Don't talk nonsense," said Johann as he took Karl's queen. "I told you once before: you could be sitting in Cologne right now, waiting to be burned at the stake."

"Then why can't I at least go up to the third floor? Or up on the platform? That thing you use to watch the stars with . . . does it really bring them that much closer?"

"I said no, and that's my final word on the matter." Johann checkmated his student with his next move, turned the board around, and sorted the pieces anew. "From the beginning. You're black this time."

In fact, Johann didn't really know why he wouldn't allow Karl upstairs. There was nothing there. Only a faded brownish pentagram that wouldn't go away. Just like the bad memories.

A pile of dirty, torn children's clothes.

Johann had tried to wash away the pentagram many times—in vain. It remained a steady reminder that Tonio might return at any moment.

Satan died during one particularly cold night in December. The evening before, she had rested by the fire and lapped up a bit of theriac, and the following morning, Johann found her cold and stiff like a log—a giant skeleton held together by a bit of shaggy fur.

Johann knelt down beside her and stroked her for a long time. He remembered all the wonderful moments they'd shared. Satan had been his companion since his escape from Heidelberg, and even though she was only a dog, Johann loved her more than he'd loved most people. He curled up beside her and tried to feel the last bit of warmth. But there was nothing.

Over the last few weeks, he'd tried everything he could to help Satan. He had collected spruce sprouts and brewed a medicine from them, and he had palpated Satan's abdomen. Toward the back he had found a hardened area, and from then on he had known there was no hope. All he could do was try to ease her pain. Despite his grief, Johann was relieved that Satan had died naturally that night. If the dog had suffered for much longer, he would have had to put her down. He didn't think he would have been capable of cutting her throat.

They buried her behind the tower, in the hole where the crate with the tube and the books had been hidden. Praying seemed inappropriate to Johann, but he remained standing at the grave for a long while, in spite of the bitter cold and the icy wind that cut through his clothes like knives. Karl stayed with him for a while before sighing deeply, giving Johann one last sympathetic look, and returning to the tower's warmth.

Johann was like an empty shell for the following days. Not even chess brought him joy, and he gave up watching the stars. He had placed all his hopes on finding the secret of his life here at the tower, but he found nothing. He had been wrong. Now that Satan was dead, he had lost all remaining willpower, the force that had kept him going and pushed him on since childhood. All he ever did now was stare into the fire. He felt so tired—so many years of traveling that had been nothing but an attempt to run from himself. What had all his cleverness, all his knowledge brought him? He stayed sitting in front of the fireplace until late at night and watched the embers die.

On the third day, Karl disappeared.

He hadn't come downstairs in the morning, and when Johann checked in his chamber he found the bed empty. Karl must have sneaked past him in the early hours, when Johann had nodded off, and left him for good. Johann couldn't blame him. He knew full well that the years had turned him into a choleric, imperious, and sometimes plainly unbearable man. Now that his will to live had left him, he wasn't even a good teacher any longer. What was the young man supposed to hang around with him for? If he didn't get caught for sodomy, Karl had a promising future. He was intelligent and inquisitive, though perhaps a tad too soft for this world. When Johann thought of him, he suddenly felt real affection.

Too late.

The only thing that puzzled Johann was the fact that Karl had taken neither provisions nor blankets. And the horse was still there. How did the boy think he was going to get by in the mountains?

Johann remained sitting in front of the cold fireplace for hours while a blizzard raged outside. He considered ending his life. He would simply have to go out into the snow, lie down, and go to sleep. Although it would be more appropriate to cut his wrists with the knife Tonio had given him.

The master seemed to pursue him right until death, just like Gilles de Rais, this foreign-sounding name that had never left him in peace. The mystery about that man remained unsolved. Once again Johann asked himself whether Agrippa may have known something about Gilles de Rais after all. But now it was too late to ask him.

It was too late for everything.

A raven cawed outside. Three times, like a knock on the door.

Johann stood up abruptly, hesitated for a moment, then walked over to one of the chests.

You damned beast! You won't get me!

Never again would Tonio have any power over him! There was only one way to get away from him, and Johann was ready to choose that way. The knife with the strange initials sat at the very bottom of the chest. Johann lifted it out and ran his thumb over the razor-sharp blade. It looked like it was as old as the world, forged from the molten lava of volcanoes.

One cut and all his searching would come to an end.

Then he would finally join Margarethe, Valentin, Martin, his mother— everyone he had left and disappointed.

Only one cut.

Johann gripped the knife hard and raised it as if he were performing a ritualistic sacrifice.

You won't get me.

Just then, he heard a noise. A soft creaking of the door. Johann felt certain that it was Tonio. The master had come to get him.

But it wasn't Tonio. It was Karl. He was covered in snow from head to toe like a white monster, and his cheeks glowed red. Water dripped to the ground and formed a small puddle.

Johann lowered the blade with a trembling hand. He fought back tears. For the first time in a long while he was deeply touched. Something had burst through the cold armor of his heart, and it hadn't been a knife. The boy hadn't left him! Karl was standing in the door with a shy smile on his lips and a dirty rag in his hands that seemed to be wrapped around something woolly. The bundle whimpered and squirmed. Karl gently set it down and unwrapped it.

It was a puppy with wiry pitch-black fur. It wagged its tail and started to explore the room on unsteady paws.

"I couldn't bear your gloomy face any longer," said Karl. "So I went out to look for something that would make you happy again." He gestured at the little dog, which was awkwardly making its way toward Johann. "I found it with a shepherd not far from the village. It's a wolfhound. I know—it doesn't look like much now. But apparently it's going to grow to be an enormous beast. You could name him Satan." Karl winked. "It's a boy this time. I checked."

"Little Satan," said Johann softly, leaning down to the puppy and holding out his hand. The animal cautiously walked up to him and licked his palm. It tickled, and Johann couldn't help but smile.

"Thank you," he said to Karl. "I . . . I'll never forget this." He cleared his throat, which felt awfully dry. He realized that he hadn't uttered a word in days.

Karl shrugged, his eyes flickered, and he looked down. "To be honest, I don't like dogs very much. But I was looking for a gift for you, and the pup seemed like a sign from God."

Johann picked up the little creature and patted it. "A sign from God?"

"Don't you know, Master?" Karl said with a grin. "It's Christmas Eve. I wish you a merry Christmas!"

Outside, the snow continued to fall.

In hindsight, Johann thought that Karl's return had also been a sign from God. He had been only a second away from ending his life—on the day of Christ's birth. But the little puppy and Karl's return gave him renewed hope. Johann remembered how sad it had been to spend Christmas at the tower alone with Tonio while the church bells of the village tolled in the distance. This time, the two men were drinking sweet Rhenish wine and eating pickled eggs and ham. Even the pup got a few mouthfuls.

Johann liked the idea of calling him Little Satan, just as if the old Satan was living on inside this pup. And the young dog lived up to its name: it destroyed pillows, chewed on chair legs, and ruined the fabric of the valuable four-poster bed. It was clear he'd be a very vivacious dog. During the days following Christmas, he and Johann formed a strong bond. Little Satan would lie on his lap while Johann once more studied books for answers to his questions; the dog played around Johann's feet when he gazed at the stars from atop the tower. Johann now allowed Karl on the platform, too. Together they watched the constellations of the winter sky.

"The stars are much brighter in the winter," explained Johann on New Year's Eve. "Do you see the winter hexagon over there? Sirius, Pollux, and Procyon in

Canis Minor. If you look through the tube, you'll see more constellations behind it—constellations we would never see with our bare eyes."

Karl stared through the tube into the night sky; his jaw dropped with amazement. "There are so many," he muttered. "And there are more and more behind them. The sky is endless."

"Yes. It's enough to make you dizzy."

"Ha!" Karl cried out with surprise. "I saw a shooting star! My mother—God rest her soul—always used to say I could make a wish if I saw one."

"Well, then, make a wish," said Johann with a smile. "But don't tell me— that would bring misfortune."

Karl shot a quick look at him before shaking his head with a sigh. "What I wish for won't come true anyhow." He turned back to the tube. "The shooting star has already disappeared. I wonder where it is now?"

"I heard that some of them fall down onto the Earth. Sometimes people find remains of strange rocks. Apparently a shooting star fell to the ground somewhere in the Alsace years ago. The emperor himself owns pieces of it—so they say. As for the others . . ." He gave a shrug. "Perhaps they simply burn out."

"Couldn't it be possible that they return? Like the stars and constellations that travel across the sky?"

"The scholars say that shooting stars—like comets—are merely evaporations in the sky, like gases that sometimes come out of the ground and start to burn. Agrippa doesn't agree, but—" Suddenly Johann broke off. Karl's questions had set off something inside him; thoughts that had hitherto been as unyielding as rocks suddenly began to flow like a river.

That they return . . .

"I must check something," he said curtly. He rushed down the stairs to the bookshelf in the bottom chamber. He pulled out the books with Tonio's notes and feverishly leafed through them. Suddenly all the numbers and formulas that had posed such a riddle to him were beginning to make sense. Johann closed his eyes and pictured the starry winter sky he'd just seen from the rooftop. He tried to visualize a grid against it. When he opened his eyes again and studied the numbers, it became obvious. The numbers and letters were coordinates. They described positions, but apparently not of stars. Dates and times were written down, and even today's date was among them. The positions on the paper changed much faster than would be the case with stars. And finally Johann realized what Tonio's coded records were about. He sat down as the weight of the realization sank in.

They described the paths of comets.

Johann spent the next few hours bent over the books in deep concentration, completely unaware of anything else around him, while Little Satan played and frolicked at his feet. Karl had gone to bed.

Johann went through the numbers row by row. What Tonio had done here was incredible! Comets were considered messengers of ill omens, warnings of wars or epidemics, or signs of good fortune. But it was impossible to predict when they would come. Tonio, however, had written down countless paths of comets spanning decades. Most of them couldn't be seen with the naked eye, but it was Tonio's theory that they returned, just like the moon and stars, which also had their regular paths. But the time spans between each visit were so great that no one had ever noticed. Some comets came every seventy years, others every ten, thirty, or forty. Johann wondered whether the star of Bethlehem from the day of Jesus Christ's birth also returned in a certain rhythm.

With great excitement, Johann leafed back through the tattered pages to the beginning. The first entries were dated so far back that they couldn't be from Tonio—unless they were based on more-recent calculations. They went back centuries—back to the conquest of England by the Normans; back to the times of the Romans, when Vesuvius broke out in Italy and swallowed a whole city. And indeed, the star of Bethlehem was also recorded and even marked with red. Tonio had written the word *Messiah* above it. Johann couldn't remember ever seeing any records like the ones he was looking at. He took notes, compared entries to books on astronomy, and finally, when dawn was already breaking, he came across the one entry he'd been looking for all along. The secret of his day of birth.

There had been a comet in the heavens on the day he was born. And Tonio had given it a name.

Larua.

Johann shuddered. *Larua* was an Old Latin word for an evil spirit. A comet that brought evil. When Johann followed the rows of numbers with trembling fingers, he found that Larua returned in regular intervals, namely every sixteen years and eleven months—every seventeen years, roughly speaking.

Every seventeen years.

Johann counted. If he was born in April 1478, the comet must have next appeared in late March of 1495. A shiver ran down his spine. That was precisely when he'd been at Nördlingen and Tonio had given him the black potion. He remembered Tonio telling Poitou that they couldn't wait any longer because the stars were favorable. Johann continued to count with a thumping heart. He wrote down the date and stared at it.

End of February 1512.

That was in two months! Was that the explanation for the feeling of being watched all the time? The tense expectation that something was about to happen? But what?

Larua . . . evil spirit . . .

Johann remembered Margarethe talking about the boogeyman in Heidelberg. *He will return,* she'd said. *He will return and change the world.*

Johann had always assumed that she'd only imagined this boogeyman, or perhaps that it was some sort of scoundrel—a rogue in the woods.

But he'd never have guessed it was a comet.

He put down his quill and leaned back. His eyes hurt from all the reading. Could it be possible? And if so, what did he have to do with it all? What was the meaning of being born on Larua's day, on the day of the prophet, and why had Tonio given him the black potion on the day of the comet's return?

And most importantly, what was going to happen in two months' time?

Johann spent the following days and weeks pondering the matter and consulting the books. He found no further answers, but at least he knew now that he had to wait. Something was going to happen. His will to live had returned. During the day, he often went for walks with Little Satan and Karl and spent time atop the platform. He enjoyed the fresh air stimulating his thoughts and the easy conversations with Karl as they roamed through the woods. He still spotted crows in the branches of trees, and one time even a raven, but they no longer frightened him. They were envoys of an event that would inevitably arrive, and he would be prepared—for whatever might happen.

And then something really did happen. It was a day in early February, and Johann was standing atop the tower, wrapped in his warm coat and wearing his floppy hat, gazing at the mountains through the tube. An ice-cold wind was blowing hard into Johann's face, but there could be no doubt.

A horseman was approaching from the edge of the woods.

At first it was just a dark spot, as if a fly had landed on the front of the tube. But the spot was growing as it moved along the road. Then the figure turned off the main road and took the narrow dirt track that led to the tower.

Johann was still standing on the rooftop. Now he watched the rider's approach with his bare eyes. He was a tall man wearing a coat and a sparkling cuirass underneath. A longsword was fastened to a bag behind the saddle. The horse was black and powerful, no cheap nag but a destrier that probably cost as much as a whole tavern.

Now the man had spotted Johann. He raised his hand in greeting, galloped the last few yards up the hill, and climbed off his horse.

Then he waited.

Pensively, Johann climbed down the stairs. He didn't know who the stranger was or what had brought him to the tower. At least the man had come alone—so clearly this wasn't about arresting him and taking him to jail. Could he be a delegate from the bishop of Cologne? Johann doubted the power of the Cologne Inquisition reached this far. And the horseman looked not like a man of the church but more like a knight.

Could he be the first messenger of what was to come? A first sign of Larua's return?

"What's happened?" asked Karl, who was sitting at the chess table with a book. He looked up with confusion as Johann strode past him toward the door.

"We have a visitor. And it isn't anyone from the village."

He took one last deep breath before opening the door and stepping outside. The man awaiting him indeed seemed to be a knight. He was wearing armor, and now Johann also saw the black cross on his coat. It was the cross of the Teutonic Knights—an ancient order that had been formed in the times of the Crusades and that still wielded a lot of influence at courts throughout the empire. Johann was startled.

What in God's name could the Teutonic Knights want from him?

"Are you Doctor Johann Georg Faustus?" asked the knight, who looked like an old battle-axe with countless scars on his face. He was at least six feet tall and of impressive stature. Johann nodded and said nothing.

"I've been sent by Wolfgang von Eisenhofen," said the knight, his harness creaking in the cold. "The commander of the Nuremberg Teutonic Knights. He asks you to come to Nuremberg. An old friend is waiting for you there."

"An old friend?" Johann raised an eyebrow. "His name?"

"I'm not permitted to say. You will be told everything else at Nuremberg."

Johann watched the man closely, but his expression gave away nothing. An icy gust swept across the hilltop and rattled the shutters. Karl had come up next to Johann and was studying the knight with curiosity. Behind them, Little Satan growled almost like a grown dog sensing danger.

"And you think that just because some mysterious friend wants to see me I'm going to follow you all the way to Nuremberg?" asked Johann sharply. "You'll have to give me a little more."

The knight nodded. "Your friend anticipated you would say something along those lines. That's why I have another message for you."

"Which is?"

"He said he could tell you more about Gilles de Rais."

Johann felt as though he had been struck by lightning. He stood rooted to the spot as the name echoed through his head. The name that had been pursuing him for more than fifteen years.

Gilles de Rais.

Now he was certain that the man from Nuremberg was the first sign of Larua.

The game had begun.

It took quite a while for Johann to regain the power of speech. Finally he cleared his throat.

"Give us an hour," he told the knight. "We're coming with you."

24

THE KNIGHT'S NAME WAS EBERHART VON STREITHAGEN, BUT
they wouldn't learn much more about him in the following days. With Little
Satan in the wagon, they followed him to the north, having packed the laterna
magica, the stargazing tube, and some of the books on astrology. At first Karl had
tried to ask Johann about the reason for their hasty departure, but he'd received
only vague answers. Eventually, Johann said no more on the subject at all.

Johann had no idea what to expect in Nuremberg. The only people who
knew about his interest in Gilles de Rais were Agrippa and Conrad Celtis, but
the latter had died a few years ago, and Johann hadn't seen him since their last
conversation at the castle in Heidelberg. Who else might know about it? The
mysterious person knew that Gilles de Rais preoccupied Johann—and he'd sent
for Johann just when a very special comet was about to return after seventeen
years.

They traveled easily with Eberhart von Streithagen by their side. No high-
wayman was stupid enough to challenge an armored knight with a longsword
on a warhorse. And even the robber knights, who had multiplied in recent years,
steered clear of them. Streithagen didn't talk much, but from the little he told
them, they learned that the Nuremberg command of the Teutonic Knights was
one of the emperor's last strongholds inside the city. The free imperial city of
Nuremberg, which answered only to the emperor, had increasingly turned away
from its former benefactor in the last few years. But the Teutonic Knights stood
firmly behind the regent, and their grounds within the city were untouchable.

Johann smiled grimly. At least he'd be safe from persecution by the Cologne
Inquisition there. But what might the emperor or the Teutonic Knights want
from him? And who was this strange old friend?

After ten very quiet days of traveling, and with terribly sore behinds from getting bounced around on the box seat, they finally arrived in Nuremberg around noon.

From afar, they could see the mighty castle rising like a crown above the double ring of the wall, as well as churches and many neat half-timbered houses. Johann gazed at the massive city wall; it was three miles long and contained over eighty towers, and Johann was filled with awe. He had visited so many cities, and during the last year he and Karl had crisscrossed the country—from the east to the north to the west to the south—but Nuremberg was something special. Augsburg might have been the wealthiest city in the empire, and Cologne the holiest; Erfurt was the most studious and Hamburg the most adventurous, but Nuremberg was the most inventive of all, with the most intelligent, witty, and resourceful citizens. The city was both the soul and the head of the empire at once—the unofficial capital in a country that didn't have a fixed political center. Not long ago a Nuremberg man named Peter Henlein had built a spring-driven clock small enough that it could be carried in the pocket of a vest. A certain Martin Behaim had ordered the construction of a globe here that showed the world as a ball and not as a flat disc. Many other technical inventions also came from Nuremberg, and many outstanding artists called this city home, including the famous Albrecht Dürer—one more reason for Karl to be excited about Nuremberg.

"Maybe we could even visit Dürer," he said to Johann as they, along with many other rattling wagons, oxcarts, and feisty merchants, neared the city. "A handsome man, by the way, this Dürer. I saw a self-portrait of him once. He painted himself almost like our savior, with long hair and a beard. I'd love to know what the church thinks of it." Karl laughed and shook his head. "I doubt the pope would appreciate man turning himself into God."

It was February, and in all directions the fields were still covered in snow. The land was barren and the Pegnitz River impassable, but several of the major routes through the empire met at Nuremberg, making the city like a spider in the center of a web. The merchants and smaller tradesmen the group passed were dressed in heavy coats and shapeless woolen hoods.

"I mean, you're not just anybody," Karl continued, "so a visit shouldn't be—"

"I'm not just anybody but a wanted sodomite and devil worshipper, remember?" said Johann, cutting him off. "I don't really think the Cologne Inquisition has any power here, but knowing people and their love of gossip, the story might have made it to Nuremberg, beefed up into a real horror story."

"Indeed, the doctor doesn't have the best reputation in town," said Eberhart von Streithagen, riding beside them on his large destrier. "They talk about necromancy and quite a few instances of fraud. And many churchmen disliked your friendship with Agrippa. Therefore, we won't enter through the large Frauentor Gate but through Spittlertor Gate. It's close to our headquarters and not as heavily guarded."

They followed a narrower road through the icy fields until they came to the moat and one of the smaller but solid city gates, which was flanked by an equally solid tower. Displayed above the gate was the double-headed eagle, the emperor's coat of arms. When the guards saw the badge of the Teutonic Knights, they waved through Streithagen and the wagon he accompanied without questions.

It was lunchtime, and the whole city seemed to be on the move despite the cold. Peddlers with their crates rushed past them; they could hear the cries of market women from a nearby square, and the steady hammering from a smithy rang in Johann's ears. The churches of Saint Sebaldus and Saint Lorenz rose above the sea of houses and the maze of narrow lanes and alleys, and right in among this maze flowed the Pegnitz, dividing the city in roughly even halves. The air smelled of fires, braised cabbage, and horse dung. Johann thought about the horrific stench of Hamburg in the summer; by comparison, the smell of Nuremberg in the winter was almost pleasant.

From the city wall, Eberhart von Streithagen led them a short distance through the noisy crowds into the city. It wasn't long before they came to a walled-in complex holding several houses and a small church. A kind of roofed walkway bridged the lane to a second, larger church. Johann had climbed off the wagon and now led the nervous horse by the reins. His hand instinctively shot to his purse when a few pedestrians bumped into him.

"We used to be outside the city, but since the last wall extension we are like an island in a sea of disbelievers," explained Streithagen with a dark expression as they neared a gate in the wall. "The last island of the German emperor, it seems to me. Leave the wagon here. Someone will bring it in later."

He knocked on a heavy portal that had been reinforced with iron. A guard eyed them suspiciously through a hatch before letting them in. On the other side of the wall, they found themselves in a large green courtyard from which further gates led to stone houses, gardens, and even fields. In contrast to the noise outside, it was peacefully quiet within the walls, and even the air was better. Little Satan jumped out of Johann's arms and peed against one of the bushes.

"What a lush piece of land you have here," said Johann appreciatively. "The emperor was most generous."

"In return we run the largest hospital in the city, aside from the Hospital of the Holy Ghost on Pegnitz Island," replied Eberhart von Streithagen. "As I'm sure you're aware, our motto is *Help, defend, and heal.*"

"Probably more defending than helping and healing," whispered Karl to Johann. "The Teutonic Knights laid waste to the east of the empire once upon a time."

Johann shot him a glance of warning. He whistled Little Satan back, and they followed Streithagen through several guarded doors until they came to a large hall. Shields with various coats of arms decorated the walls, and mighty columns held up the elaborately carved oak ceiling. A round oak table stood in the center of the hall, and bent over a few documents at the table sat a haggard old knight with a bushy beard and a monk-like, half-bald head. His expression looked serious and grim. But when he looked up and noticed the visitors, a smile spread across his careworn face.

"My dear Eberhart!" he called out happily, rising to his feet. "The guards informed me of your arrival." His eyes turned to Johann and his smile vanished. "And this must be the famous Doctor Faustus—magician, astrologer, and necromancer by trade."

"Doctor is plenty," said Johann in reply and bowed his head. "Some titles are earned, while others are bestowed without one's asking for them." He tried to keep his tone neutral; he didn't know what game was being played here. He gestured at Karl. "This is my assistant, an itinerant scholar."

The older man gave Karl a brief nod without really looking at him, and then he continued to speak to Johann. "Well, Doctor, I only know you from a few hair-raising stories that I don't particularly like. The latest come from Cologne. But it would seem there are people who think very highly of you." He motioned for his guests to take a seat at the large table, which was covered in parchment scrolls and papers. Little Satan crawled under the table and started to gnaw on one of its legs.

"My name is Wolfgang von Eisenhofen, and I am the commander here," the older man continued. "I have asked you to Nuremberg because . . . well, because we have a problem. And an old friend of yours reckoned you were the only man in the empire who might be able to solve this problem."

"We shall see," replied Johann with a shrug, trying not to let his unrest show. "It would be kind if I were allowed to meet this old friend. I traveled a long way for him, after all. Perhaps I won't even recognize him."

"You're right. It is possible he . . . changed somewhat since you last met. He told me it was a while ago that you last saw each other." With a smile, the commander turned to Knight Eberhart, who had been waiting behind them. "Very well—bring him in."

Eberhart von Streithagen walked to the double doors on the opposite end of the hall and opened them. A hunched figure had been waiting on the other side.

Johann winced and felt the blood drain from his face.

"What in God's name—" he burst out.

Behind the door stood Valentin.

Johann's former friend from Heidelberg was almost completely bald. He looked like a wrinkly old man, much older than the thirty years he must be by now. He looked as though life had sucked him dry and tossed him aside.

Only Valentin's eyes still looked as intelligent and alert as they used to. They scrutinized Johann with a mixture of disgust, curiosity, and . . .

Affection . . . Could it be true?

Johann still sat at the table, unable to move. Was he dreaming? Last time he saw Valentin, his friend was being taken to the Inquisition at Worms inside a prison cell. That had been almost fifteen years ago. Back then, Valentin was most likely going to be charged with satanism—a crime that was invariably punished with death by fire. And now here he was, approaching Johann. Changed, perhaps, but alive.

Valentin's posture was strangely bent, like a hunchback; scars disfigured his face, and his right arm hung down limply. But then he raised the hand in greeting. It was bent like a claw and missing two fingers.

"Thumbscrews are a nasty instrument," Valentin said and waved the hand as if it were a scrap of meat. His voice sounded dry and hoarse—burnt, almost. "Nearly as bad as the glowing pincers, the smoldering pokers, and the rack they use to break your back very slowly."

"You . . . you're alive . . . ," whispered Johann.

"Well, part of me." Valentin shrugged, whereby one shoulder went higher than the other. "They tortured me for three weeks, twice a day, morning and afternoon. But I stayed strong. I had no idea what hidden strengths lay inside me." He gave a lopsided grin, and Johann saw that two of his front teeth were missing. "It was probably my hatred for you that kept me alive and made me deny everything. In the end they had to let me go. That's the beauty of torture: if you make it through without confessing, you're free sooner or later." He flinched with pain as he came closer to the table with dragging steps. "But not a day goes by when my back and my hand don't remind me of that time."

"I guess it wouldn't help if I said how sorry I was," said Johann.

"No, it wouldn't." Valentin gave a dry laugh. "But do you know what, old friend? Hatred doesn't make for good company. Just like love, it can consume a man. And so I buried my hatred. And I hope it will never rise from its grave again."

"It was *you* who asked me to come here?" said Johann with a shake of his head. "How in God's name did you find me?"

Valentin hesitated briefly. "One time in Heidelberg you told me about a tower near Füssen, remember? You said you spent a winter there once. When I heard about your trouble in Cologne, I thought the tower might be a good place to hide. And so I asked the commander to search for you."

Johann ran his hand through his hair, his fingers trembling slightly. He could hardly believe that his old friend was standing in front of him—alive. Evidently, he had been mistaken at the tower when he thought the knight was the first sign of the comet.

"I kept myself above water as a traveling scribe for a while, here and there, always on the move," Valentin continued after he sat down with them. "Three years ago, the Teutonic Knights offered me a permanent position here. We were happy here."

"We?" Johann frowned. "Who?"

"I guess you're wondering how I know about your interest in Gilles de Rais," said Valentin, ignoring Johann's question. "I must admit, the thought of you never quite left me in peace, Faustus. Like a flea that bites and itches. Even years later, when you were roaming the country as the famous Doctor Johann Georg Faustus, I still wanted to know what it is that drives you. Your hunger for knowledge that was never satiated no matter how many books you read, your constant musing. In your dreams in Heidelberg you often whispered the name Gilles de Rais. Sometimes you even screamed it. You used to scream a lot." Valentin smiled sadly. "You learn a lot from sharing a room with someone. A few years after my release I had the opportunity to speak with the great Conrad Celtis once more. It was shortly before his death. The name Gilles de Rais never ceased to fascinate him, either. He told me never to say that name out loud again."

"The name is mere noise and smoke," replied Johann weakly.

"Is it?" Valentin smirked. "In any case, Celtis told me that it was the same for you. I knew the name would bring you to Nuremberg. If I'd told Eberhart von Streithagen to give my own name, your bad conscience might have stopped you from coming. Therefore I decided on Gilles de Rais—and voilà, here you are." He hesitated. "I'm afraid Celtis didn't tell me everything about that villain back then. But a scribe has plenty of time to look around old monastery libraries, and over the years I've discovered a few things."

"So you know about the children," whispered Johann. Now he noticed his own trembling fingers.

"Yes, I know." Valentin nodded. "And that is also the reason you're here."

"Excuse me," said Karl, clearing his throat. "I hate to disturb two old friends, but maybe it's about time someone explained—"

Severe looks from both Valentin and Johann cut him off.

"Gilles de Rais was a knight," said Wolfgang von Eisenhofen. "Not a Teutonic Knight, or a templar, or a knight of Saint John, but still a man who at some point lived according to the laws of chivalry and Christian virtue. He fought against a dozen knights during the liberation of Orléans and won, and he was a brave companion to the famous Joan of Arc—allegedly they were something like friends. The French king even made him a marshal of France. All the worse, what he did later." The old man bit his lip and made the sign of the cross.

"But that's hardly the reason I'm here, is it?" asked Johann with growing irritation. "Just to hear what crimes that damned Gilles de Rais committed years ago? Conrad Celtis already told me."

"No." Valentin shook his head. "You're here because it looks as if Gilles de Rais has returned."

Johann froze. The hairs on the back of his neck stood on end as if an evil beast had entered the hall.

Had he heard right?

Gilles de Rais has returned . . .

"How can you say that—" he started.

"Of course, he hasn't actually returned." Valentin gestured dismissively. "I know the monster has been dead for seventy years. But his atrocities are happening again, now, here at Nuremberg. And no one knows who might be behind them."

Wolfgang von Eisenhofen pushed a document toward Johann. About two dozen names were written on the paper. "These are the names of Nuremberg children who have gone missing in the last few months," explained the commander with a shaking voice. "Some are the children of patricians, while others are the children of common citizens and even of day laborers. None of the children was older than ten. Some of them were later found dead in the alleys, tossed aside like trash. Their throats were slit. They had been bled dry. There wasn't a single drop of blood left inside them, and a dried toad was placed in their open mouths. Gilles de Rais used to murder children in a similar manner. He slit them open, bathed in their blood, and drank it. A strange coincidence, don't you think?"

"My God, how awful!" exclaimed Karl. "How can a person do such a thing?"

"There are those who say Gilles de Rais wasn't a person," said Valentin. "Three words were written beside each body—in blood." His rough voice echoed through the vaulted room. "*Homo Deus est*. Do you know them, Johann?"

Johann felt like someone had rammed a cudgel right into his stomach.

Homo Deus est . . . Man is God . . .

"Yes, I know them," he whispered.

Valentin eyed him closely. "It would seem you know more than I thought. I was right to send for you."

"I think very highly of Master Brander. He has been working for us as a scribe for a long while now. He is clever and well read, and it was his idea to find you," said Wolfgang von Eisenhofen, squeezing Valentin's good hand. "Even though he probably has his own reasons, too," he added ominously. "He reckoned you were the only one who might be able to shed light on those horrific cases. The mood in the city is worsening by the day, and the fear is almost tangible. It feels as if we are all sitting atop a powder keg that might explode at any moment."

"I still don't understand what I can do for you," said Johann. "I'm just an itinerant doctor, a stranger in Nuremberg—"

"If what your old friend says is true, you're not just any doctor but one of the most intelligent men in the empire, and one of the shrewdest." Eisenhofen gave him a sharp look. "And you're a magician. Children who've been bled, dried toads, words written in blood . . . Clearly, we are dealing with black magic." The commander paused, choosing his next words very carefully. "So, God help us, I fear only a magician can help us now. The city—the entire empire, even—is at stake! If word gets around that the devil is on the loose in Nuremberg, the emperor's power might become seriously threatened. And he has his hands full holding both the French and the Turks at bay. Yes, we need magic!"

"Magic? You don't believe that yourself," snarled Johann, shaking his head. "I may be a scholar with unusual methods, an astrologer, healer, and chiromancer. But I'm certainly not a magician who can stand up to the devil like Archangel Michael."

"Aren't you calling yourself a magician?" asked Eisenhofen sharply.

Johann sighed. "Only to impress the simple folk. A commander and nobleman should really know better."

"Well, if you prefer, I can hand you over to my knights, who will take you and your assistant to Cologne. The reward for your capture is several hundred guilders now—did you know that?"

"That's blackmail!" Johann jumped up and slammed his fist on the table. "Has the Order of Teutonic Knights sunk this low? Blackmail?"

"Watch your tongue, Doctor!" Eisenhofen also stood up, his eyes flashing angrily. Behind the commander, Eberhart von Streithagen took a step forward, his hand on the pommel of his sword. Below the table, Little Satan growled and bared his small, sharp teeth.

"Perhaps it's better if I speak with my friend alone for a moment," Valentin said and raised his arms in a placating gesture. "A walk in the fresh air would do us both good."

Eisenhofen hesitated, but then he nodded. He turned to Valentin. "Go into the garden and tell him the rest—everything. It might change his mind. I'm expecting an answer when the bells strike one o'clock." He raised a finger and gave Johann a stern look. "And don't forget, Herr Magician: it's only a week's ride to Cologne."

A short while later, Johann and Valentin were alone in a large, tidy garden that reached from behind the knights' hall to the western wall. Paths led in a star-shaped pattern past bushes, withered roses, and pruned young fruit trees. Little Satan ran about happily, lifting his leg against a bush occasionally. The plants and trees were covered in a thin layer of frost. Their footsteps made a crunching sound as the two former friends walked along the narrow paths. They said nothing for a long while, each lost in his own memories. Eventually Johann stopped.

"Believe me, Valentin, if I could turn back time—"

"Not even God can do that." Valentin stared straight ahead. "It took me a long time to understand. But now I know that love can sometimes be destructive."

"My love for Margarethe, you mean?" asked Johann quietly.

"Do you still love her?" Valentin asked and turned toward him.

Johann hesitated. "She . . . she visits me in my dreams. But unlike years ago, they aren't happy dreams."

Valentin nodded slowly. "I understand why you can't forget her. I would have loved to paint her." With a grimace of pain, he lifted up his crippled right hand. "I took a long time to learn to draw with my left. I'm not too bad at it now."

"You still draw?"

Valentin smiled, looking at the garden, at the trees and bushes and the stone benches that would make lovely places to rest awhile in spring and summer. "I spend a lot of time here in the garden. The light is excellent." He tilted his head and studied Johann. "Perhaps I should draw you, too. You're famous now, after all."

"Why did you want to speak with me alone?" asked Johann. "The commander said you ought to tell me everything. What did he mean?"

Valentin's face darkened. "I'm sure you wonder why I asked the commander to have you of all people brought here. It is true that I believe you're the only one who might be able to help. And you owe me a favor."

Johann nodded. "Any favor in the world. I would do anything to atone for my guilt."

"Then help me to free a child."

"A child?" Johann was confused. He thought perhaps he'd misheard. "How do you mean?"

Valentin swallowed hard. "Now we come to the real reason you're here. The reason Eisenhofen hasn't told you about."

He gestured for Johann to sit on a bench in the garden's center. Blackbirds were singing all around them, and sparrows argued in the branches. It seemed like spring had already arrived here, while outside the walls winter still reigned.

"Eisenhofen said that I had my own reasons for asking you to Nuremberg," said Valentin bitterly. "And it is true. There is a girl I've grown very fond of. A child from the gutter whom I took in a few years ago. I named her Greta."

"Greta?" whispered Johann. "You named her after—"

"It seemed appropriate," said Valentin gruffly. "Maybe because I love the girl just as much as you used to love Margarethe. But not as a man. I love Gretchen—that's my nickname for her—like a father loves his child. I raised her, and she's just turned fourteen. Don't they say the love for one's children is the most powerful of all? She calls me uncle. She has no one else in this world, and . . ." He paused. "And she is in grave danger."

"What do you mean?"

"She has never enjoyed a particularly good reputation in town. Since we've moved in at the command, she's been known as a bit of a tramp, and she's even stolen the odd apple or egg at the market. When they found her near one of the dead children by the Pegnitz one night a few weeks ago, the authorities made short shrift of her. They"—Valentin's voice trembled—"they put her in Loch Prison. Not least because they found something from the devil on her—a ram's horn with some sort of strange symbols. Someone must have slipped it in her pocket."

"And now the authorities believe the child has something to do with those devilish murders?" asked Johann with disbelief.

"Don't you get it?" His old friend fought back tears. "They are trying to pin something on my Gretchen! They want her to confess that she has been with Satan and want her to tell them what she knows about the murders. But she doesn't know anything! She's still a child! They just . . . they just need a scapegoat." Valentin squeezed Johann's hand with his uninjured left. "That is the real reason I wanted you to come to Nuremberg, Johann Georg Faustus. Please help me get my Greta out of jail!"

Johann bit his lip. So that was why he was here. Not because of some comet, not to find answers to his questions, but because of a child from the gutter. Or, to be more precise, to help a friend. The only friend he'd ever had.

To atone for my guilt, he thought.

"How long?" he asked.

Valentin wiped the tears from his scarred face. "What do you mean?"

"How long until they put her on trial, damn it?"

"I . . . I don't know. She's been in jail for nearly a month. Maybe they forgot about her, or maybe they've started with the torture by now. She's only fourteen, but I heard that even with younger children . . . I know what it's like. I know the pain." Tears streamed down Valentin's cheeks now, and he trembled all over. "I told the guards that Greta is a distant niece of mine, and so—with the help of the commander—I'm allowed to visit her every few days. Until now Eisenhofen has been able to prevent the worst from happening to her. He doesn't believe she is guilty of anything. But even the power of the Teutonic Knights is limited. We can't waste any more time!"

Johann ran his hands through his hair. "And what do you imagine I can do about it? I've heard about the Loch Prison—it's heavily fortified and lies deep below the city hall. I'd gladly do anything for you, but this is impossible!"

"There must be a way!"

Johann gave a desperate laugh. "Do you want me to make a demon appear with the laterna magica to chase the guards away? That might work in a small backwater, but not here."

Valentin eyed him sharply. "So you have a laterna again? I'd heard something along those lines. My laterna . . ." He closed his eyes for a moment. "No, it probably won't work with the laterna magica. But perhaps we'll think of something else." He leaned forward. "I've got a suggestion for you, Johann. Tomorrow I'm allowed to visit Gretchen again, and I want you to come with me. If you can take a look at the prison, we might come up with an idea. I will tell them that you're a medical expert and I want you to examine her. The commander will put in a good word."

"I'll see what I can do." Johann sighed and took Valentin by the hands. For a moment they were the old friends they used to be in Heidelberg. "But I can't promise anything. Perhaps—"

He broke off when they heard footsteps on the gravel. Then the bell of the order's church tolled once, and Eberhart von Streithagen appeared.

"The commander wishes to know how you have decided, Herr Doctor," he said.

Johann exchanged a glance with Valentin.

"I will try to help you," he replied at last. "With or without magic."

～

Deep down below the city, not far from the Teutonic Knights' gardens, something rumbled.

A monotonous humming followed, echoing against the walls of the corridors until it sounded like the howling of a hundred hungry wolves. In the ancient vaults below, a man wearing a black robe stood in front of a copper basin, his hands spread far apart, his head leaning back, as if he was worshipping something lurking much deeper still below. The man's robe was covered in old symbols, and it was woven from dried sinews and tiny veins that had been cut from young bodies with sharp knives. The humming grew louder, and the man dropped something slippery into the dark waters of the basin, causing the surface to ripple.

The man smiled.

Quite a peculiar juice is blood.

He was about to continue with his invocation when a cawing disturbed his litany. The man looked up with irritation.

"Baphomet, Azazel, Belial, stop it! Or I'm going to drown you in this basin!"

The two crows and the raven stared at their master from small, nasty eyes. They shuffled back and forth excitedly on the perch in their cage, like children who can no longer hold still. The man smiled.

"You're hungry, aren't you? Not long now."

The master reached into a bag, pulled out another slippery scrap, and tossed it to the birds.

They hacked into it, tearing the scrap apart with their sharp beaks and devouring the lumps of meat.

They were surprisingly tender.

25

VALENTIN WAS ALREADY WAITING IN THE GARDEN FOR Johann shortly after sunrise. He looked like he hadn't slept much; his scarred face was pale and unshaven, and dark shadows lay beneath his eyes. He got up from the bench he'd been sitting on as soon as he spotted Johann, and limped toward him.

"Good news from the commander! Eisenhofen managed to arrange for you to accompany me as a physician. Gretchen kind of belongs to the command staff, after all, and Eisenhofen has a right to know how she is doing."

"I still can't believe the Nuremberg authorities want to put a fourteen-year-old girl on trial for witchcraft. That's ludicrous!"

"She wouldn't be the first," replied Valentin with a sigh. "But thankfully it hasn't gone that far yet. Still—the long imprisonment is getting to her. Gretchen is such a lively, inquisitive child, you know. My heart breaks every time I think about her sitting down there in the prison cell, all alone . . ." Valentin's voice trembled.

"You must love her very much," said Johann sympathetically.

"There's something about her . . . something familiar." Valentin hesitated. "You'll meet her yourself soon."

They walked out the gate and headed north toward the Pegnitz. Valentin was carrying a small leather pouch containing a few treats for the girl, and Johann had brought a bag with medical instruments. The lanes were still quiet; only the hammering from the blacksmiths at the armory near the old city moat echoed through the city. A group of nuns walked toward the Klara nunnery, their lips moving in silent prayer. Up at the castle, last night's watch fires still burned, bathing the sandstone in a warm light.

Johann hadn't slept much, either. The commander had given him permission to set up his stargazing tube in the tower of Saint Jakob's Church. He'd spent hours searching the night sky for any sign of the approaching comet, but without any luck. Maybe he was mistaken and there was no connection between him and Larua at all? His trip to Nuremberg seemed to be for different reasons altogether.

They walked across a stone bridge that separated the Lorenz quarter from the wealthier Sebaldus quarter, where merchants had built their houses as close to the main square as possible. This square, which was just beginning to grow busy, was flanked on one side by another large church with an elaborately adorned facade. There also was a fountain like no other Johann had seen in the empire, with a tall, thin tower of sculptures in its center.

"There is something else you should know," said Valentin slowly as they crossed the large square. "Last night another child went missing. The eight-year-old son of a bailiff from the castle. The boy was playing in a dry part of the moat. When his mother went looking for him a few moments later, he was gone. It truly hearkens to the time in France when that malicious French knight was at large." Valentin bit his lip. "I'm afraid our time is running out. The people are becoming more and more nervous—they want an explanation. It won't be long before they torture Greta."

North of the fountain stood the city hall, a gloomy, Gothic building that seemed to be from a different era. The entrance to the infamous Loch Prison lay at its rear.

Johann was glad that he had left Little Satan with Karl. The dog was eating as if he had been starved for weeks, and it was truly amazing how fast he grew. He was already as big as a full-grown poodle, and he wasn't even ten weeks old yet. Little Satan's discipline wasn't coming along quite as fast as his size, however; last night he'd defecated inside the knights' hall, much to Eisenhofen's disgust. Johann didn't want to imagine what they'd do to him and the dog should he do the same inside the city hall.

In front of a small but solid gate, two guards armed with halberds and pikes watched the two arrivals with surly, tired expressions. With his crippled hand, Valentin pulled out a folded document and handed it to one of the men. The man studied the seal of the Teutonic Knights for a long while. Clearly, he couldn't read but didn't want to admit to it.

"Valentin Brander from the command," said Valentin after a while. He gestured at Johann. "This is a physician charged with the task of examining my niece."

"The cripple and the devil's girl." The guard grinned and scratched his unkempt beard. "Best the doctor examine the wench for witches' marks, too. I bet he'll find some."

"That is just what I am here for," replied Johann with the imperious voice of a physician who still has many other patients to visit that day. "So better let us in. Promptly, if you will."

Grumbling, the guards stepped aside, and Johann and Valentin entered a paved courtyard. To the left was another guarded door, and then stairs led them down below. After a third, ironclad door, they finally stood in the antechamber to the prison. Heavily smoking torches barely managed to light up the low, vaulted room. A cold breeze swept up from a well in the center of the chamber. It smelled of smoke, watery cabbage soup, and stale air. More guards were posted here.

We'll never get in here undetected, thought Johann. *Not with all the magic in the world.*

The prison keeper, a stooped, unwashed fellow who was responsible for the welfare and feeding of the prisoners, shuffled toward them and cast a bored glance inside their bags.

"They told me you were coming," he grumbled. "Not many prisoners get visited by two gentlemen with treats at once. First the lantern and now ham and cheese. Must have cost you a fortune. My food ain't good enough for the high-class lady, is that it?"

"The girl is my niece," replied Valentin curtly. "Please direct any further questions to the Order of Teutonic Knights."

The prison keeper waved dismissively and led them down a narrow corridor past several cell doors. Johann could hear moaning from behind some of the doors. He caught a few glimpses through the windows in the cell doors and saw that the pitiful creatures on the other side were chained to bench seats or had their hands and feet locked in wooden blocks. Symbols above the doors indicated the nature of the crime the inmate was accused of: a red rooster for an arsonist, a black cat for a traitor, and so on. In regular intervals, they had to pass through more locked doors, and each time the keeper had to find the corresponding key on a large ring.

Johann looked over at Valentin, who was impatiently waiting for them to go on. He had to see the hopelessness of their endeavor—they would never get anyone out of here. Not out of a prison as heavily secured as this one. But Valentin merely gave him a tired smile, his eyes flickering with something that bordered on obsession.

Their progress was slow. Every few yards there were barred holes just below the ceiling of the narrow corridor, allowing in a few rays of morning sun and the noise from the market square. Outside, the day was starting, but inside this prison, it was forever dusk.

Finally they stopped outside a cell door almost at the end of the corridor. An upside-down pentagram had been drawn above the door—a sign for witches, Johann guessed. The prison keeper pulled out the heavy key ring one last time and unlocked the door.

"Half an hour," he said. "Not a minute longer."

The door swung open, and Johann froze.

The cell was entirely clad in timber, which was worm-eaten and covered in stains that looked like dried blood or excrement. There was a cot, as well as a small bench seat and a bucket to relieve oneself with a board on top that doubled as a table.

A sooty lantern hung from the ceiling and dispersed a little light.

A girl was sitting on the bench with her legs crossed, engrossed in a string game. She was wearing a dirty dress but no shoes, and her toes were blue with cold. Wrapped around her fingers was a thin string, which she twisted and spun into various patterns. When the two men entered, she lifted her face and looked straight at Johann.

That's impossible! he thought. *My God! How on earth . . . ?*

"Uncle Valentin!" cried the girl happily, jumping off the bench. "You're here, finally! I've been waiting for so long!"

"My little girl, let me give you a hug!" Valentin put down his pouch and wrapped his arms around Greta.

The girl closed her eyes with happiness. "Don't leave again," she whispered. "Ever."

In the dim light of the cell, the two of them merged into one single body, and for a while all that Johann heard was the moaning of the other prisoners.

Meanwhile, he studied Greta's face. It was quite dark in the cell, but still—there could be no doubt. The freckles, the soft mouth that always seemed to smile a little, the pronounced cheekbones, the flaxen hair . . . only the eyes were different. Black and mysterious like ponds in the forest.

His eyes.

Johann felt as though he were paralyzed. *Impossible,* he thought. *This must be a dream . . .*

Finally, Greta freed herself from Valentin's embrace and looked at Johann.

"Who is that?" she asked with curiosity.

"An old friend," replied Valentin with a smile. He eyed Johann closely, expectantly. "We were very close once. We were scholars in Heidelberg together."

"What are scholars?" asked Greta.

"Oh, young lads who drink too much wine and beer and think that they're immortal," replied Valentin with a wink. Then he turned to Johann. "That's right, isn't it? Immortal."

Johann didn't reply. He was still staring at Greta. She was just on the brink between girlhood and womanhood. Her stature was tall and athletic, and tiny breasts were showing beneath the dress, but her face was still childlike. Johann remembered the summer days in Knittlingen, playing in the hay, hide-and-seek in the woods. It could only be coincidence—there was no other possibility. Still, the resemblance was astonishing. Now he understood what Valentin had meant.

There's something about her . . . something familiar . . .

Greta appeared to have lost interest in Johann again.

"Did you bring me something?" she asked Valentin excitedly.

"What do you think?" Valentin held out the pouch with his crippled, pincer-like hand. "See for yourself."

Greta immediately started to rummage through the pouch. With a cry of delight she pulled out a chunk of cheese, half a loaf of bread, and a few shriveled apples. She stuffed her mouth with bread and pushed in the cheese after.

"Don't eat so fast, child," said Valentin. "You'll only make yourself sick."

The two men watched in silence as the girl ate. She was frightfully skinny, and her face and arms were dirty and covered in fleabites and scabs, but Johann couldn't see any serious injuries. Evidently the hangman hadn't started the torture yet. Johann was amazed at how well the girl looked, given the circumstances. It must be awful for her, alone in the cell at night, listening to the screams of other inmates and having not one person to talk to, apart from the hunchbacked keeper and a few surly guards. It would seem Greta possessed an inner strength that many adults lacked.

When Greta was finished eating, Valentin cleared his throat. "I brought you something else, too. I thought you could use it when you feel lonely. I know you're probably too old now, but still . . ."

From under his coat he pulled a tattered doll with matted, woolen hair and button eyes, one of which was dangling by a thin thread. Greta cried out with joy and squeezed the doll to her chest.

"My little Barbara," she whispered. "Did you miss me? I know, I didn't take good care of you in the last few years. I'm sorry." She stroked the doll, and suddenly she seemed much younger than her fourteen years.

"My friend is a physician," said Valentin. "He would like to examine you so we know how you are doing. His name is Johann."

"Hello, Greta." Johann thought his voice sounded as if it weren't his own. He tried to smile encouragingly. "May I . . . may I take a closer look at you?"

Greta pressed her lips together and gave him a frightened look. "That's what the keeper said, too," she whispered. "I don't like it."

Johann raised his hands. "I won't hurt you. I promise. I'm a physician. And I can do magic," he added mysteriously.

Greta looked at him with surprise. "Magic?"

Johann nodded. "Give me the doll. I'll show you."

Greta hesitated and looked at Valentin, who gave her a nod. Then she handed the doll to Johann. "But don't hurt her."

The idea had come spontaneously to Johann. He remembered well how much he'd loved magicians and jugglers as a little boy. Now he sat Barbara on his lap and held her little hands.

"Good day, little Barbara," he said.

"Good day, Johann," said the doll.

"I hear Greta hasn't been playing with you lately. What have you been up to, all alone?"

"Oh, I sneaked into the kitchen at the command and stole a pot of honey," the doll replied in a high-pitched voice. "And then I painted the commander's beard with it while he was sleeping. Such fun!"

The doll clapped her hands and Greta's jaw dropped with amazement. She looked up at Johann and then back at Barbara on his lap. Johann stifled a smile. He had taught himself ventriloquy all those years ago so that the archangel could speak to Margarethe—for purely selfish reasons, as he'd realized later. Now he used the trick to cheer up a girl in a prison cell.

"I would like to sing a song for Greta," said the doll. "Maybe she can join in." Johann hummed a tune in the high-pitched voice, slowly at first, then steadier and louder until the words came back to him.

"Growing in our garden are parsley and thyme." Barbara the doll clapped her small, tattered hands to the beat. *"Our Gretchen is the bride, she's looking so—"* Johann broke off. Without really thinking about it, he had chosen the song Margarethe always used to sing. The same song she'd hummed when the guards had arrested her inside the cave at Heiligenberg Mountain.

"Don't stop!" pleaded Greta. "Keep singing!"

"Do you know what, little Barbara?" said Johann to the doll, placing her on the bed beside Greta. "I think I might show you what I can do with apples."

He took the apples from the bag and started to juggle. Both Greta and Valentin watched him with amazement.

"You see five apples," said Johann, using the mysterious and seductive voice of jugglers and tricksters. "Hocus, pocus, locus—now there are just four!" One of the apples had suddenly vanished. "Hocus, pocus, three black cats—now there are just three!" Then three apples became two, and eventually Johann was only holding one last apple in his hand.

"You see," he told Greta. "You can juggle apples, you can make apples disappear, and . . . you can eat them." With the last words, he took a bite from the apple.

"Hey, that's my apple!" called out Greta and laughed.

Johann startled. Greta was laughing! The sound was as out of place inside this prison cell as the singing of angels.

And the laughter was so familiar.

"You can keep the apple if you let me examine you," replied Johann hesitantly.

Greta agreed, and Johann came closer. He examined her limbs for broken bones, cleaned the fleabites, and treated her frostbite with an ointment. Eventually he tore his overcoat to shreds and wrapped them around her feet. His hands trembled, and it wasn't because of the cold. Greta's laughter had removed any remaining doubts.

It was a laughter he hadn't heard for many years.

"Will you come back?" asked Greta with her mouth full. She was devouring her third apple since Johann had made the fruit reappear. "You must come back and do magic for me. Please!"

"I . . . I'm going to try," said Johann haltingly. He looked away when he felt his eyes well up. "And I'll bring you shoes next time."

"You can examine my little Barbara, too," said Greta. "I think one of her eyes is sick."

Johann nodded. "I will. I—"

Someone knocked on the door, and the gruff voice of the prison keeper rang out. "Half an hour is up! Come out now or you'll have to stay for good."

"I'll be back, I promise," said Johann again. He stood up, and he and Valentin walked out of the cell. He turned to catch one last glimpse of Greta waving at him, her eyes full of silent grief and hope at once.

"Come back," she said quietly.

Then the door slammed shut.

They didn't say a word as they walked the long way back out of the prison. When they stepped out into the morning sunshine in front of the city hall, Johann turned to Valentin.

"You . . . ," he said in a shaking voice. "You—"

"Let's go sit down at a tavern," said Valentin quickly. "And I'll explain."

They hurried across the square, where several grocers had set up their stalls in the meantime. There was salted meat for sale, as well as venison, eggs, poultry, and geese gaggling away in their cages. But Johann registered none of it. His whole life had been turned upside down by what had just happened in the prison cell.

They entered one of the cheaper taverns in an alley leading away from the main square and chose a quiet table in an alcove. Once a buxom serving maid had brought them two mugs of mulled wine, Valentin finally started to talk.

"Yes," he said in a low voice. "Margarethe's daughter. *Your* daughter. Did you see her eyes? They are your eyes, Johann Faustus. There can't be any doubt."

Johann sat as if he had turned to stone; all the noise around him, the loud conversations of the other people, the chinking of crockery—it all sounded like it came from behind a thick wall.

My daughter.

But how was that possible? Margarethe had hanged herself at the jail in Heidelberg—Valentin had said so himself. Even if she had been pregnant, there could have been no child, because she died.

Johann looked at Valentin, who was clutching the hot mug with his crippled hands, which were red from the cold. He kept his head low, avoiding Johann's eyes.

"Margarethe never hanged herself," whispered Johann. "You . . . you lied to me."

"Just like you lied to me for weeks and months." Valentin sighed. "I was so full of hatred for you, Johann. I wanted to hurt you where it hurt the most. And so I told you Margarethe was dead, when in reality she had been taken away shortly before me. I saw her again in Worms; she was in the cell next to mine. Twice a day when they dragged me to the torture chamber I saw her briefly, and her beauty helped me bear the pain." He blew on his mulled wine and took a sip. "During the nights, we had long whispered conversations. I learned much about you, Faustus. About little Johann in Knittlingen and his dreams and juggling tricks. I see you still know them." Valentin smiled. "You must have been a nice boy once."

"But Margarethe . . ." Johann's voice failed him. "Why . . . ?"

"Why she was spared? During her very first interrogation in Worms they found out that she was with child." Valentin gave a sad laugh. "She had known for a while, and she knew whose child it was. There could be no one else, of course—she was a nun, and you were the only man she saw." His finger traced an invisible line on the tabletop as if he was drawing her face. The sun stood above the rooftops by now and shone through the tavern windows.

"They spared her until the child was born," continued Valentin. "That's the law. Even torture has its rules, and they are recorded in the Bamberg book on the punishment of capital crimes. Shortly before I was released, Margarethe made me promise that I would care for the child when she was no more."

"And?"

"As soon as the child was born, Margarethe confessed to being in league with the devil. But the hangman took pity on her and throttled her with the garrote before the flames consumed her. She didn't suffer much."

Valentin gazed into the distance again. Men laughed, mugs clanked. The atmosphere was so peaceful that Johann felt like screaming out loud. He wanted to wail and cry, but no tears came. The last time he cried was a long time ago. It had been in Heidelberg when he'd learned of Margarethe's death.

Now she had actually died.

And been reborn at the same time.

"Margarethe seemed like she wasn't really in this world anymore during the last few weeks of her life," said Valentin. "She was convinced to the last that the devil would return to earth. She always spoke about the boogeyman she'd seen in the woods. And about Archangel Michael, who had abandoned her and all of us."

Johann closed his eyes.

The boogeyman . . . Archangel Michael.

Would this horror never end? No matter where he went, evil always got there first and waited for him.

Because you carry it within you . . .

"Greta isn't from the gutter," explained Valentin with a sigh. "I found her in an orphanage in Worms. It wasn't hard to get her out of there. No one likes to raise the child of a witch. I never told her who her mother was, and she knows nothing about her father. She thinks that her mother died while giving birth and that I'm a distant relative." He smiled, and for a moment Valentin looked like the zealous young student from their Heidelberg days. "She calls me Uncle Valentin. Isn't that beautiful? We had wonderful times together, even though she's been a little rascal at times since we took up residence at the command. She's stubborn and has an inclination for tricks and fibs. In that regard she takes after you."

Johann sat on the bench at the tavern and tried hard to remain calm. So many unexpected things had happened in the last hour. If Valentin was right, his daughter was in danger of suffering the same fate as her mother. He had to focus and find a solution. All his intelligence and all his knowledge were for nothing if he couldn't protect his daughter now.

The child he didn't even know.

26

IN THE FOLLOWING DAYS, JOHANN DESPERATELY TRIED TO figure out a way to get Greta out of Loch Prison. He felt like he was trying to square a circle—the legendary problem even the great Archimedes failed to solve.

He would often sit with Valentin and Karl at the command in the evenings. They met in the order's library, a bare room inside the church, rarely used by the knights. Valentin spent most of his time here. The only furniture was a wobbly table and a few shabby stools, but there were so many books and scrolls on the shelves along the walls that some had fallen off. More books were piled on the table. Wax from the candles of a candelabra dripped onto the tabletop, forming mounds of tallow. Little Satan lay curled up at Johann's feet.

Johann and Valentin had agreed that they wouldn't tell Karl the whole truth—not yet. As far as Karl was concerned, Valentin was Greta's uncle and an old friend in need. They didn't tell him that Greta was in fact Johann's daughter or about what had happened between the two men back in Heidelberg. Johann wanted to wait for the right moment to confess the sins from his past to his assistant. Thankfully, Karl was preoccupied with all the wonderful paintings, sculptures, and art treasures inside the churches of Nuremberg. Johann was under the impression that Karl was almost a little jealous of the effort his master put into trying to save a girl he didn't even know.

"Loch is probably the most heavily secured prison in the entire empire," said Valentin glumly. Lying on the table was a layout plan of the city hall that Valentin had secretly copied. "I visit the city hall regularly on administrative business. That building alone is heavily guarded, not to mention the jail below! All those doors . . ."

"Where do they keep the keys?" asked Johann.

"I've asked myself the same question." Valentin sighed deeply. "The prison keeper always carries one set on his belt, and there's another in the guards' chamber."

"Which is heavily guarded," said Johann. He fell silent again and thought hard, but try as he might, he couldn't work out a solution.

"What about bribes?" asked Karl.

"We might be able to bribe the keeper and one or two guards, but not all of them," said Valentin. "There are too many."

"Maybe we just have to accept that we can't save the child," said Karl with a shrug.

"If I'd said the same thing back in Warnheim, you wouldn't be here now," retorted Johann angrily. "I don't need to mention in which circle of Dante's *Inferno* you would be roasting right now."

Karl said nothing.

"There must be a solution," muttered Johann after a while as he rubbed his temples. "There simply has to be!"

By now he was convinced that it was no coincidence that Valentin had called him to Nuremberg. He had been watching the stars from the top of Saint Jakob's Church every night. The comet couldn't be far off now. It would be the third time Larua would enter Johann's life. The first time had been at his birth, the second time he'd nearly joined an occult group of devil worshippers, and now God was giving him one last chance. Because of his selfishness and arrogance, Margarethe—the love of his life—had been tortured and executed.

But now his daughter had entered his life, as unexpectedly as an angel. As if Margarethe were reaching out to him in forgiveness.

God had given him a key to turn back the wheel of time.

Now or never.

"We keep thinking," he said, staring at the map. "Worst case, we have to wait until they convict Greta. There might be a chance to free her on her way to the gallows."

But he knew that he couldn't wait that long. Every day down in that cell was one day too many for the child. It was strange that the Nuremberg authorities were holding Greta for so long without commencing torture.

Wolfgang von Eisenhofen inquired nearly every day whether Johann had found a lead regarding the devilish murders. Johann strung him along and garbled something about constellations he needed to observe more closely. He didn't really care who was behind the murders—he only wanted to free his daughter and get out of Nuremberg as fast as he could.

With the help of the commander's connections and some silver coins, Johann and Valentin managed to visit Greta most days. A few times Johann even went alone. He brought playing cards, coins, and colorful leather balls to show her all the juggling tricks he used to perform for her mother. He hoped it would distract Greta from the horror she was going through. The girl always loved it when he made her doll speak or coins appear from her ears.

But what she loved the most was Little Satan.

For a pile of hush money, the prison keeper allowed Johann to bring in the dog. Little Satan sniffed at the privy bucket, jumped onto the small bed, and licked Greta's face until she laughed. When he'd calmed down, he let her pat him while he sat quietly on her lap.

"I've always wanted a dog," she said. "But Uncle Valentin says the commander wouldn't allow it."

"He's probably afraid the dog will make a mess in the great hall." Johann smiled. "If you teach him properly, you might be allowed to keep one someday."

Suddenly Greta looked very serious. "The guards say that I'm a witch. And that I'm going to burn at the stake. I'm scared, Johann! Does it hurt to burn?"

"You . . . you're not going to burn." Johann swallowed hard. "Because you haven't done anything wrong."

"But they say that I'm a witch." Greta started to cry, and Johann's heart broke. "And I didn't even do anything! I was just by the river, by the bridge near the Hospital of the Holy Ghost, and then there was that dead little boy, and there was blood everywhere." She sobbed. "It was horrible! And I didn't even want to go to the river. But the man told me to go."

"The man?" Johann straightened up. Valentin had never mentioned this before. "What man?"

"I don't know. He wore a black coat and he . . . he was so dark, as dark as the night. And his eyes . . . his eyes looked like they were on fire, like glowing pieces of coal. He told me there were children playing down by the river and that there was music and food. When I got there, there was no one except for the dead boy under the bridge." Greta's eyes looked empty and her hands shook as she stroked the dog. "Then the guards came and found that thing in my pocket. A stinking ram's horn. They said the devil gave it to me."

"And he probably did," muttered Johann to himself. He shuddered.

His eyes . . . like glowing pieces of coal . . .

He, too, had seen such a man, first in Erfurt and then on the way to Hamburg. Evidently, someone had sent Greta to the dead boy on purpose, and the same man probably slipped the ram's horn into her pocket. But why? This case was getting stranger by the day.

Johann said nothing for a while, watching Little Satan snuggle with Greta. The dog rested his head in her lap as if he'd known her forever.

"You're not a witch," said Johann eventually. He rose to his feet when they heard the heavy steps of the prison keeper. It was time to go. "You're not a witch," he repeated. "And I promise I will get you out of here." He forced himself to smile. "Don't forget—I'm a magician. Nothing is impossible for a magician."

He hugged her so tightly that he felt Greta's pounding heart under her dress. He gave her one last smile on his way out and hoped she didn't notice the fear in his eyes.

On his way down the corridor, Johann continued to think about what Greta had just told him. A man in black with glowing red eyes had sent her to the bridge. It must have been a trick of her childish imagination, just like he once thought a scarecrow was a man on the way to Hamburg. Nature sometimes played nasty tricks on one's mind. It would be very strange indeed if someone had *wanted* Greta to find the body under the bridge. Who would want an innocent girl to be arrested as a witch?

Deep in thought, Johann didn't notice that Little Satan had run ahead. He startled when he heard wild barking and shouts in front of him. In the vaulted room at the end of the corridor, some guards were standing around the well. They were looking down the hole and laughing. Johann rushed up to the well and saw Little Satan treading water about seven paces below. It seemed he had jumped over the well's edge and was now in danger of drowning.

"Get him out right now!" ordered Johann.

"What do I care about the mutt?" jeered one of them. "Is it my dog? Maybe you shouldn't have brought it."

Little Satan whined and howled pitifully.

"If you don't, he'll keep howling like this for hours," said Johann, glaring at the guards. "Is that what you want?"

"The doctor's right, damn it," said the prison keeper from behind him. "Get the mutt out of there before the noise drives me insane."

The guards exchanged doubtful looks, and finally one of them grasped the chain holding a bucket in the center of the well and used it to climb down. He grabbed the whimpering Little Satan by the scruff of his neck while the other guards winched him up. When the dog arrived at the top, the keeper kicked Little Satan so hard that he flew across the room. He shrieked almost like a child and huddled underneath Johann's coat.

"Don't ever come here with that mutt again!" snarled the keeper. "And who are you, anyhow? I'm going to make some inquiries about your person and give notice upstairs that your visits are no longer acceptable. The brat has been spoiled for long enough!"

Johann fought back the urge to shout out loud when he left the prison. He held the trembling dog in his arms and soothed him while his thoughts raced in circles. He felt certain that the prison keeper would make sure he couldn't visit his daughter any longer. But that wasn't important right now.

What was important was the fact that he'd found a way to get Greta out of there.

"The well." Johann was pointing at the plan of the city hall spread out on the table before them. The three men had met sooner than usual, and Valentin and Karl could tell by Johann's excitement that it was urgent.

"When the guard pulled Little Satan from down there, I saw a barred door in the wall of the well," continued Johann. "I should have thought of it sooner. The well isn't a cistern, and so the water must come from somewhere!"

"The underground passages," murmured Valentin, studying the map. "You . . . you might be right."

Johann looked at him impatiently. "What are you saying?"

"Large areas of the city—on the north bank of the Pegnitz, at least—have cellars," replied Valentin slowly. "Many cellars serve to store beer, but there are also dozens of passages for the town's water supply. I once saw a map of them at the city hall. The water flows into the city from the outside—small trickles at first, which are caught in drains and directed into channels. The streams are then directed to the various wells around town, including the Schöner Brunnen fountain on the main square."

"And one of those passages leads directly beneath the city hall?" asked Karl skeptically.

Valentin sighed. "I don't know, damn it! I didn't study the map properly. They keep it closely guarded, together with the keys for the underground passages, because they don't want it to fall into the wrong hands—an entire army might be able to enter the city that way."

"When will you be at the city hall next?" asked Johann.

"Hmm." Valentin thought. "The day after tomorrow. The Hospital of the Holy Ghost is bursting at the seams, and the city wants us to take on more patients. I am supposed to report the number of beds available at the command. Why?"

"Do you remember how we took a print of a key back in Heidelberg? I want you to make prints of the keys here, too. And take another look at the map—we need to find out where those passages start!"

"Even if we find the particular passage that leads below the city hall and into the well of the prison," said Karl, "there are more guards, more doors—"

"I know that, God damn it!" shouted Johann. He thumped his fist on the table. "But it's our only chance. It's just the first part of a plan so far, but it's a start." He bit his lip. The plan was ludicrous. Karl was right. Even if they managed to get to the well, then how would they get to Greta? To his innocent daughter who had evidently been lured into a trap?

"There's something else, too," said Johann eventually. "Greta told me today that a man had persuaded her to go to the river, where she found the dead boy. Someone wanted her to be there. Why? Because the authorities needed a scapegoat? But then why a fourteen-year-old girl—why not a midwife or someone like that who normally gets accused of witchcraft?" He shook his head. "There are so many odd parts to this story. Why Greta? Why has she been sitting down there for so long without being tortured and without a trial? Something isn't right, but I just can't figure out what."

He would have liked to pat Little Satan, because he always felt calmer when the dog sat on his lap. But Little Satan had broken a paw when the prison keeper kicked him. Johann had put the leg in a splint and given the dog a little theriac, and now the animal slept peacefully inside the room the commander had assigned to Johann and Karl.

No one said anything for a while. Eventually, Valentin cleared his throat.

"I'm going to get the keys from the city hall for us," he said. "And I think I know the ideal time to break into the prison." He paused. "In four days."

"Why in four days?" asked Karl.

"It'll be the night before the Nuremberg Schembartlauf, a carnival parade where many citizens wear masks and get drunk before the start of Lent. The guards won't be as vigilant as usual, especially in the early hours of the morning."

"In four days' time." Johann nodded. "It's agreed." He looked at Valentin, who was sitting hunched over at the table. "Pray that I return with Greta."

"If you think you're going alone, you're mistaken," replied Valentin. "I may be a cripple, but I'm not going to let you free Greta on your own. I'm getting the keys, so I'm coming."

"If that is what you wish," said Johann with a sad smile. "I can hardly tie you up here." Deep down he was happy Valentin would be coming along. They'd need all the help they could get.

For a few moments the library was silent; somewhere outside, a solitary raven cawed. Then Karl gave a desperate chuckle.

"So . . . you're saying you're actually going to crawl through those dark passages? And then? Are you going to frighten off the guards with magic tricks?"

"Something like that," said Johann, standing up. "You heard it—we still have four days. Plenty of time to make plans and preparations."

The next few days were frenzied. Each night, Johann stood atop the spire of Saint Jakob's Church and watched the stars, which now almost matched their position on the day of his birth. Jupiter was nearly in the same sign as the sun, but the comet hadn't appeared yet. Could his calculations be wrong? Johann knew there could always be slight deviations, but he was all but certain that Larua would appear in the sky very soon.

Perhaps even precisely on the date of Greta's liberation.

During the days, Johann was running about town procuring things. Most of what he needed he found with merchants on the main square or at the craftsmen's quarter. When he wasn't on an errand, he roamed the lanes aimlessly, thinking and pondering until his plan took shape. Outside Frauenkirche Church on the market square at midday, he watched the *Männleinlaufen*—with the strike of the bell, a mechanical clock moved a procession of the seven prince electors around a figure of the Holy Roman emperor high above the portal—a never-ending circle. Johann felt like he, too, was coming full circle. In contrast to his usual habits, he even prayed. He visited the famous Lorenz Church with its heavily adorned western portal, sat down in one of the rear pews, and asked God for help as soft light fell through the stained-glass windows.

Lord, I have committed many sins in my life. I mocked you and I doubted you. Please help me to free my daughter. I swear I will watch over her for the rest of my life.

He imagined Greta huddled on her cot right now, afraid and confused because Johann and Valentin weren't visiting anymore. The Loch keeper had ensured that neither of them was allowed at the prison any longer. But Johann wanted to avoid the city hall in any case—he didn't want anything to happen at the last moment. Another child had vanished the previous day, down by river, near the hangman's house this time. The residents of Nuremberg were growing more upset. People whispered in the streets, and suspicions and rumors spread like a bad smell. The citizens of Nuremberg demanded a culprit—they didn't care who, just as long as the evil in town was banished.

The uncanny atmosphere affected Johann, too. During his walks through the city he sometimes thought he was being followed. But it was probably just the masks, which were becoming a common sight in the streets in the days leading up to the carnival and which reminded him of a man with glowing red eyes.

His eyes looked like they were on fire.

On the afternoon of the fourth day, Valentin asked Johann to the library, looking agitated. Johann's old friend went to one of the shelves and picked out a book. The book was cut out on the inside and contained a key ring with about a dozen keys. Valentin held it up triumphantly.

"Don't ask me what it cost to have these made. And I even managed to catch another glimpse of the map with the passageways and draw up a copy from memory."

Johann exhaled with relief. Valentin had done it! Johann hadn't really believed it would happen; his friend always used to be so nervous. The thought that Valentin had to steal a closely guarded key ring from the city hall had caused Johann many sleepless hours—hours he spent atop the church tower with his stargazing tube, but without success. The comet he anticipated so eagerly still hadn't arrived.

"Was it difficult to get your hands on the originals?" asked Johann.

"I . . . I caught an unobserved moment upstairs," said Valentin hesitantly. For a brief moment Johann thought his old friend was keeping something from him.

"All that matters now is that we have the keys," said Valentin a little too quickly. "The keys and the map. Did you get everything you needed?"

"Everything but one item. I need you to steal one more thing for me. It's not very big, and I've seen it on the commander's desk."

Johann gave Valentin the details, and his friend nodded. "That should be fine—I carry documents to his room all the time. Although the commander is starting to get impatient. He wants to know how your investigation is coming along."

"Tell him I'm preparing some very complicated magic that will help put an end to these murders once and for all," replied Johann with a tired smile. "That's not wholly false, and he is superstitious enough to buy it." He gave Valentin a thoughtful look. "You can still decide to stay here."

"I'm coming with you, and that's my final word."

"Very well," said Johann reluctantly. He was left with the strange feeling that something was awry.

"Show me the map," Johann asked Valentin to take his own mind off his worries. "Perhaps we'll find a good entry point to the passages. One that's not under constant surveillance."

Valentin pulled out the map. "I think I've already found one. It's not the nicest spot, but at least we have nothing to fear there." He indicated a particular point on the map. "No guards, at least."

Johann nodded. Valentin had chosen the spot well.

"It's decided," he said. "We're setting out tonight. And if we fail, at least we'll burn together."

"Old friends, united in the flames."

~

In the infinite vastness of the universe above them, a comet was hurtling along its path. It was nearing Earth like it did every seventeen years, though it couldn't be discerned by the naked eye. The comet was trailed by a bright fiery, bushy tail.

It was the tail of Lucifer, the light bringer, causer of chaos, he who fell from the heavens. Of the spirit that denies. The gloom that brought forth light.

There was someone who couldn't wait for this darkness to arrive.

Larua.

Not far from the command, the master closed his eyes, listening. He almost thought he could hear the rushing of the comet through the eight spheres. Then he sat down at a table and wrote messages for his crows and the raven to carry. He was gathering his followers. There were many of them, as many as the number of the beast, and their ranks were increasing.

It was the night before February 24 in the year of the Lord 1512.

A night that would change the world forever.

27

BELOW THE CLOUD-COVERED MOON, THREE FIGURES IN
dark coats hurried through the lanes of Nuremberg's Lorenz quarter.

All three wore hoods that concealed their faces. One of the figures carried a
cloth-covered crate on his back. The other two—one of whom was limping—
carried heavy packs. They looked like itinerant peddlers or knife sharpeners. No
one would have guessed that the cloths were hiding a laterna magica and that
one of the figures was a famous doctor and magician. Johann was wearing his
magnificent star cloak inside out, and it was blacker than a starless night.

Johann had given Karl the choice of coming or staying, and to his surprise
the young man wanted to come. Johann felt deeply grateful. He wasn't sure why
exactly Karl wanted to help him—perhaps he still felt indebted to Johann. In
any case, he was a good fellow who didn't deserve a master who treated him as
poorly as Johann had. If they came out of this business unscathed, Johann would
give him back the letters and pay him handsomely.

But he struggled to believe that they would make it out unscathed.

They had left Little Satan behind at the command, hopping back and forth
in Johann's chamber with his broken foot and probably relieving himself on the
floor at that very moment or chewing on the furniture and rugs. The dog had
sensed that something was going on. He had been restless and howled when
they closed the door.

Earlier that evening, Johann had passed several men in costumes in the
streets around the main square. The people of Nuremberg eagerly anticipated
the Schembartlauf procession, which would lead through the entire city the following morning. The masked men all wore the same tight-fitting white-and-red
garb embroidered with licking flames. They were armed with blunt pikes and

wore rings of little bells around their ankles. Their faces were hidden behind smooth masks that made them look like varnished puppets.

"The timing for our plan couldn't be better," whispered Valentin to Johann and Karl as they made their way through the dark lanes. "Tomorrow, dozens of those dressed-up jesters will dance through the streets—it's an old tradition."

"Are they all hired jugglers?" asked Karl.

"Oh, no! Many of those masks are hiding the faces of wealthy patricians. They're all from respectable, influential Nuremberg families." Valentin smiled grimly. "I heard that this year, the hell is going to be an elephant—you know, one of those long-nosed monsters from beyond the sea."

"The hell?" asked Johann.

"That's what the Schembart runners call a huge wagon that, at the end of the procession, is stormed by the crowds outside city hall in a mock battle. People sometimes get hurt or even killed. Like I said—it's a raucous affair."

A door banged, and someone gave a shrill laugh. Johann looked around suspiciously and saw one of the costumed men dance across the lane and vanish in the darkness of a doorway. A second, younger man with a pike went after him, giggled girlishly, and took a mock bow in their direction. Then he, too, was swallowed up by the dark of night. Only the jangling of their little bells could be heard for a while longer, like the cackling of kobolds. Not for the first time Johann wondered whether it wasn't those masked men who had brought back his old fear of being followed these last few days. He felt for the knife that—after lengthy deliberation—he had decided to bring. The accursed knife! He was wearing it on a thin string around his neck like he used to, ready to rip it off and throw it at any moment. He didn't like it, but he knew it was the weapon he could handle the best, especially in narrow corridors and prison cells. He had given Karl the pistol and the sword, but he doubted the student was much good as a fighter.

Johann eyed the dark houses near the city wall. Once again he felt an itch between his shoulder blades as if someone was watching him. But every time he turned around, there was nothing.

Meanwhile, they had crossed the Pegnitz west of the Hospital of the Holy Ghost and were headed toward the main square. Now, in the middle of the night, the stalls of the market women and grocers had been taken down. An icy wind swept across the open space in front of the city hall. Despite the late hour, guards with pikes and halberds were on patrol outside the building.

Johann thought about his daughter, who was just a stone's throw away. How was she feeling right now? He hoped she was asleep and dreaming something pleasant. If his plan succeeded, he would be able to wrap his arms around her in just a few hours. And if he failed, they would soon see one another again in paradise. Margarethe, Greta, Valentin, Karl. But Johann didn't know whether God would have a spot for him in paradise, too.

They turned left behind the Sebaldus Church and headed toward the city wall again.

"I still don't understand why we have to leave the city to get back inside the city," grumbled Karl. "Are there no other places to access those passageways?" He groaned and tugged at the straps of the crate on his back. "The laterna is damned heavy. I don't want to carry it halfway to Fürth."

"Most access points inside the city are guarded or lie below houses of burghers who have cellars," explained Valentin. "I found an entrance that is more or less freely accessible. Probably because folks avoid it."

"And where is this entrance?" asked Karl.

"At a cemetery," replied Johann.

"At a—?"

"Shh!" Johann gestured for Karl to be quiet. "We have nothing to fear from the dead—only from the living! So be quiet."

Cautiously, they approached Neutor Gate near the castle; the gate was closed at this time of night and was guarded by a solitary watchman.

"Wait here," whispered Valentin.

He approached the guard and, after a few moments, handed him some coins. The man opened the door and let them pass through with a nod.

The highway stretched before them, desolate and empty. Some crows flew up from the icy fields. The moon emerged from behind the clouds and painted the sparsely wooded landscape with a silvery-gray light. About half a mile to the west, a few lights sparkled.

"Sankt Johannis," said Valentin, pointing at the lights. "The city's plague cemetery. Ever since the last great epidemic, Nuremberg prefers to leave its dead outside the gates."

"The entrance is at a plague cemetery?" asked Karl.

"Just yesterday they dug out a new mass grave and scattered lime over the bodies." Valentin gave a shrug. "Lucky for us. Folks avoid the place."

"And so they should," said Karl.

Johann glanced at his young assistant, wondering whether he already regretted having come along. But Karl still strode on at a fast pace with the heavy crate on his back. The laterna was part of the plan Johann had worked out in the last few days. It was a plan that required a huge dose of luck and a crucial moment of surprise.

After a while they reached the lights, which belonged to a handful of low houses. A little off to the side stood a small church surrounded by the gray silhouettes of tombstones. A low stone wall enclosed the cemetery; dry rosebushes had grown over the wall in places. Valentin stopped in front of a rusty gate and pulled out a piece of parchment that had been folded several times.

They lit a lantern, and Valentin held it close to the map, which was covered in scribbled lines and arrows.

"The entrance is in a crypt inside the plague chapel," said Valentin, pointing to the map. "It has to be somewhere in the family crypt of the Holzschuhers, who are influential patricians in Nuremberg." He looked up and gestured at the chapel among the graves nearby.

"Let's go." Johann opened the rusty gate. For a brief moment, he thought he heard the jingle of bells, but then the squeaking of the gate drowned out all other sounds. More slowly now, they walked past the old, crooked grave markers that rose out of the ground like the teeth of giants. There were several fresh mounds of dirt, including one very large one. Several black birds sat on top of it, but Johann couldn't make them out very well in the dark. Even in the chill of winter, the sweet smell of decay lay in the air.

Soon they reached the plague chapel, a small, towerlike building. Johann pushed against the door and entered the dark room on the other side. In the light of the lantern he saw wooden choir stalls and an altar farther back. The floor in front of them was covered in grave slabs with the likenesses of many long-dead Nuremberg patricians.

"The Holzschuher crypt," whispered Valentin, gesturing toward one of the slabs. "We need to get down there."

He slipped his pack off his hunched shoulders and pulled out a crowbar. Karl took it and wedged it beneath the edge of the stone slab. There was a crunching noise, and the slab lifted a tiny bit.

"Wait." Johann rushed down the apse toward a plain cross that was about as tall as a man. It took all his strength to lift it down and drag it over to the grave slab.

"Do it again," he said to Karl while sweat ran down his forehead despite the cold.

The young man groaned as he pushed up the slab, and Johann pushed the long beam of the cross into the gap. Then he walked to the other end of the cross and levered the stone slab until it crashed to the floor on the side. A cloud of fine stone dust spread through the chapel, along with a musty smell from inside the hole.

"The law of the lever, by Archimedes," Johann declared with a smile and wiped his forehead. "The mechanical advantage is proportional to the length of the lever. Yet more proof that science gets a man further than mere muscle power." He took the flickering lantern from Valentin and held it in the room below them for a few moments. Then he gathered up his cloak. "Well, then—in the beginning was the deed!"

Clutching the lantern tightly, he jumped into the crypt below.

The chamber beneath the church floor was about as high as Johann's shoulders and full of stone sarcophagi, each one bearing the emblem of the Moor with the red hat and a wooden shoe—the family crest of the Holzschuhers. The air smelled of rot, soil, and fungi.

Karl and Valentin had also climbed into the crypt by now, the younger man helping the older one. The three of them started to feel along the walls, almost completely in the dark despite the lantern.

"Over here!" called out Karl after a while. He'd found a small, narrow door that had been reinforced with pieces of iron. A rusty lock hung on the door.

"This must be the entrance," said Valentin. "Now we need this." He fished the key ring from his pack and tried one key after another. Finally, on the seventh attempt, they heard a click and the lock opened. They pushed on the little door, and on the other side lay a pitch-black corridor.

"The entrance to the Nuremberg underground passages," murmured Valentin. "We actually found it." He stared into the darkness. "From now on, we must place our trust in God. In God and in my map."

Carrying the lantern in one hand and the map in the other, he limped ahead; Karl and Johann followed.

The passageway was about as wide as two arms' lengths and just high enough for them to walk with bent knees and hunched shoulders. It had been dug into the sandstone without any bracing. Water dripped from the ceiling, and Johann tried to avoid touching the drops. The bodies of plague victims were buried above them, and their juices of putrefaction probably seeped through coffins and sand. Small puddles had formed on the ground, and Johann saw wood splinters and pieces of bone.

Their steps echoed through the tunnel. No one spoke. After what felt like an eternity, the passage ended in a small, round chamber with three doors. All three were locked. Valentin raised the lantern and studied the map.

"I believe we're near the Tiergärtner Gate now," he said. "Back inside the city and not far from the castle. I think . . ." He hesitated. "Let's take the right-hand passage."

"And if we get lost?" asked Karl.

"We won't get lost," said Johann. He had produced a black coal pencil from his pack and used it to draw a sign next to the door on the right. "Miners use such signs below ground," he explained. "If we leave a mark at every fork, we shouldn't get lost."

Valentin smiled. "I knew it was right to bring you to Nuremberg, Johann. You may have lied to me and betrayed me, but I still admire your wit and your nerve."

You have no idea, thought Johann. Inwardly, he was shaking and his fingers trembled. His whole life seemed to be coming to a head in these crucial hours.

He had to free his daughter and right an old wrong.

Valentin pulled out the key ring again, and soon they'd opened the door. The tunnel on the other side led slightly downhill. The walls and ceiling dripped and gurgled, and trickles ran down the walls like a network of veins inside a giant stone organism. A drain enclosed with bricks stretched down the center of the passageway. The water collected in the drain and rushed into the tunnel below their feet.

"Yes, it's the old Loch water supply!" said Valentin triumphantly. "The drains collect the water and direct it to the wells. Hmm . . ." He studied the map again. "The city hall should be southeast of here—"

"And this tunnel runs southeast, indeed," said Johann. "I think we're on the right track."

"How do you know that?" asked Karl.

Johann pulled his hand out from underneath his cloak and held up a small box about the size of his palm. The top of the box was covered with glass, and inside sat a quivering needle. "This is the commander's," he said. "It's a compass. It shows us our direction, even underground and without the stars. We really must return it when we're done here. It is constructed with a gimbal mounting, according to Leonardo da Vinci's design, and it's worth about as much as a destrier." He shook his head and focused on the needle. "Until very recently, the church condemned compasses as witchcraft—a terrible thought."

Using the compass and leaving pencil marks, they continued to move southeast, passing through several more chambers with doors. Each time, Valentin pulled the key ring from his pack and found the right key. Every now and then they heard rustling and scuffling noises in the dark—rats, they assumed. On one occasion Johann thought he heard the jingle of small bells again, but he guessed it was only the key ring.

They came to yet another door. Valentin unlocked it, and this time, there wasn't another corridor on the other side but a round reservoir. Johann held his breath. He lifted the lantern through the door and looked down. The black surface of the water was about three paces below them, and a bucket was floating on it. The bucket was attached to a chain that disappeared somewhere in the dark above them. Johann thought he could make out the hint of a flickering light up there, like from smoking torches.

"This is the Loch Prison well," whispered Johann as quietly as he could. "I recognize it."

"But what about voices? Or the cries of the inmates?" whispered Karl. "Shouldn't we at least be hearing a couple of guards talking to each other?"

"We have no choice but to climb up if we want to find out," said Johann.

"But then we run right into the guards' arms!"

"You forget I came prepared." Johann took the pack from his shoulders and started to rummage inside. Then he produced a small wooden keg that stank of sulfur.

"Once I light this keg, we must act fast," he whispered. "It's going to cloak everything in smoke. Karl and I climb up the chain. Valentin, you wait here." He looked at his old friend. "You said there was a set of keys in the guards' chamber?"

"I . . . I think so." Valentin nodded slowly.

"We'll take yours just in case."

"But these are just for the underground passages, not for the prison. And how are you going to get to her cell with all the guards?" asked Valentin. "The keys won't help you against those."

Johann smiled. "You brought a magician, Valentin. Remember?"

Johann lit a pine chip on the lantern and then used it to light the contents of the keg. Instantly, dense rust-colored smoke started to pour from the keg and drifted up the sides of the well in thick clouds. Johann carefully set down the keg at the edge of the reservoir and tied his damp kerchief around his nose and mouth.

"Now!" he said, and he grabbed the chain and started to climb up it.

The rusty chain links dug into his fingers, and every single muscle in his body ached. It had been years since he'd last climbed up a rope—since his time with the jugglers, in fact.

Inch by inch, Johann pulled himself up. Below him, Karl panted as he followed him with the laterna on his back. The dense smoke made Johann's eyes water, and he tried to inhale as little as possible. The mixture inside the keg included cinnabar and ocher, coloring agents he'd bought from a Nuremberg dyer. The powder produced red, almost purplish smoke, which looked particularly devilish. And the smoke was a perfect screen for projecting heinous images with the laterna magica.

Finally Johann reached the edge of the well and pulled himself up over the side. He paused cautiously and looked around. He'd expected to encounter some guards. It had been his plan to use the general chaos and the cover of the smoke to rush over to the guards' chamber and steal their keys—or to knock down the prison keeper and take his. Meanwhile, Karl was supposed to distract the other guards with images from the laterna magica. It was a terribly poor plan, but it was the only one he'd managed to come up with. Johann had calculated that it would take him five minutes to open the doors, run down the corridor, fetch Greta, and disappear back down the well with her.

But there were no guards.

The room was empty, and there were no sounds coming from the guards' chamber upstairs, either. Johann stood still and listened. No laughter, no shouts, nothing.

What on earth?

Meanwhile, Karl had also reached the smoke-filled chamber with his heavy pack. He coughed and looked about, blinking rapidly. Like Johann, he'd covered his nose and mouth with a damp cloth.

"Where are the guards?" he asked quietly.

"I don't know, damn it! And I don't have time to worry about it—let's go!"

An eerie feeling made Johann's skin crawl. What was going on here? The oil lantern in his hand, he started to run down the corridor. All the doors stood open and every cell was empty. What was happening? With rising panic, Johann raced toward Greta's cell.

He threw himself against the unlocked door, and it slammed against the wall inside.

The cell was empty.

28

THE RUST-COLORED SMOKE HAD SPREAD DOWN THE COR-
ridor and flowed into the cell, but everything was still and silent as the grave.

"Damn it, what's going on here?" asked Karl, standing behind Johann in the open door. "Is it the wrong cell?"

Johann said nothing and walked inside. A few rats squeaked as they scattered. The bucket with the board had been knocked over. Greta's doll was lying on the cot. Johann picked it up and stared at it, as if little Barbara could tell him what had happened.

What in God's name was going on?

Had the guards taken Greta to the scaffold? But Valentin would have heard of it. And why were all the other cells open and empty? Where had all the prisoners gone, and the guards? Johann's thoughts raced. Something was wrong here, very wrong. Suddenly he remembered several strange incidents from the last few days—warning signs he had overlooked in the rush. He'd wanted to rescue his daughter and stormed along blindly, looking neither left nor right. He still wasn't sure exactly what was being played here, but the eerie feeling from earlier was growing stronger and stronger.

It was the feeling of having walked into a trap.

"Get back!" he shouted. "Out of here!"

He dropped the doll and they ran back up the corridor. The red smoke was so thick that they hardly saw anything. Almost blind, they reached the edge of the well, and Johann grabbed hold of the chain. He climbed down as fast as he could and entered the doorway that led into the room above the water. He'd already guessed what he was going to find there, but the reality still hit him like a blow.

Valentin was gone.

You're so stupid! he thought. *So terribly stupid! All your brains, all your knowledge didn't help. You didn't see the forest for the trees!*

Silent despair filled his body. He had failed—completely and utterly failed.

You lost everything. You lost your daughter. You fool, you—

Johann paused his silent tirade when he heard something.

It was a humming and lamenting that drifted down the depths of the tunnels. The sound rose and ebbed, and after a while, Johann thought he could make out a few strange words.

"O Mephistophiel . . . Jesum . . . Escha . . . Eloha . . . Penothot . . ."

Johann signaled to Karl behind him to be silent. He listened. Then the two of them started to walk toward the source of the sound.

"Rolamicon . . . Hipite . . . Mephistophiel . . . Koreipse . . . Loisant et Dortam . . ."

Johann walked faster, hurrying to meet his destiny. He needed certainty, even though he had a fair idea where his path was leading him.

Or, rather, to whom.

"O Mephistophiel, prasa Deus . . . O Larua . . ."

~

Fear crept up in Karl; he was almost as terrified as he'd been on the pyre in Warnheim.

While he followed the doctor down the dark passages toward the eerie chanting, Karl tried to figure out what it was that frightened him so. His heart was pounding in his throat and he struggled to breathe. His hand clutched the hilt of the sword Faust had given him, but he had a feeling that he wouldn't know what to do with the weapon, or with the wheel-lock pistol he'd stowed in the casing of the laterna magica. He still carried the laterna on his back, like a last souvenir from the old world above them.

The doctor had changed in the course of the past week. Karl was certain that this had something to do with Valentin. Something awful must have happened between the two men, something the doctor felt deeply guilty about. Ever since Faust had visited Valentin's niece at the prison, he'd acted like a man possessed. What was happening to him? The plan to free the girl had been doomed from the beginning. But still Karl had gone with the doctor, because . . . well, because he loved him. Because he couldn't allow this gifted mind, this extraordinary human being, to run straight into perdition.

Although right now it looked as though they were headed for it together.

Back in Cologne, Karl had wanted to ask Faust to release him. But then they'd had to flee the city and spent the next few months at the tower, where their bond had strengthened. Karl had almost confessed his love to the doctor there, even though he knew that he would only end up heartbroken. He was bound to Faust with an invisible tie.

The events of the last few hours had been more and more puzzling. Why in God's name was the entire prison empty, as if the plague had befallen the city? Why had Valentin run away when it was so important to him to free his niece? And what was this awful humming and chanting mixed with Latin-sounding words? He felt like his head was going to burst.

But what frightened Karl the most was the doctor.

Karl had never seen him like this. Johann Georg Faustus, the famous magician, was a sharp-witted, wise man who always kept his cool, even in the worst situations, and invariably parried every attack, every surprise with his brains alone. But now the doctor's face showed something Karl had never seen on it before.

The doctor was scared.

Sweat was running down Faust's forehead, and his face was ashen. He mumbled individual words that made about as much sense to Karl as that accursed chanting.

"The tower," whispered Faust. "He knew about the tower and told him . . . It was his raven all along . . . It must have been his raven . . . Baphomet . . . I have failed."

The last words frightened Karl the most. If the doctor had failed, then this was the end for him, too. No one could save them now—they would be buried alive.

On their way toward the mysterious voices, they passed through more chambers and cellars, and each time one of the doors stood open, almost as if someone was showing them the way. They had long left the passage they'd come from earlier. Karl thought they were heading west, but he felt quite disoriented. The humming and singing were getting very loud now. They entered a spacious cellar room with old barrels stacked up against the damp, moldy walls on both sides.

At the other end of the cellar was a large double door with strange runes carved into the wood.

And on the other side of the door, they heard the chanting of many male voices.

"*O Adonai . . . prasa Deus et praesant Deus . . . O Spiritus Mephistophiel Deuschca . . . O Larua . . .*"

Karl's fear took his breath away. He thought he was going to pass out. What was going on with him? He felt as though an invisible force was holding him back, and the feeling of being unable to breathe grew worse with every step. It was as if deep down inside, he knew that death was waiting for him beyond those doors.

Or something even worse than death.

Faust strode toward the portal.

"No!" cried Karl. "Don't open it! Don't—"

But it was too late.

The doctor had already opened the doors.

~

Johann pushed against the doors with both hands, and they swung open soundlessly.

On the other side was a large hall that was at least ten paces high and twice as long. Torches and candles bathed the room in a flickering light, and the walls were lined with glowing braziers. Johann's first impression was that he was standing in an underground church. There was a choir, a nave, a transept, massive columns holding up the painted ceiling, and a pulpit. There were an altar and a baptismal font in the apse and a cross beyond. A monk standing behind the altar had raised his arms in prayer and was preaching to his congregation in the pews before him.

"*O Mephistophiel . . . Obdesca mihy Aglam . . . O Christe meschca . . . O Larua . . .*"

On second glance, Johann saw the differences from a regular church: the paintings on the ceilings showed no tales of saints but blood, murder, torture, and wars. The cross in the apse hung upside down.

And lying on the altar was a young girl, either unconscious or dead.

"Greta!" screamed Johann. The sight of his daughter on the altar was too much for him. His knees buckled and he clung on to the doorframe to keep himself from falling.

The monk, who was wearing a black robe with a black hood, lowered his arms, and the congregation stopped singing.

"Greetings, Johann," said the monk, his voice echoing through the hall. "It's been a while since we last saw each other. Didn't I tell you back on the old post road that our pact is valid until I dismiss you?"

Johann was shaking all over, and he was unable to move, like a rabbit at the sight of the snake's open mouth. He knew that voice—he'd last heard it seventeen years ago. Since then he'd been running away from it, again and again, but it never stopped following him in his dreams.

Now it had caught up to him.

"Come, Johann," said Tonio del Moravia. "My disciples would like to take a closer look at you. They've been waiting a long time for your return. Seventeen years."

The heads of thirty men turned to face him, and Johann stared at blank masks. Beneath their shapeless black cloaks, which seemed to melt into the dark twilight, they all wore the colorful costumes of the Schembart runners. Faint jingling rang out here and there.

The bells. They followed us the whole time!

Then he noticed another figure. He had been hiding behind a column near the altar, but now he emerged, shaking.

"Valentin!" spat Johann. "You traitor!"

"Forgive me," pleaded Valentin. "They . . . they made me do it. They said it was the only way for me to save Greta. Believe me—I love your daughter just like you do."

The anger gave Johann back his strength. With a furious roar he started to storm to the front, but immediately some of the Schembart runners jumped up and stopped him. Strong muscles showed beneath the costumes of the men, and they had no trouble forcing Johann to the ground.

"Bring him to me!" commanded Tonio.

The Schembart runners dragged Johann like a sack of flour into the apse, where they forced him to his knees before his former master. Finally, Tonio took off his hood.

The sight of his face made Johann gasp.

"By all the saints," he whispered.

"Don't pray," said Tonio. "It doesn't suit you, and it won't help you."

Tonio had barely aged. His face was just as haggard and pale as seventeen years ago, his stature still tall and athletic. There might have been a few additional wrinkles, and the skin of his face seemed taut like that of a reptile. But other than that, he looked as though no more than a year had passed since they'd last met.

It's impossible!

"Pleased to see you haven't forgotten me after all these years, Johann," said Tonio. "I must admit, following your unfortunate decision to run away in Nördlingen, it took a while to find you again. At first it seemed you had vanished into thin air. But then friends from Venice told me about a handful of jugglers at the Fondaco dei Tedeschi who called themselves Johann Faustus's Fabulous Troupe. An unusual name, don't you think?" Tonio smiled his old wolfish smile. "I thought I'd pay you a visit. I always had a talent for playacting."

"You . . . you were Signore Barbarese!" gasped Johann. "They were your books!"

"Of course they were my books, you fool!" Tonio laughed. "No one else owns an original copy of *The Sworn Book of Honorius*, let alone so many manuscripts by Leonardo da Vinci. I was letting you mature like a good wine—you were supposed to find your own way back to me. I understood that you needed more time. It was beautiful to watch you grow and flourish, and entirely without the Krakow University I had intended for you." He gave a shrug. "Seventeen years is nothing if you've been waiting for as long as I have. But then the old fellow in Venice found me out."

"You murdered Magister Archibaldus!" Johann struggled against the masked men, but they held him firmly. "You . . . you . . ."

"Devil?" Tonio grinned. "Is that what you're trying to say? If it makes you feel any better—I didn't kill your drunken friend. Not personally, anyhow—followers of my order did it."

Johann said nothing. Did Tonio know that Archibaldus had left him a message in blood back then? The powerful arms of the Schembart runners still held him down. He tried to catch a glimpse of Greta on the altar from the corner of his eye. Pain shot through him worse than being stabbed with a knife.

Greta was wearing the same linen dress she had worn in her cell. Her eyes were closed, and her childlike face pale, almost translucent. Johann noticed that her chest was rising and falling ever so slightly. She was still alive. He guessed they had sedated her with some kind of herb or potion. What were these lunatics going to do to her?

Johann struggled against his captors with all his might, but in vain. Furious, he glared at Valentin by the column. The man's eyes went back and forth between Johann and Greta.

"Goddamned traitor!" snarled Johann again.

Valentin cowered as if he'd been struck. "They are powerful, Johann! What was I supposed to do?" His gaze turned to the unconscious girl again. "Just look at what they've done to my dearest treasure. *They* arranged everything. Greta was only the bait—they were after you all along!"

Johann flinched.

Only the bait.

He felt like punching himself in the face. He couldn't believe he hadn't seen this coming much sooner. He should have noticed when he first arrived at the command. Everything had been too easy. The underground passages leading straight into the prison, the key ring Valentin had stolen without a hitch, the map. It was so obvious—nothing but a cheap farce, and he, the oh-so-clever doctor, had fallen for it. He had followed the bacon like a mouse, and the trap had snapped shut.

"The tower," he whispered, looking Valentin straight in the eyes. "I told you about a tower back in Heidelberg, but never about its exact location. I only remembered later. There was just one person who could have told you where to find the tower—someone who lives there himself from time to time."

"You still don't understand how powerful this man is," said Valentin in a whisper. He trembled as he looked over to Tonio del Moravia.

"Oh yes, I do."

I've always known. I just didn't want to see.

He had never truly escaped the master; Tonio had always been one step ahead of him. That explained the prevailing sense of being watched. Tonio had never stopped watching him over all these years. But there must have been a reason for the master to bring Johann back to him now. After seventeen years.

At that moment, Johann understood.

Seventeen years.

Once again, Larua was in the sky, as on the day of his birth and as it had been in the clearing near Nördlingen. The comet was probably over Nuremberg right now. They had chosen this day for a reason. That was why Valentin hadn't stolen the key ring until now, and that was why Greta had been detained at the prison for so long. They had been waiting for this particular day.

Valentin seemed to read his thoughts. "They wanted you to figure out the plan with the tunnels yourself," he said in a shaking voice. "If you hadn't thought of it in time, I would have helped you. But it was more believable this way." He gave a sad smile. "I always knew you'd find the solution. Now you're precisely where they wanted you—where *he* wanted you."

Johann gazed at the upside-down cross in front of him. Back in the clearing near Nördlingen, he'd thought a horde of lunatics was going to kill him, sacrifice him for some satanic ritual like so many children and youths before him had been. But evidently they had different plans for him.

Something that would come to a close here in Nuremberg.

"Why didn't you just abduct me and bring me here if I'm so important to you?" asked Johann, looking at his former master. "Why this farce?"

"Well, I thought a farce was appropriate for a juggler and magician," replied Tonio nonchalantly. "Didn't you enjoy it? It allowed you to trick and perform and show off your clever mind as you always like to do. But you're right—that's not the true reason. The true reason is that you must return to me of your own free will. It is an ancient law, set down in the times before time."

Tonio studied him with black eyes, his pupils as sharp as needles.

"Back when you drank the black potion, you were almost mine. But then you got away at the last moment. Finding your daughter in Nuremberg was a stroke of luck. I'd only wanted to speak with your old friend here. I knew his name from the list at Heidelberg University." Tonio pointed his finger at Valentin, whose scarred face had lost all color. "He was very talkative. No one wants to undergo torture for a second time, do they? All we needed to do next was lure you to Nuremberg, this resourceful city where I have the most follow-ers in the empire. And finally we needed to get you here, into the womb of the beast. I knew you wouldn't abandon young Greta. Not after what you did to her mother." Tonio smiled coldly and took a step toward Johann. "You had to come of your own free will, and now you're here. Right time, right place."

"Where are we?" asked Johann.

"Directly underneath the Sebaldus Church, one of the city's oldest churches. The original building was dedicated to Saint Peter." Tonio smirked. "How appro-priate, considering good old Peter founded the Roman Church. We've been using this buried crypt as a gathering place for a few years now. I've had the hall renovated, bit by bit, whenever I stopped here on my travels. Every mass needs the right setting, don't you think?"

"And what do you want with my daughter?" asked Johann. "If you want to take revenge on me—for whatever—then—"

Tonio waved dismissively. "Your daughter is unimportant. We want you." He leaned down close enough so Johann could smell his sweetish breath. "*I* want you." Tonio sniffed at him and shuddered with lust. Almost lovingly he stroked Johann's cheeks. "You're the right one, Johann. I sensed it back in Knittlingen when we first met—when you were just a little boy. Everything happened just the way it was foretold."

Johann turned his face away with disgust. He realized where the smell on Tonio's breath came from.

It was the smell of fresh blood.

"I have a suggestion for you, Johann," said Tonio. "You sit down among my disciples and behave. And then I will tell you how you can save your daughter. It isn't difficult—it's entirely up to you. Are you going to behave and listen, Johann? Are you?"

Johann nodded, and the Schembart runners dragged him over to the front row of the pews, where they sat him down in their midst. Valentin had also been brought there, and he trembled and shook as he sat between two masked men. Johann looked at the empty, smooth masks around him. Now he was grateful that Greta was unconscious and didn't have to see this horror show.

Meanwhile, Tonio had walked over to the column with the pulpit and took the narrow, winding stairs to the top. When he stood beneath the black canopy, he paused for a moment, drinking in the ecclesial atmosphere, which was heavy with anticipation. Then he addressed his followers.

"You've been waiting for a long time," he shouted into the hall, looking like an angry, emaciated preacher. "But now the time has finally come. The reign of God ends and the age of man begins! *Homo Deus est!*"

"*Homo Deus est!*" chanted the masked men.

Johann winced at the words he'd heard again and again over the years without really understanding their full meaning. Magister Archibaldus had known who was hiding behind those words, and he'd had to die for this knowledge. It took Johann a moment to realize what Tonio's tone reminded him of. It was the same tone of voice the sorcerer had always used to seduce the crowd at the market squares.

"For hundreds of years, the church led us to believe that there was but one truth and one teaching," Tonio went on. "The church forbade you to read books and, yes, even to think! The church tried to lull you to sleep and condemned any scientific progress as heresy. They placed their obstinate, narrow-minded God at the center of the universe instead of man—but enough is enough!"

"*Homo Deus est, Deus homo est!*" chanted the masked men. Several of them had risen to their feet.

"Why has this city come so far? Why is it wealthier and more glamorous and better known than any other in the empire? Why is all the world praising Nuremberg wit and Nuremberg cleverness?" Johann could tell how much his former master and teacher enjoyed himself in the role of the zealous priest; his eyes gleamed with relish. "Because you have recognized that you can achieve greatness by yourselves! With the help of science, knowledge, inventions—you don't need a God, because you are gods yourself! Men can create paradise right here on earth. Starting from Nuremberg, our movement will conquer the world. The rebirth of man begins here!"

The masked men cheered, and Johann looked around with wonder. Who were those people? Lunatics? Followers of some dark, satanic sect? But then he remembered what Valentin had said about the participants of the Schembartlauf parade.

They're all from respectable, influential Nuremberg families.

Could that be true? Were all those masks hiding the faces of Nuremberg patricians? That would explain the lack of guards at the prison. Some powerful people had arranged for the cells to be cleared for him to walk into the trap. Who might belong to this creepy order? Patricians, merchants—perhaps even the burgomasters? And who was to say the Teutonic Knights weren't also part of this plot?

Johann wondered what Tonio was getting out of all of this. Johann had fought for science all his life, for reason and rationality instead of bigotry and dull-witted superstition, just like he had been taught by Conrad Celtis, Jodocus Gallus, and Archibaldus. He had seriously believed that a new age was dawning: independent thought instead of dogma, a society created by men instead of an angry God whose outdated rules were set down for all eternity. And now Tonio was perverting all those ideas that Johann had always championed with fervor. The rebirth of man celebrated as a satanic mass—what a mockery! Tonio was showing him a nasty caricature of man celebrating himself as God.

Homo Deus est.

Did these people truly believe that the age of God was coming to an end? Could anyone be so stupid? A horrible thought struck Johann and slowly became certainty: the lunatics surrounding him must be behind all those horrific child murders in Nuremberg.

Perhaps not only here in Nuremberg, but all over the empire?

But whether or not these madmen believed the world was coming to an end and killed innocent children—they had his daughter. He had walked into their trap like a donkey following a carrot.

Now Tonio addressed Johann from the pulpit. He was leaning down to him over the banister, smiling encouragingly with his pointed teeth. A wolf on the hunt.

"My dear Johann, the hour you've long been waiting for has finally arrived. Now you shall learn the truth—the truth that has been written in the stars since the day of your birth. I read it in your palm then. You were born on the day great prophets are born. Your mother also told you about that, remember? And she was right. You are the great prophet!"

The crowd clapped and cheered while Johann gaped at Tonio. He couldn't believe what he was hearing.

"You are the wizard Solomon's testament speaks of! You are the prophet who arrives with Larua and who we've been waiting for. *Because you're the son of a great sorcerer yourself.*" Tonio raised his voice as if reciting some ancient text.

"And when the day arrives and the great beast awakens, give it a coat. And a wizard will come when the sun and Jupiter are in the same sign, and he will be that coat. And he must give himself willingly and make the three sacrifices. Then the beast will come and no god can stop it."

Johann sat in the pew as if he'd turned to stone while Tonio gazed down at him with genuine affection. It was the loving gaze of a father upon his long-lost son. "This is your destiny, Johann. You are the wizard we have been waiting for. Many times I thought I'd found him, but every time, I was mistaken. Children who turned out to be false promises. We had almost given up hope—but then you came along! You needed more time, and I let you go. But now the moment has finally arrived—it is written in the stars! Larua, give us the strength for the three sacrifices!"

"You . . . you're insane!" gasped Johann. "I've always had an inkling. You're nothing but an insane fool!"

"Am I? A fool? Well, why not?" Tonio bared his teeth, climbed down from the pulpit, and walked to the still body on the altar. His spidery fingers brushed over her dress and slowly pushed it up over her knees.

"She is pretty, no doubt. I would love to mount her like a ram, despite her young age. It is the same as with lambs—the younger, the better tasting." Tonio licked his lips. "Perhaps I will take her with me on Walpurgis Night in a couple of years, and we can share her. We will make a child with her—your grandchild. And he will also bear the sign inside him. Who knows—maybe he would make a better coat than you? The stars will be favorable again in seventeen years' time. Seventeen years, more or less . . . We've been waiting for so long. Centuries. Millennia. Seventeen years don't matter. Even though I'd really like to choose you. I've grown very fond of you, Johann. Whether you believe it or not." Tonio's voice suddenly became icy and cutting, like hardened steel. His fingers had arrived at Greta's small breasts.

"You have the choice, Johann. Your daughter or you."

A piercing scream cut through the tense atmosphere. It came from Valentin, who had surprised his keepers and was heading for Tonio. "You monster!" screamed Valentin. "I should never have agreed to this deal. You . . . you devil!"

Tonio watched the small hunchbacked man with amusement. When Valentin reached him, Tonio made a small turn and kicked Valentin's feet out from under him. The crippled man fell to the ground with a whimper, but he started to crawl toward the altar on his elbows, trying to reach for Greta. Tonio kicked him again, this time with the heel of his boot and all his might, as if trying to squash a giant bug. There was a loud crack, and the little man lay still.

"Take him away," ordered Tonio. "I don't want his blood to soil the ceremony."

They carried off Valentin like a dirty bundle, and Tonio stepped toward Johann.

"Your daughter or you," he repeated.

Johann closed his eyes and opened them again in the hope of waking from a nightmare. But this was no nightmare—it was reality. He wanted to cry, but no tears came. What was happening here was beyond grief, beyond pain . . .

It was hell on earth.

What did these lunatics want from him? If he understood correctly, he was supposed to be sacrificed to something unfathomably evil. Something so unimaginable that men had given it a name so they might grasp it better. Just like they had done with God. But the name of this unimaginable creature wasn't God or Christ; nor was it Jahveh or Jehovah.

It was Satan. Lucifer. Light bringer.

In the old stories, Lucifer was the archangel who rose against God and was banished from heaven. Since then he'd been roasting in the depths of hell, hoping for the day he would rise again. He was the night before the day, chaos before order, the spirit that denies.

Only now did Johann fully comprehend what was going on here: these people, all of them respected citizens of Nuremberg, were awaiting Lucifer's return. They had murdered those poor children for some terrible ritual whose culmination was himself.

Johann had known for a long time that such people existed. But just as he had always taken God to be a principle of order, the devil, too, had been nothing but an abstract concept to him. His devil had no horns, no goat's foot, and he didn't stink of sulfur, even if that was what the church taught to frighten its flock. And that was why Satanists couldn't be anything other than misled fools who belonged in the madhouse or on a pyre.

That was the one side.

But if Johann was entirely honest, he had seen the devil in his dreams many, many times. Satan had seemed very real.

And now he stood in front of Johann.

"Your daughter or you," said Tonio for the third time. "You have my word that I won't touch her if you decide to join me."

Johann didn't speak. He didn't know what to believe. His entire conception of the world had been shaken. All he knew was that he had to save Greta. It was the only clear thought he could form.

The silence was broken by the cawing of a raven who was circling around the columns.

"You can have me," replied Johann quietly.

"Good choice. For you and for the world." Tonio smiled and nodded, then he snapped his fingers. "Bring me the black potion!" he commanded. His smile was certain of victory. "And believe me, Johann. This time, I'm going to make sure you drink every last drop of it."

The drink arrived in a chalice that had been cut from perfectly black obsidian and that sparkled in the light of the torches. Johann guessed it had probably been standing in the darkness between the columns the whole time. Two masked men solemnly carried the vessel to the altar and passed it to Tonio. The master held out the drink to Johann with both hands.

"You came to us of your own free will and decided to accept the black potion," he declared. "Know that it is for your best. Three painful sacrifices you must give, just like the accursed Son of God gave his sacrifice. The drink will expand your spirit and you will understand." Once again he raised up the chalice, and the congregation took up a prayer-like murmuring.

"O Satanas, O Mephistopheles, O Phosphoros!" The chanting echoed through the crypt. The master bowed to Johann, then Tonio gave him a nod.

Johann reluctantly accepted the cup, which felt cold and foreign. It was filled with a foul-smelling liquid.

"Drink," said Tonio.

Johann hesitated for another moment. He knew there would be no going back after the first sip.

For Greta, he thought. *For my daughter. May she lead a happier life than her father.*

He brought the vessel to his lips and drank. Like the last time, seventeen years ago, he retched immediately. The potion tasted like fire, burning his throat and spreading through his insides like scorching lava. Johann stood still for a while with his eyes closed, and then something seemed to explode inside him. An intense numbness spread through his body and he swayed; every sound suddenly seemed enormously amplified.

"Follow me, Johann," boomed Tonio's voice through the hall. "I am going to show you the truth. Only very few are granted this privilege."

The sorcerer led him to the baptismal font beside the altar, and Johann struggled to stay on his feet. He stumbled and caught himself by putting his hand straight into one of the braziers, but he hardly felt the pain. A very big masked man came up behind him and picked him up. Effortlessly, as if Johann were a bundle of kindling, the giant carried him toward his fate. The man conversed quietly with Tonio, and Johann thought the two were speaking French. But the words sounded strangely distorted, as if he were underwater.

The basin in front of him was a roughly hewn rock with notches and runes chiseled into the sides. Within, a dark liquid gleamed at him like a monstrous eye.

"Look into it," said Tonio.

Johann leaned over the baptismal font with great difficulty. He blinked and squinted, struggling to focus his eyes. After a while he realized that the liquid was red.

As red as blood.

Then he understood.

He was gazing into the blood of all those children who'd disappeared over the last few months.

"Quite a peculiar juice is blood," said Tonio. He dipped his finger into it and licked it off. "The tricky part is stopping it from curdling—it must remain fresh." He licked his lips with relish. "We need a lot of blood for the big day. The beast hasn't drunk in a long time. But I think we have enough now."

Tonio's lips suddenly looked a little bit fresher than before, his pale skin rosier and with less wrinkles. The red surface in the basin rippled, and Johann saw his own reflection. Then the image disappeared, and blurred forests appeared instead, partially hidden by wafts of mist. Muscular warriors wrapped in furs, their faces painted with blue streaks, stormed out of the woods, raising their swords and lances against an army on horseback. Horses neighed in panic; knights with helmets came crashing to the ground. Burning in the trees of a forest of oaks were wooden cages holding people who screamed as they hurled themselves against the bars like human torches. More warriors appeared, followed by burning pyres, blood, mouths opened in screams of agony, crying children, blood, houses on fire, ravaged fields, blood . . .

Blood everywhere.

Johann blinked. He knew it was the potion creating the illusions in his mind, but still—the images seemed as real as if everything were happening right before his eyes. He reached out with both hands and dipped his fingers into the surprisingly warm liquid. The images vanished and were replaced by a familiar face. It was Tonio and yet it wasn't—he looked younger, more handsome, almost seductive.

"Welcome, Johann Georg Faustus," said the younger Tonio with a smile. "Are you ready for the first sacrifice?"

Now Johann saw the whole figure in the basin. He was a knight in full armor on a magnificent horse, and he had the most beautiful eyes and fullest lips Faust had ever seen on a person. His mouth and cheeks looked red and healthy, as if he'd just returned from a fast ride; his body was brimming with strength and vitality. In the same instant Johann knew that this was the man he'd been looking for all these years.

Gilles de Rais.

"The little finger of the right hand," said the knight. The image shuddered, and the beautiful face was contorted into a grimace.

"*Faites vite.* The end and the beginning are close."

29

WITH A POUNDING HEART AND A METALLIC TASTE IN HIS mouth, Karl ran through the underground passages. He needed to get out of here as fast as possible! He'd left the laterna magica behind—he wouldn't have any more use for it. What he had seen and heard inside that mockery of a church was so horrific that he thought he might go insane.

After Faust had walked into the underground crypt, Karl had hidden behind the entrance. From the darkness of the cellar he had watched as the leader of the Satanists had kicked Valentin to the ground and handed Johann a chalice. He hadn't been able to understand much of what was being spoken, but the few words he'd heard made Karl's blood curdle. Then Faust had collapsed over the baptismal font.

It had taken everything Karl had to prevent himself from crying out loud during the next part of the ceremony. He had almost thrown up with fear and disgust.

With a large, curved knife, the leader had cut off Faust's little finger and tossed it into the basin.

That had been the moment Karl started to run.

He looked around in panic. The lantern in his hand barely gave off any light; the oil was almost used up. Once it went out, the darkness would swallow him up like the whale had swallowed Jonah. Which way should he turn? He wasn't sure how many forks and chambers he had crossed by now. Those damned tunnels all looked the same—it was like a labyrinth! Sometimes he thought he could hear the chanting again in the distance, and he ran even faster. He needed to get away from this hellish place of madness! At least he still had Valentin's key ring, so he could open doors if he needed to. But what good was that if he didn't know which doors led to the top?

Karl finally collapsed at the next corner. Panting heavily, he cowered down and closed his eyes. This was the end. Well, at least he wouldn't die of thirst down here—only starve to death slowly. In front of his feet flowed another one of the small streams that crisscrossed the underground like veins of the city.

When Karl looked up, he saw a sign in the flickering light of the lantern.

He cried out with surprise. It was one of the coal marks Faust had drawn on the walls to help them find their way back. Karl had completely forgotten about them in his blind panic. He jumped up and felt his strength return. If he followed the marks from here he would find the exit to the cemetery. From there he could turn west on the highway and leave this cursed place behind for good.

This cursed place and the doctor.

The doctor he loved.

Karl bit his lip. He pictured how he'd left Faust in the crypt. Like a calf at slaughter.

Like a sacrificial lamb.

He'd known the doctor for nearly two years. It hadn't always been easy with him—Faust was arrogant, cynical, and hot tempered—and yet Karl had learned much from him. The doctor had been almost like a father to him, and much more understanding than his own forbidding father, who had called him soft and never treated him with respect.

But there was more to it. Karl had had several relationships with men in his life. The first one had been at Latin School, but the other boy's parents sent him to a monastery before the affair came to light. None of his relationships had ever lasted very long—mainly because it was just too dangerous. But it was different with the doctor. The longer Karl was with him, the stronger the bond between them became. Karl thought Faust was somewhat frightening, but he was also fascinating. There seemed to be a deep, inscrutable secret in the doctor's black eyes. Karl's love for him consumed and nourished him at the same time. He knew the doctor would be his downfall, but he couldn't bring himself to leave him. And that was why Karl couldn't abandon him down here.

Karl leaned his head back and groaned. It was enough to drive a man insane! If he turned left, freedom and a fresh start awaited him. Together with Faust, the letters that threatened his safety would vanish. And the fire that was burning so hot inside him now would go out sooner or later. But if he turned right . . .

The coal marks could lead him back to the cemetery, but they also showed the way to the prison. Karl felt certain he'd be able to find the way back to the underground hall from there. It hadn't been far.

Left or right.

Swearing under his breath, Karl stood up. He cursed God, the world, and the doctor in particular, and turned right.

The marks on the walls led him back to the well below the prison. There still were no sounds coming from above. Karl turned around and tried to remember which way they'd gone earlier. The humming and chanting led him in the right direction. A few minutes later he was back in the cellar in front of the double doors. The crate with the laterna still sat where he'd left it in his panic.

Cautiously he sneaked back to the open door and peered into the crypt. The masked men were humming and murmuring strange-sounding spells, while their leader in the apse had pulled his hood back over his head.

On the altar, Greta had been replaced by the doctor.

Karl clenched his fists. Was his master already dead? Blood was dripping from Faust's right hand, which someone had bandaged after that madman had cut off his finger. His head had flopped to one side, and his eyes and forehead were also bandaged with rags. What in God's name had those men done to the doctor?

Now the leader was raising the curved dagger he had used to cut off Faust's little finger. The chanting stopped.

"The first and second sacrifice are complete!" bellowed the man in the robe. "The beast is awakening from its sleep—I can hear it! I can hear it stir deep in the innards of the earth. *Homo Deus est!*"

"*Homo Deus est, Deus homo est!*" chanted the masked men in a frenzy.

The leader held the dagger high up in the air, just like a priest lifting the cup during the Eucharist. It looked as though he was asking for the weapon to be blessed.

"O Spiritus Mephistophiel, Madeschea, Diabola, Larua . . . threefold spirit from hell . . . *Sanguis tuus, cor tuum . . .*"

Karl had given up trying to make any sense of the twisted Latin terms and names, but the last phrase he understood without a problem.

Sanguis tuus, cor tuum . . . Your blood, your heart.

He had a horrible suspicion about what would come next. The black monk would ram the dagger into Faust's body and slit him open like a fish so he could tear out his heart. Dark spells and invocations still poured from the leader's mouth, but it couldn't be long before the dagger shot down. Karl looked around with panic. Was there no way to stop the ritual or at least disrupt it for a while?

His eyes fell upon the laterna magica sitting on the ground, and from there to the small lantern in his hand. The flame was very weak, but it still burned. Karl's hands shook. He had plenty of practice setting up the apparatus quickly. Would there be enough time?

He yanked the crate closer, opened it, and pulled out one of the oil-drenched cloths they had brought along. He held it to his lantern, which had just about gone out. When the rag was alight, he used it to light the oil lamp inside the laterna magica. Then he adjusted the tube until the glowing circle of light was directly on the back wall of the apse.

The men in the underground church cried out with surprise, and their leader broke off in the middle of his litany. Annoyed, he turned around and spotted the circle, which was hovering and flickering like a supernatural being.

A not very human sound escaped the monk's throat. It sounded like the angry growl of a wolf.

Then Karl inserted the first glass plate his hands could find.

~

Johann woke up and stared into the darkness.

Where was he? What had happened? Scraps of memory returned and slowly came together to form a complete picture. Tonio . . . the underground hall . . . the black potion . . . a baptismal font with blood . . . his daughter, almost naked and lifeless on an altar . . .

Greta!

He shot up and was overwhelmed by a wave of nausea. He threw up and retched, and still everything around him was black. Had he gone blind? Was he in hell?

He tried to focus on his body. The ground below him was cold; it appeared he was lying on a stone floor. Carefully he tried to move his limbs, first his legs, then his hands. He felt damp straw. A sharp pain shot up from his right hand and made him scream out. Something had happened to his hand but he couldn't remember what. An image flashed through his mind.

A curved dagger glinting in the light.

He screamed again. It was strange to hear his own voice, as if it didn't belong to him. It echoed as if he was deep below ground. He had a terrible headache and trouble breathing, as if something was blocking his nose. Why on earth couldn't he see a thing?

With his left hand—burnt from reaching into the glowing brazier—Johann gently touched his face and found that it was almost completely wrapped up in a bandage. He started tugging at the rags and was instantly punished with excruciating pain in his head, worse than the pain in his hand. He threw up again, and his mouth burned like fire as he spat out the caustic bile.

"I would leave the bandage where it is," uttered a hoarse voice nearby. "It may be dirty, but they soaked it in oil of Saint-John's-wort to prevent inflammation. I can smell it from here."

Johann froze. He knew the voice.

"Va . . . Valentin?" he said with a raspy voice. "You . . . you're alive?"

"More dead than alive. That monster broke something inside me. I . . . I can't move. But yes, I'm alive."

"What happened?" asked Johann quietly.

"You really want to know?"

When Johann didn't reply, Valentin spoke slowly.

"After you drank the black potion, the leader cut off your little finger. He said that was the first sacrifice."

Johann winced. The wound on his hand throbbed, and he thought he could still feel his finger. But he knew it was no longer there. Another image emerged in his memory: Tonio had thrown the finger—his little finger that used to hold playing cards and make coins disappear—into the baptismal font.

But that wasn't all.

"And the second sacrifice?" he asked quietly. "What was the second sacrifice?"

Silence spread through the room, a heavy silence that was almost harder to bear than the darkness around him.

"Speak up, damn it!" gasped Johann. "What was the second sacrifice?"

"They . . . they cut out your left eye."

Johann groaned. He felt sick again but he had nothing left to throw up. He was tempted to touch the bandage with his hand, but he knew that every touch would result in agonizing pain and could lead to infection. He probably suffered from fever already.

"They went about it very professionally," said Valentin with a shaking voice. "They used proper surgical instruments—I'm guessing one of the masked men was a Nuremberg physician. I think they wanted you alive."

"For the third sacrifice," whispered Johann.

"Yes, but it never came to that. Something happened. I must have passed out for a while, but I heard shouts and swearing, and then they locked us up in here. I suspect we're in some forgotten cellar below the Sebaldus Church. I don't know what happened next."

Silence descended over their prison chamber again while Johann's eye socket throbbed. The pain was surprisingly bearable—probably an aftereffect of the black potion. Johann guessed the drink contained henbane or devil's trumpet, or both. That would also explain the hallucinations. Johann remembered seeing people in the glistening surface of the basin. First Tonio—or a younger version of Tonio—and then a knight. He'd thought the man was Gilles de Rais—a name that had been haunting his dreams for years. No wonder that it should appear in his hallucinations.

"May I ask you something, Johann?" Valentin's voice roused him from his musings. "That potion they gave you. I thought it was poison and you would never regain consciousness. And yet you're awake, you speak—"

"Ash," said Johann tiredly.

"What did you say?"

"Ash. I ate ash. When they dragged me to the basin, I held on to one of the braziers. I pretended to stumble, grabbed some cold ashes from the edge, and stuffed them into my mouth."

Johann ran his tongue along his gums and teeth. He could still feel the foul-tasting crumbs in his mouth. "The ancient Greeks knew that ash is detoxifying. I hoped it would lessen the worst effects of the potion." He added bitterly, "Even if it couldn't save my eye."

With a trembling hand he felt for the bandage again. Then he adjusted it on one side until his right eye was unobstructed. For a few moments, everything remained pitch black, and Johann was beginning to think he had gone completely blind. But then he started to make out a few outlines around him. He was lying on the floor of a dark cellar, and there was a closed door on the wall opposite him. A shivering bundle lay on the ground beside him—Valentin. His old friend looked even more miserable than Johann felt. Valentin's body was strangely twisted, like a puppet whose strings had been cut.

"I . . . I'm so sorry, Johann," stammered Valentin. "Believe me, I only wanted to save Greta. They forced me to bring you down here, and it had to be tonight. Something to do with the stars, some comet—"

"I think we're even," said Johann, cutting him off. "You—"

A noise made him jump with fright. It was a key turning in the lock.

Johann took a deep breath.

They had come to fetch him for the third sacrifice. His body stiffened and his pulse raced. He didn't want to show fear, but he knew he couldn't prevent it. Hopefully his sacrifice would at least save Greta.

"God is great and powerful," he uttered instinctively. "God, give me strength . . ." He realized he hadn't prayed for his own immortal soul in a very long time. Perhaps now was a good moment to start.

"The Lord is my shepherd," he started. It was the psalm that had comforted so many dying and frightened men before him. "I shall not want. He maketh me to lie down in green pastures—"

"Doctor, it's me!"

Johann broke off and turned his bandaged head to the door.

There were no masked men, no insane devil worshippers, no Tonio.

Just Karl Wagner.

His assistant's outline was stark against the light of a torch from behind him.

What on earth? Johann thought. For the first time he wondered whether God might be a real person made of flesh and blood, standing in front of him in the shape of Karl.

His jerkin was filthy and torn, his hair looked ruffled and wild, and in his hand he was holding Valentin's key ring.

"One of them was for this door," he said with a tired smile. "First one I tried. Lucky I took this when we climbed into the prison." He looked back down the dark corridor nervously. "I don't think we have much time. They'll return for you soon."

Johann's throat was making a rattling sound. After a few moments he realized that he was trying to laugh—a circumstance so strange given their situation that he thought he must be dreaming.

"My God, boy—heaven sent you!" he exclaimed eventually.

"I have to agree with you for once," replied Karl. "I disrupted that horrific devil's mass with an image of our savior. Jesus Christ inside a glowing circle of light—the leader of those Satanists wasn't overly thrilled. It didn't take them long to discover the laterna and destroy it, but at least they had to pause their ceremony for a while to search for me."

"And now you have come back," mumbled Johann. "You could have fled."

Karl lowered his eyes. "I still owed you something, remember? I think now I've earned the right to get back my letters."

"You certainly have." Johann struggled to his feet, and Karl stared at the bandage on Faust's face. He hadn't seen it in the dim light until then.

"What in heaven's name have they done to you?"

"That isn't important right now. The only thing that matters is where they've taken Greta."

"When I set off the turmoil with the laterna, some of those masked madmen took the girl away." Karl hesitated. "That creepy fellow at the front shouted something about taking her up to the church."

"Probably the Sebaldus Church. I guess they want to keep Greta as a pawn," said Valentin from his corner. He moaned softly. "They'll only let her go once the third sacrifice has been given—if they don't simply kill her as an undesirable witness."

"He gave me his word," said Johann pensively, more to himself. "He's bound by it." He hesitated. "We need those people to feel secure. I can't leave. If they find that I've escaped, they will kill Greta or do even worse things to her."

He thought about Tonio's words at the altar.

It is the same as with lambs—the younger, the better tasting . . . Perhaps I will take her with me on Walpurgis Night in a couple of years, and we can share her.

"Damn it!" he swore. "There must be a solution. There always is one!"

But no matter how hard he thought, he couldn't find one. Whether he stayed or whether he went—he wouldn't see his daughter again. He was doomed. Down here in this hell on earth, all his knowledge was for nothing.

"I know a solution," said Valentin all of a sudden. His voice was firm and determined.

"Which is?"

"You go and I stay."

"And how is that supposed to help?" said Karl. "They'll see right away that the doctor has fled."

"Not if I am the doctor."

"You the doctor?" With his one remaining eye Johann stared at his friend in confusion. "What are you talking about?"

"You're wearing a bandage that covers most of your face," explained Valentin. "I'm a fair bit shorter than you, but I don't think they'll notice in the dark. Not if I'm wearing your star cloak. We'll stuff my clothes with straw and put them in the corner. They won't take much notice of the dummy—most likely they assume I'm already dead. They want you, Johann!"

Johann shook his head. "You can't be serious."

"Listen, Johann. I'm dying! I can feel it. My whole body is numb, and the coldness in my limbs is spreading. I was already a cripple beforehand, but that monster broke the last few bones that weren't broken inside me. Even if I lived— I'd be a living corpse." Valentin gave Johann a pleading look. "All I have left is Greta! You must find her and save her. It is the last thing I'm asking of you. One last favor as a friend."

"I've let you down before," muttered Johann. "I might do it again."

"You won't let me down, Johann. I forgave you for lying to me and using me all those years ago. But I would never forgive you if anything happened to Greta. You would never forgive yourself, I know that."

Johann didn't reply. His head hurt, and his eye socket and his right hand burned like fire. There was a high probability that he wouldn't survive this. If those lunatics didn't kill him, fever probably would. He had made sacrifices, but now his friend was going to give his life for him.

"I'm not doing it for you, Johann," Valentin whispered. "I'm doing it for Greta."

For Greta.

Johann nodded slowly. Neither he nor Valentin mattered—all that mattered was the girl.

His daughter.

"I'm going to need a new bandage," Johann said with a heavy voice.

Then, slowly and carefully, he unwrapped the dirty rags from around his head.

30

RUSHING DOWN THE CORRIDOR A SHORT WHILE LATER, Johann felt as though he were trudging through a swamp. His legs kept giving way beneath him, and Karl had to hold him up. Despite the ash he'd swallowed, the poison of the black potion was still wreaking havoc in his body. Shadows would leap at him from the walls, and he thought he could hear the voice of the handsome knight.

Faites vite . . . faites vite . . . faites vite . . .

The only thing keeping him going was the thought of Greta.

Before they'd gone, he and Valentin had embraced one last time, and Johann had sensed that the strength was draining from his old friend's body. When he looked down at Valentin with his healthy eye one last time, Johann had seen himself on the stone floor. Bandaged head, star cloak, and the shell of a body, nothing more.

He had learned one thing from Valentin: what really mattered wasn't what could be seen on the outside, nor the blind pursuit of knowledge, of power.

All that mattered was love.

What use was all his cleverness if he couldn't protect those he loved? Valentin had shown him what love was capable of by sacrificing himself for Greta. In that moment, Johann had realized that it was love alone that gave meaning to life. That was something Tonio would never understand.

It was this revelation that spurred him on now.

Johann staggered more than he walked. He felt as cold as ice. He wore only a thin shirt that reached to his knees; they'd put everything else on Valentin. Somehow he managed to climb up a steep set of stairs that led to another door. With one of the many keys from Valentin's key ring, Karl opened the lock, and they found themselves in a room that, unlike all the previous ones, had a window. Early morning light fell through the bluish crown-glass pane.

They were back on the surface.

Shaking with fever, Johann looked around. The door was so smoothly set into the wall that it was almost invisible from the outside. A narrow walkway lined by columns led into another room. Elegant oak chests with veneer decorations lined the walls, and gold and silver cups stood on a table in the center. Karl opened one of the chests and gasped. Reverently, he held up a gemstone-studded cross—clearly a monstrance.

"We're in the inner sanctum," he whispered. "The sacristy of the Sebaldus Church. The masked men probably took Greta the same way." Karl put down the cross and looked around. "Hmm. Somewhere in here should be . . ." He opened another chest, rummaged around for a while, and, grinning triumphantly, pulled out two musty-smelling priests' robes. "Ha, I knew it. We'll hardly find a better disguise inside a church."

With much difficulty, Johann pulled on one of the robes, the hood scarcely concealing his poorly bandaged face. He was still shaking, but at least he felt a little warmer. He could tell the fever was still spreading, however.

When Karl had also put on his robe, he gave Johann a questioning look. "And now? What is your plan?"

Johann closed his eye. He wanted to put off the moment when he'd have to admit that he had no plan. The renowned and wise doctor was nothing but a poor, half-blind fool.

"You . . . you said before that they were taking Greta to the church," he said. "Did they say anything else? Any particular place—anything at all?"

"The leader only yelled that they ought to take the girl up to the church. I guess they went into the city from here. Nuremberg is a big place."

Johann sighed and reached for the tabletop to brace himself. "Then . . . then let's go into the church, at least. Maybe we'll find a clue as to Greta's whereabouts." But even while he spoke the sentence, he knew how helpless he sounded.

They walked down another walkway, crossed another room, and came to a door whose bolt had been left open. Slowly, Karl opened the door.

The nave of the Sebaldus Church lay in front of them. The sacristy wasn't far from the altar with the silver chest containing the relics of Saint Sebaldus. The slanted light of dawn fell through the tall glass windows and bathed the many columns, arcades, and side chapels in an unearthly light.

There were no churchgoers yet, but it couldn't be long until morning mass. Farther back, an old sexton was sweeping the floor. He was hunched low over his broom and didn't notice the two strange priests.

Johann looked around desperately.

He saw nothing. No clue, nothing.

Greta had disappeared from his life as suddenly as she'd entered it.

Karl gently touched him on the shoulder. "I know you want to find this girl for your friend," he said. "But you must see that it is pointless. They took her away hours ago. She could be anywhere by now."

"We must look for her," muttered Johann. "Look . . . for her . . ." The fever and the potion made him feel so heavy, so awfully heavy.

"Listen." Karl paused. "When I told you they didn't say anything else about where they were taking the girl, I wasn't telling the whole truth. The leader shouted something else—it was rather hard to understand. But I think he said, 'Take her up to the church and then . . .'" Karl swallowed. "'And then straight to hell.'"

"To hell?" asked Johann, his voice shaking.

"To hell." Karl nodded. "Those were his words. I didn't tell you earlier because I can see that the girl means a lot to you. But I think it's safe to assume that they killed her. But we survived! We only have to go out the church door and—"

Johann slid down against a column, his consciousness fading.

To hell.

Karl crouched down beside him with concern. "You must think about yourself now, Doctor. Forget the girl, forget—"

"I can't forget her, damn it!" shouted Johann with his last strength. Then he managed a hoarse whisper. "I can't forget her. She . . . she is my daughter."

Karl gaped at him. "Your daughter? But how?"

Then Johann passed out.

~

Deep down below, a lock clicked open and Valentin Brander spoke his final prayer.

Crunching footsteps approached, and then he was picked up like a rag doll. Underneath his bandage, a smile spread across Valentin's face.

They haven't noticed.

There must have been four of them. He could feel their hands as they lifted him onto some kind of stretcher and carried him out of the chamber. Soon he heard the strange litany again as they neared the underground hall. Valentin smelled burnt oil and smoke, a lot of smoke. He couldn't cough or his voice would give him away.

The men set him down, and the chanting stopped.

"We'll catch that scoundrel soon, I swear!" hissed someone not far from Valentin. The voice reminded him of a snake. "What a pity the cripple never told me that Faust's assistant was with him. My birds need food, and he's a handsome young man. But that doesn't matter now. All that matters is the last ritual—the third sacrifice."

Valentin held perfectly still. When he'd sent word to the man named Tonio del Moravia a few hours beforehand that he was bringing Faust to the agreed place, he hadn't mentioned anything about Karl Wagner. He wasn't sure why—a whim, one last tiny attempt of resistance against the enormously powerful, inexplicable evil. Who was Tonio? A madman who had gathered followers who were just as mad as him, or was he more than that? In the few conversations Valentin had led with him at night in some foggy alleyway, he hadn't come any closer to figuring out the man's mystery. Something incredibly cold radiated from him; he seemed like an ancient reptile in a human body. Only his eyes had glowed.

Who are you?

Valentin had hoped to learn the answer before his death. But then he realized that he didn't need any more answers after death, because there would be no more questions. Nothing mattered anymore. Nothing but Greta, the girl he loved like his own daughter, the girl who had enriched his poor, pathetic life a thousandfold for the last few years. Images started to appear before his mind's eye, giving him strength.

Greta laughing on a swing, her little hands clasping the hemp ropes tight, her legs dangling . . . Greta with a bleeding knee snuggling up to him . . . Greta with her doll on her lap, her mouth smeared with honey . . . Tell me a story, Uncle Valentin! Just one more story before bedtime—please!

He wanted to leave this life with those images in his mind.

The litany rose again, and Valentin heard the snake's voice above the chanting.

"O Mephistophiel, O Satanas, O Diabolos, O Larua . . ."

Valentin no longer trembled; his body and mind felt calm. He was no longer afraid, because he knew that his life had had meaning. And that he wasn't dying for nothing. Because of him, Greta would live, and she'd even have a father. More memories rose to the surface; there were so many of them.

Greta, stark naked in a wooden tub, giggling, her little arms stretched out for him . . .

"O Samael, O Azazel, O Beelzebub . . ."

Greta and him on a horse, riding together across the fallow fields outside Nuremberg, and she laughs—oh, how she laughs!

"O Iris, O Scheitan, O Urian . . ."

Greta dancing for him, spinning around, her dress a whirling circle . . . Her laughter . . . oh, her ringing laughter . . .

"O Lucifer, accept the third sacrifice!"

Something was driven deep into Valentin's chest, but he felt no pain, only a pleasant warmth spreading all through his body.

He laughed as his soul traveled heavenward.

Far down below, in a world that was no longer his, someone screamed out loud with rage and disappointment, and Valentin knew that the devil had lost the game.

$\sim$

Johann was dreaming.

The August sun fell on him warmly from a cloudless blue sky; bees and flies buzzed around him, and the ears in the grain field were brushed by a wind as gentle as if someone were stroking his cheek. Margarethe was lying next to him, singing the old, familiar nursery rhyme.

Growing in our garden are parsley and thyme; our Gretchen is the bride, she's looking so fine . . .

Together they dozed in their favorite hiding place in the rye field, not far from the walls of Knittlingen. The grain was trampled flat in a circle around them, and in the center stood the weathered stone cross.

"Will you marry me when we're grown up, Johann?" asked Margarethe softly in his dream. "Will you look after me? Now and forever?"

Johann smiled and squeezed her hand. "I promise I will look after you. Now and forever."

"Just like you . . ." Margarethe hesitated. She brushed a strand of flaxen hair from her face; the air shimmered with heat. "Just like you . . ." Suddenly her voice took on a different tone, low and jarred as if she were speaking from inside a well, as if she were someone else.

Someone profoundly evil.

"Just like you looked after Martin, right? You bloody coward! You piece of dirt!"

Clouds moved in front of the sun and a shadow covered Margarethe's face, which ceased to be hers. It became that of Martin, then of Signore Barbarese, of Tonio, then of Gilles de Rais.

The face of Gilles de Rais, the handsome knight.

"I like to catch two children at once. Then I kill the first one and make the other one watch," said Margarethe, and her lips melted onto the ground like hot wax.

Johann wanted to scream but only managed a gargle. His tongue had been ripped out and was lying in the dirt before him.

A thunderclap announced an impending storm, and the wind whipped waves through the rye field. He could hear footsteps now, as loud as the cutting of a scythe. They plowed through the field toward him—swish, swoosh.

Closer and closer.

Swish, swoosh.

"Who's afraid of the boogeyman?" asked Margarethe in a hoarse whisper. It was the opening line of a children's game of catch. And every child knew what to answer.

"No one," replied Johann.

"And what if he comes?"

"Then we run!"

Swish, swoosh . . . swish, swoosh . . . swish . . .

He jumped up and ran across the field as the first raindrops struck his face. After a while he noticed that he hadn't thought of Margarethe. He had forgotten all about her in his fear and had simply run away.

When he turned around, she was gone.

"Margarethe!" he shouted into the rain, thunder, and howling wind. "Margarethe, where are you?"

He searched everywhere with growing desperation. There she was! She was standing among the ears, waving. But when he looked again it was only a scarecrow. The scarecrow's eyes were black, black, dead, button eyes, as piercing as needles.

"Where are you?" screamed Johann again.

"I'm in hell," said Greta, his daughter, the scarecrow with the button eyes. "Search for me in hell."

Then she stalked away on broomstick legs, a shrinking spot on the horizon until the rain washed her away. Only her words still echoed across the windswept fields.

"Search for me in hell."

The boy who used to be called Johann a long time ago—in another life— awoke with a feverish scream. His face was bathed in sweat, and his mouth as dry as a brittle Eucharist host.

"Margarethe!" gasped Johann. "Stay with me! Greta."

"You're safe, Doctor," said a voice from next to him. "All will be well."

Johann opened his one eye and the memories returned instantly. The worried face of Karl hovered above him. He was holding a wet rag, which he used to wipe Johann's forehead. From the corner of his eye, Johann saw some old wooden beams on a ceiling, a narrow window covered in cobwebs letting in some milky sunlight, a small bed, and reeds on the floor with a foul-smelling chamber pot in the middle. From afar he heard shouting and cheering, and the music of fanfares, drums, and bells.

"Where are we?" asked Johann. He was a little dizzy and his head ached, but he felt better than earlier.

"In the attic room of a tavern," replied Karl. "Not far from Sebaldus Church. You passed out and I carried you here. You slept for a few hours." He gave an exhausted smile. "The tavern keeper thought we were two drunken itinerant preachers and gave me this chamber under the roof. It's not the best room in the house, but at least I didn't have to answer any nosy questions."

Johann groaned as he felt the bandage on his face and the empty eye socket below. Carefully he touched the left side of his face; the cloths seemed fresh.

"I might not have studied medicine for very long, but I remembered a few things," said Karl, eyeing his patient with concern. "There was a pharmacy not far from here, and I used the last of my money to buy a few herbs to stanch the bleeding. Lady's mantle, shepherd's purse." He paused. "Our professor at the university said that we ought to cauterize the wound and smear it with a paste of egg and ash, but I didn't. At least your hand and face are bandaged properly now. We'll see what happens."

"Th . . . thank you." Johann slowly rose from the musty-smelling bed. He still felt nauseated from the potion Tonio had given him. "Water."

Karl handed him a jug, and he drank in long gulps.

"What's all the noise outside?" asked Johann eventually, wiping his cracked lips.

"It's the Schembartlauf parade. It started about an hour ago—the whole of Nuremberg is in the streets," Karl said. "Those masked jesters dance through town and tease the spectators, and I think at the end they storm a life-sized elephant made of wood and linen. I saw the giant contraption briefly on our way here—it was standing next to the Sebaldus Church. A truly impressive—"

Johann dropped the jug to the ground and it shattered into a hundred pieces.

"Hell," he said.

Karl put his hand on Faust's forehead. "You still have a strong fever, Doctor. You better lie down. I'll bring you a fresh—"

"Hell," said Johann again.

He stood up on shaky legs and walked to the door.

"For heaven's sake, what are you doing? You can't go outside! Where do you think you're going? You are hurt—you're hallucinating!"

"I've never been clearer in my head," said Johann as he started to climb down the stairs. "I'm going down to hell to fetch my daughter."

~

Soon they were both standing in the street. The carnival raged all around them. Throngs of people lined the sides of the lane, waiting for the costumed dancers to pass them by.

Johann squeezed through a gap and watched as half a dozen Schembart runners skipped past, with bells on their ankles and pikes in their hands. From time to time they would rush at the hooting crowd and pretend to stab them with their blunt weapons. People laughed and cheered, and the air was rich with the delicious smells of fried and boiled food.

Many musicians and jugglers who weren't Schembart runners had also joined the procession. Troupes from all over the region used this day to show off their tricks or to roam the streets playing flutes or bagpipes. Johann looked around searchingly.

Where is the hell? he thought. *Where is it?*

A hand tapped his shoulder. It was Karl, who had pushed his way through to Johann. "You have a fever," he urged. "You must go back to bed!"

Johann said nothing and continued to watch the procession. He struggled to focus. He was trembling and sometimes thought he was still dreaming. A huge, strong man wearing a costume made of dead leaves and moss was just walking past him. His face was hidden beneath a fake bushy beard, and he was swinging a tree trunk that had something tied to it that was impossible to make out in the jostle. Johann's hood covered most of his face, but still he thought the giant looked at him.

The large man slowed down.

"Any one of those masked men could be one of the lunatics from the crypt," whispered Karl, tugging at Johann's robe. "If they spot us, we're done. We must get away from here!"

Johann still wasn't reacting, staring instead at some artificial horses that came after the dancers. He could tell by the feet under the furs that inside each costume were two men. The wild man had vanished behind the next corner, and the parade was proceeding. Noise and laughter rose and fell like water on a mill.

"The elephant," uttered Johann all of a sudden, more to himself. Then he finally turned to Karl. "Where is the elephant?"

"The elephant? It was standing right next to the portal when we left the church. Why?"

"Damn, don't you get it?" Johann was almost shouting now. "The elephant is the hell! That's what the Schembart runners call their big parade wagon. Remember? Valentin told us last night. It's the hell!"

"You . . . you're saying . . ."

"By Christ, *that's* the hell Tonio was talking about. No inferno or Last Judgment, but the parade wagon!" Johann grabbed Karl by the sleeve, his one eye glaring angrily. "Take her up to the church and then straight to hell—isn't that what he said? That's where they are hiding her. Every street in town is busy because of the Schembartlauf, so they couldn't drag her away unnoticed. But it's no problem inside the parade wagon—they can smuggle her right through Nuremberg and no one will ever know." Johann's sweaty face was right up close to Karl's now. "Where is this elephant now? Where is the hell?"

"The . . . the tavern keeper said the parade would end on the main square at noon," Karl said, trying to free himself from Johann's grasp. "There'll be a huge spectacle with dancing and fireworks, and at the end they storm the elephant."

Johann looked up and saw that the cool winter sun stood high in the sky. Damn it, how long had he slept?

On the main square at noon.

"Let's go!" he shouted. "We don't have much time."

He pushed his way through the crowd, jabbing people left and right with his elbows. His right hand burned like fire, and the pain in his head nearly drove him insane, but he pressed on.

"Hey! Wait for me!"

Karl rushed after him, his robe billowing. Johann shoved aside a burly older man who cried out angrily and kicked Johann. He staggered, caught himself, and carried on, struggling to find his bearings. His field of vision was impaired by the bandage, and he fought against dizzy spells; sledgehammers seemed to thump in his temples.

Suddenly he found himself right in the middle of a group of masked Schembart runners, dancing and jumping and cartwheeling all around him. Grinning masks stared at him, bells jingled everywhere, and someone pushed Johann to the ground. Towering above him was the wild man in his costume of moss and ferns, swinging his enormous tree trunk like a club. Now Johann saw what was tied to the trunk.

It was a doll made to look like a child, about as long as his forearm and very lifelike.

The wild man was aiming his giant cudgel straight at Johann's head.

"Bienvenue en enfer!" he growled in French, and Johann thought he'd heard the voice before.

Suddenly the huge man staggered and cried out angrily as someone gave him a shove. The tree trunk missed Johann's head by an inch.

"Run!"

Karl pulled Johann up and pushed him away from the eerie giant with the club and into a throng of laughing, dancing spectators who thought Johann's stunt was part of the show.

Johann stumbled on, partly pushed by the crowd and partly dragged by his assistant. He could hardly breathe in the stench of sweat, alcohol, and horse dung; everything was so loud, so terribly loud—the drums, the bells, the shouts of the spectators, everything mixing into a monotonous mess. Behind him, Johann caught a glimpse of the wild man flanked by other masked men, the giant waving his tree trunk violently. But then Karl maneuvered the doctor around a corner, and the parade moved past them. Instantly, it was much quieter.

"They recognized us," gasped Karl, leaning against the wall of a house. "I can't really see their eyes underneath those masks, and I don't know if they are the same men as down in the crypt—but I'm certain some of them recognized us. That huge fellow just tried to kill you! We're not even safe in the crowd any longer." He shot Johann a look of warning. "Do you still want to find that elephant?"

Johann gave a curt nod. He was too exhausted for words.

"All right, then. Let's go straight to hell." He gestured to the right. "This way. The parade takes a longer loop to the main square. If we hurry, we might get there before the Schembart runners."

The narrow, filthy alleyway went around a bend, crossed a courtyard full of barrels, and finally ended on the main square. The parade was nearing from the east. There was no sight of any dancers yet, but Johann and Karl could hear the music and cheering. Something cracked and hissed, as if fireworks were going off somewhere. Johann blinked a few times; his one eye was blinded by the noon sunshine. A large crowd had already gathered, waiting for the procession to arrive. People stood tightly packed, from the city hall to the Schöner

Brunnen fountain, with its gilded towers and manifold statues, all the way over to Frauenkirche Church; even the balconies of the patricians' houses were full of people. Johann's eye scanned the crowd, his heart racing.

Where?

There! Right next to the Schöner Brunnen fountain, surrounded by a knot of people, stood the elephant. It was at least three paces high, on wheels, and crowned by a wooden tower that was surrounded by mock battlements. Four tiny cannons were fastened on the corners, and a handful of jesters stood behind the battlements, including a priest with dozens of letters of indulgence sewn onto his robe, fools with playing cards or dice patterns on their costumes, and a hunchbacked witch with a long nose and a pack on her back. The crowd cheered for the dressed-up figures when their little cannon spouted red sparks. There was cracking, smoke, thunder, and hissing.

"Hell on earth," said Johann. "We found it."

"And what do you propose we do now?" asked Karl. "Even if Greta is somewhere inside that wagon, you can't just climb up there and—hey!"

He broke off when Johann stormed toward the elephant.

The train of Schembart runners arrived from a lane next to Frauenkirche Church and was received with much fanfare. The main square was so full that Johann struggled to get through. Several of the jugglers also arrived on the square and showed their tricks and acts. The elephant swayed like a reed in the wind among all the people, and the costumed men atop the tower threw small treats into the crowd. They grabbed the treats out of the pack of the witch, who stared at the people below from nasty little eyes. Again the cannons were lit and spat out red fire.

Johann pushed through the crowd; he was close to the elephant now, but he still hadn't figured out what to do next. He was certain that Greta must be somewhere inside the structure, probably bound and gagged. He didn't think the masked men had had an opportunity to get her away yet. But what was he supposed to do? Karl was right. He couldn't climb the tower on his own, especially since it was guarded by several costumed men—and he couldn't be sure the men weren't Tonio's.

Unsure of what to do next, he paused just a few steps away from the elephant. Then, suddenly, a horde of colorfully clad soldiers in slit trousers approached from the direction where the Schembart runners had entered the square. They yelled and shouted as they carried ladders toward the elephant. Johann startled. Yelling soldiers, like in battle? Was he having another fever dream? But then he remembered what Karl had told him earlier.

At the end they storm the elephant.

Those soldiers were part of the show. They were going to storm hell.

When the men ran past them, accompanied by the cheers and hoots of the crowd, Johann joined them. He saw from the corner of his eye that Karl had caught up to him, his face a grimace of fear and determination. Johann was surprised the soldiers let them run along just like that, but then he caught another glimpse of the preacher atop the tower. The men probably thought he and Karl were also in costume.

Screaming and shouting wildly, the false mercenaries braced their ladders against the elephant and started to scale its sides. The masked men at the top bombarded them with treats and lit their cannons again and again until Johann's ears were ringing. Panting, he struggled to climb one of the ladders when he noticed that a man at the top had started to push it away from the elephant. The ladder swayed dangerously and almost toppled, but Karl managed to hold it and started to climb up himself.

Johann studied the elephant as he climbed the rungs of the ladder. It was made of wood and linen that had been painted gray, and attached to the feet were wheels on which the giant contraption could be moved through the city. He estimated there was enough room in the elephant's belly for a person, if not several. If there was an access point to the belly, then it was probably in the tower, which was about two paces taller than the top of the elephant.

Johann and Karl reached the top of the ladder and climbed over the balustrade surrounding the tower. Several soldiers had also reached the top, and they waved to the crowd, who celebrated them as conquerors. The priest with the letters of indulgence squirmed in the arms of a mercenary, squealing like a pig and rolling his eyes, and the crowd hooted with laughter. The hunchbacked witch still stood motionless, staring into the crowd.

The tower swayed under the weight of all the people; it wouldn't be long before it toppled. Johann unsteadily crept toward an artificial arch made of thin, painted wood that led inside the tower. The archway wasn't quite three feet high.

Johann peered inside but couldn't see any way into the belly of the elephant. He slammed his fist against the wall with disappointment and ripped the linen.

Damn!

Suddenly his idea seemed absurd to him, the spawn of a fever dream. How could he have thought Greta would be in here? The masked men had probably taken her away long ago—perhaps she wasn't even in the city anymore.

Perhaps she's already dead.

Johann's good hand clutched the linen, and it ripped further. He had been forcing the thought aside with all his might, fighting the unavoidable, but now it rushed back at him with a vengeance.

He had lost his daughter only a few days after meeting her.

Below him, the crowd heaved, people clapping and cheering. The first spectators were starting to tear at the gray fabric of the elephant. It wouldn't be long before the Nurembergers would shred the beast to pieces until the hell was conquered and the Schembartlauf over.

Everything would be over.

Johann looked around desperately for Karl but couldn't find him anywhere. Maybe it was just as well that his assistant didn't see him in this dark hour. Johann decided to throw himself off the elephant in the hope of putting an end to his life—just like the time he leaped off the Heidelberg bridge into the Neckar. Was the height sufficient to break his neck? As he went to look over the balustrade, his gaze was caught by the witch, who was still standing rigidly in the same spot. She wore a dress, an apron, and a headscarf like all old women, and her body was hunched over, making her seem short. For the first time Johann noticed the eyes behind the mask.

He winced as if he'd been slapped.

Eyes as black as pools in the woods.

They were his eyes.

The witch's hunchback was artificial, and Johann realized that she wasn't crippled but in fact a small person. Her hands were crossed on the balustrade and tied with thin ropes. Gray, almost invisible strings also ran up her dress and to the tower, holding her upright like a life-sized puppet; only the head beneath the mask rocked gently from side to side. Her eyes gleamed with pain and despair.

"Greta!" screamed Johann. His voice was drowned out by the noise of the crowd. "Greta!"

He tried to rush toward his daughter when someone yanked him back abruptly. A rope was thrown around his neck and pulled tight, and then someone dragged him up as if he were a rabid dog. A huge hand lifted him over the edge of the tower, and Johann treaded thin air. Panting and gasping for breath, he tried to catch a glimpse of the figure behind him.

It was the wild man.

Underneath his fake beard, the giant gave an evil grin. His black hair hung into his pockmarked face like rotting reeds. And finally Johann recognized him.

It was Poitou, Tonio's French friend he'd met in Nördlingen all those years ago.

Johann had heard his voice down in the crypt, too. Like his master, Poitou didn't seem to have aged much, although it was hard to tell with the fake beard and the wig. His strength, at least, was just as incredible as seventeen years ago.

The giant was still holding his victim over the balustrade. Johann made out a handful of masked men with their pikes below him, but unlike the ones from the parade, their lances weren't blunt. The sharp points glinted in the noontide sun, and they were aimed directly at Johann. He gagged and wheezed. If Poitou let go of him now, he'd be skewered like a rabbit. But if the giant hung on to him, he'd choke.

The crowd roared with laughter. Evidently, they thought the squirming monk was another funny stunt. Johann gasped for air and clutched the rope around his neck with his good hand, but he was far too weak to put up a fight. The voices of the spectators began to sound farther away, and his eyesight became blotchy and blurred. The world was narrowing into a tunnel, and at its end stood the loveliest apparition, glowing, surrounded by a halo . . .

Margarethe, I'm coming . . . I'm almost there . . . I . . .

Something grunted, and it took Johann a few moments to understand that it was Poitou. Then there was a crash as the hulk of a man fell backward against the tower, pulling Johann with him. The rope loosened a fraction, and Johann coughed and spluttered. From the corner of his eye he saw Karl wrestling with Poitou and guessed that his assistant must have attacked the giant from behind. One of the masked men that had followed the soldiers up the tower was just about to point one of the little cannons at Karl. And among all the chaos, Greta was still standing at the railing, stiff and quiet.

Johann tugged at the rope around his neck but it wouldn't loosen any further. It was fastened around his throat like an iron ring, and he was running out of breath. If only he had—

The knife!

Frantically he fingered for the knife under his robe—the same knife that Tonio had given him long ago. He found it, ripped it off, and cut the rope.

Fresh, life-giving air streamed down his throat.

Johann looked around, trying to grasp the situation. Karl was still grappling with Poitou, but the young man's strength seemed to fade. The giant's eyes sparkled devilishly.

"C'est la fin et le début," he snarled. *"Bienvenue en enfer!"*

At that moment, as the crowd howled and raved and the cannon next to Karl exploded into a blazing shower of red sparks, a profound calmness spread inside Johann. And even though he knew that only a few seconds passed by, he felt as though time were stretching out forever.

Greta's fearful eyes behind the mask . . . The knife cutting through her ties . . . Poitou's angry outcry . . . The blade in Johann's hand, as cold as ice . . . One last calculating look, then the throw—the one throw he had been waiting for all his life.

The knife cut through the air like an arrow.

Then the blade entered Poitou's left eye without a sound.

"An eye for an eye, and a tooth for a tooth," breathed Johann.

With a gasp of surprise, Poitou collapsed against the wall of the tower, felled by the knife of his master. His remaining eye stared lifelessly at the raven and the two crows circling in the blue sky above them. The birds cawed loudly; it sounded like laughter. Then they flew off.

The spectators hadn't yet realized what had just happened. Johann grabbed Greta under her arms and dragged her toward a ladder. The witch's mask slid to one side, and her pale face appeared beneath it. She was no longer unconscious, but she wasn't fully in her right senses, either.

"What . . . ?" she muttered. "Who . . . ?"

"Don't worry, my dear. We'll get you out of here," said Johann softly.

Meanwhile, Karl had thrown one of the masked men by the cannon over the balustrade, but part of the tower had caught on fire from the shower of sparks.

The dry timber crackled and smoked—so it would all go up in flames. Costumed men stood leaning over the dead Poitou; someone was shouting for help.

"Quick—take Greta on your back and let's get out of here!" shouted Johann.

Karl looked confused for a moment, but then he recognized the girl.

"The hell," he whispered. "You were right, Doctor."

He heaved the girl onto his back, and she clung on as he scrambled down the ladder. Johann followed. The soldiers and other masked men were too busy with the fire to notice them.

As chaos erupted all around them, they pushed their way through the crowd, away from the elephant, which by now burned like a giant torch.

The farther away they got from the main square, the quieter the streets became. It seemed as if the whole of Nuremberg was watching the grand finale, and they hardly saw a soul as they rushed through the lanes. Karl still carried Greta on his back. She sighed from time to time and cried out, barely aware of what was going on around her. Johann suspected that Tonio had also given her a potion, but unlike him, she hadn't eaten ash. What sort of nightmares were torturing the girl right now?

As Johann looked at his daughter, he felt a fire burn in his heart unlike anything he'd ever felt before. And he felt relief. It was as if he'd paid an ancient debt. But then the pain and the fever returned. His whole body started to tremble; the fight with Poitou had drained the last of his strength. His bandage and the robe were torn. He dragged himself over the cobbled streets like a walking corpse, knowing it wouldn't be long before he'd collapse. And this time he wouldn't get back up.

"We . . . we . . . must leave town," he gasped. "Tonio . . . He'll be looking for us . . . His . . . his followers will tell him what happened."

Karl didn't reply as he carried Greta through the lanes. Sweat was pouring down his face, and he was bleeding from a wound on his forehead. His strength, too, was coming to an end; he stumbled more than he walked. He stubbornly stared straight ahead to where the lane was ending in a small market square near the Hospital of the Holy Ghost. The stalls that usually sold expensive spices, loaves of bread, cheese, and salted meat stood empty. Everyone, even the market wives, had rushed over to the main square, where a column of black smoke rose to the sky. The news of the burning elephant had probably lured even the last Nuremberger out of the house.

Utterly exhausted, Karl stopped by the bridge east of the hospital. "We should go back to the command," he said. "I can't carry Greta much further. The Teutonic Knights will give us shelter and tend to her—and you."

"Out of the question." Johann shook his head and started trudging across the bridge. "Who is to say that the command isn't full of traitors? Many of Tonio's followers are patricians. Why would the command be an exception? It's too dangerous."

"But we need shelter!" said Karl urgently. "Some kind of hiding place. Just look at you!" He gave a desperate laugh. "A feverish one-eyed man who can barely walk in a straight line."

Johann looked down at himself. Karl was right. He was a shivering bundle wrapped in filthy bandages. There was nothing left of the proud, famous doctor.

"Very well," he said. "Let us . . . rest for a while. We'll find somewhere."

He knew he probably wouldn't be able to get back up once he sat down. But they couldn't keep going, either, and so he looked around for a hiding place. In the center of the bridge, stairs led down to a long, narrow island in the Pegnitz. Its sandy shores were lined with brown foam and trash washing down the river from the mills. There was a grove in the middle of the island, which probably served as a secret meeting place for lovers during the warmer months. Low trees and shrubs would offer some shelter. They walked onto the island from the west and pushed their way into the undergrowth, where they finally collapsed with exhaustion. Greta was no longer making any sound.

"I wonder if she'll recover." Karl carefully opened Greta's torn dress and leaned over her. "Her breathing is very weak."

Johann felt a stab in his chest. The thought hadn't even crossed his mind until then. Maybe the potion Tonio had given his daughter was too strong. Maybe she'd never return to him, forever caught in the twilight? But then Greta suddenly opened her eyes—his black eyes.

"Where . . . where are we?" she asked with a feeble voice.

"Somewhere safe," replied Johann and held her cold hand.

"Johann." Greta gave a tired smile. She seemed to recognize him only now, underneath his bandage. "I . . . I feel so heavy. Everything is so heavy. Can you do magic for me? I . . . I like it when you do magic."

Johann brushed her cheek with his fingers, and then he pulled a small pebble from her ear like he used to do with coins. "Your head is full of stones," he said, trying his utmost to sound calm and cheerful. "No wonder you feel heavy." He continued to pull pebble after pebble from her ear. She smiled once more.

"Are you . . . are you a real wizard?"

I am your father, my child, he thought. *I am the man who drove your mother to her death. And I am the man who loved her more than anything. Will you ever be able to forgive me?*

"Where . . . where is Uncle Valentin?"

Johann swallowed. He couldn't tell her—not yet. What should he say? But then Greta closed her eyes, and her breathing became stronger and more regular. And as Johann watched her, he felt himself grow calm, also. It was strange. He had studied so many subjects, attended so many lectures, become a master of all seven liberal arts, but there was one art no scholar in the world had taught him—not the magisters and doctors at Heidelberg, not Archibaldus, and least of all Tonio. It was a discipline that was usually hidden behind dry words in the Latin and Greek writings, as difficult to chew as stale bread. To experience it firsthand was an entirely different story. Ovid had once called it *Ars amatoria,* even if he'd meant something slightly different.

The art of loving.

The eighth liberal art.

Yes, he had loved Margarethe, and he always would. But that love rested on experiences from their childhood, from a long, common history, and also on expectations that probably would never have been fulfilled. His love for this child, however, for his daughter, had no goal. It simply existed. It filled him and gave him an inner peace he'd never experienced before. Johann wondered how his life would have evolved if he'd met Greta sooner, if he'd been her father from the start. Would it have put an end to his endless searching, his unquenchable thirst for knowledge? Probably not. But it would have steered his life down calmer roads.

Johann jutted out his chin with determination. This life—their life together—couldn't be over yet.

It had only just begun. And he would fight for it.

The noises of the spectacle on the main square blew over to them on the breeze—the crashing of a cannon, shouting, the metallic ringing of a bell.

Johann guessed the people of Nuremberg had put out the fire by now. The feast was over and folks would go home.

Johann dozed and soon nodded off, soothed by the feeling of having saved his daughter—for the moment, at least. Soft music caressed his ears, heavenly fanfares, angelic, almost . . .

So tired . . . so awfully tired . . .

"Wake up, Doctor!" Karl's voice tore him out of his dreams.

"Leave me . . . ," he said weakly. "So warm, the music . . ."

But Karl wouldn't give up. He pulled at the doctor's robe like an irritating mutt, and finally he gathered the few handfuls of snow left under the shrubs and rubbed them on Johann's chest.

"How dare you, you insolent . . ." Johann shot up, his good hand ready to strike, but as soon as he saw Karl he knew where he was. His daughter was sleeping beside him, her chest rising and falling steadily. He shook himself to dispel the fatigue.

"Those madmen are going to search for us," said Karl imploringly. "We can't stay here forever."

"Forgive me. You . . . you're right." Johann brushed the snow off his robe and felt awake again. "We need to get out of Nuremberg as fast as we can."

"Only question is, How?" Karl looked around skeptically. He shivered underneath his thin robe. The sun had moved on and stood low above the nearby city wall. The icy waters of the Pegnitz flowed past them lazily. "If it's true what you say and Tonio has men everywhere, then he's probably watching the city gates. We won't get out of town the way we look. Most likely, not even the regular city guards would let us pass. We look like outlaws."

"We must at least try. We can't stay in Nuremberg—it's much too . . ."

Johann faltered when he heard the music again. When he was half-asleep, he'd thought he was imagining it, but now he realized it was real. Flutes, drums, tambourines—soft, but clearly there. Even the quaking sound of a bagpipe was among the instruments. The music was coming not from the main square but from somewhere to the northeast, where the Laufer Gate led onto the road to Prague.

A quiet suspicion sprouted in Johann's mind.

"Quickly—follow me," he ordered.

"What's your plan?"

But instead of replying, Johann shook Greta awake. "Child, wake up! You must try to walk—just for a short while!"

"What . . . what . . . ?" she murmured. She opened her eyes and looked around with confusion.

"Pick her up and run!" said Johann to Karl. "Before it's too late!"

Without another word he hurried back to the bridge. Breathing hard, Karl lugged Greta up the narrow, steep stairs. Staggering along slowly, they headed northeast, past wells, taverns, and smaller markets that gradually filled with people again. They walked around a corner by the old Egidienkirche Church and finally reached the wide, cobblestoned street that led to the Laufer Gate. The music had steadily grown louder and sounded very close now.

And then Johann saw them.

There were about a dozen flautists, several drummers, and a short fellow playing an ancient march on the bagpipe. Never before had the quaking, mind-numbing noise sounded so sweet to Johann's ears. The musicians were followed by jesters in red-and-blue costumes doing cartwheels and juggling balls, a real camel, and a series of colorfully painted wagons hung with all sorts of household items. Striding with self-important expressions between the wagons were several itinerant preachers who probably made a living as traveling scribes and relic trad-ers. They all headed toward the Laufer Gate like one big, glittering snake. There was no sign of any Schembart runners.

"The jugglers from the square!" cried Karl. He and Johann were holding Greta between them now, and she managed to stumble along in small steps. She was still very sluggish. "That's where the music was coming from!"

Johann nodded. "The Schembartlauf parade is over, and the jugglers move on to the next city, like they always do." He sighed. "I saw them earlier but forgot all about them."

Karl watched the bright, noisy train passing by. One of the jugglers, wearing a red fool's cap, took a mock bow and showed them his backside, making an unappetizing sound. Karl turned away in disgust.

"What are we doing here?" he asked. "I've truly had enough of jesters and masks."

"Well, I'm going to ask them if we can come along." Johann gestured at the traveling preachers in their worn-out robes. "No one is going to notice us among all those quacks and fraudsters. And I'm sure we can find a spot in one of the wagons for Greta. Wait here."

He limped toward a wagon and soon returned with a smile on his face.

"They said we can come. All the way to Prague, if we like. There's going to be a huge feast in the summer, apparently."

"Just like that?" Karl gaped at him. "How did you wrangle that so quickly? You don't have any money, so how on—?"

"I speak their language. A few words in thieves' cant, a few old tales, and the usual coin trick." Johann grinned. "We jugglers know one another."

"The great Doctor Johann Georg Faustus, a dishonorable juggler?" Karl laughed in disbelief. "Are you serious?"

Johann winked at his assistant with his one eye. "I've had many lives, my boy. You don't even know the half of it, and I'll never tell you which half is true. Now come before they move on without us."

Johann led them to one of the colorful wagons, and Greta was allowed to lie down inside. Karl joined the itinerant priests walking ahead of the wagon, while Johann sat down on the box seat with his hood pulled over his face. The driver, a young lad with red curls and a red gugel, gave him a cheeky grin.

"Got into some trouble, old man?" he jeered. "Wouldn't be the first to join the traveling folk. What do you know?"

"Oh, a few things." Johann smiled and gazed at the road that led through the Laufer Gate. The gates stood wide open, and the guards watched the lively train with dark expressions, pleased the dishonorable folks were leaving town.

When the jugglers danced through the gate, the musicians played their farewell tune and the wagons rattled across the drawbridge. Johann looked back one last time. Next to the gate stood a small boy, watching the noisy procession with his mouth open.

He looked spellbound, and Johann knew why.

Epilogue

"BEHOLD THIS DRINK AND BE AMAZED! IT IS THE SAME drink the Greek king Mithridates used, once upon a time, to protect himself from snakebites, and which Heracles used to capture Cerberus, the hound of hell. Thanks to this drink, Emperor Friedrich lived for more than a hundred years! The bottle is yours for just two hellers. And for three more I'll read your future in your palm. Come and learn what fate holds in store for you with the great Doctor Johann Georg Faustus!"

The people on the small market square pointed and stared. Standing in front of them on the box seat of a wagon was a man wearing a blue-and-black star-spangled cloak, watching them from beneath his floppy hat with a pair of piercing black eyes. The left eye in particular seemed to fix on the crowd ominously, gleaming like a black diamond from the depths of hell.

"The first of you to buy a bottle of the drink receives a horoscope for the whole year!" the doctor promised. He raised his hands, and the crowd saw that he wore a black leather glove on the right. "Come closer! Don't be afraid. What I foretell always comes true—the good things, at least," he added with a wink.

The people whispered and nudged one another. They knew this uncanny man from tales and from tattered, cheaply printed leaflets that made the rounds at taverns. Apparently, not long ago, the doctor flew upon a swan that he'd fed with his theriac in Basel. In Braunschweig, he made the wheels on the cart of a wealthy farmer disappear, and in the faraway Orient, he conjured deer antlers on the helmet of an imperial knight, whereupon the heathens fled in droves.

And now this widely traveled man had actually come to their small town, like a messenger from a distant world. The famous Doctor Johann Georg Faustus. He was real!

Johann stifled a smile as he gazed at the gawking crowd from atop his wagon. Here in the Breisgau region, near the Alps, the audience was especially grateful. Maybe that was because they were so far away from the big cities—from Cologne, Frankfurt, Nuremberg, and Augsburg, where the world was changing more rapidly than ever before.

"We only have a few bottles of the miracle potion left," declared Johann, making a sweeping gesture toward his wagon. "My loyal assistant, a widely traveled scholar from the University of Paris, will fetch them for you."

Ducking out of the wagon came Karl Wagner, carrying a heavy crate full of corked bottles of theriac in his arms. Karl had perfected the recipe with a mix of juniper, gentian root, a pinch of henbane, and a lot of strong brandy. People loved the brew, just like they loved Karl's painted canvases that hung down the sides of the wagon like flags. They showed fire-spitting dragons, monstrous creatures with long snouts, people with wolf heads, and a lion with the tail of a scorpion. Doctor Faustus had encountered all those creatures in the course of his travels, and there was a story to tell about each one. Karl was rightly proud of his artworks. They might not have been as perfect as those of Albrecht Dürer or the great Leonardo da Vinci, but they amazed people and transported them to another world. What more could an artist wish for?

While Karl handed out the bottles of theriac and pocketed the money, Johann invited individual spectators up onto the box seat, where he read their palms. Mostly he spoke in flowery words about happy events, like a good harvest or an impending marriage. He never foretold someone's death—even if he saw it. And he never read his own future.

All that mattered was the present.

"Good day, Herr . . . Herr Doctor. Um, may I call you 'Doctor'?" The voice of the fat farmer's wife who'd just taken a seat beside him trembled with awe. The hand she held out to him was marked by hard work, wrinkled, and covered in lines and craters like a barren field. "My dear Hans died last year," she said quietly. "All I've left is my daughter, Else. How are we going to fare in the coming years?"

"Hmm. Let me see." Johann leaned over the hand and squinted. His eyesight wasn't as good as it used to be, and the glass eye itched. It had been custom made by a Venetian craftsman and had cost him a fortune. With the false eye, his gaze appeared even more piercing and eerie. Thanks to Karl's bandaging, Johann's eye socket had healed well, as had his right hand, on which he wore a glove with an artificial finger. Following their escape from Nuremberg, Johann had remained in the grip of fever for three long weeks and only just managed to cheat death. Every now and then, a dull pressure reminded him of his little finger—the finger he'd lost in Nuremberg over a year ago.

The first sacrifice.

"I see a good summer and a rich harvest," he muttered and tapped a spot on the woman's palm. "Your Life line is as deep and wide as the Rhine."

As he continued to study the hand of the worried farmer's wife, his thoughts returned to Nuremberg. Tonio del Moravia had vanished from his life once more; Johann had never heard anything about him again. He still didn't know what exactly had happened that night in the crypt below the Sebaldus Church. His memories were sketchy—probably because of the black potion as well as the fever.

Or because he didn't *want* to remember what Tonio and his followers had tried to invoke in the underground hall and what role he had played in it.

Had Nuremberg patricians actually been involved in the madness? Had they really believed they could bring the devil to earth?

Or was the devil already among them?

"Your Head line is as straight as an arrow," said Johann in a mysterious-sounding voice. "It shows that you pitch in on your late husband's farm and that you know how to assert yourself."

"It's true!" The woman nodded. "You're incredible!"

Johann smiled inwardly. These days he knew right from the beginning what people wanted to hear. He prattled on and on while his thoughts were miles away.

The horrific child murders had stopped following their departure from Nuremberg, or so travelers had told them. He'd felt relieved, even though he still didn't know what he'd had to do with it all. Why had Tonio chosen him?

Why did the sorcerer believe that Johann was special? Just because of a comet that appeared every seventeen years? Sometimes, during the long nights on his travels through the empire, Johann woke up screaming because he'd dreamed of a beautiful knight—a knight whose French name he no longer spoke out loud.

On those nights, he thought about a phrase that Tonio the sorcerer had voiced down in the crypt and that, when he remembered it later on, struck him as deeply disturbing. He couldn't stop thinking about it.

Because you're the son of a great sorcerer yourself.

His mother had never told him who his father was. His stepfather had spoken about a traveling scholar and juggler, and that was all he knew. What did Tonio know about his father?

The son of a great sorcerer.

"Karl has finished setting up the booth stage and people are waiting for the puppet show. Are you coming, Uncle?"

Johann started up from his palm reading. It still felt strange when Greta called him by that title. He looked up and saw her cheerful face with the ever-smiling lips of her mother and the dark, mysterious eyes of her father. Greta was fifteen years old now and almost a woman. She was strong and nimble with full blonde hair to her shoulders and a constellation of freckles on her face that gave her a slightly impertinent look.

The traumatic events from a year ago didn't seem to have left a lasting effect on her—probably helped by the fact that she hardly remembered anything about them. Johann had told Greta that she'd been given a potion at the Loch Prison back then to make her docile for torture and questioning. He, Karl, and Valentin had rescued her. Whatever had happened in between was nothing but a bad dream for Greta.

And he hadn't told her about Valentin's sacrifice.

"Are you all right?" asked Greta, still smiling.

"Of course," he replied after a few moments. "I'm just focused on a particularly difficult chiromancy, that's all."

The farmer's wife nodded gravely.

In his stories by the evening campfires, Valentin was an old friend and nothing more. He had been stabbed to death while freeing Greta. The girl had cried for many nights, but now she had gotten over it. And she'd called Johann "Uncle" ever since.

One day he would tell her the truth—he just didn't know when.

"Um, you're going to get a grandson." He concluded the reading abruptly and gave the corpulent woman a pat on the back. "A healthy boy who will carry on the farm."

"When?" asked the woman, trembling with excitement.

"Oh, certainly this fall—"

"But my daughter isn't even expecting!"

"Are you absolutely sure?" Johann grinned and left the dumbfounded woman where she was.

He jumped down from the box seat and let Little Satan lick his hand. The huge wolfhound had waited patiently for his master and trotted alongside him now. Little Satan was fully grown, a giant of a dog standing more than three feet at the shoulder. Superstitious folk truly believed he was the devil.

When the commander Wolfgang von Eisenhofen had found out that Johann had left Nuremberg, he'd sent his knight Eberhart von Streithagen after him. "A gift from the commander," Streithagen had growled and, with an expression of disgust, handed him the squirming puppy as well as the box with the stargazing tube and Johann's books. "His Excellency believes that it is bad luck to keep the possessions of a wizard, most of all his dog. His only request is that you never set foot in Nuremberg again."

Johann had nodded and held Little Satan tightly. Even without the commander's request he would have given Nuremberg a wide berth in the future.

He walked around the wagon, where Karl had set up a wooden booth. There was no laterna magica—times had become too dangerous for that. People were burning at stakes far and wide as the church tried to defend itself against false preachers but also rebels with honest intentions. Johann sometimes thought the world was sitting on a powder keg that might blow up at any moment. And he wasn't planning on ending his life prematurely as a black magician and necromancer. Besides, he preferred the puppet theater to the laterna magica—there was more room for dreams.

And it didn't remind him of Margarethe.

He hadn't returned to the tower by the Alps. He feared Tonio might be there. In his dreams, the sorcerer was standing atop the platform, the strange stargazing tube that was now in Johann's possession pointed at some distant object. Tonio's eye was as big as a whale's.

I can see you, Johann . . . Always, every day . . . You can't escape me . . . Only seventeen years . . .

"Gather around!" shouted Greta to the people on the market square. She used the booming, praising tone Johann had taught her. "Be amazed at Doctor Faustus's fantastic journeys that took him to faraway lands!" cried the girl in a rhythm that seemed to entrance people. "Prepare to experience miracles you've never seen before!"

Greta called the booth her little theater, and she loved it. Karl had painted the crate with colorful exotic depictions. There was a little red curtain, along with several different backdrops and even an oil lamp that acted as the sun in the desert. With admiration Johann studied Karl's paintings of the scorching desert in the East and the distant lands they called America, named after a Florentine seafarer and explorer who believed he'd discovered a new continent. Karl had painted a green jungle and small people with spears who rode on dragons.

Johann couldn't help but grin. Karl was utterly useless as a juggler, but his talents clearly lay elsewhere. Johann was occasionally irritated by Karl's glances—looks that were more than those of an admiring assistant. One time Johann had heard Karl mutter his name in his sleep: *Faust, oh, my Faust.* But Johann hadn't said anything, because he didn't want to embarrass the young man.

They had set up wooden benches using bricks and planks of spruce in front of the small stage, and about three dozen spectators had gathered. Full of anticipation, they watched Greta as she juggled five balls at once, attracting even more people to their show. Johann nodded appreciatively. Despite her young age, it was clear that Greta was a highly talented performer—she could even play the bagpipe. What they had to offer wasn't the spectacular show Johann used to present with his laterna magica. It was smaller and less dramatic, but it made people happy.

And he was happy, too.

Karl was already crouching behind the booth, and now Greta caught her balls one by one, made them magically disappear in her dress, and joined him. Several young men in the audience made rude remarks and gestures, because Greta had developed a womanly figure. Sometimes she reminded him a little of Salome, the insatiable dancer who had bewitched him on their journey to Venice so long ago. Perhaps he would fall in love again someday, but for now his love for his daughter was enough for him.

"Watch how I, the widely traveled Doctor Faustus, once fought a lion in Africa and defeated it with the aid of white magic alone," announced Johann, who had walked up to the theater. As always, he acted as the narrator while Karl and Greta worked the puppets.

In front of a desert backdrop, a lion with a golden mane appeared, roaring so loudly that the audience gasped with fright. A second puppet materialized— clearly the doctor with his star cloak and floppy hat.

"You terrible beast," sounded Karl's voice from behind the stage. "Here— drink my theriac!" The Faust puppet threw a miniature bottle at the lion, and the animal staggered from side to side as if drunk, eventually collapsing with a grunt. The audience laughed and applauded.

"I once met the beautiful Helen herself," continued Johann. "I abducted her from Hades, where she had been sorrowfully waiting for her Paris since Troy."

The backdrop was quickly changed to a canvas showing menacing flames. The puppet of a princess with blonde hair appeared on stage and cried heartrendingly.

"Oh, poor me," wailed Greta's voice. "The devil himself has dragged me down to hell—I may never see my beloved Paris again!"

Some spectators sighed while others giggled; the Faust puppet appeared from the right, this time with a book in its hands.

"I am going to free you, beautiful Helen," announced Karl. "Not even the devil stands a chance against my book of magic spells."

"Harr, harr! We shall see about that," said Karl with a different, darker voice. At the same moment, a tinny thunderclap rang out and the devil emerged from the depths of the booth. He had goat's horns and a long tail, and there was smoke, along with the stink of sulfur. The audience screamed with horror.

"Now both of you must remain in hell!" snarled the devil and tugged at Helen. "You are mine!" The puppets fought one another, and the crowd booed the devil.

"Ha! Now you will feel the force of magic," shouted the Faust puppet at the devil. "This is my book of magic. *Vade, Satanas!*"

Doctor Faustus struck the devil on the nose with his book, and the hellish puppet disappeared with a wail. The audience hooted and clapped as the curtain fell, and Karl and Greta stepped in front of the booth and took a bow.

Johann stood next to them, smiling, pensively gazing at the devil puppet in Karl's hand. It was a cheap wooden thing with horns made of tin, a red cloak made of rags, and a scruffy tail—the butt of jokes that people laughed at, now vanquished.

But at the bottom of his heart, Johann knew that the devil would one day return.

Faust and I

A Sort of Afterword

This book exists thanks to the German silent-film director F. W. Murnau, my former German teacher Kurt Weiß, and the German Train Drivers' Union. Why? Well, I better start at the beginning . . .

I must have been about six years old when I saw Murnau's interpretation of Goethe's *Faust* on television—a masterpiece of expressionist film. I was home alone, flicking through the channels as children do. The eerie black-and-white images of a huge devil with a billowing cape, maimed plague victims, and a bearded old man wandering through foggy landscapes disturbed me more than any horror movie I watched later in life. (Take it as a warning to all parents who think they have to introduce their children to art at a young age—art can cause nightmares!)

At the start of the film, the word *Faust*—meaning "fist"—was written in old-fashioned letters, and for years I wondered what that meant. I always assumed it was about a fist punching someone's face, but eventually I learned that it was the name of the bearded old man who is later turned into a handsome youth who falls in love with a girl named Gretchen. I was less interested in the love story back then—the devil was much more fascinating, and the fog, and the terrifying grimaces of the era of silent film. Those movies still hold an almost magical fascination for me.

Years later, in high school, I happened across Faust again. This time it came from my German teacher, Kurt Weiß—one of the few teachers who truly helped to shape me. (Every one of us knows one of those—they aren't all bad, are they?)

Herr Weiß was a movie buff, and he regularly showed old Lubitsch and Chaplin movies at his home. One day, he dragged us to a matinee showing of *Faust*—the well-known 1960 adaptation by Gustaf Gründgens. Bored seventeen-year-olds never say no to getting out of the classroom, even if that means having to watch a dusty old postwar film.

Much to my surprise, the movie captivated me at once, evoking old memories from Murnau's *Faust*. I was moved by the story, but most of all I was fascinated by Goethe's verses, which have stayed with me ever since. Not long after our field trip to the cinema, I bought the drama on a dozen cassette tapes and listened to it again and again. I realized just how many of Goethe's lines had become part of everyday German language. To this day I love quoting from *Faust*, and this novel, too, is spiked with quotations. (During pub crawls, I never fail to impress by shouting "Uncertain shapes—again you haunt me" at my drinking buddies. And whenever we go hiking, I like to torture my family with excerpts from the Easter walk or the opening monologue, frowning broodingly and looking altogether Faustian.)

And I often do feel like Faust—never satisfied, forever searching for something. The beauty lies right before my eyes, but I don't see it. That's probably one of the reasons Faust is considered the most German of all mythical characters.

And this is where the German Train Drivers' Union comes into play.

In 2015, I was on a book tour near Karlsruhe when the German train drivers decided to go on strike. As a result, I got stuck in a small town called Bretten and couldn't get home. Any and all rental cars had been snatched up by wily businessmen who had smelled the rat before me. And there were no buses.

So I made the best of a bad situation, extended my hotel stay, rented a bicycle, and started to explore the beautiful Kraichgau region. That's how I came upon a small place called Knittlingen. There was an old stone church, a tiny church square that didn't really deserve to be called a "square," and next to it, a house with a sign. The sign read:

BIRTHPLACE OF DR. JOHANNES FAUST, 1480 TO 1540.

Intrigued, I climbed off my bike and looked more closely. Until then I'd always thought Faust was nothing but a myth. Had he really existed?

A small museum stood next door to the house where Faust was born, and thankfully it was open. I went inside and met a quack, astrologer, clairvoyant, alchemist, charlatan, wise doctor, and cunning conjurer who had lived around the year 1500 and made an astonishing international career following his death. Almost forty years after my first encounter with Faust, the doctor entered my life as a real person, a historical figure!

From that moment I knew that I would write a novel about him.

At this point I'd like to extend my sincere gratitude to the German Train Drivers' Union. Maybe sometimes the world needs to stand still for inspiration to sprout.

There are only a handful of sources about the historical Faust, but plenty of speculation. As a novelist I have the privilege of picking and choosing what I like from the existing literature on the subject without getting a rap on the knuckles from historians.

Knittlingen is considered the most likely birthplace for Faust. I decided on his date of birth because of a source that quotes Faust as having said to the prior of the Rebdorf Augustinian collegiate church that "when the sun and Jupiter stand in the same degree of a zodiac . . . prophets are born." I put that together with Faust's middle name, Georg—Saint George's feast day is April 23, so I got April 23, 1478. The name Jörg Gerlach (Faust's stepfather in my book) came from a farmer who lived in that very house in Knittlingen. A piece of paper with a magic spell was found in one of the thresholds, and a star-shaped alchemist's cupboard also allegedly belonged to this property.

There isn't much known about where Faust went from Knittlingen. It is possible that he studied at Heidelberg, because there is a corresponding name in the records. Then he probably roamed the empire, and the legends frequently mention a black dog and a companion by the name of Wagner. Faust cast a horoscope for the Bamberg prince-bishop Georg III; he spent time in Erfurt, at the Rebdorf monastery, in Nuremberg, and in Ingolstadt. The famous Sponheim abbot Johannes Trithemius (a type of magician himself) wrote nasty things about a charlatan and sodomite by the name of Faust in a letter. *Sodomy* was a term for homosexuality back then—a theme I pick up in my novel. A meeting between the historical Faust and polymath Heinrich Cornelius Agrippa von Nettesheim, as described in my novel, is possible but not proven.

Faust's demise is a well-known legend. Allegedly, during an alchemy experiment in the town of Staufen in the Breisgau, he blew himself up in a rather gruesome manner: "Brains stuck to the wall . . . and his eyes and teeth were strewn about." Unsurprising that people deduced the devil must have been at play, with such a theatrical exit. And thus the tale of Faust's pact with Satan was born—a topic as old as mankind.

The large number of stories and legends that started to circulate following his death show just how well known the figure of Doctor Johann Georg Faustus was in the German empire. In the year 1587, the book printer Johann Spies published the *Historia von D. Johann Fausten*, which became the first German bestseller and even sold abroad.

And now the story really gets interesting.

Toward the end of the sixteenth century, a certain Christopher Marlowe in London happened across that book. His competitor, William Shakespeare, had published one hit play after the other, and Marlowe needed a good story. Faust's suited him perfectly. The plot had everything a good play needed: action, blood, special effects, the dramatic downfall of the protagonist, and, of course, the devil. For theater owners back then, the devil was as valuable as comic-book superheroes are to the film industry today. You couldn't go wrong with the devil.

The play, *The Tragical History of Doctor Faustus*, was a great success in England. But there were too many directors and actors on the island, and so some of them immigrated to other countries, including the German empire. They brought with them Marlowe's play and performed it at fairs. But since barely any of the English actors spoke German, they introduced a comic figure who summarized the plot between acts. That was the birth of the Harlequin, also called Hanswurst or Kasper.

The play became very popular in the German empire, especially as a puppet show, and so about a hundred and fifty years later, a young boy named Johann Wolfgang—who would become famous under his last name, Goethe—was fascinated by the story. Just like me with Murnau's disturbing film, Goethe couldn't stop thinking about the material. From August 1771 until May 1772 he worked as a young lawyer in Frankfurt, where he witnessed the trial of a child murderess. In her desperation, a certain Susanna Margaretha Brandt had killed her newborn child. Goethe was deeply moved by the case, and by adding this sad story to the Faust theme, he created the Faust tragedy that is now considered the most German of all German tragedies—loved, venerated, canonized, and told and retold again and again.

An ancient story about the eternal battle between man and evil, about love and temptation, about a rise and a fall, and about a pact with the devil—the archetypal parable that was probably already known to the cavemen by their campfires.

Oh, yes, and finally my favorite joke on the matter:

The devil comes to the writer and says, "I promise you a bestseller in the millions! You will publish countless editions, enjoy fame, interviews, television appearances, and bathtubs full of money! All you have to do in return is this." The devil raises one finger and grins nastily. "You must sell me your soul."

The writer eyes the devil with suspicion for a long while. Then he says, "OK. And what's the catch?"

There is a little Faust in every one of us—and in writers, a rather large one.

This novel cost me more sweat and effort than other books, and it exists only because a whole bunch of people helped me.

First up, I'd like to thank Gerd Schweizer and Berit Bräuer, who supplied me with great amounts of literature on the topic of Faust and contributed many important details. Berit Bräuer has written an excellent nonfiction book on Faust (*Im Bann der Zeit*), which I recommend highly.

Eva-Maria Springer led me through the Faust museum in Knittlingen and Faust's birthplace; Brit Veith showed me through Knittlingen, and Barbara Gittinger was my expert for Maulbronn Monastery. Thank you also to Richard Dietz from the International Society for Faust (Internationale Faust-Gesellschaft e.V.), which manages Faust's heritage and regularly invites the public to interesting talks.

Alexander Kipphahn from the Bretten city archive supplied me with the names of wealthy Bretten merchants; Horst Kaufmann from the Schembart Society (Schembart-Gesellschaft Nürnberg e.V.) told me everything I needed to know about the Nuremberg Schembartlauf, which served as my showdown. The Nuremberg city archive was a helpful partner on the topics of Loch waterways, Loch Prison, and the Hospital of the Holy Ghost. As they have so often, the

Latin translations came from Dr. Manfred Heim; my rather poor Italian was corrected by Barbara Lambiase and Christian Platzer, and my French was checked by Alexandra Baisch. Helmut Hornung answered my questions on the subjects of comets, laterna magica, and telescopes. He pointed out to me that a telescope of the kind Tonio and later Faust own in my novel wasn't in fact invented until 1608 in Holland. Well, I think the devil was ahead of his time—in my book, at least. As always, any mistakes are on my own muddleheadedness, not on my expert helpers.

Thank you also to my father, who—being a doctor—knows how fingers and eyes are amputated. Thank you to Gerd, Martina, and Sophia from the Gerd F. Rumler Agency; they support me in every which way, from coffee to emotional support. Thank you to the entire team at Ullstein Publishing—you do a great job—and to my favorite editor, Uta Rupprecht. My son, Niklas, helped me to remove anything childish and corny from the beginning of the novel. My daughter, Lily, a keen artist, gave her blessing for the beautiful cover of the book's first edition.

A second and important editor in this project was my wife, Katrin, who was the first to notice that the final act wasn't quite working yet. I'm sorry if I was being a drama queen at first. You were right, as always!

Faust for Beginners

Are you a Faust expert? Below are quotations I borrowed from Goethe's famous tragedy *Faust* (translation by Charles T. Brooks). Did you find them in the book?

- Name is but sound and smoke. (Verse 3456)
- Quite a peculiar juice is blood. (Verse 1740)
- The mass can only be impressed by masses. (Prelude in the Theatre)
- Am called Magister, Doctor, indeed . . . (Verse 3600)
- Remember then! Of one make ten, the two let be, make even three, there's wealth for thee. (Verse 2540)
- That I may know what the world contains in its innermost heart and finer veins, see all its energies and seeds, and deal no more in words but in deeds. (Verse 382)
- Philosophy and medicine, and law, and ah! Theology, too. (Verse 354)
- The spirit that denies . . . (Verse 1338)
- Well, art is long! And life is short and fleeting. (Verse 558)
- [Part of the part am I, which once was all,] the Gloom that brought forth Light [itself from out her mighty womb.] (Verse 1350)
- In the beginning was the deed! (Verse 1237)

About the Author

Oliver Pötzsch worked for years as a journalist and scriptwriter for Bavarian television. He is the author of seven books in the international bestselling Hangman's Daughter Tales historical series, the children's novel *Knight Kyle and the Magic Silver Lance*, and the Black Musketeers series, including *Book of the Night* and *Sword of Power*. His work has been translated into more than twenty languages. Oliver lives in Munich with his family. For more information, visit www.oliver-poetzsch.de.

About the Translator

Lisa Reinhardt studied English and linguistics at University of Otago and lives with her family on the beautiful West Coast of New Zealand. Her most recent work includes *The Council of Twelve*, the seventh book in Oliver Pötzsch's Hangman's Daughter Tales series.